Smith & Keenan's

COMPANY LAW

Thirteenth Edition

Denis Keenan

LLB(Hons), FCIS, CertEd

of the Middle Temple, Barrister
Formerly Head of Department of
Business Studies and Law at what is now
Anglia Polytechnic University

Harlow, England • London • New York • Boston • San Francisco • Toronto
Sydney • Tokyo • Singapore • Hong Kong • Seoul • Taipei • New Delhi
Cape Town • Madrid • Mexico City • Amsterdam • Munich • Paris • Milan

Pearson Education Limited
Edinburgh Gate
Harlow
Essex CM20 2JE

and Associated Companies throughout the world.

Visit us on the World Wide Web at:
www.pearsoneduc.com

First published under the Pitman imprint in 1966
Second edition published 1970
Third edition published 1976
Fourth edition published 1981
Fifth edition published 1983
Sixth edition published 1986
Seventh edition published 1987
Eighth edition published 1990
Ninth edition published 1993
Tenth edition published 1996
Eleventh edition published 1999
Twelfth edition 2002
Thirteenth edition published 2005

© Kenneth Smith and Denis Keenan 1966
© Denis Keenan and Mrs K Smith 1970, 1976, 1981, 1983
© Denis Keenan 1986, 1987, 1990, 1993, 1996, 1999, 2002, 2005

The right of Denis Keenan to be identified as author of this work has been asserted by him in accordance with the Copyright, Designs and Patents Act 1988.

All rights reserved. No part of this publication may be reproduced, stored in a retrieval system, or transmitted in any form or by any means, electronic, mechanical, photocopying, recording or otherwise, without either the prior written permission of the publisher or a licence permitting restricted copying in the United Kingdom issued by the Copyright Licensing Agency Ltd, 90 Tottenham Court Road, London W1T 4LP.

ISBN 1 40581158 7

British Library Cataloguing-in-Publication Data
A catalogue record for this book is available from the British Library.

Library of Congress Cataloging-in-Publication Data
Keenan, Denis J.
Smith & Keenan's company law / Denis Keenan.–13th ed.
p. cm.
Includes index.
ISBN 1-4058-1158-7
1. Corporation law–England. 2. Corporation law–Wales. I. Title: Smith and Keenan's company law. II. Title: Company law. III. Title.
KD2079.S55 2005
346.42'066–dc22

2005040731

10 9 8 7 6 5 4 3 2 1
06 05

Typeset in 9½/12pt Stone Serif by 35
Printed and bound by Bell & Bain Ltd, Glasgow

CONTENTS

PREFACE TO THE THIRTEENTH EDITION

This edition includes important changes in company law between 2002 and 2005. Of particular importance are the changes brought about by The Companies (Audit, Investigations and Community Enterprise) Act 2004 which is designed to strengthen the hand of the auditor in terms of information received from the directors of a company and now also its officers and managers. However the Act brings in other important changes such as the new power given to companies to provide and indemnity for the directors in terms of legal claims against them both by third parties and in a more restricted way by the company itself. The Act also creates a new kind of corporate structure the Community Interest Company intended to make it simpler and more convenient to establish a business whose profits and assets are to be used for the benefit of the community.

Significant changes have been made by the Enterprise Act 2002 in the field of insolvency law especially in the appointment of administrators and their functions and powers. The 2002 Act will eventually bring about the demise of the office of administrative receiver and significant changes have been made to prefential debts.

There is also much more material on the Limited Liability Partnership that operates in a corporate mode.

Other changes include material on Treasury Shares and the EU Prospectus Directive that will be implemented in the UK during the lifetime of this edition. As regards loans to directors there is additional material on directors' loan accounts that form for many practitioners their only contact with the restrictive loan provisions of the Companies Act 1985. This is particularly so in the private company.

There is as usual much more case law.

In spite of all the changes my publishers and I have managed to produce a text which is but a few pages longer than the last.

We have continued to give an Appendix outlining likely areas of company law reform some of which has been enacted in the Companies (Audit, Investigations and Community Enterprise) Act 2004 but much remains to be brought into a comprehensive Bill. At the time of writing we are approaching a general election – sometime in 2005. The most recent Government statement is to the effect that a Bill will be presented to Parliament early in a third term should the Government get one. So an estimate of earliest enactment would be 2007 with the Bill being brought into force over the following one or two years.

Finally I would like to thank those members of staff at Pearson Publishing who have helped produce this edition, particularly Michelle Gallagher, Acquisitions Editor – Law and Criminology. My thanks are also due to those who designed, set, printed and bound the book.

In this edition as before I have had the invaluable assistance of my wife in terms of the collation of sources of material that should be considered and in terms of my library. No lawyer can operate without this kind of backup.

Any errors and omissions at the level at which the text is aimed are down to me.

Denis Keenan, Maenan, January 2005

LAW REPORT ABBREVIATIONS

The following table sets out the abbreviations used when citing the various series of certain law reports which are in common use, together with the periods over which they extend.

AC	Law Reports, Appeal Cases, 1891–(current)
ATC	Annotated Tax Cases, 1922–75
All ER	All England Law Reports, 1936–(current)
All ER (D)	All England Direct (an online service)
All ER Rep	All England Law Reports Reprint, 36 vols 1558–1935
App Cas	Law Reports, Appeal Cases, 15 vols 1875–90
BCC	British Company Law and Practice (CCH editions)–(current)
BCLC	Butterworths Company Law Cases, 1983–(current)
B & CR	Reports of Bankruptcy and Companies Winding-up Cases, 1918–(current)
CL	Current Law Monthly Digest, 1947–(current)
CLY	Current Law Yearbook, 1947–(current)
CMLR	Common Market Law Reports, 1962–(current)
Ch	Law Reports Chancery Division, 1891–(current)
Com Cas	Commercial Cases, 1895–1941
Fam	Law Reports Family Division, 1972–(current)
ICR	Industrial Court Reports, 1972–74; Industrial Cases Reports, 1974–(current)
IRLB	Industrial Relations Law Bulletin, 1993–(current)
IRLR	Industrial Relations Law Reports, 1971–(current)
ITR	Reports of decisions of the Industrial Tribunals, 1966–(current)
KB	Law Reports, King's Bench Division, 1901–52
LGR	Local Government Reports, 1902–(current)
Lloyd LR or (from 1951) Lloyd's Rep	Lloyd's List Law Reports, 1919–(current)
LRRP	Law Reports Restrictive Practices, 1957–(current)
LSG	Law Society Gazette Reports
NLJ	New Law Journal
P	Law Reports, Probate, Divorce and Admiralty Division, 1891–1971
P & CR	Planning and Compensation Reports, 1949–(current)
PIQR	Personal Injuries and Quantum Reports
QB	Law Reports Queen's Bench Division, 1891–1901; 1953–(current)
SJ	Solicitors' Journal, 1856–(current)
STC	Simon's Tax Cases, 1973–(current)
Tax Cas (or TC)	Tax Cases, 1875–(current)
TLR	Times Law Reports, 1884–1952
WLR	Weekly Law Reports, 1953–(current)

TABLE OF CASES

TABLE OF STATUTES

Coventions

European Directives

Statutory Instruments

Overseas Companies (Accounts) (Modifications and Exemptions) Order 1990 (SI 1990/440) 63
Public Offers of Securities Regulations 1995 210, 441
Public Offers of Securities (Amendment) Regulations 1999 210
Stamp Duty and Stamp Duty Land Tax (Consequential Amendments of Enactments) Regulations 2003 (SI 2003/2868)
Reg 2 222
Uncertified Securities Regulations 2001 (SI 2001/3755) 223, 238
SI 1982/1771 360
SI 1992/2452 14
SI 1993/564 552, 561
SI 1999/2770 169

Treaties

Treaty of Rome
Art 81 393
Art 82 393
Art 189 55
Art 235 139

Miscellaneous

City Code
s J 497, 500
Rule 2 499, 500, 501
Rule 2.5(c) 501
Rule 4 499, 500
Rule 6.2 505
Rule 7.1 505
Rule 8.1 505
Rule 9 501
Rule 9.7 502
Rule 21 498
Rule 23 500
Rules 23–27 497
Rule 24.2 497
Rule 36 501
Rule 36.8 501
Principle 7 497, 498

1

THE NATURE OF A COMPANY

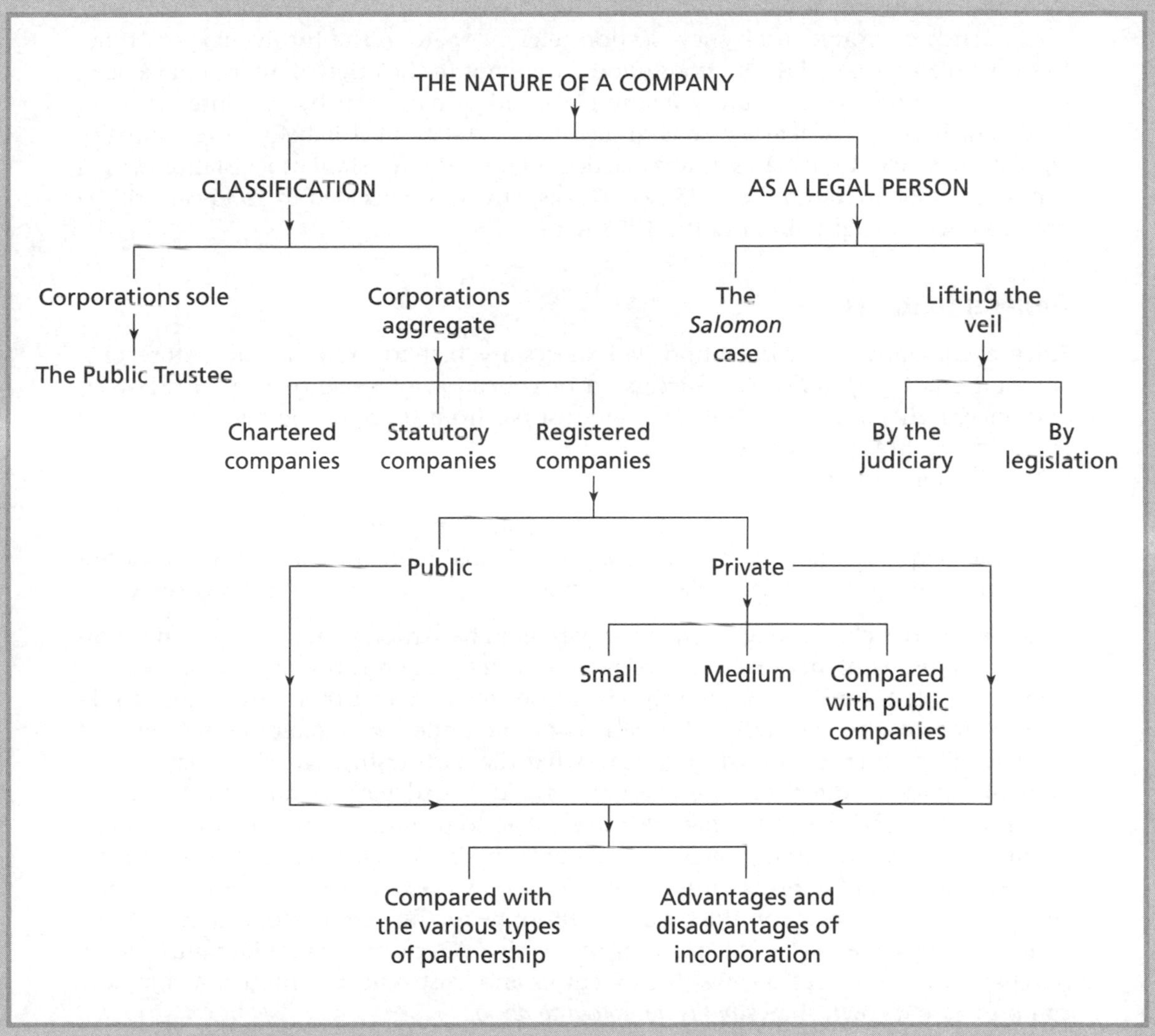

This text is concerned almost entirely with the law relating to *registered companies*. These are governed in the main by the Companies Act 1985 and relevant case law. Section references have been cut to a minimum, but those that do appear relate to the Companies Act 1985 unless otherwise indicated. It should be borne in mind, however, that a section or schedule number quoted as from the 1985 Act is not necessarily the one which appeared in the original Act. Many sections and schedules were revised and reinserted in the 1985 Act by the Companies Act 1989. Later statutory instruments have also added new sections to the 1985 Act.

As regards corporate insolvency, section references are to the Insolvency Act 1986. Here again a number of the sections quoted were not in the original Act but have been inserted by subsequent statutory instruments and in particular by the Enterprise Act 2002. Furthermore, where a case is quoted and the date of it is before the company legislation which it illustrates, it was decided on identical (or similar) legislation which is now consolidated into the 1985 Act. This is why a case decided in 1936 can still be used to illustrate a provision in the 1985 Act.

General features

Since a company is a corporation, it is necessary first to examine the nature of a corporation. A *corporation* is a succession or collection of persons having at law an existence, rights and duties, separate and distinct from those of the persons who are from time to time its members.

The distinguishing features of a corporation are:

(*a*) It is a *persona at law*, i.e. an artificial not a natural person.
(*b*) It has perpetual succession, i.e. its existence is maintained by the constant succession of new persons who replace those who die or are in some other way removed.

This means that even though a member dies, goes bankrupt, or retires from the company by transferring his shares, the company carries on and is not dissolved.

By contrast, an ordinary partnership is dissolved when a partner dies or goes bankrupt, or retires. The business will usually continue under the remaining partners but the retiring partner is entitled, subject to what the partnership agreement says, to be paid his share in the firm. The executor of a deceased partner and the trustee in bankruptcy of a bankrupt partner are also entitled to payment of the relevant share.

This results in a return of capital in a partnership. This can result in some dislocation of the business, and although this can be reduced by clauses in the articles of partnership, e.g. deferred payment, the problem cannot be totally eliminated: provision must be made. The same does not happen in companies. A retiring shareholder must find a purchaser for the shares, as must the executors and trustee in bankruptcy. A company can purchase its own shares *but is not forced to do so.*

A limited liability partnership (LLP) registered under the Limited Liability Partnerships Act 2000 is more like a company than an ordinary partnership in that it has a separate existence at law, i.e. is a persona at law with its own property and liabilities separate from its members (not partners). The retirement of a member will not therefore effect a dissolution of the LLP but there may be problems in terms of the repayment of the retiring member's capital. It is therefore important that the members of the LLP make an effective and valid agreement between themselves before the LLP is registered and incorporated. That failing, the default provisions of *Regs* 7 and 8 of the Limited Liability Partnerships Regulations 2001 apply under which all members of a LLP are entitled to share equally in the capital and profits of the firm, and in the absence of a special member agreement would be entitled to the return of it on retirement. The members of a LLP do not hold saleable shares in the LLP and the procedure for the retirement of members and the admission of new members should appear in the pre-registration agreement, otherwise the retirement of a member and the admission of a member take place 'in accordance with any agreement made in a particular case with the other members of the LLP'.

CLASSIFICATION OF CORPORATIONS – THE COMPANY AS A CORPORATION

The main classification is between corporations sole and aggregate.

Corporation sole

A corporation may be a corporation sole, i.e. it may consist of only one member at a time holding a perpetual office. Here the office is personified to distinguish it from the person who is from time to time the holder of it.

The concept has little commercial application but a useful and practical example is provided by the Public Trustee which is a corporation sole created by the Public Trustee Act 1906. The Public Trustee is a civil servant who, while in post, is the sole member of the corporation. The corporation is trustee of much property and it would be inconvenient if all the trusts had to be transferred into the ownership of the new holder of the office every time there was a change. The office of Public Trustee was therefore personified as a corporation sole and the trust property is vested in the corporation and is not affected when the human holder of the office changes.

The role of Public Trustee has now been assumed by the Official Solicitor and the Public Trust Office no longer exists. The posts of Official Solicitor and the Public Trustee are held by the same person though some types of work can only be accepted by that person in the role of Public Trustee and other types of work only in the role of Official Solicitor. The Office of the Official Solicitor and Public Trustee handles relevant business.

Corporation aggregate

A corporation aggregate consists of a number of persons so associated that in law they form a single person, e.g. a registered company. Here the undertaking is personified so that it may be distinguished from its members. A registered company is, like any other corporation, an entity separate from its members as the following cases illustrate.

Salomon *v* Salomon & Co Ltd [1897] AC 22

Salomon carried on business as a leather merchant and boot manufacturer. In 1892 he formed a limited company to take over the business. The memorandum of association was signed by Salomon, his wife, his daughter, and four of his sons. Each subscribed for one share. The subscribers met and appointed Mr Salomon and his two elder sons as directors. The company paid £39,000 to Salomon for the business, and the mode of payment was to give Salomon £10,000 in debentures, secured by a floating charge on the company's assets, and 20,000 shares of £1 each and the balance in cash. Less than one year later the company fell on hard times and a liquidator was appointed. If Salomon's debenture was valid he was as a secured creditor entitled to be paid before the unsecured trade creditors. The assets were sufficient to pay off the debentures but in that event the trade creditors would receive nothing. The unsecured creditors claimed all the remaining assets on the ground that the company was a mere alias or agent for Salomon. *Held* – The company was a separate and distinct person. The debentures were perfectly valid, and Salomon was entitled to the remaining assets in payment of the secured debentures held by him.

Comment

There was no fraud upon creditors or shareholders. The creditors of the old business had been paid off. The unsecured creditors concerned in this case were creditors of the new company. The House of Lords took the view that they must be deemed to know the risk they were taking if the company went into liquidation with insufficient funds. The members who had fully-paid shares could not be required to pay more. Any profit which Mr Salomon might have made as a promoter selling his business to the company, and in fact the price of some of the assets was fixed prior to sale at figures exceeding their balance sheet value by some £8,000, was fully disclosed and approved by the shareholders, i.e. his family.

Macaura *v* Northern Assurance Co Ltd [1925] AC 619

Macaura was the owner of a timber estate in County Tyrone and he formed an estate company and sold the timber to it for £42,000. The purchase money was paid by the issue to Macaura and his nominees of 42,000 fully-paid shares of £1 each. No other shares were issued. He also financed the company and was an unsecured creditor for £19,000, its other debts being trifling. Macaura effected an insurance policy on the timber in his own name, and not in that of the company or as agent for the company, and on 23 February 1922 most of the timber was destroyed by fire. Macaura claimed under his policies, but he was *held* not to have an insurable interest. He could only be insuring either as a creditor or as a shareholder of the company, and neither a simple creditor nor a shareholder has an insurable interest in a particular asset which the company holds, since the company is an independent entity.

Comment

Unlike a shareholder, a debenture holder can insure the property of the company on which his debenture is secured (*Westminster Fire Office* v *Glasgow Provident Investment Society* (1888) 13 App Cas 699). The difference in the debenture holder's position is justifiable since as a secured creditor he has an interest by way of a charge on the company's property which, of course, the shareholder does not have.

Lee (Catherine) *v* Lee's Air Farming Ltd [1960] 3 All ER 420

In 1954 the appellant's husband formed the respondent company which carried on the business of crop spraying from the air. In March 1956, Mr Lee was killed while piloting an aircraft during the course of top-soil dressing, and Mrs Lee claimed compensation from the company, as the employer of her husband, under the New Zealand Workers' Compensation

Act 1922. Since Mr Lee owned 2,999 of the company's 3,000 £1 shares and since he was its governing director, the question arose as to whether the relationship of employer and employee could exist between the company and him. One of his first acts as governing director had been to appoint himself the only pilot of the company at a salary arranged by himself. *Held* – Mrs Lee was entitled to compensation because her husband was employed by the company in the sense required by the Act of 1922, and the decision in *Salomon* v *Salomon & Co* was applied.

Comment

(i) In *AG's Reference* (*No 2 of 1982*) [1984] 2 All ER 216 the Court of Appeal held that two directors who were also shareholders of several companies were capable of stealing from those companies. Money from the companies, which had raised large loans from various institutions, had been used, it was alleged, to support the extravagant lifestyle of the directors and their wives. There had, it was alleged, been a spending of the company's money in hotels and restaurants and on cars, yachts, and house improvements, silver and antiques. The effect on creditors was obviously uppermost in the mind of the court, which felt that a criminal sanction was needed. By applying the rule of corporate personality the directors could, as a matter of law, be liable for stealing from a company which they owned.

(ii) This case has been distinguished in employment/insolvency law. When a company becomes insolvent, directors, who are regarded for many purposes as employees, i.e. the executive directors such as the finance director, are preferential creditors for salary due up to defined limits. These will be discussed in later chapters on company charges and insolvency. If the insolvent company cannot meet these payments, there may be a claim through the DTI, which in turn will try to recoup any payments made from the company. However, where the director concerned is also a controlling shareholder, the Employment Appeal Tribunal has refused to support claims on the DTI. *Lee*'s case has been distinguished because claims on the DTI are met from public funds whereas in *Lee*'s case the funds were supplied by the company's insurers (see *Buchan* v *Secretary of State for Trade and Industry* (1997) 565 IRLB 2). The tribunal approach is based upon the fact that the definition of an employee still requires an element of employer control which is not present where the worker in effect controls himself. However, in *Fleming* v *Secretary of State for Trade and Industry* (1998) 588 IRLB 10 the Scottish Court of Session rejected the view expressed in *Buchan* that a controlling shareholder/director could *never as a matter of law* be an employee. However, the director's claim in *Fleming* was turned down on the facts. He worked alongside the employees but was a majority shareholder and had guaranteed the company's debts. The *Fleming* approach was also approved by the Employment Appeal Tribunal in *Secretary of State for Trade and Industry* v *Bottrill* [1998] IRLR 120 where Morison J said that the reasoning in *Buchan* was 'unsound'. The decision of the EAT was affirmed by the Court of Appeal in *Secretary of State for Trade and Industry* v *Bottrill* (1999) 615 IRLB 12. In *Connolly* v *Sellers Arenascene Ltd* (2000) 633 IRLB 15 the EAT ruled that the controlling shareholder of a company could be an employee. He had a contract of employment with the company. The contract was not a sham and he had been treated and rewarded as an employee.

It seems then from the case law that a director/controlling shareholder will be regarded as an employee where there is a written contract of employment and all the usual hallmarks of employment are present. Certainly the original, almost blanket, ban on controlling shareholder/directors as employees has been much eroded.

(iii) The courts continue to be willing to draw aside the corporate veil where the circumstances warrant it. Thus in *Secretary of State for Trade and Industry* v *Backhouse* [2001] *The Times*, 23 February, Mr Backhouse was ordered to pay the costs of the Secretary of State in connection with a winding-up petition presented by him against North West Holdings plc, a company controlled by Mr Backhouse. It appeared that Mr Backhouse had caused the company to defend the petition not in the interests of the company but in order to protect his own personal reputation. His personal business affairs were bound up with those of the company and money the company earned had been treated as if it belonged to Mr Backhouse. The court drew aside the corporate veil so as to make the company's liability to pay costs that of Mr Backhouse personally. The court would obviously bear in mind that if the company was required to pay the costs, they would in effect be paid by the company's creditors who would be denied access to the funds required to pay them.

Again, in *Trustor AB* v *Smallbone* [2001] *The Times*, 30 March, Mr Smallbone, a director of Trustor AB, opened a bank account in London for the company and without the approval of the board paid money belonging to Trustor AB from its account in Sweden to the London account. Mr Smallbone then paid £38 million from Trustor AB's account in London to the account of a company called Introcom (International) Ltd that he controlled. When this was discovered by the members of the board of Trustor AB, they caused the company to claim the funds back from Introcom and also claimed that Mr Smallbone should be regarded as having received the money personally so that he was liable to repay the money personally if Introcom did not. The High Court ruled that the corporate veil could be drawn aside in this case to make Mr Smallbone personally liable.

On the other hand, the Court of Appeal refused to draw aside the veil in *Ord* v *Belhaven Pubs Ltd* [1998] 2 BCLC 447. The Ords purchased a 20-year lease of a pub, the Fox Inn. Belhaven Pubs Ltd owned the freehold and was the landlord. The Ords later alleged misrepresentation by Belhaven as to the turnover and profitability of the Fox Inn. They wished to make a claim. However, the holding company of the group in which Belhaven was a subsidiary carried out a reconstruction of the group, leaving Belhaven with only the Fox Inn as an asset. Belhaven ceased trading. The Ords wanted to claim against Ascot Holdings as the true owner (they said) of the Belhaven business. The Court of Appeal refused to draw aside the Belhaven veil and the Ords were unable to make Ascot a defendant. The reconstruction was genuine, ruled the Court of Appeal. There was no justification for ignoring the *Salomon* principle.

Corporations aggregate may be further divided by the method of their creation as follows.

1 Chartered companies

A chartered company is formed by grant of a charter by the Crown operating under either prerogative powers or special statutory powers. The procedure for the formation of such a company is for the promoters to petition the Privy Council for the grant of a charter. The petition is addressed to the Lord President and asks for the grant, a draft of the charter being attached to the petition.

Charters are used to incorporate learned societies, professional bodies such as the Institute of Chartered Accountants in England and Wales, the Association of Chartered

Certified Accountants, the Chartered Institute of Management Accountants, the Institute of Chartered Secretaries and Administrators, the BBC, public schools, and colleges of universities.

This form of incorporation is not now used by trading concerns, for whom registration is a better method, but some trading companies still operate under charters, one of the better known in recent times being P & O, the ferry company which was incorporated as the Peninsular & Oriental Steam Navigation Company by Royal Charter in 1840.

It is possible to have a *corporation by prescription*, and this occurs where it is presumed that a charter was granted but it has been lost. The City of London is a corporation by prescription.

A chartered company can have any number of members but not less than two. There is generally no personal liability in the members unless the charter otherwise provides. The creditors must rely on the company's assets.

The articles of the charter usually set out procedures for surrendering it to the Crown on a winding-up. This includes the necessary meetings of members and the majorities required.

2 Statutory companies

Such companies are formed by special Act of Parliament. This method of company formation was formerly used for public utilities such as electricity, gas, water and railways, because these undertakings need special powers, e.g. for the compulsory acquisition of land, and these powers can only be conferred by legislation. Further, such undertakings initially needed a pipeline monopoly in the area in which they operated pipelines. It would have been intolerable to have, say, ten gas companies supplying gas in one area through separate pipelines.

To ensure that there was some uniformity in the regulations controlling these companies, various public general Acts, called *Clauses Acts*, e.g. the Companies Clauses Acts 1845–89, were passed containing general corporate powers and duties. These were deemed to be incorporated in the Private Act setting up a company, unless the Act provided to the contrary.

The public utilities were then nationalised by public Acts under which their functions were taken over by public corporations. In more recent times these public corporations have been replaced, on privatisation, by registered companies under the public limited company (plc) mode, e.g. British Gas. The privatisation legislation in general continues the utilities' powers of compulsory purchase but they are no longer entirely protected from competition.

It should be mentioned that various other organisations owe their existence to statute; these include friendly societies, building societies, and industrial and provident societies (co-operative societies). These are not our concern and will not be dealt with.

3 Registered companies: generally

Such companies are either formed under the Companies Act 1985 or were formed under previous Acts. In either case they are governed by the Companies Act 1985 (as amended) and relevant case law, except that the articles of association of the company, if based on *Table A*, are those of *Table A* in the Act under which it was formed. Thus a company formed under the Companies Act 1948 is governed by *Table A*, appearing in that Act as the First Schedule to it. Such a company will have had to amend its articles if it wishes to take advantage of more recent legislation since, e.g. *Table A* to the 1948 Act forbids a company from buying its own shares, whereas the 1985 Act permits it subject to certain conditions explained in Chapter 7. The first Act allowing the registration of companies was the Joint Stock Companies Act of 1844, though they were not allowed limited liability until the Limited Liability Act of 1855.

4 Registered companies: community interest companies

The Companies (Audit, Investigations and Community Enterprise) Act 2004 establishes the community interest company for use by social enterprises which wish to operate through the corporate structure. Part 2 also provides for a Regulator of Community Interest Companies whose major role will be to maintain public confidence in this kind of company. The CIC is intended for use by enterprises that do not distribute profits in areas such as childcare, social housing, leisure and community transport and which do not wish to use the form of charitable organisations.

CICs are subject to the general framework of company law but are a new variant of existing forms of registered company. They may be companies limited by guarantee or companies limited by share capital and existing companies with these forms of limitation of liability are able to become CICs. New CICs are registered with the Registrar of Companies in the usual way and are subject to regulatory constraints and powers of registered status. They are overseen by the Department of Trade and Industry's Companies Investigation Branch.

Distinguishing features of a CIC are as follows:

- It must satisfy a community interest test to confirm that it will pursue purposes that are beneficial to the community and will not benefit an unduly restricted group. The test is wider and simpler than the charitable company test, which is public benefit. It is whether a reasonable person would consider the activities of the CIC to be beneficial to the community.
- Some companies, such as political party organisations, may be excluded from CIC status by regulations.
- CICs will not be allowed charitable status even where their objects are all charitable. However, charities and all other organisations except political parties may set up CICs as subsidiaries.
- CICs must produce an annual community interest company report giving key information relevant to CIC status, such as what the CIC has done during the year to benefit the community. The remuneration of the directors must also be shown.
- CICs will have an asset lock, i.e. they will ordinarily be prohibited from distributing any profits made to their members. CICs limited by shares have the option of issuing 'investor shares' that pay a dividend but subject to a financial cap.
- On winding-up residual assets are not distributable to members. They will pass to another suitable organisation with restrictions on profit distribution, e.g. another CIC or a charity.
- The Regulator approves applications for CIC status, receives the annual report and polices the CIC including the asset lock, in liaison with Companies House.

Since the concern of this text is with registered commercial companies the CIC will not be considered further.

CLASSIFICATION OF REGISTERED COMPANIES

Public companies

Section 1(3) defines a public company as a company limited by shares or by guarantee with a *share capital* whose memorandum states that the company is a public company. Two persons are required to form a public company, which must also have two directors. The name of a public company must end with the words 'public limited company', or the Welsh equivalent if the registered office is situated in Wales. The abbreviation plc may be used and the equivalent in Welsh may be given where the registered office is to be in Wales.

If the company is to be a public company, the authorised capital must be at least £50,000, or such other sum as the Secretary of State for Trade and Industry may, in the future by statutory instrument, specify instead. The certificate of incorporation of a public company states that it is and is conclusive evidence that the Acts have been complied with and that the company is a public company.

Under s 117 a public company formed as such cannot commence business or borrow money unless the Registrar has issued a s 117 certificate, which private companies do not require. The certificate is issued if the company's allotted share capital is at least £50,000 and not less than one-quarter of the nominal value of each issued share and the whole of any premium has been received by the company whether in cash or otherwise. A share allotted under an employees' share scheme cannot be taken into account in determining the company's allotted share capital unless it is paid up as to one-quarter of the nominal value and the whole of any premium on the share.

In order to show the extent to which the company's starting capital might be watered down, the obtaining of a s 117 certificate requires disclosure to the Registrar of the amount of preliminary expenses (including the cost of allotting shares) and by whom these were paid or are payable because if not by the company such persons will normally require reimbursement and the benefits given or intended to be given to the company's promoters.

The s 117 certificate is conclusive evidence that the company is entitled to do business and exercise any borrowing powers. It is unusual for a company to incorporate as a public company. It is more common to incorporate as a private company and go public at a later stage, e.g. when the business has expanded sufficiently to benefit from going to the market so that the public can subscribe for its shares. This obviates the need for a s 117 certificate in most cases.

In order to have evidence that the company's capital is as required by the 1985 Act, s 117 requires a statutory declaration to that effect to be submitted to Companies House signed by a director or secretary of the company. A false statement in the declaration can lead to prosecution and a fine or imprisonment for perjury.

The Companies Act 1986 (Electronic Communications) Order 2000 (The Electronic Communications Order), made under the Electronic Communications Act 2000, allows the Registrar to accept electronic statements as a substitute for the paper declaration. There are penalties under the order for making false statements.

Private companies: generally

These are intended for the smaller business and may be formed by two or more persons.

However, the EC Twelfth Company Law Directive on single-member private companies was adopted by the European Communities Council in 1989. UK regulations (SI 1992/1699) were made implementing the Directive from 15 July 1992. From that date a private company limited by shares or guarantee may be formed with only one member or allow its membership to fall to one (see below). The management requirement is only one director though more can be appointed if required. A private company is a company which is not a public company. There are no restrictions on the right to transfer the shares of the company or on the number of its members unless the articles contain such restrictions.

The Financial Services and Markets Act 2000 (Official Listing of Securities) Regulations 2001 (SI 2001/2956) prescribe bodies whose securities cannot be admitted to listing on the Stock Exchange as including private companies. The effect is to prevent private companies from offering their shares to the public. A private purchaser must be found. The previous prohibition in the Financial Services Act 1986 is repealed.

The single-member private limited company

We have noted the regulations which permit single-member private limited liability companies. The regulations also amend relevant parts of company legislation to accommodate such companies. It is now no longer necessary to have an 'artificial' member, who exists in many private companies which in fact have a sole proprietor but where, e.g., a spouse holds a nominee share to fulfil the previous two-member requirement.

The same is true of subsidiaries whether trading or dormant where someone such as the group secretary or a separate nominee company has in the past had to hold a share or shares in the subsidiary, normally under a declaration of trust and a blank transfer form in favour of the parent company so that the shareholding can be recalled from the nominee at any time.

A further useful application is that where one shareholder in a two-member company dies, the remaining shareholder can seek to acquire the deceased's shares from the personal representatives and covert the company into a single-member private company.

Registration of single-member companies

The documents which are sent to Companies House are the same as those required for multi-member companies. One subscriber to the memorandum is required who must take at least one share where there is a share capital so that the minimum share capital of the company is £1, and not £2 as in the case of multi-member companies. Other members can be added in future if desired. The necessary amendments to company legislation are considered below but it should be noted at this stage that there is no amendment to s 283 so that, although the sole member can be the sole director under s 282, he cannot act also as the company secretary. Therefore, a single-member company must have at least two officers, i.e. a director (A) and a secretary (B).

Conversion to single-member status

There are no re-registration requirements. Conversion is achieved by transferring the nominee holding to the then sole proprietor. No resolutions of the company are required and there are no filing requirements at Companies House. However, the regulations add a new s 352A to the 1985 Act, under which, when the number of members falls to one, a statement that this is the case must be entered on the Register of Members at the side of the name and address of the sole member, together with the date on which this occurred. No special form of words is given but a statement saying 'The company became a single-member company on . . . (date–month–year)' would appear to suffice. If the membership increases to two or more, then when that happens, a statement that the company has ceased to have only one member must be entered in the Register of Members alongside the name and address of the person who was formerly the sole member. The date when this occurred is also required. A statement saying 'The company ceased to be a single-member company on . . . (date–month–year)' would suffice. A default fine is imposed on the company and its officers in default if the relevant statement is not made.

Accounts and audit

The requirements are no different from those applying to other private companies.

Meetings of the single-member company

The regulations add a new s 370A to the 1985 Act. This provides that notwithstanding any provision to the contrary in the articles (so that no changes in the articles are required) one member present in person or by proxy shall be a quorum. New s 382B is also added and this provides that if the sole member takes any decision which could have been taken in general meeting he shall (unless it is a written resolution) provide the company with a written record of it and although it would seem desirable for the sole member to sign it in case of dispute there is no requirement of signature in the regulations. New s 370A is not a significant change since all the formalities of calling and holding a meeting will have to be gone through. However, s 382B is significant in that it allows the sole member to conduct business informally without notice or formal minutes.

Filing requirements still apply when, for example, the articles are altered informally, and an annual general meeting must still be held unless the company has opted out of this requirement by elective resolution. Where this has been done and the company has also dispensed by elective resolution with the requirement to lay its accounts and reports before a general meeting, it will mean that no member meetings will be required, although board meetings and board resolutions are still required. Even here, however, subject to the articles, the written resolution procedure for directors provided for by *Reg* 93 of *Table A* to the 1985 Act may be used.

Single-member companies may conduct business by written resolution. However, in multi-member companies written resolutions cannot be used to remove a director or auditor from office. In single-member companies the s 382B procedure would seem to be available. Removal of a non-member director or the auditor without a meeting and without receiving representations from them could be achieved in that way, although the regulations are silent on this.

Contracts with a sole member who is also a director

The regulations add a new s 322B to the 1985 Act. This provides that the terms of a contract with a sole member/director must either be set out in a written memorandum or be made the subject of a report to the next available board meeting and be recorded in the minutes.

This provision does not apply if the contract is in writing or if it is entered into in the ordinary course of business, as where the company buys raw materials from the sole member/director.

Other main changes in company legislation

Section 24 provides that when the membership falls to one the sole member may in certain circumstances become liable for its debts as we shall see later in this chapter. It is also a ground for compulsory winding-up of the company under the Insolvency Act 1986, s 122(1)(e). The regulations make clear that these sections do not apply to *any* private company but only to public companies.

The articles of single-member companies

Questions have been raised as to the need for special articles for these companies. Regulation 2 of the single-member company regulations provides that any enactment shall (in the absence of any express provision to the contrary) apply with such modifications as may be necessary in relation to a single-member company. The word 'enactment' covers statutory instruments such as *Table A* to the 1985 Act. If, therefore, *Table A* carries conflicts with the company's structure as a single-member company, it will be read to fit the single-member status. However, this would not affect any express provision in the company's special articles as where it had not adopted *Table A* though, as we have seen, s 370A specifically overrides provisions in special articles by allowing a quorum of one for general meetings. Therefore, any special articles should be reviewed and changed if required to suit single-member status.

Death of the sole member

If a sole member/director dies, there is no board to approve the transfer of his or her shares under the terms of the will or on intestacy. The company is then in effect paralysed, being without a board or shareholders. The articles should therefore be altered so as to allow, e.g., the company secretary to authorise a transfer or allow the personal representatives of the deceased member to appoint a director if the company has none. The director could then approve the transfer and the business of the company could proceed.

There is also a common law rule that the directors must actively refuse a transfer within a reasonable time. Under *Reg* 25 and s 183 any power of veto vested in the directors must be exercised within two months after the lodging of the transfer and after that time the court can compel the registration of the transfer, as is further described in Chapter 11. Nevertheless, it is better that the articles address this matter.

Small and medium-sized companies

Private companies are further subdivided by ss 246–249, which introduce the accounting exemptions. They give the benefit of confidentiality of information but involve the preparation of two sets of accounts – one for members and one for the Registrar of Companies. These exemptions then draw a distinction between the reporting requirements in regard to the accounts which small or medium-sized companies prepare for their members and those which they file with the Registrar of Companies. They are allowed to file what the Act refers to as 'abbreviated' and 'modified' accounts with the Registrar.

The 1985 Act permits (but does not require) a small company to dispense with the filing of its directors' report and profit and loss account and allows the filing of an abbreviated balance sheet only. Fuller particulars of the exemptions are given below, but the major result is that members of the public examining these abbreviated accounts at Companies Registration Office will have no trading information and will know nothing about directors' emoluments or the company's dividends.

A medium-sized company may modify only its profit and loss account. Apart from this, full accounts and reports must be filed.

The modifications to the profit and loss account of a medium-sized company are as follows:

- Instead of showing turnover, cost of sales, gross profit or loss and other operating income as *separate* figures they can be combined into one figure under the heading *Gross Profit or Loss*.
- In addition, the analysis of turnover and profit among different classes of business and different markets (see para 55 of Sch 4 to the 1985 Act) need not be given in the notes to the profit and loss account.

The reason for this is that the details of turnover profits and markets were sometimes used to the unreasonable disadvantage of medium-sized companies by their larger competitors. It should, however, be noted that the Companies Act 1985 (Miscellaneous Accounting Amendments) Regulations 1996 (SI 1996/189) removes this requirement for all companies where in the opinion of the directors the disclosure of such information would seriously prejudice the company's interests and the fact that it has not been disclosed is stated.

In the case of medium-sized companies, a full and unmodified set of accounts and directors' and auditors' reports must be laid before the members of the company in general meeting unless the company has passed an elective resolution (as it is called) dispensing with the need to do this. The full accounts and reports will then be sent to the members, though any member, or the company's auditor, is given the right to require the accounts and reports to be laid before a general meeting of members.

It may be taken as a general view that there is in many cases little benefit in filing abbreviated accounts for medium-sized companies. Unless there are special reasons for not disclosing details of turnover and cost of sales, the cost of preparing such accounts may outweigh the benefits.

Summary of abbreviations applicable

The following abbreviations are applicable where the accounts of small and medium companies are filed at Companies House.

	Directors' report	*Profit and loss a/c*	*Balance sheet*	*Cash flow statement*	*Notes to the accounts*	*Auditors' report*
Small	Not required	Not required	Required with special directors' statement	Not required	Limited information only	Special report (unless audit exempt)
Medium	Required in full	Required but may start at 'Gross Profit'	Required with special directors' statement	Required	All except analysis of turnover and profit	Special report

Note: Companies that are audit exempt do not need any form of audit or accountants' report, though exempt charitable companies must file a copy of the statutory accountants' report (see p 18).

Small company shorter form financial statements

In summary the position is as follows:

- In 1992 the government issued SI 1992/2452 which *applies to small but not medium-sized companies*. Under the 1992 regulations small companies can opt to send to shareholders a shorter form of directors' report and accounts. This exemption is distinct from and additional to the facility to file abbreviated accounts at Companies House.
- The 1992 provisions were then incorporated in the Companies Act 1985 (Accounts of Small and Medium-Sized Companies and Minor Accounting (Amendments) Regulations 1997 (SI 1997/220). These contain the current law.
- The expression 'small company' as defined for the purposes of the abbreviated accounts rules applies so that a plc is not included.
- The shorter form of directors' report and accounts is a balance sheet with fewer sub-headings and fewer notes to the accounts and a shorter form of directors' report.
- Certain of the exemptions may be out of line with particular SSAPs (Statements of Standard Accounting Practice) but, as will be appreciated, the Foreword to the latest edition of the Standards gives permission for departure. Also, the impact of the Financial Reporting Standard for Smaller Entities must be considered (see below).

Financial Reporting Standard for Smaller Entities

The Accounting Standards Board (see now the Financial Reporting Council) decided to free small companies from the burden of complying with many of the accounting standards. By conforming to the Financial Reporting Standard for Smaller Entities (FRSSE) such companies will be able to ignore other accounting standards. They may choose not to adopt it, in which case they remain subject to the full range of standards and abstracts.

There is no general change to a small company's abbreviated accounts but the requirement to disclose auditors' remuneration (if any) in the abbreviated accounts is withdrawn. The directors' report to which the members are entitled (but which need not be filed) is also shortened by removing the requirement to give information regarding fair review of the business, amount to be paid as dividend and amount to be carried to reserves, asset values, insurance effected for officers or for auditors (if any), Sch 7, para 6 (miscellaneous disclosures), health and safety and employee involvement. The 1992 regulations allow translation of the amounts in the accounts into ECUs either in the same accounts or in a separate copy.

As in the case of a medium company, the accounts and reports will be laid before a meeting of members unless the company has opted out of this requirement by elective resolution and even if it has a member or the auditor has a right to require the accounts and reports to be laid before a general meeting of members. Further details appear in Chapter 19.

Standard accounting formats

The DTI is considering the provision of standard form accounts for small companies. The use of the standard form will be an option for such companies.

Small and medium-sized companies: definitions

(a) Small companies

A small company is one which has been within the limits of *two* of the following thresholds since incorporation or, if not within the limits at incorporation, then for the current financial year and the one before:

Turnover £5.6 million or less
Balance sheet total (i.e. total assets) £2.8 million or less
Employees 50 (average) or less.

(b) Medium companies

A medium company is one which has been within the limits of *two* of the following thresholds since incorporation or, if not within the limits at incorporation, then for the current financial year and the one before:

Turnover £22.8 million or less
Balance sheet total (i.e. total assets) £11.4 million or less
Employees 250 (average) or less.

As regards both small and medium companies, the employee average is to be ascertained on a monthly basis and not a weekly basis as it was initially. The average is derived by dividing the sum of the number of employees employed under contracts of service in each month by the number of months in the financial year.

The authority for the above thresholds is the Companies Act 1985 (Accounts of Small and Medium-Sized Enterprises and Audit Exemption) (Amendment) Regulations 2004 (SI 2004/16).

Subsequent failure to qualify

If a company ceases to satisfy the exemption requirements for two successive years, it must file full accounts for the second year.

Exemptions inapplicable: small and medium companies

The exemptions do not apply if the company concerned is or at any time during its financial year was:

(i) a public company (whether listed or unlisted),
(ii) a banking or insurance company,
(iii) an organisation authorised to conduct investment business under the Financial Services and Markets Act 2000,
(iv) a member of an 'ineligible group', i.e. a group containing any of the companies in (i) to (iii) above.

Under s 247A a company which has subsidiaries, i.e. it is a holding or parent company, although *it* satisfies the definition of a small or medium company, cannot be treated as one unless the group as a whole is small or medium within the definitions given below. Thus if the parent company qualifies as a small company but the group is medium-sized, the parent would only be entitled to the exemptions available to a medium-sized company when preparing individual accounts.

Small and medium-sized groups

This is a further division into small and medium groups of private companies. Normally, where a company, say A Ltd, is the holding (or parent) company of B Ltd, e.g. because A Ltd owns more than half of the voting share capital of B Ltd – generally more than half of B Ltd's ordinary shares – then A Ltd and B Ltd have to prepare individual accounts. However, A Ltd has an extra duty which is to prepare group accounts (or consolidated accounts) showing, for the benefit of outsiders who might invest in or do business with either company, the financial position of A Ltd and B Ltd together in one set of financial statements.

However, a parent company, such as A Ltd, need not prepare group accounts for a financial year in relation to which the group headed by that company qualifies as a small or medium group and is not an ineligible group. This is a further example of the deregulation of private companies running the smaller business.

The qualifying conditions are met by a group which satisfies two or more of the following thresholds (a) in the parent company's first financial year as a parent company, and (b) in its second or subsequent financial year as a parent company in that year and the preceding year. If it fails to satisfy the exemption requirements for two successive years, it must prepare group accounts in the second year. The thresholds under SI 2004/16 are:

	Small	*Medium*
Aggregate turnover	£5.6m (net) or less	£22.8m (net) or less
	or	*or*
	£6.72m (gross) or less	£27.36m (gross) or less
Aggregate balance sheet total	£2.8m (net) or less	£11.4m (net) or less
	or	*or*
	£3.36m (gross) or less	£13.68m (gross) or less
Number of employees	50 (average) or less	250 (average) or less

A group can choose to meet the gross or net formula for any item; thus, say, turnover may be gross and balance sheet total net. The net formula is calculated after adjustments are made in the consolidation of the accounts, e.g. elimination of inter-company balances. Thus if B Ltd owes A Ltd £20,000, this £20,000 will be shown as an asset in A Ltd's individual balance sheet and as a liability in the individual balance sheet of B Ltd but not at all in the group balance sheet. The transaction is cancelled out on consolidation because it is of no interest to outsiders. Where there are extensive inter-company balances, it may be difficult for the group to meet the gross formula but the exemptions apply if the net formula is complied with.

In the case of a small or medium group, the average number of persons that the company employs can now be calculated on a monthly average basis instead of a weekly average as before.

Where a parent company is not exempt and is therefore required to prepare group accounts, it is not required to file a profit and loss account with the annual accounts (s 230(3)). However, where a small or medium company is exempt but chooses *voluntarily* to prepare group accounts, it must file a profit and loss account. It is not able to take advantage of the exemption because it is not 'required' to prepare group accounts as s 230 states.

Exemptions inapplicable

A group is ineligible if any of the companies in it is a plc (listed or unlisted) or a company carrying on an insurance market activity or an authorised person under the Financial Services and Markets Act 2000. A special auditors' report is required for accounts delivered to the Registrar when small and medium companies and groups take advantage of the exemptions referred to above. The purpose of the report is to say that the company concerned is entitled to them. This report is not required where the company has taken advantage of the audit exemption referred to below.

Audit exemption

The Companies Act 1985 (Accounts of Small and Medium-Sized Enterprises and Audit Exemption) (Amendment) Regulations 2004 (SI 2004/16) currently apply. The accounts aspect came into force in relation to financial years ending on or after 30 January 2004. The audit thresholds took effect in relation to financial years ending on or after 30 March 2004.

Criteria for exemption

The following conditions must apply in respect of the financial year:

- The company must **qualify as a small company** though even where it does it need not take advantage of the exemption and can have an audit.
- If the company **is a charity** then its gross income from all sources during the financial year must not be more than £90,000 and its balance sheet total (assets) must not be more than £1.4 million.
- For companies that are **not charities** then:

  (*a*) turnover must not be more than £5.6 million, and
  (*b*) the balance sheet total (assets) must not be more than £2.8 million.

- The company must not at any time during the financial year have been:
  (*a*) a public company (listed or unlisted);
  (*b*) a parent or a subsidiary undertaking unless a member of a small group (see below) or where the subsidiary is dormant (s 249A(1A), (1B) and (1C));
  (*c*) a company carrying on an insurance market activity;
  (*d*) an authorised person or appointed representative under the Financial Services and Markets Act 2000;
  (*e*) a trade union special registered body under the Trade Union and Labour Relations (Consolidation) Act 1992, s 117(1), which are treated as corporate entities.

Members holding 10 per cent or more of the issued share capital (or any class thereof) may require the company to have an audit for the financial year by depositing a written notice at the company's registered office not later than one month before the year end.

Audit exemption and small groups

A parent or non-dormant subsidiary company can claim exemption from audit if the group of which it is a member satisfies all of the following conditions throughout the financial year into which the period of group membership falls (s 249B (1B) and (1C)):

- the group qualifies as a small group for the purposes of s 249 and is not at the time of preparing accounts or at any time in the financial year an ineligible group (see above);
- the group's aggregate turnover in that year is not more than £5.6 million net (or £6.72 million gross);
- the group's aggregate balance sheet total for that year is not more than £2.8 million net (or £3.36 million gross); and
- in the case of groups that are charities the group's turnover must not exceed £350,000 net or £420,000 gross.

Charities: an exemption via the accountant's report

A company that is a charity and meets all the conditions set out below in the financial year is exempt from audit of its accounts provided the directors obtain an accountant's report in regard to the company's individual accounts for the year to be made to the members. The exemption is not available where the company is a public company. The conditions are:

- the company must qualify as a small company;
- its gross income in the financial year must be more than £90,000 but not more than £250,000;
- its balance sheet total (assets) must not be more than £1.4 million.

Individual charitable companies that exceed the above threshold of £250,000 must have an audit. An audit exemption report which is obviously not a full audit must be prepared by an accountant qualified as the regulations require. All the major accountancy bodies are included, as are members of the Institute of Chartered Secretaries and Administrators. Small charitable companies that are parent or subsidiary companies may claim exemption from audit if they are members of a small group meeting the requirements set out in the preceeding section.

Effect on dormant companies

The 1997 regulations make clear that exemption from audit is available to dormant companies under the dormant company provisions (see below) or the audit exemption procedure. The audit exemption provisions had the advantage that they do not require a special or written resolution of the members.

However, *Reg* 3 of the Companies Act 1985 (Audit Exemption) (Amendment) Regulations 2000 (SI 2000/1430) inserts s 249AA making provision for dormant companies under which they are no longer required to pass a special resolution in order to qualify for exemption from audit. Instead they automatically qualify by being dormant and so long as 10 per cent of the members do not request an audit.

Disclosure in annual report and accounts

The balance sheet of a company taking advantage of the relevant audit exemptions must include a statement to the effect that:

- the company is eligible to claim the exemption;
- no notice has been deposited at the company's registered office by members holding 10 per cent or more of the issued capital (or a class thereof) requiring that the company shall have an audit for the financial year; and
- the directors acknowledge their responsibilities for:

  (*a*) ensuring that the company keeps proper accounting records; and
  (*b*) preparing accounts which give a true and fair view.

The statement must appear on the face of the balance sheet above the signature required by s 233, i.e. by a director of the company on behalf of the board. The name of the signatory must also be stated.

Format of accounts

Even if the accounts are not audited they should comply with the provisions of the Companies Act 1985. The format should follow the relevant Schedules, i.e. Companies Act 1985, ss 246 and 246A and Sch 8.

References to audit in the articles

Companies with articles based on the 1985 version of *Table A* are unlikely to have problems in dispensing with the audit requirement since the 1985 version does not impose an obligation to appoint auditors. Article 130 of *Table A* to the 1948 Act does and companies with that or a similar article should review the contents of their articles to see that they are not precluded from implementing the audit exemption. Furthermore, Art 127 which requires that the accounts be sent to members accompanied by an auditor's report will also require amendment.

Dormant companies

When is a company dormant?

Under s 249AA a company is dormant if:

- it has been dormant since its formation; or
- it has been dormant since the end of the previous financial year; and

- it is a small company; and
- it is not required to prepare group accounts;
- during the dormant period there have been no significant accounting transactions that, by s 221, are required to be entered in the company's accounting records.

Transactions that are exempt from the above and do not prevent dormant status are transactions arising from the taking of shares in the company by a subscriber to the memorandum as a result of an undertaking in the memorandum, a fee to the Registrar of Companies on a change of name under s 28, a fee to the Registrar on the re-registration of a company under CA 1985 Pt II, e.g. limited to unlimited, a penalty under s 242A for failure to deliver accounts, or a fee for the registration of the annual return under Ch II of Pt XI.

Ineligible companies

A company cannot be regarded as dormant if it has permission under the Financial Services and Markets Act 2000 Part IV to carry on one or more regulated activities or is a person who carries on insurance market activities. A public company can qualify as a dormant company if it meets the basic s 249AA requirements and is a small company but cannot prepare small company accounts because of its public company status (see s 249AA(2)(a)) or because it is a member of an ineligible group. This means that free standing public limited companies may have dormant status. If they are members of an ineligible group because the group contains one or more plcs they may become dormant only if they are subsidiaries. Parent companies cannot be dormant because no company can be dormant under the general definition (see above) if it is required to prepare group accounts. Examples of transactions which could prevent dormant status are as follows:

- bank charges even where the account is inactive;
- payment of audit fee for the audit of the last period during which the company traded.

The problem can be solved by, say, a holding company or an individual paying the relevant fees.

Loss of exemption

The directors, or failing them the members, must appoint auditors if the company ceases to be dormant or otherwise becomes ineligible. Details of the method of appointment appear in s 388A, which should be referred to.

Form of dormant accounts

The accounts must include:

- a profit and loss account but only if the company traded in the previous period, the comparative figures being put in;
- a directors' report to include a statement that the company has not traded during the financial year. It should also state, if relevant, that a profit and loss account has not been prepared for the year;

- in place of the previous requirement on directors to make a statement on the balance sheet that the company has been dormant throughout the year, they must now make the following statements which bring them into line with the requirements on other trading audit exempt companies:

  1. For the year ended . . . the company was entitled to exemption under s 249AA(1) of the Companies Act 1985.
  2. Members have not required the company to obtain an audit of its accounts for the year in question in accordance with subsection (2) of s 249B.
  3. The directors acknowledge their responsibility for:

     (i) ensuring that the company keeps accounting records which comply with s 221; and

     (ii) preparing accounts which give a true and fair view of the state of the affairs of the company as at the end of its financial year in accordance with s 226 and which otherwise comply with the requirements of the Companies Act 1985 relating to accounts so far as applicable to the company.

Standard format for accounts

Provided the company has been dormant since it was incorporated, it may use Companies House Form DCA to file its accounts. The form which is available free is only suitable for dormant companies where the only transaction has been the issue of subscribers' shares and the company is not a subsidiary.

A dormant company can file abbreviated accounts in which case there is no need to file the directors' report or the comparative profit and loss account if applicable.

Articles of association

The company's articles should be referred to. *Regulations* 127 and 130 of *Table A* to the CA 1948 require the appointment of auditors unless altered by special (or written) resolution. There is no similar provision in *Table A* to the CA 1985.

Provisions of company law applicable to dormant companies

These are as follows:

(*a*) rights to receive or demand copies of accounts and reports under ss 238 and 239 continue but there is obviously no need for a non-existent auditors' report;

(*b*) it is not necessary to lay or circulate a copy of the auditors' report nor deliver a copy to the Registrar.

Dormant companies: agency arrangements

It is common in a wide variety of businesses to operate under agency arrangements where the agent company has no economic interest in the transactions but merely brings together the principal company and the third party into a contractual arrangement. Where the agency is disclosed to the third party, no entries need to be made in the agent company's accounting records and it may submit dormant company accounts. If the agency is not disclosed, the agent company should record the transactions in its records and cannot therefore submit dormant company accounts. Where the agency is disclosed, the agent company will have to submit memorandum accounts to the principal and will therefore need to record transactions but this does not give rise to entries in its own records and so it can be regarded as dormant. Financial Reporting Standard 5 applies and should be referred to.

The Companies Act 1985 (Audit Exemption) (Amendment) Regulations 2000 (SI 2000/1430) require dormant companies that act as agents to disclose this in their annual accounts. This applies also to the abbreviated accounts.

Distinctions between a public and a private company

(i) In a private company proxies may speak at meetings, as well as vote on a poll, though not on a show of hands unless the articles provide.

(ii) As we have seen, a private company need have only one director and a secretary; a public company must have at least two directors and a secretary. The secretary of a private company need not be qualified in the terms required of a secretary of a public company.

(iii) In a private company two or more directors may be appointed by a single resolution.

(iv) The statutory age limit of 70 placed upon directors does not apply to a private company, unless it is a subsidiary of a public company.

(v) *As regards registration.* The name of a public company must include 'public limited company' or 'plc'. A private limited company's name must only include 'limited' or 'Ltd'. The memorandum of a public company must state that it is. Furthermore, a public company can only commence business and borrow on the issue of a s 117 certificate by the Registrar of Companies, whereas a private company can commence business and borrow on incorporation. The minimum number of members is two for a public company but private companies may, as we have seen, be single-member.

(vi) *As regards share capital.* The minimum allotted share capital of a public company is £50,000, whereas there is no minimum capital requirement for a private company. A public company has an unrestricted right to offer shares or debentures to the public, whereas this is prohibited in the case of a private company. The pre-emption rights of the 1985 Act apply to public companies which must offer equity share capital first to existing shareholders. These provisions apply also to a private company though they may be excluded by the memorandum or articles. Where a public company has lost half or more of its share capital it must call an extraordinary general meeting, whereas this provision is not applicable to private companies. Finally, as regards a lien or charge on its own shares, this is restricted in the case of public companies (see Chapter 10). The provisions are not applicable to private companies which may take a lien or charge on their shares.

(vii) *As regards payment for shares.* In the case of public companies, any agreement under which shares are to be allotted by an undertaking to carry out work or perform services is prohibited but is allowed in the case of private companies. The subscribers to the memorandum of a public company must pay for their shares in cash, whereas in a private company payment may be in cash or some other consideration. In public companies there is a minimum payment for shares whenever issued, i.e. at least one-quarter of the nominal value plus the whole of any share premium must be paid up, but in private companies there is no minimum payment requirement. Where shares are to be paid for by a non-cash asset, public companies are required to ensure that the asset is to be transferred by contract within five years of the allotment, whereas there is no special requirement for private companies. Furthermore, public companies must have an independent accountant's report on the value of the non-cash asset used as consideration for an issue of shares. This requirement does not apply to private companies.

(viii) *Acquisition of non-cash assets.* A public company cannot validly acquire non-cash assets valued at one-tenth or more of the company's issued share capital from subscribers to the memorandum in the first two years of its existence as such unless an independent accountant's report is received and the members approve by ordinary resolution. These restrictions do not apply to private companies.

(ix) *As regards distribution of profits and assets.* Where interim accounts are used to support a proposed distribution these accounts must, in the case of a public company, be filed with the Registrar of Companies, whereas there is no filing requirement for private companies. Private companies need only fulfil the basic requirement of profits available for distribution. Public companies must also comply with the capital maintenance rule whereas private companies need not (see further Chapter 8).

(x) *As regards loans to directors, etc.* Quasi-loans and credit transactions, etc. for directors and the directors of the company's holding company are prohibited with certain exceptions in the case of public companies, as are loans, etc. to persons connected with the directors and the directors of any holding company. Quasi-loans and credit are not so restricted in private companies nor are, in general, such dealings with connected persons (see further Chapter 16).

(xi) An essential feature of more recent company legislation has been the move towards the deregulation of private companies. In particular, company legislation now provides for unanimous written resolutions of private companies which can be passed by members without the need to call or hold a meeting. Private companies may also pass what are called 'elective resolutions' to dispense with certain requirements of company law relating to the allotment of their shares; the holding of the annual general meeting; short notice of resolutions; the annual appointment of auditors and the laying of accounts and reports before a general meeting. Private companies may also be single-member and in appropriate circumstances opt out of the audit requirement. These matters are considered in more detail in appropriate parts of the text. Obviously these statutory provisions are not available to public companies.

Limited and unlimited companies

A registered company may be:

(i) *Limited by shares.* First it should be noted that limitation of liability refers to the members and not to the company itself. The liability of the company is always unlimited in the sense that it must discharge its liabilities so long as it has assets to do so.

Limitation of liability by shares may occur on formation, i.e. the company is registered as such. Where this is so the liability of each member to contribute to the capital of the company is limited to the nominal value of the shares that he has agreed to take up or, if he has agreed to take up such shares at a premium, i.e. at more than their nominal value, to the total amount agreed to be paid for such shares. Once the member has paid the company for his shares, his liability is discharged completely and he cannot be made responsible for making up the deficiencies of the company or of other shareholders. Furthermore, he has no liability whatever in respect of unissued shares. However, in the case of a small private company, the advantages of limited liability tend to be illusory, since those who give the company a significant amount of credit and bank overdraft facilities will in practice require personal guarantees from its directors and major shareholders.

(ii) *Limited by guarantee*. Formerly, companies limited by guarantee could be registered with or without a share capital. Companies limited by guarantee with a share capital may now not be registered, though, of course, companies which had registered with a share capital before the 1985 Act remain in existence. Since they cannot now have a share capital, they must of necessity be formed as private companies because the presence of a share capital is fundamental to the definition of a public company. Where there is no share capital the members have no liability unless and until the company goes into liquidation. When this happens those who are members at the time are required if necessary to contribute towards the payment of the company's debts and liabilities and the costs of winding-up in accordance with the guarantee. The amount guaranteed will be whatever sum is stated in the memorandum and it is frequently a small sum such as £100 (see *Table C* to the 1985 Act), although in some cases the agreed liability may be substantial and much depends upon the type of company.

The guarantee is not an asset of the company but a mere contingent liability of its members until winding-up. Consequently it cannot be charged by the company as a security nor can it be increased or reduced by an alteration of the memorandum or by agreement with the members or by any procedure equivalent to the increase or reduction of share capital (*Hennessy* v *National Agricultural and Industrial Development Association* [1947] IR 159).

If those who are members at the date of winding-up cannot meet their obligations under the guarantee or the debts exceed what they are liable to contribute, then the liquidator may have access to those who were members during the year prior to the commencement of the winding-up but only in respect of debts and liabilities incurred while they were members.

If a company limited by guarantee has a share capital, its members have two liabilities. They must pay the issue price of their shares, and must honour their guarantee in the event of the company being liquidated (Insolvency Act 1986, s 74(3)). There is no benefit to the company in having such a dual liability and in practice companies limited by guarantee with a share capital were not formed. The device of the guarantee company is only used where no share capital is to be issued but the members of the company wish to limit their liability to contribute towards the company's debts and liabilities. Obviously the members are not shareholders (except in some of the earlier companies) and membership will often be acquired by application. Provision is usually made in the articles for a member to resign. These companies provide a suitable organisation for professional bodies and trade associations which have not received a Royal Charter, particularly since under certain circumstances there is no need to show the word 'limited' – which denotes commerciality – as part of the name (see further Chapter 3).

Once incorporated as a guarantee company, there is no provision in company legislation for re-registration as a company limited by shares or vice versa.

It is worth noting that unless the guarantee company is an earlier one with a share capital, each member has one vote at general meetings (s 370(1) and (6)) but is not entitled to appoint a proxy to represent him (see s 372(2)). Special articles must provide for the appointment of proxies and unless they do the directors are neither required to send out proxy forms for general meetings nor to indicate in the notice that voting may be by proxy and therefore failure to do this will not invalidate proceedings at the meeting.

As regards accounts and audit, accounts must be prepared and audited, and filed at Companies House. The audit report is similar to that required for other companies but is addressed to the members, not the shareholders. The audit exemption is available as for other companies on the turnover, etc. basis.

(iii) *Unlimited.* The personal liability of members of this type of company is the reason why not many of them exist. They are sometimes formed by those who wish to keep the company's accounts away from the public gaze (see below). In addition, there are advantages in having separate corporate status and perpetual succession even though these are not accompanied by limited liability.

Unlimited companies must be private companies since a public company is by definition a company limited by shares (or by guarantee with a share capital).

Unlimited companies may be formed as such, either with or without a share capital. A share capital may be used, for example, if the company is trading and making profits, since the shares are a basis for the distribution of that profit. As regards liability, where there is a share capital, the members must, even while the company is a going concern, pay for their shares in full, and if on a liquidation this is not adequate to satisfy all the debts and liabilities of the company together with the costs of winding-up, the members must contribute rateably according to the nominal value of their shareholding. Where there is no share capital, the members contribute equally until all the debts and liabilities of the company plus the costs of winding-up are paid. In the event of any members defaulting the others are liable to make good the deficiency as much as is necessary to pay the whole of the company's liabilities and the costs of liquidation.

If the members at the time of commencement of the winding-up cannot collectively contribute enough to pay off the debts and liabilities, the liquidator can go to those who were members during the 12 months prior to winding-up, but only in respect of debts incurred while they were members.

Special features of unlimited companies

There are certain special features relating to unlimited companies. For example, an unlimited company may reduce its capital by extinguishing liability on partly paid shares or even repaying capital to the members by passing a special resolution to that effect *and the permission of the court is not required.* In addition, although an unlimited company cannot issue redeemable shares it may, if its articles permit, reduce its capital by buying back the shares of its members even from out of its capital.

These practices do not, in theory at least, reduce the funds available to creditors on a winding-up because the members are liable to pay the debts and liabilities of the company in full on winding-up. However, as regards reduction of capital by purchase of shares, if the company knew at the time of purchase that the members would not be able to meet their liabilities on winding-up, the purchase would be set aside as a fraud on the creditors (*Mitchell* v *City of Glasgow Bank* (1879) 4 App Cas 624).

It will be noted in Chapter 7 that limited companies can also purchase their own shares under the provisions of Part V, Chapter VII of the 1985 Act. However, limited company purchases are subject to the not inconsiderable restrictions of that Act. Unlimited companies are not subject to these restrictions and require only permission in the articles.

In addition, an unlimited company enjoys privacy in regard to its financial affairs because it need not deliver copies of its annual accounts and the relevant reports to the Registrar, not even abridged or modified ones, though it must prepare audited accounts for its members unless it has taken the audit exemption when unaudited accounts will suffice. The company's articles cannot override the requirement to supply accounts to members. Section 239 which requires *all* companies to supply accounts to members is not 'subject to any provision in the articles' and therefore supersedes any contrary provision in the articles.

However, the price of privacy is the unlimited liability of its members. The provision in regard to the annual accounts does not apply if the company concerned is a subsidiary or holding company of a limited company or is *potentially* under the control of two or more limited companies, including a foreign company, because of share or voting rights which they hold even though these have not been exercised in concert for the purposes of control.

European company

The EU Council (formerly the Council of Ministers) reached agreement on 20 December 2000 on the legislative framework necessary to establish a European Company Statute. The legislation came into force on 8 October 2004. Under the statute a European Company (called a Societas Europaea (SE)) will operate on a Europe-wide basis governed by Community law directly applicable in all member states. The statute provides for the creation of European companies in one of four ways:

- by merging two or more existing public companies from at least two different member states;
- by forming a holding company promoted by public or private limited companies from at least two different member states;
- by forming a subsidiary of companies from at least two member states;
- by the conversion of a public limited company which for at least two years had a subsidiary in another member state.

Each SE will be registered on the same register as national companies. Registration will be in the member state in which the SE has its administrative head office. SEs do not have to have a public quotation. The minimum capital requirement is 120,000 ECUs to enable medium-sized companies from different member states to create a SE.

The creation of a SE requires negotiations on worker involvement. If it is not possible to negotiate a satisfactory arrangement with worker representatives, a set of standard principles laid down in an annexe to the legislation will apply. Employment contracts and pensions are subject to national law in the member states where headquarters operate. The *European Public Limited Liability Company Regulations 2004* implement the above materials in the UK from 8 October 2004.

LIFTING THE CORPORATE VEIL

The principle set out in *Salomon* v *Salomon & Co Ltd* (1897), i.e. that a body corporate is a separate entity, separate that is from its members, led to the use of the phrase *the veil of incorporation*, which is said to hang between the company and its members and, in law at least, act as a screen between them.

However, the principle can cause difficulty and in a number of cases is lifted by the law so that the human and commercial reality behind the corporate personality can be taken account of. The veil may be lifted by the judiciary or by statute.

The judiciary

It is difficult to be precise about the circumstances in which a judge will lift the corporate veil. However, it may be said that the power to do so is a tactic used by the judiciary in a flexible way to counter fraud, sharp practice, oppression, and illegality.

Examples of special areas of application are as follows:

(i) *Groups of companies: the human and commercial reality of the group.* The court has on occasion lifted the veil of incorporation to allow a group of companies to be regarded as one, because in reality they were not independent either in human or commercial terms.

Re Hellenic and General Trust Ltd [1975] 3 All ER 382

A company called MIT was a wholly-owned subsidiary of Hambros Ltd and held 53 per cent of the ordinary shares of Hellenic. A scheme of arrangement was put forward under which Hambros was to acquire all the ordinary shares of Hellenic for a cash consideration of 48p per share. The ordinary shareholders including MIT met and over 80 per cent approved the scheme, MIT voting in support. However, the National Bank of Greece, which was a minority shareholder, opposed the scheme because it would be liable to meet a heavy tax burden under Greek law as a result of receipt of cash for its shares. Templeman J refused to approve the scheme on a number of grounds. However, the one which interests us here is that he ruled that there should have been a separate class meeting of ordinary shareholders excluding MIT; thus in effect regarding the holding company, Hambros, and the subsidiary, MIT, as one economic unit in the class meeting and not two independent companies with independent interests.

DHN Food Distributors *v* Tower Hamlets London Borough Council [1976] 3 All ER 462

DHN Food Distributors (DHN) was a holding company which ran its business through two wholly-owned subsidiaries, Bronze Investments Ltd (Bronze) and DHN Food Transport Ltd (Transport). The group collected food from the docks and distributed it to retail outlets. Bronze owned the premises in Bow from which the business was conducted and Transport ran the distribution side of the business. Tower Hamlets compulsorily acquired the premises in Bow for the purpose of building houses. This power of compulsory acquisition arose under the Housing Act 1957 and compensation was payable under the Land Compensation Act of 1961 under two headings: (a) the value of the land, and (b) disturbance of business.

Tower Hamlets was prepared to pay £360,000 for the value of the land but refused to pay on the second heading because DHN and Transport had no interest in the land. This was unfortunate for the group as a whole since the loss of the premises had caused all three companies to go into liquidation, it being impossible to find other suitable premises. The practical answer would have been, of course, to have conveyed the premises from Bronze to DHN when compulsory acquisition was threatened. This had not been done, although the conveyance would have been exempt from stamp duty since it would have been a transfer between associated companies. However, Lord Denning in the Court of Appeal drew aside the corporate veil and treated DHN as owners of the property whereupon Tower Hamlets became liable to pay for disturbance of business. The basis of Lord Denning's judgment was that company legislation required group accounts and to that extent recognised a group entity which he felt the judiciary should do also. Lord Denning did not feel that it was necessary to imply an agency between the holding and subsidiary company.

Comment

(i) It cannot be said from this case that there is a *general principle of group entity*. Much depends upon the circumstances of the case. Thus in *Woolfson* v *Strathclyde Regional Council* (1978) 38 P & CR 521 the House of Lords did not follow *DHN Foods* in what was a similar situation because in *Woolfson* the subsidiaries were active trading companies and not, as in *DHN Foods*, mere shells. Again, in *Multinational Gas and Petrochemical Co* v *Multinational Gas and Petrochemical Services Ltd* [1983] 2 All ER 563 the Court of Appeal held, following *Salomon*, that wholly-owned subsidiaries in a group were separate entities and not the agents of the holding company or each other in the absence of a specific agency agreement. Furthermore, in *Dimbleby & Sons Ltd* v *NUJ* [1984] 1 All ER 751, a group of companies was regarded as a series of separate entities so that the picketing of one company within the group by workers employed by another company within the group was regarded as unlawful secondary picketing for the purposes of s 17 of the Employment Act 1980. (See now s 224 of the Trade Union and Labour Relations (Consolidation) Act 1992.)

(ii) Additional examples in the group situation are to be found in *Re H and others* [1996] 2 All ER 391 where in an action by Customs and Excise to restrain defendants who had been charged with various offences of evading excise duty from dealing with assets pending trial the Court of Appeal was prepared to restrain subsidiary companies' assets, refusing to regard the companies as separate entities under the *Salomon* rule even though the evasions were alleged to have been committed by the holding company. However, in *Re Polly Peck International plc* (*in administration*) [1996] 2 All ER 433 the High Court applied the *Salomon* rule in a corporate insolvency, holding that the separate legal existence of group companies was important where the companies were creditors of the holding company and each wished to make a separate claim in the holding company's insolvency and be paid what is called a dividend on that claim.

(ii) *Groups of companies: the concept of agency.* The concept of agency has sometimes been used by the courts under which a subsidiary is regarded as the agent of its holding company, even though there is no agency agreement as such between them in regard to the transaction concerned. The effect is that transactions entered into by a subsidiary are regarded as those of the holding company for which the holding company is liable. This doctrine has been implemented for purposes of liability to tax.

Firestone Tyre & Rubber Co Ltd *v* Lewellin [1957] 1 All ER 561

An American company formed a wholly-owned subsidiary in England to manufacture and sell its brand of tyres in Europe. The American company negotiated agreements with European distributors under which the latter would place orders with the American company which the English subsidiary would carry out. In fact the distributors sent their orders to the subsidiary direct and the orders were met without any consultation with the American company. The subsidiary received the money for the tyres sold to the distributors and, after deducting its manufacturing expenses plus 5 per cent, it forwarded the balance of the money to the American company. All the directors of the subsidiary resided in England (except one who was the president of the American company) and they managed the subsidiary's affairs free from day-to-day control by the American company. *Held* – by the House of Lords – that the American company was carrying on business in England through its English subsidiary acting as its agent and it was consequently liable to pay United Kingdom tax.

Comment

(i) The principle of presumed agency, or agency in fact, of the subsidiary was used in *Smith, Stone & Knight Ltd* v *Birmingham Corporation* [1939] 4 All ER 116. Premises belonging to Smith, Stone were compulsorily acquired by the Corporation. The question to be resolved was whether the business of waste paper merchants, for which the premises were used, was carried on by Smith, Stone or by its subsidiary, Birmingham Waste Co Ltd. This was vital because an owner/occupier could get compensation, but a tenant/occupier like the waste company could not. The court decided that the waste company occupied the premises as a mere agent of Smith, Stone because, among other things, it was a wholly-owned subsidiary and the directors were the same in both companies. Smith, Stone was entitled to compensation. This case can be distinguished from *DHN Food Distributors* because, as we have seen in the *DHN* case, Lord Denning did not find it necessary to imply an agency.

(ii) The theories of the economic reality of the group and the implied agency approach have not been used to control abuses in the area of holding and subsidiary companies in regard to trade creditors. If a subsidiary is insolvent, only public and stock market opinion prevents the holding company from liquidating the subsidiary leaving its creditors' claims unsatisfied even though the group as a whole is solvent. In some cases even public and market opinion and criticism do not prevent it. The EC Ninth Directive, which has yet to be implemented, does in certain situations make the dominant company within the group liable for losses incurred by a dependent company.

(iii) *Illegality*. The courts have been prepared to draw aside the veil of incorporation in order to establish that a company was owned by nationals of an enemy country so that to do business with it would be illegal because it would be trading with the enemy.

Daimler Co Ltd *v* Continental Tyre & Rubber Co (Great Britain) Ltd
[1916] 2 AC 307

After the outbreak of war with Germany, the tyre company, which was registered in England and had its registered office there, sued the Daimler Company for money due in respect of goods supplied to Daimler before the outbreak of war. Daimler's defence was that, since the tyre company's members and officers were German, to pay the debt would be to trade with the enemy, and that therefore the claim by the tyre company should be struck out, i.e. not allowed to go to trial. Evidence showed that all the members of the tyre company save one were German. The secretary of the company, who held one share, lived in England and was a British subject. He brought the action in the name of, and on behalf of, the company. *Held* – by the House of Lords – that the action must be struck out. Although the place of registration and the situation of the registered office normally governs the company's nationality and domicile for the purposes of actions at law, the court has a jurisdiction to draw aside the corporate veil in some cases to see who the persons in control of the company's affairs are. If, as here, the persons in actual control of the company were enemy aliens, the company could be so regarded for the purposes of the law relating to trading with the enemy.

(iv) *The personal relationship company*. A breakdown in the management of the company or the complete exclusion of a member director from participation in management have been redressed by winding up the company on the just and equitable ground by regarding the company as in fact, if not in form, a partnership.

Ebrahimi *v* Westbourne Galleries [1972] 2 All ER 492

Since 1945 Mr Ebrahimi and Mr Nazar had carried on a partnership which dealt in Persian and other carpets. They shared equally the management and profits. In 1958 they formed a private company carrying on the same business and were appointed its first directors. Soon after the company's formation, Mr George Nazar, Mr Nazar's son, was made a third director. By reason of their shareholdings, Mr Nazar and George had the majority of votes at general meetings. The company made good profits, all of which were distributed as directors' remuneration and no dividend was ever paid. In 1969 Mr Ebrahimi was removed from the position of director by a resolution at a general meeting in pursuance of what is now s 303. Mr Ebrahimi presented a petition seeking an order under s 210 of the Companies Act 1948 (see now s 459, 1985 Act) that Mr Nazar and George should purchase his shares or, alternatively, an order under what is now s 122(1)(g) of the Insolvency Act 1986 that the company be wound up. At first instance Plowman J refused the order under s 210 because the oppression alleged was against Mr Ebrahimi in his capacity as director and not that as member. However, the petition for a compulsory winding-up was granted because, in the opinion of Plowman J, it was just and equitable that the company should be wound up. The Court of Appeal affirmed the decision of Plowman J under s 210 but dismissed the petition for a compulsory winding-up, regarding it as an unjustifiable innovation in the company situation. On further appeal, the House of Lords reversed the Court of Appeal and restored the decision of Plowman J that an order for winding-up should be made. The major points arising from the case are as follows:

(*a*) The majority shareholders, Mr Nazar and George, had made use of their undisputed right under what is now s 303 to remove a director, namely Mr Ebrahimi. Could such use of a statutory right be a ground for making a compulsory winding-up order under what is now s 122(1)(g) of the Insolvency Act 1986? In other words, could the exercise of a legal right be regarded as contravening the rules of equity which are the basis of what is now s 122(1)(g)?

(*b*) The House of Lords answered these questions in the affirmative, at least for companies founded on a personal relationship, i.e. for companies which in essence were partnerships, though in form they had assumed the character of a company: '. . . a limited company is more than a mere judicial entity, with a personality in law of its own: . . . there is room in company law for recognition of the fact that behind it, or amongst it, there are individuals, with rights, expectations and obligations *inter se* which are not necessarily submerged in the company structure. That structure is defined by the Companies Act . . . and by the articles of association by which shareholders agree to be bound. In most companies and in most contexts, this definition is sufficient and exhaustive, equally so whether the company is large or small. The "just and equitable" provision does not, as the respondents suggest, entitle one party to disregard the obligations he assumes by entering a company, nor the court to dispense him from it. It does, as equity always does, enable the court to subject the exercise of legal rights to equitable considerations; considerations, that is, of a personal character, arising between one individual and another, which may make it unjust, or inequitable, to insist on legal rights, or to exercise them in a particular way,' said Lord Wilberforce.

(*c*) The decision makes an important contribution to the movement for harmonisation of European company law. The concept of the private company founded on a personal relationship has been approximated to the continental European concept. For example, it is accepted in Germany and France that the private company is a special association and not merely a variety of a general concept of companies and they are governed by different enactments.

(*d*) The partnership analogy is an example of the drawing aside of the corporate veil, i.e. treating a company as a partnership. Once this has been done, partnership law applies and under this each general (not salaried) partner is, in the absence of contrary agreement, entitled to a say in management (see Partnership Act 1890, s 24(5)). The same is true of a limited liability partnership under *Reg* 7 of the Limited Liability Partnership Regulations 2001. Furthermore, the definition of partnership requires that the partners be in business 'in common' which they obviously are not if one or more of them is deprived of a say in management. A general partner who is deprived of a say in management is, in the absence of a contrary agreement, entitled to dissolve the firm.

However, the partnership analogy would not necessarily be applied to all private companies. The analogy is most likely to be used where, as in the *Westbourne* case, the proprietors (members) and the managers (directors) are one and the same, as full general partners in a partnership are.

Comment

(i) For the possibility, in more recent times, of using the more versatile remedy of 'unfair prejudice' under s 459, see Chapter 14.

(ii) It should also be noted that the Nazars did not offer to buy Mr Ebrahimi's shares. If they had done so, e.g. at a fair price to be decided by the company's auditors, the court may not have wound the company up so that Mr Ebrahimi could get his share capital back. A pretty drastic remedy, though, to wind up a solvent company just to achieve this (see also Chapter 14).

(v) *Sharp practice*. There is also the 'facade' or 'sham' concept which seems to apply where the company concerned has been formed primarily to evade existing liabilities or to defeat the law. Here the courts have been prepared to investigate sharp practice by individuals who are trying to hide behind a company front. Thus in *Gilford Motor Co* v *Horne* [1933] Ch 935 a former employee bound by a restraint of trade set up a company in order to evade its provisions, claiming that he as a person might be bound by the restraint but the company, being a separate entity, could not be. An injunction to prevent solicitation of Gilford's customers was granted against both him and his company which the court described as 'a device, a stratagem . . . a mere cloak or sham'.

Statutory provisions

(*a*) Under s 24 if a company carries on business without having at least two members and does so for more than six months, a person who, for the whole or any part of *the period* that it carries on business *after* those six months, (i) is a member of the company, and (ii) knows that it is carrying on business with only one member, is liable jointly and severally with the company for the payment of the company's debts contracted *during the period*, i.e. after the first six months, or, as the case may be, that part of it. In addition, as soon as the membership falls below the statutory minimum there is a ground on which a petition may be presented for winding-up by the court (Insolvency Act 1986, s 122). This ground is provided to enable a member to escape personal liability for the company's debts which he will incur if the membership remains below the statutory minimum for more than six months.

Liability may arise on the death of a member since the personal representatives do not become members unless they are on the register (*Re Bowling and Welby's Contract* [1895] 1 Ch 663). Liability may also arise by transfer of shares from one member to the only other member. This liability may be avoided by the transfer of some shares to a trustee, or nominee, for the benefit of a member or members before the six months has elapsed.

As regards the nature of the liability, a creditor may sue the member personally and there is no need for him to ask for a winding-up. Thus the situation is rather different from that pertaining in the case of an unlimited company where the creditor must ask for the winding-up of the company before the liability of the members arises. If the member is required to pay a debt or debts, he may ask for a contribution from the company. Additionally, because he has paid the company's debt, he may at common law have a complete indemnity against the company, though the Act gives a mere contribution.

It is possible for two persons to be liable for different periods and if there are no members, as where the sole member has died and the company is being run by a salaried director, the section does not apply at all.

The above provisions present a difficulty for holding companies where the holding company owns all the shares in a subsidiary. In these circumstances there is a potential risk in the holding company of liability for the debts of the subsidiary. In practice, holding companies take precautions to prevent this by having a few shares transferred to nominees, at least to make up the minimum number of members.

As we have seen, the Companies (Single Member Private Limited Companies) Regulations 1992 make clear that s 24 will not apply to any private company, nor will s 122 of the Insolvency Act 1986.

(*b*) *Section 117, Companies Act 1985*. It will be recalled that by reason of s 117 a plc cannot commence trading or exercise borrowing powers unless and until it has received a s 117 certificate from the Registrar. If it does so, the transactions are enforceable against the company but if the company fails to meet its obligations within 21 days of being called upon to do so the directors are jointly and severally liable to indemnify a person who has suffered loss or damage by reason of the company's failure to meet its obligations. This is a further example of liability in the directors to pay, e.g. the company's debts, and no proof of fraud is required.

(*c*) *Section 306, Companies Act 1985*. Under this section the memorandum of a company may provide that the liability of its members shall be limited but the liability of its directors shall be unlimited.

Under s 307 a limited company, if authorised by its articles, may by special resolution alter its memorandum in order to make unlimited the liability of its directors or managers, or of any managing director. This alternative is hardly ever adopted in practice.

(*d*) *Section 229, Companies Act 1985*. This provides that where there is a holding and subsidiary relationship between companies the holding company is required, subject to certain exceptions already referred to, not only to prepare its individual accounts but also group accounts. This suggests that for financial purposes the companies within a group are one.

(*e*) *Section 349, Companies Act 1985*. This states that if an officer, e.g. a director or secretary, signs a bill of exchange (e.g. a cheque) on which the correct name of the company is not stated he will be required to pay the amount of it, on the basis of personal liability, if the company does not pay it (but see further Chapter 3).

Finally, there are a number of examples to be found in the law relating to corporate insolvency. Thus, when a company goes into liquidation and the evidence shows that the directors have negligently struggled on for too long with an insolvent company in the hope that things would get better but which has, in the end, gone into insolvent liquidation, there are provisions in the Insolvency Act 1986 under which the directors concerned are jointly and severally liable for the company's debts. Further and more detailed considerations will be given to this concept, which is called wrongful trading, and others in the chapters on directors and corporate insolvency which is where they really belong.

It is worth noting that when offering ss 117, 306, 307 and 349 together with the insolvency situations as examples of drawing aside the veil to make the members liable for the debts of the company, these are examples of director liability. They are therefore only truly legitimate examples if the directors are also members. Since most of the problems in this area occur in private companies where the directors are normally also members, the examples can be given provided it is made clear that we assume we are dealing with director/members.

COMPANIES AND PARTNERSHIPS COMPARED

In this chapter we are considering the nature of a company. Sometimes examiners ask students to show an understanding of that by making a comparison with another business organisation – the partnership. In this connection, it is necessary to note that there are three forms of partnership in current law. The first and the oldest form is governed by the Partnership Act 1890 and is referred to here as the *ordinary partnership*. There is also the *limited partnership* governed by the Limited Partnerships Act of 1907, and finally the *limited liability partnership* governed by the Limited Liability Partnerships Act 2000. Really the only sensible comparison in terms of illustrating a knowledge of the nature of a company is with the ordinary partnership, but the main points of the other two might be included in an answer. A comparison with the relevant organisations appears below.

THE ORDINARY AND LIMITED PARTNERSHIP

Formation. A company is created by registration under company legislation. A partnership is created by agreement which may be express or implied from the conduct of the partners. No special form is required, though partnership articles are usually written, and, in the case of a limited partnership, must be written.

Status at law. A company is an artificial legal person with perpetual succession. Thus a company may own property, make contracts, and sue and be sued. As we have seen, it is an entity distinct from its members. A partnership is not a legal person though it may sue and be sued in the firm's name. Thus the partners own the property of the firm and are liable on the contracts of the firm.

Transfer of shares. Shares in a company are freely transferable unless the company's constitution otherwise provides; restrictions may, of course, appear in the articles of a private company. A partner can transfer his share in the firm, but the assignee does not thereby become a partner and is merely entitled to the assigning partner's share of the profits.

Number of members. A company whether public or private has no upper limit of membership. The maximum permitted membership for a partnership including, by reason of s 46 of the Banking Act 1979, those carrying on the business of banking is 20.

The limit is waived in some cases so that it is permissible for a partnership of more than 20 members to be formed to carry on practice as solicitors or accountants if all the members are professionally qualified, which so far as accountants are concerned means that they must be members of one of the chartered institutes in England and Wales, Scotland or Ireland, or of the Association of Chartered Certified Accountants, or to carry on business as members of a recognised stock exchange if all the members are members of a recognised stock exchange.

The Department of Trade and Industry has power to make regulations extending these provisions. Under regulations made to date it is possible, for example, for a partnership of patent agents or actuaries to have more than 20 members if they are all registered patent agents or fellows of the Institute or Faculty of Actuaries; in addition, a partnership of more than 20 persons may carry on the practice of surveyors, auctioneers, valuers, estate agents, estate managers or building designers if at least three-quarters of the partners are members of certain designated professional bodies; furthermore, a partnership of consulting engineers may have more than 20 members if a majority of them are recognised as chartered engineers. Exemption has also been extended to partnerships in other fields, e.g. loss adjusters and town planners.

An association which does not comply with the above provisions is illegal and void. Nevertheless, if the managers of the association make contracts in its name with a person who does not know that its membership is in excess of the permitted number, the managers are deemed to contract as agents for all its members and every member is personally liable to the other contracting party. However, so far as the association is concerned, the contract is affected by the illegality and is not enforceable by the association or by its members. In addition, an association with a membership in excess of the permitted number is only made void if it is formed to carry on some *business* for the purpose of *gain*. This definition covers most forms of commercial undertaking but an interesting exception is provided by the unit trust which is not an association affected by the above prohibitions. The members of such a trust deposit their funds with the managers for investment but are not in 'business' with them (*Smith* v *Anderson* (1880) 15 Ch D 247).

Management. Members of a company are not entitled to take part in the management of the company unless they become directors. General partners are entitled to share in the management of the firm unless the articles provide otherwise.

Agency. A member of a company is not by virtue only of that membership an agent of the company, and he cannot bind a company by his acts. Each general partner is an agent of the firm and may bind the firm by his acts.

Liability of members. The liability of a member of a company may be limited by shares or by guarantee. The liability of a general partner is unlimited. In a limited partnership one or more of the partners may limit his liability for the firm's debts to the amount of capital he has contributed, though even a limited partnership must have at least one general partner. In this connection it should be noted that a partnership can consist entirely of limited companies in order, e.g., to further a joint venture between them which stops short of merger, and a limited company can be a partner with individuals as the other partner(s). This will not in either case make the partnership a limited partnership unless the firm is registered as such under the Limited Partnerships Act 1907. The liability of a limited company for debt is unlimited in that it is liable for debt down to its last asset. It is the liability of the members which is limited.

Powers. The affairs of a company are closely controlled by company legislation and the company can only operate within the objects laid down in its memorandum of association, though these can be altered to some extent by special resolution. Partners may carry on any business they please so long as it is not illegal and make what arrangements they wish with regard to the running of the firm.

Termination. No one member of a company can wind up the company (but see exceptionally *Ebrahimi*), and the death, bankruptcy or insanity of a member does not mean that the company must be wound up. A partnership may be dissolved by any partner giving notice to the others at any time unless the partnership is entered into for a fixed period of time. However, dissolution by notice depends upon what the partnership agreement, if any, says. If as in *Moss* v *Elphick* [1910] 1 KB 846 the agreement says that dissolution is only to be by mutual consent of the partners, then dissolution by notice as described above does not apply. A partnership is, subject to any agreement between the partners to the contrary, dissolved by the death or bankruptcy of a partner. The partnership agreement will normally provide that the business is to continue under the remaining partner(s), so the dissolution is only a technical one, though it does leave the continuing partner(s) to deal with the paying out of the former partner's share in the business, usually in line with provisions in the partnership agreement.

LIMITED LIABILITY PARTNERSHIPS – THE ACT

The position is as follows.

Formation. A limited liability partnership (LLP) is created by registration of an incorporation document with the Registrar of Companies.

Status at law. A LLP is a body corporate and exists as a separate entity from its members in the same way as a limited company does. It has unlimited capacity to act and may enter into contracts and hold property. It continues in existence even though its individual members may change.

Transfer of membership. New members may be admitted by agreement with the existing members. A person ceases to be a member by following procedures agreed with the other members. Where there is no formal agreement, a person ceases to be a member by givng reasonable notice to the other members. Changes in membership must be notified to the Registrar within 14 days.

Number of members. There is no limit on the number of members in a LLP.

Management. There is no requirement for management powers to be set out in a formal document but it is usual to have one. In the absence of an agreement, the regulations made under the Act of 2000 set out default provision under which every member may take part in the management of the LLP.

Agency. Each member is an agent of the LLP and, therefore, can represent it and act on its behalf in all its business. However, the LLP will not be bound by the actions of a member where that member does not have authority to act and the person dealing with the member is aware of this or does not know or believe the member to be a member of the LLP.

Liability of members. The LLP and its assets are primarily liable for the debts and obligations of the firm, and in the ordinary course of business and in respect of debts, for example, the members will not be personally liable. They could, however, lose the capital that they had invested in the LLP if its assets were exhausted in paying its debts. LLPs can be set up for any business, but there is perhaps an additional risk for partners in professional organisations such as accountants and lawyers. Here the individual member has a duty of care at common law for negligent work, and under the LLP legislation a negligent member, e.g. an accountant causing loss by negligently prepared accounts, may have his personal assets taken in a payment of damages if the LLP's assets are insufficient. The non-negligent members would not be at risk of this. However, it should be noted that this personal liability will be rare since the claimant will have to show that the member concerned was accepting personal liability. In most cases the evidence will show that he was intending only to act for the LLP, in which case only the assets of the LLP will be available to satisfy the claim.

Powers. A LLP has unlimited power to act and will not face any problems of *ultra vires* (beyond the powers) even in the restricted sense that it applies to modern companies.

Termination. A LLP can be dissolved by agreement of the members. In the situation where the LLP is insolvent, creditors can initiate a winding-up and company insolvency procedures are followed including administration, administrative receiverships and voluntary arrangements. In a winding-up past and present members are liable to contribute to the assets of the LLP to the extent that they have agreed to do so in the LLP agreement.

LIMITED LIABILITY PARTNERSHIPS – THE REGULATIONS

The Limited Liability Partnerships Regulations 2001 (SI 2001/1090) came into force on 6 April 2001. They support the Act and are vital to an understanding of the operation of the law. They are quite detailed but in the end, and broadly speaking, apply company provisions to LLPs with appropriate and necessary change of wording. The regulations provide as follows.

Accounts and audit exemption

Most of the relevant provisions of the Companies Act 1985, the Company Directors Disqualification Act 1986, the Insolvency Act 1986 and the Financial Services and Markets Act 2000 are applied to LLPs with appropriate modifications. In particular the requirements relating to the keeping and retaining of accounting records and the preparation and publication of annual accounts, the form and content of annual accounts and the audit requirement are applied to LLPs in the same way as to companies with the members of the LLP taking on the duties of directors and their responsibilities.

There is, however, no requirement to prepare the equivalent of a directors' report. A period of ten months is given for delivery of accounts to the Registrar of Companies from the end of the financial year. Small LLPs and medium-sized LLPs will be able to take advantage of the provisions of CA 1985 applying to small and medium-sized companies, and the qualifying thresholds are the same. The usual company audit exemptions will apply as will the dormancy rules.

Financial disclosure: a disadvantage

So far as clients are concerned, one of the major disadvantages to the adoption of LLP status is the company-style financial disclosure. Even under the regime of abbreviated accounts financial disclosure may make an LLP vulnerable to commercial pressure. Furthermore, where it is necessary to disclose the income of the highest paid member of the LLP (which is where the aggregate profit exceeds £200,000) there may be repercussions from clients, creditors and staff. The government is being pressed to remove the disclosure requirements and, in general terms, the company analogy is not perfectly made out because disclosure and audit and accounting rules in a company are to a large extent to protect the shareholders against the directors. This is not the case with the members/managers of the LLP. In this connection it is worth noting that US LLPs do not need to disclose financial information at all, although some states do not permit the formation of LLPs.

Limited liability: alternatives

For those clients who do not wish to move into LLP financial disclosure and find the unlimited liability of one partner an off-putting feature of the limited partnership, there are only the following alternatives, given the rules of company disclosure:

- to ensure *heavy supervision of competent staff* to avoid actionable errors;
- to *negotiate with customers* a contractual exclusion or limitation of liability, following careful drafting of the relevant clause and preferably a price reduction for those customers who accept the clause;
- the back-up of insurance where this can be obtained and is not prohibitive in terms of premiums, as it has become so far as professional indemnity insurance is concerned.

Other provisions

Execution of documents. Instead of the company rule of signature by the company secretary and a director, it is provided that two members of an LLP are to be signatories for valid execution.

Register of debenture holders. An LLP must keep a register of debenture holders and debenture holders have a right to inspect it.

Registered office. The Registrar will receive notice of the address of the registered office on incorporation and must be notified of changes.

Identification. The name of the LLP is to appear outside its place of business and on correspondence and on its common seal if it has one.

Annual return. The regulations provide that an LLP must deliver an annual return to the Registrar of Companies and set out the requirements as to contents.

Auditors. Subject to the applicability of the audit exemption rules, an LLP is in general required to appoint auditors. Provision is made for the Secretary of State to appoint auditors where an LLP is in default. The auditors have various rights including the right to have access to an LLP's books, accounts and information as necessary, the right to attend meetings of the LLP and certain rights in the event of being removed from office or not being re-appointed. Provision is also made for the resignation of auditors and the making of a statement by a person ceasing to hold office.

Registration of charges. An LLP is required to register charges with the Registrar of Companies. The relevant sections of CA 1985 apply unless and until amended (see Chapter 20).

Arrangements and reconstructions. An LLP has power to compromise with its members and creditors.

Investigations. An investigation of an LLP may be made following its own application or that of not less than one-fifth in number of its members.

Fraudulent trading. This is punished in the case of an LLP in the same way as a company trading fraudulently.

Wrongful trading. The law relating to wrongful trading is applied with the necessary changes in nomenclature to members of an LLP who trade on with an insolvent LLP as it is to the directors of a company.

Unfair prejudice. Schedule 2 of the regulations applies CA 1985 so that in general there is a remedy for the members of an LLP who suffer unfair prejudice. The members of an LLP may, however, by unanimous agreement exclude the right set out in s 459(1) for such period as may be agreed.

Matters arising following winding-up. There are provisions dealing with the power of the court to declare a dissolution void, the striking out by the Registrar of Companies of a defunct company and Crown disclaimer of property vesting as *bona vacantia*.

Functions of the Registrar of Companies. These are set out in Sch 2 and include the keeping of records of LLPs' filed documents on the same lines as for registered companies.

Miscellaneous provisions. These include the form of registers, the use of computers for records, the service of documents, the powers of the court to grant relief and the punishment of offences.

Disqualification. Part III of the regulations applies the provisions of the Company Directors Disqualification Act 1986 to LLPs with appropriate modifications. Under the provisions members of an LLP will be subject to the same penalties that apply to company directors and may be disqualified from being a member of an LLP or a director of a company under those provisions.

Insolvency. Under Part IV of and Sch 3 to the regulations the insolvency provisions applied to LLPs include procedures for voluntary arrangements, administration orders, receivership and liquidation. There are two notable modifications to the company rules, i.e.:

(i) a new s 214A under which withdrawals made by members in the two years prior to winding-up will be subject to clawback if it is proved that, at the time of the relevant withdrawal, the member knew or had reasonable grounds to believe that the LLP was or would be made insolvent;
(ii) a modified s 74 providing that in a winding-up both past and present members are liable to contribute to the assets of the LLP to the extent that they have agreed to do so with the other LLP members in the partnership agreement.

In effect, therefore, this gives members of an LLP protection in terms of limited liability. However, the matter is not straightforward. There is no obligation either in the Act of 2000 or the regulations to have a written agreement and the default provisions in *Reg* 7 do not deal with the extent of the liability of each member on liquidation. The position is therefore left ill-defined, there being no relation between capital contributed and liability to contribute to deficits as there is with companies. In these circumstances insolvency practitioners may find difficulty in determining the liability of members of an LLP on liquidation. This problem area underlines once again the need for a written agreement to be made in an LLP governing the maximum liability of each member on liquidation or stating that a member is to have no liability so that creditors would have to rely on the assets of the LLP alone. Unfortunately this situation would not necessarily be known to creditors since there is no requirement to file LLP agreements so that they are not open to public inspection.

It should be noted that the insolvency provisions relating to limited liability partnerships are subject to s 14 of the Insolvency Act 2000 since they follow corporate procedures. This means that if an LLP does business in other countries of the EU and becomes insolvent it may find that insolvency proceedings may be brought in regard to a place of operations in a particular EU territory.

LLPs authorised under the financial services regime. There are in corporate law special insolvency provisions for companies involved in the financial markets because of the special problems of corporate failure in that field. These provisions contained in Parts XV and XXIV of the Financial Services and Markets Act 2000 are applied to relevant LLPs.

Default provisions. Part VI of the regulations contains 'fall-back' provisions that apply where there is no existing limited liability partnership agreement or where the agreement does not wholly deal with a particular issue. The provisions represent a modification of s 24 of the Partnership Act 1890. There are provisions relating e.g. to profit share, remuneration, assignment of partnership share, inspection of books and records, expulsion and competition.

LLP OR PRIVATE LIMITED COMPANY? – A CHECKLIST

Legal uncertainty. The company structure is a long-standing business organisation that is tried and trusted by advisers. It is set in a well-developed body of law which, over the years, has acquired a high degree of legal certainty. By contrast, the LLP is a new structure that has not been tried and tested in terms of its legal framework and legal uncertainty is often undesirable in business organisations.

Limited liability. This is, for all practical purposes, the same in the corporate and LLP organisations.

Internal flexibility. Greater flexibility in internal matters and management is claimed for the LLP as against the private company law requirements involving formal meetings and management structures. However, this problem is often overstated in the case of the private limited company where company law now allows a high degree of flexibility in decision making, e.g. by the calling of meetings at short notice and by using the written resolution procedure. Also, the *Duomatic* principle operates to validate the informal unanimous consent of all the members, even where there has been no written resolution.

The private company does not require the equivalent of an LLP agreement. The memorandum and articles of association provide standard default arrangements. However, these documents are filed with the Registrar of Companies on incorporation, as are alterations to them, so that privacy is lost. The LLP agreement is not filed nor are any alterations that may be made to it. However, these LLP agreements have not yet been challenged by disputing parties in the courts and their operation is not certain.

In conclusion, the number of LLP registrations continues to be small compared with the private limited company registrations. Business in general would seem to prefer the corporate route though LLPs have found favour with organisations of professionals because they provide for a form of limited liability within the partnership ethos.

REFORM – AN ORDINARY PARTNERSHIP WITH LEGAL PERSONALITY

The Law Commission has issued a Consultation Paper on Partnership Law in response to a request from the DTI. There are also proposals regarding partnerships in Scotland made by the Scottish Law Commission that are not considered here. The review is being conducted in respect of the provisions of the *Partnership Act 1890*, many but not all of which operate as default provisions in the absence of a contrary agreement of the partners, and the *Limited Partnerships Act 1907*. The Limited Liability Partnerships Act 2000 (see above) is not involved. The reforms would however, if implemented, narrow the present distinction between ordinary partnerships and the new limited liability partnership.

Main reform proposals

The three main proposals are:

1 Proposals to introduce separate legal personality.
There are two sub-proposals here:
   (*a*) *to confer legal personality on all partnerships without registration.* There would be a transitional period to allow the parties to a partnership agreement to organise their affairs or to opt out of the continuing aspect of separate personality of the firm.
   (*b*) *to make legal personality depend on registration.* Under this sub-proposal only a registered partnership would have legal personality capable of continuing regardless of changes in the membership of the firm. Under this option non-registered partnerships would not have legal personality.

   The Commission feels that having a system of registration would create a more complex situation in which there would be a legal environment for registered partnerships and another for non-registered firms. The Commission also feels that many small firms would not register and so lose the benefits of legal personality.

   On balance therefore the provisional view of the Commission is the first option, i.e. continuity of legal personality without registration, and views are invited on this. The creation of a registered partnership regime would bring partnership law in the UK closer to those legal systems in Europe in which legal personality is conferred by registration.

2 Proposals to avoid the unnecessary discontinuance of business caused by the dissolution of the firm under the 1890 Act default rules when one person ceases to be a partner.

3 Proposals to provide a more efficient and cheaper mechanism for the dissolution of a solvent partnership.

Other reform proposals

The following suggestions for reform are according to the Commission intended to clarify some of the uncertainties in the 1890 Act; to update provisions which are outdated or spent and to propose adaptations of existing provisions if in the event consultees support the separate and continuing legal personality of the firm.

(*a*) *Partnership and agency*. With the concept of legal entity the partners would be agents of the firm but not each other.

(*b*) *Ownership of property*. With separate personality the firm would be able to hold property in its own name. It would not be necessary, as now, to use the device of the trust. Also the firm and not the partners would have an insurable interest in partnership property.

(*c*) *Partners' liability for the obligations of the firm*. As a result of separate personality the firm would be primarily liable.

A partner's liability would be subsidiary but unlimited. Creditors would normally need to get a judgment against the firm before enforcing the claim against the assets of the firm or the partners. The liability of partners would be joint and several for the debts and obligations of the firm.

(*d*) *Partners' duties*. Partners have a duty to act in good faith in Equity already. The Commission proposes to include the duty in a reformed statute and possibly also a duty of skill and care in negligence. There is a suggestion that partners be relieved of the duty of good faith when, on the break-up of a firm, they are competing for its client base provided they act honestly and reasonably.

(*e*) *Litigation*. A partnership with a separate legal personality would be sued in its own name and the partners could be sued in the same action.

(*f*) *Information about the firm* including former partners who may have subsidiary liability at the time of a claim would be available if the partnership was registered. If this is not so the Commission proposes an extension to the Business Names Act 1985 requiring display of such information by the firm administratively.

(*g*) *Floating charges*. Currently partnerships cannot grant floating charges over the firm's assets. The Commission makes no proposals on this but invites views.

ADVANTAGES AND DISADVANTAGES OF INCORPORATION

The main advantages put forward by professional advisers for the conversion of a business into a limited company **for those who do not wish to incorporate as an LLP** can be summarised as follows:

1 Perpetual succession of the company despite the retirement, bankruptcy, mental disorder or death of members.

2 Liability of the members for the company's debts limited to the amount of their respective shareholding.

3 Contractual liability of the company for all contracts made in its name.

4 Ownership of property vested in the company is not affected by a change in shareholders.

5 The company may obtain finance by creating a floating charge (see Chapter 20) with its undertaking or property as security yet may realise assets within that property without the consent of the lenders during the normal course of business until crystallisation (see Chapter 20) occurs. *As we shall see, no other form of business organisation except an LLP can sensibly use such a charge.*

It is generally thought that the above advantages outweigh the suggested disadvantages of incorporation which are:

1 Public inspection of accounts (with exceptions in the case of some unlimited companies and abbreviated or modified disclosure in the case of small and medium companies).
2 Administrative expenses in terms, e.g., of filing fees for documents.
3 Cost of compulsory annual audit (unless the company is a dormant company or in a position to opt out).

COMPANIES AND HUMAN RIGHTS

The Human Rights Act 1998 came into force on 2 October 2000. It implements the European Convention on Human Rights into UK law. The Convention is available to companies in terms of their dealings with emanations of the state, e.g. government and local authorities. This is because the initial effect of the Act is vertical. Whether the Convention will be extended by the courts horizontally into areas of private business remains to be seen, though s 6 of the 1998 Act provides that the courts and tribunals of the UK must not act contrary to the Convention. Problems have arisen in connection with the lack of independence in UK courts and tribunals in that Crown Court recorders were appointed part time and paid by the state and removable by the state with no security of tenure. The same was true of appointments to employment tribunals in cases involving the state as an employer or an emanation of the state, such as a local authority. The solution here has been to give these part-time judicial officers fixed-term contracts of, say, five years during which time they are not dismissable except for misconduct, and this gives some security of tenure. That a company can complain about the infringements of its human rights in this context (and others no doubt) is illustrated by *County Properties Ltd* v *Scottish Ministers* [2000] *The Times*, 19 September, which, although a Scottish case, is applicable in the rest of the UK. The company, in effect, had been refused permission by the Crown to obtain the release of the listed building restrictions on one of its properties and the matter was referred for decision to an inspector appointed by the Crown. The company objected to this procedure because it infringed Art 6 of the Convention that provides: 'In the determination of his civil rights and obligations . . . everyone is entitled to a . . . hearing . . . by an independent and impartial tribunal.' The Court of Session held that this was an infringement of the company's rights. That part of the procedure was invalid and the matter would have to be dealt with by appeal to the courts as the relevant legislation allowed. The case was overturned on appeal (*County Properties Ltd* v *Scottish Ministers* 2002 SC 79) the court following the same line as in the *Barnes* case, brackets below.

The House of Lords took a different view in an appeal from the Divisional Court of Queen's Bench in England. Their Lordships felt that the hearing of planning matters by a government-appointed inspector did not flout Art 6 of the Convention because the inspector's decision could always be brought before the ordinary courts by means of a procedure called judicial review (see *R* v *Secretary of State for the Environment, etc., ex parte Holding and Barnes plc* [2001] *The Times*, 10 May). Nevertheless, the cases show that companies can argue human rights matters before our courts.

Action against companies based on human rights

Implementation of the Human Rights Act 1998 on 2 October 2000 raised the spectre of the litigation floodgates opening since it made the European Convention on Human

Rights available to litigants in UK courts, thus avoiding the need to take the matter to the European Court of Human Rights at Strasbourg, previously the only option. It has already been noted that the initial effect is *against public authorities* with the possibility of some expansion into the private sector through s 6 of the 1998 Act. In this connection, a statement by the Lord Chief Justice in *Daniels* v *Walker* [2000] 1 WLR 1382, CA is of interest. He expressed the hope that judges would be robust in resisting attempts to allow inappropriate arguments on human rights. These he defined as arguments that lead the court down blind alleys. There has also been the suggestion that adverse costs may be awarded against those who raise spurious questions and points on human rights. Furthermore, the Court of Appeal observed in *Barclays Bank plc* v *Ellis* [2000] *The Times*, 24 October that legal representatives seeking to rely on the Human Rights Act 1998 should supply the court with any decisions of the European Court of Human Rights on which they intend to rely or which might assist the court. This should operate as a deterrent to those lawyers who may think of raising human rights issues unless, where possible, supported by authority.

The specific effect of the Convention on directors is considered, in terms of their functions as individuals and managers, in Chapter 18.

GRADED QUESTIONS

Essay mode

1 (*a*) In the celebrated case of *Salomon* v *Salomon & Co Ltd* [1897] AC 22, Lord Halsbury LC observed:

> 'Either the limited company was a legal entity or it was not. If it was, the business belonged to it and not to Mr. Salomon. If it was not, there was no person and no thing to be an agent at all and it is impossible to say at the same time that there is a company and there is not.'

Comment.

(*b*) Tiedeman was the owner of a large bulk-carrier called *Ocean-Star*. The ship was valued at £1 million and was insured for that sum with Lloyd's in Tiedeman's name. Subsequently Tiedeman incorporated Tiedeman Ltd in which he held all the shares but one which was held by his wife as his nominee. *Ocean-Star* was then sold to Tiedeman Ltd and the purchase price was secured by a debenture issued in favour of Tiedeman giving as a security a fixed charge on the only asset of the company *Ocean-Star*. While carrying a valuable cargo on charter to a Kuwait company the *Ocean-Star* was attacked by Iranian gun-boats and sunk.

Consider whether Tiedeman or in the alternative Tiedeman Ltd could claim to be indemnified by Lloyd's for the loss of the bulk-carrier.

(*University of Plymouth*)

2 The principle of law set out in *Salomon* v *Salomon & Co Ltd is* not always applied. Give the facts of this case and give its principle of law, and discuss when the judiciary or statutory provisions will not take account of that principle.

(*University of Paisley*)

3 '... a fundamental attribute of corporate personality ... is that the corporation is a legal entity distinct from its members': *Gower*. Which do you consider are the two outstanding advantages of incorporation? Give reasons for your choice and explain their dependence upon this fundamental attribute.

(*The Institute of Chartered Accountants in England and Wales*)

4 Explain by reference to statutory and common law examples what is meant by the term 'lifting the veil of incorporation'.

(*The Chartered Institute of Management Accountants*)

5 John, who runs Trent Ltd, a small manufacturing company, has heard that he may not have to appoint auditors in regard to future accounts and is keen to save the audit fees. Advise John as to the relevant law.

(*Author's question*)

Objective mode

Four alternative answers are given. Select ONE only. Circle the letter beside the answer which you consider to be correct. Check your answers by referring back to the information given in the chapter and against the answers at the back of the book.

1 The members of a social club wish to form a legal entity. There is no commercial risk but they do not want too much disclosure of their affairs to the public. What type of company should they form?

A A company limited by guarantee.
B An unincorporated association.
C A private company limited by shares.
D A private unlimited company.

2 Under the Companies Act 1985 what is the result of the number of members of a public company falling below two?

A The company must cease trading during the course of the next six months.
B The sole member becomes jointly and severally liable with the company for the company's debts incurred after six months where the sole member is aware that the membership is down to one.
C The company must notify the Registrar, but subject to this can continue trading.
D The remaining member immediately takes over personal liability for the debts of the company.

3 Fred has been allotted 200 £1 ordinary shares in Ark Ltd with a nominal value of £1 and a premium of 0.40 pence. Fred has paid 0.85 pence. What is Fred's maximum liability if the company is wound up?

A £30.
B £110.
C £2,000.
D £280.

4 What is the minimum number of persons who must subscribe a public company's memorandum?

A Three.
B Two.
C One.
D Twenty.

5 To what extent is a member of a company which is limited by guarantee personally liable for the company's debts?

A He is personally liable for all the company's debts at any time.
B He is personally liable for all the company's debts if the company is wound up.
C His personal liability is limited to the amount set out in the memorandum on a winding-up.
D His personal liability is limited to the amount set out in the memorandum at any time.

6 Three friends own and are also directors of a limited company carrying on the family business. They have it in mind to change the organisation to an ordinary partnership. What aspect of the business would be affected if this change were carried out?

A The right to sue in the business name.
B The right to mortgage the business assets.
C The right of the partners to examine the firm's accounts.
D The ability to create a floating charge over the business assets.

The answers to questions set in objective mode appear on p 576.

2

PROMOTION AND INCORPORATION

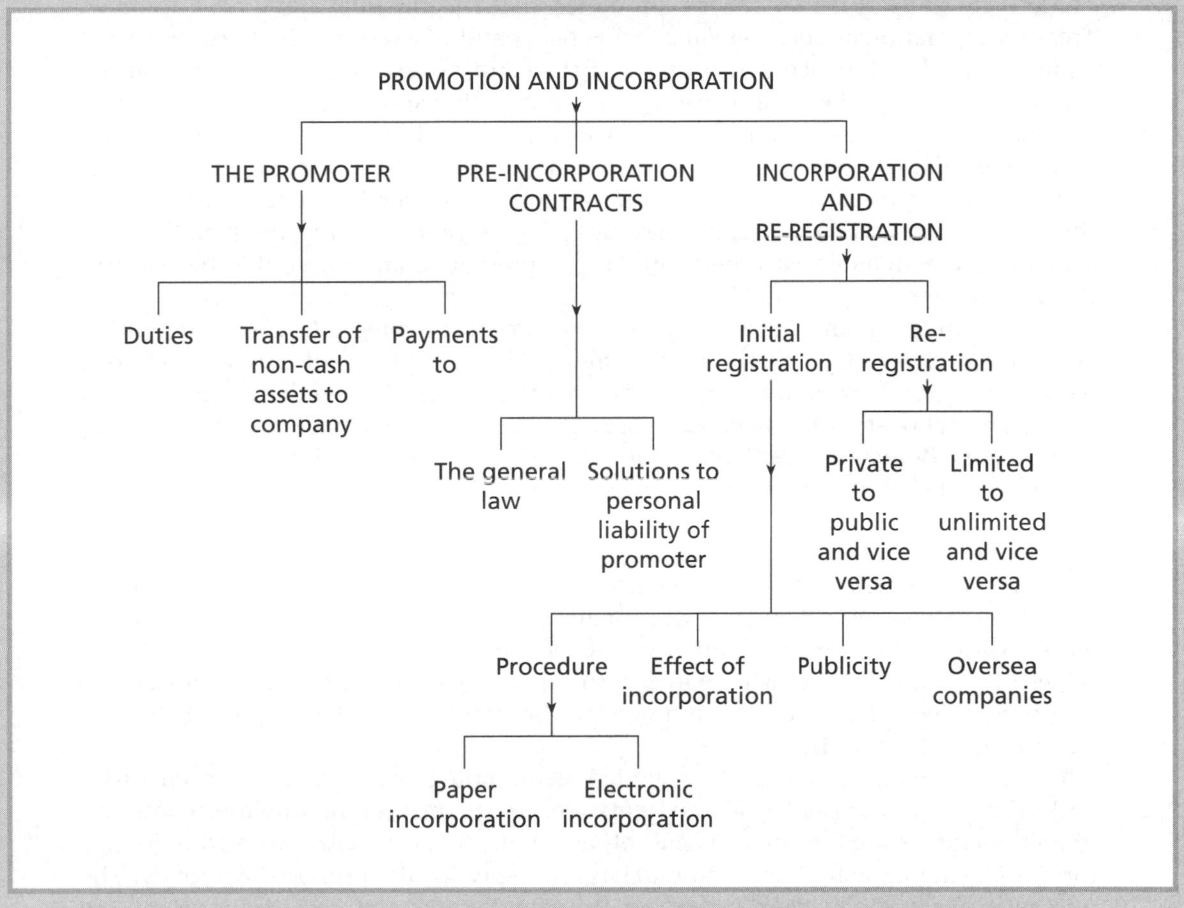

The promotion of a company consists in taking the necessary steps to incorporate it by registration under the Companies Act, to see that it has share and loan capital, and to acquire the business or property which the company is formed to control.

THE PROMOTER

There is no general definition of a promoter in the Companies Act 1985. However, Treasury regulations under the Financial Services and Markets Act 2000 exempt from liability for false statements in listing particulars, or a prospectus, those who merely give advice in a professional capacity but do not give specific reports for inclusion as experts. Thus a solicitor or accountant who merely advises the promoters on legal and financial matters respectively will not be considered as a promoter in respect of misrepresentations which appear in any prospectus issued to raise capital. Nevertheless, accountants in particular may be liable as experts if any of their financial statements are included with their consent in a prospectus and turn out to be false (see further Chapter 9).

In addition, the courts have not given the expression 'promoter' a precise definition although Cockburn C J, in *Twycross* v *Grant* (1877) 2 CPD 469, called a promoter 'one who undertakes to form a company with reference to a given project, and to set it going, and who takes the necessary steps to accomplish that purpose'. In addition, Bowen J in *Whaley Bridge Printing Co* v *Green* (1880) 5 QBD 109 said: 'The term promoter is a term not of law, but of business, usefully summing up in a single word a number of business operations familiar to the commercial world by which a company is generally brought into existence.'

Thus it can be said that whether a person is a promoter or not is a matter of *fact* and not of *law*. However, a promoter will usually be in some sort of controlling position with regard to the company's affairs, both before it is formed and during the early stages of its existence and will be in a position analogous to that of a director during that period. Basically a promoter is a person who promotes a business project through the medium of a company.

Those who would normally be regarded as promoters would include persons who authorise the drafting of legal documents such as the memorandum, and who nominate directors, solicitors, bankers and other agents, together with those who arrange for the placing of shares and who purchase property for the proposed company. The purchaser of a ready-made company is a promoter because such a person is promoting a company through the medium of a company.

During the nineteenth century there was in existence a class of professional company promoters whose methods of raising capital from the investing public were often unscrupulous and thus it was necessary for the legislature and the courts to impose rigorous duties upon such persons to protect the public from fraud.

Those days have gone and in modern times most companies are promoted as private companies by persons with an interest in the business who become directors and remain so. Obviously some protection is still required because such persons could defraud the company by, for example, selling property to it at exorbitant rates. However, they are not likely to do so because in the modern situation the promoter retains an interest in the company and would merely be defrauding himself, whereas the old professional promoter either did not take any shares in the company at all or if he did unloaded them to others shortly after its incorporation.

If, after incorporation as a private company, there is a need to raise capital from the public then there would be a conversion to a public company. In such a situation there is no need for a promoter but there would be a need for the services of a specialist organisation such as a merchant bank to raise the necessary capital from the public.

Duties of a promoter

In equity a promoter stands in a fiduciary relationship towards the company he is promoting but is not a trustee. Thus he is not absolutely forbidden to make a profit out of the promotion so long as he has disclosed his interest in the transaction out of which the profit arose and the company consents to the retention of the profit. As a general rule any profits which he makes on the promotion and fails to disclose must be surrendered to the company. This is illustrated by the following case.

Gluckstein *v* Barnes [1900] AC 240

In 1893 the National Agricultural Hall Co Ltd owned a place of entertainment called the Olympia Company which was being wound up. A syndicate was formed to raise funds to buy Olympia and resell it, either to a company registered under the Companies Act for the purpose, or to another purchaser. If a company was formed, the appellant Gluckstein and three other persons, Lyons, Hart and Hartley, who were members of the syndicate, had agreed to become its first directors and to promote it. In the event a company was formed, called the Olympia Company Ltd, and the promoters issued a prospectus stating that the syndicate which was promoting the company had purchased Olympia for £140,000 and was selling it to the company for £180,000 thus quite properly disclosing a profit of £40,000. What they did not disclose but referred to vaguely as 'interim investments', was the fact that they had purchased certain mortgage debentures in the old Olympia Company for less than their face value, and that these mortgage debentures were to be redeemed at their face value out of the proceeds of the issue of shares. This meant that the syndicate made a further £20,000 on the promotion. The company afterwards went into liquidation, Barnes being the liquidator, and he sought to recover the undisclosed secret profit. *Held* – the profit of £20,000 should have been disclosed and the appellant was bound to account to the liquidator for it.

Comment

The following points of interest arise from this case:

(i) There had been disclosure by the promoters in regard to the £40,000 and £20,000 profit to themselves as directors but of course this was useless because disclosure must be to an independent board (see below).

(ii) The prospectus said that the £40,000 profit did not include profits on 'interim investments' but the court held that this was not a disclosure of the profit of £20,000.

(iii) The case also illustrates that liability of promoters is joint and several for recovery of profit because Mr Gluckstein tried to defend himself by saying he was only liable for a proportion of the profits. The House of Lords held him liable to account for it all with a right of contribution against his fellow promoters.

In *Erlanger* v *New Sombrero Phosphate Co* (1878) 3 App Cas 1218, the House of Lords took the view that the disclosure mentioned above had to be made to an independent board of directors. This view was, however, too strict. The boards of private companies, for example, are unlikely to be entirely independent of the promoter of the company and since *Salomon*, where it was held that the liquidator of the company could not complain of the sale to it at an obvious over-valuation of Mr Salomon's business, all the members having acquiesced therein, it has been accepted that disclosure to the members is equally effective. Thus, if the company issues a prospectus disclosure to the shareholders may be made in it and the shareholders give their consent by conduct when they apply for the shares being issued under the prospectus. Disclosure by a person, in his capacity as promoter, to himself, in his capacity as director, is not enough (*Gluckstein* v *Barnes*, 1900, above).

A promoter will perhaps most often make a secret profit by selling his own property to the company at an enhanced price and this is further considered below. However, other forms of profit are possible, e.g. where the promoter takes a commission from the person who is selling property to the company (and see also *Gluckstein* v *Barnes*, 1900). All such profits are subject to the rules of disclosure. The liability of promoters as vendors of property may be considered under two headings:

***(a) Where the property was purchased by the promoter before he began to act as a promoter*.** If the promoter does not disclose his interest in the sale, the company may rescind the contract, i.e. return the property to the promoter and recover the purchase price. If the company wishes to keep the property it may do so, but cannot recover the profit as such (*Re Cape Breton* (1887) 12 App Cas 652). The remedy is to sue the promoter for damages in tort at common law for negligence if damage has been suffered, as where the company has paid a price in excess of the market price. That this can be done follows from the decision of the court in *Jacobus Marler Estates Ltd* v *Marler* (1913) 114 LT 640n, and also *Re Leeds and Hanley Theatres of Varieties Ltd* [1902] 2 Ch 809.

There may, according to circumstances, be an action for fraud, or under s 2 of the Misrepresentation Act 1967 where the promoter's misstatements, e.g. as to value, are made negligently. Therefore, if P acquired some land in 2004 for £10,000 and became the promoter of X Co in 2005, selling the land to the company for £20,000 through a nominee and without disclosing his interest, then the company may:

(i) rescind the contract; or
(ii) keep the property and recover damages for P's breach of duty of skill and care.

If the property was worth only £18,000 in 2005, the company could recover £2,000, but in no circumstances could it recover the £10,000 profit.

***(b) Where the property was purchased by the promoter after he began to act as a promoter*.** Here again the remedy of rescission is available, but if the company does not wish to rescind it is possible to regard the promoter as agent for the company when he purchased the property, and the company can recover the profit made by the promoter. Thus, in the example given above, if P had been the promoter of X Co when he purchased the land, the company could have recovered the profit made, i.e. £10,000.

One of the first acts in promotion is normally to negotiate for the purchase of property. However, the courts have been reluctant to hold that the promoter's contract to buy property is the start of his promotion and this has deprived the rule about secret profits of much of its practical value. Obviously, if the public has been invited to subscribe for shares when the property is purchased, the courts will regard the promotion as having commenced, but things rarely happen in this way.

The remedy of rescission is not in general available against the promoter if it is not possible to restore the company and the promoter to the position they were in before the contract was made, as where the company has resold the property to a third party. In such a case the company must go on with the contract and sue the promoter for the profit made, depending on the promoter's position when he bought the property which he later sold to the company. However, where the property has been merely used and not sold, as where the company has worked a mine purchased from a promoter, the rule of full restoration to the former position does not appear to operate as any real restriction on rescission in view of the wide powers now exercised by the courts to make financial adjustments when granting rescission. This is particularly true where the promoter has been fraudulent.

The duties of a promoter to the company *at common law* have not been fully developed by the judiciary. They are not contractual duties because the company is not incorporated and cannot contract with the promoter. Nevertheless, a promoter can be regarded as a quasi-agent working without a contract and as such would at common law owe a general duty in negligence to exercise reasonable skill and care in the promotion, i.e. to show reasonable business acumen in regard to transactions entered into.

Thus if he allows the company to buy property – including his own – for more than it is worth, he may be liable to the company in damages for negligence (*Re Leeds and Hanley Theatres of Varieties Ltd* [1902] 2 Ch 809).

Again, if a promoter issues a prospectus which he knows to be false so that the company is liable to be sued by subscribers, the company may sue him at common law for damages. In the *Leeds* case the court proceeded on the basis of fraud but since the company does not itself act upon the fraud by subscribing for shares, the decision is felt to be based on negligence.

In other areas, e.g. the purchase by a promoter of a business which loses money, the standard required presumably depends upon the experience and/or qualifications of the promoter in business fields. A higher standard would be expected of a promoter who was, e.g., an experienced and/or qualified accountant, than would be of a person of no great experience or qualification in the field of business. The duty may well be analogous to that of directors (see Chapter 17).

The equitable and common law duties of a promoter are owed to the company, which may enforce them by a claim form served by the company on the promoter. Also, by s 212 of the Insolvency Act 1986, the court may in a liquidation, on the petition of the liquidator or a creditor, or a member, order a promoter to repay or restore property obtained by breach of duty. A shareholder may also bring a derivative action on behalf of the company against a promoter. However, because of the decision in *Foss* v *Harbottle*, 1843 (see Chapter 14), such an action can only be brought if the shareholder can bring his complaint within one of the exceptions to the rule in *Foss* as where the promoters are also the company's directors and majority shareholders and are preventing an action being brought in the company's name.

However, a claim by a member of the company under ss 459–461 (unfair prejudice) does not have the *Foss* restrictions and may, in modern company law, be a better way to proceed. Under these sections a member may, regardless of the size of his shareholding, ask the court to authorise a claim to be brought by the company against a person who has caused loss to the generality of its members. An action by the company authorised by the court is not a derivative action and the rule in *Foss* does not apply to restrict it (see further Chapter 14).

The duties are not owed to shareholders who are unable to bring a personal action unless this relates to false statements made by the promoter in a prospectus.

Trade creditors and debenture holders cannot sue for breach of duty. There was, for example, no action by trade creditors in *Salomon* although he did not disclose to them his interest in the promotion. However, secret profits or damages recovered by the liquidator in a winding-up are used to pay the company's debts.

The duties of disclosure and skill and care upon promoters do not end on the incorporation of the company, nor indeed on the appointment of a board of directors. However, once the company has acquired the property and/or business which it was formed to manage, the initial capital has been raised and the board of directors has effectively taken over management from the promoters, the latter's duties will terminate. Thus, in *Re British Seamless Paper Box Co* (1881) 17 Ch D 467, a promoter disclosed a profit which he had made out of the company's promotion to those who provided it with share capital when it commenced business. It was held that he was under no duty to disclose that profit to those who were invited to subscribe further capital some 12 months later and in these circumstances the company could not recover the profit from him by reason of his failure to do so.

Promoters' dealings with the prospective company: rules of capital maintenance

Although a promoter is not bound to be a subscriber to the memorandum on incorporation of a public company, it is very likely that he will be. In these circumstances certain provisions of the Companies Act 1985 relating to capital maintenance apply. These are as follows:

Section 104 provides that for two years following the date of issue of the certificate that a company *registered as a public company* is entitled to commence business, the company may not acquire (whether for cash or shares) non-cash assets *from subscribers to the memorandum* having an aggregate value equal to one-tenth or more of the nominal value of the issued share capital unless:

(*a*) the valuation rules set out in s 109 are complied with. This means that the asset must have been valued by an independent accountant who must state that the value of the consideration to be received by the company is not less than the value of the consideration to be given by it; and

(*b*) the acquisition of the asset and the terms of the acquisition have been approved by an ordinary resolution of the company.

The above provisions also apply when a private company converts to a public company and the non-cash asset is acquired from a person who is *a member of the private company on the date of conversion*, i.e. re-registration. The period is two years beginning with that date. Such members are also, in a way, promoters of the public company.

The above matters are considered in more detail in Chapter 7 but it will be appreciated that they do operate as a form of control on promoters/subscribers/members, as the case may be, off-loading property on the company at above its real value, since if the transaction has gone through in breach of s 104 the company can recover what it has paid for the asset and, if it has not gone through, it is not enforceable against the company.

Payment to promoters

Since a company cannot make a valid contract before incorporation, a promoter cannot legally claim any remuneration for his services, or an indemnity for the expenses incurred in floating the company.

Re National Motor Mail Coach Co Ltd, Clinton's Claim [1908] 2 Ch 515

A company, called the Motor Mail Coach Syndicate Ltd, promoted another company, called the National Motor Mail Coach Co Ltd, to acquire the business of a motor mail contractor named Harris. The promoters paid out £416 2s 0d in promotion fees. The two companies were subsequently wound up and Clinton, who was the liquidator of the syndicate, proved in the liquidation of the National Motor Mail Coach Co Ltd for the promotion fees. *Held* – Clinton's claim on behalf of the syndicate could not be allowed because the company was not in existence when the payments were made, and could not have requested that they be made. The syndicate was not acting as the company's agent or at its request, and the fact that the company had obtained a benefit because the syndicate had performed its promotion duties was not enough.

The law remains unsatisfactory because, although it is usual for the promoters to include, as *Table A* does, a provision in the articles which allows the directors of the company to pay promotion expenses under their general management powers, this does not bind the company to pay the promoters whether the provision is in the articles or the memorandum (*Re English and Colonial Produce Co Ltd* [1906] 2 Ch 435). Furthermore, even if the directors resolve to make the payments, the promise is not enforceable against the company unless it is made by deed because the promoters' services are by then past consideration which will not support an oral or written contract unless the latter is expressed to be a deed. However, since the promoters or their nominees are likely to be the first directors, the payment will usually be made.

Pre-incorporation contracts: generally

Another consequence of the company having no legal existence and therefore no capacity to make contracts is that if a promoter, or some other person purporting to act as its agent, makes a contract for the company before its incorporation then:

(i) the company when formed is not bound by it even if it has taken some benefit under it (see *Re National Motor Mail Coach, etc.* above);
(ii) the company is unable to sue the third party on the agreement unless the promoter and the third party have given the company rights of action under the Contracts (Rights of Third Parties) Act 1999 (see below);
(iii) the company cannot ratify the agreement even after its incorporation (*Kelner* v *Baxter* (1866) LR 2 CP 174);

(iv) unless the agreement has been made specifically to the contrary, it will take effect as one made personally by the promoter or other purported agent and the third party (s 36C). This is illustrated by the following case.

Phonogram Ltd *v* Lane [1981] 3 All ER 182

In 1973, a group of pop artists decided that they would perform under the name of 'Cheap Mean and Nasty'. A company, Fragile Management Ltd (Fragile) was to be formed to run the group.

Before the company was formed, there were negotiations regarding the financing of the group. Phonogram Ltd, a subsidiary of the Hemdale Group, agreed to provide £12,000, and the first instalment of £6,000, being the initial payment for the group's first album, was paid. Fragile was never formed; the group never performed under it; but the £6,000 was not repaid.

The Court of Appeal was asked who was liable to repay it. It appeared that a Brian Lane had negotiated on behalf of Fragile and a Roland Rennie on behalf of Phonogram Ltd.

A letter of 4 July 1973 from Mr Rennie to Mr Lane was crucial. It read: 'In regard to the contract now being completed between Phonogram Ltd and Fragile Management Ltd concerning recordings of a group . . . with a provisional title of "Cheap Mean and Nasty", and further to our conversation of this morning, I send you herewith our cheque for £6,000 in anticipation of a contract signing, this being the initial payment for initial LP called for in the contract. In the unlikely event that we fail to complete within, say, one month you will undertake to pay us £6,000 . . . For good order's sake, Brian, I should be appreciative if you could sign the attached copy of this letter and return it to me so that I can keep our accounts people informed of what is happening.'

Mr Lane signed the copy 'for and on behalf of Fragile Management Ltd'. The money was paid over, and went into the account of Jelly Music Ltd, a subsidiary of the Hemdale Group, of which Mr Lane was a director.

The court had first to consider whether or not Mr Lane was personally liable on the contract. Clearly, Fragile could not be sued, since it never came into existence. Lord Denning took the view that Mr Lane was, as a matter of construction, liable on the contract without recourse to what is now s 36C, because the letter, which was in effect the contract, said: 'I send *you* herewith our cheque for £6,000', and 'in the unlikely event that we fail to complete within, say, one month, *you* will undertake to repay us the £6,000'.

However, Mr Justice Phillips at first instance had decided on the basis of a lot of evidence which he had heard that Mr Lane was not, as a matter of construction, liable personally, and Lord Denning and the rest of the Court of Appeal proceeded on the assumption that Mr Lane was not liable on the basis of intention and construction.

Lord Denning then turned to what is now s 36C. This states: 'Where a contract purports to be made by a company, or by a person as agent for a company, at a time when the company has not been formed, then subject to any agreement to the contrary the contract has effect as one entered into by the person purporting to act for the company or as agent for it and he is personally liable on the contract accordingly.'

This seemed to Lord Denning to cover the case before him and render Mr Lane liable. Mr Lane made the contract on behalf of Fragile at a time when the company had not been formed, and he purported to make it on behalf of the company so that he was personally liable for it.

Mr Lane's counsel drew the attention of the court to the Directive (68/151) on which s 36C is based. This states that its provisions are limited to companies *en formation* (in course of formation), whereas Fragile never commenced the incorporation process.

Lord Denning rejected this submission saying an English court must under Art 189 of the Treaty of Rome abide by the statute implementing the Directive, and that contained no restriction relating to the need for the company to be *en formation*.

Article 189 states: 'A Directive shall be binding, as to the result to be achieved, upon each member State to which it is addressed, but shall leave to the national authorities the choice of form and method.'

Counsel for Mr Lane also suggested that the word 'purports' must mean that there has been a representation that the company already exists. Lord Denning did not agree with this, saying that a contract can purport to be made on behalf of a company, or by a company, even though both parties knew that the company was not formed and was only about to be formed.

The court also decided that the form in which a person made the contract – e.g. 'for and on behalf of the company' as an agent, or merely by signing the company's name and subscribing his own, e.g. 'Boxo Ltd, J Snooks, managing director', where the form is not that of agency – did not matter and that in both cases the person concerned would be liable on the contract.

As regards the words 'subject to any agreement to the contrary', the court dealt with academic opinion which had suggested that where a person signs 'for and on behalf of the company' – i.e. as agent – he is saying, in effect, that he does not intend to be liable and would not be on the basis of the words 'subject to any agreement to the contrary'.

On this, Lord Denning said:

> 'If there was an express agreement that the man who was signing was not to be liable, the section would not apply. But, unless there is a clear exclusion of personal liability, [the section] should be given its full effect. It means that in all cases such as the present, where a person purports to contract on behalf of a company not yet formed, then however he expresses his signature he himself is personally liable on the contract.'

Comment

(i) The court did not consider, because it did not arise, whether an individual such as Mr Lane could have *sued* upon the contract. Section 36C talks about the person or agent being 'personally *liable*' on the contract. Perhaps it should say 'can sue or be sued'. However, lawyers have generally assumed that the court would give an individual like Mr Lane a right to sue if it arose, since it is, to say the least, unusual for a person to be liable on a contract and yet not be able to sue upon it.

(ii) In fact, the matter was raised in *Braymist Ltd* v *Wise Finance Company Ltd* [2001] *The Times*, 27 March. In that case a solicitor signed a pre-incorporation contract for the sale of land to be owned by Braymist before that company was incorporated. Later the other party, Wise Finance, refused to go on with the contract and Braymist after incorporation sued for damages. The solicitor was also a party to the action as a claimant. The High Court ruled that the claim succeeded. The solicitor was not merely liable on the contract but could also sue for its breach. Such a ruling, said the court, was workable and fair. Furthermore, the contract did not infringe s 2(1) and (3) of the Law of Property (Miscellaneous Provisions) Act 1989, which requires a contract concerning land to be in writing and signed by the parties to it. It was signed by the solicitor who was, under the provisions of s 36 of the CA 1985, a party to it.

(iii) As we have seen, s 36C can apply to make the promoter or other purported agent liable even though the company has not actually begun the process of formation. However, it was held in *Cotronic (UK) Ltd* v *Dezonie* [1991] BCC 200 that there must at least be a clear intention to form the company as there was in *Phonogram*. In the *Cotronic* case a contract was made by Mr Dezonie on behalf of a company which had been struck off the register for five years at a time when nobody concerned with its business had even thought about re-registering it. The Court of Appeal held that the contract was a nullity and Mr Dezonie was not personally liable on it under s 36C.

The above difficulties do not worry, for example, a garage proprietor in a small way of business who is promoting a limited company to take over the garage business. Such a person will obviously be a director of the new company and will usually hold most of the shares in it. Being in control, he can ensure that the company enters into the necessary contracts after incorporation. However, where the promoter is not in control of the company after its incorporation, the difficulties outlined above are very real.

Pre-incorporation contracts: the Contracts (Rights of Third Parties) Act 1999

Under the above Act the promoter and the third party are able to give the company when it is incorporated the right to sue and be sued upon a pre-incorporation contract. The Act makes clear that a party given such rights in a contract (in this case the particular pre-incorporation contract(s)) does not have to be in existence when the contract is made. Third-party rights may be applied by the court even in the absence of an express provision in the contract between the promoter and the third party if a term of the contract confers a benefit on the company which, of course, it will do. Nevertheless, an express term should be used to avoid doubt.

Pre-incorporation contracts: solutions to promoter's liability

A promoter may overcome the difficulties facing him in the matter of pre-incorporation contracts in the following ways:

(i) He may incorporate the company before he makes contracts, in which case the problems relating to pre-incorporation contracts do not apply. There is no reason why a promoter should not take this course since the expenses of incorporation are not prohibitive. There is, of course, no problem in the case of a ready-made or shelf company. The company exists and contracts can be made which will be binding on it from the beginning.

(ii) He can settle a draft agreement with the other party so that when the company is formed it enters into a contract on the terms of the draft; but the parties are not bound other than morally by the draft. However, in order to ensure that the company does enter into the contract after incorporation the memorandum or articles of the new company can be drafted to include a provision binding the directors to adopt it. The promoter is never liable here because there is never any contract with him.

(iii) The promoter may make the contract himself and assign the benefit of it to the company after it is incorporated. Since English law does not allow a person to assign the burden of his contract, the disadvantage of this method is that the promoter remains personally liable for the performance of his promises in the contract after the assignment to the company. Thus it is desirable for the other party to the contract to agree that the promoters shall be released from their obligations if the company enters into a new, but as regards terms identical, contract with the other party after incorporation. Since the promoters will usually control the company at this stage, they should be able to ensure that the company does make such a contract with the other party and so procure their own release.

(iv) Where the promoter is buying property for the company, he may take an option on it for, say, three months. If the company, when it is formed, wishes to take over the property, the promoter can assign the benefit of the option to the company or enforce the option personally for the company's benefit. If the company does not wish to take the property, the promoter is not personally liable to take and pay for it, though he may lose the money he agreed to pay for the option.

(v) It should also be noted that s 36C states that the promoter is personally liable 'subject to any agreement to the contrary'. Thus the promoter could agree when making the contract that he should not be personally liable on it. (See the remarks of Lord Denning in *Phonogram Ltd* v *Lane*, 1981.) This may not satisfy a third party who wants a form of initial binding agreement but it is sanctioned by the 1985 Act.

Nevertheless, the general legal position is unsatisfactory and the Jenkins Committee on Company Law Reform which reported in June 1962 (Cmnd 1749) recommended legislation under which a company when formed could validly adopt a pre-incorporation contract by unilateral act, and Clause 6 of the Companies Bill 1973, which never became law, permitted a company after incorporation to ratify contracts which purported to have been made in its name or on its behalf before incorporation without the consent of the other party involved. At the present time such an act or ratification operates only as an offer to be bound which the other party must accept if there is to be an enforceable contract.

Natal Land and Colonization Co *v* Pauline Colliery and Development Syndicate [1904] AC 120

Prior to incorporation, the P Company contracted to take an option to lease land belonging to Mrs de Carrey if it was coal bearing. After incorporation, the company entered on the land and made trial borings. The land was found to be coal bearing and the P company asked for a lease. Mrs de Carrey had by then transferred her interest in the property to the N company and it would not grant a lease. The P company sued at first instance for specific performance of the contract. *Held* – the P company could not enforce the option because:

(i) its own conduct in merely boring did not unequivocally evidence an intention to take a lease; *and*

(ii) even if it had, it was merely an offer, and there was no evidence of acceptance either by Mrs de Carrey or the N company.

Comment

United States courts are more generous. They take the view that a contract made before incorporation is an offer open for acceptance by the company. So any act done by the company after incorporation which is unequivocally referable to the offer operates as an acceptance and not an offer as in English company law.

Promotor's liability and the Contracts (Rights of Third Parties) Act 1999

It should be noted that the provisions of the above Act are no help to the promoter in avoiding liability on the pre-incorporation contract because, where third-party rights are given, in this case to the company when formed, the original parties, of whom the promoter is one, remain liable on the contract.

PAPER INCORPORATION – INITIAL REGISTRATION

Application for registration is made by filing certain documents with the Registrar of Companies. The main Registry is in Cardiff. The documents are as follows:

(i) *Memorandum of association.* If the company is a public company, the memorandum must be in accordance with *Table F* of the Companies (Tables A–F) Regulations 1985 (SI 1985/805), i.e. it must state that the company is a public limited company and its name must end with the words 'public limited company' and its authorised share capital must be at least £50,000.

(ii) *Articles of association.* Public and private companies limited by shares need not file special articles but may adopt *Table A* as set out in the 1985 regulations.

The contents and purposes of the above documents will be dealt with later.

(iii) *A statutory declaration* made by a solicitor engaged in the formation of the company or by a person named as a director or secretary of the company in the statement of first directors and secretary (see below) to the effect that s 12(1) (see below) has been complied with must be delivered to the Registrar on registration and he may accept it as sufficient evidence of compliance with the Act. The statutory declaration is made before a commissioner for oaths and if it contains false statements the person making those statements is liable to be prosecuted for perjury.

Section 12(1) provides that the Registrar shall not register the memorandum of a company (in effect shall not register the company) unless he is satisfied that all the requirements of the Companies Acts in regard to registration have been complied with.

A certificate of incorporation of a public company states that it is a public company and is also conclusive evidence that the requirements of the Act have been complied with and that the company is a public company. A certificate of incorporation issued to a private company is also conclusive evidence that the Act has been complied with.

(iv) *The address of the registered office and a statement of directors and secretaries.* All companies are required to file on registration a notice of the address of the registered office and a statement of the first directors and secretaries. The latter shows in respect of individual directors their names and any former names which they have used, their residential address, their nationalities, their business occupations, any other directorships which they hold, or have held during the previous five years and, if the company is a public company or a subsidiary of a public company, the dates of their birth. Where a director is a corporation the notice must show its corporate name and the address of its registered or principal office (see further Chapter 15).

The statement must be signed by or on behalf of the subscribers of the memorandum and must contain a consent signed by each of the directors and secretaries named in it to act in the relevant capacity.

Those persons named in the statement are deemed, on the incorporation of the company, to have been appointed as the first directors or secretary or joint secretaries of the company. Any appointment by the articles delivered with the memorandum of a person as director or secretary of the company is void unless he is named as a director or as a secretary in the statement.

If the Registrar is satisfied with the contents of the documents, he will, on payment of certain fees, issue a certificate of incorporation. It should be noted that if the documents are in order and the company's objects appear legal, the Registrar has no discretion in the matter. He must grant a certificate and, since the Registrar is here acting in a quasi-judicial capacity, the subscribers may enforce registration through the courts by asking the court to order the Registrar to make the registration (*R* v *Registrar of Companies, ex parte Bowen* [1914] 3 KB 1161).

Confidentiality orders

What is said above in regard to the details to be given in respect of directors and secretaries must be considered in the context of confidentiality orders. These may be granted by the Secretary of State for Trade and Industry to individual directors and secretaries who have been or may be under threat from protest groups because of the company's activities or because of previous corporate association, e.g. animal rights groups and genetically modified food protestors. Where the company will be involved in any area likely to be subjected to protest and where fringe elements might threaten harm the usual residential address is not given. Instead the address notified by the individual to the company is given. This may be the registered office of the company. A separate statement with the usual residential address is filed separately and kept by the Registrar on a secure (not public) register available only to restricted users, e.g. the police.

ELECTRONIC INCORPORATION – INITIAL INCORPORATION

Companies House has introduced a service whereby presenters who incorporate companies regularly can conduct the process electronically. Companies House also plans to introduce an incorporation service from its Website. This citizens' incorporation service is not yet available. There is a system of electronic authentication of the memorandum and articles where these documents are delivered electronically. There is a provision for electronic statements of compliance with company legislation to replace the relevant statutory declarations, with penalties for false statements. This procedure for electronic incorporation is permitted under the Electronic Communications Act 2000 and the Electronic Communications Order 2000 as part of the Registrar's general power to accept documents electronically.

EFFECT OF INCORPORATION

The issue of a certificate of incorporation incorporates the members of the company into a *persona at law* (legal person), and limits their liability if the memorandum requires this. The certificate of incorporation is *conclusive* evidence that all the requirements of the Companies Act as to registration have been complied with, and if any irregularity had occurred in the registration procedure, it would not be possible to attack the validity of the company's incorporation. The evidence which was available to prove the irregularity would not be admissible (*Cotman* v *Brougham*, 1918, see Chapter 3). This provision means that all English companies registered under the Act are companies *de jure* (as a matter of law). In the United States of America, where this rule does not apply in every state, actions have been brought in the courts attacking the validity of a company's formation many years after incorporation. This cannot happen in England and Wales.

However, the certificate of incorporation is not conclusive evidence that all the objects of the company are legal; and if a company is registered with illegal or immoral objects, the House of Lords decided in *Bowman* v *Secular Society* [1917] AC 406 that the Crown could apply, through the Attorney-General, for the prerogative *order of certiorari* to cancel the registration made by the Registrar. In *Attorney-General* v *Lindi St Claire (Personal Services) Ltd* [1981] 2 Co Law 69 the High Court quashed a decision by the Registrar of Companies to register the business of a prostitute as Lindi St Claire (Personal Services) Ltd. The name was registered in 1979 after the Registrar had rejected Miss St Claire's alternative titles, i.e. Prostitutes Ltd, Hookers Ltd and Lindi St Claire French Lessons Ltd. Miss St Claire's accountants advised her to register a company after receiving a letter from the Revenue's policy division stating that it considered prostitution to be a trade. The Attorney-General contended that the company should not have been registered because it was formed for sexually immoral purposes and was consequently against public policy and illegal. The High Court agreed and the registration was quashed.

In addition, a company incorporated with unlawful objects may be ordered by the court to be wound up on the petition of a creditor or member, the ground for the petition being that it is just and equitable that the company should be wound up (Insolvency Act 1986, s 122(1)(g)), or on the petition of the Department of Trade and Industry (DTI) where it has appointed an inspector to investigate the company's affairs and he has reported adversely on the legality of the objects for which it was formed.

From the date impressed upon the certificate the company becomes a body corporate with perpetual succession, and with the right to exercise the powers given in its memorandum. The company's life dates from the first moment of the day of incorporation (*Jubilee Cotton Mills* v *Lewis*, 1924, see below).

There is no statutory requirement that the certificate should be displayed at the registered office or kept at any particular place.

Jubilee Cotton Mills *v* Lewis [1924] AC 958

Lewis was a promoter of a company formed to purchase a cotton mill and to carry on the business of cotton spinning. The memorandum and articles of the company were accepted by the Registrar of Companies on 6 January 1920, and the certificate of incorporation was dated on that day. However, the certificate, it appeared, was not signed by the Registrar until 8 January 1920. On 6 January a large number of fully-paid shares were allotted to the vendors of the mill, and they were later transferred to Lewis. The question of the validity of the allotment arose in this case, and it was *held* that the certificate was conclusive as to the date on which the company was incorporated. A company is deemed to be incorporated from the day of the date on its certificate of incorporation, and from the first moment of that day. Therefore, the allotment was not void on the ground that it was made before the company came into existence.

READY-MADE COMPANIES

It will be appreciated that where a ready-made company is used the registration procedures will have been gone through. The promoters may wish to change the ready-made company's name and will have to appoint directors and a secretary and notify these appointments to the Registrar. The ready-made company will have had directors and a secretary on formation but these persons will have resigned on the purchase of the ready-made company.

The notification of the new directors and secretary is under s 288 as changes in the directorate and secretariat since they are *replacements* and *not original* appointments.

PUBLICITY IN CONNECTION WITH INCORPORATION

The Registrar is required to publish in the *London Gazette*:

(*a*) the issue of any certificate of incorporation (but there is in fact no statutory requirement to display the certificate at the registered office, though it is often so displayed);
(*b*) any report as to the value of a non-cash asset under s 104 where a non-cash asset has been acquired from a subscriber.

OVERSEA COMPANIES

A company which is formed in a country outside Great Britain, whether incorporated by the law of that country or not, may carry on business in Great Britain without being incorporated under our legislation relating to companies, however large or small its membership may be (*Bateman* v *Service* (1881) 6 App Cas 386). However, if the company is an incorporated one and *establishes a place of business in Great Britain*, then it must within a month of so doing file with the Registrar:

(*a*) a certified copy of the instruments defining the constitution of the company, and a certified translation if not in English;
(*b*) a list of directors and secretary (the arrangements regarding confidentiality orders already referred to apply to directors and secretaries of oversea companies);
(*c*) the name and address of at least one person resident in Great Britain authorised to accept service of notices on behalf of the company;
(*d*) the date on which the company's place of business in Great Britain was established.

Any alteration in the above particulars must be filed within 21 days of the alteration and the company must file annually the same accounts as a registered company.

The company's name and country of incorporation (and, if the liability of its members is limited, a statement of that fact) must be stated on every place of business, every prospectus, and on all letterheads, notices, and official publications of the company in Great Britain. It should be noted that the oversea company must register under the name by which it is registered oversea and the name will be subject to the statutory restrictions on registration of company names in s 26. If the corporate name offends s 26, the oversea company will have to register a non-offending business name under which the place of business will operate in the UK.

An oversea company is also subject to the same restrictions under the Financial Services and Markets Act 2000 as a registered company in regard to the issue of listing particulars or a prospectus within Great Britain, and as to its name. If an oversea company ceases to have a place of business in Great Britain, it must notify this fact to the Registrar who will remove the company from the Companies House index.

Companies incorporated in the Channel Islands or the Isle of Man, which establish a place of business here, are thereafter subject to all the provisions of the Act as if they were registered companies, and must deliver to the Registrar all documents which would be required to register a company if it were incorporated in Great Britain.

The above provisions have increased in importance since our entry into the European Community with the consequent increase in the number of foreign companies establishing manufacturing premises here.

Oversea companies: branch registration

The above long-standing regime relates to places of business registration. However, more recently a regime of branch registration has been introduced to comply with the Eleventh EC Company Directive. The relevant regulations are the Companies and Credit and Financial Institutions (Branch Disclosure) Regulations 1992 which came into force in 1993. The distinction between a place of business and a branch gives rise to difficulties. Companies House Guidance Note CHN 25 lists warehouse facilities, administrative offices, share transfer registration offices and internal data processing facilities as types of activity which fall into the place of business registration requirements. The regulations do not define 'branch' other than to say that the definition in the EC Directive applies. This says that a branch must be able to negotiate directly with third parties who may transact business direct with the branch without having to deal with another office, e.g. head office. Anything below that is not affected by registration procedures, e.g. a foreign company with an office in Great Britain purely for prestige reasons (*CPG Products Corporation* v *Shroder Executor and Trustee Co*, Chancery Division (1980) 21 April, unreported).

A new form BR1 must be submitted to the Registrar of Companies within one month of opening the branch. The form requires company details and branch details. A certified copy of the constitution together with a copy of the latest accounts and certified translations if applicable must be submitted with BR1 plus the registration fee.

The requirement for a place of business to show its corporate name and the country of incorporation on all places of business and on all billheads, notices and official publications applies also to branches. The branch stationery must give the place of registration of the oversea company and its registration number. If the liability of the company's members is limited this must also be stated. If the oversea company is incorporated outside the EU the place of registration of that company, its legal form and the registration number must be stated together with the head office location and if it is being wound up if this is applicable, e.g. as on merger or reconstruction.

Accounting requirements for branches

The requirements are dependent on the home state of the company's incorporation. The position is as follows:

(*a*) if the accounts are required to be disclosed and delivered in the home state, then copies of the accounts should be delivered to the Registrar within three months of the date for delivery in the home state;
(*b*) if accounts are required to be disclosed but not registered in the home state, copies of the relevant accounts must be delivered within six months of the first date of disclosure in the home state; or
(*c*) if no disclosure or delivery is required by the home state, accounts must still be delivered within 13 months after the end of the relevant accounting reference period. The accounts must be accompanied by a filing fee.

As regards (*a*) and (*b*) above, accounts must be prepared and disclosed to accord with the requirements of the home state law. If that law permits modified accounts, they may be filed in respect of the branch. In regard to (*c*), accounts must be prepared in accordance with the Oversea Companies (Accounts) (Modifications and Exemptions) Order 1990 SI 1990/440.

In regard to companies setting up a branch in Great Britain, there is a new service provided by Companies House for same-day registration. This is not available for companies that merely establish a place of business here.

A company cannot register both a branch and a place of business. If this happens the branch regime takes precedence and this is the regime that must be complied with.

POST-INCORPORATION PROCEDURES FOR RE-REGISTRATION

Conversion of companies from private to public

A private company may be re-registered as a public company if not previously re-registered as an unlimited company if:

(*a*) the members pass a special or written resolution which alters the company's memorandum and articles so that they fit the statutory requirements of a public company. The name will change on conversion. Companies House will only permit a change to the suffix plc under the re-registration procedure. If any other change in the name is required the members must pass a special resolution (which may be in written form) and file the resolution with the re-registration documents with the relevant name change fee. The re-registration certificate will carry the new name;
(*b*) the requirements as regards share capital are met. This means that the nominal value of the allotted share capital is not less than £50,000 and in respect of all the shares, or as many as are needed to make up the authorised minimum, the following conditions are satisfied:

   (i) no less than one-quarter of the nominal value of each share and the whole of any premium on it is paid up;
   (ii) none of the shares has been fully or partly paid up by means of an undertaking to do work or perform services where this has not already been performed or otherwise discharged; and

(iii) where any share has been allotted as fully or partly paid up for a non-cash consideration which consists solely or partly of an undertaking to do something other than to perform services, i.e. usually an undertaking to transfer a non-cash asset, either the undertaking has been performed or otherwise discharged or there is a contract between the company and the person involved under which the undertaking must be performed within five years.

Shares allotted under an employees' share scheme which are not one-quarter paid up can be disregarded for the purpose of deciding whether the above requirements have been met;

(*c*) an application for the change is made to the Registrar on a form signed by a director or secretary of the company;

(*d*) the application is accompanied by the following documents:

(i) a printed copy of the memorandum and articles as altered and added to by the special or written resolution;

(ii) a copy of a balance sheet prepared as at a date not more than seven months before the date of the application, but not necessarily in respect of an accounting reference period. The balance sheet must be accompanied by a copy of an unqualified report of the company's auditor in relation to the balance sheet. If there is a qualification, the auditor must state in writing that it is not material in determining whether at the date of the balance sheet the company's net assets were at least equal to the sum of its called up capital and non-distributable reserves, such as its share premium account and capital redemption reserve;

(iii) a copy of a written statement by the company's auditors that in their opinion the balance sheet referred to in (ii) above shows that the amount of the company's net assets at the date of the balance sheet was not less than the aggregate of its called up share capital and non-distributable reserves;

(iv) a statutory declaration by a director or secretary of the company that: (a) the requirements in regard to the making of necessary changes in the company's constitution have been complied with; and that (b) between the balance sheet date and the application for re-registration there has been no change in the financial position of the company which has caused the net assets to become less than the aggregate of called up share capital plus non-distributable reserves.

It should be noted that audit exemption regulations do not dispense with the requirement of an audit report on the balance sheet. This means that small companies can exempt themselves from the requirement to appoint an auditor unless and until it becomes necessary to do so for certain purposes other than the audit of financial statements. Re-registration is one of those purposes. Other areas where an auditor is required will be picked up as they occur.

Additional requirements relating to share capital

If between the date of the balance sheet and the passing of a special (or written) resolution to convert to a public company the company has allotted shares which are wholly or partly paid for by a non-cash consideration, then it shall not make an application for re-registration unless before application is made:

(*a*) the consideration has been valued in accordance with s 103, i.e. by a person or persons who are qualified by law to audit a public company's accounts who may themselves appoint other suitable persons to assist them;

(*b*) a report regarding the value has been made to the company by the persons referred to in (*a*) above during the six months immediately preceding the allotment of the shares.

If the Registrar is satisfied with the application for re-registration and provided that there is not in existence any court order reducing the company's share capital below the authorised minimum, he will on payment of a fee retain the documents which have been sent to him and issue a certificate of incorporation stating that the company is a public company.

The company then becomes a public company and the alterations in its constitution take effect. The certificate of incorporation is conclusive evidence that the re-registration requirements have been complied with and that the company is a public company.

Conversion of companies from public to private: generally

This is permitted and the procedure is as follows:

(*a*) the members must pass a special resolution altering the memorandum so that it no longer states that the company is a public company and also in terms of the name. The provisions regarding change of suffix from plc to Ltd and any further name change are with the necessary changes the same as those set out above for private to public conversion; and

(*b*) application is then made on the prescribed forms signed by a director or secretary. The application is delivered to the Registrar together with printed copies of the memorandum and articles as altered or added to by the special resolution.

It should be noted that because this type of conversion may well result in the loss of a market (i.e. a listing or quotation on the Stock Exchange) in which to sell the shares there are as regards the special resolution dissentient rights. Within a period of 28 days after the passing of the resolution dissentient holders of at least 5 per cent in nominal value of the company's issued share capital or any class thereof, or not less than 50 members, may apply to the court to have the resolution cancelled and the court may cancel or affirm it. If there is no application to the court or if it is unsuccessful and the court affirms the special resolution, the Registrar will issue a new certificate of incorporation as a private company.

It should also be noted that the court may, in addition, adjourn the proceedings brought by dissentients in order that satisfactory arrangements may be made for the purchase of the shares of those dissentients. The purchase may obviously be by other shareholders but the company's money may also be used for this purpose and if this is the intention the court will make the necessary order to provide for the purchase by the company of its own shares and to reduce its share capital. The order may also make any necessary alterations in or additions to the memorandum and articles of the company.

Conversion of companies from public to private: reduction of share capital

If the court reduces the share capital of a public company to below £50,000, it must re-register as a private company. To speed up this process the court may authorise re-registration without the company having followed the above procedures and the court order may specify and make the necessary changes in the company's constitution. Thus a reduction of capital may now have the further consequence of changing the company's status from public to private.

Conversion of private limited company to private unlimited company

A company limited by shares or by guarantee may be re-registered as an unlimited company.

However, no public company may apply to be re-registered as an unlimited company because a public company cannot be an unlimited company and therefore such a conversion involves a reduction in status from public to private. A public company which wishes to re-register as unlimited must use the procedure laid down in the 1985 Act for conversion of a public company to a private company.

If, however, the company is private, all the members must consent in writing and if this can be achieved there must be sent to the Registrar of Companies a statutory declaration by the directors that all the members of the company have consented together with copies of the memorandum and articles as altered. The Registrar will then issue a new certificate of incorporation which is conclusive evidence that the conversion is in all respects valid. In addition, the Registrar must publish the issue of the new certificate in the *London Gazette*. There can be no conversion back to a limited company. In addition, a company is excluded from re-registering as unlimited if it has previously re-registered as limited.

As we have seen, unlimited companies do not in general have to file accounts and re-registration back and forth between limited and unlimited status is not allowed in order to prevent selective filing of accounts, e.g. by re-registration as unlimited in a year in which the directors did not wish to file accounts and then back to limited status subsequently.

Conversion of private unlimited company to private limited company

It is also possible to re-register an unlimited company as a limited one but, as we have seen, this does not apply to a company which was previously a limited company but has re-registered as an unlimited one. If the conversion is *to a private limited company*, the conversion must be authorised by special or written resolution of the members. Following this copies of the memorandum and articles as altered are sent to the Registrar who will issue a new certificate of incorporation which is conclusive evidence that the conversion is in all respects valid. The Registrar will also advertise the issue of the new certificate in the *London Gazette*.

If an unlimited company wishes to re-register *as a public company* which is by definition a company limited by shares, the procedure to be followed is that for the re-registration of a private company as a public company except that the special resolution to convert must include two additional matters as follows:

(*a*) it must state that the liability of the members is to be limited by shares and what the share capital of the company is to be; and

(*b*) it must make such alterations in the company's memorandum as are necessary to bring it in substance and in form into conformity with the requirements of the Companies Act in regard to the memorandum of association of a public company limited by shares. This involves, e.g., changes in the company's name and capital clauses.

The re-registration as a public company is not available to unlimited companies which have re-registered as such having been previously limited companies.

The effect on the liability of members of such a conversion is that those who become members after conversion are liable only to the extent of capital unpaid on their shares. Those who were members at the date of the conversion, and are still members at the date of winding-up, are fully liable for debts and liabilities incurred before conversion. Those who were members at the date of conversion but have transferred their shares after conversion and before winding-up are liable for debts and liabilities incurred before conversion up to three years after it took place (Insolvency Act 1986, s 77(2)).

GRADED QUESTIONS

Essay mode

1 The directors of Bullian Ltd have decided that it is necessary to convert their company into a public limited company.

Advise them on:

(*a*) the differences between a private and public limited company.

AND

(*b*) the procedures to be followed during re-registration.

2 Brian, who had decided to transfer his existing wholesale food business to a private limited company called Brian Foods Ltd, delivered the necessary documents to the Registrar of Companies and received the Certificate of Incorporation (dated 1 April) on 6 April 2005.

On 15 March 2005, Brian agreed to purchase a quantity of coffee from Benco Ltd in a letter which he signed 'For and on behalf of Brian Foods Ltd, B Brian, Director'.

At the first meeting of the board of directors of Brian Foods Ltd the contract with Benco Ltd was approved and the company took delivery of the first consignment. The board later found that the Benco brand of coffee was more difficult to sell than had been anticipated and decided to cancel any subsequent consignments.

(*a*) Advise Brian Foods Ltd on its liability to Benco Ltd.

AND

(*b*) How far, if at all, will your answer to (*a*) differ if on 10 April 2005 the two companies re-negotiated the contract and agreed on a different contract price?

AND

(*c*) How far, if at all, will your answer to (*a*) differ if in the letter of 15 March 2005 Brian expressly excluded his personal liability?

(*Glasgow Caledonian University*)

3 Bill and Ben trade in partnership as garage mechanics. They are considering changing their form of business association and trading as a private registered company limited by shares.

Explain to them the legal procedures that they must follow in order to form such a company, and advise them on the advantages of trading as a private company as opposed to a partnership.

(*The Association of Chartered Certified Accountants*)

4 Philip, who is in the process of forming a company, wishes to avoid personal liability upon any contracts he may enter into on behalf of the proposed company. Advise Philip.

(*The Institute of Chartered Accountants in England and Wales*)

Objective mode

Four alternative answers are given. Select ONE only. Circle the answer which you consider to be correct. Check your answers by referring back to the information given in the chapter and against the answers at the back of the book.

1 When a private company wants to re-register as a public company it must file a balance sheet with the Registrar. The balance sheet must be one which is not more than:

A 15 months old at the date of re-registration.
B 7 months old at the date of re-registration.
C 15 months old at the date of application.
D 7 months old at the date of application.

2 Thames was re-registered from a limited to an unlimited company. It wishes to re-register as a public company.

A It must apply to the Registrar to be registered as a public limited company.
B It must re-register as a private limited company and then re-register as a public company.
C It must pass a special resolution to convert into a public company.
D There is no procedure whereby Thames may become a public limited company.

3 Fred is a member of a private company at the date of its re-registration as a public company. Fred cannot profit by selling non-cash assets to the public company within an initial period of two years from the date of re-registration unless:

A the sale is approved by a resolution of the board and the consideration is not an allotment of shares.
B the property is valued by an independent accountant and the members approve the sale by ordinary resolution.
C the property is independently valued and approved by a resolution of the board.

D the sale is approved by an ordinary resolution of the members and the consideration is not an allotment of shares.

4 Before the incorporation of Ouse Ltd its promoter Bob entered into a contract on behalf of the company. The contract gave the unformed company third-party rights. Who is liable if the contract is later breached?

A Ouse Ltd.
B Bob and Ouse Ltd.
C The shareholders of Ouse Ltd.
D The directors of Ouse Ltd.

5 Joe and Fred wished to form a company. On 1 March 20XX they filed the appropriate documents with the Registrar. On 10 May 20XX they received a certificate of incorporation dated 1 May 20XX. Later they found out that the company had been registered on 4 May 20XX.

On what date was the company incorporated?

A 1 March 20XX.
B 1 May 20XX.
C 10 May 20XX.
D 4 May 20XX.

6 Meg used to be employed by Trent Ltd. Her contract contained a clause under which she agreed not to compete with Trent Ltd. The clause was reasonable in terms of its duration and area. Meg has now formed a company called Meg (Corporate Services) Ltd and has started to compete against Trent Ltd through the company. Will Trent Ltd be able to obtain an injunction to prevent Meg (Corporate Services) Ltd from competing against Trent Ltd?

A No, because Meg (Corporate Services) Ltd is a separate entity.
B Yes, because the company has been formed as a device to avoid the restraint clause.
C No, since the company is not liable for the actions of its shareholders.
D Yes, because Meg (Corporate Services) Ltd is engaged in wrongful trading.

The answers to questions set in objective mode appear on p 576.

3

THE CONSTITUTION OF THE COMPANY – THE MEMORANDUM OF ASSOCIATION

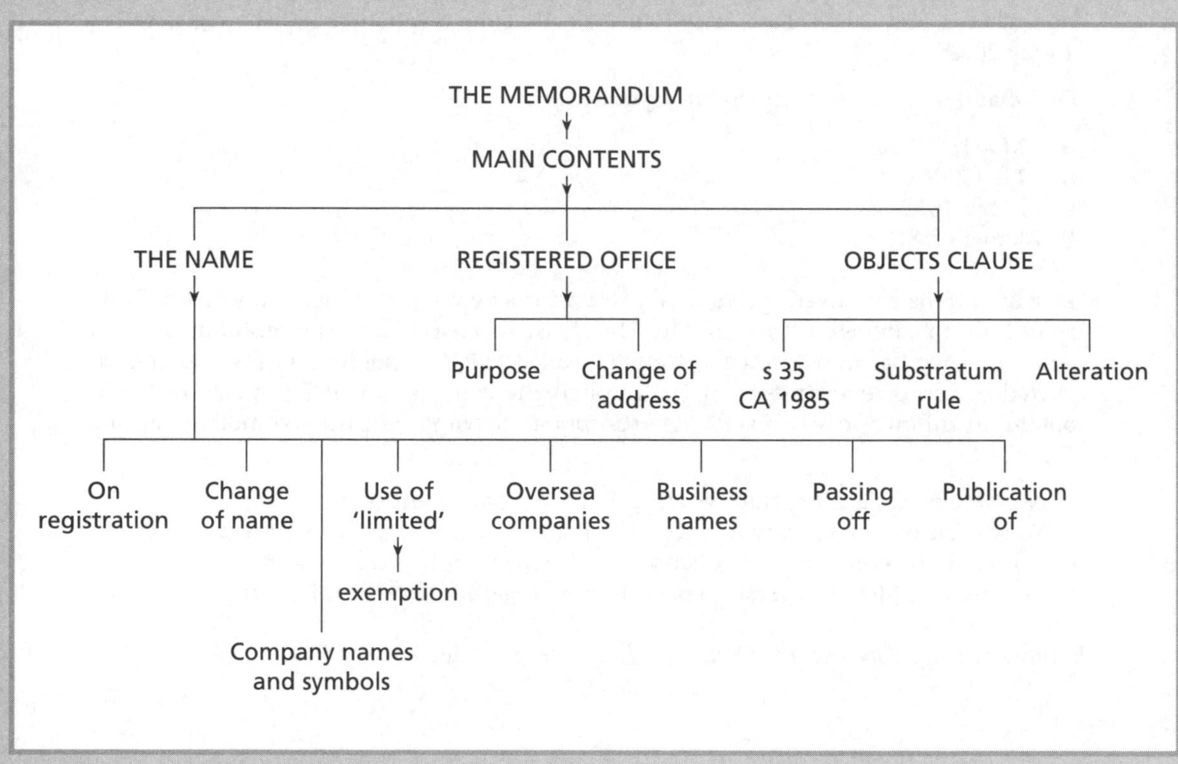

The constitution of a registered company consists of two documents called the *memorandum of association* and the *articles of association*. The memorandum contains the most important provisions setting out as it does the sort of activities which the company can carry on. The articles contain rules governing the internal management of the company such as the appointment of directors and the powers of the board, the rights of different classes of shareholders, and the holding of meetings of the company. The memorandum is of interest to outsiders who wish to deal with the company, while the articles are of interest mainly to shareholders and directors. However, since the powers of directors are, as we have seen, in the articles, they are on occasions also of interest to outsiders.

CONTENTS – GENERALLY

The memorandum must contain clauses setting out the following information:

(*a*) the name of the company with 'Limited' as the last word if the company is a private limited company. If the company is a public company, the liability of its members must be limited and its name must end with the words 'public limited company';

(*b*) in the case of a public company, the statement 'The company is to be a public company';

(*c*) whether the registered office is to be situated in England and Wales. Alternatively the memorandum may state that the registered office is to be situated in Wales;

(*d*) the objects clause;

(*e*) a statement that the liability of the members is limited by shares (or by guarantee) where this is the case;

(*f*) the amount of the share capital (if any) with which the company proposes to be registered and its division into shares of a fixed amount. This does not apply to unlimited companies. Where the company is a public company, the share capital must be at least £50,000.

In the case of a company limited by guarantee, the memorandum must state that each member undertakes to contribute to the assets of the company in the event of its being wound up, such amount as may be required, not exceeding a specified amount. The above, being statutory clauses, must appear in the memorandum and not, for example, in the articles, but the memorandum may contain other clauses (e.g. the rights attaching to different classes of shares), since the persons responsible for drafting the company's constitution have a choice between the memorandum and articles in the case of other provisions.

The memorandum is completed by the *Association Clause* in which the subscribers declare their intention to be associated as a company. Under s 1 the memorandum must be subscribed by at least two persons, whether the company is public or private, except in the case of single-member private companies where one subscriber is enough. Subscribers must take at least one share and each subscriber must show opposite his name the number of shares he takes. Each subscriber must sign the memorandum in the presence of at least one witness who must also attest the signature. The same witness may attest all the signatures.

The regulations which are designed to implement the EC Twelfth Directive make clear that s 1 does not apply to a private company so as to prevent it having one member and therefore one subscriber to its memorandum.

Reference has already been made in Chapter 2 to the fact that the memorandum can be filed electronically, subscription being by electronic signature where there is an electronic incorporation under the Electronic Communications Order 2000.

Since the memorandum is such an important document, it will now be examined in more detail.

THE NAME

Chapter II of Part I of the 1985 Act sets up a system for controlling company names.

COMPANY NAMES

On registration

A new company may not be registered by a name which:

1 includes, otherwise than at the end of the name, any of the following words or their permitted abbreviations: 'limited', 'unlimited' or 'public limited company' (or their Welsh equivalent);
2 is the same as a name already on the index of names kept by the Registrar of Companies;
3 in the opinion of the Secretary of State would, if used, constitute a criminal offence or be offensive, e.g. a name which was obscene or blasphemous. This category of restriction will not often be met with in business but the Registrar turned down the names 'Prostitutes Ltd', 'Hookers Ltd' and 'Lindi St Claire French Lessons Ltd' when application was made for the registration of the business of a prostitute (*Attorney-General* v *Lindi St Claire* (*Personal Services*) *Ltd* [1981] 2 Co Law 69).

In addition, the consent of the Secretary of State for Trade and Industry is required to the registration of a company by a name including certain words. These are words implying national or multinational pre-eminence, e.g. 'International' and 'European', though for 'International' a letter confirming that the proposed company will trade with at least two foreign countries is enough to get approval; government connection, patronage or sponsorship, e.g. Board or Council as in 'County Council Supplies'; business pre-eminence or representative status, e.g. 'Federation' or 'Institution'; certain specific objects or functions, e.g. 'Insurance' or 'Trust'. A company wishing to use the words 'association' or 'society' in its name must be limited by guarantee. Its constitution must provide for one member one vote and it must have non-profit distribution clauses in its memorandum.

There are also sensitive names which will only be registered if the applicant has obtained a letter of non-objection from the relevant government department or other body, e.g. 'Royal' or 'Royalty' requires a letter of non-objection from the Home Office, while 'Charity' or 'Charitable' requires a letter from the Charity Commission. Plural and possessive forms of the names set out are included so that 'Charities' and 'Charities'' are covered.

The above provisions apply to an existing company which wishes to change its name.

A company may also wish to use the word 'holding' or 'holdings' in its name and, since this indicates that the company is the parent company of a group of companies, it is necessary to send a letter to the Registrar together with or containing evidence of, e.g., shareholding in the other company or companies that are its subsidiaries.

Where the approval of the Secretary of State is required, the necessary evidence must be submitted with the incorporation documents or with the relevant resolution on a change of name. Where the approval of a particular body or organisation is required, a statement that an approach to that body or organisation has been made, together with a copy of any response received, must be included. This would be the case where the word 'charity' was to be used and the Charity Commissioners had been approached.

Trade marks

The name must not include a registered trade mark unless the consent of the owner of the trade mark is obtained. Possible infringement is a matter for the promoters and not the Registrar. The promoters should therefore make a search in the Trade Marks Index at the Patent Office in London or in Newport, Gwent.

In this regard, it is worth noting that the mere registration of a trade mark does not prevent the use of that name by a company that is already registered with it. The company can use the defence of 'honest practices in industrial or commercial matters' in s 11(2) (a) of the Trade Marks Act 1994, provided that the company is not using the name to deliberately exploit the goodwill of the owner of the trade mark. (See *Scandecor Developments AB* v *Scandecor Marketing Ltd* [1998] 12 LSG 28 where a passing-off action concerned the use of the name 'Scandecor'. The action failed.)

Use of own name

If the promoters experience difficulty in getting the Registrar to accept a name it may be acceptable for the promoters, if they are to remain associated with the company, normally as member/directors, to use their own names. The Registrar may require some addition to the name if a person has already registered his or her own name that is the same at Companies House, e.g. Bloggs and Snooks (Furnishings) Ltd. This will not necessarily prevent an action for passing off at common law leading to damages and/or an injunction to prevent the use of an own name. Thus in *Asprey & Garrard Ltd* v *WRA (Guns) Ltd* (2001) High Court 18 May (unreported) the claimants in a passing-off action and infringement of trade mark rights are a well known and established trader in luxury goods. The defendant traded in the same line of business in London, the same location as the claimants, in the business name of William R Asprey Esq. William Asprey who was formerly an employee of the claimants effectively controlled the defendant company. The High Court granted an injunction against passing off and infringement of trade mark. The court dismissed the own name defence saying that it was exceptional and must not be used as in this case to cause deception. It will be noted that the problems here arose from the use of a business name but the principles are applicable to corporate own names, though in such a case there might have been more difficulty in getting it registered in the first place.

Change of name

A company may change its name voluntarily, or the Secretary of State may direct a change, as follows.

(a) Voluntary change

A company may, by special or in the case of a private company written resolution, change its name and the Registrar will issue an altered certificate of incorporation. The new name must comply with the above-mentioned provisions relating to the prohibition on registration of certain names, and the change does not take effect until the altered certificate of incorporation is issued.

When considering the change of name, the practical point of cost should be borne in mind since it will be necessary to change letterheads and signs, and generally inform customers and bankers.

(b) Compulsory change

(i) Within 12 *months* of registration in a particular name the Secretary of State may direct a change in name within such period as he may specify if a registered name is the same or 'too like' that of a pre-existing company which appears (or should have appeared) on the index.

A complaints procedure exists and guidelines have been published but a major example of the 'too like' situation will be names with a distinctive element in common, e.g. Widget Holdings Ltd and Widget Ltd.

In all cases the type of business carried on, the geographical location and the area of the operation of the business are factors that the Registrar will take into account. The procedure for an organisation aggrieved is to lodge an objection with the Registrar with a request that the offending company's name be changed, together with evidence of the confusion that has arisen or will arise. If the grounds are sufficient, the Registrar will direct the company last registered to change its name.

After the passing of 12 months (and during the first 12 months) the common law action for passing off is available where the offending name is the same or too like that of the company concerned.

In a way these provisions are unsatisfactory because a newly registered company and one which has changed its name will be in doubt for 12 months as to the right to its name.

(ii) Where it appears to the Secretary of State that a company has given misleading information in connection with its registration in a particular name, the Secretary of State may *within five years of registration* direct a change of name within such period as he may specify. Names obtained by deception are, e.g., sensitive names where false information has been given to the approving authority. Thus the use of the words 'Charity' or 'Charitable' requires the approval of the Charity Commissioners and if promoters gave false information to the Commissioners in order to get permission to use, say, 'Barchester Charities Ltd' which they intended to use for personal gain rather than charitable purposes, the name would have been obtained by deception.

(iii) In addition, the Secretary of State has power to direct a company to change its name if it gives so misleading an indication of its activities as to be likely to cause harm to the public. The section is designed to deal with 'shell' companies as where a company named, e.g., 'Prosper Investments Trust' is acquired and used for the purpose of making cheap washing machines. The power is exercisable at any time. The company must comply with a request to change within six weeks but has a right to appeal to the court within three weeks after the DTI requirement is notified to it. The court may set aside the direction or confirm it.

Directions under the above provisions are rare but such a direction was given by the Secretary of State in regard to the Association of Certified Public Accountants of Britain which the Secretary of State considered to be a registered name which was likely to mislead the public. The direction was based on the word 'certified' which is already in the title of the Association of Chartered Certified Accountants. An application to the Court of Appeal to set aside the direction was dismissed (see *Association of Certified Public Accountants of Britain* v *Secretary of State for Trade and Industry* [1997] *The Times*, 12 June).

Where a company changes its name either voluntarily or compulsorily under the above provisions, the change will not affect any of its rights or obligations or render defective any legal proceedings.

On a change of name a new certificate of incorporation is issued by the Registrar who must publish the fact of issue in the *London Gazette*.

Only the members can change a company's name

The Court of Appeal has considered whether the court has jurisdiction to order and empower the Registrar of Companies to change the name of the company as it appears on the register in a situation where no special resolution of its members to that effect has been passed. The Court of Appeal ruled that there is no such jurisdiction.

Halifax plc *v* Halifax Repossessions Ltd (2004) *The Times* 11 February

The claimants had brought proceedings against the defendants for infringement of trade mark and passing off and the court granted relief in terms preventing the defendant group companies from using the word 'Halifax' in their names. However, there was no change of name. The claimants then sought a court order under the Civil Procedure Rules to order the Registrar to change the names to any name not including 'Halifax'. Two such orders were made but not acted upon by the Registrar. In the Court of Appeal it was decided that the relevant rule did not give the court jurisdiction to make such a change in the absence of a special resolution of the members. The Companies Act scheme for change must be followed. There were serious consequences to a change of company name. Signing company cheques where the company's name was not properly stated could result in personal liability in the signer. There were penalties for failing to display the proper name on places of business and on stationery and so on. The Registrar could not effectively be required to go beyond her statutory functions. She could not become involved in private litigation.

Company names and symbols

The increasing use of symbols in company names, such as '@', has led Companies House to revise its policy on registration of company names. There are two major possibilities as follows:

- *On incorporation or change of name*. Here the name must not be the same as that of an existing company. Here the use of a symbol may be sufficient to allow registration of the name. Thus, if there was already on the register a name such as 'Florists at City House Ltd', it would seem that a company called 'Florists @ City House Ltd' would be registered;
- *Challenge to a name said to be 'too like' an existing one*. Here apparently the mere use of a symbol may not be enough so that in the example given above the second registration may be challenged as 'too like'. This also applies to words such as 'UK' or 'GB' or 'com', the addition of which to a name will not prevent a 'too like' challenge. However, each case will be considered on its merits.

Companies exempt from requirement to use the word 'limited'

Companies eligible

Certain companies are exempt from the requirement to use the word 'limited', or the Welsh equivalent or any abbreviation meaning the same, in their names. The exemption applies:

1 to private companies limited by guarantee, which are the only type of company to be allowed to apply for the exemption;
2 where the objects of the company are to promote commerce, art, science, education, religion, charity, or any profession and anything incidental or conducive to any of those objects;
3 where the company's memorandum or articles require that the company's profits or income be applied in the promotion of its objects. They must also prohibit payment of dividends and require all surplus assets on a winding-up to be transferred to another body with similar or charitable objects.

Formalities to obtain the exemption

These are as follows:

1 The making of a statutory declaration *in the case of a company to be formed* by a solicitor engaged in the formation of the company or by a person named as a director or secretary of the company in the statement delivered under s 10(2) (statement of first directors and secretary) or, *in the case of a company changing its name to omit 'limited'*, by a director or secretary of the company.
2 The statutory declaration is made to the Registrar and states that the company is one whose memorandum and articles are appropriately limited so that the exemption applies.
3 Where an existing company is changing its name to omit the word 'limited', a special (or written) resolution must be passed and sent to the registrar with the statutory declaration.

The Electronic Communications Order 2000 allows the Registrar to accept an electronic statement as a substitute for a statutory declaration of compliance referred to above.

Provisions applicable after exemption

1 An exempt company may not alter its memorandum and articles so that they no longer comply with the exemption requirements.
2 If it appears to the Secretary of State that the company is breaking the limitations in its constitution, as where it is carrying on business for a profit, he has power to direct the company to change its name by adding 'limited'. There are fines on the company and its officers for contravention of the exemption provisions. If subsequently the company wishes to drop the word 'limited' from its name, it requires the permission of the DTI. The concession is no longer available as of right as it is on a first incorporation or change.
3 A company which is exempt from the requirements relating to the use of the word 'limited' and does not include the word as part of its name is also exempt from the requirements of the 1985 Act relating to the publication of its name and the sending of lists of members to the Registrar of Companies with the annual return (see Chapter 13).

It should be noted that the exemption is not fully effective because s 351 requires a limited company exempt from the obligation to use 'limited' as part of its name to mention in all business letters and order forms that it is a limited company, even though its name does not reveal that it is. However, the company at least avoids the need to use the word 'limited' *as part of its name*. The word 'limited' generally means to the general public that the organisation is commercial and profit orientated which these companies are not.

NAMES OF OVERSEA COMPANIES

The rules relating to company names and business names apply to oversea companies carrying on business here provided they have a place of business here.

BUSINESS NAMES

The Business Names Act 1985

The Business Names Act 1985 deals with the control of business names and applies to companies which carry on business in Great Britain under a name which does not consist of the corporate name without addition. An addition indicating that the business is carried on in succession to a former owner does not make the name a business name. This allows the company to benefit from the goodwill of the business for which it will have paid. Thus 'Boxo Ltd (formerly H & C Brown)' is not a business name. However, if a company uses a business name, that name must not be one which would be likely to give the impression that the business is connected with local or central government, nor must the name consist of or contain sensitive words, as already described, unless permission has been granted by the appropriate authority, or the written approval of the Secretary of State has been obtained.

The business names controls apply to oversea companies carrying on business here, provided that they have a place of business here.

Disclosure of names of those using business names

If Boxo Ltd trades through a number of retail outlets under the name 'Paris Fashions', then the rules relating to business names apply to Boxo Ltd. These rules require the company to state in legible characters on all its business letters, written orders for goods or services to be supplied to the business, invoices, receipts, and written demands for payment of debts, the corporate name and an address within Great Britain at which service of any document relating in any way to the business will be effective. This will normally be the address of the registered office of the company. The corporate name and an address for service of documents must also be disclosed in a prominent position, so that it may easily be read by customers or suppliers, in any premises where the business is carried on *and to which* the customers and suppliers of any goods or services to the business have access.

Furthermore, the Act requires that the corporate name and an address for service be given immediately, in writing, to anyone who is doing or negotiating business with the company and asks for them. This would be complied with by ensuring that relevant company representatives have a business card with appropriate information on it.

Where a registered company uses its business name rather than its corporate name all stationery must comply with the statutory requirements set out in the Companies Act 1985 regarding publication of the business name (see page 84).

Judicial interpretation of disclosure requirements

The above material sets out the generally understood view of the law and is in line with Department of Trade and Industry thinking on it. However, the courts have taken a more restricted view of the disclosure requirements as the following case illustrates.

Department of Trade and Industry *v* Cedenio (2001) *The Times* 22 March

Trevor Cedenio who was trading under a business name 'Employment Advice & Tribunal Service' was charged with an offence under the Business Names Act 1985 s 4 in that he wrote a business letter and merely signed it and the address in the letter did not state that it was the address for service of documents nor specifically that he was the proprietor of the business. The Administrative Court (a Divisional Court of Queen's Bench) ruled that s 4 did not require the above statements to be made. The section only required a statement of the individual's name or in the case of a company its corporate name and the address need not be pointed up specifically as the document serving address. Mr Cedenio was not guilty of an offence.

Comment

Section 4 states in regard to the address 'In relation to each person named an address in Great Britain at which the service of any document relating in any way to the business will be effective'. Thus in the company situation the address of the registered office will be enough without a statement that it is the address for service. However, the above case is a criminal trial and criminal offences are always interpreted strictly and not liberally. There are civil consequences of infringement (see below) and it may be prudent to identify the proprietor and point up the address for service in case in a civil dispute the court rules that these disclosures are required.

Breach of the provisions relating to business names

The criminal sanction consists of default fines on the company and also its directors and officers, e.g. secretary.

So far as the civil law is concerned, a company which has failed to make disclosure of the corporate name on business documents (as listed above) or has failed to give information to a person doing or discussing business, may be unable to enforce the resulting transaction as where, e.g., it has supplied goods on credit. In such a case the company might not be able successfully to claim the unpaid debt. However, the person being sued by the company must show:

1 that he has been unable to pursue a claim against the company himself because the company has failed to disclose the information required, *or* that he *has* suffered some financial loss as a result of failure to disclose; but
2 the court may allow the company's claim to proceed if it considers it just and equitable to do so.

Furthermore, a counterclaim by the company is not barred if it is sued by, e.g., a customer.

An example to illustrate the operation of the above provisions would be to suppose that Joe Soap bought goods from Paris Fashions which were defective, and that Joe Soap was unable to pursue a claim against Boxo Ltd because he could not find out who was behind Paris Fashions. If Boxo Ltd sued Joe Soap for the price, the court may decide that Boxo's claim should not proceed. The same might be true where Joe Soap had suffered financial loss, as where he had sought a refund on goods returned but had been unable to get it, and of course financial loss could presumably consist merely in the expense incurred in trying to trace the true owner of Paris Fashions. However, if Joe Soap were to sue Boxo Ltd for damages because, e.g., goods supplied by Paris Fashions were substandard, then Boxo Ltd could counterclaim for the price if they had not been paid.

Protection of business names

As we have seen, the Registrar keeps an index of company names and a company cannot be registered in a name which is the same as a name already on the index. In addition, we have noted that the Secretary of State can direct a company to change its name within 12 months of registration if it is 'too like' the name of a company on the index. These provisions do not apply to business names and a passing-off action would have to be brought (see below). This is a difficult and often expensive claim. However, if the name is in the nature of a trade mark it can be registered and protected more easily. The Trade Marks Act 1994 has extended this possibility since it provides that the principal criterion for the registration of a mark is that it is capable of distinguishing the goods and services of the particular undertaking from those of others and registration of geographical locations is allowed. Thus if Boxo Ltd trades as 'The Barbican Tandoori', it could register that as a mark and protect it much more easily. It is essential to a successful action for passing off that the claimant proves an intention to deceive the public. This is not required to restrain the use of a registered trade mark by another.

Other provisions not in company legislation

Statute has prohibited the use of certain names which have an association with recognised charitable organisations, in order to prevent private individuals from profiting by the goodwill which attaches to them. Thus, for example, a company's name may not comprise the words 'Red Cross' without the authority of the Army Council (Geneva Conventions Act 1957, s 6).

Oversea companies

The rules relating to company names and business names apply to oversea companies carrying on business here provided they have a place of business here.

At common law: passing off a name

As we have seen, apart from the special case of 'shell companies' where the DTI can direct a change of name 'at any time', the Registrar has only 12 months from incorporation or change of name to direct a change because a name has been registered which is the same or too like that of an existing company.

Once that time has passed and, say, the existence of a company with a 'too like' name has not been discovered by the first company to have the name, then the first company is left with the only other remedy, i.e. to seek redress at common law in the law of tort.

A company or other business organisation which carries on or proposes to carry on business under a name calculated to deceive the public by confusion with the name of an existing concern commits the civil wrong (or tort) of *passing off*, and will be restrained by injunction from doing so from the moment of incorporation. Where the offending business is a proposed company, an injunction can be obtained to prevent registration, if information is available in time. If an injunction is made against an existing company for passing off, it must either change its name or its business or wind up.

It has already been noted that the mere fact of using one's own name in business will not necessarily prevent a successful passing-off claim by an organisation already in business under that name (see *Asprey & Garrard Ltd* v *WRA (Guns) Ltd* (2001).

Société Anonyme des Anciens Etablissements Panhard et Lavassor *v* Panhard Levassor Motor Co Ltd [1901] 2 Ch 513

In this case, which we can call the *Panhard* case, the claimant was a French company and its cars were sold in England. The French company wished to set up an English company to act as an agent in England to improve the sales of its cars there. To try to stop this the defendant English company was registered, its promoters hoping that the French company would not be able to register its name for its English corporate agent, there being a company of 'too like' name on the register already, and that this would prevent increased competition in the car market. It was *held* that the members of the English company must change the name of their company or wind it up or the company would be taken off the register.

To constitute the tort of *passing off* the business carried on by the offending concern must be the same as that of the claimant, or it must be likely that custom will come to the offending concern because the public will be deceived and associate it with the claimant. An interesting contrast is provided by the following cases.

Ewing *v* Buttercup Margarine Company Ltd [1917] 2 Ch 1

The claimant had since 1904 been carrying on a business dealing in margarine and tea, and had upwards of 150 shops of his own selling 50 tons of margarine a week in all. The claimant's concern was called 'The Buttercup Dairy Co'. The claimant's shops were situated in Scotland and in the North of England, but he was planning to expand his business into the South of England. The defendant company was registered in November 1916, and as soon as the claimant heard about it, he complained to the management of the concern, and later brought this action for an injunction to prevent the defendant company from trading in that name. It appeared that although the defendant was in the business of selling margarine, it was a wholesaler, whereas the claimant was a retailer, and the defendant put this forward as a defence suggesting that there would be no confusion. Another defence was that the company would operate only around London and there would be no confusion with a Northern concern. *Held* – by the Court of Appeal – that an injunction would be granted to the claimant restraining the defendant company from trading in that name. Although the defendant was at the moment a wholesaler, the objects clause of the memorandum did give power to retail which it might exercise in future. Further, the claimant intended to open up branches in the South of England where there would be confusion.

Aerators Ltd *v* Tollitt [1902] 2 Ch 319

The claimant company was formed to work a patent for the instantaneous aeration of liquids. The defendants were the subscribers of the memorandum and articles of a proposed new company to be called Automatic Aerator Patents Ltd. The claimant sought an injunction to restrain the defendants from registering that name because it would deceive the public, the word 'Aerator' being associated with the claimant company. The claimant's patent was a portable aerator for use in siphons, whereas the defendants' company was concerned with large installations in public houses where a large amount of aeration of beer was required. *Held* – there was no evidence of the probability of deception, and an injunction would not be granted. The action was an attempt to monopolise a word in ordinary use and must be dismissed.

As a general rule, an injunction will not be granted where the offending concern is trading in the name of its *proprietor* though where a company is trading in a name which is merely that of one only of its members then an injunction will be granted if confusion with an existing concern is likely to result. Neither will an injunction be granted where a company uses a name which consists of that of the person from whom the company bought its business, even though confusion results.

Waring and Gillow Ltd *v* Gillow and Gillow Ltd (1916) 32 TLR 389

W and G Ltd, well-known furniture, carpet and rug dealers and auctioneers, sought an injunction restraining G and G Ltd from carrying on a business as auctioneers of carpets (formerly the business belonged to L C Gillow, an auctioneer, who continued to be actively concerned with the business).

The court held that on the facts the two businesses were not likely to be taken one for the other and the injunction sought was not granted. In addition, since L C Gillow was actively concerned with the business, the company was allowed to incorporate his name. Furthermore, since the defendant company had purchased the business from L C Gillow, it was allowed to use his name in order to take advantage of the goodwill purchased.

Comment

There is no similar protection for a first name or nickname. In *Biba Group Ltd* v *Biba Boutique* [1980] RPC 413 the defendant whose surname was Gill had been known since infancy by the nickname 'Biba' and she ran a boutique in that name. The claimants, who were in a similar line of business, obtained an injunction against her. Whitford J said that whatever the right of a person to use his own surname, it did not extend to the use of a first name or nickname.

Miscellaneous provisions of the 1985 Act regarding name

A company which is not a public company is guilty of an offence if it carries on any trade, profession or business under a name which includes, as the last part, the words 'public limited company' or their equivalent in Welsh.

A public company is guilty of an offence if it carries on any trade, profession or business under a name which is likely to give the impression that that company is a private company.

Abuse of names by Internet users

Persons can select any name for their Internet address, provided it has not already been registered. If an unauthorised individual or business registers an Internet address which includes the business name or trade mark of a company, this may prevent that company from using its own name in its Internet address. Action which could be taken by the company in such a situation is set out below:

- The company could offer to purchase the address from the user.
- Complaint could be made to the Internet service provider.
- Legal action could be taken if the name is a registered trade mark and the offending Internet address is used in the course of trade in the UK.
- The company may rely on the law of passing off, provided that it can be shown that there is goodwill attached to the name in the UK and that the use of the name by the Internet user is a misrepresentation made in the course of trade in the UK to customers and prospective customers of the company.

The best solution is for the company to register its name first. This can be done through a provider of Internet service at a cost of some £100.

In this connection the High Court has had to resolve a dispute between two companies where both had been allocated the same Internet domain name.

Pitman Training Ltd *v* Nominet UK [1997] 8 CL 538

Pitman Training Ltd and PTC Oxford Ltd, together with Pearson Professional Ltd (Pearson), were all entitled to use for their respective trading purposes the name 'Pitman'. The Pitman business originally included not only publishing, but also a training and examination business, and the Pitman name was associated with each of the businesses. When they were sold, the publishing business was acquired by Pearson and the training business by Pitman Training Ltd.

In February 1996 Pearson registered its chosen domain name (Pitman.co.uk.) with Nominet UK, the body responsible for allocating UK domain names. The name was for the benefit of its Pitman Publishing Division. Pitman Publishing did not intend making any immediate use of the domain name apart from for advertising purposes. It intended to set up a Website some months later and in December 1996 it tried to connect its Website to its domain name. It then discovered that the domain name had been reallocated to PTC Oxford Ltd (PTC), a computer and office skills training company, which is a franchisee of Pitman Training Ltd. Unknown to Pitman Publishing, its domain name had been removed and re-registered in the name of PTC. PTC had begun actively using its domain name and advertising using an e-mail address with that name.

Nominet tried unsuccessfully to mediate between the parties. Solicitors acting for Pitman Publishing pointed out that, as their client had been first in time in applying for the domain name and that the rules of Nominet gave priority on a first-come, first-served basis, the name should be reallocated to Pitman Publishing as soon as possible.

Nominet reinstated the name and this led to Pitman Training seeking and obtaining an injunction restraining Nominet from removing PTC's Internet services or e-mail address. PTC was joined as a second claimant and Pearson was the second defendant. There were three causes of action alleged by the claimants. First, passing off, second, interference with contract and third, abuse of process.

Sir Richard Scott said that there was no evidence that the public associated the domain name with PTC and therefore there was no passing off. With regard to the second cause of action, it was held that there was no interference in the contract between PTC and its Internet service provider. That contract included a term whereby the service provider purported to guarantee that the allocated domain name could not be withdrawn or transferred. However, the service provider in this case was not in a position to give such a guarantee since Nominet was the body with control over the allocation of UK domain names. Pearson's action in urging Nominet to reallocate the domain name to its publishing division would not constitute an interference with the agreement between PTC and the service provider, since such a term could not be implied into the agreement between PTC and its service provider, and it was not an express term. Pitman Publishing was entitled to try and persuade Nominet to restore to it its chosen domain name, of which it had been deprived by error. Sir Richard Scott considered it was following its normal and legitimate business interests by doing so.

Finally, it was not an abuse of process for Pitman Publishing's solicitors to send a letter threatening to sue Nominet if it did not restore to Pitman Publishing its domain name. The judge said that it was a legitimate letter before action written to assert their client's rights. Pitman Training and PTC had no cause of action and their application was dismissed.

Comment

(i) The case indicates that a genuine registration of a name to which the organisation applying is entitled will be protected by the courts. The case confirms that the rule of first-come first-served applies.

(ii) An additional problem which has arisen because of the rapid growth of the Internet and its use by business organisations for e-mail and commerce generally, is the parallel growth of a breed of speculators who register domain names which form a crucial part of a particular business Website and e-mail address, in the hope, for example, of offering it for sale to the business concerned with the possibility of receiving a high price for exclusivity. In *BT plc* v *One in a Million Ltd* [1997] *The Times*, 2 December, the High Court granted injunctions to restrain defendants who had registered company names and/or trade marks as domain names on the Internet on the basis of passing off and trade mark infringement. The court also said that since the names were now of no use to the defendants, they should be assigned to the claimants. The decision means that, at least in the UK, it should be easier to protect Internet domain names.

Publication of the name

The Companies Act 1985 provides that the company's full name must appear legibly and conspicuously:

(*a*) outside the registered office and all places of business;
(*b*) on the common seal (if it has one);
(*c*) on all business letters, notices, and official publications; and
(*d*) in all bills of exchange, cheques, promissory notes, orders for money or goods, receipts, and invoices signed or issued on its behalf.

The company's business letters and order forms must also show the place of registration, the registered number and registered office address and a statement that the company is limited where it is exempt from using that word in its name and a statement that the company is an investment company as defined in s 266 where this is the case.

For the purposes of the Companies Act requirements, external e-mails should be considered as letters and contain the items referred to above. This can be done by including a standard e-mail 'header' sheet or attachment with every external electronic message.

Business letters and order forms sent by fax are also to be treated in the same way as the conventional written or typed document and should therefore comply with the above-mentioned disclosure requirements. It is also good practice to include the information given on business letters with an order form placed on a Website.

The above provisions are in addition to the Business Names Act 1985 requirements. Furthermore, companies are not required to state the names of their directors on their business stationery. If a company decides to do so except as a signatory to or in the text of a letter then the names of all the directors must be shown. There is no need to show share capital but if it is shown it must be the paid-up capital.

Fines may be imposed on the company and its officers for failure to comply, and, in addition, the officers of the company may incur personal liability for any amount due unless it is paid by the company.

This liability may arise where an officer of the company signs or authorises the signature, on behalf of the company, of any bill of exchange, promissory note, cheque or order for money or goods, and the name of the company is not mentioned thereon in legible characters. The rule of personal liability, which applies even though the officer signs as an agent, arises most often in connection with bills of exchange or cheques. It is probably not necessary to show that the third party concerned has been misled (*per* Lord Hunter in *Scottish & Newcastle Breweries Ltd* v *Blair*, 1967 SLT 72).

Thus officers have been held personally liable in the following circumstances.

(*a*) The word 'limited' was omitted, though the abbreviation 'Ltd' can be used.

Penrose *v* Martyr (1858) EB & E 499

A limited company was described on a bill of exchange as 'The Saltash Watermen's Steam Packet Company, Saltash'. The bill was drawn on the company and was accepted by the secretary in the following form – 'Accepted. John Martyr, Secy. to the sd. Coy'. The bill when presented for payment was dishonoured by the company and in this action it was *held* that the secretary was personally liable because the company's correct name did not appear on the bill. 'The intention of the enactment plainly was to prevent persons from being deceived into the belief that they had a security with the unlimited liability of common law when they had but the security of a Company Limited', *per* Crompton J.

Stacey & Co Ltd *v* Wallis (1912) 28 TLR 209

A bill was drawn on a company as 'J & TH Wallis Ltd' and accepted by three persons in the following form – 'James Wallis, Thomas Wallis, Henry Bowles, Secty'.

It was *held* that the correct name of the company was mentioned in the bill as required by the Companies Act. The name appeared on the face of the bill as drawee and in these circumstances it did not matter that it did not appear on the acceptance. Furthermore, the abbreviation 'Ltd' could be used for the word 'Limited'. The persons who had signed the acceptance were not liable on the bill.

Comment

(i) It was *held* by Goff J in *Banque de l'Indochine et de Suez SA* v *Euroseas Group Finance Co* [1981] 3 All ER 198 that the abbreviation of 'company' to 'co' on a cheque is an appropriate mention of the company's name within what is now s 349 and an officer of the company is not liable on the instrument if it is not met by the company. The judge applied the approach of *Stacey*. 'Co' is a commonly accepted abbreviation as 'Ltd' is.

(ii) Section 27(4) of the Companies Act 1985 also provides that the alternative of 'limited' is 'Ltd'.

(*b*) The company was described by the wrong name, though the rule of equitable estoppel may prevent a person from enforcing his claim where he has himself written the words containing the misdescription.

Hendon *v* Adelman (1973) 117 SJ 63

A cheque signed on behalf of L & R Agencies Ltd omitted the ampersand in the company's name so that the company's name was printed on its cheques as 'L R Agencies Ltd', the bank having left out the ampersand. *Held* – that the directors who had signed the cheque had not complied with the Companies Act and were accordingly personally liable on it.

Durham Fancy Goods Ltd *v* Michael Jackson (Fancy Goods) Ltd
[1968] 2 All ER 987

On 18 September 1967, the claimants drew a bill of exchange on the first defendants, Jacksons, which was accepted by M Jackson who was a director and company secretary. The bill and form of acceptance, both of which were drawn up by the claimants, referred to 'M Jackson (Fancy Goods) Ltd', whereas the proper name of the company was 'Michael Jackson (Fancy Goods) Ltd'. The bill was dishonoured and the claimants brought an action against Mr Jackson contending that by signing the form of acceptance he had committed a criminal offence under the Companies Act and had made himself personally liable on the bill because he should either have returned the bill with a request that it be readdressed to Michael Jackson (Fancy Goods) Ltd and the form of acceptance changed, or he should have accepted it 'M Jackson (Fancy Goods) Ltd'. It was *held* – by Donaldson J – that the misdescription was in breach of what is now s 349 and that Mr Jackson was liable under the section. However, as the claimants were responsible for the misdescription, they were estopped from going back on their implied representation that it was acceptable to them.

Comment

(i) A holder other than the claimants might have been able to bring an action against Mr Jackson under what is now s 349 since such a holder would not have been affected by the equity in that he would not have drawn the bill in an incorrect name.

(ii) This case was distinguished in *Lindholst & Co A/S* v *Fowler* [1988] BCLC 166, where the claimants drew bills of exchange on Corby Chicken Co without adding 'Ltd'. They did not, however, write a form of acceptance on the bill as was done in the *Durham* case. Mr Fowler, the managing director of Corby, accepted the bills and drew the form of acceptance without adding 'Ltd'. He was subsequently sued upon the bills under s 349(4) and was held liable.

(iii) In *Blum* v *OCP Repartition SIA* [1988] BCLC 170, Mr Blum, a director, had signed a cheque on behalf of Bomore Medical Supplies Ltd for goods received from OCP, but the word 'Ltd' did not appear on the cheque as part of the company's name. Mr Blum was sued under s 349(4) and asked the court to rectify the cheque by inserting 'Ltd'. His grounds were that all parties to the contract intended it to be between OCP and Bomore Medical Supplies Ltd. In equity where parties agree but write that agreement down incorrectly, the court may rectify the written agreement to accord with the parties' true intentions. The Court of Appeal decided that this was not a situation in which rectification could be used. Equity could not be applied to allow a person to escape the consequences of s 349. Mr Blum was liable.

(*c*) Where the bill was drawn and accepted in the company's business name and not its corporate name.

Maxform SPA *v* B Mariani & Goodville Ltd [1979] 2 Lloyd's Rep 385

Maxform was an Italian company which agreed to sell furniture to Italdesign, which was the name under which the defendant, an English company, carried on business. Mariani was the sole director of the defendant company. Maxform drew a bill of exchange on 'Italdesign' for the price of the furniture. The bill was accepted by Mariani without any addition to his signature and there was no mention of the defendant company. The price was not paid and so Maxform brought an action to recover the sum due under what is now s 349(4). The defendant contended that the appearance on the bill in legible characters of 'Italdesign' was sufficient compliance with the Act, and also that Maxform was estopped from arguing that there had been a breach of it by reason of the wording used by Maxform in drawing the bill. *Held* – by Mocatta J – that there would be judgment for Maxform since it was not possible to take the view that the word 'name' in what is now s 349(4) meant other than the registered corporate name of the company, and furthermore the facts were not sufficient to found an estoppel and in this regard *Durham Fancy Goods Ltd* v *Michael Jackson* (*Fancy Goods*) *Ltd* was distinguished.

Comment

The decision of Mocatta J was affirmed by the Court of Appeal [1981] 2 Lloyd's Rep 54.

The basis of this personal liability derives from the fact that the legislature introduced limited liability on the understanding that persons dealing with the company would know that the liability of its members was limited. Since the officials of the company are the only persons who can ensure that the company's documents convey this impression, it seems right to subject them to fines and personal liability where this is not so. However, the section has been interpreted in a strict, rigid and Draconian fashion, as cases such as *Hendon* show.

However, the most recent case takes the view that so long as the outsider knows that he is dealing with a company and that the liability of its members is limited, trifling errors in the name will not trigger liability.

Jenice Ltd *v* Dan [1993] BCLC 1349

The defendant, who was a director of Primekeen Ltd, signed a cheque incorrectly printed by the bank in the name of 'Primkeen Ltd'. The company went into liquidation and did not meet the cheque. Nevertheless, Mr Dan was not liable on it. There was no doubt, said the judge, that outsiders would have known they were dealing with a limited company and no harm had been done.

THE REGISTERED OFFICE

Generally

The second clause of the memorandum must state whether the company's registered office is to be situated in England and Wales or Wales or Scotland (see below). If it is to be in England and Wales or Wales, then registration is effected by the Registrar of

Companies in London, and if in Scotland, by the Scottish Registrar of Companies in Edinburgh. The situation of the registered office in England and Wales or Wales or Scotland fixes the company's nationality as British and its domicile as English or Scottish, as the case may be (but see *Daimler Co Ltd* v *Continental Tyre & Rubber Co Ltd*, 1916), though not its residence. Residence is fixed by ascertaining where the company's centre of control and management is. Thus a company may be resident in a number of countries where it has several centres of control in different countries. The residence of a company is important in connection with its liability to pay UK taxation.

Swedish Central Railway Co Ltd *v* Thompson [1925] AC 495

The company was incorporated in 1870 to construct a railway in Sweden, the registered office of the company being in London. Later the management of the company was moved to Sweden but the registered office remained in London, dealing only with formal administrative matters such as share transfers. All dividends were declared in Sweden, and no part of the profits was ever sent to England, except payment of dividend to English shareholders. The Commissioners of Income Tax assessed the company for tax on income received in Sweden. *Held – a* company could have more than one residence, though only one nationality and domicile. This company was resident in Sweden and London, and since residence was relevant for income tax purposes, the assessment of the Commissioners was affirmed.

A company must in all its business letters and order forms state whether it is registered in England or Scotland, the registration number assigned to it (as shown in the certificate of incorporation), and the address of its registered office. Furthermore, if reference is made on letters or order forms to the amount of the company's share capital, this must represent the paid-up share capital (s 351). There are penalties in case of default.

The actual address of the registered office is not set out in the memorandum but must be sent to the Registrar with the other documents required on incorporation (s 10(6)).

A company's registered office may be, and often is with private companies, the office of its accountants, and this is where formal communications will be sent. A Post Office Box address cannot be used because people (members and in some cases the public) have a right to visit the registered office to inspect documents.

Purpose of registered office

The registered office is the company's official address. It provides a place where legal documents, notices and other communications can be served. A document can be served on a company by leaving it at, or sending it by registered or ordinary post to, the registered office. (*T O Supplies Ltd* v *Jerry Creighton Ltd* [1951] 1 KB 42.) If the company has no registered office, claim forms and summonses may be served on the directors or the secretary at an office which is not registered. Thus in *Re Fortune Copper Mining Co* (1870) LR 10 Eq 390 the registered office of the company had been pulled down and a writ (now claim form) was served on the secretary and the directors at an unregistered office. The court held that this was good service.

In an interesting development a change in the County Court Rules allows service of claim forms, and other legal process, on a company not only at the company's registered office but also at any place of business, such as a branch, which has some real connection with the cause or matter at issue. So if business has been conducted through a branch office which has resulted in the supply of defective goods or services, legal process could be served on the branch office. This assists the consumer, in particular, who will probably be more familiar with the branch through which he has dealings than the situation of the registered office.

When the Registrar of Companies receives a communication returned as undeliverable at the registered office, he will eventually set in motion the procedures for striking the company off the Register as a defunct company (see further Chapter 24).

The following registers and documents which can be inspected by shareholders, creditors or the public are also kept at the registered office:

(*a*) *The register of members* and, if the company has one, *the index of members*, unless the register is made up elsewhere, in which case they can be kept where they are made up. Where the register and index (if any) are made up by an agent, they may be kept at the agent's office.
(*b*) *A copy of any instrument creating any charge* requiring registration under Part XII, Chapter I, of the 1985 Act.
(*c*) *The company's register of charges* affecting the property of the company.
(*d*) *The minute books* containing minutes of general and directors' meetings.
(*e*) *The register of directors and secretaries.*
(*f*) *The register of directors' interests* in shares in, or debentures of, the company or associated companies, together with the index of names in the register unless it is in the form of an index. Where the register of members is not kept at the registered office, the register of directors' interests may be kept where the register of members is kept.
(*g*) *The register of interests in shares.* This is a register of substantial shareholders' interests in three per cent or more of the nominal value of any class of issued share capital which is quoted and has unrestricted voting rights, together with an index of names in the register unless it is in the form of an index. If the register of directors' interests is not kept at the registered office, the register of shareholders' interests must be kept where the register of directors' interests is kept.
(*h*) *The register of debenture holders*, if the company has one. If the register is made up at another office, it may be kept where it is made up, and where it is made up by an agent, it may be kept at his office.
(*i*) *A copy of each director's service contract or a memorandum thereof.* These may be kept at the registered office, or where the register of members is kept, or at the company's principal place of business if this is situated in the country in which the company is registered. The Registrar of Companies must be told where these documents are kept if they are not at the registered office. The directors referred to now include those directors who are employed by subsidiaries and those who work wholly or mainly outside the United Kingdom. Contractual arrangements with shadow directors are also included.
(*j*) *A copy of the report, if any, following an investigation by a company of interests in its shares on the requisition of its members.* This report must be available for inspection at

the company's registered office for a period of six years from the date on which it first became available.

(*k*) *The company's accounting records.*

The above registers and documents must be kept open to inspection by members free of charge during business hours, subject to reasonable restrictions leaving not less than two hours a day for inspection. The minute books of general meetings are only open to the inspection of members. The accounting records can only be inspected by the officers of the company. Copies of instruments creating a charge and the register of charges are also open to the inspection of debenture holders and creditors without charge.

The register of directors and secretaries, the register of directors' interests and the register of debenture holders are open to inspection by the public on payment of a prescribed fee. The register of interests in shares and any report following an investigation of interests in shares (see (*j*) above) are available for inspection by any member of the company or any other person without charge and copies of the register or report must be given on request, though the company may charge a prescribed fee.

The actual location of the registered office is usually decided by the promoters and the address is filed with the memorandum and articles when these documents are presented for registration.

The registered office and insolvency proceedings

In order to implement EU regulations on insolvency proceedings UK regulations entitled The Insolvency Act 1986 (Amendment) (No 2) Regulations 2002 were put into law. Before these regulations came into force it was possible for a UK court to deal with insolvency proceedings in regard to foreign companies provided the company concerned had assets here. Under the 2002 regulations that are numbered SI 2002/1240 the territory in which the corporate debtor has its *centre of main interests* will have jurisdiction to open insolvency proceedings against it. These are referred to as *the main proceedings* and the registered office is presumed but not conclusively to be the centre of main interests. The courts of other countries can institute insolvency proceedings but only in regard to assets of the corporate debtor that are within the jurisdiction of the court. These are called *territorial proceedings* which would not result in, e.g., the winding-up of the company. This would be a matter for the main proceedings. These matters receive further consideration in the chapters on corporate insolvency and company rescue. However, the importance here is the role of the registered office in deciding which country is entitled to conduct the main proceedings. The main thrust of the regulations is to deal with companies within the EU but as will be seen in the insolvency chapters a UK court has regarded itself as entitled to deal with insolvency matters where the corporate debtor was an American company ruling that its centre of main interests was the UK even though its registered office was in the United States (see *Brac Rent-A-Car International Inc.* [2003] All ER (D) 98 (Feb)).

Change of address of registered office

The actual address of the registered office may be changed within the domicile. Thus it is possible for a company whose memorandum states that its registered office is to be situated in 'England' or 'England and Wales' to change its registered office to somewhere else in England and Wales since 'England' includes Wales for this purpose. In spite of the fact that the law of England and Wales is the same, a company which has chosen to have its registered office situated in Wales, either initially or by a change in its memorandum, cannot change its registered office address to a place in England. Under the 1985 Act a company's memorandum may state that its registered office is to be situated in Wales and a company with a registered office in Wales may by special (or written) resolution alter its memorandum so as to provide that its registered office is to be so situated. In any case an English or Welsh company cannot change its registered office to a place in Scotland. The law is different there and the move would take the office out of the domicile set out in the company's memorandum. The change of address can be done by an ordinary (or in a private company, written) resolution of the members, i.e. a resolution passed by a simple majority (or unanimously). Quite often the power to change the address of the registered office is given to the directors by the articles, and where this is done, a resolution of the board will suffice. *Table A, Reg* 70, which gives the directors of a *Table A* company wide management powers, would appear to give them, by implication, power to change the address of the registered office. The company must notify the Registrar of the change. The Registrar must publish in the *London Gazette* notice of the receipt by him of a change in the situation of the registered office (s 711). The change takes effect when the notice is registered by the Registrar but until the end of the period of 14 days beginning with the date on which it is registered a person may validly serve any document on the company at its previous registered office (s 287).

THE OBJECTS CLAUSE

Generally

This clause lists the things which the company can do. If it enters into a transaction which is not included in the clause, that transaction will, at least at common law, be *ultra vires* (that is, beyond its powers) and void (that is, of no effect).

It should be noted that what we are looking at in this chapter is the company's *capacity* as revealed by the objects clause of its memorandum. It will be discovered that even where the company has *capacity* a transaction made on its behalf may still not be enforceable against it because the agent who made it had no *authority* to do so. The problems presented by lack of authority in the agent are looked at in Chapter 5 but the reader should, even at this early stage, bear in mind the distinction between the two areas of company *capacity* and agent *authority*.

The leading case on the operation of the *ultra vires* rule at common law appears below.

Ashbury Railway Carriage and Iron Co *v* Riche (1875) LR 7 HL 653

The company bought a concession for the construction of a railway system in Belgium, and entered into an agreement to finance Messrs Riche to construct a railway line. Messrs Riche commenced the work, and the company paid over certain sums of money in connection with the contract. The company later ran into difficulties, and the shareholders wished the directors to take over the contract in a personal capacity, and indemnify the shareholders. The directors thereupon repudiated the contract on behalf of the company, and Messrs

Riche sued for breach of contract. The case turned on whether the company was engaged in an *ultra vires* activity in financing the building of a complete railway system because, if so, the contract it had made with Messrs Riche would be *ultra vires* and void, and the claim against the company would fail. The objects clause of the company's memorandum stated that it was established:

> 'to make or sell or lend on hire railway carriages, wagons and all kinds of railway plant, fittings, machinery and rolling stock; to carry on the business of mechanical engineers and general contractors, to purchase and sell as merchants timber, coal, metal and other materials, and to buy and sell such materials on commission or as agents.'

Held – by the House of Lords – that the financing of the concession to build a complete railway system from Antwerp to Tournai was *ultra vires* and void because it was not within the objects of the company. The words empowering the company to carry on the business of general contracting must be construed *ejusdem generis* with the preceding words, and must therefore be restricted to contracting in the field of plant, fittings and machinery only. In other words, the company could use its funds to make things for railways, but not make railways as such. The contract with Messrs Riche was therefore void, and the directors were entitled to repudiate it.

Understanding the modern objects clause

By way of explanation of the above decision, it should be said that the *ultra vires* rule of the common law was brought in by the courts to protect shareholders. It was thought that if a shareholder bought shares in a company which had as its main object publishing and allied activities, he would not want the directors of that company to start up a different kind of business because he wanted to put money in publishing.

In more recent times it has been realised that shareholders are not so fussy about the business the directors take the company into so long as it is ethical and makes profits from which to pay dividends and the price of the company's shares rises on the Stock Exchange as a result of its success.

The people most affected by the *ultra vires* rule of the common law in more recent times were creditors who had supplied goods or services to a company for a purpose not contained in its objects clause. If the company was solvent, no doubt such creditors would be paid, but if it went into insolvent liquidation, they would not even be able to put in a claim. The liquidator would reject it as being based on a void transaction. Other creditors might get paid some part of their debts if the company had some funds but the *ultra vires* creditors would get nothing.

For this reason it became, and has remained, usual to put in the objects clause a large number of objects and powers so that the company can do a wide variety of things apart from its main business, if at any time it wishes to do so. It also became, and remains, common to insert a paragraph in the objects clause which states that each clause contains a separate and independent main object which can be carried on separately from the others. The House of Lords decided in *Cotman* v *Brougham* [1918] AC 514 that this type of clause was legal so that, for example, a company whose main object was publishing could use a clause giving investment powers for any kind of investment and not just investment in publishing.

Also the decision of the Court of Appeal in *Bell Houses Ltd* v *City Wall Properties Ltd* [1966] 2 All ER 674 is to the effect that a subjective objects clause can be drafted in such a way as to allow the company to carry on any additional business, not provided for in the objects clause, which the directors think can be conveniently pursued by the company. If this is thought to put too much power in the hands of the directors, the objects clause may make the decision depend upon an ordinary resolution of the members.

In this way the limitations which are placed by the common law on a company's business activities by the *ultra vires* rule have been much reduced, though of course the control by the members over the activities pursued on behalf of the company by the directors has also been lessened. In fact, with a large number of clauses in the objects clause, as a typical memorandum has, with an independent objects subclause and/or a type of *Bell Houses* clause, the modern company's contractual capacity approaches that of a natural person. The *ultra vires* rule as a method of controlling the activities of the board of directors on behalf of the company has been largely abandoned for quite a long time.

In addition, there has been, during the last few years, considerable intervention by Parliament to make the *ultra vires* rule ineffective.

Companies Act 1985

Section 35 (as inserted by the Companies Act 1989) now represents the United Kingdom's response to Art 9 of the First Directive issued by the European Community for the harmonisation of company law in the member states. It is intended largely to eliminate the effect of the *ultra vires* rule on the claims of creditors, though it has less of an impact today than it would have had in the past since, as we have seen, fewer transactions are likely to be *ultra vires* at common law. However, on the assumption that the narrow scope of a particular company's objects clause may still allow for this, a review of certain of the statutory provisions appears below.

We shall deal at this stage only with the effect of legislation upon the rules relating to the company's *capacity*. It should also be borne in mind that legislation only reforms the *ultra vires* rule – it has not been abolished, though so far as trade creditors of a company are concerned little should now be heard of it. There is a continuing relevance of the rule in other areas as we shall see.

(a) The company's capacity

Section 35 (as amended) provides that the validity of an act of a company shall not be called into question by reason of anything in the company's memorandum. Thus in the *Ashbury* case the *contents* of the objects clause only allowed the company to make things for railways and not railways as such. The contract with Messrs Riche should now have been enforceable against the company, since so far as outsiders are concerned, the contents of (what is in) the memorandum do not affect the validity of the transaction in terms of the company's *capacity* to enter into it.

(b) The rights of members

At common law any member could ask the court for an injunction to prevent the directors from making (or continuing with) an *ultra vires* transaction. Subject to some amendments by the 1985 Act, any member still can. The present position is that any member can ask the court for an injunction to prevent the directors *from entering into* an *ultra vires* transaction but not if the members have ratified it by special resolution. Thus if the directors have made an *ultra vires* contract, no action can be brought, though it can if they are contemplating doing so. In addition, no action can be brought if the members have passed a ratifying special resolution (or written resolution in a private company). The members could not ratify at common law even if they were unanimous in wishing to do so. However, if the transaction has not been entered into and there has been no ratification, normally because there is insufficient member support, then an action for an injunction can go ahead; and if it does, the *ultra vires* rule and the various protective clauses in the memorandum will be relevant in deciding whether or not an injunction will be granted. So the rule is reformed here, not abolished.

(c) Transactions with directors of the company or its holding company

Under s 322A transactions with the directors of the company or its holding company are voidable (can be avoided) by the company if they are *ultra vires*, and, once again, the contents of the objects clause and not s 35 will be relevant because s 322A says so. Transactions with directors' connected persons are included, as are transactions with directors' associated companies. We shall deal fully with 'connected persons' in Chapter 16 but as an example the spouse of a director is a connected person and transactions with a spouse or an associated company would be judged by the objects clause and not s 35. An associated company is one in which the director has 20 per cent or more of the issued share capital or controls 20 per cent or more of the votes. Sometimes if there are weighted voting rights, a person may own less than 20 per cent of the shares but have more than 20 per cent of the votes.

The above transactions are not voidable by the company if the members have ratified them by a special (or written in private companies) resolution, where the problem is that the transaction is *ultra vires* the company. For the position where the transaction is beyond the directors' powers, see Chapter 5.

(d) Liability of directors

Directors have always been liable to pay damages to the company if they entered into an *ultra vires* transaction which caused the company loss. This is still the position and the objects clause and not s 35 is relevant in deciding the liability of the directors. However, the new law, i.e. s 35(3), allows the members to relieve the directors of this liability by passing a separate special (or written in a private company) resolution. A resolution ratifying the transaction itself is not enough.

(e) Special regime for charities

Obviously charities need to be dealt with specially because people give not to the charity but to its objects. Under s 65 of the Charities Act 1993, s 35 is not available to a person dealing with a charity unless:

(*a*) he has given full consideration to the charity in money or money's worth, i.e. it is a deal in which the charity gets proper value for its money; AND
(*b*) he is unaware that the transaction was beyond the company's objects or the directors' powers; OR
(*c*) he was unaware that the company was a charity.

Unless the above matters are satisfied, the Attorney-General can ask the court to set the transaction aside. The powers of ratification referred to above do not apply.

(f) The position of outsiders such as trade creditors

So far as the company's *capacity is* concerned, there are few problems for ordinary creditors whose transactions with the company should be enforceable against it by reason of s 35. Also of assistance to ordinary creditors are the following:

(*a*) They do not have *constructive notice* of the company's objects as they did at common law (s 711A). This means that they are not assumed to know that a particular transaction is not within the objects.
(*b*) They have no duty to enquire as to the capacity of the company to enter into the particular transaction, nor as to the authority of its agents to make it on behalf of the company (s 35A).
(*c*) Their transactions with the company are enforceable against it even if they have *actual knowledge* that the transaction is not within the company's objects (s 35A(2)(b)). Thus, even if a creditor had read the memorandum and realised that the transaction was not within the objects, he could still enforce it against the company.

The *substratum* rule

This rule states that although a company may include in the objects clause a large number of objects, these objects cannot be pursued unless the main object (or *substratum*), usually the first clause, is being carried on. Thus if the main object or *substratum* fails, the company cannot continue to operate a business under another object. Furthermore, the shareholders can petition for the winding-up of the company where the whole *substratum* has gone and the court can order a liquidation under its power to do so whenever it is just and equitable (Insolvency Act 1986, s 122(1)(g)). The leading case appears below.

Re German Date Coffee Co (1882) 20 Ch D 169

According to the memorandum of association, the company was formed to work a German patent for manufacturing coffee from dates, and also to obtain patents for improvements and modifications of these inventions, and to acquire or purchase other inventions for similar purposes together with other powers. The intended German patent was never granted, but the company did purchase a Swedish patent and established a works in Hamburg, where they made coffee from dates without a patent. When it was found that the German patent could not be obtained, many shareholders withdrew from the company, but a large majority of those who remained wished to carry on the company, which was solvent. On a petition presented by two shareholders, one of whom held 100 shares and the other ten, it was *held* that the *substratum* of the company had failed, and it was impossible to carry out the objects for which the company was formed. Although the petition was presented within a year of incorporation, it was just and equitable that the company be wound up. The case was a marginal one, but the name German Date Coffee Co Ltd was material in determining the real object of the company, and on a consideration of the memorandum, the company was basically formed to work a German patent in Germany.

Comment

(i) This sort of interpretation is restrictive and has not always been followed. Thus in *Re Kitson & Co Ltd* [1946] 1 All ER 435 the company was formed to carry on a particular engineering business at the Airedale Foundry at Hunslet in the city of Leeds. The second object was to carry on the business of general engineering. Many years later the company sold the Hunslet business but the directors wished to carry on engineering through another company. The court held that both objects were main ones and the company could not be wound up.

(ii) It should be noted that the fact that the objects clause states that each object is separate and independent does not affect the *substratum* rule. Lord Parker said in his judgment in *Cotman* v *Brougham* (1918) that although such a clause would make each clause an object, it did not make each clause the *substratum*.

Altering the objects clause

The objects clause can be freely changed, or amended, by a special (or written) resolution. This type of resolution has been considered in dealing with changing the company's name. In addition, we have emphasised a number of times that legislation and practicality confines the unanimous written resolution to private companies and future references will be merely to a written resolution as above, the reader being aware that reference is to a private company procedure.

In precise terms the Companies Act 1985 confines the written resolution procedure to private companies but *Table A* to that Act provides in *Reg* 53 that *all* companies may use the procedure. In general terms this would be impracticable in public companies because of the number of member signatures required, the written procedure requiring members to be unanimous.

Furthermore, a company may alter its objects (or be registered with objects) which merely state that it is to carry on business as a general commercial company. This means that it can carry on any trade or business whatsoever. The company will also have power to do all such things as are incidental or conducive to that end, without listing them in the objects clause.

If a company does register with or change its objects clause to this formula, it will have quite effectively opted out of the *ultra vires* rule even for internal purposes, i.e. shareholder injunctions to restrain the directors from acting beyond the company's objects. However, in the case of an existing company, the change will have to be approved by a special resolution of the members. The new formula seems ideal for the private company running a family business where the owners (shareholders) and the management (directors) are often one and the same, so that the wide powers given to the directors under the formula are not of great concern. It appears that company formation agencies will, unless told otherwise, use the 'general commercial company' formula in their ready-made companies.

It should be noted that additional objects would be required if the company wished to make charitable or political donations since these would not seem to be covered by the phrase 'general commercial company'.

Once a special resolution to alter the objects clause has been passed, it stands unless, within 21 days of it being passed, the holder(s) of 15 per cent of the company's issued share capital, or if the share capital is divided into classes, say A ordinary and B ordinary, 15 per cent of the holders of any class, apply to the court to cancel it. These dissentients must not have voted for the resolution (s 5).

The court need not cancel the resolution and, in view of the fact that it has been passed by a three-quarters majority, is not likely to do so. However, it can order the purchase of the dissentients' shares from the company's funds thus reducing its capital. Alternatively, the other members may buy the shares in which case capital is not reduced.

Obviously the dissentient rights will not be exercised where the resolution is written, because such resolutions must be unanimous.

The resolution altering the memorandum must be filed with the Registrar within the usual 15 days, and if no application is made to the court, the company must within 15 days from the end of the period for making an application, i.e. within 36 days of the resolution, deliver to the Registrar a printed copy of the memorandum as altered. If an application to the court is made, the company must immediately give notice to the Registrar.

LIMITATION OF LIABILITY

The memorandum of a limited company states that the liability of the members is limited and where the company is limited by guarantee this clause may contain the terms of the guarantee, though this may appear in the articles of association. Even though the company has an exemption from the DTI allowing it to dispense with the word 'Limited' as part of its name, the memorandum must still contain a statement that the liability of the company's members is limited.

The procedure for re-registration of limited companies as unlimited and vice versa has already been considered (see Chapter 2).

CAPITAL

Under s 2, the memorandum of a company which is limited by shares must state the amount of the share capital which the company can issue *and* its division into shares of a fixed amount, e.g. 'The share capital of the company is two hundred thousand pounds divided into two hundred thousand shares of £1 each.' Shares may also be divided into classes, e.g. ordinary shares and preference shares, though it is usual to do this in the articles. Guarantee companies formed since 1980, when the law was changed, cannot have a share capital, but since such companies are not usually formed to carry on business activities this is not a disability.

The nominal value of a company's shares is left to the discretion of those promoting it. Nominal values are rarely more than £1.00 because holdings of shares of high nominal value are difficult to sell, and it is not unusual to find shares with a nominal value of 50p, 25p, or even as low as 5p.

The amount of capital stated in this clause is known as the company's *nominal* or *authorised* capital and it can be of any amount in a private company but must be at least £50,000 if the company is a public company. The requirement of s 2 that the nominal capital be divided into shares of a fixed amount means that English companies cannot issue *no-par value shares*.

A *no-par value share* has no nominal value; its *no-par value* is the price at which the share can be sold and not merely what the original owner paid for it, and since many shares are issued at a premium today, even current *par values* do not represent what was paid for shares in the first place. Few other items of property are still referred to by their original cost since it is their current market price which is of interest. Thus a *no-par value* share would have certain advantages. Having no nominal value, dividends are expressed as so much per share, e.g. £0.20 per share, and not as a percentage of a nominal value.

Suppose P buys a share in the X Co Ltd for £4, the nominal value of which was £1, and the company declares a dividend of 20 per cent which is £0.20 per share. This is only a return of 5 per cent on P's current investment, and the only person who actually gets 20 per cent on his money is an original purchaser of a share, if any such person exists who has retained the shares since issue. The rate of 20 per cent is therefore misleading in relation to the actual yield. A dividend of £0.20 per share declared in such terms is more realistic, and indeed although a company cannot issue *no-par value shares*, there is nothing to prevent it declaring dividends in such terms.

Other advantages which would accrue if *no-par value shares* could be issued would be the elimination of the need to open a share premium account when shares are issued for more than their nominal value and also the elimination of the need for provisions forbidding the issue of shares at a discount (see Chapter 12).

It is of interest to note that, since s 2 does not require an unlimited company to divide its share capital into shares of a fixed amount, an unlimited company seems to be able to issue *no-par value shares*.

A limited company may increase, reduce or reorganise its share capital but the requirements of company legislation in this regard can only be fully appreciated in the context of other rules relating to share capital and they are therefore dealt with in Chapter 7.

The effect of the introduction of the euro by certain member states of the EU in terms of UK companies is considered in Chapter 6.

OTHER CLAUSES

The clauses which have been dealt with above *must* appear in every memorandum. However, other clauses may be included, the ones most commonly found providing for the special rights of different classes of shareholders. Where such rights are included in the memorandum, and no provision for the variation of rights is made either in the memorandum itself or in the articles, such rights can be varied either with the approval of the court under s 425 (see Chapter 22) or with the consent of all the members (s 125). However, they are not alterable by special resolution under the provisions of s 17 (see below). Where class rights are contained in the *articles*, they can always be altered by special (or written) resolution, and any provision in the company's constitution to the contrary is void. Alteration is, of course, subject to the requisite consent of the holders of the shares where there is more than one class of shares (see further Chapter 6).

The memorandum is the superior document and where shareholders' rights are contained in the memorandum, any contrary provisions in the articles do not apply. However, the articles may be looked at *but only to explain any ambiguities in the memorandum, or to supplement it,* e.g. where the voting rights of certain shares are in the memorandum and dividend rights are included in the articles. This is to be expected because the contract which the shareholder makes with the company is contained in two documents, i.e. the memorandum and the articles, and they must be read together subject to the rule that in case of conflict the memorandum prevails.

Re Duncan Gilmour & Co Ltd [1952] 2 All ER 871

The company had ordinary and preference shares, and the memorandum provided that the holders of the preference shares should have a preferential right to repayment of their capital in a winding-up. The usual construction put upon such a provision by the court is that, if the preference shareholders have a preferential right to repayment of capital in a winding-up, they have no right to participate in surplus assets in a winding-up, where these exist. However, in this case, the company's articles provided that in a winding-up the surplus assets should be divided among all the members in proportion to the capital paid up on their shares, both preference and ordinary. The company was not being wound up, the point having been raised by a scheme of arrangement which was designed to alter the rights of the shareholders. *Held* – the rights conferred by the memorandum on the preference shareholders were exhaustive. They were limited to a preference in the distribution of assets, and had no right to participate in the distribution of surplus assets in a winding-up or otherwise. Although the articles may be used to clarify ambiguities in the memorandum, they could not be referred to here, because the memorandum was clear and so no question of ambiguity arose.

ASSOCIATION CLAUSE

It is in this clause that the subscribers to the memorandum declare that they desire to be formed into a company and agree to take the shares opposite their names. Their signatures must be witnessed by at least one person who is not a subscriber. It is usual for the subscriber(s) to take one share in the memorandum, and contract by another agreement for the balance of the shares they intend to take up.

ALTERATION OF THE MEMORANDUM GENERALLY

In addition to the methods of alteration of certain clauses already given, s 17 provides that any condition contained in the memorandum which could have been contained in the articles, i.e. any clause other than the statutory ones, can be altered by special (or written) resolution unless the memorandum provides for some other method, or prohibits the alteration of the condition, or the condition relates to *class rights*, i.e. the special rights of any class of members. Since provisions dealing with class rights are the only important provisions which could be in either the memorandum or the articles, the result is that s 17 is not very important in practice. Section 17 contains the same provisions as to cancellation of an alteration as we have seen for the objects clause.

Neither the memorandum nor the articles can be altered so as to require a member, after he became a member, to take up more shares, or otherwise increase his liability, unless he consents in writing, either before or after the alteration is made (s 16). Thus if a company is proving to be a bad investment and cannot get fresh capital from the public, it cannot coerce its present members into supplying more capital, by an alteration in the articles requiring this.

Where there is a court order under s 461 to relieve a minority of shareholders, and in order to relieve the minority it was necessary for the order to alter the company's memorandum or articles, then the company cannot make a further alteration inconsistent with the order without leave of the court. The rights of minorities will be further considered in Chapter 14.

When a company has altered its memorandum in any respect, all copies of it issued thereafter must contain the alteration in the sense that the text must be altered to include the amendments (s 20).

GRADED QUESTIONS

Essay mode

1 'There are occasions when the courts will look behind the formality of legal personality and will appear to disregard it, but it is impossible to find any consistent principle upon which they will do so.'

Discuss.

(*Kingston University*)

2 In 2005 Archie, Bert, Colin and David, as shareholders and directors, set up a company to acquire a disused mill to renovate into single person flats. David had bought the mill in 2004 and sold it to the company once it was formed. Bert has now become concerned that this deal has caused the company to suffer a loss. Advise Bert on what the common law position is regarding the company, the transaction and the protection of his interests.

(*University of Paisley*)

3 Eric and Stanley have been carrying on business in partnership as building contractors in a small town for some years. They carry out most of the work themselves and only occasionally employ labour. They have no plans to enlarge the area of their operations. It has been suggested to them that they ought to trade as a private registered company limited by shares. They ask your advice on the following matters.

(*a*) What are the alleged advantages of trading as a private registered company limited by shares? Are there any disadvantages in so trading?

(*b*) At present they trade as 'Ericstay'. They would like to retain the name because of the business connection attached to it.

Advise them on their suggested choice of name.

(*c*) They have been informed that as a registered company they will need a certificate to commence business.

Explain to them what a certificate to commence business is and advise them whether they will need such a certificate.

(*The Association of Chartered Certified Accountants*)

4 The objects clause in the memorandum of association of Calder Ltd has a sub-clause providing that each sub-clause shall constitute a separate and independent object of the company. What is the purpose and effect of such a provision?

(*The Institute of Chartered Accountants in England and Wales*)

5 Jane is a promoter dealing with the formation of a private limited company. You are required to advise Jane on the following matters.

(*a*) The restrictions which exist upon the choice of corporate name.

(*b*) The documentation which must be sent to the Registrar of Companies in order to obtain incorporated status.

(*c*) The liability for Jane personally if she enters into any contracts on the company's behalf before the issue of the certificate of incorporation.

(*The Chartered Institute of Management Accountants*)

6 Explain the term 'business name' and describe the relevance of the Business Names Act 1985.

(*The Institute of Company Accountants*)

7 For several years Jay Ltd has been carrying on the business of managing discotheques. The directors are now proposing that the company should operate a chain of pizza restaurants but, because some of the shareholders are objecting to the proposal, they wish to know if it would be permissible.

Advise the directors.

(*The Institute of Chartered Accountants in England and Wales*)

8 (*a*) What are the statutory requirements regarding the particulars to be disclosed on a company's correspondence?

(*b*) Why is a company required to have a registered office and how may the situation of the registered office be changed?

(*The Institute of Chartered Accountants in England and Wales*)

Objective mode

Four alternative answers are given. Select ONE only. Circle the answer which you consider to be correct. Check your answers by referring back to the information given in the chapter and against the answers at the back of the book.

1 A transaction with a trade creditor which falls outside a company's express objects set out in the memorandum is:

A valid under s 35 of the CA 1985.
B void as being *ultra vires* the company.

C void as being *ultra vires* the directors.
D void at the instance of the members.

2 Fred is a minority shareholder who did not vote in favour of an alteration to the company's objects. He holds 16 per cent in nominal value of the company's share capital and wishes to challenge the alteration. He must petition the court within how many days of the passing of the resolution?

A 7.
B 14.
C 21.
D 28.

3 On 1 February Mersey Ltd passed a special resolution changing its name to Trent Ltd. On the same day the managing director made a contract with Thames Ltd to sell it some goods. On 1 March the company received its new certificate of incorporation and on 1 April Trent Ltd failed to deliver the goods in breach of contract. What is the effect on the contract of the change of name?

A It is enforceable against the managing director as a pre-incorporation contract.
B It cannot be enforced because Mersey Ltd no longer exists.
C The contract is enforceable against the company and proceedings can be commenced against it in its new name.
D The contract cannot be enforced unless ratified by the company in the new name.

4 Ribble Ltd has a share capital of 1,000,000 ordinary shares. The holders of 800,000 shares vote on a resolution to change the company's name. The minimum number of votes which must be cast in favour of the resolution for it to be effective is:

A 400,001.
B 500,000.
C 600,000.
D 750,000.

5 Promoters wish to form a company to be called 'Barchester City Council Tuition Services Ltd'. What is the legal position as to the permissibility of that name in company law?

A The name cannot be registered because it is unlawful.
B It can be registered if the Secretary of State gives permission.
C Permission must be obtained from the Department for Education and Employment.
D The name may be registered with the permission of the Barchester City Council.

6 Derwent Ltd has passed a resolution altering its objects clause. It must deliver a printed copy of the altered memorandum to the Registrar within how many days of the passing of the resolution?

A 15 days.
B 21 days.
C 42 days.
D 36 days.

The answers to questions set in objective mode appear on p 576.

4

THE CONSTITUTION OF THE COMPANY – THE ARTICLES OF ASSOCIATION

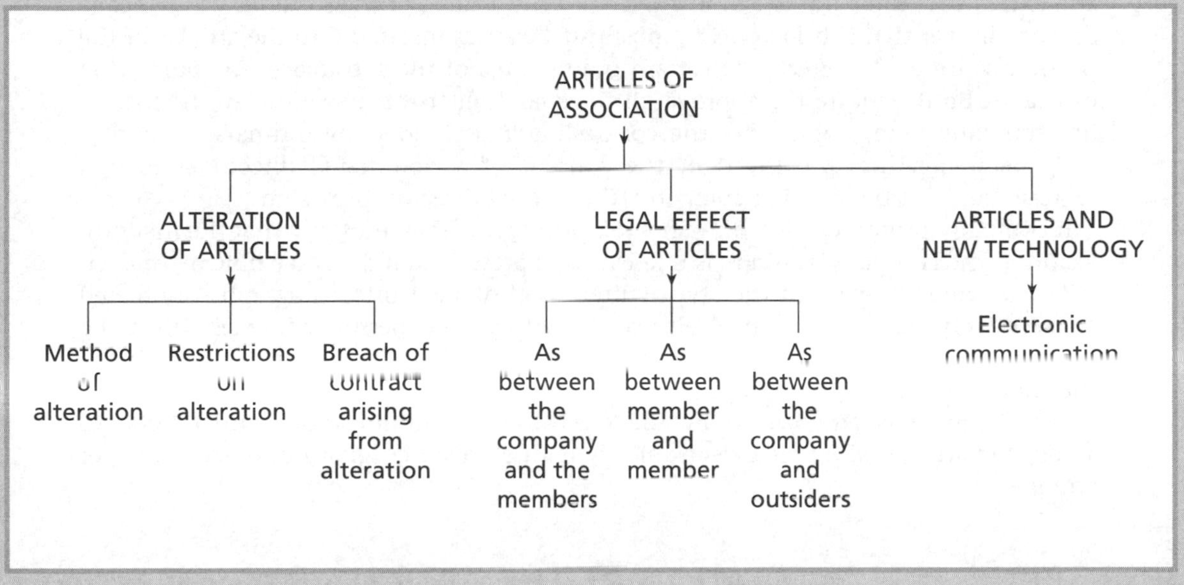

The articles of association regulate the rights of the members of the company *inter se* (among themselves), and determine the manner in which the business of the company shall be conducted. The articles deal with such matters as the appointment and powers of directors, general meetings of the company, the voting rights of members, the transfer of shares, and dividends. The rights of the different classes of shareholders may also be found in the articles though not in *Table A*.

A company may have its own articles or may adopt *Table A* as set out in regulations. However, even where a company (public or private) has its own articles, *Table A* will still apply, except where it is excluded or modified expressly or by implication in the company's special articles. A not uncommon use of special provisions in the articles of private companies is where they are subsidiaries and the holding company wants to add extra provisions, not found in *Table A*, to the articles of the subsidiary as a means of control over that subsidiary. The most usual clauses inserted into the articles of the subsidiary are to the effect that certain transactions of the subsidiary, e.g. borrowing over a set limit, require the approval of the shareholders of the subsidiary (the holding company being, of course, the controlling shareholder) by ordinary resolution (a 'general meeting' provision) or the consent of a nominated director who is a representative of the holding company (the 'special director' provision).

If company promoters do not wish *Table A* to apply, they must see that the first provision in the company's articles is one which expressly excludes the whole of *Table A*.

Articles must be printed (not typewritten) and divided into paragraphs numbered consecutively. The articles must also be signed by each person who subscribed the memorandum, and the signature must be attested, though one witness for all the subscribers' signatures is enough.

The Registrar is empowered by the Electronic Communications Order 2000 to accept the articles when filed electronically with electronic signatures replacing paper arrangements.

ALTERATION OF THE ARTICLES

The articles may be altered by a special resolution in general meeting or alternatively, and normally only in private companies, by a unanimous written resolution (see Chapter 19). A copy of the resolution together with a printed copy of the revised articles must be filed with the Registrar within 15 days of the date of the resolution. The company should also arrange for copies of the revised articles to be sent to those known to be in possession of the existing memorandum and articles, e.g. directors, auditors, accountants, company's solicitors and bankers. They need not be sent to members unless they ask, and a fee not exceeding five pence may be charged (see ss 19, 20 and 380). The fee is hopelessly out of date and few companies would consider charging it.

The alteration is as valid as if it had been in the original articles and can only itself be changed by the special resolution or written resolution procedure, though the court is given power by the Companies Act 1985 to change the articles, for example as part of assisting minority shareholders to overcome the unfairly prejudicial conduct of the majority (see Chapter 14). It is impossible to entrench a provision in the articles. All articles can be altered freely by following the above procedure. Any attempt to make particular articles unalterable or to provide for alteration by a greater majority than 75 per cent is contrary to s 9(1) and void.

An alteration of the articles may operate retrospectively and so affect the *existing* rights of members. Thus, in *Allen* v *Gold Reefs of West Africa Ltd* [1900] 1 Ch 656 the articles originally gave the company a lien on partly-paid shares. The claimant was the only member with fully-paid shares but he also owed calls on certain other partly-paid shares which he owned. The company altered its articles to give itself a lien on fully-paid shares, thus putting itself in a position where it could refuse to transfer the claimant's fully-paid shares unless and until he had paid calls owing on his partly-paid shares. It was held that the alteration was valid and for the benefit of the company, even though it operated retrospectively so far as the claimant was concerned.

There are, however, the following restrictions on alteration

(i) The articles cannot be altered so as to include an illegal clause. Thus an alteration would be invalid if it tried to overrule the general law. For example, an article giving exemption to an officer of the company from liability for negligence or breach of duty would be void as contravening s 310 which does not allow this.

(ii) An alteration to include a clause which contravenes a provision in the memorandum is of no effect. Thus, if the memorandum provides that holders of preference shares should have a preferential right to repayment of their capital in a winding-up (which the courts can construe as meaning that they have no right to participate in surplus assets in a winding-up), and the articles are altered to provide that in winding-up the surplus assets should be divided among all the members in proportion to the capital paid up on their shares, both preference and ordinary, the alteration would be of no effect.

(iii) No alteration of the memorandum or articles can impose a liability on members of the company at the date when the alteration is made to take more shares than they already hold, or to contribute more share capital or pay more money to the company than they have already agreed to contribute or pay, unless the member concerned agrees in writing. The effect of the rule is to deny power to the company to raise further capital by coercing its members when it cannot raise the capital from them voluntarily.

(iv) Where the rights of different classes of shareholders are contained in the articles, then, obviously, these rights can only be changed, so far as the articles are concerned, by special resolution of the members of the company. However, this is not enough since such a resolution is ineffective unless holders of three-fourths of the issued shares of that class consent in writing, or by means of an extraordinary resolution passed at a separate general meeting of holders of the shares of the class, or by means of a written resolution. In addition, 15 per cent of the class not voting for the variation may apply to the court within 21 days of the consent of the class being given, whether in writing or by resolution. Obviously no application will be made where there has been a unanimous written resolution. Once such an application has been made, usually by one or more dissentients on behalf of the others, the variation will not take effect unless and until it is confirmed by the court.

So far as private companies are concerned, there is no objection to the use of the unanimous written resolution to alter the shareholders' rights in the articles, if this can be obtained, and then, as we have seen, there would be no dissentients. If it could not be obtained, the company would have to proceed by special resolution in general meeting or written consent.

(v) The alteration must not deprive members of rights given to them by the court. Thus if the court has by order made an alteration in the articles in order to assist minority shareholders to overcome acts of unfair prejudice by the majority, that article cannot be altered without the approval of the court. This is considered in more detail in Chapter 14.

(vi) Finally, as Master of the Rolls Lindley said in *Allen* v *Gold Reefs of West Africa Ltd* [1900] 1 Ch 656, the court has a jurisdiction to regard an alteration of the articles as invalid unless it is made for the benefit of the company as a whole, i.e. the whole body of members. It may make it easier to understand this idea if we spend a little time in describing the position taken by the court because it does not in fact look solely at the company as it is at the time of the action (which would be a subjective test) but tries to see the company in equilibrium. That is to say the court envisages the company in a hypothetical situation in which shares and voting power are evenly distributed among the members, and assumes that members will vote independently of each other and not, as it were, combine to coerce other members.

Having viewed the company in this situation, the court then decides on the validity of the alteration. This is an objective test and is really the only one the court can adopt. If it were to test the validity of the alteration against the present state of the shareholding, then the day after the resolution was approved the shareholding may alter and there may be a shift in the centre of power in the company. Rather than cope with so many imponderables, the court decides the question by putting the company into a state of equilibrium (hypothetically at least) and then looking at the alteration.

However, the objective test is not altogether satisfactory and can sometimes operate unfavourably towards particular shareholders. The difficulty is that the court sometimes assumes, probably rightly, that those who are managing the company's affairs and, on occasion, a majority of the shareholders, know better than the court what is for its benefit. Thus shareholders may sometimes feel that they have not been dealt with fairly and yet the court will accept the alteration to the articles as valid and for the benefit of the company as a whole. This approach is illustrated by the following case.

Greenhalgh *v* Arderne Cinemas Ltd [1951] Ch 286

The articles of the company originally required any member who wished to sell his shares to offer them to his fellow members before selling them to a stranger. A majority group of the shareholders procured an alteration enabling a member to sell his shares without first offering them to his fellow members if the company so resolved by ordinary resolution. The purpose was so that the majority could sell their shares to an outsider, a Mr Sheckman, for 6s per share and so give Mr Sheckman a controlling interest. Mr Greenhalgh, a minority shareholder, objected to the alteration although Mr Sheckman was prepared to pay 6s per share to any shareholder of the company, including Mr Greenhalgh. *Held* – by the Court of Appeal – that the alteration was valid even though its *immediate* effect was to enable the majority group to sell their shares to outsiders without first offering them to the minority shareholders, though the minority shareholders, not being able to pass an ordinary resolution, were still bound to offer their shares to the majority group before selling elsewhere.

Comment

(i) Perhaps the alteration of the articles could be justified in this case under the objective test adopted by the courts since the hypothetical member might benefit equally with any other member in the future by the extension of his power to sell his shares to strangers. Furthermore, the alteration represented a relaxation of the very stringent restrictions on transfer in the article which had existed before the change.

(ii) In earlier litigation between the same parties [1946] 1 All ER 512 what would now be 10p ordinary shares had one vote per share and so did each 50p ordinary share. Greenhalgh held 10p shares and controlled 40 per cent of the vote and could block special resolutions. The holders of the 50p shares procured an ordinary resolution (as company legislation requires), to subdivide each 50p share into five 10p shares with one vote each, thus reducing G's voting power. It was held that the voting rights of the original 10p shares had not been varied. They still had one vote per share. (See also Chapter 6.)

The result of the objective test which the court uses is that most alterations are allowed, though alterations which give the company power to expel members without cause are not acceptable to the court. However, expulsion is allowed where it would benefit the members as a whole, as where the member expelled is competing with the company or defrauding it.

Dafen Tinplate Co Ltd *v* Llanelly Steel Co (1907) Ltd [1920] 2 Ch 124

The principal shareholders of the defendant company were other steel companies, and it was hoped that the member companies would buy their steel bars from the defendants, though there was no contract to this effect. In the main the member companies did buy their steel from the defendants, but the claimant company began in 1912 to get its steel from a concern called the Bynea company in which the claimant had an interest. The defendant company then sought to alter its articles to expel the claimant company. The alteration provided that the defendant company could by ordinary resolution require any member to sell his shares to the other members at a fair price to be fixed by the directors. The claimant sought a declaration that the alteration was void. *Held* – by Peterson J – that the claimant company was entitled to such a declaration. The power taken by the articles was a bare power of expulsion, and could be used to expel a member who was not acting to the detriment of the defendant company at all. Therefore, whatever its merits in the circumstances of the case, it could not be allowed.

Comment

This power of expulsion was to be written in the articles and would last indefinitely. In addition, it would permanently discriminate between shareholders of the same class and as such could not benefit the future hypothetical member and was therefore void.

Sidebottom *v* Kershaw, Leese & Co [1920] 1 Ch 154

The defendant company, which was a small private company, altered its articles to empower the directors to require any member who carried on a business competing with that of the company, to sell his shares at a fair price to persons nominated by the directors.

The claimant was a member of the defendant company, and ran mills in competition with it, and this action was brought to test the validity of the alteration in articles. The court of first instance found for the claimant, regarding the alteration as a bare power of expropriation, though there was no dispute that the price fixed for the purchase of the shares was fair. *Held* – by the Court of Appeal – that the evidence showed that the claimant might cause the defendant company loss by information which he received as a member, and as the power was restricted to expulsion for competing, the alteration was for the benefit of the company as a whole and was valid.

Comment

(i) It was obviously in the interest of the company as a whole and of the 'hypothetical member' that the company's trade secrets should not be available to its competitors.

(ii) As Lord Sterndale MR made clear in his judgment in this case, the power of compulsory purchase of shares is valid if contained in the original articles. Such a provision would not be set aside on the 'benefit' ground; the concept is applicable only to changes in the articles as *Phillips* v *Manufacturers' Securities Ltd* (1917) 116 LT 290 decides.

Shuttleworth *v* Cox Brothers & Co (Maidenhead) Ltd [1927] 2 KB 9

The company's articles provided that Shuttleworth and four other persons should be permanent directors of the company, to hold office for life, unless disqualified by any one of the events specified in Art 22 of the company's articles. These events were bankruptcy, insanity, conviction of an indictable offence, failure to hold the necessary qualification shares, and being absent from meetings of the board for more than six months without leave. The company conducted a building business, and Shuttleworth, on 22 occasions within 12 months, failed to account for the company's money which he had received on its behalf. The articles were altered by adding another disqualifying event, namely, a request in writing by all the other directors. Having made the alteration, the directors made the request to Shuttleworth, and he now questioned the validity of his expulsion from the board. *Held* – by the Court of Appeal – that the alteration and the action taken under it was valid, because it was for the benefit of the company as a whole since Shuttleworth was defrauding it. Shuttleworth also claimed that no alteration of the articles could affect his contract with the company, but the Court of Appeal held, on this point, that since part of his contract (the grounds for dismissal) was contained in the articles, he must be taken to know that this was in an alterable document and he must take the risk of change.

Breaches of contract arising out of alteration of the articles

A company cannot by altering its memorandum or articles escape liability for breach of a contract into which it has entered. The difficulty has arisen with regard to the remedies of the other party to the contract. In *Punt* v *Symons & Co Ltd* [1903] 2 Ch 506 it was said that the other party to the contract could sue the company for damages for breach, but could not obtain an injunction to prevent the alteration taking effect. Then followed a series of cases which revealed considerable judicial indecision on this point. For example, in *Baily* v *British Equitable Assurance Co Ltd* [1904] 1 Ch 374 the Court of Appeal seems to have been prepared to grant an injunction to restrain an alteration of the articles in breach of contract although in fact it was only asked to give a declaratory judgment as to the state of the law. However, in *Southern Foundries* v *Shirlaw*, 1940 (below), Lord Porter in an *obiter dictum* gave support to the view that the other party to the contract can sue the company for damages only, and cannot obtain an injunction to prevent the alteration from taking effect. It may be said, therefore, that a company is quite free to alter its articles, though if in doing so it breaks a contract which it has made, it must face an action in damages by the party aggrieved. There may also be an action against those who voted for the alteration.

Southern Foundries (1926) Ltd *v* Shirlaw [1940] AC 701

The appellant company was incorporated in 1926 as a private company, and was engaged in the business of iron founders. The respondent, Shirlaw, became a director of the company in 1929 under a provision in the articles. In 1933 he became managing director under a separate contract, the appointment to be for ten years, and containing restraints under which Shirlaw agreed that he would not, for a period of three years after leaving the employment of the appellants, engage in foundry work within 100 miles of Croydon. In 1935 there was a merger between the appellant company and ten other concerns, and the group was called Federated Industries. The members of the group agreed that they should make certain alterations in their articles regarding directors; the articles of each member were altered, and in their new form gave Federated Industries power to remove any director of the company, and also stipulated that a managing director should cease to hold office if he ceased to be a director. In 1937 Shirlaw was removed from office as a director, under the provision in the articles, by an instrument in writing, signed by two directors and the secretary of Federated Industries. This meant that Shirlaw could no longer be managing director of Southern Foundries, and since his contract had still some time to run, he brought this action for wrongful dismissal. The trial judge found for Shirlaw and awarded him £12,000 damages, and the Court of Appeal affirmed that decision. The company now appealed to the House of Lords. *Held* – by a majority – that Shirlaw's contract as managing director contained an implied term that the article making him a director would not be altered. Since it had been altered, there was a breach of contract and the company was liable for it. Lord Wright took the view that since there was no privity of contract between Shirlaw and Federated Industries, it was difficult to see how they could dismiss him. Lord Romer, dissenting, did not think a term against alteration of the articles could be implied and thought that Shirlaw took the risk of alteration. Lord Porter lent support in this case to *Punt* v *Symons*, 1903, and said that a company could not be prevented by injunction from altering its articles but that the only remedy for an alteration which has caused a breach of contract was damages.

Comment

(i) From statements made in this case it appears that any member who votes for the alteration will also be liable to the claimant for inducing the company to break its contract if the inevitable consequence of the alteration is that the contract will be broken.

(ii) This case shows how to remove a managing director. *Table A* states that a board of directors may appoint 'one or more of their number' to be managing director (or directors). Therefore in most companies, because of the adoption of *Table A*, a managing director will automatically lose his office if he ceases to be a director, e.g. by removal under s 303 or under a provision in the articles.

(iii) In *Shirlaw* the articles said that a managing director was to be subject to the same provisions for removal as any other director 'subject to the provisions of any contract between him and the company'. There was an implied term in the contract of service which overrode the power of removal without compensation in the articles.

(iv) In *Nelson* v *James Nelson & Sons Ltd* [1914] 2 KB 770 a service contract appointing the claimant to act as managing director 'so long as he shall remain a director of the company' was also held to override an article giving a power of removal without compensation. Damages were awarded to the claimant because his contract was terminated by his removal from office as a director. That was a breach by the company of his contract as managing director which he could then no longer perform.

The position is different where a person contracts with a company and the contract incorporates a provision of the memorandum or articles by implication. In such a case the other party is deemed to know that the company may alter its memorandum or articles, and therefore takes the risk of the contract failing because of such an alteration, even to the extent of failing in an action for damages (*Shuttleworth* v *Cox Bros & Co (Maidenhead) Ltd*, 1927, see above). However, there are certain limitations upon the above rule:

(i) Rights which have already accrued under the contract cannot be disturbed by the alteration.

Swabey *v* Port Darwin Gold Mining Co (1889) 1 Meg 385

Swabey had served the company as a director under a provision in the company's articles which provided for his salary. The articles were altered so as to reduce that salary and it was *held* – by the Court of Appeal – that, although the alteration was effective to reduce the salary for the future, Swabey could not be deprived of his salary at the original figure for the period he had served prior to the alteration of the articles.

(ii) As we have seen, no alteration of the memorandum or articles can affect the *express* terms of the contract. If a contract expressly provides for, say, the salary of a director, and the articles also carry a salary provision, then the contract would not be affected if the company altered the salary provision in the articles. In addition, the court may sometimes *imply* a term against alteration of the articles into a separate contract and then allow the party aggrieved to sue on the separate contract for a breach of this implied term (*Southern Foundries* v *Shirlaw*, 1940, see above).

(iii) It is felt that the obligations of the other party cannot be made more onerous by an alteration of the articles. Thus, if the articles appoint a director to serve for a period of years on a part-time basis, he cannot be required to give his full time to the company by the company altering its articles so as to require him to do so.

(iv) As we have already seen, where the company has shares of more than one class, it cannot vary the rights of a class of shares merely by altering them in the memorandum or articles. Section 125 applies and requires the consent of three-quarters of the class and there are dissentient rights.

The articles can, of course, be altered by a special (or unanimous) resolution of the members, but the rights of the class are not affected by such changes made by the membership as a whole.

Alteration of the articles by the court

As the text describes below the articles are a contract between the company and each member and in this connection the court has power to rectify contracts. For example, if parties have agreed for a lease of land for 25 years that is written down in the lease by mistake as 21 years then if one of the parties is not prepared to co-operate in changing this provision of the lease the court can be asked to rectify the lease by an order inserting 25 years as the term of the lease provided the evidence shows to the satisfaction of the court that this was the intention of the parties. The court has ruled however that it does not have power to rectify the statutory contract set out in the articles.

Scott *v* Frank F Scott (London) Ltd [1940] Ch 794

The defendant company was a private company with three members, Frank, Stuart and Reginald Scott, the business of the company being that of butchers. On the death of Frank Scott, his widow, Marie Scott, became entitled under his will to certain preference shares and ordinary shares in the company, as executrix. When she sought to be registered in respect of the shares, Stuart and Reginald Scott claimed that under a provision in the articles the shares must on the death of a member be offered to the other members at par, but the article was not so well drafted as to make this clear beyond doubt. This action was brought to interpret the article, and also to ask the court to rectify the article to carry a right to pre-emption if the article was not so drafted as to achieve this. *Held* – by the Court of Appeal – that the article did give the right of pre-emption claimed by Stuart and Reginald Scott. However, if it had not done so, the court could not have rectified it; the alteration could only be carried out by special resolution.

However, the High Court departed from this general ruling when faced with an absurd result of bad drafting.

Folkes Group plc *v* Alexander [2002] 2 BCLC 254

The Folkes family held a substantial proportion of the voting shares in the listed plc. The other shareholders had no voting rights unless the Folkes family holdings fell below 40 per cent. An article to ensure that this could never happen was drafted and agreed and became part of the articles. Later it was noticed that certain holdings of the Folkes family were excluded from the voting category so that their voting holdings fell to 23.9 per cent, thus triggering the voting rights of the other members. The former non-voting shares would not use their newly acquired voting power to change the articles to what was originally intended. The court did however do so by ordering the insertion of five words into the altered article to give it the effect intended. The judge's justification was that to leave the article as it was would flout business common sense and legal decisions might on occasion have to yield to business common sense following comments in the House of Lords in *Investors Compensation Scheme Ltd* v *West Bromwich Building Society* [1998] 1 BCLC 493.

THE LEGAL EFFECT OF THE MEMORANDUM AND ARTICLES

The memorandum and articles when registered bind the company and its members in contract as if these documents had been signed as a deed by each member and contained covenants on the part of each member to observe the provisions of the memorandum and articles (s 14).

The results of this statutory contract are as follows:

(*a*) The memorandum and articles constitute a contract between the company and each member. Thus each member *in his capacity as member* is bound to the company by the provisions in the articles. Furthermore, although s 14 does not state that the articles bind the company to the members but only the members to the company, the company is regarded as bound to each member in his capacity as member to observe the provisions in the articles.

Hickman *v* Kent or Romney Marsh Sheepbreeders' Association [1915] 1 Ch 881

The defendant company was incorporated under the Companies Acts in 1895. The objects of the company were to encourage and retain as pure the sheep known as Kent or Romney Marsh, and the establishment of a flock book listing recognised sires and ewes to be bred from. The articles provided for disputes between the company and the members to be referred to arbitration. This action was brought in the Chancery Division by the claimant because the Association had refused to register certain of his sheep in the flock book, and he asked for damages for this. It also appeared that the Association was trying to expel him, and he asked for an injunction to prevent this. *Held* – by Astbury J – that the Association was entitled to have the action stayed. The articles amounted to a contract between the Association and the claimant to refer disputes to arbitration. However, Astbury J, after accepting that the articles were a contract between a company and its members, went on to say: '. . . No right merely purporting to be given by an article to a person, whether a member or not, in a capacity other than that of a member, as for instance, a solicitor, promoter, director, can be enforced against the company.'

Comment

(i) It was held, by the Court of Appeal applying *Hickman*, in *Beattie* v *E and F Beattie Ltd* [1938] Ch 708, that a provision in the articles that disputes between the company and its members must be referred to arbitration did not apply to a person whose dispute was between the company and himself as *director* even though he was also a *member.*

(ii) In *Pender* v *Lushington* (1877) 6 Ch D 70, the chairman of a meeting of members refused to accept Pender's votes. The articles gave one vote for every ten shares to the shareholders. This caused a resolution proposed by Pender to be lost. He asked the court to grant an injunction to stop the directors acting contrary to the resolution. *Held* – Pender succeeded. The articles were a contract binding the company to the members.

(*b*) The memorandum and articles are also by reason of case law a contract between the members themselves. Thus one member can sue another if that other fails to observe a provision in the memorandum or articles. There is no need to call upon the company to sue.

Rayfield *v* Hands [1958] 2 All ER 194

The articles of a private company provided by Art II that 'Every member who intends to transfer his shares shall inform the directors who will take the said shares equally between them at a fair value.' The claimant held 725 fully-paid shares of £1 each, and he asked the defendants, the three directors of the company, to buy them but they refused. He brought this action to sue upon the contract created by the articles without joining the company as a party. *Held* – by Vaisey J – that the directors were bound to take the shares. Having regard to what is now s 14, the provisions of Art II constituted a binding contract between the directors, as members, and the claimant, as a member, in respect of his rights as a member. The word 'will' in the article did not import an option in the directors. Vaisey J did say that the conclusion he had reached in this case may not apply to all companies, but it did apply to a private company, because such a company was an intimate concern closely analogous with a partnership.

Comment

(i) Although the articles placed the obligation to take shares of members on the directors, Vaisey J construed this as an obligation falling upon the directors in their capacity as members. Otherwise the contractual aspect of the provision in the articles would not have applied. (See *Beattie* v *E and F Beattie Ltd* [1938] Ch 708.)

(ii) The company's Art II was a pre-emption clause. Many such clauses use the expression 'may take the said shares'. If so, no contract is formed. The word 'may' indicates that there is an option whether to accept or not.

(*c*) No right given by the memorandum or articles to a member in a capacity other than that of member, e.g. as solicitor or director, can be enforced against the company. The memorandum and articles are not a contract with outsiders but merely with the members in respect of their rights as members.

Eley *v* Positive Government Security Life Assurance Co (1876) 1 Ex D 88

The articles contained a clause appointing the claimant as solicitor of the company. The claimant was not appointed by a resolution of the directors or by any instrument under the seal of the company, but he did act as solicitor for some time and took shares in the company at a later stage. The company ceased to employ him, and he brought an action for breach of contract. *Held* – by the Court of Appeal – that the action failed because there was no contract between the company and Eley under the articles. He was an outsider in his capacity as a solicitor, and presumably even though he was also a member, he could not enforce the articles since they gave him rights in his capacity as solicitor only, though his rights as a member to enforce the articles are not dealt with specifically in the judgment.

Comment

It was held by the court of first instance that a service contract on the terms set out in the articles was created because Eley had actually served the company as its solicitor. However, the contract was unenforceable because the articles contemplated his employment for an indefinite period of time, possibly longer than a year, and there was no written memorandum of the contract signed on behalf of the company as was then required by s 4 of the Statute of Frauds 1677. This statute is now repealed so that the case may have been decided differently today. This view is reinforced by the decision in *Re New British Iron Co, ex parte Beckwith* (see below) because surely when Eley took office he did so on the terms of the articles and had an implied contract based upon the terms of those articles. Thus if a term as to tenure could be implied in the way that a term as to salary was in *Beckwith*, then Eley should have been able to sue for breach of the implied contract. *Read*'s case (see below) suggests also the tenure of office may be based on the articles.

However, a provision in the memorandum or articles can become part of a contract between the company and a member or outsider in the following ways:

(*a*) where there is an express contract and a provision in the memorandum or articles is *expressly incorporated* into that contract by a provision therein;

(*b*) where a provision in the memorandum or articles is *incorporated by implication* arising out of the conduct of the parties, or where an express contract between the parties is silent on a particular aspect, e.g. in the case of a director, the length of his appointment. In such a case reference may be made to the memorandum or articles to fill the gap, if those documents contain a relevant provision.

Re New British Iron Co, ex parte Beckwith [1898] 1 Ch 324

Beckwith was employed as a director of the company, relying for his remuneration on the company's articles which provided that the directors should be paid £1,000 per annum. In this action by Beckwith for his fees, it was *held* – by Wright J – that, although the articles did not constitute a contract between the company and Beckwith in his capacity as director, yet he had accepted office and worked on the footing of the articles, and the company was liable to pay him his fees on that basis. Actually the company was liable on an implied contract, the articles being merely referred to for certain of its terms.

Read *v* Astoria Garage (Streatham) Ltd [1952] Ch 637

The defendant company was a private company which had adopted Art 68 of *Table A* of the Companies Act 1929. The articles provided for the appointment of a managing director, and said that he could be dismissed at any time and without any period of notice, if the company so resolved by a special resolution. The claimant's contract made in 1932 appointed him managing director at a salary of £7 per week but said nothing about notice. The directors dismissed him on 11 May 1949 at one month's notice, and later called an extraordinary general meeting of the shareholders and got the necessary resolution. The special resolution was passed on 28 September 1949, and Read's salary was paid until that date but not afterwards. Read now sued for wrongful dismissal, suggesting that he ought to have had more notice because a person holding his position would customarily have more notice than he had been given. *Held* – by the Court of Appeal – that since the claimant's contract was silent on the point, Art 68 was incorporated into the express contract. Once this was done, the notice he had been given was most generous and his claim therefore failed, his tenure of office being based on the articles.

Although the above decisions are concerned with a member enforcing or being bound by a provision in the articles which was personal to himself as member, e.g. a right to the vote attaching to his shares as in *Pender* v *Lushington*, 1877, the principles involved may go further than this. There is some authority for the view that *each member has a right under the articles to have the company's affairs conducted in accordance with the articles.*

Salmon *v* Quin & Axtens Ltd [1909] 1 Ch 311

The memorandum of the company included among its objects the purchasing of real or personal property. By the articles the business was to be managed by the directors, but no resolution of the board to purchase or lease any premises of the company was to be valid unless two conditions were satisfied, namely notice in writing must be given to each of the two managing directors named in the articles, and neither of them must have dissented therefrom in writing before or at the meeting at which the resolution was to be passed. In August 1908 the board passed resolutions for the purchase of certain premises by the company, and for leasing part of the company's property. The claimant, who was one of the managing directors, dissented, but at an extraordinary general meeting of the company held in November 1908, resolutions similar to those passed by the board were passed by an ordinary resolution of the members. The claimant brought this action for an injunction to stop the company from acting on the resolutions as they were inconsistent with the articles. *Held* – eventually by the House of Lords (see *Quin & Axtens* v *Salmon* [1909] AC 442) – that an injunction would be granted.

Comment

The claimant sued on behalf of himself and *other shareholders* to prevent the majority and the company from acting contrary to the company's constitution.

Could the above decision be used to enable a solicitor who was also a shareholder indirectly to enforce a provision in the company's articles that he is to be the company's solicitor by saying to the company 'conduct business in accordance with the articles'? (See *Eley* v *Positive Government Security Life Assurance Co*, 1876.)

THE EFFECT OF THE CONTRACTS (RIGHTS OF THIRD PARTIES) ACT 1999

The above Act does not apply to the statutory contract between a company and its members in terms of the provisions in a company's memorandum and articles, as set out in s 14. The Act specifically excludes it to prevent third-party rights from arising. Thus the decision in *Eley* v *Positive Government Security Life Assurance Co*, 1876 still stands and would not or could not be affected by the 1999 Act.

THE ARTICLES AND NEW TECHNOLOGY

New articles can be drafted for member approval which take into account the use of new technology as follows:

- notices of meetings of shareholders can be sent by e-mail;
- voting on a poll can be done electronically;

- proxies can be appointed by e-mail;
- board meetings can take place through a series of video conferences or telephone calls from the chairman.

As regards the AGM, the Companies Act 1985 allows companies to provide how notice of meetings shall be given. However, there is no point in sending the notice by e-mail where the company, as is commonly the case, sends the directors' reports and accounts with the notice. In this connection, the Electronic Communications Act 2000 received Royal Assent on 25 May 2000. At that time also s 8 of the Act came into force. This allows ministerial orders to modify existing legislation where paper documents are required in terms of allowing communication of documents and the documents themselves to be in electronic form.

In this connection, the Companies Act 1985 (Electronic Communications) Order 2000 now applies. It modifies certain provisions of the Companies Act 1985 and *Table A* to that Act for the purpose of authorising or facilitating the use of electronic communications between the company and its members, and Companies House has arranged for electronic incorporation under its provisions.

So far as *Table A* is concerned, the order carries amendments to enable proxies and notices to be sent electronically. In this regard, the order recommends guidance entitled *Electronic Communications with Shareholders: A Guide to Recommended Best Practice*, that is obtainable (price £10 with order) from The Policy Unit, The Institute of Chartered Secretaries and Administrators, 16 Park Crescent, London, W1B 1AH. The Articles (or *Regulations*) of *Table A* that are automatically changed to allow electronic communication are:

- *Regulation* 1 (interpretation): so that 'communication' includes electronic communication;
- *Regulation* 60 (appointment of proxy);
- *Regulation* 61 (instructions to proxy);
- *Regulation* 62 (lodging of proxy appointment);
- *Regulation* 63 (determination of proxy appointment);
- *Regulation* 111 (form of notices);
- *Regulation* 112 (giving of notices);
- *Regulation* 115 (when notices deemed to be given).

Special articles are overriden but *not* amended, but amendment, though not strictly necessary, is advised. The 2000 order is not mandatory and companies are not in any sense required to use electronic communication. It should be remembered that some 90 per cent of companies are private companies and the vast majority of these have fewer than five members. They tend to operate rather informally anyway and may see the cost of setting up and maintaining electronic communication with members *who must consent and be equipped to take part* as an unnecessary expense.

The memorandum and articles and shareholders' agreements

Before leaving the law relating to the company's constitution as expressed in the memorandum and articles it is worth noting the increase in shareholders' agreements which often, in private companies, supplement the statutory documents. These agreements operate as binding contracts, as do the memorandum and articles, and they deal with the rights and duties of members of a particular company to which they apply. The great advantage of them is that they *remain secret* since they are not registered and are not therefore subject to public inspection. The courts are, of course, available to adjudicate upon disputes relating to them because they have contractual force and in *Euro Brokers Holdings Ltd* v *Monecor (London) Ltd* [2003] applied the *Duomatic* principle to such an agreement. The principle which is derived from the decision in *Re Duomatic* [1969] 2 Ch 365 states that the informal and unanimous assent of all the company's shareholders can override formal requirements as where a particular course of action requires a meeting and resolution of the shareholders, either under statutory provisions or because of the requirements of the company's articles, and no such meeting and/or resolution has been held or passed or written resolution made. Nevertheless, if there is evidence that the shareholders were unanimously agreed on the matter, the court may accept the resulting transaction as valid.

Euro Brokers Holdings Ltd *v* Monecor (London) Ltd [2003] 1 BCLC 506

So far as the facts of *Euro Brokers* are concerned, the matter in issue was a call made on the company's two shareholders requiring them to advance more capital. The finance director made the call by means of an e-mail though the shareholders' agreement required that the call be made by a notice from the board. Nevertheless, both shareholders regarded the call as valid and agreed to send the sums required to the company. Later one of the shareholders failed to forward the full amount. Under the shareholders' agreement this triggered a right in the other shareholder to acquire the shares of the defaulter at an agreed price. The defaulter was not prepared to accept this situation and challenged the validity of the call in terms that it had not been made by the formal notice of the board. This defence was rejected by the Court of Appeal. The shareholders had accepted the call in the manner in which it was made and the *Duomatic* principle could therefore be applied. In consequence, the defaulting shareholder could be required to sell his entire holding to the claimant.

Typical contents of shareholders' agreements

A typical shareholders' agreement may include:

- Undertakings and agreements from prospective shareholders before the company is formed.
- Matters that it would be inappropriate to put on the public record such as confidentiality undertakings and non-competition restrictions, the right of certain shareholders to appoint directors and dispute resolution.
- Protection of minority shareholders if required. Thus, although alteration of the articles requires a special resolution, i.e. a 75 per cent majority of votes, a shareholders' agreement can require written consent from all shareholders so protecting those with minority holdings.
- Internal management issues which the members wish to keep off the public record, e.g. choice of bankers, and the policy of the company on loans and borrowing together with cheque signatories.

GRADED QUESTIONS

Essay mode

1 Discuss how the memorandum of association and the articles of association form the constitution of a registered company with specific reference to their respective contents.

Explain how *Table A* can be utilised.

(University of Paisley)

2 Success Limited has been trading profitably for ten years, with capital provided by each of its four directors and their families. The directors consider that the company could be even more profitable, if it were able to make a public issue of securities, and they are advocating the re-registration of the company as a public limited company. However, some of the members are not enthusiastic, as they believe that there are disadvantages to trading as a public company.

Explain to the members the advantages and disadvantages of trading in the form of a public company, and the statutory procedure for re-registration of a private limited company as a public limited company.

(Napier University)

3 (*a*) Section 14(1) of Companies Act 1985 provides that the memorandum and articles of association constitute an agreement between the company and its members as if they have signed and sealed a contract to abide by its provisions.

Comment.

(*b*) A, B & C are members of X Ltd. The company has now discovered that C is also a major shareholder in a rival company. It is causing concern that C might be extracting information about X Ltd's business which could confer unfair advantage on its rival. X Ltd wishes to alter its articles of association so as to require any member competing with X Ltd, to sell his or her shares as required to any person or persons named by the directors of the company, or to the directors themselves.

Advise X Ltd.

(University of Plymouth)

4 'The articles form a contract between a company and its members. This contract is, however, an unusual one, limited both in its scope and permanence.'

Discuss.

(The Institute of Chartered Secretaries and Administrators)

5 Describe the procedure for alteration of articles and detail the considerations made in determining the validity of the alteration.

(The Institute of Company Accountants)

6 H plc wishes to change its articles of association to add a clause which states 'any director of the company may be removed from office if all other directors give notice in writing of their desire that the named directors be so removed'.

You are required to explain the procedure for alteration and discuss the difficulties the company might encounter in adding this new clause.

(*The Chartered Institute of Management Accountants*)

7 (*a*) Why must every company have a registered office? What information about the registered office must be published? To what extent can the registered office of the company be changed and what procedures must be observed when it is so changed?

(*b*) In the absence of a company taking advantage of alternative provisions under the Companies Act 1985, what statutory records must be kept at a company's registered office?

(*The Association of Chartered Certified Accountants*)

8 As the company secretary of Marcus plc, write a note for the board of directors outlining what advantage can be taken of electronic communication legislation in terms of communication with the members.

(*Author's question*)

Objective mode

Four alternative answers are given. Select ONE only. Circle the answer which you consider to be correct. Check your answers by referring back to the information given in the chapter and against the answers at the back of the book.

1 Fred bought some shares in Tyne Ltd on 1 February 20xx. To whom does Fred become bound in contract?

A The company only.
B The members of Tyne on 1 February 20xx.
C Tyne and those who are at present its members.
D Tyne and those who were members of Tyne on 1 February 20xx.

2 *Table A* will apply automatically except where it is excluded or modified by special articles of association in the case of:

A private companies limited by shares only.
B public companies limited by shares only.
C all companies limited by shares.
D all limited companies.

3 The articles of association of a company on a paper incorporation must be signed by:

A each one of the directors.
B a majority of the directors.
C all the subscribers to the memorandum.
D one of the subscribers to the memorandum.

4 A private company limited by shares must include in its memorandum a clause which states that:

A the company is a private company limited by shares.
B the liability of the members is limited.

C the company is not a public company.
D the company is a private company.

5 An ambiguity in the memorandum of a company may be resolved by reference to the:

A articles.
B Companies Act 1985.
C directors.
D shareholders.

6 The capital clause of a company limited by shares is contained in the memorandum. What does it state?

A The amount of share capital which the directors can issue.
B The amount of the share capital presently issued.
C The amount of share capital which the company is entitled to issue.
D The amount of share capital currently paid up.

The answers to questions set in objective mode appear on p 576.

5

THE COMPANY AND ITS CONTRACTS

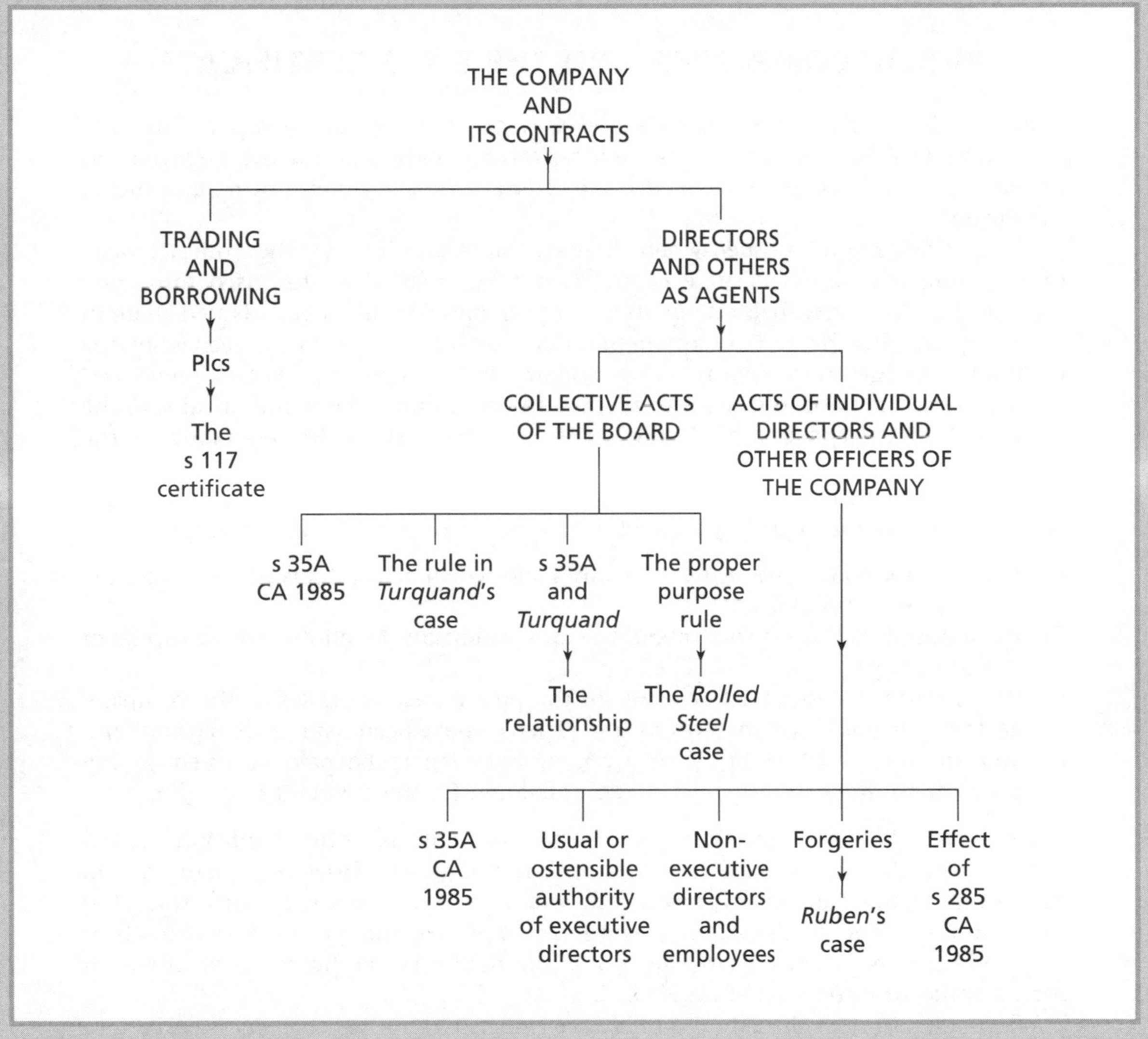

A company necessarily contracts through agents such as its directors and other officers, and senior employees. This chapter is, in the main, concerned with the problems which can arise when these agents enter into transactions which they are not authorised to make or use their powers for an improper purpose, or exercise them by irregular procedures. First, however, this is an appropriate place to deal with transactions entered into by public companies before receipt of a s 117 certificate from the Registrar.

PUBLIC COMPANIES AND THE S 117 CERTIFICATE

Under s 117 a *public company*, registered as such on its initial incorporation, cannot commence business or exercise any borrowing powers unless the Registrar has issued what is known as a s 117 certificate. A *private company* does not require such a certificate.

The certificate will be issued when the Registrar is satisfied that the nominal value of the company's allotted share capital is not less than the authorised minimum (£50,000) and not less than one-quarter of the nominal value of each issued share in the company plus the *whole* of any premium on such shares has been received by the company, whether in cash or otherwise. A share allotted in pursuance of an employees' share scheme may not be taken into account in determining the nominal value of the company's allotted share capital unless it is paid up at least as to one-quarter of the nominal value of the share and the whole of any premium on the share.

In order to obtain a s 117 certificate, the company must file with the Registrar a statutory declaration signed by a director or secretary of the company stating:

(*a*) that the nominal value of the company's allotted share capital is not less than the authorised minimum;
(*b*) the amount paid up at the time of the application on the allotted share capital of the company;
(*c*) the amount, or estimated amount, of the preliminary expenses of the company and the persons by whom any of those expenses have been paid or are payable; and
(*d*) any amount or benefit paid or given or intended to be paid or given to any promoter of the company and the consideration for the payment or benefit.

The object of the s 117 provisions is to ensure that a plc has some significant starting capital, though £12,500 plus any premium is not much. However, there was no minimum capital requirement before this and a plc could be set up with, say, £100 initial capital. The disclosure of preliminary expenses and promoter payments is required because if these are large and paid from the initial capital, then the provision for a significant initial capital is defeated.

When a certificate is issued it is conclusive evidence that the company is entitled to commence business and exercise borrowing powers. Failure to comply with s 117 may result in a fine on the company and any officer in default.

If a public company has not obtained a s 117 certificate within a year of registration, the Secretary of State for Trade and Industry may present a petition to the court to wind it up.

If a company does commence business or borrow without a s 117 certificate, transactions with traders and lenders are nevertheless enforceable against the company. However, if the company cannot meet its obligations in terms of payment of a debt or repayment of a loan incurred during the period of unlawful trading, within 21 days of being called upon to do so, the directors of the company are jointly and severally liable to indemnify the trader or lender in respect of his loss resulting from the company's failure to meet its obligations. Therefore, s 117 leaves the company liable and the directors become personally liable if the company does not pay, as where it goes into insolvent liquidation without discharging its liability on a transaction.

DIRECTORS AND OTHERS AS AGENTS

If the board acting together (that is collectively), or one director or other officer of the company acting on his own, has *actual authority* to make a particular contract on behalf of the company, and that contract is within the company's powers (or if not the transaction is protected by s 35 – see Chapter 3), then the contract, when made, will be binding on the company. However, where the directors act together, or as individuals, beyond their authority the position for them and other officers is as set out below.

Collective acts of the board

(a) Companies Act 1985

Section 35A provides that in favour of a person dealing with the company in good faith, the power of the board of directors to bind the company or authorise others to do so shall be deemed free of any limitation under the company's constitution including any special restrictions placed on the directors by resolution of the members (see further Chapter 15), and a person shall not be regarded as acting in bad faith just because he knows that an act is beyond the powers of the directors. Under s 35B there is no duty to enquire as to the directors' authority and there is no constructive notice of any provision of the company's constitution limiting authority. Therefore, provided the above requirements are met, a transaction entered into by the board beyond its powers will bind the company. This applies not only where the directors are acting beyond their powers but also where they are within their powers but have failed to observe proper internal procedures.

TCB *v* Gray [1987] 3 WLR 1144

A company issued a debenture to secure a loan. The transaction was within the company's powers and within the authority of the board. The debenture was issued under the company's seal. On this the articles of the company said 'every instrument to which the seal shall be affixed shall be signed by a director'. In this case it was signed by a solicitor to whom one of the directors had given a power of attorney to act as his agent. The question of the validity of the debenture arose and the court *held* that it was valid under s 35A which protected not only against lack of authority but also against the use of incorrect procedures.

In addition, it will be noted that the section deals with a situation where the directors authorise other persons to make contracts on behalf of the company. This is to overcome the common law rule that a company can only act through organs of the company. At common law the board of directors is an organ of the company but only if acting collectively. Section 35A overcomes this by making it clear that an act done by a person authorised by the board is in effect an act of the board and therefore an act by an organ of the company. For example, if the board authorises the company's purchasing officer to buy materials from outsiders for use in the company's manufacturing process, *each purchase within the officer's authority* will be a transaction decided upon by the directors and therefore a transaction decided upon by a common law organ of the company. There is no longer an assumption as in previous legislation that all commercial decisions are made at boardroom level. If, therefore, the board collectively makes a decision and enters into a transaction which is beyond its powers, s 35A will make the transaction enforceable, and the same is true if an individual authorised by the board exceeds the powers of the directors by a contract which he as an authorised individual has made.

Good faith. Under s 35A a person is to be regarded as acting in good faith unless the contrary is proved. Thus the burden of proof will be on the company if it wishes to avoid a transaction on the 'bad faith' ground. Section 35A also provides that a person is 'dealing' with a company even though the transaction is gratuitous in that no consideration has been provided to the company. This protects, for example, charitable donations by the directors beyond their powers.

Member injunctions. A member of a company is not prevented by s 35A from asking the court for an injunction to stop the directors from acting beyond their powers, but this cannot be done if the transaction has been entered into, *or* if the members have ratified the transaction by an ordinary (or written) resolution.

Director liability. The directors are liable to compensate the company as they always have been if they cause the company loss by acting outside their powers. Relief from this liability can be given by the members by a special (or written) resolution.

Charities. Once again, there are special rules for charities. Section 35A will not protect a person dealing with a charity unless he has given full consideration *and* did not know that the transaction was beyond the powers of the board *or* did not know he was dealing with a charity.

Section 35A: use by shareholders. The section has been viewed as essentially an outsider's protection as where a creditor relies on the section to validate a contract entered into by the directors without authority. However, in the following case it was held to be available to shareholders in regard to a disputed issue of bonus shares.

EIC Services Ltd *v* Phipps [2003] 3 All ER 804

A shareholder in the company challenged a bonus issue of shares that it had made by capitalising the sum standing to the credit of its share premium account because, if his claim had succeeded, he would have owned a substantially greater proportion of the company. The challenge was based upon the company's articles which provided that the bonus shares should be applied in proportion to the amounts paid up on the shares and following an ordinary resolution of the members. The contention was that a very substantial number of the bonus shares were issued to shareholders whose shares were not paid up and that no resolution of members was passed but only a resolution of the board. The High Court ruled, however, that the bonus issue was enforceable. The relevant shareholders were entitled to rely on CA 1985 s 35A which provides that, in favour of a person dealing with the company in good faith, the power of the board of directors to bind the company or authorise others to do so shall be deemed free of any limitation under the company's constitution, e.g. its articles. Regarding the fact that certain of the recipients of the bonus shares were directors, the judge referred to the further provisions of s 35A which state that a person shall not be regarded as acting in bad faith because he knows that the act is beyond the powers of the directors. The judge felt that they did not know that the issue of the bonus shares was beyond their powers, though as directors they should have done. In any case the judge felt that they had acted in good faith.

The issue of all the bonus shares was therefore valid.

Comment

The issue was also challenged on the ground that the directors made it under a misapprehension of their powers. The contract for the shares, therefore, was void at common law for operative mistake. The court rejected this on the grounds that the mistake was not sufficiently fundamental to avoid the contract.

Section 35A: use by directors. Section 35A states that it applies 'in favour of a person dealing with the company in good faith'. The matter of whether a director could claim to be included in the word 'person' arose in the following case.

Smith *v* Henniker-Major & Co (a firm) [2002] All ER (D) 310 (Jul)

A director of a company who was in dispute with the other directors wished to bring a claim by the company against the defendant solicitors. The company was not pursuing the claim. The director, believing that he had power under the company's articles, acted alone and, without a quorate board meeting, made an agreement as agent of the company under which the company's claim against the solicitors was assigned to him personally. The assignment was later ratified by deed, presumably to prevent a ruling that the assignment was ineffective as lacking consideration. On the issue of the authority of the director to make the assignment for the company, the solicitors contended that since the company's board did not hold a quorate meeting the assignment was invalid and ineffective, so the claimant's case against them should not proceed. On the question whether a director of the company could claim to be included in the word 'person' in s 35A, the majority of the Court of Appeal said no. The words were wide enough to cover a director but not in this case. The claimant, Mr Smith, was the chairman of the company and it was his duty to see that the company's constitution was adhered to. The articles did not permit him to turn himself into a one-man board and he could not rely on his own error as to the company's constitution to validate a transaction with himself. His appeal against a decision striking out his claim against the defendants was dismissed.

Comment

It may be that a director not so senior as Mr Smith but, say, a more junior director – perhaps only recently appointed – might have succeeded. The decision does not rule this out.

(b) The rule in Turquand's *case: the indoor management rule*

This rule is best explained by looking straightaway at the facts of the case.

Royal British Bank *v* Turquand (1856) 6 E & B 327

The claimant bank lent £2,000 to a joint stock company called Cameron's Coalbrook Steam Coal & Swansea and London Railway Company, which was at the time of the action in course of winding-up. Turquand was the general manager of the company and was brought into the action to represent it. The company had issued a bond under its common seal, signed by two directors, agreeing to repay the loan. The registered deed of settlement of the company (which corresponded to the articles of a modern company) provided that the directors might borrow on bond such sums as they should be authorised by a general resolution of the members of the company to borrow. In the case of this loan it appeared that no such resolution had been passed. *Held* – by the Court of Exchequer – that the bond was nevertheless binding on the company, because the lenders were entitled to assume that a resolution authorising the borrowing had been passed. There was no need to go indoors the management to make active enquiries.

Comment

This case succeeded because the ordinary resolution involved did not have to be filed with the Registrar of Companies. Therefore, there was no constructive notice of it. During the period when there was constructive notice of a company's memorandum and articles and the contents of its file at the Registry, it was decided that *Turquand* could not apply where the resolution required was a special or extraordinary resolution because these have to be filed and an outsider would have constructive notice that they had not been. The relevant decision is *Irvine* v *Union Bank of Australia* (1877) 2 App Cas 366.

Since the 1985 Act (as amended) in general abolishes the rule of constructive notice the rule in *Turquand*'s case should now apply to situations where special and extraordinary resolutions are required. The effect is to widen the rule.

(c) The relationship between s 35A and the rule in Turquand's *case*

Section 35A gives the same protection as *Turquand* in regard to unauthorised collective acts of the board and also where correct internal procedures were not followed as in *TCB* v *Gray* (1987) (above).

On the other hand, *Turquand*'s case would appear to be wider because it applied to make a transaction by the company enforceable against it in *Mahoney* v *East Holyford Mining Co* (1875) LR 7 HL 869, where the directors who made the transaction had never been appointed at all.

Again in *Davis* v *R Bolton & Co* [1894] 3 Ch 678 the rule was applied where the directors made a transfer of shares without a quorum at the meeting. The transfer was nevertheless held valid.

Although s 35A has not been fully interpreted by the courts, it seems logical to suppose that it would not apply in the circumstances of either *Mahoney* or *Davis* because the court will presumably expect that when an English statute says 'the power of the directors to bind the company' it means directors who are properly appointed and have a quorum at the relevant meeting. Until s 35A has been more fully interpreted, it is perhaps safer to assume that *Turquand*'s case has a role to play.

(d) The proper purpose rule

The directors must use their agency powers for the proper purpose, that is for the benefit of the company. If they do not do so, the transactions which they have entered into, while not *ultra vires* themselves or the company, are not enforceable against the company provided that the person with whom the directors dealt was aware of the improper use of the power.

Rolled Steel Products (Holdings) Ltd *v* British Steel Corporation [1985] 2 WLR 908

A Mr Shenkman was a 51 per cent shareholder and director in Rolled Steel and held all the issued share capital in another company called Scottish Steel of which he was also a director. Scottish Steel owed a lot of money to BSC and Mr Shenkman had given his personal guarantee of that debt. Later BSC wanted more security and Mr S caused Rolled Steel to enter into a guarantee of the Scottish Steel debt. There was no benefit to Rolled Steel in this and BSC knew there was not.

Rolled Steel went into liquidation as did Scottish Steel, and the court was asked to decide whether BSC could prove in the liquidation of Rolled Steel on the guarantee.

Eventually the Court of Appeal decided that it could not. The transaction was not *ultra vires* Rolled Steel because its objects clause contained a paragraph giving an express power to enter into guarantees. Rolled Steel also had an independent objects paragraph on the lines of that in the *Cotman* case (see Chapter 3), so the giving of guarantees was, in effect, an object of the company which it could exercise whether there was a benefit or not. However, the power of the directors to bind the company as agents was a different matter. Mr S and the other director of Rolled Steel, Mr Shenkman's father, had exercised their powers of giving guarantees for an improper purpose, i.e. a purpose which was of no benefit to the company. The guarantee could therefore be avoided by the liquidator of Rolled Steel provided that those to whom it was given were aware of the improper purpose.

Since BSC knew that there was no benefit to Rolled Steel in the guarantee, it could not enforce the guarantee and prove in the liquidation.

Comment

(i) If BSC had not been on notice of the circumstances in which Rolled Steel had been made to enter into the guarantee, it could have claimed in the liquidation.

(ii) It should be noted that if the members of Rolled Steel had passed an ordinary resolution ratifying the making of the guarantee, then it would have been enforceable against the company. Where the directors act for an improper purpose, this can be put right by an ordinary resolution of the members even if, as here, the 'wrongdoer' can himself obtain an ordinary resolution. This would not apply if the 'wrongdoer' acted fraudulently, which was not the case here.

Acts of individual directors and other officers of the company

We must now consider the extent to which a company will be bound by a transaction entered into by an individual director or other officer, e.g. the company secretary, who has no actual authority to enter into it. There are the following possibilities:

(i) *Companies Act 1985*. As we have seen, s 35A states that in favour of a person dealing with a company in good faith the power of the board to authorise other persons to bind the company shall be regarded as free from any limitation under the company's constitution. Therefore, an individual director, company secretary, employee or other agent, authorised by the board to bind the company, will do so even if he exceeds the powers given to the board itself or other agents of the company by the articles. Once again, knowledge of the lack of power in the individual making the transaction on behalf of the company is not bad faith and does not prevent the transaction from binding the company.

(ii) The rules of agency: the doctrine of holding out. Where a director or other officer of a company has no actual authority, or authorisation under s 35A, an outsider may be able to regard a transaction entered into by such an individual as binding on the company if the person with whom he negotiated was held out by the company as having authority to enter into it, in regard to all commercial activities relating to the running of the business.

Since it is usual to delegate wide powers to a managing director and other executive directors, and *Table A* allows the board to delegate widely to such persons, an outsider will normally be protected and the transaction will bind the company if he has dealt with a managing director or other executive director (e.g. a sales director) or other officer (e.g. the company secretary) and this applies even if the person concerned has not actually been appointed to the post.

Freeman & Lockyer *v* Buckhurst Park Properties Ltd [1964] 1 All ER 630

A Mr Kapoor carried on a business as a property developer, and entered into a contract to buy an estate called Buckhurst Park at Sunninghill. He did not have enough money to pay for it, and obtained financial assistance from a Mr Hoon. They formed a limited company with a share capital of £70,000, subscribed equally by Kapoor and Hoon, to buy the estate with a view to selling it for development. Kapoor and Hoon, together with two other persons, comprised the board of directors. The quorum of the board was four, and Hoon was at all material times abroad. There was a power under the articles to appoint a managing director but this was never done. Kapoor, to the knowledge of the board, acted as if he were managing director in relation to finding a purchaser for the estate; and again, without express authority of the board but with its knowledge, he employed on behalf of the company a firm of architects and surveyors, the claimants in this case, for the submission of an application for planning permission which involved preparing plans and defining the estate boundaries. The claimants now claimed from the company the fees for the work done, and the company's defence was that Kapoor had no authority to act for the company. The Court of Appeal found that the company was liable, and Diplock LJ said that *four conditions* must be fulfilled before a third party was entitled to enforce against a company a contract entered into on its behalf by an agent without actual authority to make it:

(i) *A representation must be made to the third party that the agent had authority.* This condition was satisfied here because the board knew that Kapoor was making the contract as managing director but did not stop him.
(ii) *The representation must be made by the persons who have actual authority to manage the company.* This condition was satisfied because the articles conferred full powers of management on the board.

(iii) *The third party must have been induced to make the contract because of the representation.* This condition was satisfied because the claimants relied on Kapoor's authority and thought they were dealing with the company.

(iv) *Under the memorandum and articles the company is not deprived of the capacity either to make a contract of the kind made or to delegate authority to an agent to make the contract.* This condition was satisfied because the articles allowed the board to delegate any of its functions of management to a managing director or a single director.

The court also decided that although the claimants had not looked at the articles, this did not matter: for the rule does not depend upon estoppel arising out of a document, but on estoppel by representation.

Panorama Developments (Guildford) Ltd *v* Fidelis Furnishing Fabrics Ltd [1971] 3 All ER 16

The claimant company trading as Belgravia Executive Car Rental sued the defendant company for £570 in respect of car hiring. Belgravia had a fleet of Rolls Royce, Jaguar and other cars. Fidelis was a company of good reputation which employed a new man, X, as its secretary. He got in touch with Belgravia and booked cars which he wanted to drive for the company to meet important customers when they arrived at Heathrow Airport. On the first occasion, X wrote a cheque on his own account and it was met. In January 1970 he gave a list of dates for which he required cars on hire to Belgravia. It confirmed that the cars would be available and sent a written confirmation to Fidelis and not to X. Belgravia allowed the cars to go out on credit, asking for references. X gave references of the company which proved to be satisfactory. The printed forms of hiring and insurance agreements showed that X, the company secretary, was the hirer. These forms were signed by X or the sales manager of Fidelis. X used the cars which were never paid for. Belgravia sent the statement of account to Fidelis but it did not pay. Later the managing director of Fidelis found many unpaid bills in the company's name and disputed X's authority to act on behalf of the company. *Held* – by the Court of Appeal – that the defendant company was liable for the hire because, amongst other things, X as company secretary had ostensible authority to enter into the contracts for the hire of the cars on behalf of the defendant.

Comment

(i) The observations of Lord Denning on the position of a company secretary are of interest. He said:

> 'He is no longer a mere clerk. He regularly makes representations on behalf of the company and enters into contracts on its behalf which come within the day to day running of the company's business. So much so that he may be regarded as held out as having authority to do such things on behalf of the company. He is certainly entitled to sign contracts connected with the administrative side of the company's affairs such as employing staff and ordering cars and so forth.'

(ii) It should be noted that the judges in this case referred to the power of the company secretary to bind the company in this limited way as being based on ostensible authority. The reader should, however, be aware that it is sometimes referred to as 'usual' authority, i.e. being what, for example, a managing director or company secretary can 'usually do'.

Non-executive directors and employees

Where the outsider deals with a non-executive director or employee not occupying a designated office within the company-law structure, neither of whom have been authorised under s 35A, the position of the outsider is much less secure and there is little authority in case law which deals with the ostensible or usual authority of middle and lower management: such as there is would suggest that their unauthorised acts are unlikely to bind the company.

Of course, where the company allows an employee to hold himself out as an *executive* director, he may assume the actual ostensible or usual authority of such a director in regard to an outsider who is not aware of the true position, as the following case illustrates.

Electronics Ltd *v* Akhter Computers Ltd [2001] 1 BCLC 433

Mr David Bennett was employed by Skynet, a division of Akhter, as 'director PSU sales'. In fact, he was not a director of any company in the Akhter Group. He worked from a small sales office in Basingstoke with two other people, his assistant Andy Wall and a secretary. Mr Bennett's primary duty was to promote sales and he was paid large commissions when he was successful. He was given a very high degree of autonomy. He even had the habit, *known to and permitted by his employers*, of writing on Skynet notepaper and describing himself as a 'director'. This Skynet notepaper, in breach of s 351 of the CA 1985, omitted to contain the registered name, company number, and address of Akhter, leaving the reader no indication as to whom David Bennett might answer. Mr Bennett made a contract on behalf of Skynet to arrange for the supply of power-supply units to Pitney-Bowes and share the commission with SMC, which had passed the procurement contract on to Akhter through Mr Bennett. Later Akhter contended that it was not required to pay SMC a share of the commission because Mr Bennett had no authority to make the commission-splitting deal.

The Court of Appeal decided that since the agreement was reasonably associated with his job, Mr Bennett had actual authority to enter into the deal. In any event, he had ostensible authority to enter into commission agreements generally because that was ordinarily incidental to his duties. Furthermore, SMC was not on notice of any lack of authority.

Comment

There was no argument in the case that this contract was beyond the powers of the company or the board, so that it was presumably not necessary to use s 35A of the Companies Act 1985 to validate Mr Bennett's actions. The court was merely applying the common rules of agency. The provisions of Mr Bennett's employment contract were also of crucial importance. The relevant provision was in the following terms: 'Job title: Director PSU sales. You must perform such duties as may be reasonably associated with your job title.' Perhaps Akhter should have been more restrictive.

Kreditbank Cassel *v* Schenkers Ltd [1927] 1 KB 826

Under the articles of the company the directors were empowered to decide who should draw bills of exchange on behalf of the company. A Mr Clarke, who was the Manchester Branch manager of Schenkers, drew bills of exchange on the company's behalf in favour of Kreditbank. He had no authority to do so. The court later *held* that the bills were not binding on the company because it was, on the evidence, unusual for a branch manager to have such authority.

Where the company document which the outsider relies upon is a forgery

The rules of law laid down in *Turquand* and the other general rules of agency described above together with the statutory contribution of s 35A will not validate a forgery. A forgery is a crime and in no sense a genuine transaction.

Ruben *v* Great Fingall Consolidated [1906] AC 439

Rowe was the secretary of the company and he asked the appellants, who were stockbrokers, to get him a loan of £20,000. The appellants procured the money and advanced it in good faith on the security of the share certificate of the company issued by Rowe, the latter stating that the appellants were registered in the register of members, which was not the case. The certificate was in accordance with the company's articles, bore the company's seal, and was signed by two directors and the secretary, Rowe; but Rowe had forged the signatures of the two directors. When the fraud was discovered, the appellants tried to get registration, and when this failed, they sued the company in estoppel. *Held* – by the House of Lords – a company secretary had no authority to do more than deliver the share certificates, and in the absence of evidence that the company had held Rowe out as having authority to actually issue certificates, the company was not estopped by a forged certificate. Neither was the company responsible for the fraud of its secretary, because it was not within the scope of his employment to issue certificates. This was a matter for the directors.

The Lord Chancellor, Lord Loreburn, said:

> 'The forged certificate is a pure nullity. It is quite true that persons dealing with limited liability companies are not bound to inquire into their indoor management, and will not be affected by irregularities of which they had no notice. But this doctrine, which is well established, applies only to irregularities that might otherwise affect a genuine transaction. It cannot apply to a forgery.'

Defective authority and insiders

The rule in *Turquand*'s case, and the ostensible or usual authority rules of agency which have been considered above, are in general designed to protect persons who deal with the company from *outside* against defects in the internal management of the company's affairs. Members of a company can take advantage of the rule and in *Bargate* v *Shortridge* (1855) 5 HL Cas 297 it was held that a member could rely upon a written consent purporting to be given by the board, as required by the articles, allowing him to transfer his shares, even though it was given by the managing director alone. The company could not set aside the transfer and restore the member's name to the register.

Directors and persons who act as such *in regard to the transaction in question* are regarded as *insiders* and cannot rely on the rule. Thus, an allotment of shares made to a director at a meeting at which he was present by a board, some or all of whom were not properly appointed, would be invalid. As Lord Simonds said in *Morris* v *Kanssen* [1946] 1 All ER 586 (the case in point) in regard to directors: 'To admit in their favour a presumption that that is rightly done which they themselves have wrongly done is to encourage ignorance and careless dereliction from duty.'

However, if a director *does not act as such in connection with a transaction*, he may be able to rely on the rule. Thus in *Hely-Hutchinson* v *Brayhead* [1968] 1 QB 549 it was held that a director who lent money to his company's subsidiary, and also guaranteed loans to it by other persons, could enforce an agreement to indemnify him given in the company's name by a fellow director who had assumed the functions of managing director on an irregular basis but with the acquiescence of the board. The company was represented in the transaction only by the fellow director, and the director who made the loan was not therefore prevented from relying on the rule.

Directors acting despite defects in title to office: statutory protection

The Companies Act 1985 may also assist a person who has dealt with directors and finds that the validity of their acts is called into question. It provides that the acts of a director or manager shall be valid notwithstanding any defect that may later be discovered in his appointment or qualification. (*Table A* contains a similar provision, see s 285 and *Reg* 92.)

There are *certain differences in the protection* provided by the common law in *Turquand*'s case and that provided by the 1985 Act as follows:

(*a*) The statutory provision applies only where there is some defect in the procedure involved in the appointment; it does not cover cases where there is no real appointment at all as in *Mahoney* v *East Holyford Mining Co* (1875), though *Turquand* will apply here. Thus the statute provides rather less protection than the common law.

(*b*) The common law rule in *Turquand* operates to cure the defects only at the instance of the person dealing with the company; the company has no right to use *Turquand* to validate a transaction. However, the company can take advantage of the provisions of the 1985 Act and can claim a transaction as valid and binding on the other party, even though the director was not properly appointed or qualified.

GRADED QUESTIONS

Essay mode

1 (*a*) State the legal rules applying to a transaction within the powers of the company, but entered into by directors in excess of their authority.

AND

(*b*) Bob is chairman of Light Ltd. He functions as the company's chief executive and makes most decisions regarding its business. He reports his various decisions to the board in order to inform them of what has happened. The articles of Light Ltd provide that:

'The directors may from time to time appoint one or more of their body to be managing director. The directors may entrust to and confer upon a managing director any of the powers exercisable by them, subject to such restrictions as they think fit.'

Bob has on a number of occasions given Light Ltd's guarantee of loans from finance companies to Light Ltd's customers. Each of these transactions was later reported to the board. In June 1999 in a board room dispute, the directors resolve that in future such guarantees may only be given after approval by the full board. On 1 August Bob as a matter of urgency acts on his own initiative to give Light Ltd's guarantee to Slow Ltd, a new and potentially valuable customer. The lender is Sharp Ltd, a finance house with whom Light Ltd has had previous dealings. Sharp Ltd has a copy of Light Ltd's articles. The board refuses to adopt Bob's action and Light Ltd disclaims liability on the guarantee.

Advise Sharp Ltd on the enforceability of the guarantee.

(University of Central Lancashire)

2 The main business of Placey Planes plc is the running of a commercial airline from London's Docklands. The objects clause of the company's memorandum of association includes a power to borrow money for such purpose as the company thinks fit and states that the directors may do all things that are conducive or incidental to the general business of the company. The objects clause concludes with a paragraph stating that all the objects are to be regarded as distinct and separate objects. The airline was launched in 2001, following a blaze of publicity. It was expected that the company would not begin to realise a profit until 2008.

In 2005 the directors, faced with worsening end-of-year accounts and wishing to make the company more competitive, campaigned the government for the present runway to be extended. Government permission for the extension was refused on environmental grounds. The directors, concerned that the company was unlikely to meet its financial targets, decided that the company should build a conference and leisure complex in the Midlands.

The Finance Director negotiated with the manager of National Bank plc, the company's bankers, for the borrowing of £1.5 million to finance the development. In turn, the Managing Director contracted with Crusader plc for the construction of the complex, which Crusader has started to build but for which it has yet to receive payment.

Last month, the Managing Director, who is a local Conservative councillor, decided to donate £10,000 of company funds to Riverside Ltd, a company incorporated to pass on donations to the Tory Party.

Aviation Electronics plc is a minority shareholder in Placey Planes and is concerned at the activities of Placey Planes' management. Riverside has yet to receive the £10,000 and seeks to enforce the donation. Both National and Crusader have now expressed doubts about the validity of their respective contracts.

Advise all parties.

(University of Greenwich)

3 In what circumstances will an agent bind a company to a contract made with a third party? What effect do the memorandum and articles of association have on the power of agents to bind companies to such contracts?

(The Institute of Chartered Secretaries and Administrators)

4 B is the managing director of T Ltd. He has decided that the company should have a new factory built. He arranges for P Ltd to carry out the building work on the usual standard term contract for the building industry which requires that T Ltd makes progress payments on a three-monthly basis.

The articles of association of T Ltd provide that the directors of the company may negotiate any contract on the company's behalf up to a value of £100,000 but contracts in excess of this sum must be approved by the company passing an ordinary resolution in general meeting.

The value of this building contract is £500,000. B did not obtain the approval of the general meeting. The first progress payment has now fallen due and the other directors of T Ltd have resolved not to pay it on the grounds that the contract was not properly authorised by the shareholders.

You are required to explain whether T Ltd is bound to pay this progress payment and more generally whether T Ltd is bound to the contract with P Ltd.

(*The Chartered Institute of Management Accountants*)

5 (*a*) What is the rule in *Royal British Bank* v *Turquand* (1856), and what defences against its application are available to a company?

(*b*) Beetlecrush Ltd was a company involved in pest control. In 1999 Pellet was appointed as managing director of the company by a board resolution, which gave him exclusive power to manage the company, subject only to a requirement to get the approval of the board for all contracts in excess of £50,000.

On behalf of the company, Pellet began negotiating for the purchase of insecticides from Toxin, who had supplied the company with similar products for a number of years. Before these negotiations were concluded, Toxin accepted an invitation to become a member of the board of Beetlecrush Ltd, and thenceforth duly attended its board meetings. Some months after this, Pellet, without getting the approval of the board, signed a contract with Toxin for the supply of £80,000 worth of insecticides.

Preliminary trials with these insecticides have revealed that they are not as effective as the company had been hoping. The board, with the exception of Pellet and Toxin, is now seeking some way in which the company can claim that it is not bound by its obligations under the contract.

Advise the board.

(*The Association of Chartered Certified Accountants*)

6 Contrast the rules governing contracts purporting to be made on behalf of a company before it has been incorporated under the Companies Act with those governing contracts made by or on behalf of an incorporated company before it is entitled to do business.

(*The Institute of Company Accountants*)

7 During the course of a meeting with your client Jones, who is a director and shareholder of a small private limited company, you discover that the word 'limited' has been omitted from the company cheque book, and that since the death in July 2004 of George, the only other member and director, Jones has not only been acting as the sole director and company secretary, but has also been its only member.

Advise Jones of the legal implications of this discovery.

(*Napier University*)

8 The company secretary of Beech Ltd has in the past been permitted to order office equipment and stationery for the company but no single transaction has exceeded £500. Recently, without the knowledge of the directors, he ordered a computer installation costing £200,000. The board does not wish to proceed with the purchase but the supplier is claiming that the company is bound by the contract.

Advise the directors.

(*The Institute of Chartered Accountants in England and Wales*)

Objective mode

Four alternative answers are given. Select ONE only. Circle the answer which you consider to be correct. Check your answers by referring back to the information given in the chapter and against the answers at the back of the book.

1 Delta plc and Ullswater Ltd have each recently received their certificates of incorporation.

A Delta plc and Ullswater Ltd can now both commence trading and borrow.
B Only Delta plc can trade and borrow.
C Only Ullswater Ltd can trade and borrow.
D Neither Delta nor Ullswater can trade or borrow.

2 A transaction with another company entered into by Tom, a director of Thames Ltd, with the authority of the board is outside the authority of the board under the articles of Thames Ltd but within its objects. The transaction is:

A valid under s 35A of the CA 1985.
B void as being beyond the powers of the board.
C voidable at the option of the members.
D void at the instance of the other party.

3 Directors who act beyond their powers are liable to compensate the company for any loss thereby caused. Relief from this liability can be given:

A by the members by special or written resolution.
B by the members by extraordinary or written resolution.
C by unanimous vote of the board.
D by a majority vote of the board.

4 A managing director of a company has usual (or ostensible) authority to bind the company by his acts. Which of the following sets out the full limit of this authority?

A All commercial activities relating to the running of the business.
B All activities of the company whether commercial or not.
C Such commercial activities as the board chooses to delegate.
D Those commercial activities which the members direct in general meeting.

5 Bob, a non-executive director of Test Ltd, who has no responsibility for the purchasing department, makes a contract on behalf of Test (which is unknown to his fellow directors) to buy goods from a new supplier. What is the legal position of Test?

A It is bound because all matters decided upon by any director bind the company under s 35A of the CA 1985.
B It is not bound because a non-executive director as such does not have usual (or ostensible) authority by reason of office to bind the company.
C It is bound because all the acts of an ordinary director bind the company under *Turquand*'s case.
D It is not bound because a company is never bound by the acts of one director.

6 Clyde Ltd wishes to re-register as a plc. The members have passed a special resolution to change the memorandum and articles to comply with plc requirements. The issued share capital has been increased to 50,000 £1 shares by the allotment at a premium of 30p of 10,000 shares on which 50p was paid up immediately. On 31 December 2004 the company made its application together with a balance sheet at 1 June 2004.

On what grounds would the Registrar refuse to re-register the company?

A The balance sheet is more than six months old.
B The members should have passed an extraordinary resolution to alter the memorandum and articles.
C The nominal share capital is not enough.
D An insufficient sum has been paid up on the shares.

Answers to questions set in objective mode appear on p 576.

6

THE CAPITAL OF A COMPANY

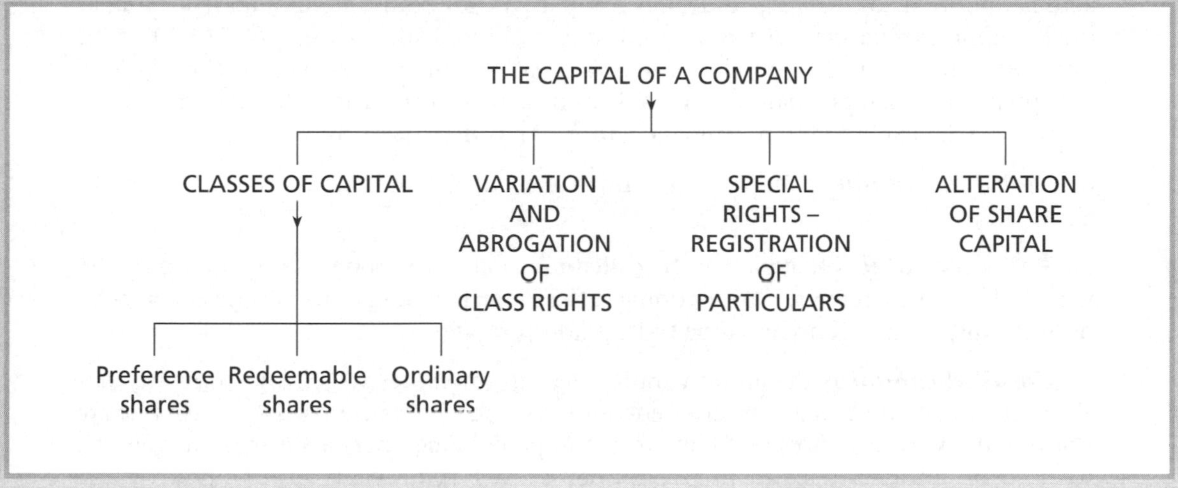

When we talk of a company's capital we may have one of many things in mind, since the word capital has several meanings.

(*a*) ***Nominal or authorised capital*** is the total amount of capital which the company is allowed to issue. The initial amount on registration, which is set out in the memorandum, can be increased or reduced.

(*b*) ***Allotted capital*** is that part of the company's nominal capital which has been actually allotted to the shareholders. A company is not bound to allot all its capital at once. Public companies must have a minimum allotted share capital of £50,000 with not less than one-quarter of the nominal value of each allotted share plus the whole of any premium on such share being paid up in cash or otherwise, though employees' shares may be excluded from this calculation. All other shares must be included.

(*c*) ***Called-up capital*** is the total amount called up by the company on the shares allotted.

(*d*) ***Paid-up capital*** is that part of the called-up capital which has been paid up by the shareholders. If a reference to a company's capital is made in its business letters or order forms, the reference must be to its paid-up capital.

(*e*) ***Uncalled capital*** is the amount not called up on shares which the company has allotted. Uncalled capital is seldom encountered today because partly-paid shares are not popular with investors in commercial companies. Such persons do not, in general, wish to be under a liability to pay money at any time when called upon by the company to do so. Thus nowadays most issues of shares are fully paid up within a very short time after allotment, and *reserve capital* (see (*g*) below) is comparatively rare.

(*f*) ***Equity share capital*** is that part of the company's allotted capital (usually the ordinary shares) which gives the holders a right to participate in dividends and distributions of capital *without limit.*

(*g*) ***Reserve capital*** is that part of the uncalled capital of a limited company which the company has by special (or written) resolution determined shall not be called up except in the event of winding-up. It is not under the control of the directors and if charged by the company, e.g. as security for an issue of debentures, the charge is void.

(*h*) ***Debentures***. Money raised by debentures is not *strictly speaking* capital, although it is often an alternative way of raising money needed for carrying on the company's business instead of issuing further shares. A debenture is distinguished from share capital in that it is a *loan* to the company; it is often *secured* by either a charge on a specific asset or assets, or a floating charge on all the assets, or a combination of both; it carries *no voting rights or any share of control*; the interest charge must be met, whether profits are made or not, and may therefore, unlike the dividends on shares, be paid out of capital. These matters will be fully treated at a later stage. Incidentally, the word 'debenture' has its origin in the Latin word for 'owing'.

(*i*) ***Multi-currency share capital***. It was decided in *Re Scandinavian Bank Group* [1987] 2 All ER 70, that a company could reconstruct its capital into four currencies so as better to reflect the composition of its assets. The capital was divided into Dollar shares

(50 per cent), Sterling shares (20 per cent), Dm shares (15 per cent), and Swiss franc shares (15 per cent).

Effect of the euro on share capital: a fresh issue

As a result of the decision in *Re Scandinavian Bank Group* [1987] 2 All ER 70, a UK company may *issue shares* denominated in euros. Normal issuing procedures will apply subject to adapting references to the euro. As regards the *conversion of existing capital*, a UK company has had, from 1 January 2002 (the date of the introduction of the euro in some member states of the EU), EU authority to convert a portion of its existing capital into euros. However, under the CA 1985 this can only be done by a reduction of capital or a purchase of own shares. The government is therefore considering reforms and the introduction of a new procedure for redenomination. There is also a proposal to introduce 'no-par' value shares which is not currently legal in the UK. This would do away with the need to round values up and down on the redenomination since the shares would have no nominal value. Currently in UK law, shares must have a nominal value. As regards the effect of the euro on *existing capital* of UK companies which is already *expressed in a foreign currency*, e.g. deutschmarks, the shares will probably continue to be referred to in that currency during the transitional period. When this ended on 31 March 2002 (under a regulation based on Art 235 of the EC Treaty), euro references took over. This could result in awkward nominal values requiring rounding up or down with a need to adjust the company's reserves.

The euro and share capital: redenomination of existing capital

Under existing UK company law, it is necessary to return existing share capital to the members and re-issue capital in euros. This can only be done by a reduction of capital or a purchase of own shares by the company. The company could also capitalise its reserves by an issue of bonus shares in euro. These methods are not satisfactory and the government continues to consult on easier methods. Amendments to the Companies Act 1985 will be introduced by secondary legislation under the Deregulation and Contracting Out Act 1994 which allows primary legislation to be repealed and amended by statutory instrument. No changes in the law have as yet been made.

CLASSES OF CAPITAL

A company may confer different rights on different classes of shares, the main types being *preference* and *ordinary* shares. It is necessary to refer to the articles, or to the terms of issue, in order to ascertain the rights attaching to the various classes of share. Although the share capital is stated in the memorandum, the types of shares and their respective rights need not be set out in it, and power may be taken in the articles to issue different classes of shares. (See *Table A, Reg* 2.) But where the rights attaching to different classes of shares *are* set out in the memorandum, they cannot be altered *unless* the memorandum or articles provide a method of alteration, or the permission of the court is obtained for a scheme of arrangement under s 425, or with the consent of *all* the members. The question of arrangements will be dealt with more fully in Chapter 22, but by way of explanation here, s 425 provides a procedure whereby the company can meet and discuss with the shareholders the question of variation of their rights so as to achieve an agreed alteration.

PREFERENCE SHARES

These shares are entitled to preferential treatment when dividends are declared. Thus a 10 per cent preference share must receive a dividend of 10 per cent out of profits before anything can be paid to the ordinary shares. Since there may be several classes of preference shares ranking one after the other, it is essential to refer to the company's articles, or the terms under which the shares were issued, to ascertain the precise rights of a holder of a particular preference share.

However, a right to preferential dividend without more is deemed a right to a *cumulative* dividend, i.e. if no dividend is declared on the preference shares in any year, the arrears are carried forward and must be paid before any dividend can be declared on ordinary shares (*Webb* v *Earle* (1875) LR 20 Eq 556). Thus, if the 10 per cent preference shares mentioned above received dividends of 5 per cent in 1999; 5 per cent in 2000; and nothing in 2001; they would be entitled at the end of 2002 to 5 + 5 + 10 + 10, or 30 per cent before the ordinary shareholders could have a penny.

However, it may be *expressly* provided by the terms of issue that they are to be non-cumulative but it is rare nowadays to find such a provision in the case of shares issued by public companies; and they may be held to be *non-cumulative by implication*, as where the terms of issue or the articles provide that dividends shall be paid 'out of yearly profits' (*Adair* v *Old Bushmills Distillery* [1908] WN 24) or 'out of the net profits of each year' (*Staples* v *Eastman Photographic Materials Co* [1896] 2 Ch 303).

Preference shares do not carry the right to participate in any surplus profits of the company unless the articles so provide (*Will* v *United Lankat Plantations Co* [1914] AC 11). However, it is possible to create *cumulative* and *participating* preference shares, conferring on the holders of such shares a right to participate in surplus profits up to a given percentage, e.g. a right to a preferential dividend of 6 per cent plus a further right, after, say, 10 per cent has been paid to ordinary shareholders, to participate in surplus profits until a further 6 per cent has been paid but no more.

Arrears of preference dividend in a winding-up

In the absence of an express provision in the articles, no arrears of preference dividend are payable in the winding-up of a company unless the dividend has already been declared (*Re Crichton's Oil Co* [1902] 2 Ch 86) and this is so even where the articles provide for the payment of dividends *due* at the date of winding-up, for a dividend is not *due* until *declared* (*Re Roberts and Cooper Ltd* [1929] 2 Ch 383). Where the articles do provide for payment of arrears, they may be paid out of the surplus assets after payment of the company's debts, *even though those assets do not contain any undistributed profits* (*Re Wharfedale Brewery Co* [1952] Ch 913). Thus the general rule that dividends must not be paid out of capital does not apply in this sort of situation. However, unless there is a specific provision which says so, the right to arrears ceases at the date of liquidation (*Re E W Savory Ltd* [1951] All ER 1036).

Even where the articles or terms of issue do contain a provision regarding the repayment of dividend and/or capital to preference shareholders in a winding-up, problems of construction arise, i.e. problems arise with regard to the meaning of the words used. For example, in *Re Walter Symons Ltd* [1934] Ch 308, preference shares were issued with 'the right to a fixed cumulative preferential dividend at the rate of 12 per cent per annum on the capital for the time being paid up thereon . . . and to rank both as regards dividends and capital in priority to the ordinary shares *but with no right to any further participation in profits or assets*'. The court took the view that the italicised words envisaged a winding-up, because it is only in winding up that the question of participation in *assets* arises. Therefore the rest of the clause must also apply in a winding-up, and the preference shares had priority in a winding-up for repayment of dividends unpaid at that date.

However, in *Re Wood, Skinner and Co Ltd* [1944] Ch 323, the preference shareholders had 'the right to a fixed cumulative dividend of 6 per cent per annum on the capital paid up on the shares', and were expressed to rank 'both as regards dividends and capital in priority to the ordinary shares'. In this case the court decided that since the latter part of the clause did not refer solely to the winding-up situation, the priority conferred was restricted to dividends declared whilst the company was in operation, and did not give the right to arrears of dividend once a winding-up had commenced.

Of course, a person drafting terms of issue today would normally make his intentions more clear than was done in the two cases cited above, and would certainly not use the phrases which were used then. Nevertheless, problems do arise out of bad draftsmanship and the cases show how the court might deal with such situations.

A typical modern clause in the terms of issue of preference shares which more clearly expresses the rights intended to be conferred is as follows. 'The holders of preference shares shall be entitled to a fixed cumulative preferential dividend at the rate of X per cent per annum upon the amount paid up thereon, and in the event of the winding-up of the company, to repayment of the amount paid up thereon together with any arrears of dividend calculated to the date of such repayment in priority to the claims of ordinary shares, but shall have no other right to participate in the assets or profits of the company.'

It should be noted that under such a clause unpaid preference dividends will be payable for periods up to the repayment of the preference capital, even though the dividends have not been declared and in spite of the fact that the company may not have earned sufficient profits to pay them while it was a going concern (*Re Wharfedale Brewery Co* [1952] Ch 913).

Repayment of capital on winding-up

Preference shares have no inherent priority as to the repayment of capital in a winding-up. If the assets are not enough to pay the preference and ordinary shares in full then, unless the articles or terms of issue provide to the contrary, preference and ordinary shares are paid off rateably according to the nominal value of their shares (*Birch* v *Cropper* (1889)14 App Cas 525). Where, *as is usual*, the preference shares have priority either by the articles or terms of issue, they are entitled to repayment of their capital in full before the ordinary shareholders receive anything by way of repayment of capital. Where there are surplus assets left after the discharge of all the company's liabilities and the repayment of capital to all shareholders, the surplus is divided among ordinary and preference shareholders unless the articles provide to the contrary. Any rights given by the articles are exhaustive. Thus, where the articles give preference shareholders priority of repayment of capital in a winding-up, but do not refer to any further rights in the capital of the company, the preference shareholders have no right to participate in surplus capital (*Scottish Insurance Corporation* v *Wilsons and Clyde Coal Co* [1949] AC 462).

The following is, therefore, a summary of the position:

(i) Where the preference shareholders have no priority in regard to repayment of capital, they share the assets rateably with the ordinary shareholders, including any surplus assets left after repayment of share capital and other liabilities.
(ii) If the articles or terms of issue give the preference shareholders priority for repayment of capital, they are repaid the nominal value of their shares before the ordinary shareholders *but no more*.

In addition, it should be noted that if the articles give preference shareholders an *express* right to participate equally with the ordinary shareholders in surplus assets, they are entitled to share in such assets even though they include ploughed back profits of former years which could have been distributed as dividend to ordinary shareholders but which instead were placed in reserve (*Dimbula Valley (Ceylon) Tea Co Ltd* v *Laurie* [1961] 1 All ER 769). The fact that the ordinary shareholders are, while the company is a going concern, in charge of the profit, i.e. they can resolve upon a distribution within the provisions of Part VIII of the Companies Act 1985, does not prevent the preference shareholders having a right to participate in those profits which the ordinary shareholders have left undistributed.

REDEEMABLE SHARES

Sections 159 and 160 of the Companies Act 1985 allow the issue of redeemable shares whether equity or preference.

The provisions are designed, amongst other things, to encourage investment in the equity of small businesses in circumstances where the proprietors, often members of a family, can at an appropriate stage buy back the equity investments without parting permanently with family control.

Issue of redeemable shares

A company limited by shares or guarantee with a share capital may, if authorised by its articles, issue redeemable shares. They may be issued as redeemable at the option of the company or the shareholder. *Table A* to the CA 1985 authorises the issue of redeemable shares. Earlier *Tables A*, e.g. *Table A* to the CA 1948 which may still govern companies formed before 1985, only authorise the issue of redeemable preference shares and must be changed if it is desired to issue redeemable equity shares.

Redeemable shares may be issued only if there are in issue other shares which cannot be redeemed. If a company's shares were all redeemable it could redeem the whole of its capital and end up under a board of directors with no members. This would circumvent provisions which have already been considered in Chapter 1 and which are designed to prevent a company continuing in existence without any members.

The redemption of redeemable shares

Redeemable shares may not be redeemed unless they are fully paid. The *issued capital* is the creditors' buffer and it is this figure and not the paid-up capital which must be replaced.

The terms of the redemption must provide that the company shall pay for the shares on redemption and not, e.g., at a later date as by creating a creditor. Creditors do not usually receive interest on an outstanding debt or a dividend so that failure to pay on redemption would give the company the resource of the share capital without cost.

Financing the redemption

Redeemable shares may only be redeemed out of distributable profits or out of the proceeds of a fresh issue of shares (which need not be redeemable) made for the purpose. Any premium payable on redemption must be paid out of distributable profits of the company, unless the shares being redeemed were issued at a premium (see below).

Private companies may redeem (or purchase their own shares not issued as redeemable) partly out of capital subject to certain restrictions (see further Chapter 7).

Where shares are redeemed out of profits, a sum equal to the nominal value of the shares redeemed must be transferred from the company's profit and loss account to a non-distributable reserve called the 'Capital Redemption Reserve'. The purpose of this provision is to preserve the capital of the company intact. The reserve cannot be utilised for the payment of dividends, but only in making a bonus issue of fully-paid shares to the members.

Shares, when redeemed, are to be cancelled and this will reduce the issued share capital of the company by the nominal value of the shares redeemed. Authorised capital is not reduced.

If the shares being redeemed were themselves issued at a premium, any premium on their redemption may be paid *out of the proceeds of a fresh issue of shares* made for the purposes of redemption up to an amount equal to:

(*a*) the aggregate of the premiums received by the company on the issue of the shares redeemed, or

(*b*) the current amount of the company's share premium account (including any sum transferred to that account in respect of premiums on the new shares) *whichever is the less*, and in that case the amount of the company's share premium account shall be reduced by a sum corresponding (or by sums in the aggregate corresponding) to the amount of any payment made out of the proceeds of the issue of the new shares, or

(*c*) alternatively, the premium on redemption can be paid for out of profits and charged to profit and loss.

The object of the above provisions is to tighten protection for creditors on a redemption (or purchase, see Chapter 7) of shares as shown in Figure 6.1.

In company law the creditors' buffer, as it is called, is the company's share capital plus non-distributable reserves, i.e. reserves that cannot be written off to pay dividends, such as the capital redemption reserve and the share premium account. Under the

If the premium on redemption is not paid for out of profits, it must be paid for out of the proceeds of a fresh issue. A company's capital consists of

	£
Ordinary shares of £1	10,000
Redeemable shares	6,000
Share premium A/c	5,000
	21,000
Profit and loss A/c	6,000
Net assets	27,000

The redeemable shares had been issued at a premium of 30p each and were to be redeemed at the same premium (£1,800). The company wishes to issue the minimum number of new shares (at par) to finance the redemption.

In this case profits available are £6,000. The total cost of redemption will be £7,800. Therefore the minimum proceeds of issue will be £1,800. This £1,800 may then be written off to share premium account and after redemption the balance sheet would read:

	£
Ordinary capital	11,800
Capital redemption reserve	6,000
Share premium A/c	3,200
Net assets	21,000

Alternatively, the premium on redemption could be paid for out of profits and charged to profit and loss and the £1,800 proceeds would be applied in paying for the shares thus reducing the transfer to CRR to £4,200, in which case the balance sheet would read:

	£
Ordinary capital	11,800
Capital redemption reserve	4,200
Share premium A/c	5,000
	21,000

In either case the creditors' buffer, i.e. share capital and non-distributable reserves, is preserved at £21,000. £1,800 *must be raised by a fresh issue of shares.*

Figure 6.1 Premium on redemption of shares

above formula the share premium account can only be written down to the extent of the amount of the new issue of shares that will replace the amount so written down, thus replacing with share capital what has been written off the share premium account and so preserving the buffer.

A company which has issued all of its authorised capital need not increase it merely to issue the new shares necessary to redeem existing ones.

Private companies may redeem (or purchase their own shares not issued as redeemable) partly out of capital (see further Chapter 7).

Miscellaneous matters relating to redeemable shares

Time of redemption

Redeemable shares can be made redeemable between certain dates. The holder thus knows that his shares cannot be redeemed before the earlier of the two dates, which is normally a number of years after the issue of the shares, in order to give him an investment which will last for a reasonable period. He also knows that the shares are bound to be redeemed by the later of the two dates mentioned.

However, there are no legal provisions requiring the company to fix the time of redemption at the time of issue though as we have seen there is no reason why this should not be done by, e.g., making the shares redeemable at the option of the company between stated dates. Section 160(3) provides that the redemption of shares may be effected in such a manner as may be provided by the company's articles. There was a proposal to repeal this provision in s 133 of the Companies Act 1989 and introduce restrictive provisions regarding the terms and manner of redemption including the setting of a date for redemption and also a formula for ascertaining the redemption price. The government has announced that it is now considered that the proposals were too restrictive and s 133 will not be brought into force and will be repealed at the first legislative opportunity.

As regards failure to redeem (or purchase) its shares, a company cannot be liable in damages for such a failure. The shareholder may obtain an order for specific performance unless the company can show that it cannot meet the cost of redemption out of distributable profits.

In addition, following statements by Megarry J in *Re Holders Investment Trust* [1971] 2 All ER 289, a shareholder whose shares are not redeemed on the agreed date may be able to obtain an injunction to prevent the company from paying dividends either to ordinary shareholders or to any subordinate class of preference shareholder until the redemption has been carried out. *Re Holders* also confirms that such a shareholder may petition for a winding-up under s 122 of the Insolvency Act 1986 – the just and equitable ground.

If the company goes into liquidation and at the date of commencement of the winding-up has failed to meet an obligation to redeem (or purchase) its own shares, and this obligation occurred before the commencement of the winding-up, the terms of the redemption (or purchase) can be enforced by the shareholder against the company as a *deferred* debt in the liquidation, *but not if* during the period between the due date for redemption (or purchase) and the date of commencement of the winding-up the company could not have lawfully made a distribution (see further Chapter 8) equal in value to the price at which the shares were to have been redeemed (or purchased).

Any money owed is *deferred* to claims of all creditors and preference shareholders having rights to capital which rank in preference to the shares redeemed (or purchased) but *ranks in front* of the claims of other shareholders.

Notice of redemption must be given to the Registrar within one month of the redemption.

Shares which are already issued cannot be converted into redeemable shares since this is not considered to be an 'issue' within the terms of the relevant legislation (*Re St James' Court Estate Ltd* [1944] Ch 6). This can, however, be done under s 425 (see further Chapter 22) by cancelling the existing non-redeemable shares and replacing them with an issue of redeemable shares.

ORDINARY SHARES

The nature of an ordinary share is perhaps best understood by comparing it with a preference share. In this way we can ascertain the distinguishing features, and the advantages and disadvantages which arise from the holding of ordinary shares.

Disadvantages

Under this heading we shall consider the fact that the ordinary shareholder is entitled to a dividend only after the preference dividends have been paid. Furthermore, where the preference shares have preference as to capital, the ordinary shares rank behind the preference shares for repayment of capital on winding-up or where there is a reduction of capital by repayment. The preference shares must be fully repaid first (see further Chapter 7).

It is perhaps because of the above priorities given to preference shareholders that the ordinary shareholders are said to hold the *equity* share capital of the company, presumably by analogy with the *equity of redemption* held by a mortgagor in the law of mortgages. A mortgagor who pays off all the charges on his property has the right to redeem or recover it by virtue of this equity; indeed it is the last right he retains, for when that is gone, he has lost his property. Similarly the *equity shareholders* are entitled to the remaining assets of the company after the claims of creditors and of preference shareholders have been met.

Advantages

Here we may observe that the voting power of the ordinary shareholders in general meetings is such as to allow them to control the resolutions at such meetings. In fact this means that *the directorate really represents*, or can be made to represent, *the ordinary shareholders*.

It is not uncommon for companies to issue preference shares with no voting rights at general meetings, though if such shares are to be listed on the Stock Exchange, they must be given *adequate* voting rights by the company's articles. It would seem, however, that the voting rights of preference shareholders are *adequate* if they can vote:

(*a*) when their dividend is in arrear;
(*b*) on resolutions for reducing share capital and winding up the company; and
(*c*) on resolutions which are likely to affect their class rights.

A further advantage of ordinary shareholders is that their dividends are not fixed and may rise considerably with the profitability of the company.

A final advantage is that a company may issue bonus shares for which the shareholder does not pay in cash, or make new issues (called rights issues) at prices lower than outsiders would have to pay, and both of these are generally offered to the company's existing ordinary shareholders.

VARIATION AND ABROGATION OF CLASS RIGHTS

If the shares of a company are divided into different classes, e.g. ordinary and preference, the expression 'class rights' refers to the special rights of a particular class of shareholder concerning, e.g., dividends and voting and rights on a winding-up. The Companies Act 1985 makes it clear that *abrogation of class rights is included.* This means that class rights can be *extinguished entirely* as well as merely varied provided the appropriate procedures of s 125 as set out below are followed.

1 Meaning of variation

Case law decided that class rights are to be regarded as varied only if after the purported act of variation they are *different in substance* from before as where the company proposes to make its existing cumulative preference shares non-cumulative. Unless this is so, consent of the particular class or classes of shareholders is not required. The courts have in general taken a narrow and, perhaps, over-literal approach to the meaning of variation of rights. An example has already been given in *Greenhalgh* v *Arderne Cinemas,* 1946. In particular, the creation of new rights in others does not amount to a variation if existing rights are preserved. Thus Boxo Ltd has 'A' ordinary shares with one vote each and 'B' ordinaries with one vote each. If the company increases the voting power of the 'A' ordinaries to two votes per share, is that a variation of the rights of the 'B' ordinary shares? From the decision in *Greenhalgh,* it would seem not. The following case is also of interest.

House of Fraser plc *v* ACGE Investments [1987] 2 WLR 1083

In this case the House of Lords decided that where a company pays off and cancels cumulative preference shares (which have priority for repayment of capital in the company's articles) in a capital reduction there is no need for a class meeting of the preference shareholders to approve this. In the circumstances their rights have not been varied but merely put into effect. One of the rights attached to the preference shares was the right to a return of capital in priority to other shareholders when any capital was returned as being in excess of the company's needs. That right was not being affected, modified, dealt with or abrogated. It was merely being put into effect. The company was granting the preference shareholders their rights, not denying them.

2 Method of variation or abrogation

The method by which the variation or abrogation is effected will depend upon the source of the class rights.

(*a*) *Where the rights are conferred by the memorandum.* The company in general meeting must change the rights by a resolution of the type laid down in the memorandum. As we have seen, the general power to alter the memorandum by special resolution does not apply to alteration of class rights. If neither the memorandum nor the articles provide for variation, they may not be varied except with the consent of all the members, or by a scheme of arrangement under s 425 (see further Chapter 22).

(*b*) *Where the rights are contained in the articles*. In the case, e.g., of an article creating a class of preference share, or a redeemable ordinary share, the rights can be changed by a special resolution of the company in general meeting. Private companies can use the unanimous written resolution procedure (see Chapter 19).

(*c*) *Where the rights are contained in a resolution setting out the terms of issue*. The articles or terms of issue must be followed. It may be that only an ordinary resolution is required. Private companies can use the unanimous written resolution procedure (see Chapter 19).

3 Permission to vary

Except in those cases where *all* the members have consented, the resolution to vary the rights is of no legal effect unless the consent of the class or classes concerned is obtained. It will be appreciated that *there must be a variation to begin with*, otherwise the following materials do not have relevance. Obviously, if the company has 'A' ordinary shares and 'B' ordinary shares and the rights of the 'B' ordinaries are to be varied, the consent of the 'B' ordinaries is required. However, the concept of a class of shareholders is more subtle than that, as the following cases show.

Cumbrian Newspapers Group Ltd *v* Cumberland & Westmorland Herald
[1986] 3 WLR 26

In this case Scott J *held* that a person who had purchased 10 per cent of the share capital of a company following an agreement by the company to grant him, by the articles, pre-emption (first purchase) rights over the other 90 per cent so that he could prevent a takeover had what were, in effect, class rights so that the articles could not be changed without his consent.

Comment

(i) The case is unusual because one generally thinks of rights attaching to a whole class of shares and not to the holder of part only of a class.

(ii) A similar and earlier decision is that in *Re United Provident Assurance Co Ltd* [1910] 2 Ch 477 where it was *held* that shareholders within a class who have paid up different amounts on their shares must be regarded as a separate class and on a variation must meet separately as a class.

Any procedures for obtaining the consent of the class specified in the memorandum or articles must be complied with. There are no such procedures in the current *Table A*.

Where class rights are not in the memorandum, as where they are in the articles or a resolution containing the terms of issue, and there is no provision in the articles under which they can be varied, they can be varied with the three-quarters' consent or extraordinary resolution procedure described in Chapter 19. A class of shareholders in a private company may use the unanimous written resolution procedure, in which case there will be no dissentients and 4 below will not apply. The rules relating to the conduct of the class meeting are considered in Chapter 19.

4 Right to dissent

Dissentient members of a class may object to variation. The holders of not less than 15 per cent of the issued shares of the class, being persons who did not consent to or vote for the resolution to vary, may apply to the court to have the variation cancelled. If such application is made, the variation has no effect until confirmed by the court. Application to the court must be made within 21 days after the date on which the resolution was passed or the consent given. It may be made on behalf of all the dissentients by one or more of them appointed in writing. The variation then has no effect unless and until confirmed by the court. The court's power on hearing a petition for cancellation of a variation of class rights is limited to approving or disallowing the variation. The court cannot amend the variation or approve it subject to conditions.

The company must send to the Registrar within 15 days of the making of the court order, a copy of that order embodying the court's decision on the matter of variation.

SPECIAL RIGHTS – REGISTRATION OF PARTICULARS

In order to ensure that the public has access to the details of a company's class rights, s 128 provides that *if a company allots shares* with rights which are not recorded in its memorandum or articles, nor contained in a resolution or agreement required to be sent to the Registrar of Companies (see Chapter 19), it must, unless the shares have rights which are in all respects the same as those previously allotted, save that they do not carry the same rights to dividend during the 12 months immediately following allotment, deliver to the Registrar within one month of allotment a statement giving particulars of the class rights attached to those shares. Newly allotted shares sometimes have restrictions as to the receipt of dividends in the first year of issue. This does not mean, however, that they must, *for that reason alone*, be treated as different from shares previously allotted.

The same procedure must be followed where there is a *variation of rights of existing shares* or *the renaming of them* by a method, e.g. an ordinary resolution as required by the terms of issue which does not require the filing of a resolution or agreement because there is no amendment of the memorandum or articles. Similar provisions apply under s 129 to the rights of members of a company which does not have a share capital.

Further publicity as to the classes of shares (or members) which a company has is provided by s 352 which states that the different classes of shares (or members if there is no share capital) must be identified in the register of members (see further Chapter 13). This is particularly useful to a minority that is trying to mount opposition to the board in seeking to get in touch only with voting shares or members.

The Registrar must publish in the *London Gazette* the receipt by him of any statement or notice delivered under the above provisions.

ALTERATION OF SHARE CAPITAL

A company's share capital may be altered or increased provided the company follows the appropriate methods and procedures.

1 Increase of nominal or authorised capital

A company may, if authorised by its articles (see *Table A*, *Reg* 32), increase its nominal or authorised capital by new shares of such amount as the resolution prescribes. Under *Reg* 32 this is done by an ordinary resolution in general meeting, or in private companies by the unanimous written resolution procedure, and this power cannot by reason of *Reg* 70 be delegated to the directors. Notice of the increase must be given to the Registrar within 15 days of the passing of the resolution. A copy of the resolution effecting the increase must also be filed with the Registrar. The resolution must state the company's number and be in a form required by the Registrar to be suitable for microfilming.

Where the articles do not give power to increase or alter capital, a special resolution to alter the articles is required, but the alteration of the articles and the alteration of the capital can be achieved by the same *special resolution*, and presumably also by the same unanimous written resolution where the company is private (*Campbell's Case* (1873) LR 9 Ch App 1). The new shares may be ordinary or preference unless the memorandum otherwise provides. It is usual to increase the nominal capital only when all the existing nominal capital has been issued, but an increase can be made before this position is reached.

2 Consolidation of capital

A company may, if authorised by its articles, consolidate its capital by amalgamating shares of smaller amount into shares of larger amount, e.g. by consolidating groups of 20 shares of nominal value 5p into shares of nominal value £1. It is rarely that a company needs to consolidate, the tendency being to subdivide and go for lower nominal values which makes the shares easier to sell, since shares in public companies generally sell on the Stock Exchange for more than nominal value.

3 Conversion into stock

A company may, if authorised by its articles, convert its *paid-up* shares into stock, or reconvert stock into paid-up shares of any denomination. Stock is the holding of a member expressed in pounds instead of so many shares of a certain value each. Instead of saying A holds ten shares of £1 each, one would say A holds £10 of stock. Stock cannot be issued direct; if shares have been converted into stock and additional capital is subsequently issued, the new capital must be issued as shares and another resolution passed converting it into stock with effect from the date on which it becomes fully paid. Stock may be reconverted into paid-up shares of any denomination and the procedure is similar to that on conversion into stock.

4 Subdivision of shares

This would occur, for example, where a company subdivides every £1 share into ten shares of 10p each. However, the proportions of amounts paid and unpaid must remain the same where the shares are partly paid. For example, if before subdivision every £1 share was 50p paid, then the new shares of 10p each must be treated as 5p paid. The company cannot regard some of the new shares as fully paid and some as partly paid. A company may wish to subdivide shares to make them more easily marketable, e.g. a share having a nominal value of £1 may have a market value of £8 and this may restrict market dealings. If the company subdivides its shares into shares of 10p each, the market price would be 80p per share and dealings would be facilitated.

5 Cancellation of unissued nominal capital

A company can reduce the amount of share capital available for issue and this does not operate as a reduction (see Chapter 7). A cancellation may be desirable following a scheme of arrangement or an amalgamation, or where a company wishes to get rid of onerous conditions attaching to a class of shares which have been created but not issued, e.g. preference shares giving the right to a preferential dividend of 30 per cent per annum.

6 Type of resolution required

The type of resolution required to make the alterations set out in 2, 3, 4 and 5 above is the one laid down in the articles. Where the articles are silent, a resolution to alter the articles to give authority and to effect the change required is necessary. *Table A* and the 1985 Act provide that an ordinary resolution is sufficient, but where a company has special articles these may require a special or extraordinary resolution to effect the change. In all cases private companies can use the unanimous written resolution procedure. When an alteration by way of consolidation, conversion, subdivision or cancellation has been effected, the company must notify the Registrar within one month of the alteration.

GRADED QUESTIONS

Essay mode

1 (*a*) Distinguish between ordinary and preference shares.

(*b*) Shark plc has an authorised share capital of £150,000. It is divided into 50,000 £1 preference shares and 100,000 £1 ordinary shares. All shares have been issued. The rights attached to the preference shares include the right to have capital repaid before the ordinary shareholders in the event of the company being wound up. The articles contain no such provision. The articles are also silent on how to vary class rights.

Advise Shark plc on whether and how it may convert its preference shares into ordinary shares.

(*Glasgow Caledonian University*)

2 Distinguish between preference shares, participating preference shares and ordinary shares.

(*The Institute of Chartered Accountants in England and Wales*)

3 'A company is contractually bound by the actions of its directors when those directors act within their authority.'

You are required to discuss this statement.

(*The Chartered Institute of Management Accountants*)

4 With specific reference to the facts and principle of law in *Salomon* v *Salomon & Co Ltd*, discuss corporate identity and the occasions when it is set aside.

(*University of Paisley*)

5 Tom and Dick wish to form a company to manufacture wooden hen houses to be called Cluck Ltd. Explain the procedure for incorporation and commencement of business.

(*The Institute of Company Accountants*)

6 'A secretary is a mere servant; his position is that he is to do what he is told, and no person can assume that he has any authority to represent anything at all . . .' *per* Lord Esher in *Barnett Hoares & Co* v *South London Tramways Co* (1887).

To what extent does the statement reflect the current status of a company secretary?

(*The Institute of Chartered Accountants in England and Wales*)

Objective mode

Four alternative answers are given. Select ONE only. Circle the answer which you consider to be correct. Check your answers by referring back to the information given in the chapter and against the answers at the back of the book.

1 Where rights are attached to a class of shares set out in a company's memorandum and the memorandum does not contain any provision regarding the way in which the rights may be varied then they may be varied by:

A a special resolution of the company.
B an extraordinary resolution of the company or the consent of the holders of three-quarters of the class of shares in question.
C the agreement of all the members of the company.
D an extraordinary resolution of the holders of the class in question.

2 Boxo Limited has varied the class rights of one of its classes of shares. What proportion of the owners of those shares who did not consent to or vote for the variation can make an application to the court to have the variation cancelled, and within what time must they apply?

A The holders of not less than 15 per cent of the issued shares of the class whose rights were varied within 21 days of the passing of the resolution.
B The holders of not less than 10 per cent of the issued shares of the class within 28 days of the resolution being passed.
C The holders of not less than 15 per cent of the issued shares of the class within 28 days of the resolution being passed.
D The holders of 21 per cent of the issued shares of the class within 15 days of the resolution being passed.

3 Where would a preference shareholder go to ascertain the rights attaching to the shares?

A To the share certificate.
B To the share certificate and the memorandum of association.
C To the articles of association only.
D To the articles of association and/or the terms of issue.

4 What type of resolution is required at a general meeting to increase the nominal (or authorised) capital?

A An ordinary resolution.
B A special resolution following special notice.
C A special resolution.
D An extraordinary resolution.

5 A private company limited by shares must state in its memorandum:

A that the company is a private company.
B that the company is not a public company.
C that the company is a private company limited by shares.
D that the liability of the members is limited.

6 What type of resolution must be passed in general meeting in order that there may be a valid alteration of the company's articles?

A A special resolution with special notice to the company.
B An ordinary resolution following special notice to the company.
C A special resolution.
D An ordinary resolution.

Answers to questions set in objective mode appear on p 576.

7

CAPITAL MAINTENANCE – GENERALLY

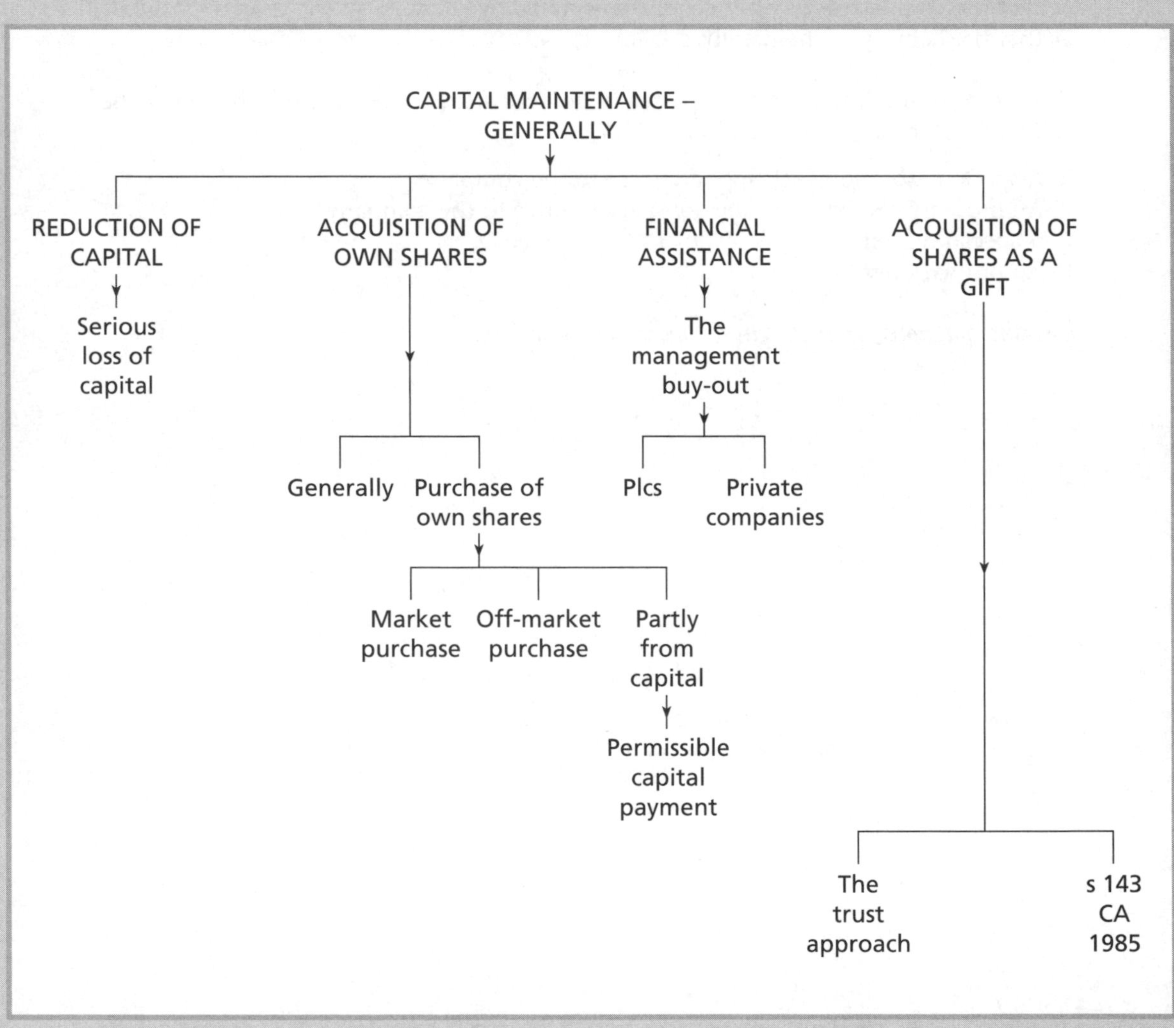

The acceptance by English company law of the concept of limited liability has led to a need to protect the capital contributed by the members of such a company since those members cannot be required to contribute funds to enable the company to pay its debts once they have paid for their shares in full.

A creditor of a company must expect that the company's capital may be lost because of business misfortune. However, he can also expect that the company's shares will be paid for in full and that the company will not return the capital to its members.

Company legislation therefore deals with the protection of the creditors' fund in two ways as follows:

(i) Provisions designed to prevent capital being 'watered down' as it comes in. These are to be found in ss 97 and 98 in relation to underwriting commission (see Chapter 9) and the rules preventing the issue of shares at a discount (see Chapter 12).

(ii) Provisions designed to prevent capital going out of the company once received. We have already considered the rules relating to the redemption of redeemable shares. We shall be considering the rules relating to distributions and share premium in later chapters, i.e. Chapters 8 and 12. The remaining capital maintenance provisions appear below.

REDUCTION OF CAPITAL

A company limited by shares may, under s 135 and if authorised by its articles, reduce its share capital or share premium account or its capital redemption reserve. The method is by *special resolution* which must be confirmed by the court, though private companies may use the unanimous written resolution procedure followed by confirmation by the court. In addition, where the share capital is divided into shares of different classes, before a reduction of capital can proceed the consent of three-quarters of each class of shareholders affected is required.

In *Re Northern Engineering Industries plc* [1993] BCLC 1151 the High Court decided that the rights of preference shareholders were to be regarded as varied by a reduction of capital in which the capital paid up on their shares was to be paid off and the shares cancelled. It could not be successfully argued that the word 'reduction' referred only to a situation in which the reduction was to a figure above zero. Therefore, the reduction had to be approved by class meetings of the company's three classes of preference shareholders.

Types of reduction

Under s 135 share capital can be reduced 'in any way'. The section, however, envisages *three* forms of reduction in particular. These enable a company to reduce for the reasons set out below:

(*a*) *It may have more capital than it needs* and may wish to return some of it to shareholders. For example, a company may wish to return paid-up capital which is in excess of its requirements where it has sold a part of its undertaking and intends in the future to confine its activities to running the remaining part of its business. The company may achieve its purpose by reducing the nominal value of its shares. Suppose that before the reduction the company had a share capital of 50,000 shares of £1 each, fully paid. On reduction it could substitute a share capital of 50,000 shares of 50p each fully paid, and return 50p per share in cash to the members.

(*b*) *Share capital already issued may not be fully paid* and yet the company may have all the capital it needs. Reduction in these circumstances may be effected as follows. If the company's share capital before reduction was 50,000 shares of £1 each, 50p paid, the company may reduce it to 50,000 shares of 50p each fully paid. However, liability for unpaid capital cannot be reduced by crediting a partly-paid share as paid up to a greater extent than it has in fact been paid up (*Re Development Co of Central and West Africa* [1902] Ch 547). Thus, it is not possible to leave the nominal value of the shares at £1 and cancel one share from every two held by shareholders, regarding the remaining one of the two as fully paid.

(*c*) *Where the assets have suffered a realised loss* as in *Re Jupiter House Investments (Cambridge) Ltd* [1985] 1 WLR 975 where the company had incurred a substantial loss on the sale of some of its property. In such a case a share capital of 50,000 shares of £1 each fully paid could be reduced to 50,000 shares of 50p each fully paid and no capital would be returned to shareholders.

(*d*) *To comply with the law relating to distributions.* The provisions relating to reduction have been increasingly used in more recent times to comply with the law relating to distributions, under which companies cannot pay a dividend unless and until any deficit on the profit and loss account is made good. In such a situation the company may wish to cancel a share premium account in order to offset a capital loss. Let us suppose that there is a balance of £5,000 in the P and L account, but the company has sold assets at a loss and suffered a realised loss of £6,000. There is, in effect, a deficit of £1,000 on the P and L account and no dividend can be paid. But if the company has a share premium account of £2,000, it can ask the court to approve a reduction in that account and write off the capital loss against it.

According to the decision in *Quayle Munro Ltd, Petitioners* [1994] 1 BCLC 410, the court in confirming such a reduction may also agree to the transfer of any balance remaining in the share premium account to a distributable reserve and allow its use to write off future losses which lead to deficits on the P and L account so that further application to the court is not necessary. The court may also be prepared to allow funds released from the share premium account to be utilised to redeem preference shares or redeemable equity shares and to purchase the company's own shares thus making it unnecessary to follow the more complex procedures of s 171 (power of private companies to redeem or purchase their own shares partly from capital). It should be noted that a capital deficit may arise and prevent payment of a dividend in a plc following a realised loss and unrealised loss as where the value of the assets has fallen but they have not been sold. Private companies are not prevented from making dividend payments where the capital loss is unrealised (see further Chapter 8).

In cases under (*a*) above, a reduction may be confirmed by the court even though the money which is to be used to make the payment is borrowed (*Re Nixon's Navigation Co* [1897] 1 Ch 872). It may even be borrowed from the same shareholders whose shares are to be reduced (*Re Thomas de la Rue & Co Ltd* [1911] 2 Ch 361). Thus if a company wishes to simplify its capital structure by replacing all its preference shares by exchanging them for loan stock, it could do so on the authority of *Re Thomas de la*

Rue. Alternatively, the company could use a reconstruction under s 425 (see further Chapter 22).

As we have seen, the permissible modes of reduction are not limited to the situations outlined above. Thus in *Carruth* v *ICI Ltd* [1937] AC 707 the company had issued £1 ordinary shares and 50p deferred shares both fully paid, and the market value of the deferred shares was a quarter of that of the ordinary shares. The court approved a reduction of the deferred shares to 25p shares fully paid so that other resolutions passed by shareholders for converting the deferred shares into ordinary shares, on the basis of four deferred shares for one ordinary share, might be more conveniently carried out.

Protection of creditors

In methods (*a*) and (*b*) above the creditors are deprived of funds which might have been used to pay off the debts in a winding-up. Accordingly, before the company's petition for confirmation of the resolution for reduction is heard the court must be asked to settle a list of creditors. Each creditor must be given by post details of the reduction and a consent form. The fact of the reduction and details of it must be advertised as the court may direct. The advertisements will give a date by which creditors not on the list must make a claim to be entered on it.

The court will not proceed to consider a company's petition for its permission to reduce unless it is satisfied by affidavit of the company's solicitor and one of its officers that all creditors who are named in the filed list, or who have notified their claims, have been paid or have consented to the reduction. If not, the company must secure the amount claimed to the court's satisfaction or satisfy the court that the disputed claims are invalid. The court may dispense with these requirements which protect creditors where, for example, the company has deposited, e.g. with a bank, sufficient funds to cover all claims which may be made against it.

In method (*c*) above the creditors are not deprived of any funds because the assets have been lost. However, the court may still require the company to take the same steps as outlined above, if it thinks this necessary to protect the creditors. This might arise where the court does not think that the reduction is necessary or genuine, e.g. where the court suspects that the supposed loss of assets has not in fact occurred, so that after the reduction the actual value of the assets might exceed the reduced capital and the company might then distribute the excess amongst its shareholders as if it were profit and so diminish the assets available to pay its debts. It is also the function of the court to see that in method (*c*) and in the other two types the reduction is operated fairly as between shareholders.

In spite of what is said above, the court may be prepared to accept an undertaking by the company that creditors will be asked to consent and if they do not will be paid off. The court may in such a case decide, as it did in *Quayle Munro, Petitioners* [1994] 1 BCLC 410, that it is unnecessary to follow the procedures outlined above in terms of creditor protection.

Nevertheless, it is wise to follow the statutory procedures because it does not follow that the court will *in all situations* approve a reduction where there is a defect in procedures. In *Ransomes plc* [1999] 1 BCLC 775 the judge approved a reduction even though there was short notice of the meeting to pass the special resolution (without formal member approval). He did so, he said, because, in fact, the vast majority of the shareholders approved of the reduction. However, he warned that other companies would not be advised to infringe the procedural rules, especially where a significant minority were likely to withhold their consent.

Serious loss of capital

In addition, with regard to method (*c*) above, it should be noted that under s 142 where the net assets of a public company amount to half or less of the called-up share capital, the directors of the company are required to call an extraordinary general meeting within 28 days of one or more of their number becoming aware of that fact. The meeting is to be held within 28 days of its being called so that it is held within 56 days of one or more directors becoming aware of the serious loss of capital. The meeting is to consider what, if any, measures should be taken to deal with the situation, i.e. winding-up, or perhaps to resolve that in view of the measures being taken by the board no further action is required.

The ordinary rules as to notice apply so that the notice of the meeting must set out verbatim any special or extraordinary resolution that is to be proposed at the meeting together with the general nature of any other business (see further Chapter 19).

If there is a failure to convene an extraordinary general meeting, each of the directors of the company who:

(*a*) knowingly and wilfully authorises or permits that failure, or
(*b*) after the expiry of the period during which the meeting should have been convened, knowingly and wilfully authorises or permits that failure to continue,

is liable on conviction by the court to a fine.

The above provision is to some extent an unsatisfactory one. It does reproduce the requirements of the EC Second Directive but leaves doubts as to procedures to be adopted. The financial position of a company may vary greatly during a financial year and it requires asset valuation to make an appropriate assessment so that a balance sheet is required as well as management accounts.

It would seem to be a reasonable approach for directors to rely on the audited annual accounts as the trigger, if any, for compliance unless, of course, they become aware, presumably as a result of some catastrophe, that the asset value is materially below 50 per cent of the called-up share capital.

The section does not state whether a reckless or uncaring director could be saddled with constructive notice. It is also silent as to what happens after the meeting if the deficiency continues. The holding of the meeting would seem to be all the section requires. Once this has been done, its force is presumably spent. However, it does force the directors out of their bunkers and make them face the shareholders if things are going so badly.

Provided the meeting is held, there is no other penalty placed upon the directors for the fact that the company is in such a parlous state. The reader may find this odd in view of the general insistence of English company law that the creditors' buffer must be maintained!

Payment of shareholders on reduction

The matter of repayment of shareholders should be treated as if the company was being wound up. Thus if the capital is being repaid for the reasons given in methods (*a*) and (*b*), the preference shareholders should be paid or reduced first if they have priority in a winding-up. If the reduction is due to loss of assets, the ordinary shareholders should be paid or reduced before the preference shareholders. This order may, however, be varied if the preference shareholders consent. The court has no discretion to confirm a reduction without separate class meetings of the shareholders affected.

It should also be noted that if a company has created reserves by the transfer of retained profits and subsequently suffers a loss of assets, it is the usual practice to write off the loss against the reserves and to reduce share capital only if the reserves are insufficient. Again, where the company has capital reserves such as a share premium account or a capital redemption reserve, the practice is to write off losses against them before reducing share capital. Losses may be written off against revenue reserves by making an appropriate adjustment in the accounts but as we have seen losses may only be written off by reducing the share premium account or capital redemption reserve if the same steps are taken as are required for reducing share capital.

Procedure after confirmation by the court

If the court is satisfied that the creditors have consented or been paid off or secured, it may make an order confirming the reduction on such terms and conditions as it thinks fit. If the reduction is confirmed, the court will approve a minute giving the new capital structure of the company, and that minute must be filed at the Companies Registry.

The Registrar of Companies, on production to him of an order of the court confirming the reduction, will issue a certificate of registration to the company. The minute when registered will be deemed to be substituted for the corresponding capital provision in the memorandum and is valid and alterable as if it had been originally contained therein. Copies of the memorandum issued after the date of registration must show the capital as altered. The reduction must be advertised as the court may direct, and the court may also require that the company shall publish reasons for the reduction, and may order the company to add the words '*and reduced*' after its name for a period of time. In practice these powers are not normally exercised by the court, but if such an order was made the words 'and reduced' would be inserted after the company's name on all documents, including business letters, on which the name of the company appears.

If the court reduces the issued share capital of a public company to below £50,000, it must re-register as a private company. The Registrar is required not to register the order confirming the reduction unless the company is first re-registered as a private one. To facilitate this the court may authorise re-registration without the company having passed the special resolution normally required, in which case the court order will also specify and in effect make the necessary changes in the company's constitution, e.g. in the company's name.

A private company can in certain circumstances purchase its own shares *partly* from capital (see later in this chapter). This provides, in effect, a much easier way of reducing capital. However, the shareholders concerned must be willing to sell their shares to the company. With a reduction, following a special resolution and court approval, the minority shareholders who dissented will have to have their capital reduced, willing or not.

In addition, unlimited companies may also reduce share capital and the share premium account but without going through a purchase procedure and without confirmation of the court. This is because the provision which requires court confirmation, i.e. s 135, applies only if the company is limited.

ACQUISITION OF OWN SHARES – GENERALLY

Section 143 prohibits a company (whether public or private) from acquiring its own shares (whether by purchase, subscription or otherwise). Exceptions are:

(i) the redemption or purchase (see below) of any shares under Part V of the 1985 Act;
(ii) the acquisition of shares in a reduction of capital duly made;
(iii) purchasing shares under a court order as, for example, under s 5 – the buying out of dissentients on an alteration of objects, or under Part XVII – buying out an unfairly prejudiced minority (see Chapter 14); or
(iv) forfeiting shares or accepting a surrender in lieu under provisions in the articles for failure to pay any sum payable in respect of those shares.

Furthermore, a company may acquire its own fully-paid shares as a gift and hold them directly in its own name or as a beneficiary under a trust where the trustees appear on the Register of Members.

Acquisition of shares by company's nominee

Under s 144, if a person has acquired shares in a company as nominee for that company, then if he fails to pay any sums due on the shares the other subscribers to the memorandum – if he acquired them as a subscriber – or the directors – if he acquired them in some other way – are, unless the court grants relief, jointly and severally liable with the nominee for payment of the sums due.

Such arrangements could in the past be engineered by the directors to keep themselves in secret control so that when faced with a takeover bid they could frustrate the bidder by arranging for shares to be acquired by nominees of the company, sometimes without too much attention as to when and how they were to be paid for, who would, of course, refuse to accept the bid. Under the 1985 Act, a person who acquires shares as nominee for the company alone is liable to pay for them and the company is not regarded as having any beneficial interest. If the nominee fails to pay the amount of any call in respect of the nominal value or the premium within 21 days of his being called upon to do so, the subscribers to the memorandum (if the shares were issued to the nominee as a subscriber), or the directors at the time of the issue or the acquisition (in all other circumstances), are jointly and severally liable with the nominee for that amount. In addition, in the case of a public company, such shares must be disposed of or cancelled within three years and in the meantime any attempt to exercise voting rights in respect of them will be void.

Relief may be granted by the court in cases where a subscriber or a director would otherwise be liable, if it appears to the court that he acted honestly and reasonably and he ought fairly to be excused, taking into account all the circumstances of the case. The relief may be granted either in any proceedings for the recovery of any amount due or upon the application of a subscriber or a director in anticipation of such proceedings.

Forfeiture, surrender and lien: public companies

Under s 146, *in the case of a public company*, where shares are forfeited or surrendered, no voting rights may be exercised by the company in respect of them and the shares must be disposed of or cancelled within three years. If the cancellation has the effect of reducing the company's allotted share capital below the authorised minimum, then the directors must apply for the company to be re-registered as a private company. In such a case there are relaxations in the conversion procedure. In particular, only a directors' resolution is required to make any alterations to the memorandum that are necessary. The company does not need to apply to the court to obtain confirmation of the reduction in capital, but any resolution to reduce capital passed by the directors must be filed with the Registrar.

Under s 150 a public company must not take a lien (see further Chapter 10) or other charge over its own shares. However, a lien is permitted over partly-paid shares for amounts called or payable on the shares. In addition, charges over its own shares may be taken by a company which makes a loan in the ordinary course of a business so that a bank may take its own shares as a security for a loan by the bank.

PURCHASING OWN SHARES

Generally

Formerly the rule of capital maintenance designed to protect creditors prevented a limited company from using its resources to purchase its own shares from its shareholders. This principle first appeared in case law, the leading case being *Trevor* v *Whitworth* (1887) 12 App Cas 409, and later in company legislation. The strictness of that rule was later relaxed and purchase by a company of its own shares is allowed subject to safeguards. The procedures to be followed are set out in ss 162–181.

Why purchase own shares?

Among the most important reasons for a company's purchase of its own shares are the following:

1 So far as private companies are concerned, it gives their shares some marketability. Individuals may be more easily persuaded to invest in private companies if they know that the company can buy them out even if the other shareholders have insufficient resources to do so.
2 In family companies a shareholder may die or want to, in effect, resign or retire. Perhaps the other shareholders cannot agree how many shares each should take, or they cannot afford to buy them anyway. In order to avoid an outsider taking them the company can buy them.
3 In the case of shareholder disputes, there is now the possibility of reaching a compromise with a member or members whereby they are bought out by the company thus avoiding the introduction of an outsider as the price of getting rid of a disenchanted member.
4 The provision is useful also in the case of executive directors who have taken shares in the company. Suppose a finance director has taken shares in the company but leaves at the end of his contract for, say, a better position. The company can buy his

shares so that he truly severs his connection with the company. The shares must be cancelled, but this does not affect the authorised capital and new shares can be issued to the next finance director on appointment.

Types of purchase: generally

There is a 'market purchase' and an 'off-market' purchase. A market purchase includes only purchases of shares subject to a marketing agreement on a recognised investment exchange.

An off-market purchase is a purchase of any other types of shares.

Any market or off-market purchases must, if they are to be legal, have authorisation in the articles. *Reg* 35 of *Table A* gives such authorisation.

Market purchase

A company may make a market purchase of its own shares provided that the purchase has been authorised by an ordinary resolution of the members in general meeting. The resolution must:

(*a*) specify the maximum number of shares which the company may acquire under the resolution;

(*b*) state the maximum and minimum prices which the company may pay for those shares. There will normally be a minimum price set out in the resolution, but for the maximum a formula would be used, e.g. an amount equal to 105 per cent of the average of the upper and lower prices shown in the quotations for ordinary shares of the company in the daily list of the London Stock Exchange on the three business days immediately preceding the day on which the contract to purchase is made;

(*c*) specify a date when the authority given by the resolution will expire. *This must not be later than 18 months after the passing of the resolution.*

The authority given may be varied, revoked or renewed by a further ordinary resolution of the members.

A company may complete a purchase after the date of the authority given by the ordinary resolution has expired, given that the contract for the purchase was made before the expiry date and the terms of the ordinary resolution cover execution of the contract after the expiry date.

The ordinary resolution giving the authority must be filed with the Registrar within 15 days of being passed and a copy must be embodied in or annexed to every copy of the articles issued thereafter.

Off-market purchases

A company may make an off-market purchase under a *specific contract* which has received advance authorisation by a special (or written) resolution of the company. That authorisation may be varied, revoked or, if subject to a time limit, renewed by special resolution *and with regard to a public company* the resolution must give a date on which the authority will expire, this being not later than 18 months after the date on which the resolution was passed. Private companies are not so restricted and if the authorisation does have an expiry date on it (which it need not) there is no particular time restriction.

The shareholder whose shares are being purchased should not vote the shares being purchased on a special resolution to confer, vary, revoke or renew an authority, though there is nothing to prevent him from voting against the resolution if he has changed his mind. If he does, the authority will not be effective unless the resolution would have been passed with the requisite majority without his votes. If he holds other shares, then he cannot vote at all on a show of hands but can vote those shares on a poll (see further Chapter 19). Any member of the company may demand a poll on the resolution.

A copy of the contract of purchase, or a memorandum of its terms if it is not in writing, must be available for inspection by any member at the registered office for at least 15 days prior to the date of the meeting at which the special resolution is to be passed and available at the meeting itself, otherwise the resolution is of no effect.

The contract, or the memorandum of it, must include or have annexed to it a written memorandum giving the names of the shareholders to which the contract relates, if they do not appear in the contract or memorandum.

The special resolution must be filed with the Registrar within 15 days of its passing and a copy of it must be embodied in or annexed to every copy of the articles issued after the resolution has been passed.

The above provisions might appear to rule out the use by private companies of the unanimous written resolution procedure, since the member whose shares were being purchased would, of necessity, be voting for the purchase in respect of all his shares. However, the provisions inserted into the 1985 Act by the Companies Act 1989 solve this by saying that the person whose shares are being purchased is not to be regarded as a person who can vote in respect of any of his shares. So, the resolution must be agreed unanimously by the other members and the one whose shares are being purchased is not included.

Furthermore, where the 1985 Act requires contracts or documents of one sort or another to be laid before the meeting at which the resolution is passed, that provision does not apply if the written resolution procedure is used. Instead the relevant documents must be supplied to each member at or before the time at which the resolution is supplied to him for signature.

A written resolution will therefore shorten the procedure since the relevant documents are sent to the members with the resolution and the 15-day display period referred to above does not apply.

Financing the purchase

The Companies Act 1985 in ss 162(2) and 159(3) (the latter in regard to redemption of share capital) require that the terms of purchase (or redemption) must provide for payment to be made at the time of purchase (or redemption). Thus a creditor cannot be created following the relevant transaction and until case law stated otherwise the provisions had generally been regarded as requiring a payment in cash at the time of purchase (or redemption). However this matter was considered in *BDG Roof-Bond Ltd* v *Douglas* [2000] 1 BCLC 401 where the company had agreed to purchase shares from one of its shareholders for a consideration involving cash and a property and a car owned by the company. The court held that in the same way as a dividend can be paid in kind so a company can pay for its own shares by a transfer of assets. The agreed amount payable for those assets could be set off against the balance of the consideration owed by the company to the shareholder in connection with the purchase of shares, provided that the transaction was bona fide (in good faith) and that there was no element of fraud.

Contingent purchase contracts

A company may enter into a contract to buy its own shares on the future happening of a certain event, e.g. a contract to buy the shares of an employee on death or retirement. This is a 'contingent purchase contract' and can only be made if approved in advance by a special resolution, or unanimous written resolution, and the following of the procedures set out above.

Assignment and release

The rights of the company under any contract to buy its own shares by a purchase or contingent purchase are not capable of assignment so that the company *cannot sell or buy back* its rights to purchase a member's shares and so create a market in purchase contracts. The company *cannot release its right* to purchase under any approved contract unless the release has been approved in advance by a special or unanimous written resolution. This is to prevent the company from providing funds to, say, selected shareholders by buying the right to purchase their shares and then later releasing that right, i.e. buying a sort of option which it is never intended to exercise.

Disclosure

A company which has purchased shares under the Act must within 28 days afterwards deliver a return to the Registrar stating the number and nominal value of each class of shares purchased and the date on which they were delivered to the company and the amount paid for them. Although there is no official transfer procedure, stamp duty is payable by the company on submission of the above return. In addition, the company must keep at its registered office any contract or contingent contract for the purchase of its shares and any variation thereof, or a memorandum of its terms if it is not in writing. These documents must be kept for ten years after the final purchase of the shares, and must be open to inspection by any member of the company and, in the case of a public company, to any other person.

Failure by company to purchase shares

The company is not liable to pay *damages* in respect of a failure to purchase (or redeem) its shares. However, a shareholder may apply to the court for specific performance of the contract of purchase (or the terms of redemption) but no order is to be made if the company can show that it could not pay the price from distributable profits.

In a liquidation a shareholder may enforce a contract of purchase (or the terms of redemption) against the company as a *deferred* debt provided that the due date for purchase (or redemption) was before the date of commencement of the winding-up, *unless* it is shown that the company could not at any time between the due date for purchase (or redemption) and the commencement of the winding-up have paid for the shares from distributable profits.

In a winding-up, because it is a deferred debt all other debts and liabilities are paid in priority to the purchase price (or redemption price) as are shareholders with a prior right to return of capital, e.g. preference shareholders. Subject to that the purchase or redemption price is paid in priority to amounts due to other members as members, e.g. share capital in a winding-up.

Provisions to ensure preservation of capital

All companies may purchase (or redeem) shares from profits or from a fresh issue of shares. Where the purchase or redemption is from profits an amount equivalent to the nominal value of the shares purchased or redeemed must be transferred to a capital redemption reserve. This reserve can only be reduced under s 135 (see earlier in this chapter), though it may be written down in the accounting records for the purpose of paying up unissued shares to be allotted to members as fully-paid bonus shares. Thus the creditors' fund is protected because the shares purchased (or redeemed) are replaced by a new issue of shares or a capital reserve.

The position regarding the financing of any premium on purchase (or redemption) has already been considered in Chapter 6.

Failure to observe the statutory rules

In this connection the decision of the High Court in *Re R W Peak (Kings Lynn) Ltd* [1998] 1 BCLC 193 should be noted. In that case an agreement by a company to purchase its own shares was declared void because the company's articles did not permit such a purchase, as s 162 requires. In addition, there was no special or written resolution authorising the purchase contract before it was entered into, as s 164 requires. Furthermore, even a waiver of the requirements by the two members of the company was not an effective dispensation of the statutory requirements because ss 162 and 164 are not, said the court, merely for the benefit of current members. The ruling in this case would also make void an issue of redeemable equity shares or a purchase from capital (see below) unless the statutory rules and procedures were followed.

Purchase or redemption partly out of capital: generally

The Companies Act 1985 gives a power to private companies to purchase or redeem shares *partly* (but not wholly) from capital when the company concerned has neither sufficient distributable profits nor the ability in the circumstances to raise all the money required by a new issue of shares. These provisions allow, in effect, a private company to reduce its capital without going to the court as the rules relating to a capital reduction require (see earlier in this chapter).

Thus a private family company could purchase the shares of a retiring member and so keep out non-family members even though profits were insufficient to make the purchase in full and the members of the family did not wish to subscribe to a fresh issue which would be enough to pay the full purchase price.

Conditions

The following conditions must be satisfied before payment out of capital can be made:

(*a*) The articles of the company must authorise it. A general power to purchase is not enough. *Reg* 35 of *Table A* to the CA 1985 allows a payment from capital. Previous *Tables A* do not allow purchase or purchase from capital and would have to be changed.

(*b*) The payment must not exceed the 'permissible capital payment'. Under this rule the company is required to utilise its available profits and any proceeds arising from a new issue, if any, before making a payment out of capital. *Only the deficiency, if any, can be met from capital.*

(*c*) A sole director or all the directors and not just a majority of them must make a statutory declaration specifying the amount of the permissible capital payment and also that they are of the opinion that:

- (i) immediately following the purchase (redemption) the company will be able to pay its debts; and
- (ii) for one year immediately following also, so that the directors are saying in effect that the company can continue as a going concern throughout the year.

(*d*) Attached to the statutory declaration is a report by the auditors addressed to the directors stating that they have enquired into the company's affairs; that the permissible capital payment has been properly determined; and that they are not aware of anything to indicate that the opinion expressed by the directors is unreasonable. The audit exemption regulations do not dispense with the requirement of an audit report on the permissible capital payment so that a company wishing to make a purchase partly from capital must have an auditor.

(*e*) The payment must be approved by a *special* (*or written*) *resolution* of the members, to safeguard the interests of those members who are not selling. There is a mandatory right for any voting member or his proxy member to demand a poll on the special resolution. The resolution must be passed on, or within one week after, the date on which the directors make the statutory declaration. The resolution will be effective only if the statutory declaration and auditors' report are available for inspection at the meeting at which it is passed. The special resolution is invalid if it was passed only because the shares being purchased were voted. However, the member whose shares are being purchased may vote other shares if he has any on a poll but not on a show of hands.

The position where a unanimous written resolution is used has already been described. Briefly, the documents which would have been available at a meeting must be circulated because there will be no meeting, and the person whose shares are being purchased is regarded as someone who is not entitled to vote. So long as there is unanimous approval by the others this is enough.

(*f*) The payments out of capital must be made not earlier than five weeks (to allow for objections; see below) nor later than seven weeks after the date of the resolution.

Permissible capital payment (PCP)

The following examples show how this is calculated in practice.

(*a*) *Where the PCP is less than the nominal amount of the shares purchased*. Here the difference must under s 171 be transferred to Capital Redemption Reserve (CRR).

Shareholders' funds before purchase

	£
Share capital	100
Share premium	10
Total capital	110
Profit and loss balance	20
Net assets	130

Assume that there is now a purchase of 20 shares of £1 each at a premium of 50p and there is no fresh issue of shares.

The PCP is – Cost of purchase £30 less *all* available profits of £20. PCP = £10. The premium is written off to P & L under s 160 and the £10 difference between the nominal value and the PCP is transferred to CRR as s 171 requires.

The journal entries would be as follows:

	£	£
Dr Share capital	20	
Dr Profit & loss A/c	10	
Cr Cash		30
	30	30

(being purchase of shares at a premium of 50%)

	£	£
Dr Profit & loss A/c	10	
Cr CRR		10
	10	10

(being transfer to CRR per s 171)

Shareholders' funds after purchase

	£
Share capital	80
Share premium	10
CRR	10
Net assets	100

Net assets are reduced because we have used £30 of our cash to buy the shares.

(b) Where the PCP is greater than the nominal amount of the shares purchased. Here under s 171 the difference is written off to CRR or share premium account or revaluation reserve (if any) or even in the last analysis share capital. Suppose that in the example given in (*a*) above the company had purchased 30 shares of a nominal value of £1 each at £2 each with no fresh issue.

The PCP is – Cost of purchase £60 less all available profits of £20. PCP = £40. The nominal amount of the shares purchased is £30, so £10 must be written off against a capital account. We shall take the share premium account because we do not have any other capital reserve, but if that had not been enough we should have had to proceed to reduce the share capital.

The journal entries would be as follows:

	£	£
Dr Share capital	30	
Dr Profit & loss A/c	20	
Dr Share premium A/c	10	
Cr Cash		60
	60	60

(being purchase of 30 shares at £2 each in accordance with s 171)

Shareholders' funds after purchase

	£
Share capital	70
Share premium	–
Total capital	70
Profit and loss balance	–
Net assets	70

The net assets have been reduced because we have used £60 of our cash to buy the shares.

The above examples apply also, with the necessary changes in nomenclature, to a redemption from capital.

Publicity

Within a week of the date of the special (or written) resolution the company must publish a notice in the *London Gazette* and either give notice in writing to each of its creditors or publish a notice in an 'appropriate national newspaper'.

Similar publicity must be given to the fact that the directors' statutory declaration and the special auditors' report thereon are available for inspection at the registered office of the company for at least five weeks after the date of the authorising resolution. A copy of the statutory declaration and the auditors' report must be filed with the Registrar by the date of first publicising the proposed payment, either in the *London Gazette*, or the national newspaper or the notice to creditors.

Dissentient shareholders/creditors

A member or a creditor may within five weeks from the resolution apply to the court for an order cancelling the resolution. The right does not extend to a member who consented to the resolution and is obviously inapplicable so far as members are concerned where the unanimous written procedure has been followed.

If an application is made, the company must notify the registrar forthwith and within 15 days of any court order (or such longer period as the court directs) deliver a copy of the order to the Registrar. The court has various powers under s 177 other than cancellation and it may, e.g., approve arrangements for the purchase of the shares of dissentient members, who rather obviously will not be the ones whose shares are being purchased.

Civil liability of past shareholders and directors

Under s 76 of the Insolvency Act 1986:

(*a*) if winding-up takes place within 12 months of a purchase (redemption) from capital and the company's assets are not sufficient to pay its debts and liabilities; *then*

(*b*) the person(s) from whom the shares were purchased (or redeemed) *and* the directors who signed the statutory declaration; *are*

(*c*) jointly and severally liable to contribute to the assets of the company, to the amount of the payment received by the shareholder(s) when the company purchased (or redeemed) the shares. There is a right of contribution between those liable in such an amount as the court thinks just and equitable;

(*d*) those in (*b*) above, are given a right to petition for a winding-up on the grounds:

- (i) that the company cannot pay its debts, and
- (ii) that it is just and equitable for the company to be wound up.

The purpose of this is to enable them to limit the amount of their liability by initiating a winding-up before the company's assets are further dissipated leading to an increase in the contribution required of them.

Directors are not liable if they had reasonable grounds for the opinion given in the statutory declaration.

Criminal penalties

There are a variety of criminal penalties on directors, e.g. for making a false statutory declaration, or refusing to allow its inspection.

Transfer

A stock transfer form is not required on completion. The seller merely hands over his share certificate(s) to the company, but the company as purchaser is still required to pay transfer stamp duty.

Investment companies

The government implemented changes to company law that allow investment companies (i.e. companies whose assets are investments in other companies) to use capital profits to repurchase their shares (see SI 1999/2770). Dropping the restriction allows investment companies to better manage their capital structure and maximise shareholder value. Creditors are protected by the existing requirement that an investment company can purchase its own shares only if it has assets at least $1\frac{1}{2}$ times its liabilities.

Treasury shares

In general terms shares which are purchased by a company must be cancelled. A company cannot usually become a member of itself.

An exception is provided under the provisions of the Companies (Acquisition of Own Shares) (Treasury Shares) Regulations 2003 (SI 2003/1116). These regulations allow companies listed on the Stock Exchange or the Alternative Investment Market (but not private companies) to buy, hold and resell their shares. The regulations apply only to 'qualifying shares'. These are shares listed on the London Stock Exchange or traded on the AIM or listed on any other European Economic Area Stock Exchange. Other main points to note are as follows.

- The shares must be purchased from distributable profits since it was thought unlikely that a company would wish to finance the purchase of shares to be held in treasury from the proceeds of a fresh issue of share capital.
- The company having bought shares to hold in treasury may cancel or sell them at any time including a sale for a non-cash consideration.
- Cancellation will involve a reduction of capital but there is no need for a special resolution of the members or authorisation by the court.
- Consideration received on a sale of treasury shares is to be treated as profits for distribution purposes.
- The maximum number of treasury shares held at any one time must not exceed 10 per cent of the nominal value of the issued share capital of the company. Where there is more than one class of shares each class is subject to a separate 10 per cent limit. Shares held in breach of the 10 per cent limit are subject to mandatory cancellation.
- A company holding treasury shares must not exercise any voting rights attached to them and if it does the votes are void. No dividend or other form of distribution can be made in respect of them.

Disclosure of dealings in treasury shares

Dealings in treasury shares must be disclosed to the market under arrangements made with the Financial Services Authority and the London Stock Exchange. The Listing Rules were amended with effect from 1 December 2003 to take account of treasury shares. The new rules state that shares in treasury will remain listed so that new applications for listing are not required when shares are sold out of treasury. However to protect the market a company will normally be prohibited from buying or selling treasury shares at a time when its directors would be prevented from dealing in the company's shares under the Model Code of Directors' Dealings (see Chapter 12). A company is prohibited from buying or selling its treasury shares when in possession of price-sensitive information as by insider dealing (see Chapter 12). Treasury shares may be included or excluded from a takeover offer and the prohibition on directors dealing in share options under s 323 will not extend to the purchase of options in treasury shares.

Informing the registrar

Within 28 days from the date shares purchased as treasury shares are delivered to the company the company must deliver to the Registrar of Companies for registration a return giving details of the purchase as required by Form 169 (1B). Cancellation, transfer or sale of shares from treasury must be similarly notified to the Registrar on Form 169A (2).

Company dealing in treasury shares: not regulated

The Financial Services and Markets Act 2000 (Regulated Activities) (Amendment) (No 3) Order 2003 (SI 2003/2822) provides that purchasing its own shares to keep in treasury and the subsequent dealing in those shares is not a regulated activity under FSMA 2000 so that the company does not require FSA authorisation, at least for these activities.

Articles

The regulations do not automatically amend a company's articles but in general listed company articles do not prevent the holding of shares in treasury.

The purchase

The purchase of qualifying shares to be held in treasury must follow the usual legal procedures for purchase of own shares whether the purchase is conducted through the market (a market purchase) or off-market.

Pre-emption rights

The pre-emption rights in existing shareholders on a new issue of shares apply to the sale of shares held in treasury. These must therefore be offered first to existing shareholders unless the procedures for disapplying pre-emption rights have been followed.

The City Takeover Panel

So far as the Panel and the City Code are concerned the position is as follows.

- since treasury shares have few rights attached to them the provisions of the City Code and the rules governing substantial acquisitions of shares will not apply to them;
- a sale and transfer by the company of treasury shares will normally be treated like a new issue.

Accounting treatment

The Accounting Standards Board has issued an abstract on the accounting treatment of treasury shares (see UITF Abstract 37 accessible at www.asb.org.uk/publications/publication412.html).

FINANCIAL ASSISTANCE FOR PURCHASE OF SHARES

Previous position

The prohibition on the giving by companies of financial assistance for the purchase of their own shares or the shares of their holding companies by someone other than the company was introduced by the Companies Act 1929 and retained in subsequent legislation until 1981.

The object was largely to defeat the asset stripper who might, e.g., acquire shares in a company by means of a loan from a third party so that he came to control it and once in control could repay the loan from the company's funds and then sell off its assets leaving the company to go into liquidation with no assets to meet the claims of creditors. The company concerned was usually one whose shares were, perhaps because of the management policies of the board, undervalued.

The sanction of the law designed to deter this sort of activity was a default fine which could be levied following *criminal proceedings*.

However, following cases such as *Heald* v *O'Connor* [1971] 2 All ER 1105 it was realised that there were civil law consequences since the transactions surrounding the acquisition of the company were illegal. Thus the loan by the third party was void and irrecoverable at law; if the company had given the lender a debenture to secure the loan, or a guarantee to repay it, these securities were void and unenforceable, as was any guarantee or other security given by anyone else including the asset stripper himself.

The same civil law consequences would apply in so far as a person infringed the present law set out below. Breach of the present law is stated to be 'unlawful' and is attended as before by criminal sanctions, the maximum penalty being a term of imprisonment of two years and/or a fine of unlimited amount.

Problems created by previous legislation

The rule against the giving of financial assistance struck potentially at ordinary commercial transactions of companies as follows:

(*a*) *Management buy-outs*. This is the disposal of a company to its management. A holding company may use a buy-out to sell off a subsidiary whose business though successful does not fit the current development plan of the group.

However, the buy-out is more common in the case of private free-standing companies. Suppose that in a family business senior management has reached the age of retirement and is unable to find any purchaser of the business, who knows and can run it successfully other than those employees who are coming up as the next generation of management. In such a case those in management below the owner/directors may use a buy-out technique to acquire the business with the blessing of the owner/directors (but see *Brady* v *Brady* [1988] 2 All ER 617, below).

A management buy-out is commonly achieved by a bank lending the managers the money to buy the shares. Typically the managers can only provide between 10 and 20 per cent of the funds required. The loan is often secured on the assets of the company which management is acquiring and this is the giving of financial assistance and was an infringement of previous legislation.

Nevertheless, it was a popular and useful technique which regrettably operated outside the law.

(*b*) *Other transactions*. It was held by the Court of Appeal in *Belmont Finance* v *Williams (No 2)* [1980] 1 All ER 393 that there was an infringement of then existing legislation when Company A bought the share capital of Company B at an over-inflated price and the former owner of Company B used the money to buy shares in Company A.

Belmont Finance was a member of the Williams group of companies and engaged in property development. The directors of Belmont were anxious to get the 'expertise and flair in property development' of a Mr Grosscurth on the Belmont board, but he wanted to be a substantial shareholder in Belmont as well. Mr Grosscurth owned

Maximum Finance which was worth £60,000. Belmont agreed to buy Maximum Finance for £500,000 and Mr Grosscurth used that money to buy a substantial stake in Belmont. In later proceedings this transaction, which obviously reduced the net assets of Belmont, was regarded as unlawful financial assistance by Belmont.

Finally, there were even lawyers prepared to state that the purchase of shares in a company by an innocent recipient of dividends from it might be infringing the financial assistance rule!

Thus some not uncommon commercial transactions were rendered illegal by a rule which was not, it seems, intended to catch all of them.

The present law

This is contained in ss 151–158 and is designed to bring UK companies into line with US and Continental companies. The provisions, which cover limited and unlimited companies, are set out below.

The prohibition

It is unlawful, as before, for a company, including both limited and unlimited companies, to give a person financial assistance for the purchase of its own shares or those of its holding company, directly or indirectly, *whether before or after or at the same time as the shares are acquired.* The reference to 'a person' is not confined to individuals but includes registered companies and other corporate bodies.

There is no prohibition on a subsidiary company providing financial assistance for the purchase of shares in its fellow subsidiaries or in a holding company providing assistance for the purchase of shares in one of its subsidiaries. As we have seen, the prohibition is extended to *assistance after acquisition* as where A borrows money to acquire shares in B Ltd and B Ltd later repays the loan or reimburses A after A has repaid the loan.

Meaning of financial assistance

(*a*) Financial assistance is provided if the company concerned *makes a gift of the shares or a gift of funds to buy them*; or *guarantees a loan* used to buy its shares; or *gives an indemnity* to the lender; or *secures the loan by giving a charge* over its assets to the lender.

A company would also give assistance if it *waived or released*, e.g., its right to recover a debt from a person A so that A could use the funds to buy shares in the company.

(*b*) The 1985 Act contains a 'sweep-up' provision which forbids any other financial assistance given by a company, the net assets of which are thereby reduced to a material extent. The test is not liquidity but net worth based on the actual value of the assets. Thus a purchase by a company for cash at market value of a fixed asset from a person who later bought its shares would not be financial assistance because the company's net assets would not be reduced and cash would be replaced by the assets.

However, the section would catch artificial transactions affecting a company's assets, as where the company paid twice the market value for an asset in order to enable the seller to buy its shares.

Thus, as we have seen, in *Belmont* the actual transaction was artificial and designed purely to assist the owner of Company B to acquire shares in A at the expense of the assets of A, because Company A paid far more for the shares of B than they were worth, i.e. £500,000 against a valuation of £60,000. The actual deal in *Belmont* would thus infringe s 152, although what happened is not otherwise a forbidden transaction.

'Net assets' is defined as the aggregate assets less the aggregate liabilities determined by reference to their actual rather than their book value.

When is financial assistance lawful?

(*a*) The giving of financial assistance is lawful if the *principal purpose* of the company's action is not to give financial assistance OR such assistance is given as *an incidental part of some larger purpose of the company*. In addition, the assistance MUST be given *in good faith* and *in the best interests of the company* giving the assistance.

The company's defence is therefore founded upon *the purpose* in giving assistance and since *this is a matter of fact* to be decided *on the evidence* it would be as well for the purpose to be set out clearly in the relevant board minutes. A purpose must be established other than the mere giving of assistance and there is also a good faith and best interests of the company requirement. This should prevent the kind of asset stripping referred to at the beginning of this section although there is little doubt that some, seeking to gain profit from purely artificial transactions at the expense of a company's assets, will try to dress up their dealings as some form, e.g., of 'reconstruction'.

However, a legitimate management buy-out is hopefully allowed and other ordinary commercial transactions are no longer threatened by illegality. For example, A acquires B. B wishes to transfer its bank balances to A to effect a more efficient disposition of funds within the group. The boards of A and B may both know that A intends to use those balances to reduce indebtedness, e.g. a loan incurred as a result of acquiring B but this is permitted because reduction of such indebtedness is merely incidental to a larger corporate purpose.

(*b*) The following are also permitted:

(i) A distribution of assets in Company A by way of *dividend* or in a *winding-up* where the distribution is used to buy shares in A or in its holding company or in the case of winding-up A's former holding company.

(ii) An allotment of bonus shares – which in a sense the company assists the shareholders concerned to acquire (the provisions relating to assistance cover acquisition of shares other than for cash but bonus shares are specifically exempt).

(iii) Any arrangement or compromise under s 425, or s 110 and Part I of the Insolvency Act 1986 (see further Chapter 22), which results, e.g., in a liquidator transferring the assets of Company A to Company B so that the shareholders of A receive shares in B into which A is merged which in a sense A's assets have assisted them to acquire.

(iv) Where the funds used for the purchase of the shares in the company or its holding company arise from:

- a reduction of its capital; or
- a redemption or purchase of its shares under the 1985 Act.

In the case where a company is reducing its share capital the money received by the shareholder in the reduction is most likely to be used to buy shares in the holding company.

(v) A company may lend money to a person which he uses to acquire shares in it or its holding company if lending money is part of the ordinary business of the company as is the case with a bank. The fact that a company has power to lend money by its memorandum does not make lending money part of its ordinary business unless making loans is one of its main business activities. Neither the loans it ordinarily makes nor the loan which facilitates the acquisition of the shares must be made for the specific purpose of acquiring the shares. The borrower must be free to use the loan as he wishes, and it must be merely coincidental that the borrower uses it to buy shares in the company. So if a person gets a general loan or an overdraft from a bank and uses it or part of it to buy shares in the bank, there is no illegal financial assistance.

(vi) The provision by a company, in good faith in the interests of the company, of financial assistance for the purposes of an employees' share scheme is permitted. This amendment to the 1985 Act, introduced by the Companies Act 1989, means that assistance is no longer limited, as before, to the provision of money for the acquisition of shares but applies to all forms of assistance for the purposes of an employees' share scheme, e.g. repaying some or all of the borrowings taken out by the scheme in order to buy the company's shares. The giving of guarantees of loans to acquire the company's shares would also be included.

A company may finance an employees' share scheme which benefits employees of the group and their dependants and not merely employees of the company. Employee/directors may be included in such a scheme.

(vii) A company may make loans to its employees, other than directors, to enable them to subscribe for or purchase fully-paid shares in the company or its holding company to be held by them in their own right.

It should be noted that the lending set out in (v)–(vii) above is permissible in the case of a public company only if the company's net assets are not thereby reduced, or, to the extent that those assets are thereby reduced, if the financial assistance is provided out of profits which are available for dividend. 'Net assets' in relation to a company for this purpose means the aggregate of that company's assets less the aggregate of its liabilities, including provisions, determined by their *book* value.

Finally, if shares are acquired by a *nominee for a public company* (not any other person) with financial assistance from the company, then (apart from any infringement of the general law) no voting rights may be exercised by that nominee and any purported exercise of such rights is void. Secondly, the company must dispose of the shares within one year and if this is not done it must cancel them. If the shares are cancelled and the cancellation has the effect of reducing the company's allotted share capital below the authorised minimum, the directors must apply for the company to be re-registered as a private company. Only a directors' resolution is required to make the necessary reduction, application and any alterations to the memorandum that are necessary. There is no need to apply to the court to obtain confirmation of the reduction but any resolution passed by the directors must be filed with the Registrar.

It is worth noting at this point that the 1985 Act does not prohibit a foreign subsidiary from giving financial assistance for the acquisition of shares in its English parent company. There is no need in such a case to follow the 1985 Act procedures. The authority for this is *Arab Bank plc* v *Mercantile Holdings Ltd* [1994] 2 All ER 74.

Reform

This text has considered for some time the possible legal invalidity of the management buy-out, and since some problems have emerged, particularly in relation to public companies, on which the DTI has consulted in regard to possible changes in the legislation, a brief mention of the difficulties follows.

As we have seen, it is necessary to find 'a larger purpose of the company' of which the giving of assistance is merely an incident. The House of Lords in *Brady* v *Brady* [1988] 2 All ER 617 said that it was not enough to show that there were 'other reasons' for the assistance being given. Reasons were not the same as 'a larger purpose of the company'. Although the decision is not concerned with a management buy-out but rather a company reconstruction, it could be said that a management buy-out is the 'reason' for the assistance and not 'a larger purpose of the company'. Clearly if A sells an asset to B Ltd at the proper market price and uses the money to buy shares in B Ltd, then the assistance is exempt because B Ltd has 'a larger purpose', i.e. the acquisition of the asset, but in the management buy-out it may be a struggle to convince the court that there is a 'larger purpose of the company'. Public limited companies are most at risk since, as we shall see, private companies can disapply the larger purpose rule by following the procedures outlined below and it is after all in such companies that most management buy-outs take place.

The DTI will propose changes in the legislation but it is likely to be some time before any reforms can be put in place because primary legislation will be required. However, the DTI has completed the process of consultation through a consultation document entitled *Company Law Reform: Financial Assistance by a Company for the Acquisition of its Own Shares*. Of particular importance is a proposal to alter for public companies the 'principal or larger purpose' test to 'whether the predominant reason was to provide financial assistance'. This is to deal with the decision in *Brady*. Clearly, in a management buy-out the predominant reason is the buy-out and not to provide financial assistance.

The consultation document also suggests that lawful commissions and indemnities for underwriting share issues should be added to the list of exemptions in s 153(3) and proposes to introduce a defence to the criminal sanctions in current legislation. There is also a proposal that unlimited private companies should be removed from the scope of the provisions and that private limited companies should be allowed to provide financial assistance so long as it is not 'materially prejudicial' to the company or alternatively the members have approved the transaction in advance. Draft legislation was scheduled to be published in the spring of 1997 for further consultation but at the time of writing has not appeared.

Relaxation of restrictions: private companies

A private company can give financial assistance in the same circumstances as a public company (see above: 'When is financial assistance lawful?'), BUT in addition *a private company is not affected by the principal purpose rule* and could therefore provide assistance as the sole purpose and object of a particular exercise, provided the assistance is given in good faith and in the interests of the company (*Brady* v *Brady* [1988] 2 All ER 617). For example, in a management buy-out it should be possible to show that the company will benefit from the introduction of younger management on the retirement of elderly director/shareholders.

However, a private company cannot give financial assistance for the acquisition of its own shares or those of its holding company if its net assets would thereby be reduced *except* that if the net assets will be reduced assistance can be provided if it comes from distributable profits.

For this purpose, net assets means the aggregate assets less the aggregate liabilities (including provisions) determined according to their *book* value.

The Court of Appeal ruled in *Hill* v *Mullis and Peake* (1999) BCC 325, that in a case of dispute as to the reduction of assets, the court would hear and normally follow the evidence of an accountant as an expert witness.

The net assets must be as stated in the company's accounting records immediately before the financial assistance is given. The directors will have to have a set of management accounts drawn up at a date immediately before the assistance is given. If the assistance is by way of *gift*, the net assets will be reduced and the assistance would have to be covered by, and made out of, distributable profits. Where the assistance is by way of a *charge* on the company's assets to secure a bank loan granted to the purchaser of the shares, as in many management buy-outs, this will not generally be regarded as a reduction in net assets.

In addition, the Court of Appeal has decided that s 151 of the Companies Act 1985, which prohibits companies from giving financial assistance for the acquisition of their own shares, does not apply in a private company where the assistance consists of the payment by the company concerned of a salary, bonus and pension (given sufficient profits) to a shareholder in return for his transferring his shares into the joint names of himself and his two sons. The point about assistance relates, of course, to the acquisition of a joint interest by the sons.

Parlett *v* Guppys (Bridport) Ltd [1996] 2 BCLC 34

Proceedings arose out of a dispute between the claimant and his two sons. Apparently, the claimant would not continue to work in what were four family companies unless certain payments were made to him. Consequently, in July 1988 it was agreed that four family companies would provide the claimant with a salary of £100,000, a bonus of one-quarter of the profits, and a pension, in return for the transfer of his £26,000 in shares in Guppy Estates Ltd, the fourth defendant, into the joint names of himself and his sons. The agreement to make these payments was subject to there being sufficient profits. In 1991 the claimant issued a writ (now claim form) claiming the balance of salary and bonus which he alleged were owed to him. The defence was that the agreement was unenforceable since it involved unlawful financial assistance contrary to s 151. The judge at first instance accepted this defence, holding that the contract was unenforceable, and there was an appeal to the Court of Appeal.

The companies were all private companies and as such were not controlled so rigidly by the financial assistance provisions as are plcs. Basically, as we have seen, private companies can give financial assistance for the purchase of their shares so long as the company's net assets are not thereby reduced to 'a material extent'. The issue really was whether in deciding the asset reduction question it was right to take into account the capitalised value at the date of the assistance of all future payments to the claimant under the agreement. If so, the defendants argued, the assumption of a liability to make future payments at the time of the agreement reduced the net assets of the company by that liability, even though it was limited to payment out of future distributable profits.

For the claimant it was argued that all that needed to be taken into account was that part of the salary and bonus which was immediately payable at the conclusion of the agreement and also it was necessary to bring into account the counter-balancing asset acquired by Guppy Estates in the shape of the claimant's services. The Court of Appeal accepted the claimant's submissions but thought that the value of the claimant's services to the fourth defendant, if objectively judged, was not worth as much as £100,00 a year plus one-quarter of the profits, so, on that footing, there was a reduction in the net assets of the group of companies. However, that was not enough to bring the 1988 agreement within s 151. The decisive question was whether there was a reduction in the net assets of Guppy Estates to a 'material extent'. Sufficient material existed for the court to decide that there was not.

Comment

This was a transfer of shares from the ownership of A into the ownership of A, B and C but this does not seem to have been vital to the decision. Presumably the ruling would support, in a private company, the payment of a salary, etc. out of future divisible profits to A, provided A transferred his shares to B, or B and C, and so on – although the Court of Appeal's comments regarding the amount of the package is worth noting. However, it would seem that in the above circumstances B (or B and C) would not be regarded as having acquired the shares with financial assistance from the company. This salary, etc. procedure might prove useful in family company arrangements, and seems to represent a relaxation of the financial assistance rule in private companies.

A private company cannot give assistance for the purpose of acquiring shares in its holding company unless it complies with the principal purpose rule, if the holding company or any intermediate holding company is a public company. This is to ensure that public companies cannot avoid the principal purpose rule by a group scheme of some sort.

The practical effect of the above provisions is that a private company can give virtually any kind of financial assistance, provided the company is solvent and the complicated procedure set out below is followed.

Procedure

Whether or not the financial assistance is the principal or only purpose or whether it is an incidental purpose, as in a management buy-out, a private company must follow a statutory procedure, known as the 'whitewash' procedure, before the assistance is given. This is set out below:

(*a*) *Creditor protection: a statutory declaration and auditors' report.* As we have seen, a private company can give financial assistance if the company's net (book value) assets will not be reduced, or if the financial assistance is provided from distributable profits. However, since *a private company is not required to take into account unrealised losses in determining distributable profits (see further Chapter 8), a statutory declaration of solvency is required.*

The directors of the company (and any holding company and intermediate holding company, if the assistance is for the purchase of shares in the holding company) giving financial assistance must make a statutory declaration in prescribed form. *It must state:*

> To the Directors of Assistance Ltd
>
> 1 December 2XXX
> *(being the date of the statutory declaration)*
>
> We have enquired into the state of affairs of Assistance Ltd as at 1 December 2XXX and are not aware of anything to indicate that the opinion expressed by the directors made pursuant to s 155 as to any of the matters specified in s 156(2) is unreasonable in all the circumstances.
>
> Accountants & Co

Figure 7.1 Auditors' Report

(i) particulars of the company's business and the assistance to be given and identifying the recipient of the assistance;

(ii) that the giving of the assistance will not prevent the company from paying its debts in the *immediate future;*

(iii) that *as regards the prospects of the assisting company for the following year*, the company will be able to carry on its business as a going concern and will be able to pay its debts as they fall due throughout the year. If the assisting company is to be put into liquidation within a year but is now, e.g., assisting a purchase of shares in its holding company, the period must be the year following the start of the winding-up.

In forming an opinion on these matters contingent and prospective liabilities, e.g. commitments under hire-purchase agreements, must be taken into account.

The statutory declaration referred to above must have an *Auditors' Report* annexed to it.

The report, which is addressed to the directors, states that the auditors have enquired into the company's affairs and are not aware of anything indicating that the directors' opinion regarding the company's ability to pay its debts is unreasonable (see Figure 7.1). The audit exemption regulations do not dispense with the requirement of an audit report on the reasonableness of the directors' opinions so that a private company wishing to give financial assistance under the procedures outlined above must have an auditor.

Whitewash procedure: powers of the court

The court has power to declare that whitewash procedures are effective even though errors appear in the documentation provided the court is satisfied that creditors have sufficient details regarding the financial assistance.

Harlow *v* Loveday, In re Hill and Tyler Ltd (in administration) (2004)
The Times 11 June

The administrators of a private limited company, Hill and Tyler Ltd, asked the court for directions as to whether certain arrangements made in the course of the purchase of shares in the company constituted unlawful financial assistance under s 151 of the CA 1985. Mr and Mrs Mills held shares in the company. Their shares were purchased by a company called Jewelrun Ltd partly by a loan from Hill and Tyler, which was itself partly financed by a loan from Royscot Trust that took a charge over the assets of Hill and Tyler. The directors of Hill and Tyler purported to comply with the whitewash procedures of the CA 1985. They: (i) decided that the proposed assistance did not reduce the net assets of the company (s 155(2)); and (ii) made a statutory declaration giving particulars of the identity of the person to whom assistance was to be given and the amount of cash being transferred (s 156 (1)). The deal was then completed.

The administrators accepted that the loan was not unlawful assistance because it did not reduce the company's net assets to a material extent but they contended that the charge was unlawful assistance being a condition of the loan without which it would not have been made. They also contended that the declaration was defective because it stated the wrong amount of cash to be transferred. The High Court ruled (i) that the charge did constitute indirect financial assistance; (ii) the whitewash of that assistance was valid notwithstanding the errors because, looked at overall, the statutory declaration gave sufficient details for creditors about the proposed assistance.

However, the judge gave a warning order in regard to the use of the whitewash procedure by noting that if the directors do get it wrong and the court feels unable to accept it, the loan is void, any security is void, and the company and any officer in default is liable to a fine and any director of the company is liable to a fine or imprisonment. Private companies wishing to use the relevant procedures must do so meticulously. The consequences of error can be serious.

Comment

The results of failure to apply the whitewash procedure properly are illustrated by the ruling of the High Court in *Re In a Flap Envelope Co Ltd, Wilmott* v *Jenkin* [2003] All ER (D) 216. In that case the purchaser of the In a Flap company received a loan from the company in order to assist the purchase of its shares. Realising that this was financial assistance the director/shareholders of In a Flap decided to use the whitewash procedure. Jenkin who was one of the director/shareholders purported to resign before the statutory declaration was made and was then reappointed after it had been made. Mr Jenkin did not sign the statutory declaration claiming that he was not a director. In a Flap then went into liquidation and the liquidator was able to recover all the money received by Mr Jenkin and the other vendors because the statutory declaration should have been signed by Mr Jenkin. His resignation and reappointment were a sham and the court regarded him as a director at the time of the declaration and since the declaration required the signatures of all the directors at the time it was unlawful and the purchase arrangements were illegal and void.

(*b*) *Shareholder protection: a special resolution.* Within a week of making the statutory declaration referred to in (*a*) above, a *special* (*or unanimous written*) *resolution* must be passed by the company (and if the financial assistance is for the purchase of shares in its holding company, by that holding company and any intermediate holding company) approving the financial assistance. If a company is a wholly-owned subsidiary, it is not necessary to pass a resolution for the reason that there are no shareholders to protect in the sense required by the 1985 Act. However, participation by the directors in the statutory declaration requirements is still necessary.

Although a 75 per cent majority of those who vote is enough to pass the special resolution, it is important in practice that every shareholder should vote in favour as would be the case with a unanimous written resolution. If not, a four-week delay is imposed to enable possible dissenting shareholders to make application to the court (see below).

The resolution must be filed with the statutory declaration (or the statutory declaration alone for a wholly-owned subsidiary which need not pass a resolution) plus the auditors' report within 15 days of passing the resolution or making the statutory declaration where there is no need for a resolution.

Giving the assistance: when can it be done?

The financial assistance can, once the procedure outlined above has been followed, be given at any time within eight weeks from the date of the statutory declaration, provided that all shareholders voted in favour of the resolution in order to avoid the minority four-week delay, which will otherwise have to come out of the beginning half of the eight-week period. If there is an application to the court, the timetable is then a matter for the court which may, if there is delay in dealing with the dissentients' claim which eventually fails, ask for another statutory declaration.

Dissentient rights

The holders of not less than 10 per cent in aggregate of the nominal value of the company's issued share capital or of any class thereof, or not less than 10 per cent of the members, if the company is not limited by shares, who did not consent to the special resolution, where that procedure was followed, may apply to the court to cancel it. The court *may require* the company to buy out the dissentients if necessary from the company's funds thus effecting a reduction of capital; *or make an order* cancelling the resolution, which will then be ineffective.

If an application is made, the company must forthwith inform the Registrar and then send a copy of any order which the court may make within 15 days of its making.

Table A

The current *Table A* does not prevent the giving of financial assistance. *Table A* to previous Acts did so. Companies covered by previous *Tables A* or having a similar restrictive regulation must remove it before giving financial assistance.

Management buy-outs and fair dealing by directors

Schemes of financial assistance given to *directors* to achieve a management buy-out would be caught and rendered illegal by Part X of the 1985 Act – loans, etc. to directors (see Chapter 16). Thus financial assistance for such a buy-out could only be given personally to management who were not at the time at board level. However, if they later became directors, the outstanding loan would not be illegal unless, e.g., unpaid interest was added to the capital sum. However, if the directors of, say, A Ltd, or some of them, wished to buy out the major shareholders of A Ltd, a legal procedure would be for the acquiring directors to form another company, say B Ltd, and borrow money from a bank in B Ltd's name, letting A Ltd give a security over its assets to the bank to secure the loan to B Ltd of which the acquiring directors would form the board. The loan would be used to buy the shares in A Ltd thus making it a wholly-owned subsidiary of B Ltd. Although A Ltd would have given financial assistance for the purchase of its own shares, this would be within the law because the assistance would not be the 'principal purpose' but part of a management buy-out.

Financial assistance: auditors' duty

In *Coulthard* v *Neville Russell* (*A Firm*) (1997) *The Times*, 18 December, the Court of Appeal decided that as a matter of principle auditors have a duty of care, not only to the company as client, but also to its directors to advise them that a transaction which the company and its directors intend to carry out might be a breach of the financial provisions of the CA 1895. It will be appreciated that the giving of unlawful financial assistance may affect the contracts concerned with it at civil law and can result in criminal proceedings under which the company may be required to pay an unlimited fine, and its officers, if convicted, may receive a custodial sentence of up to two years and/or an unlimited fine. Because auditors are often asked to advise, and do advise, directors on the treatment of items in the accounts and their likely attitude as auditors to particular future transactions, it may well be that the duty to give advice on the statutory legal position could frequently arise. The decision seems to widen the scope of potential liability of auditors for negligence. The allegations accepted as a basis for a duty of care in this case seem to depend on an *omission*, i.e. the failure to advise that a particular transaction which the directors tell the auditors they intend to do may be illegal.

Sanctions for breach of financial assistance rules

The consequences of a breach of the financial assistance rules are considerable, as the following summary shows:

- It is a criminal offence. The company giving the assistance is liable to a fine and the officers in default are liable to imprisonment and/or a fine.
- The company and its officers can be sued and required to compensate any person who suffers loss as a consequence of their unlawful actions.
- Breach of the rules is a breach of fiduciary duty by a director for which the company can claim damages.

ACQUISITION OTHER THAN FOR VALUABLE CONSIDERATION

There is nothing to prevent the transfer of shares in the company to a trustee who will then hold the shares on trust for the company, given that the transfer is voluntary and the shares are fully paid (*Kirby* v *Wilkins* [1929] 2 Ch 444); and a gift to a company of fully-paid shares in the company is apparently not objectionable, so long as the shares are held by some other person on trust for the company (*Re Castiglione's Will Trusts* [1958] 1 All ER 480).

All companies limited by shares may under s 143 acquire their own fully-paid shares by way of gift and the effect of this provision is that the company may hold the shares directly in its own name. There is now no need to put such shares in the name of a nominee or trustee for the company. There is nothing to prevent the use of such a device but it is unnecessary in view of the above provision.

However, nominee holdings, as distinct from holdings as gifts, are governed by s 144. In the case of both a public and private company, if a person has been issued with or has acquired shares in a company as nominee for that company, then if he fails to pay any sums due on the shares the other subscribers to the memorandum, if he acquired them as a subscriber, or the directors, if he acquired them in some other way, are, unless the court grants relief, jointly and severally liable with the nominee for the repayment of the sums due. If the shares have been acquired by a person as nominee for a public company, then under s 146 the shares must be disposed of and if this has not been done within three years, the company must cancel the shares and the formalities of the 1985 Act do not apply to the reduction. In addition, the company's nominee must not exercise voting rights in respect of the shares and if he does the votes are void.

GRADED QUESTIONS

Essay mode

1 Soapstone Ltd has agreed with a merchant bank that the bank is to take a £50,000 equity stake in the company in the form of ordinary shares which will be redeemable in 2008 or earlier at the option of Soapstone Ltd.

Advise the directors as to the funds which can be used for the redemption, and as to the statutory procedure for the issue of redeemable shares.

(*Napier University*)

2 Microchip is a public limited company. Allan and Bill are directors of the company who own 85 per cent of its equity shares between them. In addition, Allan also owns certain debentures issued by the company. The remaining 15 per cent of the equity shares is owned by Charles. Allan now wishes to dispose of his shares and debentures so as to enable him to retire to the south of France. Bill and Charles are concerned that the shares and debentures should not fall into the hands of strangers who might disrupt the smooth running of the company. They consult their accountant who devises the following scheme:

(*a*) Microchip uses reserves in the profit and loss account to purchase the shares and raise the necessary funds from its bank to purchase the debentures; or
(*b*) Microchip guarantees a private loan which Bill will arrange with his bank so as to purchase the shares and debentures as a gift to his wife; or
(*c*) Charles obtains a private loan, guaranteed by Microchip, to purchase Allan's shares and debentures.

Advise Microchip plc as to the legal validity of each of the proposed schemes. Would your answers be different if Microchip were a private company?

(*University of Plymouth*)

3 Identify and explain the three specific circumstances envisaged by the Companies Act 1985 for a reduction of share capital.

(*The Institute of Chartered Accountants in England and Wales*)

4 Assume you are the management accountant reporting to the finance director of a public listed company. The finance director has recently undertaken a financial review as part of the company's strategic review process. In his report he has suggested that the company has more funds than are necessary to support its planned growth and that capital should be reduced.

You are required to write a report for the finance director explaining the methods which may be adopted to reduce the capital of the company.

(*The Chartered Institute of Management Accountants*)

5 (*a*) State the exceptions to the general rule that a public company must not give financial assistance to any person for the purpose of the acquisition of its own shares.

(*b*) Milk Bottles Ltd is a profitable small family company whose principal activity is the retail distribution of milk. The elderly directors appoint Kevin, a younger man, to the board. The articles of association require each director to hold 1,000 £1 qualification shares and allow a director two months from the date of his appointment to acquire his qualification shares. Kevin has not got the money to enable him to do this and the company is willing to lend him the necessary finance.

Advise:

(i) the directors as to the procedures they should observe to effect the loan;
(ii) Steven, a director who disapproves of the arrangement, of any action he may take.

(*The Association of Chartered Certified Accountants*)

6 Section 14 of the Companies Act 1985 provides that the memorandum and articles of association of a company shall, when registered, bind the company and the members to the same extent as if they respectively had been signed and sealed by each member, and contained covenants on the part of each member to observe all the provisions of the memorandum and articles.

Explain the effect of this section on the relationships between shareholders and their company, persons acting in another capacity than that of shareholders and the company and between the shareholders themselves. Illustrate your answer with decided cases.

(*Glasgow Caledonian University*)

7 (*a*) The general legal principle is that a company has a separate legal existence from that of its members. In what circumstances does that general principle not apply? Give examples of such situations.

(*b*) Walter is employed as a managing director by Clipse Ltd whose main object is to retail office equipment. His contract of employment contains a clause which states that in the event of his leaving the employment of Clipse Ltd he will not solicit its customers for a period of two years. He resigns his employment and together with his wife Jean forms a new company, Desks Ltd, whose main object is also retailing office equipment. Bill is a salesman employed by Desks Ltd. He is given customer lists by Walter and immediately begins soliciting Clipse Ltd's customers.

In order to raise cash for his new business, Walter enters into a contract to sell his house to Wilf for £450,000. Bill, who has always admired the house, approaches Walter and makes him an offer of £460,000. Walter transfers ownership of the house to Desks Ltd, and on behalf of the company enters into negotiations to sell the house to Bill.

Advise Clipse Ltd and Wilf on any action they can take.

(*The Association of Chartered Certified Accountants*)

Objective mode

Four alternative answers are given. Select ONE only. Circle the answer which you consider to be correct. Check your answers by referring back to the information given in the chapter and against the answers at the back of the book.

1 Boxo Ltd has passed a special resolution with a 78 per cent majority to give the company the power to give financial assistance for the purchase of its own shares. Within what time from the date of the resolution must the assistance be given?

A 0–6 weeks.
B 4–10 weeks.
C 8–12 weeks.
D 4–8 weeks.

2 Jock wants Trent Ltd to give a security over its assets to the Derwent bank so that the bank may lend Jock money to buy shares in Trent Ltd. The position regarding this proposal is:

A it is lawful if the court approves.
B it is lawful if approved by an ordinary resolution in general meeting.
C it is lawful if approved by a special resolution in general meeting or a written resolution.
D it is always unlawful for a company to give financial assistance for the purchase of its shares.

3 The directors of Humber Ltd are intending that the company should purchase some of its own shares partly from capital. Amongst other things they must make a statutory declaration containing a statement that in their opinion the company will be able to carry on business as a going concern and will be able to pay its debts as they fall due during a stated period not exceeding:

A 12 months.
B six months.
C 18 months.
D two years.

4 The directors of Tyne Ltd intend a purchase by the company of its own shares from John, a member, but partly out of Tyne's capital. They have made an appropriate statutory declaration and have also called an extraordinary general meeting of the members. Which of the following resolutions must be passed to approve the proposal?

A An ordinary resolution.
B A special resolution.
C An extraordinary resolution.
D An ordinary resolution following special notice.

5 What is the maximum permitted period between the passing of a resolution sanctioning a purchase of own shares partly from capital and the date of payment?

A 15 days.
B One week.
C Five weeks.
D Seven weeks.

6 The assets of Derwent plc are less than one-half of its called-up share capital. The directors must call an extraordinary meeting of the members to be held not later than 56 days from the date:

A on which the auditor informed the directors in writing of the capital loss.
B on which all the directors became aware of the capital loss.
C on which a director became aware of the capital loss.
D of the deposit of a requisition by 15 per cent of the voting members.

Answers to questions set in objective mode appear on p 576.

8

CAPITAL MAINTENANCE – COMPANY DISTRIBUTIONS

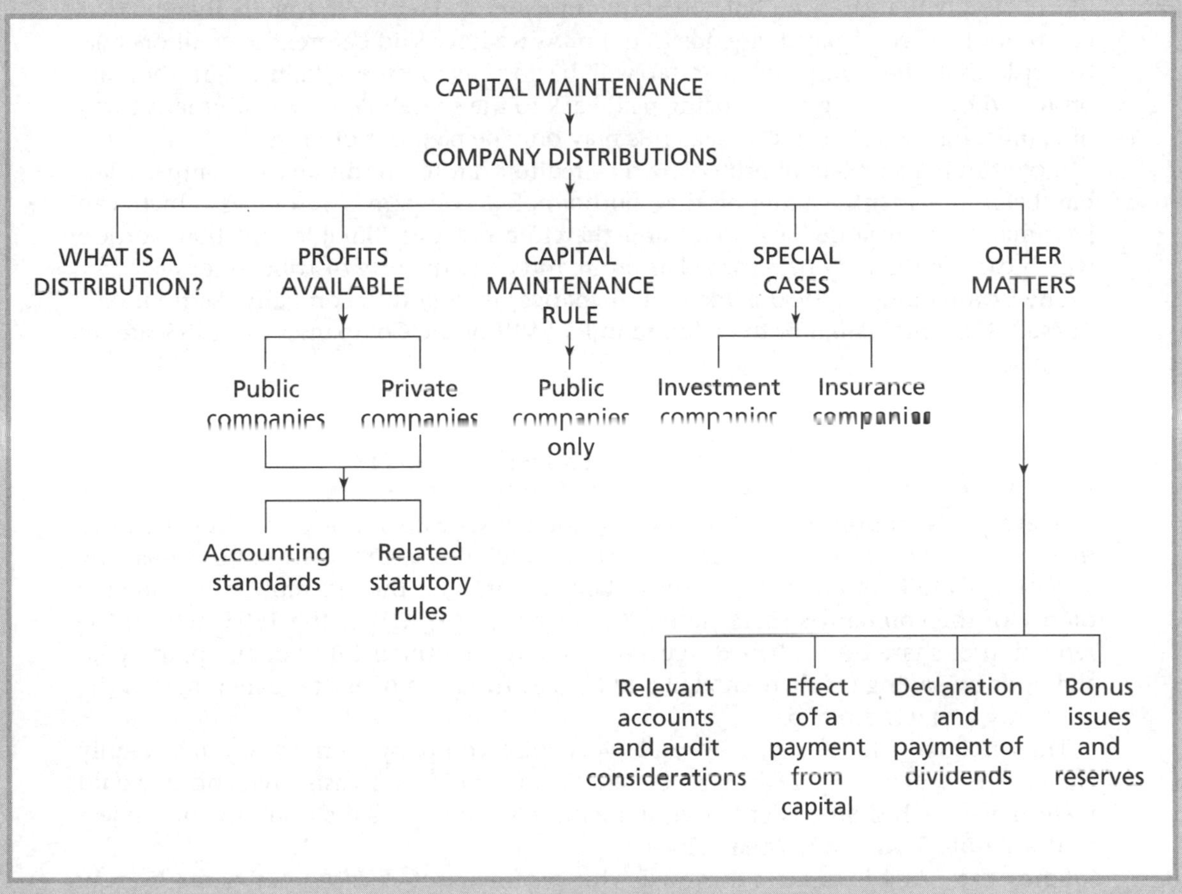

The matter of company distributions is a specific and rather special aspect of capital maintenance. The relevant rules are considered below together with the rules relating to the declaration and payment of dividends.

PROFITS AVAILABLE FOR DISTRIBUTION – GENERALLY

In earlier times when the narrower term *dividend* was used rather than the current expression *distributions*, it was said that 'dividends may not be paid out of capital'. This meant simply that share capital which the company had received from its shareholders could not be used to pay dividends to them. As we have said before, the creditors take the risk that the company's capital will be lost by business failure but they are protected by the law against it being paid back to the shareholders. An alternative way of expressing the rule is that 'dividends may only be paid out of profits'.

A continuing problem in protecting the creditors' buffer in this area of company law has been the identification of that portion of a company's resources which can legitimately be regarded as capital and therefore not distributable and that portion which can legitimately be regarded as profit and consequently distributable.

The Companies Act 1980 made radical changes in regard to company distributions. These rules, which are now to be found in Part VIII of the Companies Act 1985, are set out below.

WHAT IS A DISTRIBUTION?

It is every description of distribution of a company's assets (not only a dividend) to members of the company, whether in cash or otherwise, except distributions made by way of: (1) a fully or partly-paid issue of bonus shares; (2) the redemption or purchase of any of the company's shares under Chapter VII of Part V of the 1985 Act; (3) the reduction of share capital by extinguishing or reducing the liability of any partly-paid shares or by paying off share capital; and (4) a distribution of assets to members of the company in a winding-up.

Thus if Boxo Ltd, a television and video hire company, run by say five family shareholders, decided that instead of paying shareholders a cash dividend it would instead give each shareholder free equipment, that would be a distribution and subject to the statutory rules discussed below.

Since the provisions are concerned with payments of *dividend* payments by way of *deferred remuneration* to directors, even though there are no realised profits available, they are not caught by the distribution rules (see *MacPherson* v *European Strategic Bureau Ltd* [2000] 2 BCLC 683). However, such payments would be void and recoverable by the company if it was insolvent. Then the creditors' interests would be paramount.

In essence, these rules state that a distribution can only be made out of profits available in terms of the provisions of ss 263–269 and by reference to accounts which are properly prepared under ss 270–276.

PROFITS AVAILABLE – PUBLIC AND PRIVATE COMPANIES

The basic rule is that a company's profits available for distribution are: (a) its accumulated realised profits (both revenue and capital) not previously distributed or capitalised (as by being applied in financing a bonus issue or the purchase or redemption of the company's shares with a transfer to a capital redemption reserve), LESS (b) its accumulated realised losses (both revenue and capital) not written off in a reduction or reorganisation of capital.

In addition, para 12 of the fourth Schedule to the 1985 Act states that 'only profits realised at the balance sheet date shall be included in the profit and loss account'.

From the above provisions it follows that:

1 Unrealised profits, either revenue or capital, are no longer distributable.

2 A realised capital loss following, e.g., the actual sale of an asset at a loss will reduce the profit available for distribution. The 1985 Act requires the making good of unrealised capital losses following, e.g., the downward revaluation of an asset retained by the company, but only for public companies (see below).

   The depreciation of fixed assets is required and realised losses to be taken into account when calculating the sum available for dividend include amounts written off or retained for depreciation. This ensures that dividends will be restricted to allow for depreciation, subject to what is said below.

3 The use of the word 'accumulated' is important. It means that the position in the current year cannot be regarded in isolation. The profit and loss account is a continuous account. Thus if Boxo Ltd makes a trading loss of £1,000 in year 1 and £2,000 in year 2, but a trading profit of £1,000 in year 3, it must make a profit in excess of £2,000 in year 4 before any dividend can be paid, unless the company applies to the court for a reduction of capital, so cancelling the losses.

4 Undistributed profits of previous years cannot be brought forward and distributed without taking into account a revenue loss on the current year's trading.

5 An unrealised capital profit cannot be applied in writing off a realised revenue loss.

The provisions also introduce other concepts which are set out below. Insofar as these relate to realised profits reference should be made to the fourth Schedule which states, in effect, that references in the Schedule to realised profits are to such profits as fall to be treated as realised profits, in accordance with principles generally accepted with respect to the determination for accounting purposes of realised profits, at the time when the relevant accounts are prepared.

This implies that it is for the accounting profession to specify in more detail the meaning of realised profits and that the term may be amended from time to time so as to encompass changes in accounting practice.

REALISED PROFITS AND ACCOUNTING STANDARDS

There are several possible meanings of the expression 'realised' starting with the obvious one of realised in cash. The conclusion reached following research by the accounting bodies was that the preferable approach would be to treat an item as realised if its occurrence can be established from sufficiently reliable measurements.

The profit and loss account should be confined to *legally* distributable profits. The treatment of individual items should follow the guidance set out in the relevant Statements of Standard Accounting Practice (SSAPs) and, more recently, Financial Reporting Standards (FRSs), issued by the Accounting Standards Board.

These are not considered further here because they are part of accounting rather than legal practice and should be studied in the accounting context. As a legal point, however, it should be noted that it was stated in *Lloyd Cheyham & Co* v *Littlejohn & Co* [1987] BCLC 303 that 'SSAPs are very strong evidence as to what is the proper standard which should be adopted and unless there is some justification a departure . . . will be regarded as constituting a breach of duty'.

While the following of appropriate standards will continue to be a vital part of accountancy practice it will be possible for a court to find liability in negligence even though a relevant standard has been followed if the implication of a decision of the House of Lords in *Bolitho* v *City and Hackney Health Authority* [1997] 4 All ER 771 is taken to its logical conclusion. The law lords qualified the long-established principle laid down in *Bolam* v *Friern Hospital Management Committee* [1957] 2 All ER 118 that so long as medical practitioners relied on 'a responsible body of professional opinion' they would not be liable in negligence. The court was not bound, their Lordships said in *Bolitho*, to hold that a defendant doctor would escape liability for negligent treatment or diagnosis just because he leads evidence from a number of medical experts who are generally of the opinion that the defendant's treatment or diagnosis accorded with sound medical practice. The court has to be satisfied that the exponents of the body of opinion relied upon can demonstrate that such an opinion has a logical basis.

Although the *Bolitho* case is a medical one, it is likely to be given general application. It seems now that it will not necessarily be enough to meet an allegation of negligence with the response that the actions complained of are accepted and practised by many others. The court will wish to be satisfied that the practice stands up to logical scrutiny. Canadian courts have already pronounced on the position regarding accountants: the Court of Appeal of British Columbia in *Kripps* v *Touche Ross* [1997] held against Touche on the ground 'that the accountants had known that a simple application of (a Canadian accounting standard) would omit material information'.

While *Bolitho* is an important case, it is in practice unlikely that the courts will often find that existing accounting standards are illogical, although they have now acquired the right to do so in appropriate circumstances. The decision is perhaps not too surprising. Professional persons cannot really expect to be judges in their own cause.

RELATED STATUTORY RULES

The relevant statutory provisions, running alongside accounting practice, are summarised below.

1 An unrealised profit cannot be applied in paying up debentures or any amounts outstanding on partly-paid shares.

2 As we have seen, provisions for depreciation (and contingencies) are to be regarded as realised losses when considering profits available for distribution. In addition, a deficit on the revaluation of an asset gives rise to a provision which must be treated as a realised loss except in two situations when the provision may be treated as an unrealised loss – (*a*) where the deficit offsets an unrealised profit previously recorded on the same asset; (*b*) where the deficit arises on a revaluation of all the fixed assets. This applies even though goodwill is not revalued, notwithstanding that goodwill is treated by the formats of the 1985 Act, which deal with the way in which company accounts are to look, as a fixed asset.

The revaluation does not necessitate the changing of the amounts of every fixed asset, but that every such asset be considered for revaluation by the directors. They must be satisfied that those assets whose values have not been changed have an aggregate value not less than their aggregate amount as stated in the financial statements.

The above will not apply unless the notes to the relevant accounts state:

(*a*) that the directors have considered the value at any time of any fixed assets of the company without actually revaluing those assets;
(*b*) that they are satisfied that the aggregate value of those assets at the time in question is, or was, not less than the aggregate amount at which they are, or were for the time being, stated in the company's financial statements;
(*c*) that the relevant items affected are accordingly stated in the relevant accounts on the basis that a revaluation of the company's fixed assets which included the assets in question took place at that time.

It will be noted that the 'aggregate' approach enables losses on some assets to be compensated for by increases in the value of others.

2 Where a fixed asset is revalued upwards and subsequently depreciated only that part of the depreciation applicable to the value of the asset before its revaluation is treated as reducing realised profits. The excess may be added back to distributable profits.

The entries in accounting terms are set out in Figure 8.1.

	Dr	Cr
	£	£
Fixed asset at cost (2002)	2,000	
Revaluation (end 2002)	1,200	
Revalued amount before depreciation	3,200	
Revaluation reserve		
Fixed asset revaluation		
realised		1,200
unrealised		(120)
		1,080
Provision for depreciation		
Charge to P and L Account for 2002		
(10 per cent of revalued figure at end 2002)		320
(Excess depreciation over 2001 = £120)		

Figure 8.1 Realised profits – provisions for depreciation

4 Development costs, e.g. the costs of developing a saleable company product before any revenue is received from its sale or use, must in general be treated as a realised loss. If they are shown as an asset, i.e. capitalised, they are to be treated as a realised loss, except insofar as the development costs represent an unrealised profit made on a revaluation of those costs. The basic rule of realised loss does not apply either if the directors justify, in the light of special circumstances, that the amount carried forward shall not be treated as a realised loss. For example, the directors may feel that future benefits in terms of revenue from the product can be reasonably anticipated in the near future and may wish to set off the expenditure on development against future revenue from its sale or use rather than treat it as a realised loss in a particular year. The grounds of justification must be included in the notes to the accounts on capitalised development costs as required by the fourth Schedule.

Overriding the statutory provisions

It should be noted that the requirement to bring into the profit and loss account only realised profits can be overtaken in two ways:

1 The fourth Schedule of the 1985 Act allows the directors to depart from the realised profit principles if there are special reasons for doing so, but particulars of the reasons and the effect of departure must be given in a note to the accounts.
2 The requirement of a true and fair view overrides other requirements, so that an unrealised profit must be included if this is essential to give a true and fair view.

PUBLIC COMPANIES – A CAPITAL MAINTENANCE RULE

As we have seen, a company may make a distribution only out of realised profits less realised losses. Section 264 of the 1985 Act imposes a further restriction on public companies. Such a company cannot make a distribution in a situation where the amount of its net assets is less than the aggregate of its called-up share capital and undistributable reserves after making such distribution. This means in effect that a plc must deduct any net unrealised losses from net realised profits before making a distribution. A private company need not do so.

Undistributable reserves are:

1 the share premium account;
2 capital redemption reserve;
3 the amount by which the company's accumulated unrealised profits so far as not previously utilised by any capitalisation exceed its accumulated unrealised losses so far as not previously written off in a reduction or reorganisation of capital;
4 any other reserve which the company is prohibited from distributing by statute or by its memorandum or articles.

Although the above rule applies only to plcs, it should be noted that none of the reserves listed above is distributable by private companies.

An illustration of the capital maintenance rule appears in Figure 8.2.

		Company A		Company B
		£		£
Share capital		50,000		50,000
Surplus or deficit on revaluation of fixed assets		4,000		(4,000)
Realised profits	7,000		7,000	
Realised losses	(2,000)	5,000	(2,000)	5,000
Total share capital and reserves/net assets	=	59,000		51,000
Distributable profit				
(*a*) if private company		5,000		5,000 (no capital maintenance rule)
(*b*) if public company		5,000		1,000 (capital maintenance rule applies)

Figure 8.2 The capital maintenance rule

SPECIAL CASES

Investment and insurance companies are subject to different rules. Basically the 1985 Act gives an investment company, i.e. a public listed company whose business consists of investing its funds mainly in securities with the object of spreading investment risk and giving its members the benefits of the management of its funds, an option when making a distribution of using either the capital maintenance rule or an asset/liability ratio test under which it can make a distribution *but only out of its accumulated realised revenue profits less accumulated revenue losses* so long as this does not reduce the amount of its assets to less than $1^1/_2$ times the aggregate of its liabilities immediately after the proposed distribution.

An amount properly transferred to the profit and loss account of an insurance company from a surplus on its long-term business, e.g. life assurance, shall be considered as realised profit and available for distribution provided it is supported by actuarial investigation showing a surplus in the sense of assets over liabilities attributable to the long-term business.

RELEVANT ACCOUNTS

The 1985 Act requires companies to decide the question whether a distribution can be made and the amount of it by reference to 'relevant accounts'. The relevant accounts, which must have been prepared to give a true and fair view, will most usually be the last annual accounts. The accounts must have been laid before the company in general meeting, though a private company may elect to dispense with this requirement (see Chapter 19). In any case the accounts must have been prepared in accordance with the provisions of the Companies Act, or have been so prepared subject only to matters which are not material for the purpose of determining the legality of a proposed distribution.

AUDIT CONSIDERATIONS

The auditors of a company must have made an unqualified report on the accounts. If the report is qualified, then the auditors must state in writing whether, in their opinion, the substance of the qualification is material for the purpose of determining the legality of the proposed distribution. A copy of any statement by the auditors relating to the qualification must have been laid before the company in general meeting, or in the case of a private company, which is not laying the accounts before a general meeting, circulated to the members.

In the case of a holding company, the latest annual accounts would normally be group accounts and reported profit will have been determined by consolidation. If the consolidated accounts are qualified, it may be necessary for the auditors to state whether or not the qualification is material to the calculation of distributable profits of the holding company. From a legal point of view, the distributable profits are the realised profits of the holding company. In *Re Precision Dippings Ltd* [1985] 3 WLR 812 it was held that compliance with these provisions was not a mere procedural matter.

In this case the company paid a dividend of £60,000 to its holding company. This payment exhausted the subsidiary company's cash resources, and some months later it went into voluntary liquidation. The liquidator sought recovery of the payment plus interest since it had contravened the 1985 Act and so was *ultra vires*.

For the year in question the auditors' report contained a qualification as to the basis of valuing work in progress. The auditors had not made the statement required by the 1985 Act and the directors were unaware that it was required.

After the company had gone into liquidation, the auditors issued a statement that, in their opinion, the basis of the valuation of work in progress referred to was not material for the purpose of determining whether the dividend of £60,000 would have been in contravention of the Act. This statement was subsequently accepted by a resolution of the shareholders.

The court *held* that the distribution rules are a major protection for creditors, and the requirement for an auditor's written statement when the audit report is qualified is an important part of that protection. This statement has to be available before the distribution is made. The payment of the dividend was *ultra vires* and the holding company held the £60,000 as constructive trustee for the subsidiary.

The resolution of the shareholders could not ratify or confirm the dividend payment. The shareholders could not dispense with or waive the legal requirements.

The above provisions regarding the functions of the auditor do not apply to companies which have dispensed with the audit requirement. For these companies there is therefore no audit or reporting requirement for the last accounts on distribution of profit.

EFFECT OF PAYING DIVIDENDS OUT OF CAPITAL

Section 277(1) provides that if a member of a company knows or has reasonable grounds to believe at the time a distribution was made to him that it contravened Part

VIII of the 1985 Act he is liable to repay it (or the illegal part) to the company. Section 277 does not deal with the civil liability of the directors who made the improper distribution. However, since they have misapplied the company's property they are in breach of their fiduciary duty to the company and therefore are jointly and severally liable to the company to replace the dividend paid. This was decided in *Flitcroft's Case* (1882) 21 Ch D 519 and means that each director can be called upon to repay the whole amount, and if he does he has a right of contribution against the others. Thus there are three directors – A, B and C. The dividend wrongly paid is £3,000. A is called upon to pay and does. He may then recover by a claim at law if necessary £1,000 from B and £1,000 from C. Section 277(2) makes it clear that the liability of the members at common law is preserved, and according to the decision in *Moxham* v *Grant* [1900] 1 QB 88 directors who have repaid the dividend to the company have a right of *indemnity* against each shareholder who received the dividend to the extent of the dividend received whether the shareholder concerned *knew or not* that it was paid out of capital.

It may be possible for the directors to claim relief if they have acted honestly and reasonably (see Chapter 17), and there may be a claim against negligent auditors.

Allied Carpets Group plc *v* Nethercott [2001] BCC 81

In this case the High Court ruled that a former managing director who had received dividends that he knew were paid on the basis of inadequate accounts held the dividends on a constructive trust for the company and he was required to repay them to the company. The accounts deliberately overstated both sales and profits by the inclusion of uncompleted transactions. The accounts failed therefore to comply with ss 270 and 271 of the CA 1985, there being also no auditor's report or statement as required by s 271.

Comment

(i) In this connection, the High Court has also ruled that the directors of a plc who had authorised the payment of dividends other than out of distributable profits were personally liable to repay them to the company, regardless of whether they themselves were the recipients of the dividend (see *Bairstow* v *Queens Moat Houses plc*, High Court [2000] 1 BCLC 549). The amounts were not inconsiderable, being £27.7 million of dividend and £14 million in interest.

(ii) *In the matter of Marini Ltd (liquidator of Marini Ltd)* v *Dickinson* [2003] EWHC 334 the High Court was asked to excuse directors, who had paid dividends that exceeded available profits, under s 727 CA 1985 because they had acted honestly and reasonably on accountants' advice. The court agreed that they had so acted but would not exercise its discretion to excuse because the directors had themselves received the benefit of the dividend and could not be left with what was a default benefit.

(iii) In *Re Loquitur Ltd, IRC* v *Richmond* [2003] STC 1394 the High Court ruled that the directors of a company were liable to repay to the company certain dividends declared on the basis of improperly prepared accounts which they had drawn up. The accounts did not make provision for a potential corporation tax liability if a rollover relief scheme failed, which it did. The directors' plea to be excused because they had been assisted by what the court called 'a raft of advisers' in terms of an appropriate scheme failed because they used an alternative scheme not referred back to the advisers before declaring the dividend.

Exceptionally, shareholders can receive money out of capital in the form of interest. This can happen where interest is paid on calls in advance accepted by the company under the 1985 Act if the articles so provide; *Table A* does not.

DECLARATION AND PAYMENT OF DIVIDENDS

The question of declaration of dividends is usually dealt with by the articles. There is no absolute right to a dividend, and where the articles follow the pattern of *Table A*, the members can declare dividends by ordinary or written resolution but cannot declare a dividend higher than that recommended by the directors, and if the directors do not recommend payment of dividend, the members cannot declare one either on the preference or ordinary shares. Under such a provision the members in general meeting can reduce the dividend recommended by the directors. As regards the dividend payable in a particular year, the matter is usually already decided because the dividend has been paid before the general meeting is held. However, the members could reduce the dividend recommended and paid which would involve adjustments in the accounts for the following year.

Dividend payments have in the past been put to the members for approval at the annual general meeting but where a private company has elected not to hold annual general meetings, approval to the payment of dividend can be sought from the members at any time to suit the administrative convenience of the company in terms of the date on which a dividend payment is to be made but member approval by written resolution is required.

Table A provides that all dividends shall be declared and paid according to the amounts paid up on the shares. Under such an article, no amount credited as paid in respect of calls in advance could be counted as paid for this purpose. Where the company's articles exclude *Table A* and yet do not provide for the method of payment of dividend, dividends are paid on the nominal value of the shares.

A dividend must be paid in proportion to the shares held and at a uniform rate on all shares of the same class. The dividend can, as we have seen, be paid according to the nominal value of the shares so that a shareholder who has fully-paid shares gets no more per share than a shareholder whose shares are merely partly paid. However, s 119(c) of the CA 1985 permits companies to pay dividends in proportion to the amounts paid up on them and Art 104 of *Table A* contains a similar provision. It is therefore not possible for the holders of a majority of the shares to pass a resolution to the effect that a larger dividend (or a smaller one) shall be paid on their shares than on those of other members.

Thus if a company has two shareholders, A and B, who hold 60 per cent and 40 per cent respectively of the issued and paid-up ordinary share capital and they both agree that they should be paid the same amount of dividend in regard to the last year's accounts, this is illegal unless the shareholdings are amended to a 50/50 proportion. Thus a total dividend of £20,000 cannot be split as to £10,000 each. The split must be £12,000/£8,000 unless the shareholding is changed.

Unless the articles otherwise provide, dividends are payable in cash, but *Table A* provides that the company may distribute specific assets in whole or in part satisfaction. *Table A* also provides that payment may be made by cheque sent through the post to the registered address of the holder. In the case of joint holders, it is sent to the one whose name appears first on the register of members, or alternatively as the joint holders may direct *in writing*. Any one of two or more joint holders may give an effectual receipt.

Table A further provides that no dividend shall bear interest against the company, unless otherwise provided by the rights attached to the shares.

Dividends when declared are in the nature of a specialty debt and can be sued for up to 12 years from the date of declaration.

Interim dividends

When the directors can see that the company is going to make a sufficient profit by the end of the financial year, they may declare a dividend part way through the year which is in the nature of a part payment of the dividend for the year as a whole. At the end of the year a final dividend is declared in respect of the balance. *Table A* provides that the directors may from time to time pay to the members such interim dividends as appear to the directors to be justified by the distributable profits of the company. Under *Table A* an interim dividend does not require the approval of a general meeting of the members, and is not in the nature of a debt due from the company. Thus if it is not paid, it cannot be sued for, and there is nothing to prevent the directors subsequently rescinding or varying the dividend (*Lagunas Nitrate Co* v *Schroeder* (1901) 85 LT 22).

Where the directors propose to pay an interim dividend, reference may have to be made to interim accounts, which in the case of a public company must be such 'as are necessary to enable a reasonable judgment to be made': i.e. accounts complying with the 1985 Act (true and fair view) and signed by a director. Public companies must file these interim accounts with the Registrar before distribution. Interim accounts need not be audited.

Reference to interim accounts would be necessary if under the last annual accounts a distribution would be unlawful, as where the amount of distributable reserves calculated by reference to the last annual accounts is insufficient to make the distribution required.

Where a dividend is to be declared during the company's first accounting reference period or before any accounts have been laid in respect of that period, the dividend must be justified by reference to initial accounts.

The requirements for interim and initial accounts for plcs are more stringent than those for private companies and are dealt with in ss 272–273 of the CA 1985. These sections are not considered further in this text.

Procedure for payment of dividend

The company may close its register for a short time before payment is made in order that the register shall remain static whilst the procedure for payment is carried out. *Dividend warrants* are prepared in favour of those persons whose names appear on the register, the dividend being declared according to the recommendation of the directors. The warrants are posted to the shareholders as soon as possible after the dividend is declared. However, companies encourage the use of a dividend mandate system under which the payment is direct into the shareholder's bank account.

In the case of share warrants, the company will advertise that the dividend is payable in exchange for a coupon bearing a certain number, these coupons being attached to the share warrant. A dividend warrant is then made out in the name of the present holder of the share warrant.

It is current practice not to close registers but to declare a dividend payable to shareholders registered as at close of business on a given date (the striking date). It should be noted that companies are not concerned with equities when paying dividends. The registered shareholder (or the first named of joint holders) on the striking date or the first day on which the register is closed is the person to whom the dividend is paid. If such a person has recently sold his holding *cum* (with) dividend, the buyer's broker will claim it through the seller's broker. If the sale was *ex* (without) dividend, the seller keeps it and no claim arises. The purchase price of the share will take into account the *cum* or *ex* dividend element.

Many companies include a power in their articles to forfeit unclaimed dividends after a reasonable period. However, in the case of quoted companies Stock Exchange regulations insist that such a power shall not be exercised until 12 years or more have passed since the dividend was declared. *Table A* provides that any dividend which has remained unclaimed for 12 years from the date when it became due for payment shall, if the directors so resolve, be forfeited and cease to remain owing by the company.

In the case of public listed companies, the requirements of the listing agreement as appearing in the Listing Rules issued by the Financial Services Authority, which deals with the listing of companies on the London Stock Exchange, would have to be considered. This specialist area is considered in outline in Chapter 9.

Directors failing to declare dividends

It may well be that in a private company the directors are happy to take their salaries from the company and refuse to declare dividends. Members who are not on the board may seek advice as to the availability of remedies in this situation. Where the company has articles similar to those of *Table A* nothing can be done under the constitution. Members who find themselves in this situation are usually minority shareholders and so cannot change the articles. *Reg* 102 allows the members by ordinary resolution to declare dividends not exceeding the amount recommended by the directors. So if the directors' 'recommendation' is nil that is it.

Under s 459 (see Chapter 14) a minority could ask the court for a declaration that they have been and are being unfairly prejudiced by the conduct of the board. Any order made by the court would normally be a requirement for the majority or the company to purchase the shares of the minority at a price to be determined usually by the company's auditors or advising accountants. The court is unlikely to declare and continue to declare dividends. As a minority such members would not have sufficient power to remove the board and so s 459 is the only real way of getting out of the company with their capital.

CAPITALISING PROFITS

The company may, as an alternative to paying a cash dividend, capitalise its profits. This may be achieved by the allotment of fully-paid-up bonus shares (or scrip issue, or capitalisation issue as it is sometimes called) by transferring to the capital account undistributed profit equal to the nominal value of the shares issued.

Profits, including unrealised profits, cannot be capitalised unless the articles so provide because, as we have already seen, in the absence of such a provision a shareholder is entitled to the payment of dividend in cash. *Table A* provides for the capitalisation of profits by an ordinary resolution of the members in general meeting (or a written resolution) upon the recommendation of the directors.

Where there is an allotment of bonus shares, the company must make a return of the allotment and since the shares are allotted for a consideration other than cash, the contract constituting the title of the allottees must be registered. *Table A* allows the directors to authorise any person to enter into an agreement on behalf of the members who are to be allotted bonus shares, and this would obviate the need to make a contract with them all. However, since the 1985 Act allows particulars of the contract to be registered in lieu of the contract itself, the company need not actually file a contract but merely the particulars of it, and will in practice adopt this method.

It should be borne in mind that *an issue of bonus shares may necessitate an increase in the company's authorised capital*. The actual distribution of the bonus shares among the various classes of shareholders will be based on their right to receive dividend unless the articles or terms of issue otherwise provide.

RESERVES

A company is not in general bound to allocate certain of its profits to reserves, although it must *on a redemption or purchase of shares* out of profits set up a *capital redemption reserve*, and it may be that the company is bound under a contract with its debenture holders to set aside a certain sum by way of a reserve to redeem the debentures.

Nevertheless, the articles may provide for the directors to set up *reserve funds for dividend equalisation* or *to meet future liabilities*. *Table A* does not give such a power, it being implied that provided the reserves are distributable the shareholders are entitled to them. However, where such a power exists, the directors may decide to set aside all the profits, even if this means that no dividend is paid on the preference or ordinary shares, though in such circumstances there may be a petition under s 459 by a member or members on the grounds of 'unfair prejudice' (see Chapter 14).

AID TO LEARNING ON DISTRIBUTIONS

These objective testing questions are taken from Pilot Papers on objective testing published by the Institute of Chartered Accountants in England and Wales and are retained because of their high quality. They take the place in this chapter of the tests in objective mode devised by the author.

Question A

A dividend may not be paid by reference to a set of financial statements which carry a qualified audit report unless the auditor states in writing that the matter is not material in determining whether the proposed dividend is illegal under the Companies Act. Which of the following might be considered material?

A A qualification disagreeing with certain reorganisation costs being classified as extraordinary.
B A qualification disagreeing with the carrying forward of goodwill arising on consolidation in the consolidated balance sheet.
C A qualification for the non-disclosure of loans to directors.
D A qualification arising from a disagreement as to the book value of stocks.

Answer to Question A

The answer is D since disagreement as to the book value of stocks will affect the amount of realised profits in the profit and loss account.

A is a matter of classification, but the requirement for profits available for dividend is whether or not they have been realised.
B is a qualification affecting the consolidated accounts, but the write-off of goodwill on consolidation will not affect the distributable profits of the holding company.
C The auditors are required to disclose loans to directors if not included in the accounts or notes, but this will not affect the distributable profits.

Question B

With reference to the following information answer questions 1 to 6.

The table below shows the financial status of two companies, Alpha and Beta, at the year ending 31 March 2xxx.

	ALPHA	BETA
	£m	£m
Unrealised revaluation surplus/(deficit)	350	(300)
Realised capital profits	250	150
Realised revenue profits brought forward	150	150
Realised revenue profits/(loss) for the year	50	(50)

At all times the net assets of the companies after distribution will exceed the statutory minimum.

1 If Alpha is a limited but not a public limited company, what are the profits available for distribution as dividend of Alpha Ltd?

A £50m
B £200m
C £450m
D £800m

2 If Alpha is a public limited company, what are the profits available for distribution as dividend of Alpha plc?

A £50m
B £200m
C £450m
D £800m

3 If Alpha is a public limited company treated as an investment company, what are the profits available for distribution as dividend of Alpha plc?

A £50m
B £200m
C £450m
D £800m

4 If Beta is a limited but not a public limited company, what are the profits available for distribution as dividend of Beta Ltd if the revaluation deficit arises on a revaluation of all the fixed assets?

A Nil
B £50m
C £100m
D £250m

5 If Beta is a public limited company, what are the profits available for distribution as dividend of Beta plc?

A Nil
B £50m
C £100m
D £250m

6 If Beta is a public limited company treated as an investment company, what are the profits available for distribution as dividend of Beta plc?

A Nil
B £50m
C £100m
D £250m

Answers to Question B

Q.1 *The answer is C,* £450m.

A only takes account of the current year's realised profits but it is accumulated realised profits that are taken into account.
B excludes capital profits which are available if realised.
D includes revaluation surplus which is not available.

Q.2 *The answer is C.* There is no difference between a public and private company in such a case.

Q.3 *The answer is B,* i.e. realised *revenue* profits.

Q.4 *The answer is D,* £250m. Realised losses must be taken into account but revaluation deficit need not be so long as it relates to all the fixed assets (excluding goodwill).

Q.5 *The answer is A.* In a public company a further limitation is that the net assets must not be reduced below the capital and non-distributable reserves.

Q.6 *The answer is C,* £100m, since capital profits and losses need not be taken into account provided the company qualifies as an investment company.

GRADED QUESTIONS

Essay mode

1 Explain the rules of company law which regulate the making of distributions by public companies, private companies and investment companies. Indicate also the consequences which can follow the making of an unlawful distribution.

(*The Association of Chartered Certified Accountants*)

2 The summarised draft balance sheet of a company as on 31 March 200X was as follows:

	£'000
Fixed assets at cost less depreciation	
Land and buildings	1,500
Machinery	60
Fixtures	15
	1,575
Net current assets	925
	2,500
Ordinary share capital	1,600
Profit and loss account	900
	2,500

An independent professional valuation undertaken on 31 March 200X showed valuations of £1,400,000 and £50,000 for the land and buildings and machinery respectively which the directors decided to incorporate into the company's accounting records. They considered that the value of the fixtures was not less than £15,000.

Advise the directors of the maximum amount of profit *legally* available for distribution explaining fully the relevant statutory requirements.

(*The Institute of Chartered Accountants in England and Wales*)

3 Fred, George and Harry, who run a business buying and selling antiques, have been advised to form a private company to run the business. They seek your advice on the major differences between their present general partnership and the proposed company, and in particular as to the rules relating to company names, contracts entered into prior to the formation of the company and the concept of maintenance of share capital.

(*The Institute of Chartered Secretaries and Administrators*)

4 Explain the rules applicable to the determination and payment of dividends.

(*The Institute of Company Accountants*)

5 Give the facts in *Macaura* v *Northern Assurance Co Ltd* (1825) and explain the importance of its *ratio decidendi*.

(*University of Paisley*)

6 H plc wishes to change its articles of association to add a clause which states 'any director of the company may be removed from office if all other directors give notice in writing of their desire that the named director be so removed'. You are required to explain the procedure for alteration and discuss the difficulties the company might encounter in adding this new clause.

(*The Chartered Institute of Management Accountants*)

7 (*a*) Why must every company have a registered office? What information about the registered office must be published? To what extent can the registered office of the company be changed and what procedures must be observed when it is so changed?

(*b*) In the absence of a company taking advantage of alternative provisions under the Companies Act 1985, what statutory records must be kept at a company's registered office?

(*The Association of Chartered Certified Accountants*)

9

COMPANY FLOTATIONS

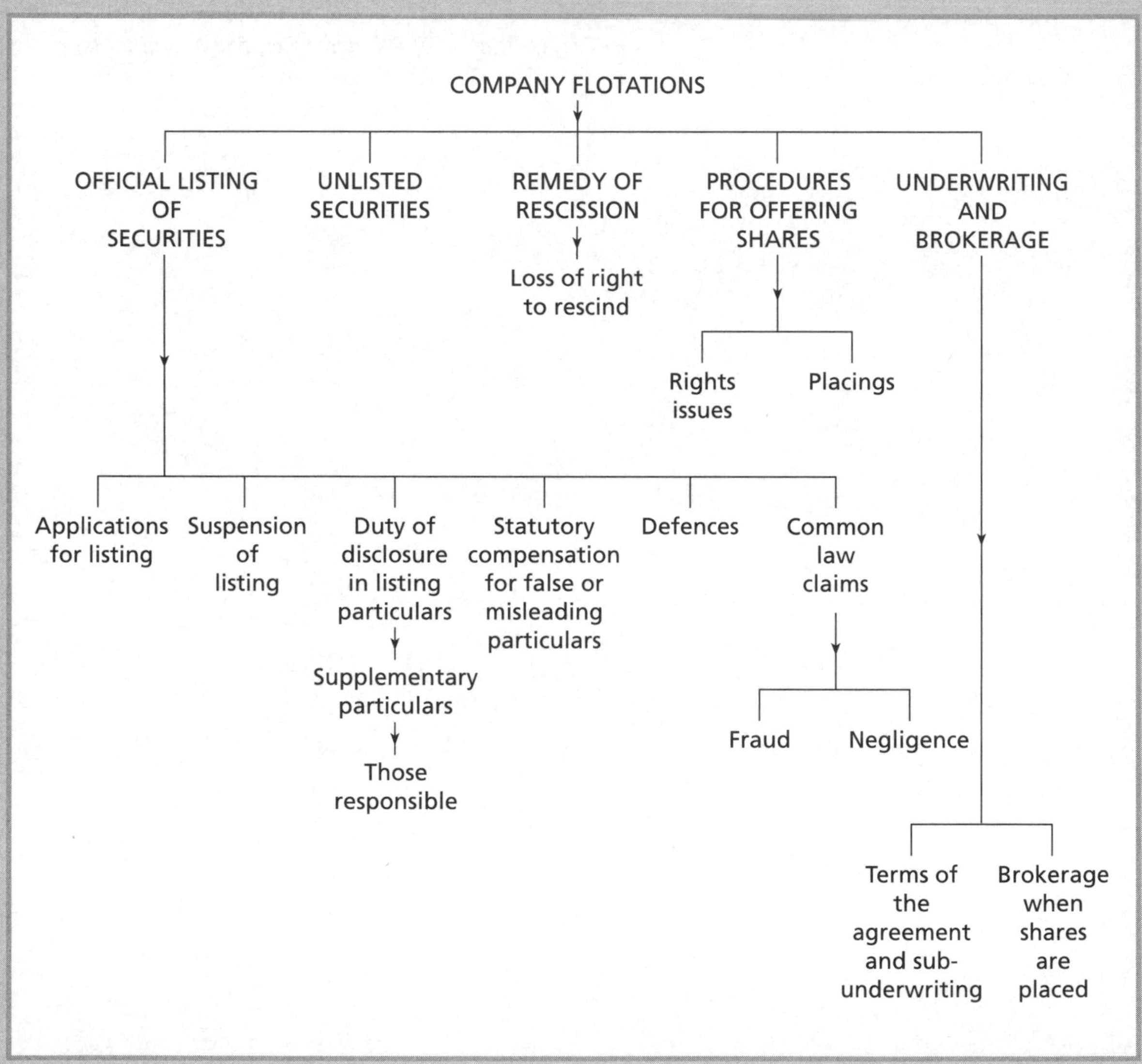

The Financial Services and Markets Act 2000 made major and important changes in the regulation of listing particulars and prospectuses as part of the new regime of investor protection. Section and other references are to the Act of 2000 (FSMA) unless otherwise indicated.

THE OFFICIAL SYSTEM FOR LISTING SECURITIES ON AN INVESTMENT EXCHANGE

Under s 72 the UK Listing Authority is part of the Markets and Exchanges division of the Financial Services Authority under the Director of Markets and Exchanges. This merger took effect in November 2003. Its main task is to determine whether securities meet the requirements to be admitted to and retained on the Official List of the relevant investment exchange, the London Stock Exchange. Permission to actually trade the securities when they have been admitted to the List is a matter for the London Stock Exchange.

Applications for listing

The application by a company must comply with the Listing Rules (The Purple Book, so called because of its colour) issued by the FSA. However, an application may be refused if granting it would be detrimental to the interests of investors (s 75). Of particular importance is that 25 per cent of the company's shares must be in public hands and not, e.g., in those of the directors. In addition the expected market value of the securities to be listed must be at least £700,000 in the case of shares and £200,000 in the case of debt securities. Securities of a lower value can be admitted to listing if the relevant authority is satisfied that adequate marketability can be expected. The Treasury, which has regulatory powers in the field of financial services, has, for example, designated private companies as being unlistable.

Decision on the application

The FSA has six months to consider an application. Where listing is granted, the applicant must be given written notice. If the FSA refuses the application, there are rejection procedures that the FSA must follow, including the right of the applicant to appeal to the Financial Services and Markets Tribunal set up under Part IX of the FSMA 2000 (ss 75 and 76).

Discontinuance and suspension of listing

The FSA has a discretion to suspend a listing for a while or discontinue it altogether where it is satisfied that there are special circumstances that preclude normal dealing in the shares, as where there appears to be insider dealing in them on the basis of inside information, e.g. a bid for the company not known to the public. The FSA will often need to act quickly and so need not use its rejection procedures, but if it refuses to cancel its decision to suspend a listing, it will have to follow rejection procedures.

In any case, the holders of the securities cannot challenge the decisions of the FSA by judicial review through the courts (see ss 77 and 78 and *R* v *International Stock Exchange of the United Kingdom and the Republic of Ireland, ex parte Else (1982) Ltd* [1993] BCC 11).

Listing particulars and other documents

Prospectuses and listing particulars must be approved by the FSA and filed with the Registrar of Companies and published and advertised before the shares can actually be listed.

General duty of disclosure in listing particulars

In addition to detailed information required by the Listing Rules and any special conditions imposed by the FSA that are beyond the scope of this text, listing particulars must contain all such information as investors and their professional advisers would reasonably require and reasonably expect to find there for the purpose of making an informed assessment of:

- the assets and liabilities, financial position, profits and losses and prospects of the issuer of the securities; and
- the rights attaching to the securities (s 80(1) and (2)).

Once a class of securities has been issued, further issues still require new listing particulars unless it is, e.g., a bonus issue.

Supplementary listing particulars

Those responsible for the original particulars are under a duty to notify any change or new matter of which they become aware (s 81). Supplementary particulars must be submitted by the issuer for approval and then filed with the Registrar of Companies and published.

Those responsible are defined by the Treasury in statutory instruments (s 79(3)). They include the issuer or sponsor, such as a merchant (or investment) bank and, of course, the directors of the issuing company.

Default sanctions

The FSA can publicly censure (name and shame) or fine anyone who was a director at the time and was knowingly concerned in the contravention of the Listing Rules. Sponsors such as investment banks may be censured but not fined (ss 89 and 91). In imposing a public reprimand or fine, the FSA must follow its disciplinary procedures (ss 89 and 92–94).

Failing to file listing particulars or a prospectus with the Registrar of Companies on or before the date on which they are published is an offence committed by the issuer and, e.g., directors, being knowingly a party, but is punishable only by a fine (s 83(3) and (4)). Offering securities to the public before a prospectus is issued is an offence punishable by up to two years' imprisonment as well as a fine (s 85(1)–(3)). Issuing advertisements in regard to a listing that have not been approved or authorised by the FSA is punishable by up to two years' imprisonment and a fine. There is a defence of reasonable belief that the advertisements had been authorised or approved (s 98(2) and (3)).

The FSA can launch an *investigation* into suspected contravention of the rules (s 97) and institute legal proceedings on behalf of investors for compensation and/or disgorgement of profits for breach of any obligation under the FSMA 2000 and can order an authorised firm to make payment without taking court action (ss 382 and 383).

So far as *investors* are concerned, there is a *separate civil action* for them against anyone responsible for misleading listing particulars and prospectuses (see below).

Prospectuses

When will a prospectus, as distinct from listing particulars, be used to make an issue of shares? A prospectus must be produced when securities are being issued to the public while the company is still seeking a listing, provided the shares are being offered for the first time.

An offer to the public includes an offer made to any section of the public including existing members or debenture holders of a company (s 84 and Sch 11, para 1). The rules applying to prospectuses are the same as those applying to listing particulars (s 86 and Sch 11, paras 2–25). A prospectus must be approved by the FSA and such approval can be given even where no listing is sought but the issuer wishes to use the prospectus to offer shares in the UK or other member states of the EU (s 287 and Sch 9).

Sponsors

The FSA requires all applicants for listing to use the services of a sponsor, e.g. a FSA-authorised investment bank, to ensure that the applicant company complies with all its obligations. The FSA may refuse an application to be an approved sponsor (s 88). Sponsors may be censured by the FSA but not fined for breaching any rules on listing imposed on them (s 89).

Compensation for false or misleading statements

Errors in listing particulars and prospectuses make any person responsible for the relevant document liable for any loss caused thereby to anyone acquiring the securities that the document covers (s 90).

Errors include:

- untrue or misleading statements in the document;
- the omission of any matter requiring inclusion by the Listing Rules, except:
  - (*a*) a case where there is no such matter; or
  - (*b*) an omission that has been authorised by the FSA.

The fact that matter required by the Listing Rules is omitted is to be taken as a statement that there is no such matter (ss 82 and 90(3)).

Statutory defences

A person responsible (see below) can avoid liability where he made such enquiries as were reasonable and reasonably believed that the statement was true and not misleading (or properly omitted) when the document was submitted for approval by the FSA, provided that when the securities were later acquired:

- he continued in that belief;
- it was not reasonably practicable to bring the correction to the attention of those likely to acquire the securities;
- he had taken all reasonable steps to bring a correction to their attention; or
- he ought reasonably to be excused because he believed it when the dealings began and now too much time has elapsed (Sch 10, para 1).

There is also a defence where, although no correction was made, the person responsible did not reasonably believe the matter was material and where he reasonably believed a correction had been published. Furthermore, no one is liable to a person who acquired the securities knowing of the error (Sch 10, paras 3, 6 and 7).

Statements by experts

If the statement is made by or on the authority of an expert, such as an accountant, valuer or engineer, and is included with his consent, other persons responsible for the document have only to prove that they reasonably believed that the expert was competent and had consented. There is no need to show that there was reasonable belief in their truth. A correction need only be to the effect that the expert was not competent or had not consented. There is no liability for statements by public officials or in official documents, provided that they have been fairly and accurately reproduced (Sch 10, paras 2, 4, 5 and 8).

The duty to report significant changes continues until dealings begin and after that there is a duty to make reasonable endeavours to issue a correction notice unless, given lapse of time, the document is no longer relevant (ss 80, 81, 90 and Sch 10).

Dealings in the after-market

Acquiring securities includes contracting to acquire them or any interest in them not merely at the time of listing but seemingly also in secondary dealings after issue called the after-market (s 90(7)).

Persons responsible

Under s 79(3) the Treasury defines by statutory instrument those responsible for listing particulars and prospectuses. Currently it is the following:

- the issuer of the securities, e.g. the sponsoring investment bank;
- the directors and proposed directors of the issuing company;
- consenting experts for their own part of the particulars or prospectus.

Common law claims

These are expressly preserved by s 90(6). The position is as follows:

- The normal contractual remedies for breach of contract or misrepresentation apply, including rescission of the contract (but see below). These remedies are against the company.
- Actions against directors, auditors or sponsors will have to be based on the tort of deceit or the tort of negligence since there is no contractual nexus with these persons.

It is not easy to prove deceit since some form of dishonesty must be shown. The burden of proof in negligence is on the claimant but is not so difficult to prove. However, the defendant will only be liable if a duty of care exists and is broken and the loss was within the contemplation of the defendant. The general rule of foreseeable loss is probably too wide for this type of case. The relevant case law appears below.

Fraud claims

Derry *v* Peek (1889) 14 App Cas 337

The Plymouth, Devonport and District Tramways Co had power under a special Act of Parliament to run trams by animal power and, with the consent of the Board of Trade, by mechanical and steam power. Derry and the other directors of the company issued a prospectus inviting the public to apply for shares in the company and stating that the company had power to run trams by steam power and claiming that considerable economies would result. The directors assumed that the Board of Trade would grant its consent as a matter of course, but in the event the Board refused permission for certain parts of the tramway, and the company went into liquidation. Peek, who had subscribed for shares under the prospectus, brought this action against the directors for fraud. *Held* – by the House of Lords – that before a statement can be regarded as fraudulent at common law, it must be shown that it was made knowing it to be untrue, or not believing it to be true, or recklessly, not caring whether it be true or false. On the facts of the case it appeared that the directors honestly believed that permission to run the trams by steam power would be granted as a matter of course by the Board of Trade, and thus they were not liable for fraud.

Comment

Fraud must be proved to the criminal standard, i.e. beyond a reasonable doubt; not to the civil standard, i.e. on a balance of probabilities. It is thus not easy to sustain an action based on fraud. Furthermore, it will be noticed from this case that the mere fact that no grounds exist for believing a false statement does not of itself constitute fraud. Dishonesty is required.

Negligence claims

As regards *claims in negligence* by those who have purchased in the market, it appears that there is no duty of care on the part of the makers of false statements in listing particulars to those who make market purchases, though there is a duty to subscribers direct from the company. This follows from the restrictive approach to liability in negligence by the House of Lords in *Caparo Industries* v *Dickman* (1990) (see Chapter 21). This restrictive approach was applied by Mervyn Davies J in the High Court in *Al-Nakib Investments (Jersey) Ltd* v *Longcroft* [1990] 3 All ER 321. The claimant company sued the directors of a company, claiming that it had bought shares in the company under an allegedly false prospectus. This it was said had induced the purchase of 400,000 shares in the newly floated company under the prospectus and directly from the company and had also induced the purchase of other shares in the company on the stock market. The judge held that since the purpose of the prospectus was to invite subscriptions direct to the company and not purchases through the stock market there was no duty of care in negligence in regard to the market purchases, though there was a duty in regard to the shares purchased directly from the company.

There has been some movement in the position at common law since *Possfund Custodian Trustee Ltd* v *Victor Derek Diamond* [1996] 2 All ER 774. Mr Justice Lightman in the High Court stated that nowadays it is at least arguable that those who are responsible for issuing listing particulars and prospectuses owe a duty of care to subscribers and those who purchase in what may be described as the after-market in reliance on the prospectus. This could place liability on the company's directors and its advisers if they are negligent.

Purchasers in the after-market following an issue with a listing are protected by s 90(7) FSMA 2000 in terms of statutory remedies. The only advantage of claiming at common law under *Possfund* is that not all of the FSMA 2000 statutory defences are available to the defendant (see page 207). The only defence at common law is a reasonable belief in the truth of the statement.

OFFERS OF UNLISTED SECURITIES

In previous editions we have discussed offers on the Unlisted Securities Market, which has been replaced by the Alternative Investment Market. These securities are not part of the FSMA 2000. The Public Offers of Securities Regulations 1995 (as amended by the Public Offers of Securities (Amendment) Regulations 1999) apply and introduce a new regime for unlisted securities. These are not considered in any detail in this text.

In any case, there are no great differences between the form and contents of a prospectus under the regulations and listing particulars under the FSMA 2000, which are covered in this chapter. In particular, the law relating to false or misleading prospectuses is covered by provisions in the regulations which again show no great differences from the rules applying to listing particulars, which are also covered in this chapter.

Obtaining a quotation on the Alternative Investment Market is less onerous since among other things there is no requirement for:

- a minimum proportion of shares in public hands; or
- a minimum aggregate share valuation at flotation.

THE REMEDY OF RESCISSION

The main remedy for loss resulting from a misstatement in listing particulars is, as we have seen, damages based either on breach of a statutory duty under the Financial Services and Markets Act 2000 and the Misrepresentation Act 1967, or at common law under the principles of liability for negligent misstatements.

The remedy of rescission involves taking the name of the shareholder off the register of members and returning money paid to the company by him. This is against the modern trend because it goes contrary to the principle of protection of the creditors' buffer which is the major purpose of the many statutory rules relating to capital maintenance.

The modern trend is to leave the shareholder's capital in the company but allow him a remedy for money compensation if the shares are less valuable because of the misstatement and against those who were responsible for the misstatement, such as directors or experts.

The cases which are illustrative of the remedy of rescission are rather old and are not referred to here. Suffice it to say that in order to obtain rescission, the shareholder must prove a material misstatement of fact not opinion (the principles in negligence cover actions for damages for opinions), and that the misstatement induced the subscription for the shares. The action can only be brought by the subscriber for the shares under the prospectus.

The right to rescind is a fragile one, being lost unless the action is brought quickly; or if the contract is affirmed, as where the shareholder has attended a meeting and voted the shares; or where the company is in liquidation or liquidation is imminent.

PROCEDURES FOR ISSUING SHARES

As we shall see in Chapter 10, shareholders in companies today have pre-emption rights, i.e. a right to have new issues offered to them first (s 89, CA 1985). The company can disapply this right by special resolution (or in the case of private companies by the articles). However, since the major shareholders of listed companies are institutions, such as insurance companies, which like to receive offers of new shares, listed companies are in general restricted to a disapplication of only up to 5 per cent of the existing shares. Therefore, *rights issues to existing shareholders* are the major way of financing listed companies in capital terms and not offers directly to the public. Nevertheless, the circular that accompanies the rights issue to shareholders is a prospectus and must be approved by the Listing Authority (an arm of the FSA). It must contain the detailed requirements set out in the Listing Rules (The Purple Book). The shares are allotted to the shareholders under provisional allotment letters and these can be traded in the market nil paid while the rights offer is open for acceptance. Thus the shareholder can sell his rights without paying the company for them. The purchaser from the shareholder will pay the market price to the shareholder and since rights issues are at a discount to the market value, but not, of course, less than par value, the shareholder will make a profit and will be left with money when he has later paid the company the discounted price. Any shares remaining, as where a shareholder does nothing, will be *placed* by the company's brokers with their clients and any not so taken up will be left with the merchant or investment bank that has underwritten the issue or any sub-underwriters. These are then the two main methods these days of raising equity finance by listed companies. A placing will be on the terms of the rights issue particulars but will not even require those, in full form at least, if the offer is to no more than 50 persons or to professional investors.

UNDERWRITING

Before a company's shares or debentures are issued, agreement is reached with an investment bank that is prepared for a commission to take up (or underwrite) the whole or a part of the shares being offered if not all of the shares are taken up.

It is usual to underwrite even when a company is sound and the shares are popular, since changes, for example in the international situation or the financial state of the country, can affect an issue adversely.

Because the payment of underwriting commission could be used as a device to issue shares at a discount, the payment of underwriting commission is controlled by s 97 of the 1985 Act, which provides:

(*a*) that the payment of such commission must be authorised by the articles;
(*b*) that the commission paid must not exceed 10 per cent of the price at which the shares are issued, or such less amount as may be authorised by the articles.

However, the requirement in (*b*) above does not apply where shares are offered under listing particulars, but the Listing Rules require that the amount of underwriting and other commissions paid shall be disclosed in the listing particulars.

If there is in existence a *share premium account*, this may be applied to pay the commission on an issue of shares or debentures (s 130(2)(b)).

As consideration for underwriting, underwriters may accept an option to buy further shares in the company at par. This will be beneficial where the issue underwritten is at a premium.

Terms of the agreement

The underwriter agrees to underwrite a stated number of shares on the terms of a specified prospectus or particulars so that an alteration in these document before issue may render the underwriting agreement void if it materially increases the risk taken by the underwriters. Thus in *Warner International & Overseas Engineering Co Ltd* v *Kilburn, Brown & Co* (1914) 84 LJ KB 365 a company altered the draft prospectus on which an underwriting agreement was based by reducing the minimum subscription to be received before allotment from £15,000 to £100 and by stating also that, instead of buying a business it was to acquire by one payment from the proceeds of the issue, it would buy the business by instalments out of future issues. It was held by the Court of Appeal that the underwriters were released from their contract.

The underwriter agrees to take up the balance of shares (if any) not taken up in the issue, and authorises a director or other agent of the company to apply for the shares on the underwriter's behalf. This means that the company can ensure the allotment of the shares to the underwriter, and thus have an action for the full price, and not merely an action for damages if the underwriter merely refuses to apply for them. The authority to apply is expressed to be irrevocable.

Finally, the company agrees to pay a certain percentage of the nominal value of the underwritten shares as commission. The amount of the commission is a matter between the parties and the UKLA, but it must be in line with the risk and not excessive in terms of it if listing is to be obtained.

The liability of the underwriter ends when persons subscribe for the shares, and he cannot be called on to pay if allottees do not meet their liabilities.

Sub-underwriting

Underwriters may enter into sub-underwriting contracts to relieve themselves of the whole or part of their liability. The underwriter pays a commission to the sub-underwriters.

BROKERAGE

This is a commission paid over to a bank, stockbroker, or issuing house for placing shares. The difference between brokerage and underwriting is that the broker does not agree to take the shares himself, but merely agrees to try to find purchasers. The payment of brokerage could also lead to an issue of shares at a discount and yet it is not controlled by the Act, s 98(3) providing that s 97 shall not affect the power of any company to pay brokerage. However, it can only be paid to a bank, market maker, or issuing house and the rate must be reasonable, though the precise rate is a matter for negotiation according to the degree of risk (*Metropolitan Coal Consumers' Association* v *Scrimgeour* [1895] 2 QB 604).

REFORM

The Prospectus Directive: EU developments

This background note is included mainly because of the possible effect of the EU Prospectus Directive on the position of the AIM. As already noted this is a market that might prove attractive to the smaller plc wishing to trade its shares on a public market perhaps on conversion from a private company.

The Prospectus Directive came into force on 31 December 2003. Member states are required to implement the new regime by 1 July 2005.

The main principle

This is that if an issuer is making an offer of securities to the public or its securities are being admitted to trading on a regulated market in the EU it must publish a prospectus and get it approved by the competent authority in what is called its 'home member state'. When the prospectus has been approved in that state it may then be used to offer shares or gain admission to regulated markets in all EU member states without the issuer having to publish any further information or having to get further approval for the document in those member states. The Directive sets out the procedure for identifying an issuer's home member state and states when a prospectus is required and what it should contain. The Directive relates only to the prospectus and does not govern admission criteria and continuing obligations. The UK and other member states will be able to impose additional obligations in those areas but cannot impose any additional disclosure requirements so far as the prospectus is concerned.

Home member state for EU issuers

The home member state for an EU issuer will be the member state in which it has its registered office.

Example

A German company decides to list its shares on the London Stock Exchange. It is not offering shares in Germany or seeking admission of the shares to a regulated market in Germany. Its home member state will be Germany and so the German competent authority will approve the prospectus. The competent authority in England will then have to accept that prospectus as approved and will not be able to require the issuer to publish any additional information. It will have discretion to assess whether the issuer satisfies any eligibility criteria for admission to listing or trading set by it.

Effect on AIM

The Directive covers secondary markets such as AIM and in fact one of the European Commission's objects is to catch start-up and high-tech companies and apply more onerous requirements to them. This could affect the AIM and some have suggested it might make it redundant. **However the London Stock Exchange made the AIM an unregulated market from 12 October 2004 in order to avoid the application of the Directive.**

Non-EU issuers

These issuers are affected now by the Prospectus Directive. In regard to non-EU issuers whose securities are already admitted to trading on an EU regulated market the issuer can choose as its home member state the member state where its securities are first offered to the public or where its securities are first admitted to trading in the EU after the Directive comes into force, i.e. after 31 December 2003. The issuer must notify its decision to the competent authority of its chosen member state by 31 December 2005.

For non-EU issuers whose securities are not already admitted to a regulated market in the EU the home member state will be the member state where the securities are offered to the public or admitted to trading in the EU for the first time (this is at the choice of the issuer whether or not the issuer has to publish a prospectus) after the date of entry into force of the Directive, i.e. 31 December 2003.

FSA Listing Rules Review

The FSA is reviewing the UK Listing Rules which will result in an overhaul of the listing regime on the London Stock Exchange. The review is to some extent driven by the Prospectus Directive.

Consultation on the draft rules was expected in the autumn of 2004 with the final rules coming into force in 2005 to coincide with the implementation of the EU Prospectus Directive.

GRADED QUESTIONS

Essay mode

1 'The Financial Services and Markets Act 2000 has provided a more rational and fair procedure to compensate investors who are misled by a misrepresentation in a prospectus (or listing particulars) on an issue of shares by a company. Nevertheless, the common law remedies remain of importance.'

Discuss.

(The Institute of Chartered Secretaries and Administrators)

2 Explain 'rescission' and the loss of the right to rescind in respect of prospectuses.

(The Institute of Company Accountants)

3 Harriet subscribed for shares in Overseas plc on the basis of the prospectus which showed that for the previous five years the company had earned substantial and increasing profits. Shortly after allotment she sold half her shares to Georgina at a large profit.

The information in the prospectus was correct but it omitted to mention that much of the business was in the Middle East and, because of various wars, the profits had been materially reduced. The shares are now worth only half the price paid by Harriet.

Compare and contrast the remedies available to Harriet and Georgina.

(*The Institute of Company Accountants*)

4 (*a*) 'The law treats a registered company as a separate legal person from its members. To this general rule there are several exceptions.'

Examine the statement, giving two examples of circumstances in which the court will look at the reality behind the legal facade.

(*b*) Dairy Products Limited employed Roundsman to distribute their products in and around Saltash. A clause in the contract of employment provided that in the event of his leaving the employment he would not solicit the company's customers for a period of three years. Roundsman assiduously collected the names and made a list of all their customers, left his employment after three months and formed a company, Farm Produce Limited, which competed with Dairy Products. All the shares in Farm Produce were allotted to Mrs Roundsman and her father, both of whom began soliciting the customers of Dairy Products with the help of the list produced by Roundsman.

Advise Dairy Products Ltd.

(*University of Plymouth*)

5 J is the managing director of Z plc, a listed company. She has recently seen the end of year accounts for Z plc which are to be published in three weeks' time. These accounts show the company to have substantial liquid assets and J believes that Z plc is likely to attract takeover bidders when the accounts are published. J has decided that she should build up her own personal shareholding in Z plc and has asked you, the company's finance director, whether she can borrow £30,000 from the company and use it to purchase more equity shares in the company.

You are required to advise J.

(*The Chartered Institute of Management Accountants*)

Objective mode

Four alternative answers are given. Select ONE only. Circle the answer which you consider to be correct. Check your answers by referring back to the information given in the chapter and against the answers at the back of the book.

1 A public company wishes to have its shares listed on the London Stock Exchange. What percentage of its shares must be in the ownership of the public?

A 10 per cent.
B 20 per cent.
C 25 per cent.
D 30 per cent.

2 Fylde plc has issued listing particulars containing a material misrepresentation in a report by an accountant who did not consent to the inclusion of the report in the form in which it was included. Fred purchased shares on the stock market from Joe who was an original subscriber under the listing particulars. Fred is now suing the directors of Fylde plc for monetary compensation.

A Fred's action against the directors will succeed because the directors are liable for all statements in listing particulars without any defence.
B Fred's action against the directors will fail because the directors have a defence under the Financial Services and Markets Act 2000.
C Fred's action against the directors will succeed because the accountant did not consent to the inclusion of his report.
D Fred's action will fail because he was not an original subscriber.

3 Tay plc has issued listing particulars containing a material misrepresentation. Relying on the particulars, Alf, Bert and Clare subscribed for shares. Alf sold half of his shares immediately. Bert went to an extraordinary general meeting of Tay and voted on a number of matters. Who can rescind the contract to take the shares?

A Clare.
B Clare and Bert.
C Bert.
D Alf and Bert.

4 Which of the following expressions best describes the relationship of company promoter to the company?

A Fiduciary.
B Equitable.
C Agent to a principal.
D Commercial.

5 Prior to the incorporation of Ouse Ltd, Mark, its promoter, made a contract on behalf of the company. Who will be liable if the contract is breached?

A Mark.
B Ouse Ltd.
C The shareholders of Ouse Ltd.
D The directors of Ouse Ltd.

6 Alf and Bert formed a company called Tyne Ltd. They became the sole directors and took up 50 per cent of the shares, the other shares being allotted to 15 other people. Alf and Bert sold their business to Tyne Ltd for £130,000, although it was valued at £120,000. How should the profit be dealt with?

A Alf and Bert may keep it.
B Alf and Bert may keep it if they disclose it to the board of directors and obtain the consent of the board.
C Alf and Bert may keep it if they disclose it to all the other shareholders and obtain their consent.
D Alf and Bert cannot keep it in any circumstances.

Answers to questions set in objective mode appear on p 576.

10

SHARES – GENERALLY

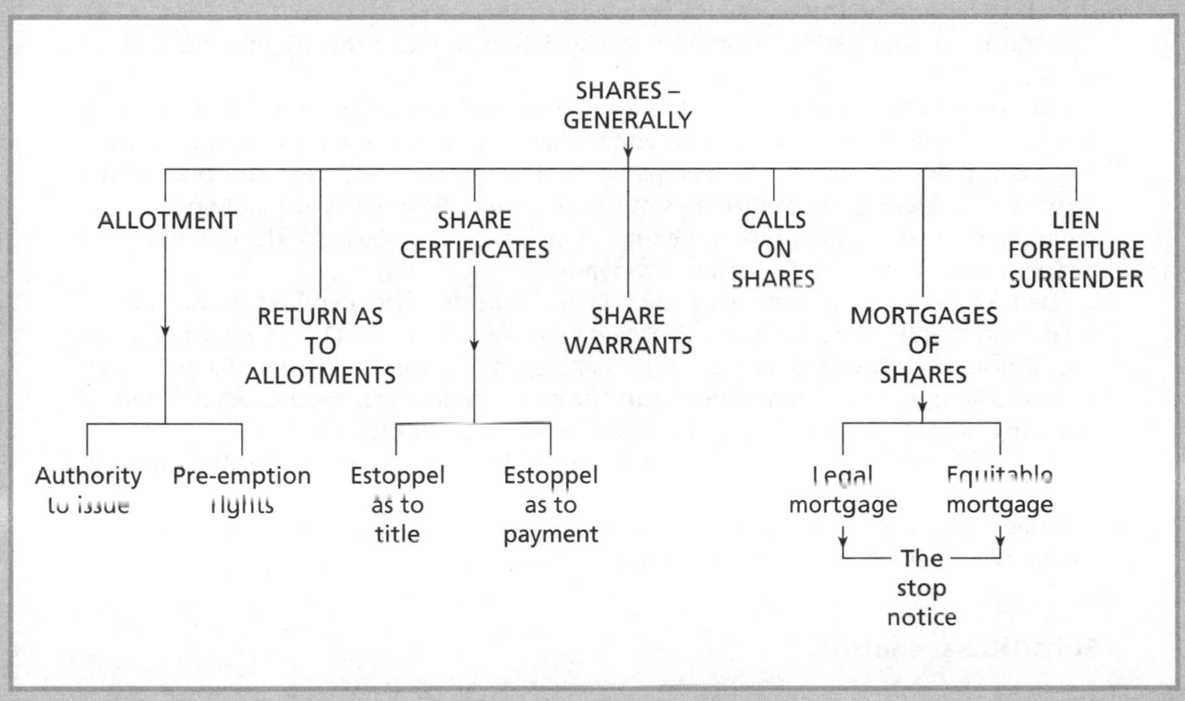

A share may be defined as a measure of the interest of the member in the company. It is clear from the judgment of Farwell J in *Borland's Trustee* v *Steel Brothers & Co Ltd* [1901] 1 Ch 279 at p 288 that this interest consists in the rights and duties given and imposed by the constitution of the company and also by company legislation. As Mr Justice Farwell said: 'A share is the interest of a shareholder in the company measured by a sum of money, for the purpose of liability in the first place, and of interest in the second, but also consisting of a series of mutual covenants entered into by all the shareholders *inter se* in accordance with s 16 of the Companies Act 1862 (now s 14). The contract contained in the articles of association is one of the original incidents of the share.'

Thus under the Companies Act 1985 shareholders have a right to requisition meetings and to put resolutions on the agenda. They also have the right to inspect certain records and documents which a company is obliged to keep and the right to appoint a proxy to represent them at meetings of the company. Financially it represents what a member must pay or has paid for the share, and it provides a basis for the calculation of distributions of profits by means of dividends.

The assets of the company are owned *by the company*. The members do not have a legal or equitable interest in them (*Macaura* v *Northern Assurance* (1925), see Chapter 1), and although share capital is in a sense a liability, it is not in the nature of a debt owed by the company, and on a winding-up the shareholders will receive what is left, if anything, after payment of the company's debts and liabilities.

Shares are personal estate and not real estate. They are, therefore, in the same category as money or goods. The section removes doubts raised by early cases as to whether shares in companies formed mainly to hold and manage land were not themselves of the legal nature of realty.

Subscribers' contract

Where shares or debentures are offered to existing members, which is obligatory unless waived by special resolution of the members in plcs, the letter of rights or *provisional letter of allotment* is an offer, and no notification of acceptance is required. Acceptance is by conduct, as where the member pays an instalment of the purchase price or renounces the allotment to another person, as where he sells his rights (*Re New Eberhardt Co ex parte Menzies* (1889) 43 Ch D 118). Where there is a *placing* of any balance not taken up, the company's brokers offer the shares to their clients who can accept the offer.

ALLOTMENT

Authority to issue

Before proceeding to the mechanics of allotment, it is necessary to note that under s 80 directors of public and private companies must have the authority of the members by ordinary resolution in general meeting, or written resolution or of the articles, before they exercise a power of allotment of shares or grant rights to subscribe for or convert securities into shares. The fact that the articles give the directors power to allot the company's shares, while vital to their power to do so, is not enough without the member approval referred to above.

The authority of the members may be given each time there is an allotment or for up to five years in advance and the ordinary (or written) resolution giving the authority is registrable at the Companies Registry within 15 days.

The authority, however given, must state the number of shares authorised, e.g. the remainder of the company's unissued share capital, and be expressed to expire not more than five years after it was granted unless revoked or varied before then. When such an authority expires, it may be renewed for a further period not exceeding five years.

Under provisions set out in s 80A which are deregulatory, i.e. designed to free smaller organisations from the regulations and formalities of company law, private companies may elect by an elective resolution (see Chapter 19) that the authority given to directors to allot shares can be given for an indefinite period or for a fixed period of longer than five years. The fixed period is renewable, and further renewable, by the company in general meeting. The authority may also be varied or revoked by the company in general meeting.

No authority is needed to allot shares to a person who is exercising an option previously approved or existing, or a conversion right, i.e. from loan stock to shares previously approved or existing, nor is it required for the allotment of shares made by the directors after the authority has expired where it was agreed during the currency of the authority that the allotment would be made and might involve the actual issue of the shares after the period of authority had expired.

Allotments made in contravention of the above provisions will not be invalid but the directors are liable to prosecution. Furthermore, the provisions do not apply to shares taken by subscribers to the memorandum or to shares allotted as part of an employees' share scheme. If members refuse to authorise directors to allot shares, the power of allotment, except in relation to employees' shares, lies in the members themselves by ordinary resolution in general meeting.

Before leaving the topic of authority to issue shares, it is worth noting that, because of the fiduciary duties which the directors owe the company, they must use the power of allotment for the 'proper purpose', which means to raise capital for the company and not, e.g., to put off a takeover bid to keep themselves in control of the company (see further Chapter 17).

Pre-emption rights

As regards ordinary (or equity) shareholders, s 89 gives a right of pre-emption. This is designed to ensure that the rights of ordinary shareholders are not necessarily affected by the issue of further ordinary shares to others, which has never been regarded as a variation of rights. The section gives pre-emption rights to all equity shareholders in both public and private companies. Each ordinary shareholder must be offered a part of the issue pro rata to his existing holding. The offer must be in writing and delivered to the shareholders personally or by post. Equity shares may be offered to outsiders if they have not been taken up by existing shareholders within the offer period, which must be at least 21 days.

If the section is not complied with, the company and any officer knowingly in default is liable under s 92 to compensate shareholders for their loss. Claims by shareholders must be brought within two years of the filing of the return of allotments under which the section was contravened.

A private, but not a public, company may disapply pre-emption rights *without a time limit* by a provision in the memorandum or articles stating this, or by having a provision in the memorandum or articles about pre-emption rights which is inconsistent with the statutory rules (s 91). The pre-emption right is disapplied until such time, if any, as the memorandum or articles, as the case may be, are amended to remove the disapplication provision.

Both public and private companies may under s 95 disapply pre-emption rights by a provision in the articles or by a special (or written if a private company) resolution of the members. *In either event, the maximum period for disapplication is five years or such shorter period as the articles or special resolution may state.*

Even in a private company which has given the directors a power of allotment for an indefinite period, the members must still approve the disapplication of pre-emption rights though the written resolution procedure can be used to do this. This assumes that the private company has not opted out of the pre-emption provisions altogether (see above).

It should also be noted that institutional shareholders, such as insurance companies and pension funds, attach great importance to the fact that they get additional shares on a fresh issue under the pre-emption provisions. Accordingly the Pre-emption Group (comprising the Investment Committees of the Association of British Insurers and the National Association of Pension Funds, the London Stock Exchange and the Association of Corporate Treasurers) requires s 89 disapplications to be limited to 5 per cent of the equity capital in issue at the date of the latest audited accounts but imposes a cumulative limit of 7.5 per cent in any three-year rolling period. In addition, listed companies have to comply with the London Stock Exchange Listing Rules. For example, until September 1997 the London Stock Exchange required that s 89 disapplications should be for a fixed period not exceeding 15 months. This was amended so that the disapplication can be effective for up to a maximum of five years (i.e. the same period as the authority in s 80 to which the disapplication relates) although it is likely that listed companies will wish to continue to make annual disapplications.

The pre-emption provisions are triggered by an issue of equity shares for *cash*. Thus pre-emption rights would not apply, e.g., to an issue of preference shares for cash or to the issue of equity shares for a non-cash consideration, as in a merger of two companies where the shares in the company to be acquired are exchanged for shares in the acquiring company and the company to be acquired is then wound up following the transfer of its assets to the acquiring company. In addition, pre-emption rights do not apply where shares are allotted under an employees' scheme. Thus, if the company allots shares to employees under an employees' scheme, it is not obliged to make an offer of shares to the ordinary shareholders who are not employees. However, employees in a share scheme are entitled to participate in the pre-emption rights where an offer of equity shares is made to shareholders generally.

Thus if a company, A, has an authorised and issued share capital of £100,000 divided into 100,000 ordinary shares of £1 each and 50,000 of those shares are held under an employees' share scheme, then on an increase of capital and a proposal to issue 50,000 additional ordinary shares, each member will be entitled to an offer to subscribe for one share for every two ordinary shares which he currently holds.

The directors must recommend the disapplication of pre-emption rights, and no special or written resolution to allow it or a special or written resolution to renew a period of disapplication previously approved may be proposed, unless with the notice of the meeting the directors have circulated a written statement giving their reasons for recommending disapplication and stating the amount which will be paid when the equity shares which are the subject of the disapplication are allotted and giving the directors' justification of that price. There are penalties for the inclusion of misleading matter in this statement.

Where the unanimous written resolution procedure is used by a private company, the statement by the directors must be supplied to each member at or before the time at which the resolution is given to him for signature.

A shareholder may waive his pre-emption rights, in which case he will not be entitled to receive shares under a pre-emptive offer. In addition, shares which are offered on a pre-emptive basis may be allotted to a person in favour of whom the shareholder entitled to the offer has renounced his rights.

The Registrar must under s 711 publish a notice in the *London Gazette* of the receipt by him of a resolution passed in connection with disapplication of pre-emption rights.

It will be seen from what is said above that even when the directors have been given authority to issue shares they must still observe the pre-emption provisions outlined above.

Public companies: the 25 per cent rule

It should also be noted that shares in a public company cannot be allotted until 25 per cent of the nominal value and 100 per cent of any premium have been received (in cash or otherwise) by the company, and also that the Companies Act 1985 contains restrictions upon the allotment of shares for a non-cash consideration (see Chapter 12).

An allottee who takes shares in a public company which are not paid up as required is liable to pay the company the balance up to the minimum the company should have received plus interest, which is at present 5 per cent per annum.

Allotment is usually made by the directors at a properly constituted board meeting, or by a committee of the board where the directors have power to delegate their powers to such a committee. The directors' powers of allotment are usually given by the articles and, even where the allotment is irregular because of some defect in the constitution of the board making it, the allotment may nevertheless be made binding on the company:

(*a*) under a clause in the articles similar to *Reg* 92 of *Table A* (see Chapter 5); or
(*b*) by reason of subsequent ratification by a properly constituted board (*Re Portuguese Consolidated Copper Mines Ltd* (1889) 42 Ch D 160); or
(*c*) under s 35A (see Chapter 5) or s 285 (see Chapter 5) or under the rule in *Royal British Bank* v *Turquand*, 1856 even without ratification.

As we have seen, allotment is effected by sending a provisional letter of allotment to the allottee. The letter of allotment gives instructions for payment of instalments and registration and, in addition, often contains provisions under which the allottee may *renounce the whole* of the allotment in favour of another by signing the form of renunciation provided, or *renounce it partially* by 'splitting' the allotment with another.

These renunciations become known to the company or issuing house when the relevant letters of allotment are returned.

RETURN AS TO ALLOTMENTS

Under s 88, whenever a company makes an allotment of its shares, it must within one month of allotment deliver to the Registrar of Companies a *return of the allotments* stating the number and nominal value of the shares comprised in the allotment, the names and addresses of the allottees, and the amount paid up and unpaid on each share, whether on account of the nominal value of the share or by way of premium.

Where shares have been allotted as fully or partly paid up otherwise than in cash, as where, for example, the shares form the whole or part of the purchase price on a sale of land to the company, the consideration must be specified in the return, and if the contract is written, it must be sent with the return. If the contract is not written, a written memorandum of its terms must be made out and filed with the Registrar. These provisions are, of course, strengthened for public companies by s 103 (requirement to file with return of allotment an expert's report on the value of non-cash consideration) (see Chapter 12).

Compliance with these requirements is enforced by a substantial fine on every director, manager, secretary or other officer of the company who is a party to the default. The court may grant relief where the omission to deliver any document within the time prescribed is accidental or due to inadvertence or it is just and equitable to grant relief, and may make an order extending the time for the delivery of the document for such period as the court thinks proper.

Return of allotments and Companies House

For the avoidance of doubt Companies House announced in the spring of 2004 that it is not necessary to file a return of allotments in respect of subscriber shares following incorporation. This view is based on legal advice that under s 22(1) of the CA 1985 shares taken by those who subscribe the company's memorandum and articles are automatically allotted on incorporation, at which point the subscribers acquire the unconditional right to be entered in the register of members. Section 738(1) of CA 1985 defines allotment as taking place at the point at which that right is acquired. The subscribers will be entered on the register of members on incorporation so that the company cannot allot the shares of the subscribers: s 22(1) does the job for it. Companies House further states that since *Reg* 2 of the Stamp Duty and Stamp Duty Land Tax (Consequential Amendments of Enactments) Regulations 2003 (SI 2003/2868) removes the requirement in s 88(2) and (3) CA 1985 to 'stamp' a contract or particulars that a company has to deliver to Companies House when it allots shares either fully or partly paid otherwise than in cash Companies House will accept for registration contracts or particulars dated on or after 1 December 2003 without stamping by the Inland Revenue Stamp Office.

Reform

Companies House has consulted on ways to simplify or remove the requirements relating to returns as to allotments issued for cash by either:

- simplifying the requirement so that only the overall amount of any allotment need be notified to Companies House within one month of the allotment. The details of new allottees would then be included in the list of members on the next annual return; or
- abolishing completely the requirement under s 88(2) to deliver a return of allotments.

It is not proposed to change the requirements relating to allotments for a non-cash consideration. No changes in law have yet been made.

SHARE CERTIFICATES

Before reading the rest of this section, it should be borne in mind that under the Uncertificated Securities Regulations 2001 a company which has a listing may amend its articles so that they allow the holding of its shares in uncertificated form, transfer being by electronic link between the operator of a new transfer system called Crest and the company's Registrar. Obviously the share certificate provisions will not apply to that part of the company's register. However, from the point of view of shareholders, holding shares through the Crest system is voluntary and they may if they wish retain their shares in certificated form, remaining on a separate part of the register.

In general terms and in the case of listed companies that are part of the Crest system the shareholder is not entitled to a share certificate unless opted out but in other cases every company must, under the penalty of a fine for each day of the default, within two months after allotment or transfer of shares or debentures have ready for delivery a certificate, unless in the case of an issue of shares the terms of the issue otherwise provide (s 185). The terms of issue usually do exclude the section because companies rarely issue a share certificate until the shares are fully paid which normally takes at least six months. Until the issue of a certificate, the subscriber has a letter of allotment which is renounceable or transferable.

The form of the certificate is governed by the articles which may provide for the issue of share certificates under seal, though a seal is not required by law. The certificate will also specify the shares to which it relates and the amount paid up on the shares. It will be signed by at least one director and the secretary. If the current *Table A* applies, every certificate must be under the seal of the company (or under the official seal kept by the company by virtue of s 40 specially for use on securities, if it has a seal).

Shares must be distinguished by an appropriate number, but if all the shares of the company are fully paid, or all the shares in a particular class are fully paid and rank *pari passu* in all respects, the distinguishing numbers can be dispensed with.

A share certificate under the common seal of the company or the seal kept (if any) by virtue of s 40 specifying any shares held by any member is prima facie, but not conclusive, evidence of the title of the member to the shares.

The articles usually empower the directors to renew share certificates which have been lost or destroyed. A small fee is charged, but the shareholder must give the company an indemnity in case any liability should fall upon it by reason of the possibility of two share certificates in respect of the same holding being in existence. Where the certificate is defaced or worn out, delivery of the old certificate to the company is required.

The doctrine of estoppel

By reason of the doctrine of *estoppel* a company may be unable in certain circumstances to deny the truth of the particulars in the certificate even though they are incorrect. Once again, it will be appreciated that the law relating to estoppel presupposes the existence of a share certificate. It will be relevant mainly in private companies whose shares will not be transferred through the Crest system. It will also be relevant to those members of public companies using Crest who have opted for a share certificate which will be transferred through the company itself by sending the certificate to the company together with an instrument of transfer.

(*a*) *Estoppel as to title*. The mere fact that at some time the company has issued to X a share certificate stating that he is the holder of, say, 100 shares does not prevent the company from denying that X is the holder at some future date. The certificate is only prima facie evidence that X was entitled to the shares *at the date of issue of the certificate*.

However, if the company recognises the validity of X's title by registering or certifying a transfer to Y on the basis of the certificate, the company is estopped from denying Y's title, because it has held out to Y that X has a title.

Where the transfer is a forgery, the original transferee under it will not normally obtain a good title and the company will not normally be estopped from denying his title even if it has issued a share certificate to him. But a purchaser from the original transferee, though not getting a good title, can hold the company estopped by the certificate issued to him because he did not take it under a forged transfer, the signature of the apparent owner being on the transfer form.

Thus if X owns some shares in a company and his clerk forges X's signature on a form of transfer and sells the shares to Y, then Y will not get a good title to the shares and the company will not be estopped by the certificate issued to him, because at this stage the share certificate is one which the company issued to the true owner, X, and the company has played no part in the deception. If, however, Y transfers the shares to Z before the forgery is discovered, and Z is issued with a share certificate, then the company will be estopped as against Z, and will have to pay him the value of the shares as damages if he chooses to sue the company rather than Y. This is because the company issued a share certificate to Y who was not the owner, thereby facilitating the deception. Nevertheless, Z will not become a member by virtue of estoppel and X's name must be restored to the register.

(*b*) *Estoppel as to payment*. In similar circumstances to those outlined above, the company may be estopped from denying that the shares are fully paid, or paid up to the extent stated on the certificate, even though the effect of this is that the shares are issued at a discount. However, the directors who issue the certificate are liable to the company for the unpaid share capital which cannot now be recovered (*Hirsche* v *Sims* [1894] AC 654). This estoppel does not apply to a person such as an original allottee under a prospectus who knows how much he has paid up on the shares.

The doctrine of *estoppel* does not operate if the certificate itself is a forgery and in addition is issued by a person without apparent authority (*Ruben* v *Great Fingall Consolidated*, 1906, see Chapter 5).

The estoppel does not seem to be defeated by the fact that the entries in the register of members show who the true owner is even though the register is accessible to the public for inspection, but there can certainly be no estoppel in favour of a person who actually knows the true facts.

Finally, there can, in general, be no claim on an estoppel without some detriment to the person making the claim. The detriment usually arises because the claimant has bought the shares or lent money on a mortgage of them. It is not normally available to a person who has received the shares as a gift.

SHARE WARRANTS (OR BEARER SHARES)

Public and also private companies may, if authorised by their articles, issue in respect of fully-paid shares a share warrant under the common seal stating that the bearer of the warrant is entitled to the shares specified in it. *Table A* does not authorise the issue of share warrants. Although share warrants could be issued under a prospectus, it has been the case in the past that they have been exchanged for registered shares and the procedures described below relate to that situation. When a share warrant is issued the company must strike out of the register of members the name of the holder of the shares and make the following entries in the register:

(*a*) the fact of the issue of the warrant;
(*b*) a statement of the shares included in the warrant, distinguishing each share by its number, if the shares had numbers; and
(*c*) the date of issue of the warrant.

The bearer of the warrant is, unless the articles provide to the contrary, entitled to be registered as a member on surrender of the warrant.

Difficulties arise as to the rights of holders of warrants because, although they are always shareholders, they are not members, since they are not entered on the register of members, though the bearer of a share warrant may, if the articles so provide, be *deemed* to be a member of the company either to the full extent or for any purpose defined in the articles. Their rights are in fact governed by the articles, but *dividends* are usually obtained by handing over to the company coupons which are detachable from the warrant, the payment of dividend being advertised.

The articles may deprive the holders of share warrants of their *voting rights*, but usually they are given the right to vote if they deposit their warrants with the company, or, if the warrant is deposited at a bank, on production of a certificate from the bank. The holding of share warrants is not sufficient to satisfy a director's share qualification.

A share warrant operates as an *estoppel* that the holder has a title now, and not that he once did when the warrant was issued. Hence, *the company must recognise the holder* unless the warrant is a forgery issued by a person without apparent authority.

A share warrant is also *negotiable*, so that a title to it passes free from defects in the title of previous holders on mere delivery (*Webb, Hale & Co* v *Alexandria Water Co* (1905) 93 LT 339).

The main advantages of share warrants are anonymity, i.e. no one can find out from the company's public records who the owner of a warrant is, and the ease of transfer. Warrants are merely handed to the purchaser avoiding the formality and expense involved in transferring a registered share. The main disadvantage is that company law leaves it entirely to the company as to how it communicates with its warrant holders. Advertisements, e.g. of meetings, may not always be seen by warrant holders who may therefore not attend and vote.

CALLS

It is usual today for a company to specify in the terms of issue that money due on the shares is payable by stated instalments. These are not really calls but are contractual instalments which the member is bound to pay on the dates mentioned by virtue of taking an allotment of the shares. Where the method of instalments is used, the company cannot ask for the money sooner by relying on a general power to make calls under the articles.

A *call proper is* made in a situation where the company did not lay down a date for payment in the terms of issue of the shares. Since shares are generally fully paid up now within a short time after allotment under a fixed instalment arrangement, calls are not common today.

The articles usually give the directors power to make calls subject to certain restrictions, e.g. *Table A* provides that subject to the terms of allotment, the directors may make calls upon the members in respect of any moneys unpaid on their shares (whether in respect of nominal value or premium) and each member shall (subject to receiving at least 14 days' notice specifying when and where payment is to be made) pay to the company as required by the notice the amount called on his shares. A call may be required to be paid by instalments.

A call may, before receipt by the company of any sum due thereunder, be revoked in whole or part and payment of a call may be postponed in whole or part. A person under whom a call is made shall remain liable for calls made upon him notwithstanding the subsequent transfer of the shares in respect of which the call was made. *Table A* must be complied with, otherwise there can be no action against the shareholders in respect of the call.

Table A also provides that a call shall be deemed to have been made at the time when the resolution of the directors authorising the call was passed. Joint holders of a share are jointly and severally liable to pay all calls in respect thereof.

If the articles do not give the directors power to make calls, then the company may make them by ordinary resolution in general meeting. The resolution of the board or the members must state the amount of the call and the *date* on which it is payable (*Re Cawley & Co* (1889) 42 Ch D 209). It is essential that calls be made equally on all the shareholders of the same class unless the terms of issue and the company's articles otherwise provide. *Table A* authorises such an arrangement, but that does not entitle directors to make calls on all shareholders except themselves (*Alexander* v *Automatic Telephone Co* [1900] 2 Ch 56) unless the other shareholders *know* and *approve* of the arrangement.

An irregularity in the making of the call may make the call invalid. Any major irregularity in procedure, as where there is no quorum at the meeting, or where the directors are not properly appointed, will have that effect, though s 285 may validate the call since it provides that the acts of a director or manager shall be valid notwithstanding any defect which may afterwards be discovered in his appointment or qualification. Minor irregularities will not invalidate a call (*Shackleford, Ford & Co* v *Dangerfield* (1868) LR 3 CP 407).

All money payable by any member to the company under the memorandum or the articles is in the nature of a *specialty debt*. This allows the company to sue for unpaid calls up to 12 years after the date upon which payment became due (Limitation Act 1980, s 8). The directors may charge interest on calls unpaid, and *Table A* provides that if a call remains unpaid after it has become due and payable, the person from whom it is due and payable shall pay interest on the amount unpaid from the day it became due and payable until it is paid at the rate fixed by the terms of allotment of the share or in the notice of the call or, if no rate is fixed, at the appropriate rate (as defined by the Companies Act and currently 5 per cent) but the directors may waive payment of the interest wholly or in part.

The company may also accept payment in advance of calls if the articles so provide. Such payments are loans, and interest is usually paid on them.

Default in payment gives the company a lien over the shares for the amount unpaid. *Table A, Regs* 20–22 provide for forfeiture of shares for non-payment of a call or instalment.

MORTGAGES OF SHARES

Mortgages of shares may be either legal or equitable.

Legal mortgages

In order that there shall be a legal mortgage, the mortgagee or lender must be entered on the register of members. To achieve this, the shares which are being used as a security must be transferred to him or his nominee. A separate agreement will set out the terms of the loan, and will also contain an undertaking by the lender to retransfer the shares to the mortgagor when the loan and interest are repaid. A legal mortgage gives the lender maximum security.

With a legal mortgage the lender (mortgagee) or his nominee is on the register and therefore appears to the outside world to be the absolute owner whereas he has a duty to transfer to the borrower on the repayment of the loan. Thus the borrower (mortgagor) should serve a 'stop notice' (see below) upon the company to prevent an unauthorised sale of the shares by the lender.

During the period that the loan is outstanding the lender will be entitled to all of the rights attaching to the shares, e.g. dividends. Because he is registered he will receive all communications from the company and is thus in a better position to reach decisions affecting the value of his security, e.g. whether to subscribe for a rights issue or cast his vote against or in favour of such important issues as reorganisation or takeover bids.

Equitable mortgages

Such a mortgage is more usual than a legal mortgage, particularly in the case of a short-term loan and in the case of shares in a private company where pre-emption provisions in the articles (see Chapter 11) may prevent the registration of the lender, and may be achieved in the following ways:

(a) Mere deposit of the share certificate with the lender. This is sufficient to create an equitable mortgage, given that the intention to do so is present, but if the lender wishes to enforce his security, he must ask the court for an *order for sale*, and having sold the shares under the order, he must account to the borrower for the balance if the proceeds exceed the amount of the loan. Alternatively, the lender can apply for an *order of foreclosure* which vests the ownership of the shares in him, and if such an order is made, the lender is not obliged to account to the borrower for any excess. For this reason foreclosure is difficult to obtain.

(b) Deposit of share certificate plus a blank transfer. Where the borrower deposits the share certificate along with a transfer form, signed by him but with the transferee's name left blank, the seller has an implied authority to sell the shares by completing the transfer in favour of a purchaser, or in favour of himself if he so wishes, and in such a case there is no need to go to the court. Once again, a separate agreement will set out the terms of the loan, and provide for the delivery of the certificate and blank transfer on repayment of the loan plus interest.

The methods of equitable mortgage outlined above do not necessarily ensure the priority of the lender as against other persons with whom the borrower may deal in respect of the shares. Where the borrower obtains another certificate from the company and sells to a *bona fide purchaser for value* who then obtains registration, that purchaser will have priority over the original lender.

It is no use the borrower in a legal mortgage or the original lender in an equitable mortgage (L) writing to the company telling it of his interest, because by s 360 and *Reg* 5 of *Table A* a company cannot take notice of any trust or similar right over its shares. However, a borrower or lender, as appropriate, may protect himself by serving on the company a stop notice under the Rules of the Supreme Court. He will file at the Central Office of the Supreme Court an affidavit declaring the nature of his interest in the shares, accompanied by a copy of the notice addressed to the company and signed by the applicant. Copies of the affidavit and the notice are then served on the company.

Once the stop notice has been served, the company cannot register a transfer or pay a dividend, if the notice extends to dividends, without first notifying L. However, after the expiration of 14 days from the lodgement of the transfer or notice of payment of a dividend, the company is bound to make the transfer or pay the dividend unless in the meantime L has obtained an injunction from the court prohibiting it.

A judgment creditor of a registered owner of shares may obtain an order charging the shares with payment of the judgment debt. Notice of the making of the order, or demand for the dividend, when served upon the company, has a similar effect to a stop notice (see above), in that until the charging order is discharged or made absolute the company cannot allow a transfer except with the authority of the court. A charging order has no priority over a mortgage created by deposit of the share certificate and a blank transfer *before* the date on which the charging order was made.

LIEN

The articles often give the company a first and paramount lien over its shares for unpaid calls, or even for general debts owed to the company by shareholders, but the Stock Exchange will not give a listing where there is a lien on fully-paid shares. Furthermore, s 150(1) prevents, subject to some exceptions, e.g. for banks, a public company from taking a lien or other charge over its own shares. However, a lien is permitted over partly-paid shares for amounts called or payable on the shares. It is usual also for the articles to give a power of sale. *Table A* gives such a power of sale, but requires 14 days' notice in writing to the shareholder or his representatives before the sale takes place, during which time the money owed can be paid and the sale prevented. Since on a sale the shareholder or his representatives will probably not co-operate in the necessary transfer, the articles usually provide, as *Table A* does, that a purchaser shall get a good title if the transfer is signed by a person nominated by the directors. If the articles create a lien but give no power of sale, the company would have to obtain an order for sale from the court.

A lien, other than for amounts due on the shares, cannot be enforced by forfeiture even if a power to forfeit is contained in the articles. Thus a company cannot enforce a lien for general debts by forfeiture even if its articles so provide.

The company's lien takes priority over all equitable interests in the shares, e.g. those of equitable mortgages, unless, when the shareholder becomes indebted to the company, it has actual notice of the equitable interest.

The Bradford Banking Co Ltd *v* Henry Briggs, Son & Co Ltd (1886) 12 App Cas 29

The respondent was a trading company carrying on the business of a colliery. The articles of the company provided that it should have 'a first and permanent lien and charge available at law and in equity upon every share for all debts due from the holder thereof'. John Easby, a coal merchant, became a shareholder in the respondent company, and deposited his certificates with the bank as security for the overdraft on his current account. The bank gave notice to the company that the shares had been so deposited. Easby owed the respondent company money, having done trade with it, and he also owed money to the bank. The question for decision was whether the company was entitled to recoup its debts by exercising a lien and sale on the shares, or whether the bank was entitled to sell as mortgagees. *Held* – by the House of Lords – that the respondent company could not claim priority over the bank in respect of the shares for money which became due from Easby after the notice given by the bank. The notice served by the bank was not a notice of trust under s 30 of the Companies Act 1862 (now s 360 of the Companies Act 1985), but must be regarded in the same light as notice between traders regarding their interests.

Comment

A company is not ordinarily bound to take notice of a trust or other equitable interest over its shares. It is, however, bound by such a notice when the company itself is also claiming an interest, e.g. a lien, over the shares in competition with the person who gives notice.

The lien attaches to dividends payable in respect of the shares subject to the lien (*Hague* v *Dandeson* (1848) 2 Exch 741).

FORFEITURE OF SHARES

Shares may be forfeited by a resolution of the board of directors if, *and only if*, an express power to forfeit is given in the articles. Where such an express power exists, it must be strictly followed, otherwise the forfeiture may be annulled. Further, the object of the forfeiture must be for the benefit of the company and not to give some personal advantage to a director or shareholder, e.g. in order to allow him to avoid liability for the payment of calls where the shares have fallen in value as in *Re Esparto Trading* (1879) 12 Ch D 191.

The articles usually provide that shares may be forfeited where the member concerned does not pay a call made upon him, whether the call is in respect of the nominal value of the shares or of premium.

The usual procedure is for a notice to be served on the member asking for payment, and stating that if payment is not made by a specific date, not earlier than 14 days from the date of the notice, the shares may be forfeited. If payment is not so made, the company may forfeit the shares and make an entry of forfeiture on the register of members. Once the shares have been forfeited, the member should be required to return the share certificate or other document of title so as to obviate fraud. A forfeiture operates to reduce the company's issued capital, since it cancels the liability of the member concerned to pay for his shares in full, but even so the sanction of the court is not required; a mere power in the articles is enough.

Shares cannot be forfeited except for non-payment of calls and any provision in the articles to the contrary is void.

Reissue of forfeited shares

Forfeited shares may be reissued to a purchaser so long as the price which he pays for the shares is not less than the amount of calls due but unpaid at forfeiture.

Suppose X is the holder of 100 shares of £1 each on which 75p per share has been called up, and X does not pay the final call of 25p per share, as a result of which the shares are forfeited. If they are reissued to Y, then Y must pay not less than £25 for them, and any sum received in excess of that amount from Y will be considered as *share premium* and must be credited to a *share premium account*. Thus, although Y appears to have bought the shares at a discount, this is not so because the company has received the full amount of the called-up capital, i.e. £75 from X and £25 from Y.

The company's articles usually provide (as *Table A* does) that if any irregularity occurs in the forfeiture procedure, the person to whom the forfeited shares are reissued will nevertheless obtain a good title.

Liability of person whose shares are forfeited

Forfeiture of shares means that the holder ceases to be a member of the company, but his liability in respect of the shares forfeited depends upon the articles.

(*a*) *Where there is no provision in the articles* with regard to liability, the former holder is discharged from liability, and no action can be brought by the company against him for calls due at the date of the forfeiture unless the company is wound up within one year of it. In such a case the former holder may be put on the *B list of contributories* in the winding-up, and may be called upon to pay the calls due at the date of the forfeiture unless they have been paid by another holder.

(*b*) *The articles may provide* (as does *Table A*) that the former holder shall be liable to pay the calls due but unpaid at the date of forfeiture, whether the company is in liquidation or not, unless they have been paid to the company by a subsequent holder.

SURRENDER OF SHARES

The directors of a company cannot accept a surrender of shares unless the articles so provide. There is no provision in *Table A* but it would seem from decided cases that directors may accept surrender:

(*a*) where the circumstances are such that the shares could have been forfeited under the articles (*per* Lord Herschell in *Trevor* v *Whitworth* (1887) 12 App Cas 409); and

(*b*) where shares are surrendered as part of a scheme to exchange existing shares for new shares of the same nominal value, the new shares having perhaps slightly different rights and the old shares being either cancelled or available for reissue.

In other circumstances surrender is not allowed (see below).

Bellerby *v* Rowland & Marwood's SS Co Ltd [1902] 2 Ch 14

Three directors of the company, Bellerby, Moss and Marwood, agreed to surrender several of their shares to the company so that they might be reissued. The object of the surrender was not that the directors could not pay the calls, the shares being of nominal value £11 with £10 paid, but to assist the company to make good the loss of one of its ships, the *Golden Cross*, valued at £4,000. The surrender was accepted but the shares were not in fact reissued. The company survived the loss and became prosperous, and in this action the directors sought to be returned to the register as members, claiming that the earlier surrender was invalid. *Held* – by the Court of Appeal – that it was invalid since the surrender was not accepted because of non-payment of calls or inability to pay them, and so the directors must be restored to the register of members.

Comment

This decision is essentially to the effect that a company cannot evade the rules relating to reduction of capital by taking a surrender of its partly-paid shares.

Treatment of forfeited and surrendered shares in public companies

The above material relating to forfeiture and surrender is still valid because it relates to the source of the power to forfeit or surrender and the surrounding circumstances. However, the treatment of forfeited and surrendered shares once this has happened is a matter for the Companies Act 1985. The Act provides that no voting rights may be exercised by the company so long as the shares are forfeited or surrendered and also that the company must dispose of the shares within three years. If they are not disposed of, they must be cancelled. If the shares are cancelled and the cancellation has the effect of reducing the company's allotted share capital below the authorised minimum, the directors must apply for the company to be re-registered as a private company. There are, however, certain relaxations in the procedures in this event. In particular, only a directors' resolution is required to make the necessary reduction application, and any alterations to the memorandum that are necessary. The company does not need to apply to the court to obtain confirmation of the reduction in capital but any resolution passed by the directors must be filed with the Registrar. If a company fails to comply with either the requirement to cancel or the requirement to re-register as a private company, the company and its officers in default become liable to a fine.

GRADED QUESTIONS

Essay mode

1 (*a*) Sam has 2,000 fully paid shares in X Ltd. The articles of X Ltd give a first and paramount lien over shares in respect of any debts owed by a member to the company. On 3 January, Sam borrowed £1,500 from George and secured the loan by giving George his share certificate and a blank transfer form. George notified the company of these facts. The company informed George they could not take cognisance of his interest as this would be contrary to s 360 of the Companies Act 1985. On 10 February, Sam became indebted to the company for goods delivered to him invoiced at £800. He has not paid for these and the company seeks to enforce its lien.

Advise George of the legal position.

(*b*) T stole M's share certificate and forged a transfer to B, who was a bona fide purchaser. B was registered and received a new share certificate from the company. He later sold the shares to C, but T's fraud was discovered and the company refused to register C.

What is the legal position of M, C and B?

(Kingston University)

2 Describe and discuss the significance of each of the following:

(*a*) The pre-emption rights of existing shareholders.
(*b*) Preference shares.
(*c*) Redeemable shares.

(The Association of Chartered Certified Accountants)

3 Dee Ltd has an authorised and issued share capital of £15,000 in £1 shares. The directors have decided to issue for cash at par a further 10,000 £1 shares.

What procedures must the directors follow to implement their decision?

(The Institute of Chartered Accountants in England and Wales)

4 'Although they may not be in the strict sense agents or trustees for the company, promoters stand in a fiduciary relation to it' – *Northey and Leigh.*

Discuss by looking at the promoter's relationship with the company he is forming and the remedies available for failure to discharge the fiduciary duty.

(The Institute of Company Accountants)

5 Explain by reference to statutory and common law examples what is meant by the term 'lifting the veil of incorporation'.

(The Chartered Institute of Management Accountants)

Objective mode

Four alternative answers are given. Select ONE only. Circle the answer which you consider to be correct. Check your answers by referring back to the information given in the chapter and against the answers at the back of the book.

1 The Companies Act 1985 gives shareholders a statutory right of pre-emption:

A on the allotment of any shares.
B where shares are transferred from one member of a company to another.
C on the transmission of shares on the death of a member of the same company.
D on the allotment for cash of equity shares.

2 The board of Mersey plc has authorised the allotment of shares to the public in contravention of the statutory pre-emption rights of Mersey's shareholders. What is the legal position as regards the allotment?

A It is invalid and the allottees have no right to compensation.
B It is valid and the shareholders can ask for compensation from the directors and the company.
C It is invalid and the allottees can ask for compensation from the directors and the company.
D It is valid and the original shareholders have no right to compensation.

3 The shareholders of Test Ltd are Ann who holds 600 shares, Barbara who has 100 shares, and Clare and Diana who have 250 shares each. The shares carry one vote each. A resolution to exclude the statutory pre-emption right of the shareholders of Test Ltd, given that all members attend the meeting and that voting is by poll, requires the minimum support of:

A Ann alone.
B Ann and Barbara.
C Ann and Barbara and Clare.
D Ann and Barbara and Clare and Diana.

4 Under the provisions of the Companies Act 1985, where there is to be an allotment of unissued share capital for cash the notice of the offer to existing shareholders must remain open for not less than:

A 28 days.
B 21 days.
C 15 days.
D 14 days.

5 Which of the following resolutions requires the directors of a private company to give a statutory declaration of solvency? A resolution to:

A commence a creditors' voluntary winding-up.
B reduce the company's share capital.
C approve the giving of financial assistance for the purchase of its own shares from distributable profits.
D approve a contract for the purchase of its own shares out of distributable profits.

6 What is the minimum percentage of shareholders required to make an application to the court to set aside an alteration of the objects clause of a company?

A Not less than 15 per cent of the total number of shareholders.

B Those holding not less than 15 per cent in nominal value of the issued share capital of the company or any class thereof.

C Not less than 15 per cent of the total number of shareholders or any class thereof.

D Those holding not less than 15 per cent in nominal value of the issued share capital of the company.

Answers to questions set in objective mode appear on p 576.

11

SHARES – TRANSFER AND TRANSMISSION

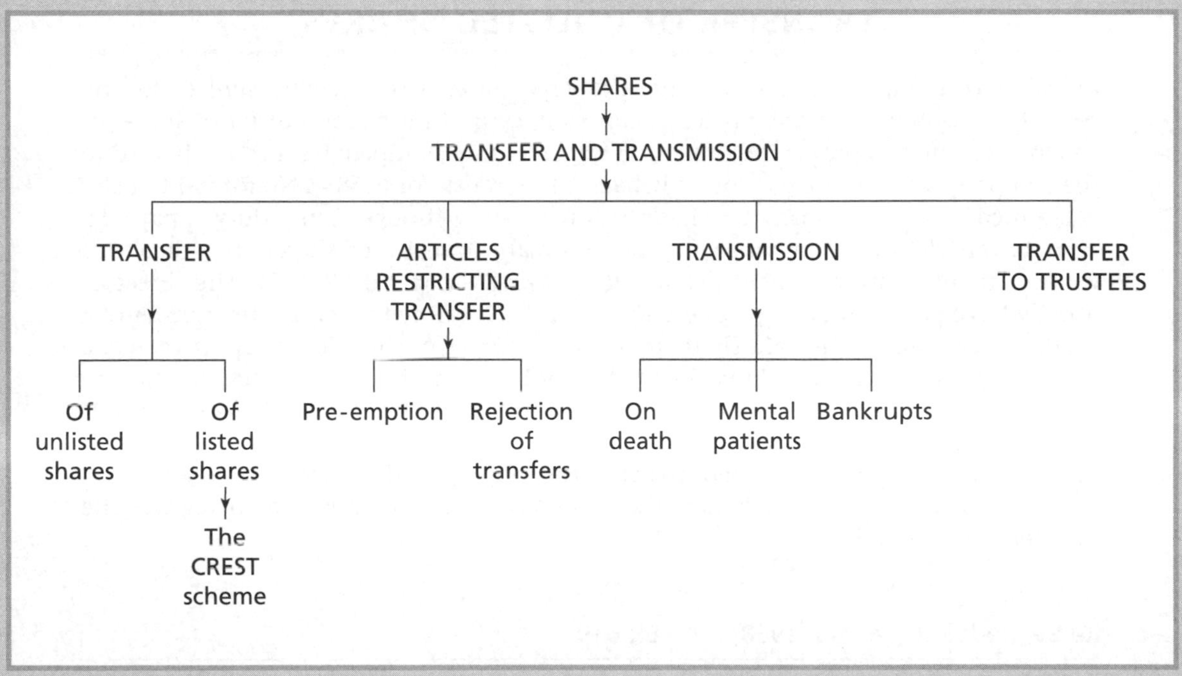

This chapter is concerned with the way in which shares are transferred from one person to another. It is necessary to distinguish between the transfer of unlisted shares and shares which are listed on an investment exchange such as the Stock Exchange. Basically the material in this chapter covers the transfer of shares in a private company which cannot have a listing on an investment exchange. The rules could, however, apply to a plc which had not sought a listing on an investment exchange.

TRANSFER OF UNLISTED SHARES

As we have seen, shares are personal property and are transferable subject to any restriction contained in the articles. A company cannot register a transfer of shares or debentures unless a proper instrument of transfer, duly stamped, has been delivered to the company and executed by or on behalf of the transferor (s 183). No formal transfer is required when a company purchases its own shares, though stamp duty is payable. Thus an article which provided for the automatic transfer of shares to a director's widow on his death was held invalid (*Re Greene* [1949]1 All ER 167). The directors usually have power under articles such as *Table A* to decline to register the transfer of a share, other than a fully-paid share, to a person of whom they do not approve, e.g. a minor or person of unsound mind who cannot be bound by the contract; and also to decline to register the transfer of a share on which the company has a lien, e.g. for calls made but not paid. Any power of veto on transfer vested by the articles in the directors must be exercised within two months after the lodging of the transfer for registration and the transferee notified. If not, the company may be compelled to register the transferee as a member.

Re Swaledale Cleaners [1968] 3 All ER 619

On 3 August 1967 the shareholding of the company was: H (deceased) 5,000; S 4,000; A (deceased) 500; L 500. S and L were directors of the company which was a private one. The company's articles provided that the quorum of directors should be two although a sole continuing director had power to appoint an additional director. At a combined board meeting and annual general meeting held on 3 August 1967, L retired by rotation and was not re-elected a director. The personal representatives of H and A had executed transfers of H and A shareholdings in favour of L, but S as director refused to register them purporting to exercise a power of refusal contained in the articles. There was no resolution either of the board or of the shareholders on the matter of refusal to register the transfers. On 11 December 1967 L began proceedings for rectification of the register, and on 18 December 1967 S appointed an additional director and the two directors formally refused to register the transfers. *Held* – by the Court of Appeal – the register must be rectified to show L as the holder of the shares of H and A. The power to refuse a transfer must be construed strictly because a shareholder ordinarily has a right to transfer his shares. Furthermore, the delay in exercising the power of refusal, i.e. four months, had been unreasonable and the power was no longer capable of being exercised.

Comment

The above case was followed by the High Court in *Re Inverdeck Ltd* [1998] 2 BCLC 242. This later case stresses the need for directors in private companies as Inverdeck Ltd was to observe the relevant corporate formalities in their day-to-day transactions. The power in private companies to refuse to register a transfer is a valuable one in that it can be used to prevent persons from acquiring rights in the company which the directors believe are contrary to its interests. Failure to observe formalities can lead to this valuable power being lost.

Court's power to rectify the register where no instrument of transfer

It was held by the Court of Appeal in *Re Hoicrest Ltd* [1999] 2 BCLC 346 that the power of the court to rectify the membership register of a company could be used to effect a transfer where there was no instrument of transfer so that the company had not had an opportunity to refuse the transfer. Although s 359 has traditionally been used in disputes between a would-be shareholder and the company where following transfer the company refuses registration, the section was not confined to that situation and could be used to settle a dispute as to the ownership of shares between two members.

The legal transactions involved

The purchase and sale of shares involves the following separate and distinct legal transactions:

(*a*) An unconditional contract is agreed between the transferor and transferee. The transferor then holds the shares as a trustee for the transferee (who has an equitable interest) until registration but is still a member of the company and retains the right to vote as he chooses.

(*b*) The transferee pays for the shares. The position remains as in (*a*) above except that the transferor must now vote as the transferee directs. An unpaid transferor has the right to vote the shares free from any obligation to comply with the transferee's requirements (*JRRT* (*Investments*) v *Haycraft* [1993] BCLC 401).

(*c*) The position remains as in (*b*) above while the transfer is approved by the directors and the transfer is stamped.

(*d*) The transferee's name is entered on the register of members. At this stage the transferor ceases to be a member of the company. The transferee becomes the member and acquires the legal title to the shares. Since membership and membership rights are only effective when the transferee is on the register of members, it may be necessary to ask the court to rectify the register of members under s 359 where the company is refusing to register the transferee, *but only if this is contrary to the powers of the board*.

The rights of persons to obtain registration or to claim under an equitable title are set out in Chapter 13. Section 127 of the Insolvency Act 1986 declares void any transfer of shares after the commencement of winding-up by the court, unless the court otherwise orders.

Form of transfer

Schedule 1 of the Stock Transfer Act 1963 introduced a new transfer form – a *stock transfer form*, which is for general use with unlisted shares.

Registrars are required to accept for registration transfers in the form introduced by the Act because it overrides any contrary provision regarding transfer, whether statutory or not. Thus the 1963 Act overrides any other provisions relating to the *form* of transfer in the company's articles. The signature of the transferor need not be witnessed, and the transferee need not sign the transfer, nor need it be in the form of a deed.

It should be noted that the 1963 Act does not override provisions in the articles relating to the rights of the directors to refuse registration.

The stock transfer form is not available to transfer partly-paid shares or shares in an unlimited or guarantee company. If such companies are encountered, reference should be made to the articles for the form of transfer to be used.

Procedure on transfer of unlisted shares

The method of transferring fully-paid shares or stock is as follows.

The shareholder executes (signs) a stock transfer form in favour of the purchaser, and hands it to the purchaser or his agent, together with the share certificate. The purchaser, or his agent, sends the stock transfer form along with the certificate to the company for registration. The purchaser need not sign the stock transfer form, nor need it be in the form of a deed. The company secretary, following approval by the board, deletes the transferor's name from the register of shareholders and replaces it with the transferee's name and, within two months, sends the share certificate to the transferee.

TRANSFER OF LISTED SHARES

Transfers of shares with a listing on the London Stock Exchange are covered by the Uncertificated Securities Regulations 2001 (SI 2001/3755). This area of the law is rather specialised and only an outline of the system called CREST is given here.

The regulations provide for the system to be run by an approved operator which is CRESTCo Ltd, a private company owned by a number of firms connected with all sectors of the equities market. The system which is known as CREST is an electronic system which allows shareholders to hold and transfer their securities in dematerialised form, i.e. without a share certificate. A statement not unlike a bank statement reveals purchases and sales by the intermediaries concerned.

CREST does not impose dematerialisation of shares on shareholders. Shareholders who wish to become or remain uncertificated are able to do so. Institutional shareholders such as insurance companies that are frequent traders will go for dematerialisation but less sophisticated shareholders will in many cases opt for the paper certificate regime, follow the method of transfer described above and be on a separate register of members.

Uncertificated shareholders will appoint a custodian broker to hold the shares. The broker will appear on the electronic register of members but can only deal with shares in accordance with the customer agreement between the shareholder and the custodian broker. Shareholders who wish to retain paper certificates in listed companies may be forced to appoint custodian brokers as nominees because of the Stock Exchange three-day rolling settlement system under which an entire share transfer transaction must be completed in three days. This is difficult to achieve under a paper certificate regime but easy under an electronic transfer regime. It is possible to opt for a ten-day settlement regime though it will be necessary to find a stockbroker who operates it – some do.

Once a nominee is installed, the shareholder will receive dividends and benefit from capital growth but rights will be lost such as the right actually to attend meetings unless the nominee can make arrangements for this, nor will the shareholder receive the annual report and accounts unless the nominee asks for enough to send out to all his members, but this would be a concession not a right.

The regulations make dematerialisation lawful and disapply s 185 of the 1985 Act under which a share certificate must be provided to the transferee within two months after allotment or transfer where the uncertificated regime applies, but not in the paper certificate regime. Companies that wish to allow their shares to be transferred via CREST will have to change their articles to add a relevant provision.

Finally, a company any of whose securities can be transferred through CREST must subdivide its register of members (or debenture holders) to show how many of those securities each person holds in uncertificated form and certificated form respectively. An issuer of securities can only rectify a register of securities in relation to uncertificated units with the consent of CRESTCo or by order of the court.

Certification of transfers: unlisted shares

The above procedure assumes that on completion of the sale of registered unlisted shares the seller delivers his share certificate to the purchaser together with the instrument of transfer. Where he is selling all the shares represented by the certificate the seller will do this, but if he is selling only part of his holding, or the whole of his holding but to more than one person, he will instead send the share certificate and the executed transfer of the shares which the purchaser is buying to the company so that the transfer may be certificated.

The company secretary or registrar or transfer agent will compare the share certificate and the transfer with the register of members and if it appears that the seller is the owner of the shares mentioned in the certificate and some of those shares are comprised in the transfer, the secretary, registrar, or agent, as the case may be, will write in the margin of the transfer a note that the share certificate has been lodged and will sign it on behalf of the company.

The certificated transfer is then returned to the seller, the share certificate being retained by the company or the transfer agents. The seller will complete the sale by delivering the certificated transfer to the purchaser who will accept it as equal to delivery of an uncertificated transfer accompanied by the share certificate. The purchaser will then lodge the transfer with the company or its transfer agents for registration and the company will issue a new share certificate to him for the shares he has bought and a new certificate showing the seller as the registered holder of the balance of the shares which he retains if he retains any. Obviously the seller will not get a new certificate where he has sold his whole holding but to more than one person.

Liability arising out of certification

This is covered by s 184 and although a certification is not a warranty by the company that the person transferring the shares has any title to them, it is a representation by the company that documents have been produced to it which show prima facie title in the transferor.

Where, therefore, the company or its agent fraudulently or negligently makes a false certification, a purchaser who acts upon the false certification may sue the company for any loss he may have incurred as a result.

For example, if the company certifies a transfer without production of a certificate, it may be that the certificate has been used to make an uncertificated transfer to another purchaser. If so, two purchasers now exist and both are eligible for entry on the register of members. If the later purchaser achieves registration first, he will establish priority over the certificated transferee who will not then be registered and the company will be liable in damages to the certificated transferee for the loss he suffers thereby. However, if the company registers the certificated transferee and refuses the other purchaser, it will not be liable to the latter because the share certificate does not operate as an estoppel except as on the date of issue, which will have been some time ago.

Forged transfers

If a company transfers shares under a forged instrument of transfer, the transferor whose name has been forged must be restored to the register, and in so far as this puts the company to expense or loss, it can claim an indemnity from the person presenting the transfer for registration, even though he is quite innocent of the forgery.

Sheffield Corporation *v* Barclay [1905] AC 392

Two persons, Timbrell and Honnywill, were joint owners of corporation stock. Timbrell, in fraud of Honnywill, forged a transfer of the stock and borrowed money from the respondents on the security of the stock. The respondents sent the transfer to the corporation asking for registration, and they were duly registered. Later the respondents sold the shares and the corporation issued certificates to the purchasers who were also registered. Honnywill, after the death of Timbrell, discovered the forgery, and the corporation replaced the stock which was the best course open to them, because if they had taken the ultimate purchasers off the register of stockholders, they would have had to pay damages to them by virtue of the doctrine of estoppel. The corporation now sued the respondents for an indemnity on the grounds that they had presented the forged transfer. *Held* – by the House of Lords – the corporation succeeded. The person presenting a transfer warrants that it is good, and the fact that he is innocent of any fraud does not affect this warranty. The corporation, therefore, was entitled to recover from the respondents the value of the stock replaced, leaving them to such remedies as they might have against Timbrell's estate.

Comment

(i) Where a person requests the registration of a share transfer which a company is under a duty to effect there is implied in that request a warranty that the transfer is genuine. The rule applies whether the transfer is in favour of the person presenting it or someone else, as where a broker presents a transfer on behalf of a client.

(ii) The company's loss, for which it needs an indemnity, will normally consist in buying in or issuing for no consideration new shares to recompense the original holder. The innocent transferee will stay on the register of members by reason of the rules relating to estoppel that are described above. The indemnity may be made by the fraudster if he presents the transfer but it may be presented by a broker on behalf of the fraudster where the company is listed. In these circumstances the broker must give the indemnity, even though he may be innocent of the fraud, leaving him to claim against the fraudster. This was the situation in the *Barclay* case and in *Royal Bank of Scotland plc* v *Sandstone Properties Ltd* [1998] *The Times*, 12 March, where the facts were similar and the *Barclay* case was followed.

If the company issues a share certificate to the transferee under a forged transfer, the company is not estopped from denying his title to the shares, but it may become estopped if it issues a new certificate to a non-owner as part of a subsequent transfer transaction.

A company may inform the transferor that a transfer has been received for registration so as to give him a chance to prevent a fraudulent transfer but a transferor is not prejudiced by the fact that he has received notice, and may still deny the validity of the transfer.

Death of a holder in a joint account

A transfer is not needed to a surviving joint holder or holders on the death of one. In such cases, it is usual for the company to receive a death certificate certified by the Registrar of Births and Deaths. Photocopies are not official documents but some companies will accept them if presented by a person of professional standing. Sometimes a grant of probate or administration may be received and this is satisfactory evidence of death. The necessary alterations in the register of members are made on the basis of these documents and not on the basis of the conventional instrument of transfer. The procedure is a form of transmission of shares which is considered later in this chapter.

COMPANIES WHOSE ARTICLES RESTRICT TRANSFER

In the case of a company whose articles restrict transfer a transfer must be submitted to and approved by the board and any restriction must be the decision of the directors.

In practice these restrictions are normally found only in the articles of private companies. Most plcs have their shares listed, or quoted, on a recognised investment exchange such as the Stock Exchange, and the rules of the listing or quotation agreement do not permit restrictions on transfer following sale. Consideration will be given to the right of pre-emption in private companies and the general rules relating to rejection of transfers.

The right of pre-emption: generally

This means that when a member of a private company wishes to sell his shares, he must, under a provision in the articles, first offer them to other members of the company before he offers them to an outsider. The price is usually to be calculated by some method laid down in the articles, e.g. at a price fixed by the auditors of the company. In this context it should be noted that the auditor can be sued by the seller of the shares if the valuation is lower than it should be because of the auditor's negligence. This is an important claim because the seller will not normally be able to avoid the contract of sale because that contract usually makes the auditor's valuation final and binding on the parties.

However, a distinction must be made where the accountant or valuer has not merely made a mistake in the valuation of the shares, but has not done what he was appointed to do. In such a case the court can intervene and set the contract of purchase aside. Thus in *Macro* v *Thompson* [1997] BCLC 626 an accountant/valuer was asked to value the shares in two private companies for the purpose of a pre-emption purchase. In reaching conclusions as to the valuation of company A's shares, he mistakenly transposed the assets of company B, which was less valuable. This transposition appeared in the judgment of an earlier decision of the court in these proceedings. The contract to buy the shares of company A at the lower price was set aside by the court even though the purchaser had paid for the shares. The accountant/valuer had been asked to value the shares of company A but by mistake had valued the shares of company B, which represented not merely an error in the valuation, but an error in terms of his instructions.

If the other members do not wish to take up the shares, the shares may then be sold to an outsider. The other members must apparently be prepared to take *all* the shares that the vendor member is offering (*Ocean Coal Co Ltd* v *Powell Duffryn Steam Coal Co Ltd* [1932] 1 Ch 654).

The right of pre-emption can, if appropriately worded, be enforced as between the members (*Rayfield* v *Hands*, 1958), and also by the company, which may obtain an injunction against a member who is not complying with the articles in this matter (*Lyle & Scott Ltd* v *Scott's Trustees* [1959] 2 All ER 661). The decision in *Lyle & Scott Ltd* could make it very difficult for a takeover bidder to take over a private company because if there is a pre-emption clause the board can ask the court for an injunction requiring a member to offer his shares to another member rather than to the bidder.

Effect of transfer of equitable interest in shares

A method of effectively transferring control over the shares without triggering a pre-emption clause can be seen in the following case.

Scotto *v* Petch [2001] *The Times*, 8 February

The company owned Sedgefield racecourse, and an offer to buy all the shares in the company was made by Northern Racing Ltd. Mrs Sotto, a 21 per cent shareholder, refused to sell. The other shareholders were willing to do so. The victim company had a pre-emption clause in its articles under which pre-emption rights in other shareholders were triggered if a shareholder 'intends to transfer shares'. The shareholders other than Mrs Sotto made an agreement under which they would remain on the register as legal owners of their shares but the equitable interest would belong to Northern Racing. The agreement went on to say that if they were ever required to transfer the legal interest, it would be to another member, i.e. it would be a permitted transfer under the article. The arrangement gave Northern Racing effective control since under the agreement the shareholders, who were parties to it, would obviously vote as Northern Racing required. Mrs Sotto said that the arrangement triggered the pre-emption clause so that the shares had to be offered to her.

The Court of Appeal ruled that the pre-emption clause was not triggered. There had been no transfer of the legal interest in the shares and if ever there was, it would be to other members and would, therefore, be a permitted transfer under the articles.

Pre-emption: members' waivers

The other members of the company may be prepared to give written waivers of their rights to pre-emption, bearing in mind that a private company will normally have articles giving the directors power to reject a transferee. However, where shares are transferred in breach of a pre-emption clause without unanimous waiver of the other members, the directors have no power to register the transfer and no question of discretion arises. A person wishing to sell his shares in a private company with a pre-emption clause will normally notify the company secretary, who will advise the other members of the wish to sell.

Rejection of transfers

Where the articles give the directors power simply to refuse or approve the registration of transfers, that power must be exercised in good faith, and this may be tested in the courts if it appears that the directors have rejected a transfer for purely personal reasons as where they simply do not like the proposed transferee (and see *Re Accidental Death Insurance Co, Allin's Case*, 1873, below); but where the power to reject is exercisable for reasons specified in the articles, the transferee need not be told which is the reason for this rejection if the articles so provide (see *Berry and Stewart* v *Tottenham Hotspur FC*, 1935, below). The position is the same where the articles merely provide that the directors may reject a transfer 'without assigning reasons therefor'. These provisions are much stronger because the directors cannot be required to give reasons and therefore it is difficult, if not impossible, to prove before a court that they acted in bad faith.

Re Accidental Death Insurance Co, Allin's Case (1873) LR 16 Eq 449

The company's deed of settlement provided that when a shareholder wished to transfer his shares, he should leave notice at the company's office, and the directors should consider the proposal and signify their acceptance or rejection of the proposed transferee. If they rejected the proposed transferee, the proposed transfer would still be considered approved unless the directors could find someone else to take the shares at market price. The company arranged to transfer its business to the Accident and Marine Insurance Corporation Ltd. The shareholders acquiesced in an arrangement to exchange their shares for shares in the corporation, but the company was not wound up. A year later, the former directors of the company reversed the procedure, and the company proposed to resume its former business. Notice of this was given to shareholders, and shortly afterwards the corporation was wound up. Under an arrangement to release certain shareholders of liability, Allin transferred 200 shares in the company to Robert Pocock for a nominal consideration. He gave notice to the directors at a meeting at which he was present, and the transfer was agreed. Later the company was wound up. *Held* – by the High Court – the transfer was invalid, and Allin must be a contributory. The clauses were not intended to be in operation for the purpose of enabling individuals to escape liability when the company had ceased to be a going concern.

Berry and Stewart *v* Tottenham Hotspur FC Ltd [1935] Ch 718

Berry held one ordinary share in Tottenham Hotspur and he transferred his share to Stewart, both of them subsequently trying to register the transfer. Registration was refused, and Art 16 of the company's articles specified four grounds on which this was allowable, and also stipulated that the directors were not bound to divulge the grounds upon which registration was declined. The claimants brought an action for a declaration that the company was not entitled to decline to register the transfer, and sought interrogatories directed to find out which of the four grounds was the basis of the refusal. *Held* – by Crossman J – Art 16 excused the directors from the need to disclose this information, and this was binding not only on Berry, as a member, but also on Stewart who was applying to be a member. An action coupled with a demand for interrogatories could not be used to oust the agreement.

Comment

A more recent example of the use of this much stronger power of rejection is to be found in *Popely* v *Planarrive Ltd* [1996] 5 CL 104. Article 14 of the articles of association of Planarrive Ltd (P Ltd), a private company, gave its directors the power 'in their absolute discretion and without assigning any reason therefor' to 'decline to register the transfer of a share'. If the directors took such an action, they were required, under Art 25, to notify the transferee of their refusal to register his interest within two months after the date on which the transfer was lodged. Darren Popely validly transferred 15 shares in P Ltd to his father Ronald. The directors of P Ltd exercised their powers under Art 14 and refused to register the transfer. Ronald Popely then applied to the Chancery Division under s 359 of the Companies Act 1985 for an order rectifying the register of members of P Ltd by registering him as the owner of the shares transferred by his son. It was not disputed that notice of the refusal to register had not been sent to Mr Popely within the time set out in Art 25. Counsel for Mr Popely attempted to argue that this breach made the whole decision void. Mr Justice Laddie said that it did not nullify the decision although it might expose the directors to some civil or criminal liability (see s 183(6)). With regard to the actual refusal to register the transfer, Mr Popely's counsel said that this refusal was based on the strong feelings of hostility felt by the directors towards his client. However, the judge said that such feelings did not render the decision invalid. Where directors have such wide powers as these in the articles, the only restriction placed on them was that they must act bona fide in the best interests of the company and not outside their powers. Mr Popely was refused his application.

When is a transfer rejected?

Where there is an equality of votes, a transfer cannot be deemed rejected, but must be accepted (see *Re Hackney Pavilion Ltd*, 1924, below), though it is usual for the chairman to have a casting vote which he can use to decide the issue. Similarly, a transferee can ask the court to rectify the register so that his name is included on it where one director, by refusing to attend board meetings, is preventing a directors' meeting from being held to consider the registration because of lack of quorum (*Re Copal Varnish Co*, 1917). In addition, the powers vested in directors to refuse to register a transfer must be exercised within a reasonable time (see *Re Swaledale Cleaners*, 1968).

Re Hackney Pavilion Ltd [1924] 1 Ch 276

The company had three directors, Sunshine, Kramer and Rose, each of whom held 3,333 shares in the company. Sunshine died, having appointed his widow as his executrix. Her solicitors wrote to the company, enclosing a transfer of the 3,333 shares from herself as executrix to herself in an individual capacity. At a board meeting at which Kramer, Rose and the secretary were present, Rose proposed that the shares be registered, but Kramer objected in accordance with a provision in the articles. There was no casting vote. The secretary then wrote to the solicitors informing them that his directors had declined to register the transfer. *Held* – by the High Court – the board's right to decline required to be actively expressed. The mere failure to pass the proposed resolution for registration was not a formal active exercise of the right to decline. The right to registration remained, and the register must be rectified.

Unless the articles otherwise provide, rights of pre-emption and rejection apply only on a transfer by a member, and do not arise on transmission through death or bankruptcy. Neither do they arise where the shares are still represented by a renounceable letter of allotment.

Re Pool Shipping Ltd [1920] 1 Ch 251

The applicants were shareholders of the company which had capitalised £125,000, part of a reserve fund, for distribution among the registered shareholders or their nominees, at the rate of one share for every four shares issued. All but one of the shareholders renounced their right to allotments, and requested the company to allot the shares to Coulson who had agreed to accept them. The managers refused to issue the shares or register them to him when he presented the letters of renunciation in his favour, so the applicants moved for rectification of the register by the insertion of Coulson's name. The company had no directors but was controlled by Sir R Ropner & Co Ltd, who were described as managers and who relied on various clauses in the articles as grounds for refusal. *Held* – by the High Court – letters of renunciation do not amount to transfers of shares so as to come within the provisions of the articles of association dealing with the transfer of shares already registered. The managers were wrong in thinking they could refuse to register Mr Coulson, and the register must be rectified.

Special articles may allow rejection of executors' transfers to themselves as members pending the winding-up of the estate as an alternative to dealing with them in a representative capacity, and where this is so, they will *not* be able to vote the deceased's shares. A trustee in bankruptcy in the same situation will at least be able to direct his living debtor on how to vote.

A restriction in a company's articles upon the transfer of shares covers only the transfer of the legal title, i.e. a transfer in the title of the person on the register of members, and does not include transfer of the beneficial interest. Thus if A and B are the only shareholders in a company and B has a majority holding, then if on the death of B his executor, C, who has obtained registration, holds the shares on trust for beneficiaries, X and Y, and C proposes to vote in accordance with the wishes of X and Y so that X and Y will control the company, then A cannot claim that there has been a transfer of the shares of B entitling A to the implementation of a pre-emption clause under which A might require the shares held by C to be offered to him (A) (see *Safeguard Industrial Investments Ltd* v *National Westminster Bank* [1982] 1 All ER 449).

Of course, if C had been refused registration under a provision in the company's articles allowing this, he could not vote and so the above situation would not apply.

TRANSMISSION OF SHARES

This occurs where the rights encompassed in the holding of shares vests in another by operation of law and not by reason of transfer. It occurs in the following cases.

(a) *Death of a shareholder*

The shares of the deceased shareholder vest, in terms of the rights they represent, in executors (or administrators if there is no will) who can sell or otherwise dispose of them, e.g. to a beneficiary, without actually being registered, subject to any restrictions on transfer which the articles may contain. Section 187 provides that the company must accept probate of the will, or in the case of administrators, letters of administration, as sufficient evidence of the title of the personal representatives notwithstanding anything in its articles.

Personal representatives can insist on registration as members in respect of the deceased's shares unless the articles otherwise provide. Under *Table A, Reg* 30, the directors have the same power to refuse to register personal representatives as they have to register transfers, provided the shares are not fully paid, i.e. *Reg* 24 applies and they may refuse the transfer on the grounds that the personal representative is a 'person' of whom they do not approve. The company cannot insist that personal representatives be registered as members, but *Reg* 30 of *Table A* allows them to elect to be registered subject to the above restriction. If they are registered as members, they become personally liable for capital unpaid on the shares with an indemnity from the estate, but they do receive the benefit of being able to vote the shares at general and class meetings and to participate in written resolutions. *Table A, Reg* 31 excludes voting rights unless personal representatives are registered. They receive all the benefits attaching to the shares without registration except voting rights. Where, under the articles, they are refused registration, they may now apply to the court for relief, e.g. an order to the company to register them under s 459 on the grounds of unfair prejudice.

(b) *Mental Health Act patients*

Transmission also occurs to a receiver appointed by the Court of Protection to the estate of a person becoming a patient under the Mental Health Act 1983. The authority of the receiver is established by production of the protection order of the court appointing him. The position of the receiver is similar to that of personal representatives.

(c) *Bankruptcy of a shareholder*

On the bankruptcy of a member, the right to deal with the shares passes to the trustee in bankruptcy, and he can sell them without actually being registered or he can elect to register subject to any restrictions in the articles. *Reg* 30 of *Table A* allows him to elect to register. He would then be personally liable to pay any calls on the shares subject to a right of indemnity against the estate. When the trustee sells the shares, the sale is effected by production to the company of the share certificate together with the Department of Trade and Industry's certificate appointing the trustee and a transfer signed by him. A trustee cannot vote unless he is registered but can direct the bankrupt on the way he must vote (*Morgan* v *Gray* [1953] 1 All ER 213).

A trustee in bankruptcy has a right of disclaimer under which he may disclaim shares as onerous property where there are calls due on them and they would have little value if sold. This power is given by s 315 of the Insolvency Act 1986. Disclaimer is effected by the trustee serving upon the company a notice in writing disclaiming the shares, and he is then not personally liable to pay any calls if registered and the estate of the bankrupt member is no longer liable as such. The company may claim damages, which in the case of shares of little value, which was the reason for the disclaimer, are unlikely to be as much as the calls due but unpaid (*Re Hallet, ex parte National Insurance Co* [1894] WN 156). Shares disclaimed may be reissued as paid up to the extent to which cash has been received on them. However, the company would have to ask the court for an order temporarily vesting the shares in the company so that it could reissue them. Section 320 of the Insolvency Act 1986 applies. This is because on disclaimer the shares vest in the Crown (Treasury Solicitor) as *bona vacantia* (property without an owner). The situation is one of legal difficulty and doubt and legal advice would have to be sought from a firm specialising in insolvency practice.

TRUSTEES

The shares, if trust property, are transferred to the trustees by the settlor (in a lifetime trust), or by his personal representatives where the trust is by will. If new trustees or replacement trustees are appointed once the trust has begun, the shares must be transferred to the new trustees by the surviving former trustees in the usual way, i.e. by stock transfer form. There is no transfer by operation of law on the appointment of the new trustee, nor under s 40 of the Trustee Act 1925 where the trustee is appointed by deed.

Section 40 provides for the automatic transfer of property without a transfer or conveyance to include a new trustee where his appointment is by deed. However, the section specifically excludes company shares, which must be transferred into the joint names of the trustees including the new one(s) in the ordinary way.

GRADED QUESTIONS

Essay mode

1 Edward owns a small number of shares in Severn Ltd, a private company. He wishes to transfer these shares to a charity but fears that the directors may object.

For what reasons may the directors refuse to register such a transfer and for how long may they delay their decision?

(*The Institute of Chartered Accountants in England and Wales*)

2 Write explanatory notes on TWO of the following:

(*a*) the doctrine of *ultra vires*;
(*b*) promoters;
(*c*) certification of transfer forms;
(*d*) ways in which shares may be mortgaged.

(*Kingston University*)

3 (*a*) What is the procedure for varying the rights attached to a class of shares if the memorandum and articles are silent on the matter? What safeguards are there for a minority of that class?

(*b*) Explain the liability of a person who presents a forged share transfer to the company for registration and is registered accordingly. Can the company ever be liable in this situation?

(*The Institute of Chartered Secretaries and Administrators*)

4 Sprouts Ltd wishes to change its name to Greenstuff Ltd and trade under the name of Brassica Wholefoods. What steps must be taken to achieve this result?

(*The Institute of Company Accountants*)

5 Write notes on TWO of the following:

(*a*) the name clause of the memorandum;
(*b*) the transfer of shares;
(*c*) variation of class rights;
(*d*) promoters.

(*The Institute of Chartered Secretaries and Administrators*)

Objective mode

Four alternative answers are given. Select ONE only. Circle the answer which you consider to be correct. Check your answers by referring back to the information given in the chapter and against the answers at the back of the book.

1 When is it necessary to certify a transfer of shares?

A Where there are pre-emption rights in the articles.
B When a part holding of shares is being transferred to the transferee(s).
C When shares are being transferred to an existing member.
D On all transfers of unlisted shares.

2 What is the legal position of a person who buys shares on the faith of a share certificate issued by a company to a transferee on the basis of a forged transfer?

A The person gets an equitable interest in the shares.
B The transfer is valid and the person gets a good title if he has acted in good faith.
C The transfer is void and the person cannot claim against the company.
D The transfer is void but the person has a claim for compensation against the company.

3 Conwy Ltd has a provision in its articles which allows a transfer of shares to be made orally. This provision is:

A invalid.
B valid.
C voidable.
D valid if the transfer is to an existing member.

4 Botham dies and leaves all his shares in Thames Ltd to Gower. Under the articles the shares in Thames 'can only be transferred by the directors'. What must Botham's executor do to pass the shares to Gower?

A Become a member and sign a transfer deed.
B Sign a transfer in the form of a deed.
C Sign a stock transfer form.
D Become a member and sign a stock transfer form once on the register of members.

5 Maurice has become bankrupt. What is the legal effect of his bankruptcy on his shareholding in Mersey Ltd?

A Maurice retains his title and control of the shares but his trustee can file a stop notice.
B Maurice retains his title but the control of the shares is transmitted to his trustee in bankruptcy.
C The title to the shares passes to Maurice's trustee in bankruptcy.
D Maurice retains his title and control of the shares.

6 In which of the following circumstances is Fred not a member of a company?

A Fred subscribed the memorandum but his name is not as yet on the register of members.
B Fred has been allotted shares and entered on the register but has not received a letter of allotment.
C Fred has lodged a transfer with the company as transferee but has not yet been entered on the register of members.
D Fred has sold all his shares in the company to Bill but Fred's name has not yet been removed from the register of members.

Answers to questions set in objective mode appear on p 576.

12

SHARES – PAYMENT FOR AND INSIDER DEALING

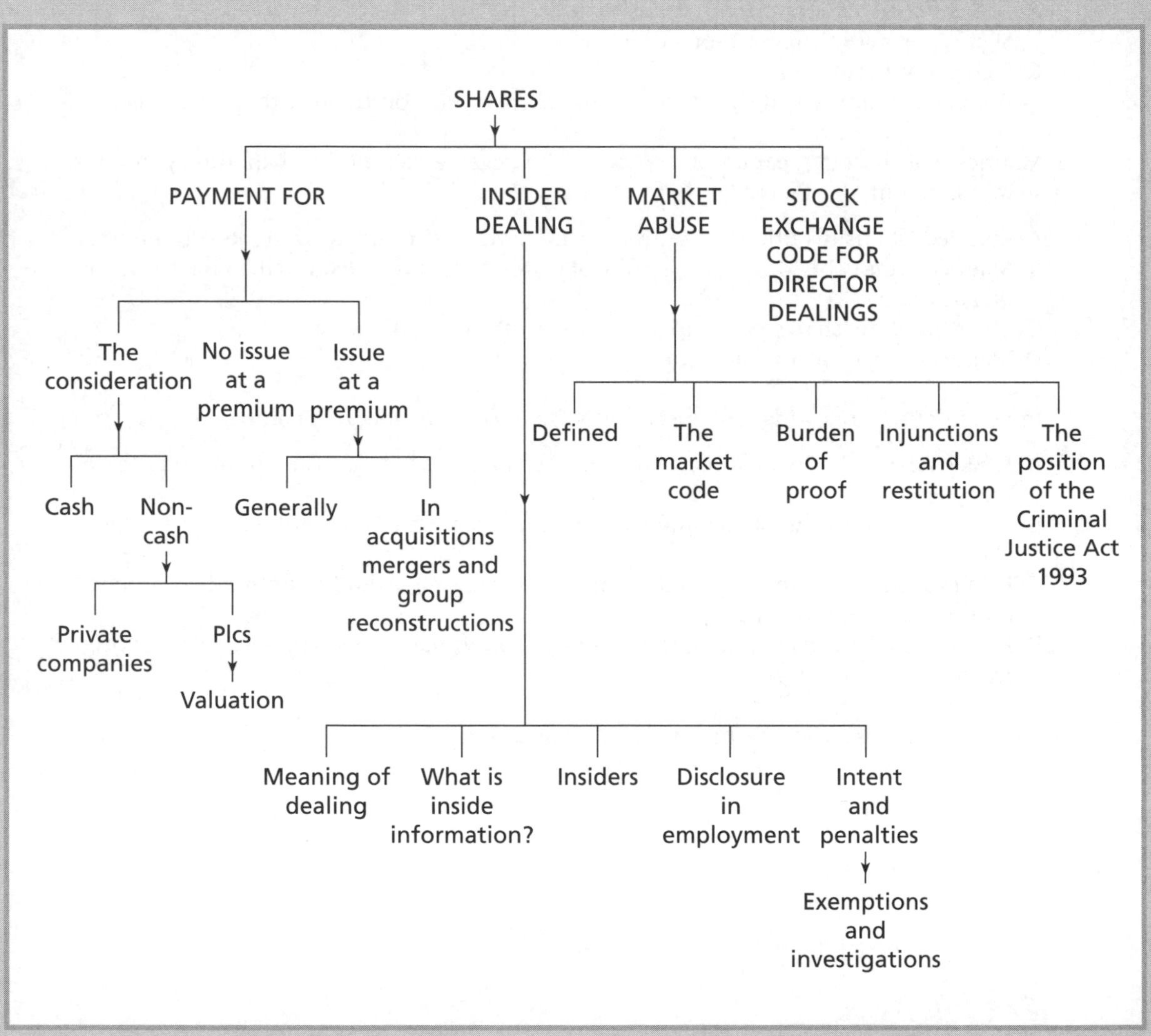

In this chapter we shall deal with the methods of payment for shares and the rules which apply according to the consideration offered, together with the rules relating to insider dealing.

THE CONSIDERATION – GENERALLY

Under s 100 a member of a company must pay for his shares in full, and no arrangement between the company and the members can affect this rule (*Ooregum Gold Mining Co of India* v *Roper* [1892] AC 125). However, payment need not be in cash but may be for some other consideration. Where this is so issues at a discount may still in effect be made in private companies.

Payment in cash

This is generally effected by handing cash or a cheque to the company, but if the company pays an existing debt by an issue of shares to the creditor, this set-off arrangement is deemed to be a payment in cash.

Re Harmony and Montague Tin and Copper Mining Co, Spargo's Case
(1873) LR 8 Ch App 407

A company purchased a mine from Spargo and he made an agreement to buy shares in the company. The moneys owed by Spargo to the company for his shares and by the company to Spargo for the mine were payable immediately. Under a further agreement between Spargo and the company he was debited with the amount payable on the shares and credited with the purchase price of the property making up the difference in cash. It was *held* by the Court of Appeal in Chancery that Spargo must be deemed to have paid for his shares in cash.

Comment

The provisions of the Companies Act relating to an issue of shares for a non-cash consideration seem not to apply to set-offs of this kind which are regarded as cash transactions. Section 739 provides in effect that the issue of shares to satisfy a liquidated sum, i.e. an existing quantified debt, as in this case, is not an issue for a consideration other than cash.

Considerations other than cash

(a) *In private companies*

Such considerations are legal, and the consideration very often consists in the sale of property to the company or the rendering of services. The consideration offered must be sufficient to support the contract in law and must not, for example, be past, though in private companies, at least, it need not be adequate.

Re Eddystone Marine Insurance Co [1893] 3 Ch 9

The company proposed to raise capital from the public, but passed a resolution before going to the public to allot £6,000 worth of fully-paid shares to the existing directors and shareholders for a consideration other than cash. A copy of the agreement was filed in which the consideration was said to be services rendered by the allottees to the company during its formation. There was in fact no such rendering of services. Eighteen months later the company was wound up, and the liquidator proposed to regard the shares as unpaid on the grounds that there was no consideration given for them. *Held* – by the Court of Appeal – the allottees must contribute the nominal value of the shares. There was in fact no consideration because the services had not been rendered, but even if they had, they would not have supported the contract to take the shares because the consideration would have been past.

Comment

Section 99 provides that a public company shall not accept at any time in payment up of its shares or any premium on them, an undertaking given by any person that he or another should do work or perform services for the company or any other person. If shares are issued for services by a public company the holder is liable to pay the nominal value and any premium to the company plus interest, which under s 107 is currently 5 per cent per annum. This applies whether the services are rendered or not. If services are rendered the person who renders them must pay for his shares and submit an account for the services.

Re Wragg Ltd [1897] 1 Ch 796

Messrs Wragg and Martin were the proprietors of a livery stable business and they agreed to sell it to a company, Wragg Ltd, which they formed. The business was sold to the company for £46,300, among the assets being horses and carriages valued for the purposes of the sale at £27,000. The company paid for the business by issuing shares and debentures to Wragg and Martin, and later, when the company was being wound up, the liquidator asked the court to declare that the shares were not fully paid up because it appeared that the horses and carriages had been overvalued and were really worth only £15,000 at the date of sale. It was *held* by the Court of Appeal that:

(i) Where fully-paid shares are allotted to vendors under a contract registered in accordance with the Companies Acts, it is not illegal for the said vendors or promoters to make a profit, though disclosure is required. In this case disclosure did not arise, since Wragg and Martin and certain nominees of theirs became the only shareholders in Wragg Ltd, and they were aware of the details of the transaction.

(ii) The court will not go behind a contract of this sort and enquire into the adequacy of the consideration unless the consideration appears on the face of the contract to be insufficient or illusory. This was not the case here for if the company had received advice on the purchase of the business, some advisers might have thought that, looking at the business as a whole, it was a good bargain at £46,300.

(iii) Where persons, as vendors, make an agreement with themselves and their nominees in the character of a limited company it is, following *Salomon* v *Salomon & Co*, 1897, an agreement between independent legal entities and is valid.

Comment

The Companies Act 1985 places restrictions on public companies in regard to the allotment of shares for a non-cash consideration by requiring, amongst other things, a valuation of that consideration. However, in private companies the company's valuation of the consideration will still be accepted as conclusive in the absence of, e.g., fraud.

It should be noted, however, that the court will enquire into the agreement where the consideration does not really exist.

Hong Kong & China Gas Co Ltd *v* Glen [1914] 1 Ch 527

The company agreed that in return for a concession to supply gas to the city of Victoria, Hong Kong, it would allot the vendor of the concession 400 shares of £10 each, fully paid; and it further agreed that if and when it increased its capital in the future, the vendor or his executors, administrators or assigns should have as fully paid, one-fifth of the increased capital. In this action the company asked the court to decide whether the part of the agreement relating to the one-fifth share of any increase in the capital of the company was binding. *Held* – by the High Court – it was not. The insufficiency of the consideration appeared on the face of the contract, for the company had agreed to give at any future time or times a wholly indefinite and possibly unlimited value for the purchase of the concession.

An agreement to allot shares for future services, even in a private company, may mean that the allottee will become liable to pay for the shares in full, since if he does not render the services, the company would otherwise be reduced to a mere action for damages, and would not have an action for the actual price of the shares, and it is doubtful whether a company can replace the liability of a member to pay for his shares in full with a mere action for damages (*Gardner* v *Iredale* [1912] 1 Ch 700).

Where shares are issued for a consideration other than cash, the contract, or if the contract is not in writing written particulars of it, must be sent to the Registrar for registration within one month of the allotment of the shares. If there is no such registration within the time prescribed, the officers of the company are liable to a fine under the 1985 Act, but the allotment is not affected. It should be noted that *mere registration* of a contract will not make it binding on the company if there is no consideration for it (*Re Eddystone Marine Insurance Co*, 1893, see above).

(b) In public companies

Under s 102 a public company is only allowed to allot shares as fully or partly paid by an undertaking to transfer a non-cash asset to the company if the transfer is to take place within five years of the date of the allotment.

In addition, under ss 103 and 108 allotment for a non-cash consideration is not to be made unless the non-cash asset has been valued by an independent accountant who would be qualified to be the auditor of the company (or by someone else approved by that independent accountant). In addition, the independent accountant must have reported to the company on his valuation during the six months prior to the allotment, and must state that the value of the consideration is at least equal to the value of the shares being allotted. A copy of the report must also have been sent to the allottee and filed at the Companies Registry with the return of allotments.

A typical report to satisfy s 103 appears in Figure 12.1.

Independent Accountants' Report issued in accordance with s 103 of the Companies Act 1985 to Dove plc

As required by s 103 of the Companies Act 1985 we report on the valuation of the consideration for the allotment to H Hawke of two hundred thousand shares of a nominal value of one pound issued at a premium of 50 pence per share. The shares and the share premium are to be treated as fully paid up.

The consideration given by H Hawke is freehold building land situated at Meadow Drift, Chelmsford, Essex. The land was valued on the basis of its open market value by R Robin, FRICS, on 1 December 2004, and, in our opinion, it is reasonable to accept that valuation. In our opinion, the method of valuation of the freehold building land was reasonable and there appears to have been no material change in the value since it was made. On the basis of this valuation, in our opinion, the value of the consideration is not less than £300,000.

Accountants & Co.

Figure 12.1

A valuation of the kind set out above is not required in a share exchange as in a takeover bid where Predator is acquiring Victim by exchanging Predator shares for Victim shares so that the consideration for Predator shares is the assets of Victim, but all the holders of shares in Victim must be able to take part in the arrangement. The valuation is not a mere formality since failure to obtain a valuation when shares in a plc are allotted for a non-cash consideration introduces the rather startling provisions of s 103(6), i.e. that the recipient of the shares must pay for them. This is in the nature of a penalty and there are no provisions in the Act for recovery of the property. This result can be mitigated under s 113(1) which allows the recipient to apply to the court for exemption.

An exemption was granted in *Re Ossory Estates plc* [1988] BCLC 213 where shares were issued for a non-cash consideration, i.e. property, without an accountant's valuation. However, there was evidence before the court that the company had sold some of the properties at a profit. This suggested that they were at least as valuable as the shares issued for them and the recipient of the shares was excused from paying the cash penalty.

Under s 104 for two years following the date of issue of the certificate that a company registered as a public company is entitled to commence business, the company may not acquire assets from subscribers to the memorandum having an aggregate value equal to 10 per cent or more of the nominal value of the issued share capital unless:

(i) the valuation rules set out above are complied with; and
(ii) the acquisition of the asset(s) and the terms of the acquisition have been approved by an ordinary resolution of the company. A copy of that resolution must be filed at the Companies Registry within 15 days of its passing.

The report under s 104 is similar to that under s 103 except that the consideration need not be shares and approval in general meeting is required.

Similar rules apply on re-registration as a public company where non-cash assets equal to at least 10 per cent of the nominal value of the issued share capital at that time are acquired from persons who are members of the company at the time of re-registration. These provisions do not apply to assets acquired in the ordinary course of business.

In addition, under s 106, the shares which a subscriber of the memorandum of a public company agrees in the memorandum to take must be paid up in cash, and under s 99 a public company must not accept at any time in payment up of its shares or any premium on them, an undertaking given by any person that he or another should do work or perform services in the future for the company or any other person.

Where the above requirements are contravened, s 112 provides that the allottee and his successors, but not purchasers for value without notice, will be liable to pay to the company the amount outstanding in respect of the allotment with interest which is currently 5 per cent per annum. The company and any officer in default may also be liable to a fine. However, as we have seen, the court may grant relief where the applicant has acted in good faith and it is just and equitable to grant relief.

PROHIBITION ON ALLOTMENT OF SHARES AT A DISCOUNT

Section 100 prohibits the issue of shares at a discount, though, as we have seen, this may happen in private companies where there is a *non-cash consideration* for the reason that the directors' valuation is accepted, so that there is in law no issue at a discount. A private company that issued shares for *cash at a discount* would be acting illegally. The power to pay underwriting commission under s 97 is not affected. Where shares are allotted in contravention of s 100, those shares shall be treated as paid up by the payment to the company of the amount of the nominal value of the shares less the amount of the discount, but the allottee shall be liable to pay the company the latter amount and shall be liable to pay interest thereon at the appropriate rate which is currently 5 per cent per annum (s 107). Persons who take the shares from the original allottee are jointly and severally liable with the original allottee to pay the amount mentioned above unless they are purchasers for value, and even a purchaser for value may be liable if he has actual knowledge of the contravention of s 100 at the time of the purchase.

Debentures may be issued at a discount, though where there is a right to exchange the debentures for shares at par value the debentures are good but the right to exchange is void.

Mosely *v* Koffyfontein Mines Ltd [1904] 2 Ch 108

The company proposed to issue to its shareholders certain debentures at a discount of 20 per cent, the debentures to be repayable by the company on 1 November 1909. The debenture holders were to have the right at any time prior to 1 May 1909, to exchange the debentures for fully-paid shares in the company on the basis of one fully-paid share of £1 nominal value for every £1 of nominal value of debentures held. The court was asked in this case to decide whether the proposed issue of debentures was void. *Held* – by the Court of Appeal – it was void, because the exchange of debentures for fully-paid shares would lead to the issue of shares at a discount whenever the right was exercised.

Comment

Issue of shares at a discount was permitted prior to the Companies Act 1980, but only if, amongst other things, there had been an ordinary resolution of the members, together with the permission of the court. Issue at a discount is now forbidden by s 100 of the Companies Act 1985.

SHARES ISSUED AT A PREMIUM

Share premiums: generally

There is nothing to prevent a company issuing shares at a premium, e.g. £1 shares at a price of £1.25p; and, indeed, where it is desired to issue further shares, of a class already dealt in on the Stock Exchange at a substantial premium, it is a practical necessity to do so except perhaps in a rights issue.

However, s 130 requires that such premium must be credited to a 'share premium account' to be treated as capital except in so far as it may be written down to pay up fully-paid bonus shares, to write off preliminary expenses, commissions and discounts in respect of new issues, and to provide any premium on the redemption of any debentures. It may also be used in a very restricted way to charge the premium on redemption of shares if this premium has been paid out of the proceeds of a fresh issue of shares made for the purpose.

The above rules prevent such premiums which are capital by nature from being paid away as dividends. Any balance on the share premium account must be shown in the balance sheet.

Section 130 in fact recognises that the real capital of a company is the price which subscribers pay for its shares and not the somewhat artificial nominal value. This results, in effect, in an admission that shares are really of no par value. If no par value shares were issued, the capital of the company would simply be the total paid for its shares by subscribers. This is known in the United States as the company's paid-in capital. Where the whole of the issued price has not been paid, the total amount paid plus the total amount remaining to be paid is in the United States called the company's stated capital.

If it were possible to issue no par shares in England, the accidental payment of dividends out of capital would automatically be precluded by the company's obligation to keep in hand assets worth at least the amount paid by subscribers plus the amount of the company's outstanding debts. However, until no par value shares are allowed, the law can ensure that the issue price of the shares is not dissipated in paying dividends only by using the somewhat inelegant device of the share premium account.

The Companies Act 1985 requires share premiums to be credited to a share premium account whether the shares are issued for cash or otherwise. In consequence, the Act always applies whether premiums are paid in cash or kind and so if a company issues shares for a consideration in kind which is worth more than the nominal value of the shares, a sum equal to the excess value of the consideration has to be transferred to a share premium account.

Henry Head & Co Ltd *v* Ropner Holdings Ltd [1952] Ch 124

Ropner Holdings was formed as a holding company, its main object being to acquire the whole of the issued share capital of the Pool Shipping Co Ltd and the Ropner Shipping Co Ltd for the purposes of amalgamation. Ropner Holdings issued the whole of its authorised capital of £1,759,606 (this being equal to the sum of the issued capitals of the two shipping companies) to the shareholders of Pool Shipping and Ropner Shipping on the basis of £1 share for each £1 share held in the two shipping companies. The value of the assets of the two shipping companies, when Ropner Holdings acquired the shares, was £6,830,972, and the difference between this figure and £1,759,606, less formation expenses, was shown on the balance sheet of Ropner Holdings as 'Capital Reserve – Share Premium Account' so as to comply with the Companies Act 1948. The claimants, who were large shareholders in Ropner Holdings, asked that the company be required to treat the reserve as a general and not a capital reserve because otherwise no payment out of the reserve could be made unless the procedure for reduction of capital was followed. *Held* – by Harman J – Ropner Holdings had, in effect, issued its shares at a premium within the meaning of what is now s 130, and was bound to retain the reserve as a capital reserve.

Comment

The case is still authority for the statement that a share premium account must be raised even where the consideration is not cash. However, in the circumstances of the case merger relief would presumably have been available.

Share premiums – acquisitions, mergers and group reconstructions

Sections 131–134 give relief, in certain circumstances, from the requirement to set up a share premium account under s 130.

Acquisitions and mergers

(i) *Acquisitions*. This involves a takeover where the predator company P makes an offer to the shareholders of the Victim company V either with or without the consent of the board of V. The price offered is usually above the market price. If V is acquired, i.e. if there are sufficient acceptances from the shareholders of V, the investment of P in V must be shown in the books of P at its *true value*, i.e. the value of the consideration given. This has the effect of treating the reserves of V as pre-acquisition and therefore as undistributable and in particular pre-acquisition profits are locked up.

This position is unchanged by the 1985 Act and pre-acquisition profits must be locked up because if V pays a dividend to P out of pre-acquisition profits and P uses it to pay dividend to its shareholders P is returning the capital it used for the purchase of V's shares to its members because the pre-acquisition profits were represented in the price which P paid for V's shares.

(ii) *Mergers*. In the case of a merger between P and V involving a share-for-share exchange, e.g. P issues its equity shares to the members of V on a one-for-one basis, in exchange for the shares of the members of V, as a result of which P becomes the holder of 90 per cent or more of the equity shares of V, then there is no need to value the investment in V at its true value. The value may simply be the nominal value of the shares exchanged and so no share premium account is created as was the case in *Henry*

Head under the old law (see above). Thus the reserves of V need not be treated as pre-acquisition and pre-acquisition profits are not locked up.

Section 131 sets out the minimum conditions which must be met before a company can use the merger method of accounting. The conditions are:

1 The parent company must acquire at least 90 per cent by nominal value of relevant shares in the target company. This is then a genuine 'pooling of assets'. Relevant shares are shares carrying unrestricted rights to participate both in distributions and in the assets of the undertaking on liquidation.
2 The 90 per cent must be achieved under an arrangement for the issue of shares by the parent company, i.e. merger accounting is appropriate only where there is substantially a share-for-share exchange. It is permissible to have a prior holding but the 1985 Act does not restrict its size.
3 The issue of equity shares must be the dominant element in the consideration offered by the parent company for the relevant shares in the company to be acquired. The fair value of the consideration which may be given in a form other than equity shares is limited to 10 per cent of the nominal value of the equity shares issued.
4 Finally, merger accounting is not available as of right even if (1)–(3) are satisfied but only where its use accords with generally accepted accounting principles and practice.

Students who are also taking accounting courses will appreciate that this area of the law is subject to Accounting Standards issued by the Accounting Standards Board. It would not be appropriate to deal with these here and an examination in company law would not require knowledge of them. They would normally be examined in accounting papers.

However some of them are so important that they have a major effect on statutory provisions and must be noted in outline here. Corporate mergers will in regard to business combinations agreed on or after 31 March 2004 always be treated as if one party is buying the other (an acquisition) under amendments to **International Accounting Standard 36** issued by the International Accounting Standards Board. As already noted merger accounting enables the enlarged group to take a full year of profits from both companies. Under amended IAS 36 companies will have to treat mergers as takeovers so the enlarged organisation can only count profits since the date of acquisition (acquisition accounting).

The need to write down goodwill following a takeover is abolished. In future all goodwill is to be valued according to the profits that are actually earned from the business and projected to be earned in the future.

Group reconstructions

Section 132 provides limited relief in the case of certain group reconstructions. The reconstructions to which the Act applies are those where the transactions are as follows:

(i) a wholly-owned subsidiary (the issuing company) has allotted some of its shares either to its holding company or to another wholly-owned subsidiary of its holding company;

(ii) the allotment is a consideration for the transfer to it of shares or any non-cash assets in another subsidiary of the holding company. This other subsidiary need not necessarily be wholly owned.

The purposes of reconstruction and the variety of changes that can be achieved by the use of the reconstruction sections of the Companies Act 1985 are further described in Chapter 22.

However, let us assume that our holding company (H) holds 100 per cent of the shares in company A and 75 per cent of the shares in company B. A allots 1,000 £1 ordinary shares (valued at £6 per share) to H; in return H transfers its 75 per cent holding in B to A. If there was no relief in this situation, A would have had to raise a share premium account in its books. However, under s 132(2) A need only transfer to a share premium account an amount equal to the 'minimum premium value'.

This is the amount, if any, by which the base value of the shares in the subsidiary (B) exceeds the aggregate nominal value of the shares that the issuing company (A) allotted in consideration for the transfer.

Base value is the lower of:

(*a*) the cost to the holding company (H) of the shares in B;

(*b*) the amount at which the shares of B were stated immediately prior to this transfer in the accounting records of H.

Thus if in our example the shares in B cost £4,000 but are standing in the accounting records of H at £3,000 the base value is £3,000. The nominal value of the shares allotted by A is £1,000 so the minimum premium value is £2,000 and this must be transferred to A's share premium account, but not, of course, the true value of the consideration it received from B by allotting 1,000 shares to H.

Finally, it should be noted that the Act of 1985 imposes no obligation on a company to issue its shares at a premium when a premium could be obtained. Consequently, the issue of shares at par is valid even though a premium could have been obtained (*Hilder* v *Dexter* [1902] AC 474) but directors who fail to require subscribers to pay a premium which could have been obtained are guilty of breach of duty to the company and will be liable to pay the premium themselves as damages (*Lowry* v *Consolidated African Selection Trust Ltd* [1940] 2 All ER 545). Nevertheless, there are some exceptions to this ruling. For example, directors may issue shares at a price below their market value to existing shareholders in pursuance of a rights offer made to all the shareholders of the company, or to all the ordinary shareholders in proportion to the nominal values of their existing holdings. The reason for this is that all the shareholders concerned can avail themselves of the offer and if they do none of them will suffer a diminution of their percentage interest in the net assets or earnings of the company and consequently none of them will be harmed.

INSIDER DEALING

Part V of the Criminal Justice Act 1993 applies and Sch 2 to that Act sets out the securities covered by its provisions. It is not necessary at this level to list all of these, but obviously shares issued by companies are covered, and the prosecutions that have been brought under the insider-dealing rules, which are very few, have been concerned with dealings in company shares. However, the 1993 Act also covers gilts, which are interest-bearing securities as distinct from shares which pay a dividend, and where insider dealing could consist of dealing in such securities with inside information as to changes in interest rates either up or down.

The securities must also be listed on a regulated market such as the Stock Exchange, but dealing in differences is covered too. Those who deal in differences do not buy shares or even take an option on them. The deal consists of a forecast of the price of a particular security at a given future time, and those who enter into such deals with inside information which helps them better to predict the price will commit an offence.

The Act does not apply to unlisted securities or face-to-face transactions, so that cases such as *Percival* v *Wright*, 1902 (see Chapter 17) are unaltered on their own facts.

Meaning of dealing

A person deals in securities if he acquires or disposes of the securities himself, whether for himself or as the agent of some other person, *or* procures an acquisition or a disposal of the securities by someone else. Therefore, A could acquire shares for himself, or acquire shares as a broker for his client or dispose of them in the same contexts. Alternatively, A may simply advise B to purchase or dispose of shares and still be potentially liable if he has inside information. B may also be liable in this situation if he is a tippee (see below).

What is inside information?

Basically this is information which relates to the securities themselves or to the state of the company which issued them. It must be specific and precise so that general information about a company, e.g. that it was desirous of moving into the field of supermarkets, would not be enough. In addition the information must not have been made public and must be the sort of information which, if it had been made public, would be likely to have had a significant effect on the price of those securities, e.g. falling or rising profits or decisions to pay a higher dividend than expected, or a lower one or no dividend at all.

Insiders

In order to be guilty of the offence of insider dealing, the individual concerned must be an insider. A person has information as an insider if:

- the information which he has is and he knows it is 'insider information';
- he has the information and he knows that he has it from an 'inside source'.

A person is in possession of information from an 'inside source' if:

- he has the information through being a director, employee or shareholder of a company or by having access to it by reason of his employment, e.g. as auditor; *or*
- the source of the information is a person within the above categories.

So A is a director of Boxo plc. He has inside information that Boxo's profits when announced in ten days' time will be up (or down). He buys (or sells) Boxo shares himself and is potentially liable. He advises his friend Fred to buy (or sell) Boxo shares but does not tell him why. A is potentially liable but Fred is not – he does not have the inside information. If A tells Fred about the future profit announcement and then Fred deals, Fred is potentially liable, as is A. If Fred advises his son to buy (or sell) Boxo shares but does not tell him why, A and Fred are potentially liable but Fred's son is not. If Fred gives his son the inside information and the son deals, then A and Fred and Fred's son are potentially liable.

Disclosure in the course of employment

Sometimes it is necessary for a person to pass on inside information as part of his employment, as may be the case with an audit manager who passes on inside information to a senior partner of the firm who is in charge of the audit. If the senior partner deals he will be potentially liable, but the audit manager will not since the 1993 Act exempts such persons.

Necessity for intent

Since insider dealing is a crime, it requires, as most but not all crimes do, an intention to see a dealing take place to secure a profit or prevent a loss. It is unlikely that an examiner would go deeply into what is essentially the field of the criminal lawyer, but consider this example: A's son was at college and broke. He asked his father for a loan and his father said, 'Look, son, you're not getting any more money from me – pity you cannot buy some shares in Boxo plc of which I am a director. Next month's profit announcement will be way up on last year's. You could make a killing.' If for some reason A's son was able to scrape up sufficient funds to buy shares in Boxo plc, it is unlikely that his father would be liable because he had no idea that his son would be in a position to buy the shares.

Penalty for insider dealing

The contract is unaffected as in *Percival* v *Wright*, 1902. The sanctions are criminal, the maximum sentence being seven years' imprisonment and/or a fine of unlimited amount. In order to be found guilty, the offence must in general terms be committed while the person concerned was in the UK or the trading market was.

Exemptions

Schedule 2 to the Criminal Justice Act 1993 sets out in particular an exemption for persons operating as market makers, so that, for example, those engaged in making a market for shares on the Stock Exchange are exempt because they would find it difficult to operate markets in shares if they had to stop dealing in them when in possession of what might be inside information about some of them. It should be noted, however, that the exemption covers only the offence of dealing. They are not exempt from the offence of encouraging another to deal.

MARKET ABUSE

The Financial Services and Markets Act 2000 introduces the concept of market abuse. Under the relevant provisions, the Financial Services Authority has power to reprimand publicly or impose an unlimited fine on authorised and unauthorised persons for engaging in market abuse. The Financial Services Authority is the sole regulator for the financial services industry and has the power to authorise persons and organisations to operate in it. Its power extends to non-authorised persons and this would include members of professions such as lawyers and accountants who are, e.g., authorised by their own professional bodies to give advice incidentally to the practice of their profession, as where an accountant gives a client advice on investments as part of a tax-planning arrangement. Such persons are not authorised by the FSA unless investment advice is their main line of business and yet are covered by the market-abuse rules. Indirect market abuse is covered as where a person requires or encourages another to engage in behaviour that if done by the defendant would amount to market abuse (s 123(1) and (3)).

Market abuse defined

Section 118(1) defines market abuse as:

- behaviour in relation to any qualifying investments;
- likely to be regarded by regular users of the market as falling below the standard reasonably expected of a person in that position; and
- that falls within at least one of three categories (see below).

In general terms, the behaviour will be in a UK investment market, such as the London Stock Exchange. The regular-user concept is hypothetical and is defined as 'a reasonable person who regularly deals on the market in investments of the kind in question' (s 118(10)). The behaviour referred to is set out in s 118(2) as:

- based on information not generally available to users of the market which, if available to a regular user, would be likely to be regarded by him as relevant in regard to the terms on which to deal in those investments. *In other words, insider dealing*;
- likely to give a regular user a false or misleading impression as to the market value of such investments. *In other words, misleading statements and practices*; or
- regarded by a regular user as likely to distort the market in such investments. *In other words, rigging the market*, as where a company makes funds available to a person so that he can buy its shares in order to raise the market price by increased demand so that the shares will be more acceptable as part of takeover consideration by an exchange of shares.

There is a major defence that the person concerned exercised all due diligence to avoid market abuse, and there is a 'safe haven' where the Takeover Panel has ruled that the dealing may go ahead, as where a person with inside knowledge deals as part of a rescue operation to save the company concerned.

The market code

The FSMA gives only a broad definition of abuse but the FSA has drawn up, as the Act requires, a Code of Market Conduct to help particularise abuse. For example, the Code mentions persons using Internet bulletin boards to post misleading information and journalists using inside knowledge to trade in shares.

Burden of proof

Unlike the provisions of the Criminal Justice Act 1993, which are obviously criminal in nature and where proof beyond a reasonable doubt is required (this being the cause of its failure to provide convictions in many cases), the FSA operates under *a civil regime* so that abuse need be proved only on a balance of probabilities. However, because the proceedings might be viewed as criminal in nature under the Convention on Human Rights, the government has excluded the admission of compelled evidence emanating, for example, from a DTI inspection. It has also granted safe harbours and a due diligence defence under the Code and made some legal aid available (ss 114(8), 122, 123(2), 134–136 and 174(2)).

Injunctions and restitution

In order not to disturb the proper working of the market when the FSA imposes a fine, the transaction is not made void or unenforceable. However, for any form of market abuse or misconduct, the FSA can seek to prevent anticipated abuse by a court injunction and ask the court for a restitution order on behalf of victims of abuse to make up their loss. There are defences of reasonable belief and due diligence (ss 382(1) and (8); 383(1), (3) and (10); and 384(1) and (6)).

Position of the Criminal Justice Act 1993

This measure is not repealed and continues to be available for the pursuit of criminal prosecutions.

MODEL CODE FOR SECURITIES TRANSACTIONS BY DIRECTORS OF LISTED COMPANIES

The Financial Services Authority set up a Model Code for Securities Transactions, to give guidance as to when it is proper for directors of listed companies to deal in the securities of the company. The Code received widespread acceptance and is part of the Listing Rules. The main principles of the Code are:

(*a*) Directors should not engage in short-term dealings, e.g. purchases and sales over short periods, because it is difficult to avoid the suggestion that such dealing is based on inside knowledge.

(*b*) Directors should not deal for a minimum period prior to the announcement of reports and results. Where results are announced half-yearly, the closed period for dealings should be the previous two months but, if announcements are more frequent, e.g. quarterly, the period is one month immediately preceding the announcement of the quarterly results.

Directors should not deal either when an exceptional announcement is to be made which would probably affect the market price of the company's shares, or when they are in possession of knowledge which when accessible to the public will affect the market price of the shares.

(*c*) A director must obtain clearance from the chairman (or other designated director) before dealing. The chairman must obtain clearance either from the board or the designated director before dealing. Clearance must not be given in a closed period.

(*d*) A written record of dealings should be kept by the company and the board as a whole should see that directors comply with a practice to be established within the company on the above lines. In this respect a director should ensure that where he is a beneficiary under a trust, the trustees notify him after dealing so that it can be recorded. In addition, a director must return dealings of a spouse or for minor children.

The above rules apply also to 'relevant employees', i.e. those whose work within the company may cause them to be in possession of price-sensitive information in regard to its securities and to dealings by a director's 'connected' person, e.g. spouse.

Full details of the Model Code appear in the Listing Rules (The Purple Book) as an Appendix to Chapter 16 of those rules.

GRADED QUESTIONS

Essay mode

1 Give an account of the statutory restrictions which seek to ensure that when shares are issued by a company, they are paid for either in money or in money's worth.

(*Napier University*)

2 'A survey of price movements . . . showed clearly that there was a general tendency for the price of shares in bid-for companies to rise sharply before the announcement of takeover bids, which is in itself *prima facie* evidence of "inside buying". And there has been a continuing series of cases in which specific allegations of improper conduct by insiders have been made. The question of control over insider trading has consequently been a matter of general concern in recent years.' (Hadden)

How far has legislation alleviated this concern?

(*University of Central Lancashire*)

3 (*a*) Druid Ltd has recently issued an additional one thousand shares. Five hundred of these were issued to its former employee, Edwin, in return for his past services and his agreement not to set up a competing business in the same locality. The other 500 were issued to Francis in return for the use for a year of his garage as storage space. Previously, Francis had let his garage for this purpose for £100 per annum.

Discuss. How would your answer be different if Druid Ltd had been a public company?

(*b*) Gorgon Ltd has an issued share capital of £2 million. In 1999 it made a trading profit of £100,000 but the value of its assets fell to £1 million. In 1998, it made a trading loss of £50,000.

Advise the directors whether, and how much of, the 1999 profit is available for distribution as dividend. How would your answer differ if Gorgon Ltd was a public company?

(*The Institute of Chartered Secretaries and Administrators*)

4 (*a*) Explain what is meant by the term 'capital maintenance'.

(*b*) Discuss how the provisions of the Companies Act 1985 attempt to ensure capital maintenance by regulating:
(i) the payment of dividends,
(ii) the issue of shares at a premium.

(*The Chartered Institute of Management Accountants*)

5 Who is an 'insider' and what is 'inside information' for the purposes of the laws relating to insider dealing? What prohibitions are imposed on the activities of insiders? State the main exemptions to these prohibitions.

(*Author's question*)

6 James agrees to pay £2m for a controlling interest in Sapphire plc providing the company transfers £3m deposited with its present bankers to Emerald Bank from which James has arranged to borrow £2m. After the transfer Emerald Bank honours the cheque drawn by James to pay for the shares in Sapphire plc.

Discuss the legality of the above transactions.

(*The Institute of Chartered Accountants in England and Wales*)

7 Rich and Wealthy are partners in a firm which they wish to convert into a limited company, but they are undecided between incorporating with private status or public status. Advise them as to the advantages and restrictions of each type of company.

(*The Institute of Company Accountants*)

Objective mode

Four alternative answers are given. Select ONE only. Circle the answer which you consider to be correct. Check your answers by referring back to the information given in the chapter and against the answers at the back of the book.

1 Boxo plc was formed five years ago. It now proposes to issue 100,000 shares of £1 each to Alan in return for freehold land in Barchester. In order that the transaction should conform with company law:

A there must be a valuation of the land by the company's auditor.
B there must be a valuation by the company's auditor but only if the land is estimated to be worth more than 10 per cent of the company's issued share capital.
C there must be a valuation by an independent accountant qualified to be the company's auditor, regardless of the estimated value of the land.
D no valuation is required.

2 Which of the following is a permissible use of the share premium account under s 130 of the Companies Act 1985?

A Writing off a premium on redemption of any ordinary shares.
B Writing off goodwill.
C Writing off a premium on the redemption of debentures.
D Writing off a deficit on the profit and loss account.

3 Trent plc has issued convertible debentures to Bill at a discount. The legal position is:

A the issue is valid but the right to convert to shares is void.
B the issue is valid and so is the right to convert to shares.
C the issue is void and so therefore is the right to convert to shares.
D the issue is valid and so is the right to convert to shares if the members of Trent agree by ordinary resolution.

4 John is a director of Derwent plc, a listed company. The board of Derwent received at its last meeting a report by Joe, the finance director of Derwent, that Derwent's profits would be up by 30 per cent and that this would appear in the press report of the annual results in two weeks' time. Next day John told Sid his golfing companion that Derwent's profits would be 30 per cent up and Sid bought shares in Derwent. On the same day Sid said to his son Ronald, who was a well-paid consultant engineer, that he 'really ought to have some shares in Derwent because they seem to be a good thing'. Ronald also bought shares in Derwent. When the results were announced the shares in Derwent increased in price by 0.5p per share. Which of the following statements represents the legal liability of the parties?

A Only John is liable.
B John and Sid are liable.
C John and Joe are liable.
D John, Joe and Ronald are liable.

5 George, who is a creditor of Tees Ltd, can object to the court, regardless of the amount of his debt, about a resolution of the company which has the effect of:

A writing off goodwill against the share premium account.
B repaying debenture holders.
C writing off a deficit on profit and loss account to share capital.
D repaying non-redeemable share capital.

6 George, a director and member, proposes to transfer his shares in Moorgate Ltd in breach of a pre-emption clause in the articles of Moorgate which provides that members will offer their shares to other members first and that the other members may purchase them. What action can the other shareholders take?

A Restrain the transfer through an action by the company.
B Bring an action against George through the company for breach of his fiduciary duties as a director.
C Bring a personal action to prevent the transfer as being in breach of contract.
D They can take no action.

Answers to questions set in objective mode appear on p 576.

13

MEMBERSHIP – CAPACITY, REGISTRATION, SUBSTANTIAL AND NOMINEE HOLDINGS, ANNUAL RETURN

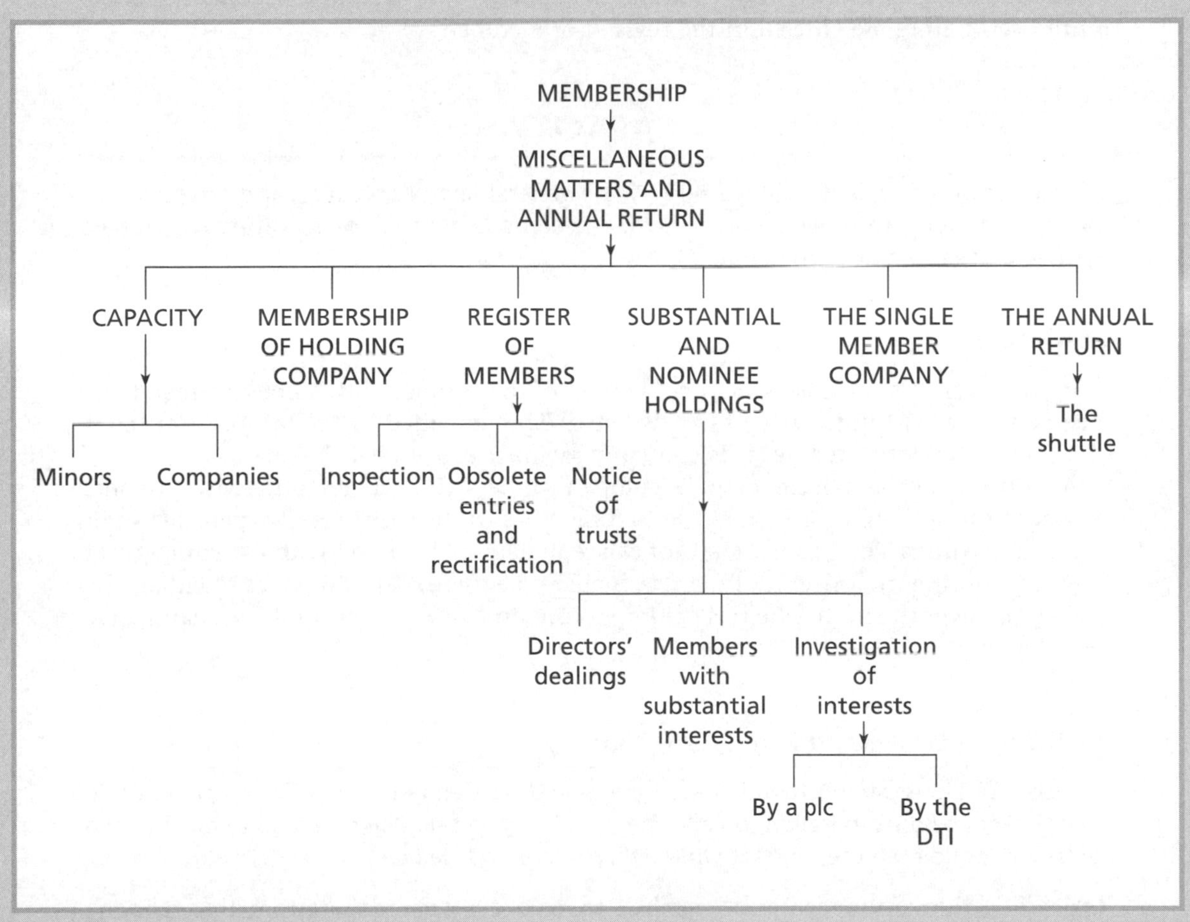

There are several ways in which membership of a company may be acquired. These are as follows:

(*a*) *By subscribing the memorandum.* When the company is registered, the persons who subscribed the memorandum automatically become members on subscription, and must be put on the register of members on registration of the company though they are deemed to be members without such an entry and even without allotment.
(*b*) *By making an application* on the basis of listing particulars or a prospectus for an allotment of shares.
(*c*) *By taking a transfer* from an existing member.
(*d*) *By succeeding to shares* on the *death* or *bankruptcy* of a member.

The persons mentioned in (*b*), (*c*) and (*d*) above do not actually become members until their names are entered in the register of members.

CAPACITY

The question of capacity is governed by the general law of contract, and anyone who has the capacity to make a contract may become a member of a company. Certain special cases must be considered:

1 Minors

The contracts of minors are governed by rules of the common law some of which have been enacted, e.g., in the Sale of Goods Act 1979 as amended by the Minors' Contracts Act 1987. The position as regards company membership appears below.

A minor may be a member of a company unless the articles otherwise provide. Registration of a minor may give rise to difficulties in the case of partly-paid shares or unlimited companies, because a minor can repudiate the contract with the company at any time during minority and for a reasonable time thereafter. If he does repudiate, he cannot recover the money he has paid up to the time of repudiation if the shares have ever had any value.

Steinberg *v* Scala (Leeds) Ltd [1923] 2 Ch 452

The claimant, Miss Steinberg, purchased shares in the defendant company and paid certain sums of money on application, on allotment and on one call. Being unable to meet future calls, she repudiated the contract whilst still a minor and claimed:

(*a*) rectification of the register of members to remove her name therefrom, thus relieving her from liability on future calls; and
(*b*) the recovery of the money already paid.

The company agreed to rectify the register and issue was joined on the claim to recover the money paid.

Held – the claim under (*b*) above failed because there had not been total failure of consideration. The shares had some value and gave some rights even though the claimant had not received any dividends and the shares had always stood at a discount on the market.

The Family Law Reform Act 1969, s 1 reduced the age of majority from 21 to 18 years. There is a general provision in the Act that a person attains a particular age, i.e. not only the age of majority, on the first moment of the relevant birthday.

A company always has power to refuse to accept a minor as a transferee or shareholder where it knows his age and can probably set aside a transfer to a minor once it learns the position (*Re Contract Corporation, Gooch's Case* (1872) LR 8 Ch App 266). However, if a company registers a minor knowing him to be such it cannot afterwards repudiate him.

2 Companies

A company may, if authorised by its memorandum, become a member of another company. It may attend meetings and vote by means of a representative (appointed by the board) or by proxy. However, a company cannot be a member of itself, i.e. it cannot purchase its own shares for a consideration because such a purchase would amount to a return of capital to the shareholders from whom the shares were bought, and would, therefore, operate as a reduction of capital without the consent of the court. A company limited by shares may acquire any of its own fully-paid shares otherwise than for valuable consideration.

This does not apply in relation to the redemption or purchase of any shares in accordance with Part V, Chapter VII of the Companies Act 1985; the acquisition of any shares in a reduction of capital duly made; the purchase of any shares in pursuance of an order of the court under s 5 (alteration of objects); s 54 (objection to resolution for company to be re-registered as private) or Part XVII (relief to members unfairly prejudiced); or the forfeiture of any shares or the acceptance of any shares surrendered in lieu in pursuance of the articles for failure to pay any sum payable in respect of those shares.

MEMBERSHIP OF A HOLDING COMPANY

Another of Parliament's attempts to prevent devices which are tantamount to an acquisition by a company of its own shares is to be found in s 23. Under that section a company cannot become a member of its holding company since the section regards this as in effect the acquisition of its own shares.

There are exceptions in the case of 'back-holdings', as where the subsidiary was a member of its holding company on 1 July 1948 (when the Companies Act 1948 brought in the rule) or on 1 November 1990 if it then became a subsidiary by reason of the revised and wider definitions of the relationship contained in the Companies Act 1989. Shares held as 'back-holdings' cannot be voted by the subsidiary at general or class meetings of members. Companies with 'back-holdings' may take further fully-paid shares where these are issued by the holding company by way of capitalisation of its reserves, whether revenue or capital reserves, such as the share premium account (a bonus issue). These additional shares cannot be voted.

There is a further exemption where the subsidiary holds the shares as a personal representative or a trustee unless the holding company or a subsidiary of it is beneficially interested under the trust, and where the shares are held by the subsidiary as a security for a loan where the subsidiary's ordinary business is lending money.

In addition, the holding company is not deemed to be beneficially interested in a trust merely because it has a subsidiary trustee company through which it runs an employees' share scheme or pension scheme and that trustee company has shares in the holding company and the surplus assets of the trustee company go under the scheme to the holding company if the trustee company is wound up.

THE REGISTER OF MEMBERS

Section 352 requires every company to keep a register of its members. The register must contain the following information:

(*a*) the names and addresses of the members;
(*b*) a statement of the shares held by each member, each share being distinguished by its number if it has one;
(*c*) the amount paid or agreed to be considered as paid up on the shares of each member;
(*d*) the date on which each person was entered in the register as a member;
(*e*) the date on which each person ceased to be a member.

Where a company has more than one class of shareholders or stockholders, the register must show to which class a member belongs and in the case of a company without a share capital having more than one class of members, the class to which the member belongs.

This useful provision enables, e.g., members who wish to maintain a campaign against the policies of the board to extract for circulation to members only the names of members holding voting rights.

Failure to keep a register of members renders the company and every officer in default liable to a fine and also to a daily fine for each day during which the default continues. However, the duty of notifying changes of address is on the shareholders and the company is not required to trace shareholders where, for example, letters are returned or dividend warrants not cashed.

The register may be kept in any form, e.g. in the form of a loose leaf system, so long as proper precautions are taken to guard against falsification. The 1985 Act allows the use of computers for company records, including the register of members, so long as the records can be reproduced in legible form. A company with more than 50 members must keep an index of its members, and if there is any alteration in the register, the index must also be altered within 14 days of such alteration. The above provisions do not apply if the register is kept in the form of an index.

The register and index are to be kept at the registered office of the company, but if the register is made up elsewhere, then it may be kept at the place where it is made up. The index must be kept where the register is kept. It is necessary to inform the

Registrar of the whereabouts of the register and of any changes if it is not kept at the registered office.

The statements required to be made in the register of members when a company's membership falls to one and if it increases again to two or more have already been considered in Chapter 1.

Inspection of register

During business hours the register and the index must under s 356 be kept open for inspection by any member free of charge, and by any other person on payment of a fee. The company must make available either to a member or to any other person a copy of any part of the register, and may make a charge for this. The company must send the copy within ten days commencing on the day after that on which the company received the request. If a company will not allow inspection of its register or give copies of it on request the company or any director or secretary who is responsible is guilty of an offence and the person asking for inspection or a copy of the register can apply to the court for an order that the company will comply with his request.

However, the relevant subsection, i.e. s 356(6) provides that the court 'may' make an order for inspection or copies. This gives the court a discretion and it may refuse to make an order, e.g. in the case of a pro-hunting charity which felt that a disclosure of members might be detrimental. A compromise might be achieved by the company offering to act as a post-box for confidential communication to and from members (see *P v F Ltd* [2001] NLJR 284). The Court of Appeal accepted a similar post-box undertaking from a company and refused to make an order for inspection in *Pelling v Families Need Fathers Ltd* [2003] [2002] 1 All ER 440 where the defendant company was a charity with the object of helping parents to stay in touch with their children after separation or divorce.

A person inspecting the register has no right himself to take extracts from or make copies of it (*Re Balaghat Co* [1901] 2 KB 665), and the right of inspection terminates on the commencement of winding-up (*Re Kent Coalfields Syndicate* [1898] 1 QB 754). Any rights then existing are derived from the insolvency rules, and not from the Act, and may require an order of court.

Power to close the register

A company may, under s 358, if it gives notice by an advertisement in a newspaper circulating in the district in which its registered office is situated, close the register for any time not exceeding 30 days in each year. This may be done to defer the entry of share transfers just prior to the annual general meeting at which a dividend is to be declared and shortly afterwards paid. It will also enable the company to prepare a list of its members as at a certain date in case a poll should be demanded at the annual general meeting.

Obsolete entries in the register

A company may remove from the register any entry which relates to a former member where the person concerned has not been a member for at least 20 years.

Rectification of the register

The register of members is under s 361 prima facie evidence of the matters which the Companies Act requires it to contain.

However, the court has power under s 359 to rectify the register if application is made to it where:

(*a*) the name of any person is without sufficient cause entered in or omitted from the register; or
(*b*) default is made, or unnecessary delay takes place, in entering on the register the fact that a person has ceased to be a member.

As well as rectification, the court may order the payment by the company of any damages sustained by any party aggrieved. Notice of rectification must be given to the Registrar of Companies under the terms of the court's order.

The circumstances set out in (*a*) and (*b*) above are not the only ones in which the court can order rectification. For example, rectification will be ordered where joint holders wish to split the holding because in general terms the rights attaching to the shares, e.g. voting rights, are vested in the first-named person on the register (see below). The company should therefore in ordinary circumstances agree to a request to split the holding.

Burns *v* Siemens Bros Dynamo Works Ltd [1919] 1 Ch 225

The claimants, Burns and Hambro, were the joint owners of shares in the defendant company. The shares were entered in the company's register in the joint names of Burns and Hambro. The company's articles provided that, where there were joint holders, the person whose name appeared first in the register of members, and no other, should be entitled to vote in respect of the shares. The result was, of course, that Hambro had no voting rights. This action was brought by Burns and Hambro asking that the register be rectified so as to show roughly half of the joint shareholding in the name of each joint holder. *Held* – by the High Court – the court had jurisdiction to make such an order, and the company was required to rectify the register, showing shares numbered 1 to 10,000 in the names of Burns and Hambro, and shares numbered 10,001 to 19,993 in the names of Hambro and Burns.

Comment

Rectification will also be granted where an allotment of shares is set aside following, e.g., a false statement in a prospectus. The consequent action for rescission – if that is the course the claimant chooses to pursue – is accompanied by a request for rectification of the register.

Minor amendments

Minor amendments not involving the identity of a member, e.g. as to a postal address, may be made without resort to the court under the authority of the company secretary or company registrar, following receipt by the company of a request for a change in a member's details.

Notice of trusts

Under s 360 and *Reg* 5 of *Table A* no notice of any trust shall be entered on the register of members of companies registered in England and Wales. The rule laid down by the section has two branches:

(i) *The company is entitled to treat every person whose name appears on the register as the beneficial owner of the shares even though he may in fact hold them in trust for another.* Thus, if the company registers a transfer of shares held by a trustee, it is not liable to the beneficiaries under the trust even though the sale of the shares by the trustee was fraudulent or in breach of the powers given to him in the trust instrument.

Simpson *v* Molson's Bank [1895] AC 270

This was an appeal to the Privy Council in England from the Court of Queen's Bench for Lower Canada. It appeared that the bank was incorporated by an Act of Parliament, and that by s 36 of that Act the bank was not bound to take notice of any trust over its shares. (The provision was similar to the one contained in s 360.) The executors of the Hon John Molson were given ten years by his will to wind up his estate. After the expiration of that time, and in breach of the terms of the will, they made a transfer of certain shares in the bank. The claimants, who had an interest in the residuary estate of John Molson, brought this action claiming damages from the bank because it had registered a transfer knowing that transfer to be in breach of trust, such knowledge being derived from the fact that a copy of the will was deposited at the bank, and that William Molson, the testator's brother, was one of the executors who signed the transfer and was also the president of the bank. *Held* – the bank was not liable for registering the transfer although it had notice that it was in breach of trust, because s 36 of the Act of Parliament incorporating the bank provided specifically that it should not take notice of any trust over its shares.

(ii) *Where persons claim rights in shares under equitable titles, such as an equitable mortgage, the company is not made into a trustee if those persons merely serve notice on the company of the existence of their equitable claims.* The correct way of protecting such an interest is by serving a *stop notice* on the company by the procedure already outlined in Chapter 10.

It follows from this branch of the 'no trusts' rule that where there are two or more lenders on the security of the same shares by way of equitable mortgage, the first in date has priority, not the first to give notice to the company.

Société Générale de Paris *v* Walker (1885) 11 App Cas 20

James Walker was the registered owner of 100 shares in Tramways Union Ltd, and he created two charges over the shares, one on 9 March 1881 in favour of James Scott Walker, who took the certificates and a blank transfer, and one on 1 December 1882 in favour of the appellants, the latter charge being created by means of a blank transfer, duly executed but without the deposit of the share certificate. The appellants tried to obtain registration first, but Tramways Union Ltd would not register the transfer without the certificates, and later the executors of James Scott Walker informed the Tramways Union that they had the certificates. This action was brought to decide who had the title to the shares. The articles of Tramways Union Ltd provided that the company should not be bound to recognise any equitable interest in its shares. The appellants claimed that because they notified first the fact of their equitable interest in the shares, they were entitled as against the executors of James Scott Walker. *Held* – by the House of Lords – they were not, because neither the company nor its officers could be treated as trustees for the purpose of notifying equitable interests over the shares. The title to the shares was in the person eventually registered by the company, and the company was right in refusing to register a person who could not produce the share certificates. The respondents were entitled to the shares.

It should be noted that s 360 only protects the company, and where directors register a transfer, *knowing it is being made in breach of trust or in fraud of some person having an equitable right*, they may incur personal liability to the person suffering loss.

The rule also means that there can be no registration of a trust as such. An entry on the register such as 'The ABC Family Trust' would be an infringement of s 360. The correct entry and the share certificate should show merely the names of the individual trustees without any reference to the fact that they are trustees or the nature of the trusts. If a note of the existence of the trust is required for administrative purposes this can be recorded outside the register possibly with a coded cross-reference.

If a trustee of shares is entered on the register, he is personally liable for the calls made by the company, though he can claim an indemnity to the extent of the trust property and, if this is not sufficient, from the beneficiaries personally. A company cannot put a beneficiary on the list of contributories in a winding-up, though it can enforce the trustee's right of indemnity against the beneficiaries by the doctrine of *subrogation* (*per* James L J in *Re European Society Arbitration Acts* (1878) 8 Ch D 679).

A company claiming a *lien* on its shares will be affected by a notice of any charge which arose prior to the debt in respect of which the company's lien is being exercised. As we have seen, this is not regarded as a notice of trust, but is more by way of a notice of lien as between one trader and another (see *Bradford Banking Co* v *Briggs*, 1886).

Table A, Reg 5 provides: 'Except as required by law, no person shall be recognised by the company as holding any share upon any trust and (except as otherwise provided by the articles or by law) the company shall not be bound by or recognise any interest in any share except an absolute right to the entirety thereof in the holder.'

Overseas branch register

A company which carries on business in some part of Northern Ireland or any part of Her Majesty's dominions outside the UK as listed in Sch 14, Part I, the Isle of Man and the Channel Islands may under s 362 keep an overseas branch register of members resident in the country where it carries on business. It seems that the purpose of such a register is to facilitate the transfer of the shares of these members. The Registrar of Companies must be informed of the situation of the office where the overseas branch register is kept within 14 days of its opening, and must receive the same notice of its closure and changes in the place where it is kept.

The overseas branch register is considered part of the company's main register and must be kept in the same manner. Copies of all entries on the register must be sent to the company's registered office as soon as possible after they are made, and the company must keep a duplicate of the register at the same place as its principal register. Rectification of the register is achieved by application to the appropriate court in the place in which the register is kept.

Termination of membership

Termination of membership is complete when the name of a former member is removed from the register. This may occur by:

(*a*) transfer of the shares to a purchaser or by way of gift (subject to liability to be put on the list of members for one year if the company goes into liquidation) (see further Chapter 25);
(*b*) forfeiture, surrender, or a sale by the company under its lien;
(*c*) the taking of a share warrant, though certain rights of membership may still be conferred by the articles;
(*d*) redemption or purchase of shares by the company;
(*e*) the registration of a trustee in bankruptcy, or by his disclaimer of the shares;
(*f*) death of the member;
(*g*) rescission of the contract to take the shares arising out of fraud or misrepresentation in the prospectus, or by reason of irregular allotment;
(*h*) dissolution of the company by winding-up or amalgamation or reconstruction under Insolvency Act 1986, s 110 (see Chapter 22);
(*i*) compulsory acquisition under s 429 (see further Chapter 22);
(*j*) under the provisions of the company's constitution, e.g. expulsion under the articles for competing with the company (see *Sidebottom* v *Kershaw Leese*, 1920).

SUBSTANTIAL AND NOMINEE SHAREHOLDINGS

As we have seen, the register of members merely gives the identity of the person in whose name the shares are registered. No indication is given of any interests in the shares which persons other than the registered holder might have. Furthermore, no notice of trust is to be entered on the register of members of a company registered in England. Where share warrants are in issue the position is, of course, worse since the names of the holders at any point of time are unknown, there being no form of registration.

This situation is capable of abuse. For example, it enables directors to traffic in the securities of their companies without this being known, or someone secretly to acquire control of a sizeable holding on which to base a bid for control.

The Companies Act deals with the above problems as follows.

The purchase and sale of the company's securities by the directors

Directors and shadow directors have under Sch 13 to notify the company in writing within five days of acquiring or disposing of *any* beneficial interest in shares or debentures of the company or companies in the group. The five days begins to run from the day following knowledge of the acquisition or disposal. Interests of a spouse or minor child of a director are treated as interests of the director, as are interests held behind a nominee. This does not apply in the case of a spouse or minor child if those persons are also directors, in which case they will disclose their own holding themselves. There is no minimum limit on the amount of the interest. A listed company must notify the Stock Exchange by close of business on the day following notification by the director.

The company must maintain a register of directors' interests and dealings and must enter thereon the information received within three days. This register is to be open to inspection by members without charge and by others on payment of a fee, and copies may be obtained on payment of a fee.

Substantial share interests

Schedule 13 also deals with disclosure of interests in shares only and not debentures. A person must notify a public (not a private) company of his known acquisition of interests or cessation of interests in the issued share capital of the company carrying the right to vote in all circumstances at general meetings of the company whether the company's shares are listed or not.

The notifiable percentage is 3 per cent or more of the aggregate nominal value of the company's voting shares. Where the voting share capital is divided into different classes of shares the obligation to notify arises whenever a person is interested in 3 per cent or more of any class of shares. Notification must also be made where having reached the 3 per cent holding or more there is a *known* increase or decrease of more than 1 per cent in the interest.

Notification must therefore be made whenever a known change brings about a known increase or decrease above or below 3 per cent or a known increase or decrease to the next percentage point occurs in an interest exceeding 3 per cent. Thus if a person has an interest in, say, 10.5 per cent of relevant capital, there is no requirement to notify a change in the interest unless and until it falls below 10 per cent or increases to 11 per cent.

No further notification is required once the interest is below 3 per cent unless and until it reaches 3 per cent or more again. A person has an interest if (*a*) he is the owner of the shares either in his own name or through a nominee; (*b*) his spouse or minor child owns them; (*c*) a company in which he controls one-third of the voting power owns them; (*d*) he is a beneficiary under a trust over the shares; (*e*) he owns them jointly with another (each owner is deemed to be interested in the entire holding); (*f*) he has a stock exchange contract to buy the shares; (*g*) he is a member of a 'concert party' (see below).

The company must be notified within two days of the change and the company must record the details in a register of interests in shares within three days of receiving the notification. The register must be available for inspection without charge by any member or by any other person.

The Act exempts market makers from the requirement to disclose holdings of 3 per cent or more. This refers, however, only to holdings in the capacity of market maker.

A person who fails to notify as required or gives false or misleading information is liable to a fine or imprisonment or both.

The Act gives a company power to remove entries from the register after six years if the person concerned has ceased to have a notifiable interest. The section does not place a duty upon the company to remove the entry.

Where the company is listed, there is an additional requirement for the company to disclose the information it has received from the member to the London Stock Exchange. Disclosure is to be made without delay to the Company Announcements Office, as provided for in the Listing Rules.

Concert parties

A major difficulty which had arisen under previous disclosure legislation of the kind set out above was that several persons had held a non-disclosable interest, say, 2.9 per cent of a company's voting shares and had acted in concert, e.g. voted together, so that a position of strength had been built up in the company without the need for disclosure.

The Companies Act 1985 deals with this situation and the relevant provisions are set out below.

A concert party is defined as an agreement between two or more persons, whether legally binding or not, to *acquire shares in a public company*, and the agreement must include a provision for that. The agreement must also include provisions containing restrictions in respect of the use of the shares, e.g. as regards voting and disposal. Finally, the shares must have been acquired because the person who bought them was doing so in order to carry out his agreement with the other or others.

Thus a group of shareholders who band together to oppose a particular plan of the board are not a concert party and therefore not subject to the provisions in the 1985 Act relating to concert parties.

If the three criteria for a concert party are established, the obligation to notify the company of the *collective holding* at 3 per cent, and of 1 percentage point increases and decreases in an interest above 3 per cent, is upon each member of the concert party and each member has an obligation to notify the other members of the concert party of his holding whether acquired under the agreement or not so that each is in a position to disclose the collective holding. The parties can appoint one of their number as an agent for the purposes of notification. The obligation to notify must be carried out within two days and there are criminal penalties for failing to do so. Once a concert party is established, the collective holding is *all* the voting shares held by each member and not merely those acquired in pursuance of the agreement.

Disclosure by those managing the investments of others

Here the Disclosure of Interests in Shares (Amendment) Regulations 1993 apply and provide for disclosure of non-material interests as they are called. Disclosure here is when a 10 per cent threshold is reached. Disclosure is first to the company and then by the company to the Stock Exchange in the case of listed companies. Thus an investment manager who has a unit trust with an interest of 3.2 per cent in Boxo plc, a managed investment trust owning 4 per cent in Boxo and other managed funds coming to 4 per cent in Boxo, must disclose his interest as a non-material interest to the company and the company must then disclose to the Stock Exchange. The rules relating to the time of disclosure are the same as those set out for the 3 per cent disclosure of material interests.

Power of public company to investigate interests

Under s 212 a public company may make enquiries of *any person* (not merely a member) whom it knows or has reasonable cause to believe to be *interested* in any of its voting shares either at the present time or at any time during the preceding three years.

This applies whether or not the company's shares are listed or dealt in on the unlisted securities market. It embraces present members, past members during the preceding three years, and others, e.g. those holding behind a bank nominee who have never been registered as members. Failure to respond to an enquiry by a person who is or was interested or the giving of an incorrect response may result in a criminal prosecution leading to a fine and/or imprisonment. In addition, the company may apply to the court for an order imposing the restrictions of Part XV on the shares involved. These restrictions may prevent transfer, voting, dividend payments, and the receipt of rights issues.

The above restrictions can be lifted on application to the court if the court is satisfied that the information has been given or the court is asked to approve a sale of the shares. However, in *Re Geers Gross plc* [1988] BCLC 140 it was held that it was not enough for a shareholder to ask the court to approve a sale. The court decided that it had power in doing so to require that the company be given the information it required as part of the approval of a sale.

As regards the imposition of sanctions, a company may, as we have seen, apply to the court. In addition, it may take power in its articles to impose sanctions, though if it is a listed company Stock Exchange rules allow only the restriction of voting rights. The rules prescribe a time limit of 14 days for notification and will not allow sanctions to be imposed on holders of less than 0.25 per cent of relevant shares. The Secretary of State has power to make rules under which restriction in the articles could extend, in the case of all plcs, to dividend and transfer rights, and to prescribe a 14-day time limit for notification. At the present time the Act merely says that the information must be supplied within a reasonable time.

Restrictions can be placed on shares in a UK company held by a foreign company if the foreign company will not make disclosure (see *Re F H Lloyd Holdings* (1985) PCC 268).

If the company (in practice the board) is not willing to commence an investigation, members who hold at least 10 per cent of the paid-up voting shares may *require the board* to exercise the powers of investigation. There are fines and/or imprisonment on any officer of the company in default if the company is not caused to exercise the powers of investigation.

In addition, if the company fails to exercise its powers of investigation the 10 per cent (or more) requisitionists may apply to the court for restrictions to be put on the shares.

Department of Trade and Industry investigations

It should be noted that the 1985 Act confers a power on the Department of Trade and Industry to appoint an inspector to investigate possible breaches by the directors of their duty to disclose share and debenture holdings in the company.

As regards the secret acquisition of control of companies, mention should also be made here of provisions which give the DTI power to investigate the ownership of a company's shares. These provisions will be dealt with at greater length, but the sections have been used quite extensively in recent times in order to ascertain whether a person operating through nominees has acquired sufficient shares in a company to give rise to the making of a bid for the remainder as is required by the City Code, once 30 per cent of the voting shares have been acquired (see further Chapter 22).

THE SINGLE-MEMBER PRIVATE LIMITED COMPANY

The Companies (Single Member Private Limited Companies) Regulations 1992 (SI 1992/699) have already been referred to in detail in Chapter 1, to which reference might be made at this point by way of revision.

THE ANNUAL RETURN

Under the Companies Act 1985, Part XI, as amended by the Companies Act 1989, a company must file an annual return with the Registrar. It must be made up to a date 12 months after the previous return or in the case of the first return 12 months after incorporation. The company may move the date of its next annual return by informing Companies House (the Companies Registration Office) on Form 363s. The new date of submission then governs future annual submissions; alternatively, a company that wishes to change the date of submission before the receipt of Form 363s can submit Form 363a (see below). The return must be delivered to the Registrar within 28 days of the make-up date. 'Delivered' means what it says: it is not enough to post it on day 28. There is no longer any link with the annual general meeting.

The shuttle concept

The usual form of annual return is a 'shuttle document' (Form 363s) which is prepared by the Registrar and is based on information which has been filed by the company. It is sent to the company for checking, signature and return with amendment if necessary. In the first year Companies House will prepare and issue Form 363b to enable shuttle documents to be issued in subsequent years. A company may as an alternative make the annual return on Form 363a which does not involve preparation and issue by Companies House.

Contents of annual return

The shuttle document (Form 363s) contains the following matters:

(*a*) the company's name and number;
(*b*) the date of the annual return;
(*c*) the date of next return. The company can put a new date in here and Companies House will send the document at the appropriate time *next year*. If the company wishes to change the submission date to a date earlier than this it must submit Form 363a before it receives the shuttle document;
(*d*) the address of the registered office;
(*e*) the principal business activity by reference to one or more codes based on the UK Standard Industrial Classification of Economic Activities published by the Stationery Office. For example the manufacture of computers and process equipment is currently 3001;
(*f*) the address where the register of members is kept;
(*g*) the place where the register of debenture holders (or duplicate) is kept;

(*h*) company type, e.g. public limited company;

(*i*) particulars of the company secretary. Particulars of a new secretary must be notified on Form 288a;

(*j*) particulars of directors which are the same as those contained in the register of directors and secretaries (see Chapter 15), though there is no need to give other directorships or previous first names. Particulars of a new director must be notified on Form 288a;

In this connection, the Criminal Justice and Police Act 2001 makes changes to the CA 1985 so that company directors at risk of serious violence or intimidation from protest groups, such as the directors of companies involved in the use of animals for medical purposes, may apply to the Department of Trade and Industry for permission (by order) to file a service address at Companies House instead of the home address. Directors still have to supply the Registrar with a home address but this is kept on a special register that is secure and open to inspection only by specific bodies such as the police. The orders are called 'confidentiality orders'. Regulations may be made under s 723C of the CA 1985 (inserted by the 2001 Act) under which private addresses may in certain circumstances be omitted from the company's own register of directors and secretaries. Confidentiality orders may be made in the case of company secretaries or a company's 'permanent representatives'.

(*k*) issued share capital;

(*l*) a list of current members and those who have ceased to be members since the last return. If full details have been given on the return for either of the last two years the company need only give new members since the last return and those ceasing to be members since then together with those whose holdings of stocks and shares have changed. If there have been no changes the company's agent ticks the appropriate box.

The return contains a certification section to be signed by the secretary or a director. A filing fee is payable. If the shuttle return reveals a change which has not been previously notified, as in the case of a change in the particulars of a director (notifiable on Form 288c), the Registrar will regard the return as giving the required notification but may take enforcement procedures where there is abuse. Consequently, separate notification as required should preferably be made.

Dormant companies must file an annual return.

Sanctions if return not made

The company and every officer in default is liable to a fine under Sch 24, and in addition the directors may become disqualified by the court if they persist in failing to file the annual return or other documents (see further Chapter 18). Furthermore, any member or creditor can, under s 713, serve a notice on a defaulting company requiring that company to file an annual return. If it fails to do so within 14 days, the member or creditor may make application to the court for a direction that the company shall make the return and the company is liable to pay the applicant's costs.

Reform

Companies House is proposing changes in the annual return as follows:

(*a*) to abolish the requirements for companies to enter on the annual return:

(i) details of transfers of shares since the made-up date of the last annual return; and

(ii) a list of persons who have ceased to be members of the company since the made-up date of the last annual return;

(*b*) there is also a proposal to store capital and shareholder information electronically enabling the information provided in the previous year to be pre-printed on the next annual return (the 'shuttle document').

The electronic shuttle

The shuttle annual return can be submitted electronically under the Companies House system called WebFiling. Electronic annual return forms are not currently available for all companies. The website gives full details (see www.companieshouse.gov.uk).

For security reasons WebFiling can only be used when registration for a security code (issued by e-mail) and an authentication code (issued by post) have been obtained. These codes are required to log in and the relevant company details can be viewed and the necessary changes made.

GRADED QUESTIONS

Essay mode

1 Describe an Annual Return and state the particulars which must be given in the Annual Return of a company which has a share capital.

(*The Institute of Company Accountants*)

2 Every public company is required to maintain a register of 'substantial holdings and interests' in shares which it has issued.

(*a*) What duties are imposed upon persons to notify such holdings and interests?
(*b*) What is the purpose of the requirement?

(*The Institute of Chartered Accountants in England and Wales*)

3 Privatus Ltd was a private company which owed the sum of £4,000 to Alex for goods which he had sold to it. As the company was short of cash, its directors allotted to Alex 6,000 £1 shares in the company credited as fully paid. The share certificate issued to Alex stated that the shares were fully paid.

Alex contracted to sell these shares to Bertram and duly handed him the share certificate and a signed stock transfer form. When Bertram sent these documents to the company in order to have the transfer registered, the directors became concerned that problems might arise over the original issue to Alex. They discussed the matter over a four-month period and then wrote to Bertram informing him that in accordance with Art 24 of the company's articles of association they refused to register his transfer. Article 24 reads, 'The directors may refuse to register the transfer of a share which is not fully paid to a person of whom they do not approve.' Bertram has now begun a court action to secure his registration as a member.

Advise the company of its position with regard to the issue of the shares to Alex and the action brought by Bertram.

(The Association of Chartered Certified Accountants)

4 The Companies Act 1985 places upon public companies certain controls over the type and value of the consideration which such companies may receive for an issue of their shares. You are required to select any three of these controls and explain in each instance how the control restricts the company and why, in your view, the provision was enacted.

(The Chartered Institute of Management Accountants)

5 The following is a summarised balance sheet of C Ltd:

	£	£
Authorised Capital		
100,000 Ordinary Shares of £1 each	100,000	
10,000 – 10 per cent Redeemable Preference Shares of £1 each	10,000	110,000
Total Assets (including Cash at Bank of £50,000)		400,000
Liabilities		200,000
Net Assets		200,000
Represented by:		
Issued Capital		
100,000 Ordinary Shares of £1 each		100,000
10,000 – 10 per cent Redeemable Preference Shares		10,000
		110,000
Capital Reserve (Share Premium a/c)	10,000	
Revenue Reserves	80,000	90,000
		£200,000

The directors seek your advice as to how they may redeem the preference shares and whether they may issue 20,000 bonus Ordinary Shares of £1 each. Advise them on these matters and redraft the balance sheet as it would appear after implementing your advice.

(Kingston University)

6 (*a*) 'A company cannot issue shares at a discount.'

Discuss.

(*b*) False Ltd and Gorgon Ltd both have an issued share capital of £500,000 and a share premium account of £50,000. The directors of False Ltd have recently decided that it is over-capitalised and wish to return £55,000 to the shareholders. Gorgon Ltd has recently made a loss of £55,000 and its directors wish to reduce the company's capital accordingly.

Advise the directors of both companies.

(The Institute of Chartered Secretaries and Administrators)

Objective mode

Four alternative answers are given. Select ONE only. Circle the answer which you consider to be correct. Check your answers by referring back to the information given in the chapter and against the answers at the back of the book.

1 A person who acquires an interest in the shares of a public company must notify the company of that interest when it equals or exceeds:

A 20% of the voting shares.
B 10% of the voting shares.
C 5% of the voting shares.
D 3% of the voting shares.

2 Tees plc has an issued share capital of £100,000 and recently issued another 100,000 £1 ordinary shares. Fred, his wife, his son (aged 18) and a private company in which Fred is the majority shareholder each acquired 10,000 shares. What is the interest which Fred must notify to the company under the Companies Act 1985 (as amended)?

A 40,000 shares.
B 30,000 shares.
C 20,000 shares.
D 10,000 shares.

3 Dodgy plc has four members as set out below. Which one of these members cannot exercise the voting rights on the shares held?

A Miss Tranter, a schoolmistress.
B Magic plc, which is the holding company of the Magic Group.
C Michael, who is a minor whose membership is permitted by Dodgy's articles.
D Mostyn Ltd, which is a subsidiary of Dodgy.

4 The Companies Act 1985 requires that when equity shares are allotted for cash they must be offered first to existing shareholders in proportion to their holding in the company. Such an issue of shares is known as:

A a rights issue.
B a preference issue.
C an issue of bonus shares.
D an issue of founders' shares.

5 How is a share warrant validly transferred?

A By any writing.
B By writing and delivery.
C By delivery.
D By instrument of transfer.

6 The articles of private companies often provide that members wishing to sell their shares must offer them first to existing members. What is such a clause called?

A An expropriation clause.
B A compulsory purchase clause.
C A pre-emption clause.
D A statutory pre-emption clause.

Answers to questions set in objective mode appear on p 576.

14

MINORITY PROTECTION

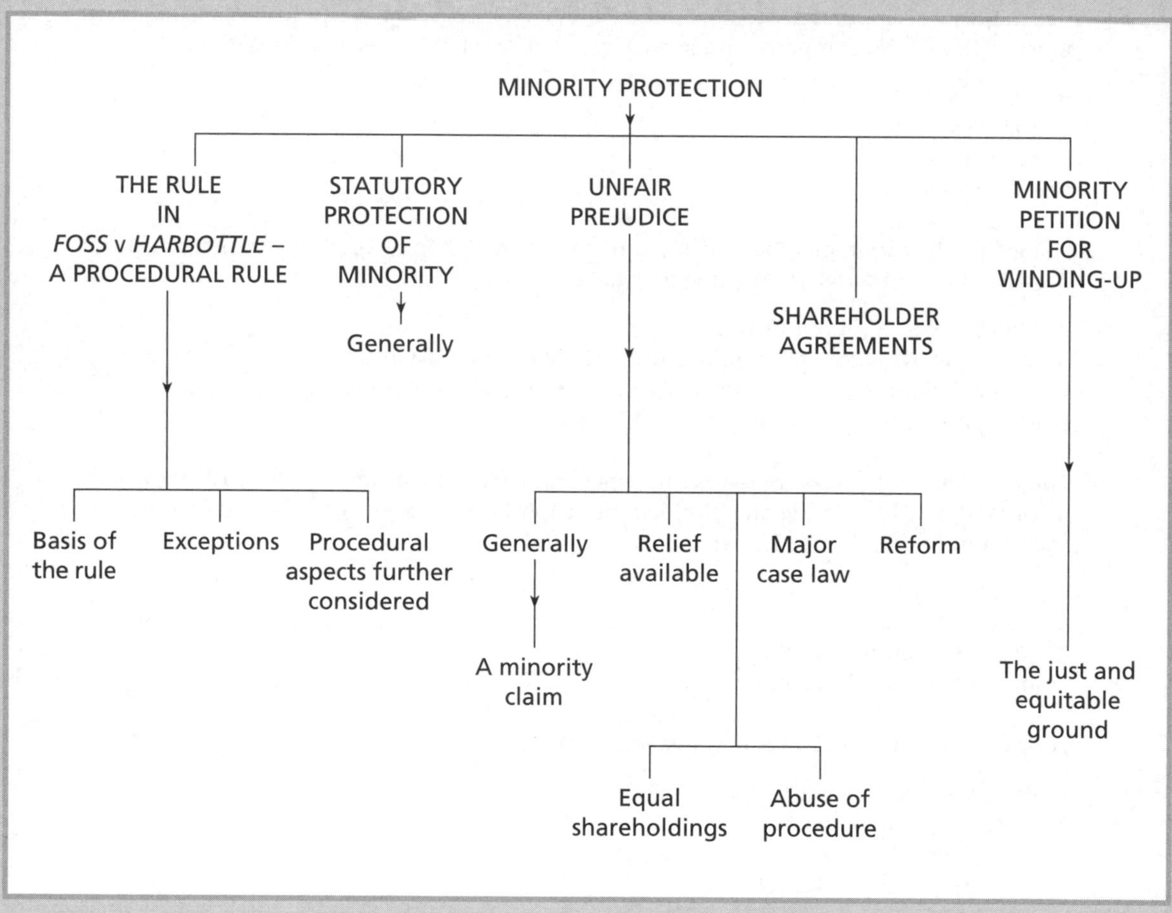

Although many functions are delegated to the directorate, the eventual power and control in a company rests with those shareholders who can command a majority of the voting power. Thus a person or group of persons controlling three-quarters of the votes would have complete control of the company, and a little more than half the votes would give considerable influence allowing, e.g., control over appointments to the board.

The principle of majority rule is well established and is emphasised in the matter of litigation by the rule in *Foss* v *Harbottle*, 1843 (see below). Generally it does little harm since most companies are managed fairly, even if at times there is not due concern for the rights of minorities which might lead to oppression. The problem is at its greatest in private companies because the shares of such companies are not listed on the Stock Exchange, the protection of the Stock Exchange rules is not available, and there is rarely any press comment on their activities.

THE FUNCTION OF PROCEDURAL RULES

The matter of minority rights is really a matter of civil procedure, rather than a principle of company law as such. Derivative claims, as they are called, are covered by the rules of court procedure. A derivative claim is an action by a minority shareholder on behalf of the company to pursue a cause of action that is vested in (or belongs to) the company where there is an abuse of power by the majority in the company, whether acting as directors or shareholders. The matter gets into court so as to give us the relevant decisions in the following way. Where, e.g., directors who are alleged to have abused their powers receive a claim form from a minority shareholder and respond to it, the minority shareholder as claimant must apply to the court to continue the claim. Hence, our case law. The application may include a request to the court by the claimant to be indemnified (paid) in costs out of the assets of the company. If the claimant fails to apply to the court for permission to continue, any defendant director may apply to the court for an order to dismiss the proceedings.

It may be helpful to understand this procedural aspect at the beginning, though the matter receives further treatment later in the chapter.

THE RULE IN *FOSS V HARBOTTLE*

The rule in *Foss* v *Harbottle*, 1843 states that in order to redress a wrong done to a company or to the property of the company, or to enforce rights of the company, the proper claimant is the company itself, and the court will not ordinarily entertain an action brought on behalf of the company by a shareholder.

Foss *v* Harbottle (1843) 2 Hare 461

The claimants, Foss and Turton, were shareholders in a company called 'The Victoria Park Company' which was formed to buy land for use as a pleasure park. The defendants were the other directors and shareholders of the company. The claimants alleged that the defendants had defrauded the company in various ways, and in particular that certain of the defendants had sold land belonging to them to the company at an exorbitant price. The claimants now asked the court to order that the defendants make good the losses to the company. *Held* – by Vice-Chancellor Wigram – since the company's board of directors was still in existence, and since it was still possible to call a general meeting of the company, there was nothing to prevent the company from obtaining redress in its corporate character, and the action by the claimants could not be sustained.

Basis of the rule

Four major principles seem to be at the basis of the rule as the decided cases show:

1 ***The right of the majority to rule***. The court has said in some of the cases that an action by a single shareholder cannot be entertained because the feeling of the majority of the members has not been tested, and they may be prepared, if asked, to waive their right to sue. Thus the company can only sue (a) if the directors pass a resolution to that effect where the power is delegated to them; or (b) if the company expresses its desire to sue by an ordinary resolution in general meeting, whether the power is delegated to the directors or not, since the power of the members to bring the company into court as a claimant is concurrent with that of the directors, and if the members wish to bring the company into court and the directors do not, the wish of the members by ordinary resolution will prevail.

2 ***The company is a legal person***. The court has also said from time to time that since a company is a *persona at law*, the action is vested in it, and cannot be brought by a single member.

3 ***The prevention of a multiplicity of actions***. This situation could occur if each individual member was allowed to commence an action in respect of a wrong done to the company. See James LJ in *Gray* v *Lewis* (1873) 8 Ch App 1035 at p 1051 – a judgment which is particularly supportive of the multiplicity problem.

4 ***The court's order may be made ineffective***. It should be noted that the court order could be overruled by an ordinary resolution of members in a subsequent general meeting, provided that the general meeting is not controlled by the wrongdoers (see below). As Mellish LJ said in *MacDougall* v *Gardiner* (1875) 1 Ch D 13 at p 25, '. . . if the thing complained of is a thing which in substance the majority of the company are entitled to do . . . there can be no use in having a litigation about it, the ultimate end of which is only that a meeting has to be called, and then ultimately the majority gets its wishes'.

It will be appreciated that we cannot substitute unanimous written resolutions here since the minority who allege oppression would not sign such a resolution.

It will be seen, therefore, that the rule in *Foss* is in no sense helpful to the minority. In fact, if there were no exceptions to the rule, the minority could never bring a claim at all. It is to the exceptions that we must now turn.

Acts infringing the personal rights of shareholders

These actions are not so much genuine exceptions to the rule in *Foss*, they are more in the nature of situations which are outside it. Thus in *Pender* v *Lushingon*, 1877 (see Chapter 4) the court dealt with the attempted removal of the claimant's right to vote without suggesting that the rule in *Foss* in any way prevented the action from being brought.

Exceptions to the rule – generally

Although the courts have not developed an entirely clear pattern of exceptions, those set out below appear to be the main areas in which the court will allow claims to be brought by shareholders as an exception to the rule in *Foss*.

1 ***Acts which are* ultra vires *or illegal*.** No simple majority of members can confirm or ratify an illegal act. Section 35 of the 1985 Act gives an individual member a *statutory* right to ask the court for an injunction to restrain the directors from entering into *ultra vires* transactions but *not* if the members of the company have ratified a particular transaction by special resolution. So far as illegality is concerned, the minority could bring an action to force the directors to comply with the law restricting, e.g., loans, quasi-loans and credit given by the company to directors and their connected persons.

2 ***Where the act complained of can only be confirmed by a special or extraordinary resolution*.** *Foss* is based on the principle that the majority, i.e. those who can obtain an ordinary resolution, should decide whether or not a complaint relating to the company should be brought before the court. Clearly, therefore, a simple majority of the members cannot be allowed to confirm a transaction requiring a greater majority.

Edwards *v* Halliwell [1950] 2 All ER 1064

A trade union had rules, which were the equivalent of articles of association, under which any increase in members' contributions had to be agreed by a two-thirds majority in a ballot of members. A meeting decided by a simple majority to increase the subscriptions without holding a ballot. The claimants, as a minority of members, applied for a declaration from the court that the resolution was invalid. It was *held* that the rule in *Foss* did not prevent a minority of a company, or as here, an association of persons, from suing because the matter about which they were suing was one which could only be done or validly sanctioned by a greater than simple majority.

3 ***Where there is a fraud on the minority*.** The rule in *Foss* would create grave injustice if the majority were allowed to commit wrongs against the company and benefit from those wrongs at the expense of the minority simply because no claim could be brought in respect of the wrong. Thus, there is a major and somewhat ill-defined exception referred to as 'fraud on the minority'. The following headings describe the main areas of fraud.

(*a*) *Where the company is defrauded*. Examples of this exception are to be found in the following cases which involved misappropriation of the company's property.

Menier *v* Hooper's Telegraph Works Ltd (1874) 9 Ch App 350

Company A (European and South American Telegraph Co) was formed to lay a transatlantic cable to be made by Hooper's, the majority shareholder in company A, from Portugal to Brazil. Hooper's found that they could make a greater profit by selling the cable to another company B, but B did not have the government concession to lay the cable which company A had. After much intrigue with the Portuguese government trustee of the concession, he agreed to transfer the concession to company B, and company B then bought the cable from Hooper's. To prevent company A from suing for loss of the concession Hooper obtained the passing of a resolution to wind up company A voluntarily and arranged that a liquidator should be appointed whom Hooper could trust not to pursue the claim of company A in respect of the loss of its contract. Menier, a minority shareholder of company A, asked the court to compel Hooper to account to company A for the profits made on the sale of the cable to B. *Held* – by the Court of Appeal in Chancery – where the majority shareholders of a company propose to gain a benefit for themselves at the expense of the minority, the court may interfere to protect the minority. In such a case one shareholder has a right to bring a derivative claim to seek relief and the claim is not barred by the rule in *Foss* v *Harbottle*. This was a blatant case of fraud and oppression and Hooper's were trustees of the profit and had to account to company A for it.

Comment

It seems that in cases like *Menier* and *Cook* (below) it is the company which is defrauded. It might therefore be better to rename the jurisdiction as 'fraud upon the company'. The claim is, after all, brought on behalf of the company and is therefore derivative (see below), and the company takes the benefit of any damages recovered. The value of the shares may fall giving a loss to individual shareholders but since the Court of Appeal held in *Prudential Assurance Co Ltd* v *Newman Industries* [1982] 1 All ER 354 that this loss was not recoverable by individual shareholders, at least where it is caused by fraud or negligence, it seems that the claim is basically for defrauding the company.

Cook *v* Deeks [1916] 1 AC 554

This action was brought in the High Court Division of the Supreme Court of Ontario by the claimant, suing on behalf of himself and other shareholders in the Toronto Construction Co Ltd, against the respondents, who were directors of the company. The claimant sought a declaration that the respondents were trustees of the company of the benefit of a contract made between the respondents and the Canadian Pacific Railway Co for construction work. It appeared that the respondents, while acting on behalf of the company in negotiating the contract, actually made it for themselves and not for the company, and by their votes as holders of three-quarters of the issued share capital, subsequently passed a resolution at a general meeting declaring that the company had no interest in the contract. *Held* – by the Privy Council:

(i) that the contract belonged in equity to the company, and the directors could not validly use their voting powers to vest the contract in themselves, in fraud of the minority;
(ii) in cases of breach of duty of this sort, the rule in Foss v *Harbottle* did not bar the claimant's claim.

Comment

In *Industrial Development Consultants* v *Cooley*, 1972 (see Chapter 17) there was a not dissimilar misappropriation of a corporate opportunity. However, in the *Cooley* case there was no need to resort to a derivative claim because Mr Cooley had made the profit for himself. The whole board was not involved and was clearly anxious to bring the company into court in order to sue Mr Cooley for recovery of the profit.

(*b*) *Where the minority as individuals are defrauded.*

(i) *Expulsion of minority*. This will amount to fraud unless it is done bona fide and for the benefit of the company.

Brown *v* British Abrasive Wheel Co [1919] 1 Ch 290

The company required further capital. The majority, who represented 98 per cent of the shareholders, were willing to provide this capital but only if they could buy up the 2 per cent minority. The minority would not agree to sell and so the majority shareholders proposed to alter the articles to provide for compulsory acquisition under which nine-tenths of the shareholders could buy out any other shareholders. *Held* – by Astbury J – that the alteration of the articles would be restrained because the alteration was not for the benefit of the company. In addition, the rule in *Foss* v *Harbottle* did not bar the claimant's claim.

Comment

A contrast is provided by *Dafen Tinplate Co Ltd* v *Llanelli Steel Co* (1907) *Ltd*, 1920, and *Sidebottom* v *Kershaw Leese & Co*, 1920 (see Chapter 4).

(ii) *Inequitable use of majority power*. An example of this jurisdiction is to be found in the following case.

Clemens *v* Clemens Bros [1976] 2 All ER 268

In this case the issued share capital of £2,000 in a small but prosperous family company was held between the claimant (45 per cent) and her aunt (55 per cent), the aunt being one of the five directors of the company. The directors proposed to increase the company's share capital to £3,650 by the creation of a further 1,650 voting ordinary shares. The four directors, other than the aunt, were to receive 200 shares each, and the balance of 850 shares was to be placed in trust for the company's long-service employees. The claimant objected to the proposed resolution to put this scheme into effect since the result would be to reduce her shareholding to under 25 per cent. At the extraordinary general meeting called to approve the scheme, the aunt voted in favour of the resolutions which were passed. The claimant sought a declaration against both the company and the aunt that the resolutions should be set aside on the ground that they were oppressive of the claimant. The defendant contended that if two shareholders honestly hold differing opinions, the view of the majority should prevail, and that shareholders in general meeting were entitled to consider their own interests and to vote in any way they honestly believed proper in the interest of the company. In giving judgment in favour of the claimant, Foster J made it clear that in the circumstances of this case Miss Clemens (the aunt) was not entitled to exercise her majority vote in whatever way she pleased. The judge found difficulty, however, in expressing this as a general principle of law, in terms, for example, of expressions such as 'bona fide for the benefit of the company as a whole', 'fraud on a minority', and 'oppressive'. He came to the conclusion that it would be unwise to try to produce a principle because the circumstances of each case are infinitely varied. He did, however, say, following a phrase of Lord Wilberforce in *Westbourne Galleries* (see Chapter 1), that the right of a shareholder to exercise voting rights in any way whatever is subject always to equitable considerations which may in particular circumstances make it unjust to exercise votes in a certain way. Dealing with the facts before him, Foster J then went on to say:

> 'I cannot escape the conclusion that the resolutions have been framed so as to put into the hands of Miss Clemens and her fellow directors complete control of the company and to deprive the [claimant] of her existing rights as a shareholder with more than 25 per cent of the votes, and greatly reduce her rights. They are specifically and carefully designed to ensure not only that the [claimant] can never get control of the company, but to deprive her of what has been called her negative control. [Here the judge is referring to her ability to block special and extraordinary resolutions.] Whether I say that these proposals are oppressive to the [claimant] or that no-one could honestly believe that they are for her benefit, matters not. A court of equity will in my judgment regard these considerations as sufficient to prevent the consequences arising from Miss Clemens using her legal right to vote in the way she has and it would be right for a court of equity to prevent such consequences taking effect.'

Comment

(i) The case is quoted to show the very wide power which equity reserves to itself to control the activities of majority shareholders. On the particular facts of this case, of course, the pre-emption rights given to shareholders by s 89 should prevent the sort of prejudicial conduct towards a minority which was alleged in this case. The claimant could, of course, have prevented the other members from effecting the disapplication of pre-emption rights under s 95 because a special resolution is required for this (see further Chapter 19).

(ii) Although Foster J was not prepared to put the case into any existing category of *Foss* exceptions, fraud on the minority seems a possible one.

(iii) The allotment was presumably also invalid because it was an improper exercise of the directors' powers.

The exception of fraud on the minority depends *where the company is defrauded* on 'wrongdoer control', i.e. the individual shareholder must show that the wrongdoers control the company as where they control the board and general meetings and will not permit an action to be brought in the company's name. Furthermore, wrongdoer control is essential because cases of misappropriation of property and breach of duty can be ratified by a 51 per cent majority of the members which is not controlled by the wrongdoers.

The wrongdoers will obviously be in the above position if they have voting control as they had, for example, in *Menier* and *Cook*. However, in *Prudential Assurance Co Ltd* v *Newman Industries Ltd* [1980] 2 All ER 841 Vinelott J held that *de facto* control was enough, i.e. the company does what the wrongdoers want even though the wrongdoers do not have voting control. They are able to persuade the majority to follow them. The Court of Appeal did not accept this reasoning because it requires a trial to see if there is evidence of control, whereas voting control is obvious from shares held and voting rights. However, they gave no guidance as to what might be meant by control.

4 *Fraud and negligence*. It is still not entirely certain whether damage caused by *negligence* can be brought under the heading of 'fraud' for the purposes of the exception of 'fraud on the minority'. In *Pavlides* v *Jensen*, 1956 (below) the court held that negligence, however gross, was not included. However, in *Daniels* v *Daniels*, 1978 (below) Templeman J, in distinguishing *Pavlides*, said that a minority shareholder who had no other remedy should be able to sue whenever directors use their powers intentionally or unintentionally, fraudulently or negligently, in a manner which benefits them at the expense of the company. Vinelott J accepted this view in the *Newman* case. The Court of Appeal in that case did not give any guidance but the general approach of the court was restrictive and suggests that negligence *which does not result in personal benefit* to the wrongdoers might still be ratifiable by a general meeting even with the votes of the wrongdoers and therefore not within the definition of fraud on the minority.

Pavlides *v* Jensen [1956] 2 All ER 518

The directors of the Tunnel Asbestos Cement Co Ltd sold an asbestos mine to the Cyprus Asbestos Mines Ltd in which the TAC Ltd held 25 per cent of the issued capital. The mine was sold for £182,000 but the sale was not submitted to a general meeting of TAC for approval. The claimant, who was a minority shareholder in TAC, claimed that the defendant directors were negligent because the mine was worth £1,000,000, and this price or something like it should have been obtained. He sued the directors with the company as a nominal defendant for a declaration that the directors were in breach of duty, and for an enquiry into the damage caused to TAC by their negligence and for payment of that sum by the directors to TAC. On the preliminary point as to the competence of the claimant as a minority shareholder to bring a derivative action in these circumstances, it was *held* – by Danckwerts J – that the action was not maintainable because the sale was *intra vires* and, since no acts of a fraudulent character were alleged by the claimant, the sale could be approved by the majority of shareholders and it was a matter for them.

Comment

(i) The claimant was alleging negligence which is a common law claim and derivative actions are creatures of equity, the judiciary being reluctant to extend them to common law claims such as negligence.

(ii) This line of reasoning was followed in *Multinational Gas* v *Multinational Gas Services* [1983] 2 All ER 563 where two judges in the Court of Appeal were of opinion that a claim for negligent mismanagement could not be brought even by a liquidator against directors whose actions had been approved by a majority of the members who were not a disinterested majority because they had appointed the directors as their nominees.

Daniels *v* Daniels [1978] 2 All ER 89

Mr Douglas Daniels, Mr Gordon Daniels and Mrs Soule, three minority shareholders in Ideal Homes (Coventry) Ltd, wished to bring an action against the majority shareholders (who were also the directors), Mr Bernard Daniels, Mrs Beryl Daniels and the company. In their claim the minority alleged that in October 1970 Ideal Homes, acting on the instructions of the majority shareholders, sold and conveyed freehold property in Warwick to Mrs Beryl Daniels for £4,250 when they knew, or ought to have known, that the correct value of the land was higher. The majority, in reply to these allegations, said that they adopted a valuation made for probate purposes in June 1969 on the occasion of the death in that month of Mr Joseph Daniels, the father of the minority shareholders and Mr Bernard Daniels. Against this the minority shareholders alleged that probate valuations were conservative as to amount and usually less than the value obtainable on open market between a willing seller and buyer.

In 1974 the land was sold by Mrs Daniels for £120,000 and although the majority had every intention of denying the allegations, they asked at this stage that the claim of the minority be struck out as disclosing no reasonable cause of action or otherwise as an abuse of the process of the court. It was argued, on behalf of the majority, that since the minority was not alleging fraud against the majority no action on behalf of the alleged loss to the company could be brought because under the decision in *Foss* v *Harbottle*, 1843 the court could not interfere in the internal affairs of the company at the request of the minority. The minority said they were unable to allege fraud because they were not able to say precisely what had happened beyond the matters set out in their claim.

Templeman J, who had not been asked to try the action but only to say whether there was an action at all, reviewed the decisions under the rule in *Foss* v *Harbottle*, 1843 and his judgment made clear that if the breach of duty alleged turned out to be a breach of fiduciary duty, then it should be allowed to proceed under the rule in *Cook* v *Deeks*, 1916 because the majority could control general meetings. Furthermore, if the breach of duty alleged was one of skill and care, i.e. negligence at common law, then it should also be allowed to proceed as an exception to *Foss* v *Harbottle*, 1843 because the alleged negligence had resulted in a profit to one of the directors which distinguished this case from *Pavlides* v *Jensen*, 1956.

Procedural aspects

When a shareholder is suing to restrain the majority from acting illegally or continuing to commit a personal wrong upon him he has a choice. He may sue in his own name or in the representative form on behalf of himself and other shareholders with whom he enjoys the right allegedly denied to him. The relief asked for will normally be a *declaratory judgment* saying what the law is and by which the parties intend to abide, or an *injunction* to restrain the conduct complained of if it is thought the majority will still continue to act unfairly.

Where the individual member is seeking a claim against third parties for the company's benefit so that he is trying to enforce a claim which belongs to the company, his claim is called *derivative*.

In a *personal* or *representative* claim the company is a real and genuine defendant. In a *derivative* action the company is joined as a nominal defendant because the directors and the majority of the members of the company will not bring the company into court as a claimant. The company is made a party to the action so that the judge may grant it a remedy by being brought in as a nominal defendant, the claimant naming the company as a defendant in his claim form.

The remedy of damages is available in a derivative claim. The damages go to the company and not to the claimant. However, the claimant is entitled to an indemnity for his costs from the company (*Wallersteiner* v *Moir* (*No 2*) [1975] 1 All ER 849).

A derivative action is not available to challenge the form in which a company's accounts are prepared. The Companies Act requires the appointment of auditors who must report upon the accounts and this is the protection which statute law gives to the exclusion of other remedies (*Devlin* v *Slough Estates Ltd* [1982] 2 All ER 273). It should, however, be noted that the courts may distinguish the *Devlin* case and intervene where the company concerned has taken advantage of the audit exemption (see Chapter 1).

A derivative claim is not available to a plaintiff whose own conduct is in some way tainted, as where he has been involved in the wrongdoing (*Nurcombe* v *Nurcombe* [1985] 1 All ER 65). This contrasts with petitions under Part XVII where, according to Nourse J in *Re London School of Electronics*, 1985 (discussed later in this chapter), there is no overriding requirement that the petitioner should come to court with clean hands.

The rule in *Foss* is a *rule of procedure*. It is a matter to be decided *before* the trial of the allegations as to whether the claimant can be allowed to proceed to a trial under an exception to the rule.

There is a firm statement to this effect by the Court of Appeal in *Prudential Assurance* v *Newman* (*No 2*) [1982] 1 All ER 354 where the court was critical of the approach of the trial judge in taking evidence in proof of the allegations for many days and at great cost to the defendants before deciding that a claim could proceed as an exception to *Foss*.

MINORITY PROTECTION UNDER STATUTE – GENERALLY

There are a number of other sections in the Companies Act 1985 which enable a number of shareholders to defy the majority. For example, under s 5 dissentient holders of 15 per cent of the issued shares can apply for cancellation of an alteration of objects (see Chapter 3). Furthermore, under s 127 where class rights are varied in pursuance of a clause in the memorandum or articles, or under s 125, dissentient holders of 15 per cent of the issued shares of the class can apply for cancellation of the variation (see Chapter 6). Furthermore, under s 54, where a public company passes a special resolution to re-register as a private company, holders of not less than 5 per cent in nominal value of the company's issued share capital or any class thereof; or not less than 5 per cent in number of the members of the company, if the company is not limited by shares; or not less than 50 of the company's members may apply to the court to cancel the resolution (see Chapter 2).

Other examples are the right given by s 157 to 10 per cent in nominal value of the company's issued share capital or any class of it, or 10 per cent of the members if the company is not limited by shares, to object to the court where a private company gives financial assistance for the purchase of its own shares (see further Chapter 7); the right given by s 176 to any member who did not consent or vote in favour of the special resolution approving the purchase by a private company of its own shares partly from capital to apply to the court for the cancellation of the resolution (see further Chapter 7); the misfeasance proceedings under s 212 of the Insolvency Act 1986 which a member may bring against defaulting officers when the company is in liquidation (see further Chapter 26).

There are also certain minority rights in regard to meetings, i.e. the right given to a 10 per cent minority to require the convening of an extraordinary general meeting (s 368), and the right of a 20 per cent minority to requisition members' resolutions at the AGM (s 376) (see Chapter 19).

As regards investigations, a right is given to a 10 per cent minority to ask the DTI, on the basis of evidence submitted, to order an investigation of the company's affairs or compel an investigation into its ownership.

The rights of a minority to petition the court on the grounds of unfair prejudice or for a winding-up are considered below.

STATUTORY PROTECTION AGAINST UNFAIR PREJUDICE

The statutory rights considered above are granted in specific areas for specific purposes, e.g. so that a minority can convene an EGM. The rights described under this heading and given by Part XVII of the 1985 Act are more general, being potentially available whenever a minority can show 'unfair prejudice'.

The main provisions of Part XVII are set out below.

Generally

Any member or personal representative, or the Secretary of State as a result of a DTI investigation, may petition the court on the grounds that the affairs of the company are being, or have been, or will be, conducted in a manner unfairly prejudicial to the interests of its members generally, or of some part of its members, including the petitioner himself. The court must, among other things, be satisfied that the petition is well founded.

The provision relating to a petition by personal representatives of a deceased shareholder is important because a major form of abuse in private companies has been the refusal by the board, under powers in the articles, to register the personal representatives of a major deceased shareholder and also to refuse to register the beneficiaries under the will or on intestacy. Although personal representatives have some rights, e.g. to receive dividends, they cannot vote unless they are registered, nor can a beneficiary. The holding is therefore rendered powerless and the motive of the board is often to purchase the holding themselves at an advantageous price.

The provisions apply to conduct past, present or future. In *Re Kenyon Swansea Ltd* [1987] *The Times*, 29 April, the High Court decided that it was sufficient to support a petition that an act had been proposed which if carried out or completed would be prejudicial to the petitioner. Thus the giving of notice of a meeting at which the directors propose to use their majority power to introduce policies allegedly unfair to the minority is probably enough for the minority to commence a claim under s 459. The court also decided that it was enough that the affairs of the company had, in the past, been conducted in such a way as to be unfairly prejudicial to the petitioner, even though at the date of the petition the unfairness had been remedied. The court could still make an order to check possible future prejudice.

The use of the word 'conduct' is important since it covers both acts and omissions, e.g. failure to pay proper dividends when profits allow.

Of even greater importance, however, at least in terms of the case law, is the interpretation placed by the courts, in particular by Mr Justice Hoffman in *Re A Company (No 00477 of 1986)* [1986] PCC 372, on 'interests of its members'. Many of the petitions presented under the unfair prejudice provisions have been in regard to the removal of a director from the board of a private company. The director concerned has been able to establish that the conduct relating to him as a director was also unfairly prejudicial to him as a member because the 'interest' of a member in a private company legitimately includes a place on the board. Some of these cases are set out later in this chapter.

The requirement that the petition be 'well founded' is to ensure that the provisions are not abused or used for a wrongful purpose. An earlier case under different legislation provides a valid illustration. In *Re Bellador Silk Ltd* [1965] 1 All ER 667 a member of the company presented a petition to the court for relief, but mainly as a form of harassment of the board in order to make them pay an alleged debt to one of his companies. The court decided that the petition had a collateral purpose and dismissed it as not a bona fide attempt to get relief.

The test for unfairness is objective and thus the fact that the minority feel that they are being unfairly treated is not enough. The starting point is whether or not the conduct of the majority is in accordance with the articles (as Hoffman LJ said in *Saul D Harrison* [1995] 1 BCLC 14). The matter often turns upon whether the powers which the shareholders have entrusted to the majority shareholder/directors which are fiduciary powers have been exercised for the benefit of the company as a whole.

Essentially a minority claim

The Part XVII provisions are essentially designed to protect the minority against unfairly prejudicial conduct by the majority. The provisions will not normally be available to enable the majority to acquire the shares of a minority under a court order, even though there is evidence that the minority concerned is acting in an unfairly prejudicial way. This is because the majority control the company and can remove directors and so on and, in effect, put matters right without the aid of the court. Thus in *Legal Costs Negotiators Ltd* [1998] CLY 695 two partners converted their business into a limited company in which one held 75 per cent of the shares and the other 25 per cent. The majority shareholder alleged that the minority shareholder was not carrying out his duties properly and obtained his resignation from the board. He was also dismissed from his employment with the company. The majority shareholder then asked the court to use the Part XVII provisions to grant him an order requiring the minority to sell his shares to him. The High Court refused the claim as an inappropriate use of the provisions. After all, the majority shareholder had removed his ex-partner from the board and from his employment, and to that extent had removed any problems to the company that might have resulted from the alleged conduct of the minority.

Relief available

(*a*) *Specific relief*. This is as follows:

(i) The court may make an order regulating the company's affairs for the future.
(ii) The court may restrain the doing of or the continuing of prejudicial acts.

The above two heads are illustrated quite validly by the following case decided under earlier legislation.

Re H R Harmer Ltd [1958] 3 All ER 689

The company was formed in July 1947, to acquire a business founded by Mr H R Harmer, who was born in 1869. The business of the company was stamp auctioneering and dealing in and valuing stamps. Two of Mr Harmer's sons, Cyril and Bernard Harmer, went into the business on leaving school. The nominal capital of the company was £50,000, and Mr Harmer senior and his wife were between them able to control the general meetings of the company, and could even obtain special and extraordinary resolutions. Mrs Harmer always voted with her husband. The father and his two sons were life directors under the articles, the father being chairman of the board with a casting vote. The sons claimed that their father had repeatedly abused his controlling power in the conduct of the company's affairs so that they were bound to apply for relief. Mr Harmer senior had, they said, always acted as though the right of appointing and dismissing senior staff was vested in him alone, and this right he also extended to the appointment of directors. He also considered that no director should express a contrary view to that expressed by himself, and had generally ignored the views of his sons and the other directors and shareholders. In particular he had opened a branch of the company in Australia in spite of the protests by the other directors, and the branch had not proved profitable. In addition, he dismissed an old servant and procured the appointment of his own 'yes men' to the board. He drew unauthorised expenses for himself and his wife and engaged a detective to watch the staff. He also endeavoured to sell off the company's American business which severely damaged its goodwill. Roxburgh J, at first instance, granted relief under s 210 (see below), and the Court of Appeal confirmed the order, saying that the relief was properly granted because the circumstances were such that the court would have been justified in ordering a winding-up. Roxburgh J's order provided *inter alia* that the company should contract for the services of Mr Harmer senior as philatelic consultant at a salary of £2,500 per annum; that he should not interfere in the affairs of the company otherwise than in accordance with the valid decisions of the board; and that he be appointed president of the company for life, but that this office should not impose any duties or create any rights or powers to him.

Comment

The court's order had the effect of changing the provision in the articles under which Mr Harmer was a director for life with a casting vote. The order also restrained him for the future from interfering with the valid decisions of the board.

(iii) The court may authorise a claim to be brought by the company. This would appear to allow a minority to obtain redress for the company where it had been injured by the wrongful acts of the majority. It seems to provide another approach to that found in *Foss* v *Harbottle*, though the claim would not be derivative because the court would authorise the company to commence the action as a claimant.

(iv) The court may order the purchase of the minority shares at a fair price either by other members or by the company itself, in which case the court would also authorise a reduction of capital. This remedy has been by far the most popular and has largely substituted for winding-up under the just and equitable rule which was formerly the only real way of compelling the majority to return the share capital of the minority (see below). The court will also give directions as to the basis of the valuation of the shares to produce a fair value. The court will often, e.g., direct that the shares should not be valued as a minority interest for this purpose since this would depress the value in view of the lack of power in minority shareholders. Since the companies being dealt with by the courts in these minority problem areas are usually private companies with no stock market share price, the valuation is normally carried out by the company's auditors.

(*b*) *General relief*. In addition to the above, the court may make such order as it thinks fit for giving relief in respect of the matters complained of. Thus in *Re a Company (No 005287 of 1985)* [1986] 1 WLR 281, the controlling shareholder took all the profits in management fees and was ordered to account for the money to the company and this although at the time of the action he had sold all his shares in the company concerned to his Gibraltar company. Thus a petition can be presented even against a person who has ceased to be a member.

Where the shareholding is equal

The court has been faced with a claim under the unfair prejudice provisions where the members of a private company were equal shareholders and in deadlock in terms of their relationship. They could not agree who should buy out whom where each had made an offer to buy the other's shares.

West *v* Blanchet and Another [2000] 1 BCLC 795

The company's business was teaching English under the name of Leicester Square School of English Ltd. It was a joint venture between Jason West, the petitioner, and Stephen Blanchet. The nominal capital was £100 divided into 100 £1 shares. The paid-up capital was £2, of which West and Blanchet held one share each. West was responsible for marketing and Blanchet for management. The second respondent, who was a director with no shares, was responsible for teaching.

The parties' relationship broke down and the respondents terminated West's employment. He played no part in management after this but continued as a director/shareholder. West later offered to buy Blanchet's shares and Blanchet made an offer for West's. However, they could not agree who should leave the company. West applied to the court for an order under s 461 that Blanchet be required to sell him the shares, alleging that the two respondents had conducted the company's affairs in a manner prejudicial to him in that they had excluded him from the company's affairs and management decisions. The respondents asked the court to strike out the claim as an abuse of court process.

The judge reached the conclusion that in a case such as this the issue was which offer was the more reasonable and realistic. Blanchet had funds readily available to buy West's shares, but West had no available personal funds and his offer was short on details. Blanchet's offer was therefore the more reasonable and realistic, so the court should strike out West's claim.

Comment

The case perhaps illustrates the need to resolve disputes such as these by alternative dispute resolution.

The High Court decision does not resolve the deadlock problem in the context of this case. It simply identifies a good defence against a s 459 claim brought with a request for an order for the purchase of the respondent's shares. To avoid being forced out of the company, all the respondent needs to do is make a more reasonable and realistic counter-offer, and then ask the court to strike out the petitioner's claim.

Maybe the petitioner in this case will now accept the respondent's offer. However, he has not been ordered to do so. The court was merely asked to strike out his claim.

The motives of the minority: abuse of procedure

The unfair prejudice procedures cannot be used where they would achieve a collateral purpose, as where the board of a company would be required to make a takeover bid at a higher price than that intended.

Re Astec (BSR) plc [1999] 2 BCLC 556

In 1989, Emerson Electric, a US company, acquired 45 per cent of the Astec shares. It made further acquisitions over the subsequent period so that in March 1997 it held 51 per cent of Astec. In January 1998, Emerson issued a press release stating that it would buy the remainder of the shares in Astec at no premium to market value, and would stop making dividend payments.

The minority shareholders petitioned the court under s 459, accusing Emerson of bullying tactics and asking the court to order it to purchase the remaining shares in Astec at a fair value – in effect, to undertake a takeover of Astec at an increased price.

Mr Justice Jonathan Parker decided, among other things, that the petition was an abuse of process and should be struck out. He said:

> 'I fully accept that the petitioners genuinely desire the relief claimed, that is to say an order for the buy-out of their own shares. Equally, however . . . they desire that relief not for itself but because they hope that, if granted, it will lead to something else, that something else being something which the court would not order under s 459, namely a takeover bid by Emerson. The petition is, in my judgment, being used for the purposes of exerting pressure in order to achieve a collateral purpose, that is to say, the making of a takeover bid by Emerson.'

Comment

The court's ruling was a severe blow for the minority, who had costs awarded against them, and should give pause for thought to those minorities who may see the unfair prejudice procedures as available, not merety to achieve their own purposes, but to accomplish wider aims.

It is also an abuse of the unfair prejudice procedures to seek to obtain an order for purchase of shares simply because the claimant has lost trust and confidence in the way in which the company is being run by the other members. There must be some breach of the terms on which it has been agreed the company should be run.

O'Neill and Another *v* Phillips and Others [1999] 1 WLR 1092

The company, which provided specialist services for stripping asbestos from buildings, employed Mr O'Neill as a manual worker in 1983. Mr Phillips, who held the entire issued share capital of 100 £1 shares, was so impressed by Mr O'Neill that in 1985 he gave him 25 shares and appointed him a director. Shortly afterwards, Mr Phillips had informally expressed the hope that Mr O'Neill would be able to take over the day-to-day running of the company and would allow him to draw 50 per cent of the profits.

Mr O'Neill took over on Mr Phillips' retirement from the board, and was duly credited with half the profits.

In 1991, the industry went into recession, the company struggled and Mr Phillips, who had become concerned by Mr O'Neill's management, resumed personal command. He told Mr O'Neill that he would only be receiving his salary and any dividends on his 25 shares, but would no longer receive 50 per cent of the profits.

In January 1992, Mr O'Neill petitioned the court for relief against unfair prejudice in respect both of his termination of equal profit-sharing and the repudiation of an alleged agreement for the allotment of more shares.

The House of Lords unanimously allowed an appeal by Mr Phillips and others from the Court of Appeal. Lord Hoffmann said that, as to whether Mr Phillips had acted unfairly in respect of equality of shareholding, the real question was whether in fairness or equity Mr O'Neill had had a right to the shares. On that point, one ran up against the insuperable obstacle of the judge's finding that Mr Phillips had never promised to give them. There was no basis consistent with established principles of equity for a court to hold that he had behaved unfairly in withdrawing from the negotiations. The same applied to the sharing of profits.

A member who had not been dismissed or excluded from management could not demand that his shares be purchased simply because he felt that he had lost trust and confidence in the others and in the way the company was run.

Comment

As seen in *Re Astec (BSR) plc* (above), the unfair prejudice provisions are not a 'cure-all' remedy for shareholders who are not satisfied for a variety of reasons with the way in which the company is run. In a quasi-partnership company, one 'partner' should not be entitled at will to require the other partners to buy his shares at a fair value. There is no support in previous decisions for such a right of unilateral withdrawal under the provisions. The courts will not construe the requirement of 'unfairly prejudicial conduct' so narrowly.

The Jenkins Committee and unfair prejudice

Part XVII results from recommendations made by the Jenkins Committee which advocated the repeal of s 210 of the 1948 Act and the substitution of new statutory arrangements. It is of value, therefore, to consider what sort of conduct the Jenkins Committee thought would be 'unfairly prejudicial'. It mentioned the following:

(*a*) directors appointing themselves to paid posts within the company at excessive rates of remuneration, thus depriving the members of a dividend or an adequate dividend – and indeed it was exactly this sort of scenario which caused the court to find unfair prejudice to a non-director member in *Re Sam Weller* [1989] 3 WLR 923;

(*b*) directors refusing to register the personal representatives of a deceased member so that, in the absence of a specific provision in the articles, they cannot vote, as part of a scheme to make the personal representatives sell the shares to the directors at an inadequate price;
(*c*) the issue of shares to directors and others on advantageous terms;
(*d*) failure of directors to declare dividends on non-cumulative preference shares held by a minority.

Obviously some matters affect all the shareholders and not merely a minority, e.g. non-payment of dividends. However, the provisions as reworded by the Companies Act 1989 clearly now include acts affecting the members *generally*.

It is not clear, however, whether failure to pay a dividend would amount to unfair prejudicial conduct in every case. Much will depend upon the circumstances. It could be argued, for example, that ploughing back profits into building up the assets of the company was not in the circumstances of the case a breach of duty by the directors.

Illustrative case law

In *Re a Company* (*No 004475 of 1982*) [1983] 2 WLR 381 Lord Grantchester QC held that no prejudice arose under what is now Part XVII of the 1985 Act simply because the directors of a company refuse to exercise their power to buy the company's shares; nor because they fail to put into effect a scheme which would have entitled the petitioners to sell their shares at a higher price than they might have been able to otherwise; nor because they proposed to dissipate the company's liquid resources by investing them in a partly-owned subsidiary. Lord Grantchester also said that it would usually be necessary for a member claiming unfair prejudice to show that his shares had been seriously diminished in value. However, in *Re R A Noble* (*Clothing*) *Ltd* [1983] BCLC 273 Nourse J said that the jurisdiction under Part XVII was not limited to such a case and that diminution in the value of shares was not essential. In *Re Garage Door Associates* [1984] 1 All ER 434 Mervyn Davies J held that a member could present a petition for a winding-up on the just and equitable ground *and* petition for the purchase of his shares under Part XVII. Such a procedure is not an abuse of the process of the court. However, there has more recently been a Practice Direction that the two claims should not be made as a matter of course but only where there is a chance that one or the other will fail.

In *Re Bird Precision Bellows* [1984] 2 WLR 869 and again in *Re London School of Electronics* [1985] 3 WLR 474, Nourse J said that the removal of a member from the board was unfairly prejudicial conduct within what is now Part XVII. He made an order for the purchase of the shares of the petitioners in both cases by the majority shareholders and decided that in valuing the shares there should be no discount in the price because the holdings were minority holdings, unless the minority were in some way to blame for the situation giving rise to the alleged unfair prejudice. However, Nourse J did decide in *Re London School of Electronics*, 1985 (see above), that there was no overriding requirement under what is now Part XVII that the petitioner should come to court with clean hands.

In *Re R A Noble* (*Clothing*) *Ltd*, 1983 (see above), Nourse J decided that a director who had been excluded from management could claim unfair prejudice but not in the particular circumstances of the case because his exclusion was to a large extent due to his own disinterest in the company's affairs so that the other members of the board felt that they had to manage without him.

In *Re a Company (No 008699 of 1985)* [1986] PCC 296, the High Court held that it was unfairly prejudicial to minority shareholders where, on a takeover bid for the company, the directors recommended acceptance of a bid by a company in which they had an interest while ignoring a much more favourable alternative offer.

In *Re Mossmain Ltd* [1986] *Financial Times*, 27 June, four persons agreed to form a company. Two of these were husband and wife. Because the husband had a restrictive covenant in a contract of employment which might be infringed if he became a member/director of the company, his shares were held by his wife for the duration of the covenant, he becoming an employee only for the time being. The wife was made a director. Later the husband was dismissed and his wife was removed from the board. Husband and wife petitioned under Part XVII and the court held that the husband's name must be struck out of the petition. He did not qualify to petition since he was not a member as Part XVII requires.

Finally, in *Re a Company (No 007623 of 1984)* [1986] BCLC 362 it was held that there was no unfair prejudice where the company made a rights issue to all members *pro rata* to their shareholding which the petitioner could not afford even though his interest in the company after the issue would be reduced from 25 per cent to 0.125 per cent. The company genuinely needed capital. The case can be contrasted with *Clemens* v *Clemens Bros Ltd*, 1976 where the fresh issue of shares was not a rights issue offered to all members but to members *other* than Miss Clemens in order to reduce her voting power in the company.

Reform

The Law Commission has published a report on shareholder remedies (see Law Commission Report No 246: *Shareholder Remedies*). The Report recommends:

- changes to simplify the s 459 remedy and in particular to reduce its cost to litigants and taxpayers by giving judges power to control and manage cases and promote out-of-court settlements – this, it is hoped, would cut down the current often drawn-out trial procedure;
- that directors of private companies which are owner-managed and who hold 10 per cent or more of the company's shares should be *presumed* to have suffered unfair prejudice if they are removed from the board by their colleagues and should be given the right to have their shares purchased at full price unless the presumption is rebutted in the particular circumstances of the case;
- that a new dispute resolution article be added to *Table A* in order to minimise the use of the shareholder remedies provided by trial in the courts.

Most of the changes will require primary legislation and may therefore not be put into effect for some time.

MINORITY PROTECTION – THE SHAREHOLDERS' AGREEMENTS

Many small private companies have converted from partnerships where a partnership contractual agreement has governed the business affairs. Such an agreement has, of course, no validity once the business is turned into a company but there is no reason why a formal shareholders' agreement should not be drawn up in similar fashion to a partnership agreement. *This is arguably a vital document to be drawn up for shareholders in private companies*. It will ensure that nobody is disadvantaged by majority voting or is unfairly treated on retirement and that the dependants of a shareholder are protected on his or her death. The agreement normally contains provisions on how decisions are to be made on matters such as directors' pay, dividends and the employment of key staff. The agreement is designed so that shareholders with big holdings cannot in all cases impose their will through majority voting power, and is of particular importance where shareholder voting can result in damaging deadlock. One of the most important aspects of the agreement will be the provisions for share valuation on the sale of shares, on leaving the company by retirement or by death.

MINORITY PETITION FOR JUST AND EQUITABLE WINDING-UP

The court has a jurisdiction under s 122(1)(g) of the Insolvency Act 1986 to wind up a company on the petition of a minority on the ground that it is 'just and equitable' to do so.

This ground is subjected to a flexible interpretation by the courts. In the context of minority rights, however, orders have been made where the managing director who represented the majority shareholder interests in his management of the company refused, e.g., to produce accounts or pay dividends (*Loch* v *John Blackwood Ltd* [1924] AC 783) and where, in the case of a small company, formed or continued on the basis of a personal relationship, involving mutual confidence and which is in essence a partnership, the person petitioning is excluded from management participation and the circumstances are such as would justify the dissolution of a partnership. This, it will be remembered, was the approach in *Ebrahimi* v *Westbourne Galleries*, 1972 (see Chapter 1). However, since the enactment of the unfair prejudice provisions and following the case of *Re a Company (No 002567 of 1982)* [1983] 2 All ER 854 other matters have been brought to the fore. These are:

(*a*) that if the majority make an offer to buy out the shares of the director who has been removed at a fair price, e.g. to be decided on by the company's auditor, the court is not perhaps likely to wind up the company because the ex-director's capital is available by other means. No such offer was made in *Ebrahimi*;

(*b*) that even if no such offer is made the better approach these days might be by petition under the unfair prejudice provisions. The court can, as we have seen, order the purchase of the ex-director's shares, at a fair price, either by the other members or by the company in reduction of capital.

However, the procedure through just and equitable winding-up is not specifically repealed and there is no rule of law preventing that approach, and indeed it was held in *Jesner* v *Jarrad* [1992] *The Times*, 26 October, that a lack of unfair prejudice under s 459 will not prevent the court from winding up a company on the just and equitable ground. In that case a family company was being run in good faith and without prejudice to the claimant who was a family member. Nevertheless, the claimant and his brother and the other members of the family had lost that mutual confidence required in what was really a quasi-partnership, and on the basis of the *Westbourne Galleries* case it was just and equitable that it should be wound up, given the disputes within the family as to how it should be run.

GRADED QUESTIONS

Essay mode

1 Ben is a minority shareholder in App plc, whose directors are Charles, David and Edward. Though not the controlling shareholders the directors control the company in practice.

(i) Last year one of the company's employees was convicted of stealing property belonging to the company and was given a suspended sentence. A general meeting instructed the directors to bring civil proceedings to recover the value of property stolen but they refused to do so.

(ii) It has also come to light that the directors have diverted to themselves contracts obtained by the company. Fearing litigation the directors called a general meeting and persuaded the shareholders to approve their actions by passing a simple resolution. The directors cast their votes in favour of the resolution.

Advise Ben whether he could sue the directors personally or on behalf of the company in respect of the two matters.

(*University of Plymouth*)

2 In certain areas the Companies Act 1985 and to a limited extent the Insolvency Act 1986 give special protection to minority shareholders with various holdings of shares. The most important of these statutory provisions seems to be s 459 of the Companies Act 1985 which gives any member the right to complain to the court on the ground that the affairs of the company are being or have been conducted in a manner which is unfairly prejudicial to the concerns of the members generally or of some part of the members including himself.

(*a*) Explain and, by making reference to decided cases, illustrate the operation of s 459 of the Companies Act 1985.

AND

(*b*) Select TWO OTHER statutory examples of minority protection and in each selected area explain the size of holding and the rights given to a minority.

(*Glasgow Caledonian University*)

3 Explain the Rule in *Foss* v *Harbottle* and describe the limits to this Rule.

(*The Institute of Company Accountants*)

4 'For a minority shareholder who has suffered a wrong at the hands of the majority to establish a case under the alternative remedy he must show both that he suffered "unfairly prejudicial conduct" and that this was suffered in his capacity as a member of the company.'

Discuss.

(*The Institute of Chartered Secretaries and Administrators*)

5 Explain how the provisions of the Companies Act 1985 attempt to ensure that majority shareholders do not conduct the affairs of a company with complete disregard for the interests of minority shareholders.

(*The Chartered Institute of Management Accountants*)

6 The directors of Merchanting Ltd, a very successful business, have allocated most of the profits to themselves as remuneration and as donations to a charitable institution established by the founder of the company. Sheila, a shareholder, wishes to challenge the amount of the directors' remuneration, to discontinue the charitable donations and to increase the dividends.

Explain how she could make her proposed challenge.

(*The Institute of Chartered Accountants in England and Wales*)

7 Give an account of the legal procedure which must be followed in order to effect the registration of a new public limited company which is entitled to do business.

(*The Association of Chartered Certified Accountants*)

Objective mode

Four alternative answers are given. Select ONE only. Circle the answer which you consider to be correct. Check your answers by referring back to the information given in the chapter and against the answers at the back of the book.

1 The directors of Ouse Ltd have been selling off certain of the company's assets negligently at what the minority shareholders regard as too low a value. The directors have not made any gain themselves. What action can the minority shareholders bring on behalf of the company?

A An action could be brought on the basis that the directors acted *ultra vires*.
B The minority could apply to the court in the company's name for rescission of the contract.
C An action can be brought if the articles allow this.
D Under the rule in *Foss* v *Harbottle* no action can be brought.

2 Tom is the majority shareholder in Ribble Ltd and is also a director. Recently Tom sold freehold land belonging to the company to his wife who is also a director, and two months later his wife sold it to the local council at a profit of £30,000. The sale was ratified by an ordinary resolution. What action can the minority bring to recover the profit for the company?

A A derivative action under an exception to *Foss* v *Harbottle*.
B A representative action against Tom on the ground of fraud.
C No action can be brought because the sale was ratified.
D No action can be brought on behalf of the company except by the majority shareholders.

3 John, who is the majority shareholder in Thames Ltd, is refusing to recommend the payment of dividends in spite of healthy profits. Instead he has recently increased his salary as a director by £40,000. What action can the minority shareholders take?

A Bring a derivative action under an exception to *Foss* v *Harbottle*.
B Petition under CA 1985, s 459.

C Bring an action under the CA 1985 which requires that the directors recommend a dividend if there are distributable profits.
D No action is possible in this situation.

4 Which of the following can petition the court for relief under CA 1985, s 459?

A The company.
B Members holding not less than 10 per cent in number of the company's issued shares.
C A member of the company.
D A creditor of the company.

5 A derivative action is one which is brought by:

A the company.
B a member of the company on behalf of all the other members.
C a member of the company on his own account.
D a member of the company on behalf of the company.

6 John has just formed a limited company. Which of the following details can John exclude from its business stationery?

A The names of all of the company's directors.
B The company's registered number.
C The full name of the company.
D The address of the registered office.

The answers to questions set in objective mode appear on p 576.

15

DIRECTORS AND MANAGEMENT – GENERALLY

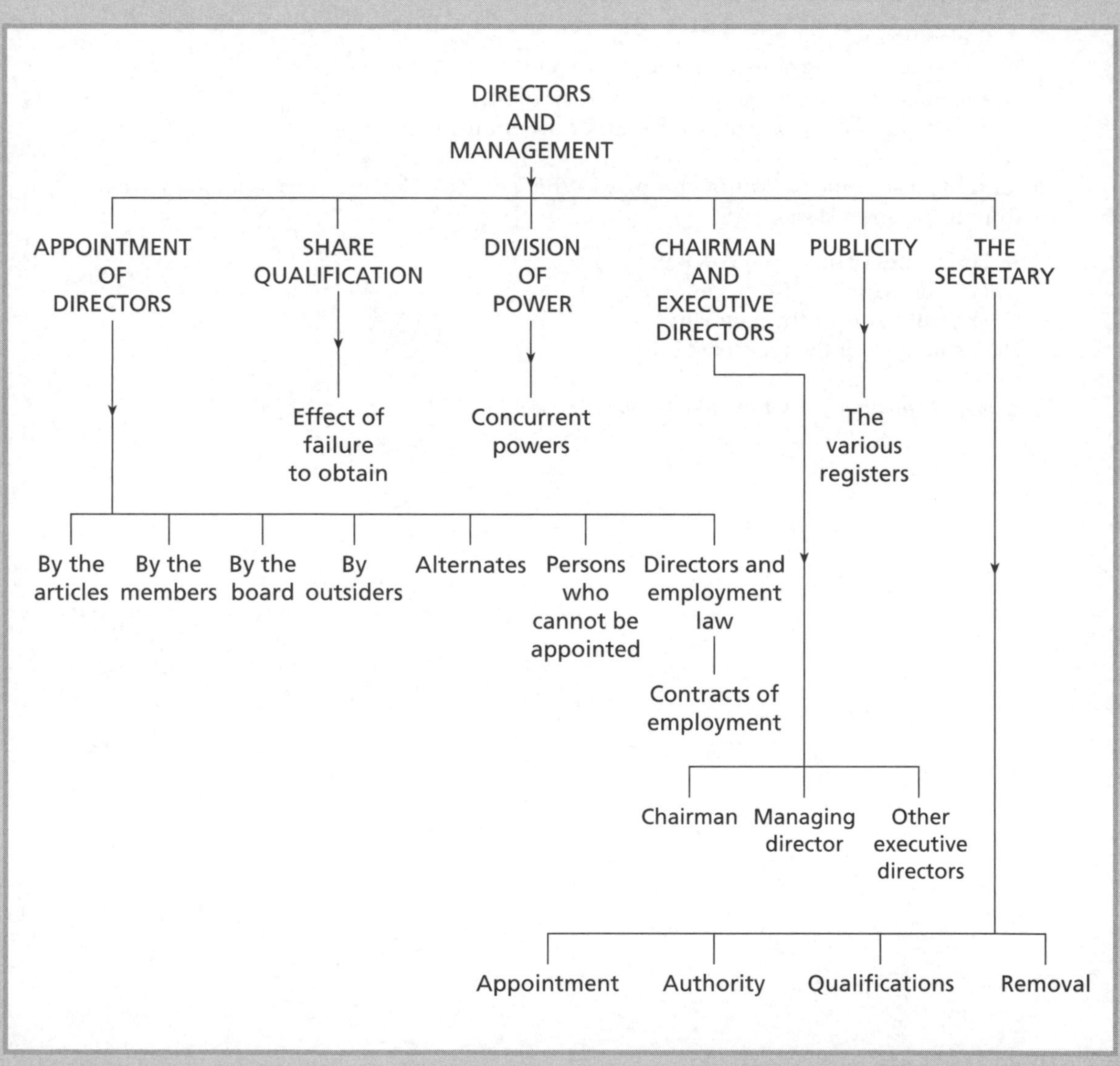

The management of a company is usually entrusted to a small group of persons called directors, supported, in the main, by the company secretary and the company accountant.

A company must have a board of directors numbering at least two in the case of a public company; one will suffice in the case of a private company. Apart from this, the number of directors and the way in which they are to be appointed is left to be regulated by the articles. *Table A* provides that unless otherwise determined by ordinary resolution, the number of directors (other than alternate directors) shall not be subject to any maximum but shall not be less than two. *Table A* provides, in effect, that the company may from time to time by ordinary resolution increase or reduce the number of directors, and determine in what rotation the increased number is to retire.

Definition

Although the persons managing the company are usually called directors, other names are sometimes used, e.g. managers, governors, or committee of management. In this connection it is important to note the provisions of s 741(1) which are that the term 'director' when used in the Act is taken to include any persons occupying the position of director by whatever name called. Thus a director is anyone occupying the role of director regardless of his title within the company. This could include a person not actually appointed to the board, i.e. a *de facto* director. Thus s 285 provides that the acts of a director are valid regardless of any defect in his or her appointment and this must of necessity apply to *de facto* directors (or directors *in fact*). A director is also an officer of the company.

It was held in *Re Sykes (Butchers) Ltd* [1998] 1 BCLC 110 that a person who denied that he was a director and whose appointment had not been notified to Companies House could nevertheless be disqualified as a *de facto* director following various defaults, including a preference in which he paid off a bank overdraft with the company's money to the detriment of other creditors where he had guaranteed the overdraft. He then went on trading with the company in a situation of inevitable insolvency. The court said that it was difficult to lay down one decisive test of whether a person is a *de facto* director. All the relevant facts relating to an involvement in management must be considered.

However, in *Secretary of State for Trade and Industry* v *Tjolle* [1998] 1 BCLC 333 a woman who called herself a director was not regarded as such for the purposes of disqualification because, on the facts of the case, she had no involvement with anything financial and did not form part of the company's real governance.

Shadow directors

It should also be noted that s 741 extends certain provisions of the 1985 Act to a 'shadow director', being a person in accordance with whose directions or instructions the directors of a company are accustomed to act unless the directors are accustomed so to act only because the person concerned gives them advice in a professional capacity. Professional advisers such as accountants and lawyers are not, therefore, for that reason alone, shadow directors. However, those who give advice other than purely in a professional capacity may be included. In *Secretary of State for Trade and Industry* v

Deverell [2000] 2 BCLC 133 the Court of Appeal gave a ruling that appears to extend the definition. The court said that the concepts of 'direction' and 'instruction' in the definition did not exclude the concept of the giving of advice. The company concerned was in the travel business. It went into voluntary liquidation owing creditors an estimated £4.46 million. Disqualification proceedings were brought against three of its directors and two of its advisers or consultants who were persons with experience in the travel business. The consultants were held to be shadow directors and disqualification orders could be made against them.

Whether a person is or is not a shadow director is a matter of fact to be decided on the circumstances of the case, but some indications are: (a) being a signatory to the company's bank account and/or attendance at interviews with bank officials; (b) the ordering by the person concerned of goods and/or services for the company; (c) the signing of contracts and/or letters in the capacity of director; (d) attendance at meetings of the board; (e) possession of detailed information about the company. However, s 741 exempts a holding company which does not become a shadow director of any of its subsidiaries for the purposes of s 309 (directors' duty to have regard to the interests of employees); s 319 (directors' long-term contracts of employment); ss 320–322 (substantial property transactions involving directors) and ss 330–346 (loans, etc. to directors and connected persons), by reason only that the directors of the subsidiary are accustomed to act in accordance with the holding company's directions or instructions.

The case of *Secretary of State for Trade and Industry* v *Laing* [1996] 2 BCLC 324 strengthens and points to the fact that it is not easy to persuade a court that a person has acted either as a shadow or *de facto* director. It is necessary to present to the court specific evidence of the alleged 'directions' given by the person concerned, plus evidence that they were acted upon by the company to satisfy the test for a shadow director and, for a *de facto* director, that there was a sufficient pattern of activities which could constitute acting as a *de facto* director. Thus in *Laing*, one of the directors had actually signed a contract on behalf of the company but the court concluded that this was not enough to make him a *de facto* director. The evidence did not establish that he had continued to act as a director for a sufficiently long period of time after that act.

The significance of being a shadow director is that such persons are caught by certain statutory provisions in the same way as a formally appointed or *de facto* director. The provisions are:

(*a*) long-term service contracts (see later in this chapter);
(*b*) substantial property transactions (see Chapter 16);
(*c*) loans and similar dealings (see Chapter 16);
(*d*) interests in contracts made with the company (see Chapter 16);
(*e*) requirements relating to disclosures in the accounts (see Chapter 16);
(*f*) the rules relating to wrongful trading (see Chapter 18);
(*g*) entry on the register of directors and secretaries (see Chapter 15).

In addition, it is necessary for a company to keep, generally at its registered office, a copy of any service contract made with a shadow director (see later in this chapter).

Different types of director may exist on a single board. There may be full-time executive directors employed for their expertise under a contract of service, e.g. a finance director. Other non-executive directors may be appointed not to work full time under a contract of service, but to give general advice and business skill and experience to the board or the goodwill attached to their name. They may also carry out a service for the company below board level as in *Buchan* v *Secretary of State for Employment* [1997] 565 IRLB 2 where Mr Buchan who was a director of Croydon Scanning Centre Ltd was also the operator of the scanner and the sales manager.

APPOINTMENT OF DIRECTORS

Directors may be appointed in the following ways:

(i) *By being named in the articles*. This method is sometimes used for the appointment of the company's first directors as an alternative to following the procedure laid down in the articles.

(ii) *By the subscribers to the memorandum*. As we have seen, the subscribers (or subscriber in the case of a single-member company) to the memorandum, or a majority of them, may appoint directors; and again this method is sometimes used to appoint the first directors of the company.

However the first appointment is made, it is not effective unless the person concerned is named in the statement of directors and secretaries which is required by s 10. This statement which is filed with other documents on incorporation must be signed by or on behalf of the subscribers (or subscriber) of the memorandum and must contain a consent signed by each of the directors named in it to act in that capacity. Any appointment by any articles delivered with the memorandum of a person as director is void unless he is named as a director in the statement.

(iii) *By an ordinary resolution of the members in general meeting*. In a public company the appointment of each director must be by a separate resolution, unless the meeting resolves with no dissentients that a composite resolution appointing several directors be put forward. This is to prevent the board from coercing members into voting for the appointment of an unpopular director by putting him up for election along with others who are more popular. The directors of a private company may by implication be appointed by a composite resolution and the written resolution procedure could be used.

In addition, subject to any restrictions in the articles, which would be improbable, all members of companies, whether public or private, can vote on a resolution for the election of directors whether they are themselves directors or not.

(iv) *By the board of directors*. The board may make appointments in two cases:

(*a*) to fill casual vacancies which may occur on resignation, disqualification, removal or death;

(*b*) to appoint *additional* directors up to a given maximum which may be set out in the company's articles. Any such appointment in excess of the permitted maximum is void.

Persons appointed in these two ways usually hold office until the next annual general meeting. However, if *Table A* applies the director concerned is not automatically eligible for re-election. The usual procedure under *Table A* requires that the director concerned be recommended by the board or that, before voting on the appointment the members have received, usually with the notice of the meeting, details of the person to be appointed which, if an appointment was made, would have to appear in the company's register of directors and secretaries. Private companies using the written resolution procedure would circulate the relevant information.

Table A, Reg 78 gives the members a concurrent power to appoint directors to fill casual vacancies and appoint additional directors, but this would involve the calling of an extraordinary general meeting unless the written resolution procedure was followed.

Qualifications

No general qualifications are required in order to become a company director. However, the Institute of Directors has introduced a professional qualification for directors. They are called 'Chartered Directors', and are able to use the letters 'CDir' after their names. There is an examination and normally three years' board experience before obtaining the title. Candidates also need a proposer and two seconders, and undergo a one-hour interview. After reaching chartered status, directors have to submit to 30 hours of professional development courses each year. The Institute of Directors also has power to discipline directors who fail to keep up proper standards. The Institute is considering offering some form of accreditation for non-executive directors. The object of the qualification is to enable qualified directors to distinguish themselves from those without any recognised training, or from those who run smaller companies, who may call themselves directors but who do not attend formal board meetings with agendas and formal procedures as would be required in larger companies.

Contractual rights to appoint directors

If by a company's articles directors are to be appointed by the members in general meeting, the board cannot make a valid contract by which an outsider is empowered to appoint directors (*James* v *Eve* (1873) LR 6 HL 335).

However, if the company is governed by *Table A* it seems that the board may delegate its power to appoint additional directors and this may prove useful when the board wishes, for example, to raise a loan or share capital from persons who are only willing to lend or invest if they can nominate a certain number of directors to the board to protect their interests.

If the articles expressly empower an outsider to appoint directors, the power to do so is undoubtedly valid, but whether the court would enforce the power by specific performance is doubtful. Generally, the court will not enforce contracts of personal service in this way.

However, if the company refuses to accept an appointee in these circumstances there is, of course, always the solution in a quasi-partnership company of asking for a winding-up. This method was adopted in the following case.

Re A & B C Chewing Gum Ltd [1975] 1 All ER 1017

The petitioners, Topps Chewing Gum, held one-third of the ordinary shares in A & B C on the basis of a shareholders' agreement that they should have equal control with the two Coakley brothers, Douglas and Anthony, who were directors of and held a two-thirds interest in the ordinary shares of A & B C. In order to achieve equality of control, the company adopted a new set of articles which allowed Topps to appoint and remove a director representing them in A & B C, and for board decisions to be unanimous. On the same day Topps, the Coakleys and A & B C signed and sealed the shareholders' agreement setting out the terms referred to above. Topps appointed Douglas Coakley to represent them but later removed him and appointed John Sullivan, their marketing director. Douglas and Anthony Coakley refused to accept the change so that Topps were effectively prevented from participating in management. *Held* – by Plowman J – that it was just and equitable that the company be wound up under what is now s 122(1)(g) of the Insolvency Act 1986. The Coakleys had repudiated the relationship in the agreement and the articles. The case was one of expulsion and *Westbourne Galleries* (see Chapter 1) applied. It is interesting to note that in applying *Westbourne Galleries* Plowman J took the view that Lord Wilberforce's judgment spoke of entitlement to management participation as being an obligation so basic that if broken the association must be dissolved, even though it is not a company arising out of a partnership.

Comment

(i) Although Plowman J purported to be applying the equitable principles of *Westbourne*, he was in fact merely enforcing the petitioner's contract rights set out in the shareholders' agreement. He could have granted an injunction to prevent the breach of that contract by the Coakley brothers, a less drastic remedy than winding the company up.

(ii) Also less drastic, if return of share capital was required, would be an application to the court by petition for unfair prejudice. It will be recalled that in Chapter 14 we gave cases in which the courts had decided that in a private company, such as this was, it was part of the interest of a member (such as Topps) to have a place on the board. Presumably this ruling would be applied to a corporate member in terms of entitling the company to have a nominee on the board where this has been agreed.

Assignment of office

The 1985 Act provides that if, under the articles or by reason of any agreement, a director or other manager of the company has power to *assign* his office to another person, such assignment will be of no effect unless it is sanctioned by a *special resolution* of the members in general meeting.

Alternate directors

These can be useful if the director has many outside commitments which may from time to time result in prolonged absences from the board. The appointment of an alternate can solve problems relating to quorum, cheque-signing and so on. There is no statutory authority for a director to appoint an *alternate* to act in his place in the event of his absence and alternate directors can only be appointed if the articles so provide. *Table A* provides that any director (other than an alternate director) may appoint any other director, or any other person approved by the directors and willing to act, to be an alternate director and may remove from office an alternate director so appointed by him. An alternate director is entitled to receive notice of all meetings of directors and of all meetings of committees of directors of which his appointor is a member, to attend and vote at any such meeting at which the director appointing him is not personally present, and generally to perform all the functions of his appointor as a director in his absence but is not entitled to receive any remuneration from the company for his services as an alternate director. But it is not necessary to give notice of such a meeting to an alternate director who is absent from the United Kingdom.

An alternate director ceases to be an alternate director if his appointor ceases to be a director, but, if a director retires by rotation or otherwise but is reappointed or deemed to have been reappointed at the meeting at which he retires, any appointment of an alternate director made by him which was in force immediately prior to his retirement continues after his reappointment. Any appointment or removal of an alternate director is by notice to the company signed by the director making or revoking the appointment or in any other manner approved by the directors. Finally, and save as otherwise provided in the articles, an alternate director is deemed for all purposes to be a director and is alone responsible for his own acts and defaults and is not deemed to be the agent of the director appointing him.

An alternate director is a director of the company in his own right and his particulars should be lodged with the Registrar if he is not already a director of the company. All the other provisions relating to directors in company legislation apply to an alternate including, e.g., disclosure of interests in shares and debentures and material contracts.

Persons who cannot be appointed

This is to some extent a matter for the articles and they may, for example, provide that a minor or an alien shall not be appointed a director of the company. *Table A* does not contain any such restrictions, but the following statutory provisions apply:

(i) *Age limit.* No person is to be appointed as the director of a public company, or of a private company which is the subsidiary of a public company, if at the time of his appointment he has reached the age of 70. However, the articles may set a higher or lower limit, or may simply exclude the section altogether. Furthermore, such a person may be appointed by the members in general meeting by an *ordinary resolution* of which *special notice* of 28 days has been given to the company. The special notice given to the company and by the company to its members must state the *actual* age of the person to whom it relates, and this is the purpose of it. Where a director over the age limit has been appointed in some other way, the members may approve the appointment by a similar resolution.

In addition to the bar on the appointment of directors who have reached the age of 70, there is also a bar on those who have reached 70 while directors from continuing in office. They must retire at the next AGM but may be re-elected to office by the special notice procedure described above. They then retire by rotation in the usual way and may be re-elected again by the special notice procedure, and so on.

Any person who is appointed or to his knowledge is proposed for appointment as a director, and is over the age limit by reason of the Act or the company's articles, must give notice of the fact that he is over age to the company.

(ii) *Bankruptcy.* The Company Directors Disqualification Act 1986, s 11 makes it an offence for an undischarged bankrupt to act as a director of a company unless the court gives him the necessary permission to act. If he has such permission, he may take up an appointment unless the articles forbid his appointment with or without permission, in which case he cannot take the appointment. *Table A* provides that a director who becomes bankrupt vacates office. The article does not prevent the appointment of a director who is already bankrupt, but such an appointment would not normally be made since the director could not act in that capacity.

The offence created by s 11 is one of strict liability which means that it does not require a guilty mind. Therefore it is no defence for the director concerned to claim that he or she did not realise that management functions were being performed.

Thus in *R* v *Doring* (2002) 33 LS Gaz R 21 the defendant said in her defence that she was only concerned with publicity and design in regard to the products of Cabouchon Europe Ltd of which she was a director. She said that she did not hire or fire staff or make financial decisions or contracts on behalf of the company. The judge directed the jury that since the offence was strict they were not required to consider whether the defendant had acted dishonestly in carrying out her duties (which she had not) but only whether her acts looked at objectively amounted to being concerned in the management of the company. The jury found her guilty and she was sentenced to 120 hours of community service. Her appeal to the Court of Appeal was dismissed.

(iii) *Persons disqualified by court order*. The court *may*, and in some cases under s 6 of the 1986 Act *must*, make a disqualification order. This is an order to the effect that a named person may not (unless the court gives leave) perform any of the following activities during the period specified by the order:

(*a*) be a director (or liquidator, or administrator receiver, or receiver and manager) of a company;
(*b*) be concerned with or take part in, directly or indirectly, the promotion, formation or management of a company (s 1 of the 1986 Act).

The 1986 Act requires the Registrar of Companies to keep a register of all persons against whom disqualification orders are made and they remain on the register for the period in which the order is in force. The register is open to inspection by members of the public. The circumstances in which a court may make an order are set out in Chapter 18.

(iv) *Articles of association*. Further disqualifications may be imposed by a company's articles. *Table A* imposes no such disqualifications, merely specifying the grounds on which directors will vacate office. Thus, unless there are such express provisions, a person is not disqualified merely because he is a minor or an alien and a company may be a director of another company.

(v) *Directors*. A person cannot be a company's sole director and its secretary at the same time nor a director and auditor at the same time. This means that a single-member company must have two officers even though it may have only one member. The sole member/director cannot also be secretary.

Directors and employment law: generally

Directors may be fee-paid supervisors acting in some ways as trustees for the shareholders, or senior executives or managers who work the whole time as directors of the company and who sometimes combine this with the giving of a professional service to the company, as in the case of an accountant who takes up an appointment as finance director. Under *Table A* directors are allowed to enter into service contracts which may be made by the board. They then become known as executive directors.

Under *Reg* 70 of *Table A* the directors are empowered to enter into a service contract with an executive director, provided that the term is not for more than five years when member approval is required (see below). In addition, the normal procedures relating to the appointment of the executive as a director must be followed.

In making the contract of appointment, the board must follow requirements of the company's articles (see below).

UK Safety Group Ltd *v* Heane [1998] 2 BCLC 208

The problem in this case arose because of a failure by the directors to observe provisions in the company's articles. In this connection, the directors of the company can in general terms bind the company and a third party in contractual rights and duties only if the provisions of the articles in regard to contractual agreements are followed.

The main relevant article of UK Safety provided as follows in terms of the appointment of directors to an executive office. 'Any such appointment, agreement or arrangement may be made upon such terms as the directors determine and they may remunerate any such director for his services as they think fit.'

It appeared that an agreement between Mr Nicholas Heane as sales and marketing director and UK Safety was made in effect by the chief executive of UK Safety, a Mr Newman, on his own initiative and not by following the relevant article of the company. In evidence he said that he did not feel it appropriate to discuss the terms at a board meeting but that the contract and its contents had been made known to, and approved by, the remuneration committee of the board – but not the full board.

Mr Heane resigned to set up another company, which was the second defendant and UK Safety was, in this action, seeking to enforce covenants in the alleged contract with Mr Heane restraining his activities after leaving the company and in particular restraining his use of confidential information.

The judge accepted that it may not be necessary for a board to meet formally in order to transact business. He said: 'I entirely accept . . . that it may not be necessary for a company to have a formal board meeting and, consistently with the decision in *Re Bonelli's Electric Telegraph Co, Cook's Claim* (*No 2*) (1874) LR 18 Eq 656 it may be possible for all the directors informally to consider the terms of a contract. . . . That, however, is not what occurred in the present case. The initiative for the contracts came from Mr Newman himself.' He went on to hold that the agreement with Mr Heane was not binding on him and therefore the restraints were unenforceable.

Comment

It is all too easy for the directors of a busy company to neglect corporate formalities but this may result in unfortunate consequences for the company, such as in this case an inability to protect the company's confidential information.

The case also makes clear that if the appointment is to the office of director or executive director of a subsidiary approval by the group board is not enough. This, of course, does not mean that the matter of the appointment by the subsidiary should not be raised with the group board in order to satisfy corporate governance requirements.

The termination of the contract of service, of itself, does not terminate the directorship. It is therefore advisable for the contract of service of an executive director to provide that the director concerned will resign the directorship on termination of the contract of employment for any reason. That failing, the director would have to be removed under a provision in the articles, if any (there is no such provision in *Table A*) or under s 303.

Removal does not prevent the director concerned from bringing an action for damages for wrongful dismissal. As regards claims for redundancy before employment tribunals, directors who are employed under service contracts may have been engaged for a fixed term of two years or more and may have been required in the contract to waive the right to claim for redundancy.

However, from 1 October 2002 it has not been possible to make a contract of fixed-term employment where the right to a redundancy payment is waived (see Fixed-Term Employees (Prevention of Less Favourable Treatment) Regulations 2002 (SI 2002/2034)).

It had been assumed that a director serving under a contract as an executive of the company could claim unfair dismissal. However in *Cobley* v *Forward Technology Industries plc* [2003] All ER (D) 175 the Court of Appeal ruled that the chief executive of a public listed company was not unfairly dismissed when the shareholders removed him from office by a resolution in general meeting. This effected his dismissal as CEO because his contract said that he could not continue as CEO unless he was also a director of the company. His dismissal was, ruled the court, 'for some other substantial reason' under s 98 of the Employment Rights Act 1996. The removal followed a successful hostile takeover and business reorganisations are capable of amounting to 'some other substantial reason'. The judgment notes that Mr Cobley had reserved his right to claim at common law for wrongful dismissal by breach of contract. This was not an issue before the Court of Appeal.

Comment

Presumably therefore where the company can establish one of the reasons justifying dismissal under the 1996 Act i.e. incapability, misconduct, redundancy, contravention of statutory provision or 'some other substantial reason' a claim for unfair dismissal will fail. Since removal from the board is a substantial reason as a 'business reorganisation' and presumably always will be the claim for unfair dismissal seems ruled out. The statutory defence of substantial reason does not apply in wrongful dismissal claims though misconduct does. Claims for wrongful dismissal can be brought before employment tribunals but there is a cap on the award of £25,000. There is no cap in claims before the County Court or High Court.

Employee/directors may claim a redundancy payment (if they have not contracted-out before 1 October 2002) or insolvency payment as a preferential creditor. The fees of an officeholder/director are not so protected. Director/employees are also covered by the Sex Discrimination Act 1975, the Race Relations Act 1976, the Equal Pay Act 1970, the Disability Discrimination Act 1995 and regulations relating to discrimination on the grounds of sexual orientation and religion or belief and employment legislation generally. The wider definition of 'employee' in the discrimination legislation brings within their scope directors who have a contract for services, as where they contract with the company to act as a consultant.

Directors' contracts of employment

As regards contracts of employment of directors, both public and private companies may not incorporate into any agreement a term under which a director's employment with the company or, if he is a director of a holding company, his employment with the group is to continue, or may be continued, except by the agreement of the members by ordinary (or written) resolution, for a period that exceeds five years, if during that period the company cannot terminate his contract by notice or his employment can be terminated by notice but only in specified circumstances.

A contract for services is included and so the provisions relating to contracts of employment cannot be circumvented by directors who enter into long-term consultancy arrangements instead of contracts of employment. These arrangements could nullify to a large extent the provisions of s 303 (see Chapter 18) in that directors could be removed from office under that section but long-term arrangements which they may have given themselves could involve massive compensation so that the company would, in practice, be unable to remove them.

The prohibition on long-term contracts applies to agreements between a director of a holding company and any of its subsidiaries. Thus a director is prevented from avoiding the provisions by entering into agreements with a company that is controlled by the company of which he is a director.

There are provisions to prevent avoidance of the long-term contracts rules by the device of entering into a series of agreements. Thus if a director during the first year of a five-year contract which cannot be terminated by notice enters into a further five-year contract which cannot be terminated by notice, the period for which he is employed would be regarded as ten years and therefore a term would be implied into both contracts making the employment terminable by reasonable notice.

The provisions do not apply if the agreement continues after five years, but once five years have passed, it can be terminated at the instance of the company by notice. In addition, a term longer than five years may be valid if it has been first approved by a resolution of the company and in the case of a director of a holding company, by a resolution of that company also. However, in such a case a written memorandum setting out the proposed agreement and incorporating the term regarding length, must be available for inspection by the members of the company at the registered office for not less than 15 days ending with the date of the meeting and also the meeting itself, or circulated in the case of a written resolution. Finally, the provisions do not apply to contracts given to the directors of a wholly-owned subsidiary. The Act regards the subsidiary as a mere unit of management of the holding company so that the directors of these management units can have their conditions of service settled by the directors of the holding company. If a director of a wholly-owned subsidiary is also a director of the holding company, any contract in excess of five years will be caught by the above provisions and will be affected unless one of the exceptions applies.

A contract which contravenes the above provisions is void and can be terminated by the company at any time after reasonable notice. Reasonable notice is not defined by the Act but in *James* v *Kent & Co Ltd* [1950] 2 All ER 1099 it was held to be an implied term of a company director's contract that he should be entitled to three months' notice.

Any term in the agreement, e.g. salary, which is distinct from the term relating to duration is valid and enforceable.

Under s 318 companies must keep copies of all written service agreements and written memoranda of oral service agreements.

Section 319 and the *Duomatic* principle

In *Atlas Wright (Europe) Ltd* v *Wright and Wright* [1999] *The Times*, 3 February, the Court of Appeal held that a term in a contract between a company and a director under which the agreement would be for life terminable only by the director and not the company was not void under s 319 because the sole shareholder of the company had consented to it, albeit without a formal meeting, and had known about the agreement for at least the requisite 15-day period. The *Duomatic* principle was applied. This states that the unanimous consent of all the shareholders who have a right to attend and vote at a general meeting of a company can override formal (including statutory) requirements relating to the passing of resolutions at those meetings (see *In Re Duomatic* [1969] 1 All ER 161).

The desirability of written contracts

As we have seen, executive directors can have a double function – one as an officer of the company and the other as an employee. However, the general attitude of the courts has been to regard them as holders of an office rather than employees unless there is satisfactory evidence to the contrary (see *Eaton* v *Robert Eaton Ltd and Secretary of State for Employment* [1988] IRLR 83 and *McLean* v *Secretary of State for Employment* (1992) 455 IRLIB 14). These cases emphasise the general desirability of executive directors, particularly in small businesses, having written contracts of service. Where this is so, the court would normally recognise the employee aspect of the dual role and, in particular, allow claims to be made under s 166 of the Employment Rights Act 1996 to the Department of Trade and Industry (DTI) for a redundancy payment if the business goes insolvent. The written contract of service should not exclude employment protection rights if it is for a fixed term. Once the DTI has made the payment, the remedies of the employee against the employing company are transferred to the Secretary of State for Trade and Industry for what they might be worth. The right of an employee to apply directly to the DTI thus becomes very important in an insolvency. However, this right only applies to employees and many directors of small family companies who are acting in an executive role but without written contracts of employment may find themselves without any financial recompense if the business fails.

Controlling members as employed directors

Before leaving the topic of directors as employees, it is worth mentioning that a director who has a controlling interest in the shares of a company may not be regarded as an employee of the company. Control is still a major factor in establishing a contract of employment and a majority shareholder is not, as a worker, subject to any effective control by the company (see *Otton* v *Secretary of State for Employment* (1995) 7 February, EAT 1150/94). More recent case law appears below. The provisions referred to above were then administered by the Department of Employment.

Buchan *v* **Secretary of State for Employment** (1997) 565 IRLB 2

Mr Buchan was one of two working directors of Croydon Scanning Centre Ltd. He was also the operator of the scanner and the sales manager and had a 50 per cent shareholding in the company. He worked full time for a salary of £35,000 pa and had an entitlement of five weeks' holiday per year. He had no written contract of service and no written record of his engagement or conditions of service. The company went into administrative receivership and Mr Buchan tried unsuccessfully to obtain from the Secretary of State a redundancy payment from the National Insurance Fund under ss 166 and 182 of the Employment Rights Act 1996. As we have seen, this course of action is available to an employee where, e.g., the employer is insolvent and the whole or any part of a redundancy payment remains unpaid. If the Secretary of State makes a payment, he takes over the employee's rights and remedies in the insolvency.

An employment tribunal upheld the Secretary of State's decision and Mr Buchan appealed to the EAT. The EAT dismissed Mr Buchan's appeal, concluding on the evidence that he was not an employee. As beneficial owner of 50 per cent of the shares, he could block any company decisions with which he did not agree, including decisions as to his own terms of service or dismissal. The appointment of an administrative receiver did not and could not alter Mr Buchan's status within the company. The EAT distinguished the case of *Lee* v *Lee's Air Farming Ltd* [1960] 3 All ER 420 (see Chapter 1) where a controlling shareholder was held to be an employee. He was killed while crop-spraying and a claim was brought against the company for workmen's compensation, the company being indemnified in this respect by an insurance company. The claim succeeded but the EAT did not think it would have done if it had been made under employment protection legislation. Policy considerations were involved. Employment protection claims on insolvency are met by the state and not by a company backed up by an insurer.

Comment

(i) The EAT followed this decision in a case heard contemporaneously with *Buchan*, i.e. *Ivey* v *Secretary of State for Employment* (1997) 565 IRLB 2 where Mr Ivey was managing director owning 99 per cent of the company shares and also had a written contract. The two decisions were then followed in *Heffer* v *Secretary of State for Trade and Industry* (EAT 355/96) where it was held that an individual with a 70 per cent shareholding in the company was not an employee.

(ii) There was a further development in *Fleming* v *Secretary of State for Trade and Industry* (1998) 588 IRLB 10. The decision in *Buchan* had carried the suggestion that there was a rule of law that a controlling shareholder could *never* be an employee. That proposition was rejected by the Court of Session in *Fleming*. The court held that the fact that a director holds a majority shareholding in the company is a relevant factor in deciding whether he is or is not an employee for the purposes of employment protection legislation but it is not in itself decisive. Nevertheless, the court held that Fleming was not an employee because, even though he worked alongside the company's employees, he was a majority shareholder and, in addition, had guaranteed the company's debts. The *Fleming* approach was also approved by the Employment Appeal Tribunal in *Secretary of State for Trade and Industry* v *Bottrill* [1998] IRLR 120 where Morison J said that the reasoning in *Buchan* and *Ivey* was 'unsound'.

(iii) The decision of the EAT was affirmed by the Court of Appeal in *Secretary of State for Trade and Industry* v *Bottrill* (1999) 615 IRLB 12. The Court of Appeal stated that whether or not a controlling shareholder could also be an employee can be decided only by having regard to all the relevant facts. His controlling shareholding is likely to be a significant fact in all situations and in some cases may be decisive. However, it is only one of the relevant facts and is not to be taken as determining the relationship without taking into account all the relevant circumstances.

(iv) Following *Bottrill*, the EAT has ruled that a controlling shareholder of a company could be regarded as an employee even though he stood to gain if the company did well. The fact that he was a skilled entrepreneur was also irrelevant to the question of whether or not he was an employee. He had a contract of employment with the company that was not a sham and he had been treated and rewarded as an employee (see *Connolly* v *Sellers Arenascene Ltd* (2000) 633 IRLB 15).

(v) It seems that a director will be regarded as an employee where there is a written contract of employment and all the usual hallmarks of employment are present. Certainly the original, almost blanket, ban on controlling shareholders as employees has been considerably eroded.

Statutory employment claims

Directors are, in general, the best paid employees in a company and they have in the past shown little interest in claims for unfair dismissal because of the existence of a cap on the amount of compensation recoverable. This limit was increased under the Employment Rights (Increase of Limits) Order 2003, to £55,000. Since a claim for wrongful dismissal may be limited to the sum which the director would have received during the relevant period of notice, there may be more claims by directors of smaller companies for unfair dismissal where this can be sustained in the circumstances of the case.

However in this context the decision of the Court of Appeal in *Cobley* and the comment thereto should be noted (see page 315).

DIRECTORS' SHARE QUALIFICATION

The articles may require the directors to take up a certain number of shares as a share qualification. The general purpose of this is said to be that, since they are to manage the company's affairs on behalf of the other shareholders, they should have a stake in it themselves to induce them to act diligently to ensure the company's progress. However, since it is not possible to ensure that directors have a beneficial interest in their qualification shares it seems that no useful purpose is served by a requirement of qualification shares.

It is the duty of every director who is required to hold a share qualification, and who is not already qualified, to obtain the necessary shares within two months after his appointment, or such shorter time as may be fixed by the articles.

A *director must be entered on the company's register* as the holder of his qualification shares, but he need not hold them beneficially and could, for example, hold them on trust for others so long as his name appears on the register of members in respect of them. A director is not allowed to hold his qualification shares in the name of a nominee, since it would involve the company receiving notice of trust which is forbidden by s 360 (see Chapter 13). A director is not qualified by holding a share warrant.

The modern trend is for articles of association not to require a share qualification for directors since it is now a generally held view that no useful purpose is served by the requirement. It does, of course, help to ensure a quorum at general meetings, though it carries a distinct risk that directors will become disqualified and therefore automatically vacate office, either by transfer, or during the currency of a takeover bid, where they have accepted an offer in respect of their own holdings.

It is almost certain that far more cases of disqualification occur than might be supposed and that when the fact comes to light the directors concerned merely buy sufficient shares and carry on as before. In fact, of course, having been disqualified, and thereby vacated office, they ought to be reappointed by the board or the members as the case may be, but probably very few are so reappointed and it is unlikely that s 285 (see Chapter 5) can be relied upon. The section does admittedly provide that the acts of a director shall be valid, notwithstanding any defect that may afterwards be discovered in his appointment or qualification. However, it is possible that s 285 does not apply if there is no attempt at reappointment, though the rule in *Turquand*'s case may be of assistance (see Chapter 5). An unqualified person acting as director may be fined for each day that he continues to act.

DIVISION OF POWER – DIRECTORS AND MEMBERS

The board of directors and meetings of members of a company can between them exercise all of the company's powers. In a private company there is the option of a unanimous written resolution of members. The distribution of those powers as between the members and the directors is, subject to the provisions of the Companies Act, left entirely to the discretion of those who frame the articles of association.

The board's powers can be as broad or as narrow as is desired, but if *Table A, Reg* 70 applies, then this confers on the board all the powers of the company, except those which the Companies Act 1985 and the articles require to be exercised by the members.

The powers reserved to the members by the Companies Act are mainly the power to alter the memorandum and articles, the power to alter share capital, the power to appoint auditors and remove directors and the power to put the company into liquidation. Additionally, *Table A* reserves to the members the power to fix the rights to be attached to a new issue of shares and to effect variations of such rights, the power to appoint directors and the power to declare dividends, though not in excess of the percentage recommended by the board, and to capitalise profits and reserves.

In addition, directors of public and private companies must have the authority of the members by ordinary resolution in general meeting, or written resolution, or of the company's articles, before they exercise a power of allotment of shares or grant rights to subscribe for, or convert securities into, shares. Furthermore, public and private companies must offer new shares to existing members before they are allotted to others. However, a private company may exclude this requirement by its memorandum or articles or by special (or written) resolution and a plc may achieve the disapplication of pre-emption rights by a special resolution of its members (see Chapter 10).

Concurrent powers

Certain powers, even though given to the directors, will be regarded as concurrent and exercisable by the members unless the articles make it clear that the power is exclusive to the directors. Thus a power for directors to appoint additional directors and to fill casual vacancies on the board or to fix the remuneration of the managing director will be treated as concurrent powers, unless the articles clearly show that it is to be exclusive to the directors (which *Table A* does not) and so resolutions passed by the members in respect of such matters will prevail over the directors' own decision. Although the directors have power to sue in the company's name, there is also a concurrent power in the members so that if the board decides not to sue in a particular case the members may by ordinary resolution resolve that the company shall sue.

Control of the company's business

If the members are dissatisfied with the way in which the directors are running the company's business, there are the following ways in which the members can deal with the situation:

(*a*) *by overriding decisions of the board by ordinary* (*or written*) *resolution* where the power is concurrent. Thus if the directors have refused to bring a claim to court on behalf of the company the members may initiate it by ordinary (or written) resolution; or

(*b*) *by altering the memorandum by special* (*or written*) *resolution to take away the company's capacity to continue the activity concerned*; or

(*c*) *by altering the company's articles by a special* (*or written*) *resolution so as to cut down the directors' powers*; or

(*d*) *by refusing to re-elect directors of whose actions they disapprove*. The procedure would involve replacing the directors by others with different policies and this would require an ordinary (or written) resolution; or

(*e*) *by recourse to the provisions of s 303*, which provides that a company may by *ordinary resolution* remove a director before the expiration of his period of office, notwithstanding anything in the articles or in any agreement between the company and him. Such a resolution requires *special notice* of 28 days to be given to the company of the intention to propose it. The section does not deprive a director so removed of any claim he may have for damages or compensation payable to him as a result of the termination of his appointment. The section would be satisfied by a majority of one, but a small minority would be unlikely to succeed in carrying such a resolution, and removal may be impossible if the directors have weighted voting rights on the resolution to remove them (*Bushell* v *Faith*, 1969, see Chapter 18). Company legislation does not allow the use of a written resolution by private companies for removal of directors.

In addition, *Pedley* v *Inland Waterways*, 1977 (see Chapter 18) decides that a minority wishing to remove a director must be of sufficient size to comply with s 376 (if the directors are to be compelled to put a resolution on the agenda for removal at an AGM), or s 368 (if the directors are to be required to call an extraordinary general meeting to consider the removal) (see further Chapter 18);

(*f*) *where there is a regulation such as Reg 70 of Table A*, the members may give a direction by a special (or written) resolution under which the directors are required to act differently for the future. *Regulation* 70 provides that subject to the provisions of the Act, the memorandum and the articles, *and to any directions given by special resolution*, the business of the company shall be managed by the directors who may exercise all the powers of the company. No alteration of the memorandum or articles *and no such direction* shall invalidate any prior act of the directors which would have been valid if that alteration had not been made *or that direction* had not been given.

Directors' irregular acts – validation

Directors who carry out acts which are initially defective can have them validated by an ordinary (or written) resolution. If the transaction is *ultra vires* the company, a special (or written) resolution is required (see Chapter 3).

Grant *v* United Kingdom Switchback Railways Co (1888) 40 Ch D 135

The articles of association of Thompson's Patent Gravity Switchback Railways Co (the second defendant) disqualified any director from voting at a board meeting in regard to any contract in which he was interested. The directors of Thompson's agreed to sell the company's undertaking to the United Kingdom Co (the first defendant) despite the fact that they were also the promoters of the purchasing company. An action was brought by a shareholder in Thompson's for an injunction to restrain Thompson's from carrying into effect the contract of sale on the grounds that they had no authority to enter into it since the articles prohibited a director from voting upon a contract in which he was interested, and here all the directors but one were interested. However, it appeared that a general meeting of the shareholders of Thompson's had been properly held and that they had passed an ordinary resolution approving and adopting the agreement and authorising the directors to carry it into effect. *Held* – by the Court of Appeal – that the contract was valid and an injunction was refused.

The directors cannot cure acts which are in breach of their fiduciary duty to the company by obtaining an ordinary resolution of the members in general meeting if they control the voting at general meetings (*Cook* v *Deeks*, 1916, see Chapter 14) or possibly control general meetings in fact, even though they do not have a majority of voting shares (*Prudential Assurance* v *Newman*, 1980, see Chapter 14).

A unanimous written resolution would presumably cure such acts in the sense that there would be no member wishing to object. However, in a situation of insolvency the creditors, through an insolvency practitioner, may wish to contest the validity of a written resolution as a cure for the directors' breach of duty.

Delegation of powers by the directors

The well-known maxim of the law of agency – '*delegatus non potest delegare*' (a delegate cannot delegate) – applies to directors, so that they cannot delegate their functions and powers to others without the permission of the members or the articles. Articles do usually allow delegation of powers to a committee of the board as *Table A* does though such delegation is revocable even if made for a fixed period of time (*Manton* v *Brighton*

Corporation [1951] 2 All ER 101). *Table A* also allows delegation to any managing director or any director holding any other executive office of such of the directors' powers as they consider desirable to be exercised by him.

In addition, *Table A* also allows the board to employ agents and professional persons to carry out any functions which the board may itself carry out.

Board unable or unwilling to act

This situation may arise in the following circumstances:

(*a*) *Where the act is beyond the powers of the board* authority for the transaction must be sought from the members in general meeting and the authorisation may be given by ordinary (or written) resolution.

The members may authorise directors to do an act which is outside the directors' own powers, but within the company's power, by passing an ordinary (or written) resolution either before or after the directors' act (*per* Bowen LJ in *Grant* v *United Kingdom Switchback Railways Co*, 1888, see above). In such a situation the members can, of course, revoke or vary the authority by ordinary (or written) resolution at any time. It is only necessary to amend the articles if the members wish to add the particular power to the powers of the board.

(*b*) *Lack of quorum at board meetings*. Directors may be unable to exercise the powers given to them by the articles because they have become so few in number that they cannot constitute a quorum, or because so many of them are, in a legal sense, interested in the transaction in question and are consequently disabled from voting by the articles, that a quorum of competent directors cannot be found.

As regards quorum, *Table A* empowers the remaining directors to fill vacancies so as to make up a quorum, but if there are no directors at all, or if the remaining directors are unwilling to fill the vacancies, the members may exercise their powers until a board is properly constituted.

When a quorum of competent directors (i.e. directors who are not interested in the transaction) cannot be found, the board's powers temporarily revert to the members who may then authorise the remaining directors to act either in advance of their acting or by ratification afterwards.

(*c*) *The proper purpose rule*. If directors are unable to exercise their powers in a lawful manner because to do so would be a breach of their duty to exercise those powers for the purpose for which they were given, i.e. for the benefit of the company (alternatively expressed as the proper purpose rule), the members may by ordinary (or written) resolution ratify what the directors have in fact done (*Bamford* v *Bamford* [1969] 2 WLR 1107), and it would seem that they may also authorise the directors in advance to do the act in question (*Bamford* v *Bamford*, 1969, *per* Russell LJ). It appears from cases such as *North-West Transportation Co Ltd* v *Beatty* (1887) 12 App Cas 589 that the directors are not under any legal duty to abstain from voting in order to achieve ratification or authorisation.

If there is no such ratification or authorisation by the members and the act of the board contravenes the proper purpose rule, it is invalid.

It is important to note that directors may fall foul of the proper purpose rule even when they are exercising a power for the benefit of the company.

Galloway *v* Hallé Concerts Society [1915] 2 Ch 233

The defendant society was registered in 1899 as a company limited by guarantee without the addition of the word limited to its name, as being formed for the promotion of art and with the intention that its profits should be applied in promoting its objects without payment of dividends to its members. Its object was the promotion of concerts known as the 'Hallé Concerts' in Manchester. Under the provisions of the memorandum each member was to contribute on a winding-up such amount as should be required to pay the company's liabilities, not exceeding £5 per member. Article 7 of the company's articles provided that each member should be liable to contribute, and should pay on demand to the society, any sum or sums not exceeding in the aggregate £100 (called the contribution) as and when called. The claimants, Galloway and Holt, were members of the society but disagreed with certain of its policies. They objected to calls being made upon them in respect of the contribution and had not paid previous calls made, although one such call had been recovered by the society in a county court. On 31 March 1915, the committee of the society resolved to call up the whole of the contributions of Galloway and Holt, but no corresponding call was made on the other members. The claimants sought a declaration that the resolution was invalid and the call unenforceable. *Held* – by Sargant J – there is an implied condition of equality between shareholders in a company, and it is generally improper for directors to make a call on part of a class of members without making a similar call on all the members of the class. Further, even if the articles give power to discriminate, the fact that the members are dilatory in paying previous calls would not be sufficient reason for enforcing a discriminatory power in the articles.

Comment

(i) It should be noted that the act of making the call was not in any sense beyond the powers of the directors and was even in a sense exercised for the benefit of the company because, having called up the whole of the share capital of Galloway and Holt, they could have been sued once and for all for its recovery if they had not paid it. However, in spite of the fact that the directors had the power and were probably motivated in the company's benefit, the power was not exercised for the proper purpose and was struck down for this reason.

(ii) More commonly perhaps the proper purpose rule is used where the directors have used their powers for a purpose which does not benefit the company as in the *Rolled Steel* case (see Chapter 5).

(*d*) *Dissension between members of the board.* If directors are unable to act because of a dissension between themselves, the members may exercise the powers of the board until a board is elected which can act. However, the dissension must result in deadlock before the members can intervene. It must, for example, be shown either that so many directors persistently absent themselves from board meetings that a quorum cannot be found, or that the dissenting parties have equal voting power at board meetings and resolutions cannot therefore be passed.

(*e*) *Powers of the court.* Where the board is unable to act because the directors are so few in number that a quorum cannot be found, or because of deadlock between the directors, the court may appoint a receiver of the company's business to manage it until a competent board can be constituted. Furthermore, if the power of the board which the members wish to have exercised is one which the court can conveniently exercise itself, the court may exercise the power and give any decision which the board could have given (see *Re Copal Varnish Co Ltd* [1917] 2 Ch 349 where the court exercised a power to approve the transfer of shares).

THE CHAIRMAN AND EXECUTIVE DIRECTORS

Consideration will now be given to the special position of the chairman and executive directors.

Chairman

Companies are not required by the law to appoint a chairman. Since, however, they are bound to hold an AGM of shareholders, unless in the case of a private company an elective resolution has been passed dispensing with this requirement (see further Chapter 19), and *Table A* envisages meetings of the board, there is obviously a need for a chairman to control proceedings.

A chairman of the company is therefore usually appointed. *Table A* gives the board specific power to appoint a chairman of the board and states that the chairman of the board shall preside as chairman of general meetings, though provisions are made in each case for the chairman's absence and in practice a deputy chairman is often appointed.

The chairman is normally regarded as a non-executive director even though he may be closely involved with the affairs of the company. Where he is in receipt of fees and is not employed at a salary but is concerned solely with running the board and representing the company as a figurehead, he is properly described as a non-executive director. However, he may not qualify as an 'independent' director where such independence may be required. There is in recent times a tendency to refer to non-executive directors as 'outside directors' and in many cases the chairman would not truly fit that description.

Managing director

It is usual to make one or more of the full-time directors managing director (or directors) and give him powers relating to the management of the business which are exercisable without reference to the full board.

Before such an appointment can be made, the articles must so provide. *Table A* provides for the appointment of a member of the board to the office of managing director, and further states that he shall not be subject to retirement by rotation, but that he shall cease to be a managing director if for any other reason he ceases to be a director, e.g. where he is removed or becomes disqualified (*Southern Foundries v Shirlaw*, 1940, see Chapter 4). Thus under *Table A*, a managing director must also be a director, as must the chairman of the board. *Table A* allows the directors to fix the managing director's remuneration and in *Reg* 72 allows the board to delegate any of their powers to him, subject to a right to review these powers from time to time. Where the articles are in the form of *Table A*, then the managing director is not wholly independent of the board, as he will be if his powers are outlined expressly in the articles. In practice, *Table A* gives the board flexibility to give a managing director a specific portfolio of powers and review the situation from time to time.

The fact that *Reg* 72 allows the board to delegate any of its powers to the managing director has given the holder of such office wide ostensible or usual authority as an agent on the assumption perhaps by the outsider that the relevant powers have been delegated. This means that the managing director may bind the company, at least in business contracts, even where he exceeds actual authority. However, the case of *Mitchell & Hobbs (UK) Ltd* v *Mill* [1996] 2 BCLC 102 decides that such ostensible or usual authority does not extend to instructing solicitors to commence an action on behalf of the company without the consent of the board.

Appointment of directors to executive posts

Under *Table A* the directors may appoint one or more of their number to any executive office, e.g. finance director, under the company and may enter into an agreement or arrangement with any director for his employment by the company or for the provision by him of any services outside the scope of the ordinary duties of a director. Any such appointment, agreement or arrangement may be made on such terms as the directors determine, and they may remunerate any such director for his services as they think fit. Any appointment of a director to an executive office will terminate if he ceases to be a director but without prejudice to any claim for damages for breach of the contract of service between the director and the company. A director holding executive office is not subject to retirement by rotation.

Furthermore, the board may delegate to any director holding executive office such of their powers as they consider desirable to be exercised by him. Any such delegation may be subject to any conditions the directors may impose and either collaterally with, or to the exclusion of, their own powers may be revoked or altered. This extension of the power of delegation to directors holding executive office may well have increased their ostensible or usual authority (see further Chapter 5).

DIRECTORS AS AGENTS

Reference should be made to Chapter 5 dealing amongst other things with the rule in *Turquand*'s case and s 35A, since these have a bearing on the power of the directors to bind the company in contract.

PUBLICITY IN CONNECTION WITH DIRECTORS

Certain provisions of the Companies Act 1985 are designed to make available details regarding the executive of the company which may be of assistance to members and persons dealing with it. The following should be noted:

(*a*) *The register of directors and secretaries*. The company must keep at its registered office a register of directors and secretaries and must notify the Registrar of any changes within 14 days of the happening thereof.

The contents of the register as to directors are as follows:

(i) Present name and nationality.
(ii) Any former name.
(iii) Usual residential address (but see below).
(iv) Business occupation (if any).
(v) Any other directorships currently held or held within the preceding five years.

The object of including past directorships is to enable members and creditors or potential members and creditors to ascertain a director's past record, e.g. have certain of the companies of which he has been a director failed or at least not done well?

There are exemptions for both *present and past* directorships in companies which, for the whole five-year period, were dormant or within the same wholly-owned group of companies. In addition, the company must include on the relevant forms sent to the Registrar on registration of a new company not only present directorships held by each director, but also those held in the preceding five years.

The register must be open to inspection by members free and to other persons on payment of a fee. Shadow directors are included in the above provisions.

Where a **confidentiality order** is in force in respect of a director the register will not contain the usual residential address but must contain instead a service address. Such an address must have a physical presence which excludes a Post Office Box number but does not preclude the use of the company's registered office as the service address.

(*b*) *Trade catalogues and circulars*. Every company registered on or after 23 November 1916 must state on all letter headings, on which the company's name appears, the names of all their directors *or none of them*. This does not apply to a name quoted in the text of a letter or to the signatory. Companies incorporated before 23 November 1916 do not come within these provisions and may, if they wish, show some and not all of the names of the directors.

(*c*) *Register of directors' interests in shares and debentures*. The provisions relating to this register were considered in Chapter 13.

(*d*) *Inspection of directors' service contracts*. Every company must keep a copy of each of its directors' service contracts at its registered office or at its principal place of business in England, Scotland or Wales (depending on where it is registered), or the place where its register of members is kept.

If a director has no written contract, a written memorandum of the terms on which he serves must be kept instead. This means, in practice, that directors are given written contracts if they are employed (or executive) directors. There is little point in employing a director under an oral contract if it is necessary, as it is, to draft a written memorandum of its terms.

The copy or memorandum must show all changes in the terms of the contract made since it was entered into.

The company must notify the Registrar of Companies where the copies or memoranda of its directors' service contracts are kept unless they are kept at its registered office.

There is no need for a copy or memorandum to be kept if the contract has less than 12 months to run, or if it can be brought to an end by the company within that time without payment of compensation.

Members of the company may inspect such copies or memoranda without charge. If inspection is refused, the person wishing to inspect the contract may apply to the court which will make an order compelling inspection.

The intention of the above provisions is to assist members who wish to remove a director under s 303. This publicity enables members to see what the cost of removal will be.

The 1985 Act also provides that:

(i) A director's service contract with a subsidiary (or a memorandum of it if it is not in writing) must also be open for inspection.

(ii) The *contract* of a director who works with the company or a subsidiary wholly or mainly outside the United Kingdom need not be available for inspection. In such a case there need only be available for inspection a memorandum containing:

  (*a*) the director's name;
  (*b*) the name and place of incorporation of the subsidiary (if any) with which the contract is made; and
  (*c*) the provisions in the contract as to its duration.

(iii) Shadow directors, i.e. persons other than professional advisers, in accordance with whose instructions directors of a company are accustomed to act, are to be treated as directors for the purposes of this section.

THE SECRETARY

A secretary owes fiduciary duties to the company which are similar to those of a director. Thus he must not make secret profits or take secret benefits from his office and if this happens he can be required to account for them to the company as a constructive trustee (*Re Morvah Consols Tin Mining Co, McKay's Case* (1875) 2 Ch D 1).

The criminal law regards him as an organ of the company and a higher managerial agent whose fraudulent conduct can be imputed to the company in order to make it liable along with him for crimes arising out of fraud and the falsification of documents and returns.

Under s 283 every company must have a secretary, and a sole director cannot also be the secretary. A corporation may be secretary to a company but a company, X, cannot have as secretary a company, Y, if the sole director of company Y is also the sole director or secretary of company X. Under s 284 a provision requiring or authorising a thing to be done by or to a director and the secretary is not satisfied by its being done by or to the same person acting both as director and secretary. The register of directors includes particulars of the secretary.

Appointment

It is usual for the secretary to be appointed by the directors who may fix his term of office and the conditions upon which he is to hold office. *Table A* confers such a power upon the board together with the power to remove him. The secretary is an employee of the company. He is regarded as such for the purpose of preferential payments in a liquidation (Insolvency Act 1986, s 175 and Sch 6). The secretary is also within the 1985 Act's definition of 'officer' of a company.

Authority

The civil courts now recognise that the modern secretary is an important official who enjoys the power to contract on behalf of the company, even without authority. This is, however, confined to contracts in the administrative operations of the company, including the employment of office staff and the management of the office together with the hiring of transport (*Panorama Developments* (*Guildford*) *Ltd* v *Fidelis Furnishing Fabrics Ltd*, 1971, see Chapter 5). However, his authority is not unlimited. He cannot without authority borrow money on behalf of the company (*Re Cleadon Trust Ltd* [1939] Ch 286). He cannot without authority commence litigation on the company's behalf (*Daimler Co Ltd* v *Continental Tyre and Rubber Co Ltd* [1916] 2 AC 307). He cannot summon a general meeting himself (*Re State of Wyoming Syndicate* [1901] 2 Ch 431) nor register a transfer without the board's approval (*Chida Mines Ltd* v *Anderson* (1905) 22 TLR 27) nor may he without approval strike a name off the register (*Re Indo China Steam Navigation* Co [1917] 2 Ch 100). These are powers which are vested in the directors.

Certain duties are directly imposed upon the secretary by statute. These include the submission of certain statutory declarations, e.g. before commencing business, in order to obtain a s 117 certificate (see Chapter 1), and the annual return; and also as an officer, the verification of certain statements, e.g. under s 131 of the Insolvency Act 1986 in relation to the statement of affairs to be submitted to the Official Receiver in a compulsory winding-up; under ss 22 and 47 of the same Act in relation to the statement of affairs to be submitted to an administrator and administrative receiver respectively (see further Chapter 23).

Qualifications of the secretary of a public company

Under s 286 it is the duty of the directors of a *public company* to take reasonable steps to secure that the company secretary or each joint secretary, where appropriate, has the requisite knowledge and experience and comes within one of the following categories:

(*a*) He was in post as the secretary or the assistant or deputy secretary of the company on the day the section was brought into force.

(*b*) He has been the secretary of a public company for at least three out of the five years immediately preceding his appointment as secretary.

(*c*) He is a member of either the Institute of Chartered Accountants in England and Wales, or the Institute of Chartered Accountants of Scotland, or the Association of Chartered Certified Accountants, or the Institute of Chartered Accountants of Ireland, or the Institute of Chartered Secretaries and Administrators, or the Chartered Institute of Management Accountants, or the Chartered Institute of Public Finance and Accountancy. In addition, he will be suitable if he is a barrister, or an advocate, or a solicitor who qualified in the UK. Furthermore, a person who 'by virtue of his holding or having held any other position or his being a member of any other body, appears to the directors to be capable of discharging' the duties and functions of a secretary is also acceptable.

Thus, the directors of a public company may appoint a person who does not hold any of the specified formal qualifications.

It would seem that the duty of the board in regard to the secretary's qualification is a continuing one. Thus, if the secretary, being a member of one of the professional bodies listed, was struck off, then the directors would probably have to reconsider his position.

The word 'person' in the above provisions includes a company.

Removal

Table A allows the directors to remove the secretary before his term of office has expired but, depending on the circumstances, the secretary will retain a right to sue for damages for breach of his contract, provided that this was a separate contract and not merely contained in the articles (see further Chapter 4).

Assistant and deputy secretary: joint secretaries

Statutory recognition of these offices is given by s 283(3), the relevant part of which provides 'Anything required or authorised to be done by or to the secretary may, if the office is vacant or there is for any other reason no secretary capable of acting, be done by or to any assistant or deputy secretary'.

Special articles may delegate the power to appoint assistant or deputy secretaries to the secretary. Otherwise the appointment and removal can be effected by the board in the same way as for the secretary but there is no need to notify appointment, removal or resignation to Companies House. Companies which have joint secretaries are required to give details of them in the register of directors and secretaries and notify Companies House of any appointments and changes in particulars within 14 days of the occurrence.

THE COMPANY ACCOUNTANT

The accountant is an officer of the company. He owes a contractual duty to the company to prepare the accounts properly and like the auditor may, in some cases, owe a duty of care to third persons who act in reliance on his skill in their preparation. Seemingly, the accountant can acknowledge a debt on behalf of the company (*Jones* v *Bellgrove Properties* [1949] 2 All ER 198).

GRADED QUESTIONS

Essay mode

1 The articles of association of a public limited company provide as follows:

A101 'the directors shall appoint a person to hold the office of company secretary at their discretion but subject to the provison that any such appointment must be made for a period of at least five years from the date of appointment.'

(*a*) Does the inclusion of A101 in the articles really mean that the directors can appoint anyone to the office of secretary?

(*b*) What could a secretary do if he were appointed and then removed from his office before the expiration of the five-year term?

(*The Chartered Institute of Management Accountants*)

2 'If powers of management are vested in the directors, they and they alone can exercise these powers . . .' *per* Greer LJ in *Shaw & Sons (Salford) Ltd* v *Shaw* (1935).

Discuss the above statement in relation to the powers of the shareholders in general meeting.

(*The Institute of Chartered Accountants in England and Wales*)

3 Write notes on TWO of the following:

(*a*) the name clause of the memorandum;
(*b*) the transfer of shares;
(*c*) variation of class rights;
(*d*) promoters.

(*The Institute of Chartered Secretaries and Administrators*)

4 Name FOUR ways in which the facility to purchase its own shares may be useful to a company and briefly outline the safeguards provided by the legislature when using this facility.

(*Kingston University*)

5 Detail the contents of the memorandum of association of a public limited company and state the importance of having a registered office.

(*The Institute of Company Accountants*)

Objective mode

Four alternative answers are given. Select ONE only. Circle the answer which you consider to be correct. Check your answers by referring back to the information given in the chapter and against the answers at the back of the book.

1 Jones is a director of Shannon Ltd which is a subsidiary of a public company. At what age will Jones have to vacate office and seek re-election at the next annual general meeting?

A No age limit.
B 75.
C 70.
D 65.

2 Fred is a director of Bray Ltd and holds 500 shares in that company. His wife is also a director and holds 400 shares. He has two children – John, aged 19 and Jane, aged 15 – who hold 50 shares each. What is the maximum number of shares which Fred must disclose as his shareholding?

A 1,000 shares.
B 550 shares.
C 950 shares.
D 500 shares.

3 The register of directors and secretaries of a company must be available to inspection by:

A members without charge and other persons on payment of a fee.
B members only.
C members and other persons without charge.
D members and other persons on payment of a charge.

4 The register of directors and secretaries contains particulars of directors and secretaries. In the case of a director these must include his:

A usual residential or confidentiality service address.
B usual residential and business address.
C usual business address only.
D usual residential address only.

5 The managing director of a company has usual or ostensible authority to bind the company by transactions he enters into on its behalf. Which of the following statements represents the limit of this authority?

A All commercial matters which relate to the running of the business.
B All activities of the company whether commercial or not.
C Such commercial activities as the company may direct in general meeting.
D Such commercial activities as the board may delegate to him.

6 Madonna was employed as a hair stylist by Manecut Ltd. She entered into an agreement not to compete with Manecut for six months after leaving the company's employment. That agreement is a reasonable restraint of trade. Madonna left and formed a company called Topcut Ltd and began to trade in hair styling 100 yards away from the Manecut branch at which she had worked. Will Manecut Ltd be able to get an injunction to prevent Madonna and Topcut Ltd from trading?

A No, since Topcut has a separate legal entity.
B No, since a company is not liable for the acts of its shareholders.
C Yes, because the Topcut company was formed as a device to cover up Madonna's trading.
D Yes, because Topcut is engaged in fraudulent trading.

Answers to questions set in objective mode appear on p 576.

16

FINANCIAL ARRANGEMENTS WITH, AND FAIR DEALING BY, DIRECTORS

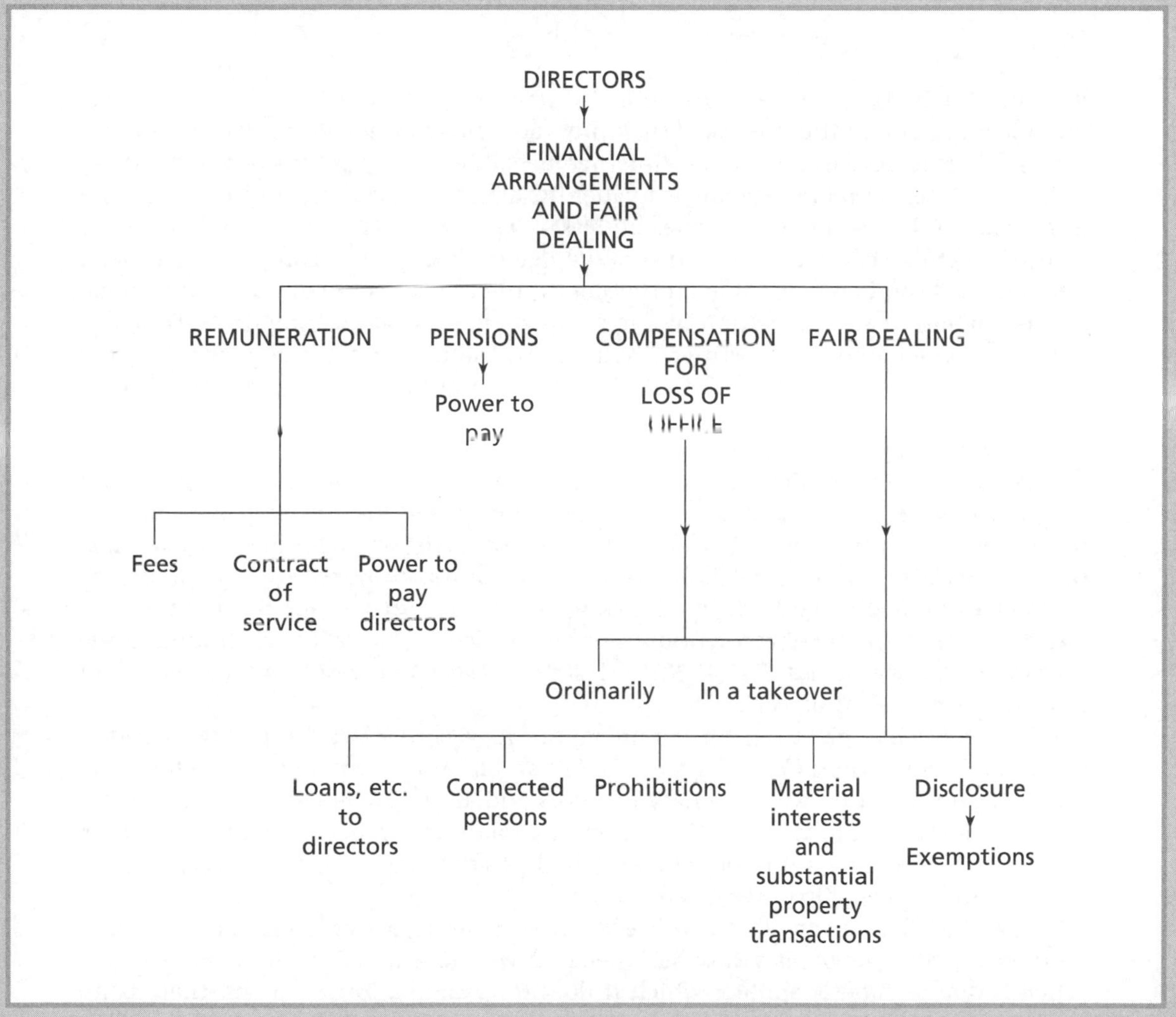

In this chapter we shall first consider those provisions of company law which relate to payments to directors, e.g. by way of remuneration and compensation for loss of office. Consideration will then be given to Companies Act requirements relating to transactions with directors and persons connected with them which provide a legal safeguard against directors abusing their position in the company.

REMUNERATION

Fees

If a director is to receive remuneration by way of fees, the articles must expressly provide for it, and in the absence of such provision, no remuneration is payable even if the members resolve in general meeting that it shall be (*Re George Newman & Co* [1895] 1 Ch 674). Their proper procedure is to alter the articles or give the director concerned a contract so that he no longer relies on fees. *Table A* provides that the remuneration of the directors shall from time to time be determined by the company in general meeting. It should be noted that a provision in the articles is not enough; there must also be an authorising resolution by the company in general meeting (*In Re Duomatic Ltd*, 1969, see Chapter 17). A written resolution will suffice. The ability to fix the fees of directors is not within *Reg* 70 of *Table A* (delegation of powers to board) (see *Foster* v *Foster* [1916] 1 Ch 532). However, special articles could allow the directors to fix their own remuneration by a specific provision.

Directors are not entitled to any remuneration unless the articles so provide and if they pay themselves remuneration out of the company's funds they may be compelled to restore it, even though they believed that the payment was permissible (*Brown and Green Ltd* v *Hays* (1920) 36 TLR 330). The directors cannot evade the rule by appointing themselves to salaried posts within the company. If they do, the appointment is valid but it appears that the director would not be entitled to the salary applicable to the post (*Kerr* v *Marine Products Ltd* (1928) 44 TLR 292). *Table A* provides for the payment of directors' expenses of office.

Where there is a provision for remuneration, it is *payable whether profits are earned or not* (*Re Lundy Granite Co* (1872) 26 LT 673), and in a winding-up the directors rank for their remuneration with ordinary creditors and are not deferred, though they are not preferential creditors, except in respect of a salary which may be payable to them as where they occupy a non-board managerial position, e.g. a company secretary, in addition to membership of the board.

Whether a director who vacates office before completing a year in office is entitled to a proportionate part of his yearly remuneration will depend upon the wording of the articles. Where *Table A* applies, which it does for examination purposes, there is no problem since under *Table A* directors' remuneration accrues from day to day so that they are entitled to a proportionate part of yearly remuneration.

If the director works for the company without a contract, he can recover a sum of money for his service under a *quantum meruit* but this remedy is not available where the director has a contract which has used inappropriate words.

Craven-Ellis *v* Canons Ltd [1936] 2 KB 403

The claimant was employed as managing director by the company under a deed which provided for remuneration. The articles provided that directors must have qualification shares, and must obtain these within two months of appointment. The claimant and other directors never obtained the required number of shares so that the deed was invalid. However, the claimant had rendered services, and he now sued on a *quantum meruit* for a reasonable sum by way of remuneration. *Held* – by the Court of Appeal – he succeeded on a *quantum meruit*, there being no valid contract.

Re Richmond Gate Property Co Ltd [1964] 3 All ER 936

The company was incorporated on 19 January 1962, and a resolution for a voluntary winding-up was passed on 20 September 1962, a declaration of insolvency being filed. Walker, one of the two joint managing directors, lodged proof of a salary claim which the liquidator rejected. Walker was appointed on terms that he should receive 'such remuneration as the directors may determine', and in fact no remuneration was fixed. He claimed £400 either in contract or on *quantum meruit*. *Held* – by Plowman J – the liquidator was right in rejecting the proof. There was no claim under the contract which was only for 'such remuneration as the directors may determine' and none had been so determined. Moreover, the existence of an express contract in regard to remuneration automatically excluded a claim on a *quantum meruit*.

Comment

Although the decision seems harsh and represents the law, in this case there had been an understanding that until the company got on its feet, which it never did, no remuneration should be paid.

Contract of service

Remuneration by way of contract of service is governed by different rules. *Table A* provides that service contracts may be made by the board with individual directors thus ousting the general fiduciary rule that a director may not contract with his company. *Table A* allows the director concerned to be counted in the quorum at the meeting at which the company through its board decides to contract with him, though he cannot vote on his own appointment. Directors have, therefore, even under *Table A*, a largely unsupervised freedom to fix their own salaries and other terms of employment by using the contract of service approach.

The DTI has issued a consultation document entided *Rewards for Failure: Directors' Remuneration – Contracts, Performance and Severance*. The basic premise of the document is that individual directors' pay is a matter for the companies and their shareholders and that the Government's role is to create a framework to allow shareholders to play their part in the process effectively and responsibly. The document is available at www.dti.gov.uk.

Taxation

Section 311 of the Companies Act 1985 provides that it shall not be lawful for the company to pay a director remuneration free of income tax, the company paying the tax.

Reporting on directors' pay – listed companies

The Directors' Remuneration Report Regulations 2002 (SI 2002/1986) apply to listed companies with financial years ending on or after 31 December 2002. Under the regulations, which take effect as CA 1985 Sch 7A, quoted companies must publish a report on directors' pay as part of their annual reporting cycle. The report must be approved by the board of directors and copies must be sent to the Registrar of Companies. Companies must hold a shareholder vote on the report at each AGM. The Report must include:

- Details of individual directors' pay packages and justification for any compensation packages given in the preceding year.
- Details of the board's consideration of directors' pay.
- Membership of the remuneration committee.
- Names of any remuneration consultants used, whether they were appointed independently, and whether they provide any other services to the company.
- A forward-looking statement of the company policy on directors' pay, including details of incentive and share option schemes, an explanation of how packages relate to performance, and details and explanations of policy on contract and notice periods.
- A performance graph providing information on the company's performance in comparison with an appropriate share market index.

Comment. The shareholder vote is advisory only and the company is not legally bound to act upon it. Nevertheless, the Government takes the view that any company that defies such a vote will face considerable criticism and pressure for change. The regulations fly in the face of calls from investor groups, such as the Association of British Insurers and the National Association of Pension Funds, for the matter to be addressed by means of corporate governance codes rather than what they regard as inflexible legislation.

The power to pay directors

As regards the power to pay, a company may remunerate its directors where this is 'reasonably incidental to the carrying on of the company's business', *per* Bowen LJ in *Hutton* v *West Cork Railway* (1883) 23 Ch D 654.

Where the power to pay remuneration is expressly set out in the company's constitution, as it is in *Table A*, it would seem that it can be made even though the company is not a going concern. There is no requirement that directors' remuneration should be paid only from distributable profits.

Re Halt Garage (1964) Ltd [1982] 3 All ER 1016

The entire issued share capital of the company was owned by a husband and wife, Mr and Mrs Charlesworth, who were also the only directors. During its early years the company prospered. Both husband and wife worked very hard. Later, the company got into financial problems and went into what eventually became compulsory insolvent liquidation.

The liquidator issued a summons against husband and wife under what is now s 212 of the Insolvency Act 1986. He wanted the court to decide that they were jointly and severally liable to repay to him certain sums paid to them both as directors under an express power now in *Reg 82* of *Table A* which provides that: 'The directors shall be entitled to such remuneration as the company may by ordinary resolution determine . . .' during the period when the company had been making a loss. In regard to the husband's remuneration, the liquidator wanted repayment of that part of it which it was alleged had exceeded the market value of the work he had done. In regard to the wife, repayment was sought of the whole of her remuneration during the periods when she could not work by reason of illness. Counsel for the liquidator said quite simply that the payments to Mr and Mrs C were presents which the company had no power to make and which could not be ratified by the shareholders. Counsel for Mr and Mrs C said that the company had an express power to determine and pay directors' remuneration and that in the absence of fraud on the creditors or on minority shareholders, the amount of such remuneration was a matter for the company.

Mr Justice Oliver (as he then was) decided that:

(i) the amount of remuneration awarded to a company director was a matter of company management. Provided there has been a genuine exercise of the company's power to award remuneration and in the absence of fraud on the creditors or minority shareholders, it was not for the court to determine it or to decide to what extent it was reasonable.

(ii) since there was no evidence, having regard to the company's turnover, that Mr C's drawings were obviously excessive or unreasonable or that they were disguised gifts of capital, the court would not enquire whether it would have been more for the benefit of the company if he had taken less. That was a matter for the company. The claim for misfeasance in regard to Mr C's drawings failed.

(iii) as regards Mrs C's drawings, the company's articles (now *Reg 82* of *Table A*) gave power to award remuneration to a director on the mere assumption of office. It was not necessary that he should be active in any sense. To this extent the liquidator's claim that he should recover everything paid to Mrs C during periods of absence failed. However, where a director was not active, the court could examine the amount of the drawings. In the circumstances Mrs C was entitled to £10 per week (she had drawn £30) merely for being a director even during the period in which she was not active. Amounts drawn in excess of this were repayable to the liquidator.

Comment

It would appear from this decision, which affirms *Re Lundy Granite Co Ltd, Lewis's Case* (1872) 26 LT 673, that there is no need for directors' remuneration to come from profits. Any requirement that it must would bring some companies to a standstill and prevent those which had fallen on hard times from being brought round. The creditors' right to have the capital kept intact is subject to the consideration that directors may be paid remuneration.

Directors and the national minimum wage

It may be that while a business is being built up a director pays himself nothing while paying other employees a reasonable wage. The director may have a spouse at work or savings, or may simply get by on very little until the business is established. What is the position in regard to the payment to the director of the minimum wage (NMW)?

Guidance on the NMW and directors and family members working for a family company is given in Issue 50 of the Inland Revenue Tax Bulletin. It is in the form of an article written by the Tax Faculty of the Institute of Chartered Accountants in England and Wales. The guidance confirms that directors and company secretaries who are paid less than the minimum wage should ensure that there is *no contract of employment with them*. That being so, the NMW is unlikely to apply. Other family members working in a family company who are not office holders may need to have their wages increased to comply with the NMW. There is, of course, the possibility that the law might *imply a contract* with a working office holder, such as a director. However, the DTI has informed the Revenue that if there is no written contract of employment or other evidence of an intention to create an employer/employee relationship, it will not contest the relationship on the implied-contract ground.

The combined code of best practice

This Code is a response to separate reports on directors' remuneration over a period of years by the Greenbury Committee and the Hampel Committee as amended to include certain recommendations of the Higgs Committee and a Committee chaired by Sir Robert Smith. It is enforced extra-legally as a code of best practice that is part of the Listing Rules. It must therefore be complied with as part of obtaining and retaining a listing for the company's shares on the Stock Exchange without which they would not be readily saleable. The Combined Code deals with matters relating to the transparency of board appointments and day-to-day administration but impinges on the composition of boards and the independence of members which has effect upon 'cozy' remuneration decisions.

Specifically as regards remuneration it requires listed companies to set up remuneration committees of independent non-executive directors to make recommendations. The remuneration of non-executive directors is envisaged as being set by the board or if the articles require it by shareholder approval. The code also states that the notice or contract period for directors should move towards one year. This is designed to cut down compensation required when a director, sometimes of a failing company, has his contract withdrawn with say two or more years to go.

The Directors' Remuneration Report Regulations 2002 deal largely with the publication in the directors' report of the workings of the remuneration committee (see page 336).

Listed companies are required under a listing rule to disclose in the annual report and accounts how they have applied the principles and complied with the detailed provisions of the Combined Code. Where a company has not complied with a provision of the Code, it is required to give an explanation.

Statutory requirements on disclosure of remuneration

Schedule 6 of the Companies Act 1985 (as amended) applies and deals with the statutory disclosures required in notes to company accounts relating to directors' emoluments. There is a division between listed and non-listed companies. The position is broadly as follows.

Listed companies

- Companies are required to show aggregate details of directors' remuneration under four headings – emoluments (i.e. basic salary and annual bonuses); gains made on the exercise of share options; gains made under long-term incentive schemes; and company contributions to money purchase pension schemes. Small companies' full accounts can show merely the total of the aggregate amounts.
- Where the aggregate remuneration exceeds or is equal to £200,000 companies will be required to show also the figures attributable to the highest paid director and the amount of his accrued retirement benefits if he is a member of a defined benefit pension scheme, i.e. a pension scheme in which the rules specify the benefits to be paid, and the scheme must be financed accordingly.
- Companies are no longer required to show the number of directors whose emoluments fell within each band of £5,000.

Thus for listed companies the regulations bring the Companies Act into line with Greenbury and the Listing Rules. For unlisted companies they streamline the former disclosure requirements.

Exceptions for unlisted companies

The above requirements apply to companies listed on the Stock Exchange and on the Alternative Investment Market. Unlisted companies must comply with the requirements with two important exceptions:

- unlisted companies do not have to disclose the amount of gains made when directors exercise share options. They have merely to disclose the number of directors who have exercised their share options;
- unlisted companies do not have to disclose the net value of any assets that comprise shares which would otherwise be disclosed in respect of assets received under long-term incentive schemes. Instead they disclose the number of directors in respect of whose qualifying service shares were received or receivable under long-term incentive schemes, together with the aggregate of:
  (*a*) the amount of money paid to or receivable by directors under long-term incentive schemes; and
  (*b*) the net value of assets other than money or shares received or receivable under the schemes.

For the purpose of highest-paid director disclosures in determining whether the £200,000 threshold has been reached, it is necessary to add the amounts set out above to the aggregate amount of emoluments.

Comparative figures

These are required for the information on directors' emoluments in the usual way.

Waiver of remuneration

If in, say, difficult times the directors wish to waive all or any of their remuneration, then in order to protect the company from possible claims, e.g. by personal representatives following the death of a director who had waived, the waiver should be absolute and by irrevocable deed since the company will not normally be able to show that it gave consideration for the waiver. A mere minute of the waiver following a resolution at a board meeting is not enough.

EXPENSES

Regulation 83 provides that the directors may be paid all travelling, hotel and other expenses properly incurred by them in attending meetings of the directors, general meetings and class meetings or otherwise in connection with the carrying out of their duties.

PENSIONS

The company has implied powers to pay pensions to employees only and not directors unless the articles so provide. *Regulation* 87 allows the directors to provide benefits by means of payment of pensions insurance gratuities, etc. for former directors of the company or its subsidiaries and for their families and dependants. They may also both during and after a particular director ceases to hold office contribute to any fund or pay premiums for the purchase or provision of any such benefit.

COMPENSATION FOR LOSS OF OFFICE

Under s 312 such compensation can be paid but the payment must be disclosed to the members in general meeting and approved by an ordinary resolution or written resolution. If it is not so disclosed, the director holds the money on trust for the company, and must repay the sum involved to the company (*In Re Duomatic Ltd*, 1969, see Chapter 17). Furthermore, a director is also by reason of s 314 under a duty to disclose payment for loss of office made in connection with a transfer of shares on an offer, for example, to take over the company. In so far as the amount a director is to receive is not disclosed and approved by the shareholders, the director concerned holds the money on trust for persons who have sold their shares as a result of the offer. The director concerned must bear the expense of distributing the compensation to them.

A payment will be treated as compensation for loss of office only if the company is under no legal obligation to make it. Thus payment of damages to a director who is dismissed in breach of his service contract, whether the damages are settled out of court or assessed by the court, does not require the approval of members. It was held in *Mercer* v *Heart of Midlothian plc* 2001 SLT 945 that payments by way of compensation are not confined to cash payments but can cover also the transfer of a company asset.

In addition, an amount which a director receives under the terms of his service contract on his resignation or removal from office in terms of severance pay is not treated as compensation for loss of office because the company is obliged by the contract to pay it. Thus it is payable unconditionally when the resignation or removal takes place and it does not require the approval of the members in general meeting (*Taupo Totara Timber Co Ltd* v *Rowe* [1977] 3 All ER 123). The decision of the Privy

Council in *Taupo* was affirmed by the Court of Session in *Lander* v *Premier Pict Petroleum Ltd* [1998] BCC 248.

The 1985 Act provisions are particularly weak in a takeover situation where the directors of the victim company remain in office within the group. The disclosure and approval provisions apply only on loss of office or retirement and if the director concerned does not lose his office or retire but continues as a director in the merged organisation managing the same assets, there is no need to disclose or get members' approval of any compensation which is paid, though the City Code contains some extra-legal rules (see further Chapter 22).

It should also be noted that para 1 of Sch 6 requires disclosure in the accounts of any sum paid to a director on joining the board, i.e. a 'golden hello' as it is called. No member approval is required however. Schedule 6 also contains disclosure requirements in terms of notes to the financial statements in regard to compensation for loss of office.

FAIR DEALING BY DIRECTORS

This section is concerned with the basic rules relating to loans, quasi-loans and credit to directors, along with material interests and substantial property transactions.

Loans, etc. to directors

The Act deals with loans, quasi-loans and credit. The sections concerned cover transactions between a company and its own directors or the directors of its holding company and their connected persons. Shadow directors are included, i.e. transactions with persons who are not on the board but are persons in accordance with whose directions or instructions the board of the company is accustomed to act. Acting on advice given in a professional capacity is excluded.

A description of loans, quasi-loans, credit and connected persons may be useful at this point.

Loans and quasi-loans

Basically a quasi-loan occurs when a director incurs personal expenditure but the company pays the bill. The director pays the company back later. In a loan situation the company would put the director in funds: he would buy, say, personal goods with the money, and then repay the loan. In some cases, for example, quasi-loans arise when the company buys a yearly railway season ticket for a director of the company or its holding company and he then repays the company; or a director uses a company credit card to pay for personal goods, e.g. a video, and the company pays the credit card company and then the director reimburses the company.

Credit

Examples are: (1) a furniture company sells furniture to a director of the company (or its holding company) on terms that payment be deferred for 12 months; (2) the company services a director's personal car in its workshops and the director is given time to pay; (3) Motor Sales plc sells a BMW to the wife of one of its directors under a hire-purchase agreement. The wife is a 'connected person' and in some cases transactions with such persons are controlled.

Connected persons

In broad terms, a person who is not a director of the company concerned is regarded as connected with a director of the company if the person is the spouse, child or stepchild (under 18 years of age) of that director. Also connected are companies (called associated companies) in which the director and his connected persons have together a one-fifth or more interest in the equity share capital or control one-fifth or more of the voting power.

Trustees of trusts whose beneficiaries include the director or the director's spouse or any child or stepchild (under 18) or any associated company are also connected, as is a partner of the director or a partner of the director's connected persons.

Prohibitions and exceptions

The Act prohibits loans to directors and, in the case of relevant companies, to connected persons. Quasi-loans and credit transactions are also prohibited in the case of relevant companies. Relevant companies are plcs or private companies which are part of a group in which one or more of the member companies is *not* a private company.

The exceptions to these prohibitions are as follows:

(*a*) A company may make a loan to a director (but not a connected person) provided that the aggregate amount of the loan does not exceed £5,000. These loans are not aggregated with other loans or with quasi-loans or credit transactions but only with other small loans.

(*b*) A company may lend money to a director, but not to a director of its holding company, to assist him in the performance of his duties, e.g. if he is moved from one part of the country to another the company may make him a bridging loan on a house. In the case of a relevant company this is limited to £20,000 and in all cases the transaction must be approved by ordinary resolution of the members *or* must contain a term that if not so approved at or before the next AGM it will be repaid within six months from the conclusion of that meeting.

A private company which has dispensed with the requirement to hold an AGM would have to get the members to approve the loan by written resolution before it was made.

(*c*) Loans may be made in the ordinary course of business on proper commercial terms. This confines the exception to companies where the lending of money is part of their business.

For relevant companies there is a limit of £100,000, except in the case of a recognised bank where there is no limit.

In all cases such companies may make loans for house purchase or for improvements to the director's only or main residence, on employees' scheme terms, with a maximum of £100,000 if they are to be on 'non-commercial' terms. These sums do not aggregate so that a director of such a company could have a loan of up to £100,000 for a boat on ordinary commercial terms and another £100,000 as a housing loan on employees' terms.

(*d*) Quasi-loans may be effected by relevant companies provided they do not exceed £5,000 and are repayable within two months.

(*e*) Credit transactions may be effected for the directors of relevant companies in the ordinary course of business (by finance companies) on proper commercial terms. Other credit may be effected up to a maximum of £10,000 at any one time.

Consequences of contravention

There are consequences in civil and criminal law as follows.

(i) *Civil remedies*. A loan which contravenes the provisions set out above is voidable at the instance of the company but no one else (s 341). In consequence, the company will be able to recover the funds from those into whose hands they have passed and there would appear to be no limit in time for avoiding the transaction. However, there are exceptions where:

- it is no longer possible to make restitution, as where the loan has been spent on a cruise;
- the company has been indemnified, e.g. by the borrowing director;
- avoidance of the loan would affect rights which were acquired in good faith and for value and without actual notice by a person other than the person for whom the loan was made. This is the usual protection for third parties and would, for example, cover the shipping company which had provided the cruise referred to above so that the loan would not be recovered from such a company.

It appears from case law that the existence of the above-mentioned tracing of funds remedies depends upon whether or not the company has actually avoided the contract of loan.

Ciro Citterio Menswear plc *v* Thakrar [2002] 2 All ER 717

In this case the High Court ruled that an illegal loan to a director which had been used to purchase a house could not be recovered by the company's administrator by an order for a sale of the property to extract the amount of the loan from the proceeds. At the time the property was purchased the company had not rescinded the loan so that the director was still the owner of the loan. Therefore no tracing remedy was available.

Comment

The administrator presumably did not rate highly his chances of getting repayment from the director and went instead for a tracing remedy into the property purchased with the loan. It would seem that the tracing remedy could be used if the loan was used to buy the property *after* the company had provided evidence, e.g. a board resolution that it had rescinded the loan.

In addition, whether or not the transaction has been rescinded, the director who is a party to it is liable to account to the company for any gain made from the loan and to indemnify the company against any loss or damage it has suffered which has not been put right by rescinding the loan. This liability is extended also to any other director who authorised the transaction, though such a person will not be liable if he can show that he did not know the relevant circumstances constituting the contravention at the time the transaction was made.

As an example of the above-mentioned civil remedies, the Court of Appeal has decided that a company is entitled under CA 1985 to demand from a director immediate repayment of an illegal loan made to the director, regardless of any other terms of the contract of loan which may provide differently.

Tait Consibee (Oxford) Ltd *v* Tait [1997] 2 BCLC 349

On 1 February 1994 the claimant company made a loan of £10,000 to the defendant, who was at that time a director of the company. In July 1994 the defendant's employment terminated and in October 1994 he ceased to be a director. By a letter dated 9 January 1995 the company demanded repayment of the loan. The defendant admitted that he received that letter of demand. Since the loan was not repaid, the company commenced an action for its recovery. The defendant said that it was agreed that the loan was to be repaid from dividends declared by the company, and since no dividends had been declared the loan was not repayable, at least at the relevant point in time.

The terms of the loan agreement, which was not recorded in writing, were disputed by the company. However, the company also contended in support of its claim that the loan was recoverable anyway, regardless of the terms of any agreement (in this case, repayment from dividends), since the loan was illegal under s 330 and therefore recoverable under s 341. The Court of Appeal accepted the company's contention. The only section that might have applied to make the loan valid was s 334 which exempts loans of small amounts but applies only to loans which do not exceed £5,000. The loan in this case, being £10,000, was prohibited and recoverable. The decision of the lower court which gave the company judgment for that sum plus interest was affirmed by the Court of Appeal.

(ii) *Criminal penalties*. These are set out in s 342 and Sch 24. It is an offence for a director to authorise or permit contravention of the Act. The company is also liable and this should encourage shareholders to take what steps they can to prevent offences. Any other person, e.g. the company secretary, who procures a prohibited transaction is also liable. A successful prosecution will require full knowledge in the defendant.

Shadow directors

By reason of s 741, shadow directors are included in both the civil and criminal sanctions.

Material interests

Material interests of directors and their connected persons must also be disclosed in a note to the accounts. A material interest could be, for example, a contract to build a new office block which the company had entered into with a building firm run by a director, or by the spouse of a director. It might also be a loan to the brother of a director. A brother is not a connected person but the loan might be a material interest.

The treatment of directors' loan accounts

The materials set out above may have to be applied in regard to a not uncommon feature of private companies: the directors' loan accounts. Two situations may arise as follows.

(a) The loan account is overdrawn

In this case the directors owe money to the company and problems may arise either during the company's lifetime, as on a director's resignation, and even more likely on its insolvent liquidation. The directors may have made drawings against the company's funds that have been allocated to a loan account. Consideration needs to be given to the following matters:

- are the drawings to be regarded as loans to directors? If so then there are issues to be addressed in terms of compliance or otherwise with CA 1985 requirements. If the drawings are unlawful loans the company or a liquidator can set them aside and require repayment to the company by the director.
- are the drawings dividends received by the director in regard to a shareholding? If so the distribution rules in CA 1985 must be addressed. Drawings may sometimes be justified on the basis that they are made in expectation of dividends though this is a risky strategy if the dividends do not materialise and it is a pointless strategy if the company was not in a position to pay dividends.
- are the drawings remuneration? If they are, as where the director has carried out work or given services to the company, then the drawings are perfectly permissible given that the work or services have been rendered, though issues of taxation must be addressed.
- are the drawings a misappropriation of corporate assets? If so the company and its liquidator can seek recovery of the sums paid.

(b) The loan account is in credit

In this case the directors have lent money to the company which has not repaid it fully or at all. The problems that arise here are in connection with impending insolvency where the directors have arranged for the repayment of the loans and have been required to repay the sums to the company upon commencement of its liquidation as preferences. Since the directors are connected persons for the purposes of the repayment any repayment that is made within two years immediately prior to the commencement of winding-up may well amount to a preference that can be challenged by the liquidator.

The case law

There is instructive case law on the above matters as follows.

First Global Media Group Ltd *v* Larkin [2003] All ER (D) 293 (Nov)

In this case a director tried to establish his drawings as remuneration but this was not acceptable to the court because there was a directors' agreement that in order to minimise tax no remuneration would be paid to directors. A further attempt to establish the drawings as dividends failed since, at the time the sums were drawn, the company was incurring losses and there were no distributable profits. The drawings were repayable to the liquidator.

Currencies Direct Ltd *v* Ellis [2003] 2 BCLC 482

Here a director was successful in establishing drawings as remuneration. He had done work and rendered services to the company and the Court of Appeal was satisfied that the drawings were the consideration. The court also stated that remuneration could take different forms and need not be in the nature of a regular wage or salary cheque or credit. Remuneration might consist in payment of the consideration to a third party in discharge of the debts of the person who had done or was to do the work or render services. It could take the form of commissions, fees or bonuses. It could be a lump sum payment or be spread over a period and the payment need not be backed by a formal contract. It might arise from the company's obligation to pay reasonable remuneration under an implied contract. The company could not recover the sums paid. They were not loans.

Re Conegrade Ltd [2003] BPIR 358

In this case the directors' loan account was in credit to the extent of some £65,000. At a time when the company was insolvent the directors purchased an asset from the company at the market value of £125,000. The consideration was a payment by the directors of £60,000 to the company and the cancellation of the credit balance on the loan account. The company went into insolvent liquidation and the liquidators challenged the transaction as a preference. The High Court ruled that it was. The directors were put in a better position in terms of their loans to the company of £65,000 than they would have been if they had been reduced to proving for that sum as unsecured creditors in the liquidation. The directors were ordered to pay the sum of £65,000 to the company. They would then have to prove as unsecured creditors in the liquidation for that sum.

Advice to directors

The following are some major points for consideration:

- Directors who have lent money to the company through a loan account should be appraised of the legal rules regarding preference. They should not repay any amounts due to them in the two years immediately prior to an insolvency.
- With regard to drawings made by directors it is important to ensure:

  (*a*) that the date and amount of the drawings are properly documented; and
  (*b*) that the basis on which they have been made is clearly stated.

Directors' contracts with the company

Under s 317 every director who has an interest, whether direct or indirect, in a contract or proposed contract must disclose his interest either at the board meeting at which the contract is first discussed, or if his interest has not arisen at that time, then at the first board meeting after his interest arises. In *Guiness* v *Saunders* [1990] 1 All ER 652 the House of lords ruled that disclosure had to be made at a full meeting of the board and not at a meeting of a committee of the board.

If the director is a member of another concern which is doing business with the company, he may give a general notice of interest, either orally to the board, or in writing to the company, and this will cover a series of contracts made with the other concern. If a director fails to make proper disclosure of his interest, he is liable to a fine.

The provisions are extended to cover any transaction or arrangement of the type set out under the loans, quasi-loans and credit heading and it should be noted that the interest of a connected person, unless the connected person is also a director, is treated for these purposes as an interest of the director. The above rules are extended to shadow directors.

Although the major sanction is a default fine, the company can in any case rescind the contract made with the director because of the fiduciary duty that exists, but it must be possible to restore the status quo (*per* Lord Denning MR in *Hely-Hutchinson* v *Brayhead* [1968] 1 QB 549). The articles may provide otherwise or the members in general meeting may, by ordinary resolution, waive the company's rights to rescind, but there can be no waiver by the board.

In this regard, *Craven Textile Engineers Ltd* v *Batley Football Club Ltd*, Transcript: B2 99/1127, CA, is of interest. A director of the claimant company was also a former director of the football club. The claimant did work for and supplied goods to the football club during the period of the dual directorship. The football club purported to avoid the contract because it appeared that the director concerned had not declared his interest in the contracts to the companies. The Court of Appeal noted that s 317 does not deal with the civil consequences of a breach but at common law the contracts could be avoided by the company. However, it must be possible to restore the parties to their pre-contractual positions before this could be done. In this case that was not possible as the goods and services had already been supplied. The claimant was therefore entitled to payment of the invoices.

In *Re Neptune (Vehicle Washing Equipment) Ltd* [1995] *The Times*, 2 March, the High Court had to decide whether a sole director must hold a board meeting and formally declare his interest in a contract with the company and record it in the minutes. The High Court said he must and if not the company could rescind the contract. So, in effect, s 317 applies in this situation even though the director is disclosing what he already knows to himself!

It should also be noted that under *Table A* a director who has disclosed an interest cannot count towards the quorum of the board on the item in which he is interested nor vote upon it. These provisions of *Table A* should be amended or excluded where a private company intends to operate through a sole director since otherwise he cannot approve any transaction in which he is interested.

In addition, in the absence of disclosure, a director who has received a payment under an undisclosed contract with his company is regarded as holding that payment in the capacity of a constructive trustee for the company and is bound to repay the sum received although he may have a claim for compensation for any services actually rendered under the undisclosed contract (*Guinness* v *Saunders* [1990] 1 All ER 652).

Substantial property transactions

Under s 320, in both public and private companies, the approval of the members by ordinary (or written) resolution of any contract to transfer to, or receive from, a director (or connected person) a non-cash asset, e.g. land, exceeding £100,000 or exceeding 10 per cent of the company's net assets, whichever is the lowest, is required. The provision does not apply, however, to non-cash assets of less than £2,000 in value.

Thus a company whose assets less its liabilities amounted to £200,000 would have to comply with this provision in respect of a transaction with a director or connected person for a non-cash asset worth more than £20,000.

The provisions are designed to prevent directors (at least without member approval) from buying assets from the company at less than their true value or transferring their own property to the company at more than market value. At least if they are to do this the members must be aware of it and approve by ordinary (or written) resolution. If the above provisions are infringed the contract is voidable by the company but not by the director.

The asset would not require valuation by an independent accountant (see Chapter 12) unless it was the acquisition of a non-cash asset by the company from a director; the company was a plc; and the consideration to the director was shares in the company.

The Scottish Court of Session has held that for the purposes of s 320 of the CA 1985 the value of a non-cash asset acquired by a director from the company (or acquired by a connected person) is the value to the director (or connected person) and not the objective market value (see *Micro Leisure Ltd* v *County Properties & Development Ltd* [2000] *The Times*, 12 January). The defendant, a corporate director of the claimant, acquired land from the claimant at its market value. However, the land was next to a piece of land already belonging to the claimant and, in effect, gave the defendant 'ransom land' on the development of the site by the claimant. This brought the plot of land acquired by the defendant corporate director within the provisions of s 320 and subject to shareholder approval.

Board minutes

Disclosure of material transactions is the responsibility of the director concerned. Such matters will be disclosed to the board of directors, and should be recorded in board minutes. Inspection of directors' minute books should identify such transactions and any discussion that took place regarding materiality.

The 1985 Act states that a transaction is not material if in the board's opinion it is not so. The Law Society's committee on company law proposed that the definition should be altered to include a 'relevance' test as follows: an interest is material if, and only if, knowledge thereof might reasonably be expected to influence the judgment:

(*a*) of a person determining whether he will enter into any transaction . . . with the company and whether he will deal in securities of the company, or

(*b*) of a member of the company in determining whether he will exercise any of his rights in that capacity.

In the last resort, if materiality cannot be agreed between the auditor and the directors, legal advice must be sought.

Disclosure: an outline

It will be appreciated that subject to certain exemptions relating to credit Sch 6 requires disclosure in notes to the accounts of transactions of non-relevant companies as reviewed above. All loans, quasi-loans and credit provided during the year to directors, shadow directors and their connected persons must be shown in the statutory accounts whether the transaction was lawful or not and irrespective of amount. Details are required of directors' current accounts with the company where these are or have been overdrawn during the relevant period. However, under para 24 of Sch 6 credit transactions need not be disclosed if they have not exceeded in respect of the person concerned £5,000 in the year in question.

Under para 22 of Sch 6 the following matters must be included in respect of each person involved:

1 the principal terms of the transaction;
2 the name of the person concerned and the nature of his interest in the transaction;
3 in the case of a loan:
   (*a*) the amount at the beginning and end of the financial year;
   (*b*) the maximum amount during the year;
   (*c*) the amount of interest due and not paid (if any);
   (*d*) the amount of any provision made for non-payment.

The above disclosures must also be included in the notes to the abbreviated accounts of small companies (para 19(3), Sch 8).

These matters must be disclosed whether or not the loan was lawful and irrespective of the amount of the loan.

Figures 16.1 and 16.2, based on published accounts, provide an example of transactions with directors and illustrate the manner of their disclosure.

The Boxo Group plc

Directors' loans and transactions

In accordance with the requirements of the Companies Act 1985, the following information is given for directors and persons connected with the directors. As a result of sundry transactions and the use of credit cards, balances exist with directors. These sums are repaid within two months.

There were no balances outstanding at either the beginning or end of the financial year but in the course of the year maximum amounts existed for Sir John Bloggs £940, Mr Allan Snooks £618 and Ms Twitchett £102.

Figure 16.1 Disclosure of quasi-loans to directors

Smith and Keenan plc

During the year the company was a lessee of the property listed below, which was sub-let to a director at a rent equal to the annual value of the property concerned as part of the arrangements, details of which are set out below.

Name of director	Lord Barchester
Property cost	£421,000
Company's tenure	Leasehold to 2027
Acquired from	Open market
Date of acquisition	23 June 2005
Length of sub-lease	7 years from 28 November 2005 with option to extend for a further 5 years but subject to an option on the tenant's part to determine at one month's notice at any time.
Annual rent payable	£9,650

Figure 16.2 Disclosure of transactions with directors

The disclosure of the above items should be agreed with the directors. There are penalties for failure to disclose and if the financial statements do not disclose the information the auditor will do so in his report. The audit exemption provisions for small companies which were dealt with in Chapter 1 are silent on the point as to whether an auditor or reporting accountant are still required in this context. It is safe to assume they are not, so that if the company concerned has no auditor there will be no audit report in which to make the disclosure and therefore the provision can be ignored. The auditor is not required to draw attention to an unlawful transaction by stating that it contravenes the Act, but he will have to consider the effect on the true and fair view.

Many published accounts include a statement to the effect that there were no transactions requiring disclosure. This would appear to be good practice to reassure shareholders and other users of the accounts.

Exemptions from disclosure

As we have seen, credit transactions not exceeding £5,000 need not be disclosed and any transaction or arrangement in which a director had a material interest need not be disclosed if it did not at any time in the financial year exceed in aggregate £1,000 or, if more, did not exceed £5,000 or 1 per cent of the value of the net assets of the company. It should be noted that although the credit limit which a director may have in a relevant company is £10,000 the disclosure limit remains at £5,000, since the government thinks that the amount of credit a director may have must be distinguished from what is material in terms of the accounts.

GRADED QUESTIONS

Essay mode

1 Dives is chairman and controlling shareholder of Cashloans plc. You are company secretary. Dives informs you he wishes to buy a seaside cottage for himself and his wife and that, to finance the transaction, he will propose to the next board meeting that the company lend him £60,000 for 10 years at 9 per cent per annum on a mortgage of the property. He asks for your comments.

Advise Dives and the board.

(*The Institute of Company Accountants*)

2 The Companies Act 1985 contains provisions regulating 'substantial property transactions' between a company and any of its directors. What are 'substantial property transactions' and what procedure is required to approve such transactions?

(*The Institute of Chartered Accountants in England and Wales*)

3 How does s 459 of the Companies Act 1985 provide an alternative remedy to a winding-up order for the minority shareholders in a company?

(*The Chartered Institute of Management Accountants*)

4 In what circumstances may a shareholder bring a derivative action on behalf of his company? What procedure is available to deal with the procedural problems presented by such actions?

(*The Institute of Chartered Secretaries and Administrators*)

Objective mode

Four alternative answers are given. Select ONE only. Circle the answer which you consider to be correct. Check your answers by referring back to the information given in the chapter and against the answers at the back of the book.

1 Test Ltd is reducing the size of the board and Fred is to leave it. Test Ltd wishes to pay Fred compensation for loss of office. This payment must be approved by:

A the Inland Revenue.
B the shareholders by ordinary or written resolution.
C the board of directors.
D the creditors.

2 Tees Ltd is engaged in the catering business. It has lent John, a director, £6,000 interest free, to buy a car. It has also lent Jane, another director, £10,000 at 8 per cent per annum interest to assist in the purchase of her place of residence. What is the legal status of the loans?

A The loans are valid.
B The loan to Jane is valid because the company has charged interest. The loan to John is voidable because it is interest free.
C The loan to John is void since a director cannot borrow from his company. The loan to Jane is valid because it is for house purchase on commercial terms.
D Both loans are illegal because each of them exceeds £5,000.

3 Amber Ltd, which is engaged in car distribution, wishes to make a loan of £16,000 to one of its directors to extend his main residence. The transaction is:

A prohibited by the CA 1985.
B permitted by the CA 1985.
C prohibited by the CA 1985 unless approved by an ordinary or a written resolution of the members.
D prohibited by the CA 1985 unless approved by a special or written resolution of the members.

4 Windermere Ltd has entered into a transaction with one of its directors to purchase from him freehold land exceeding £100,000 in value. Given that the transaction has not been approved by the members it is:

A void.
B valid.
C voidable at the instance of the company.
D voidable at the instance of the director.

5 Coniston Ltd holds board meetings once a month, on the first day of the month. At the August meeting the board discussed a contract with Ullswater Ltd. On 15 August John, a director of Coniston, bought shares in Ullswater. The contract was eventually signed between Coniston and Ullswater on 12 October. When should John declare his interest?

A On 12 October.
B On 1 October.
C On 1 September.
D On 15 August.

6 Manfred is a director of Thames Bank plc. He has borrowed £40,000 under the bank's directors' and employees' cheap loans scheme to carry out repairs to his main residence. His son, Adolf, who is aged 30 and is employed by the bank, has also got a loan under the scheme and his wife has borrowed money at normal commercial rates to set up a hair-dressing salon. In order to calculate whether the CA 1985 borrowing limits have been exceeded, which do you include?

A Manfred's loan only.
B Manfred's loan plus Adolf's.
C Manfred's loan plus that of his wife.
D All three loans.

Answers to questions set in objective mode appear on p 577.

17

THE DUTIES OF DIRECTORS

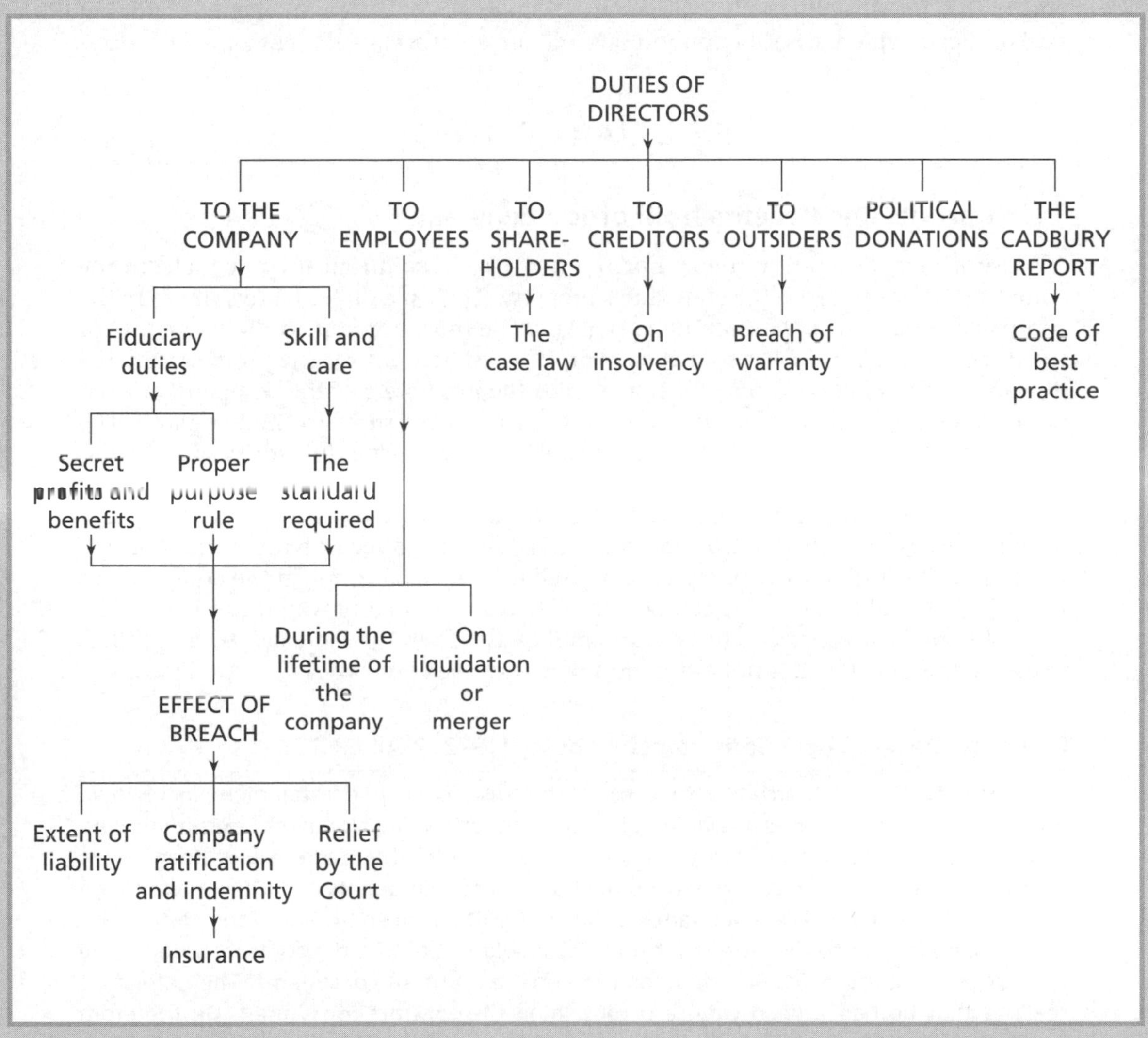

In this chapter we shall consider the duties which directors owe to the company, to employees, to individual shareholders and to outsiders.

DUTIES OF DIRECTORS TO THE COMPANY

It is convenient to categorise the duties of directors into fiduciary (or equitable) duties which arise because they are quasi-trustees of the assets of the company, and duties of skill and care which arise at common law and are an aspect of the law of negligence.

FIDUCIARY DUTIES

Secret profits and benefits from office: generally

A director must account to the company for any personal profit he may make in the course of his dealing with the company's property. Thus, if a director buys shares in the company at par when the issue price is greater, he must account to the company for the difference; where he has sold at a profit, he must account for the profit. Again, if a director receives gifts of money or shares from the promoters of the company or from persons selling property to it, he must account for these sums to the company. The reason for this is that there has been a *conflict of interest.* The director is supposed to negotiate for the company's benefit, and he can hardly have done so if he was taking gifts from the other party. He must also account for commissions received from persons who supply goods to the company. In addition, a director who in the course of his employment obtains a contract for himself is liable to account to the company for the profit he makes, even if it can be shown that the company would not necessarily have obtained the contract. The accountability arises from the mere fact that a profit is made by the director; it is not a question of loss to the company.

Industrial Development Consultants *v* Cooley [1972] 2 All ER 162

The defendant was an architect of considerable distinction and attainment in his own sphere. He was employed as managing director by Industrial Development Consultants who provided construction consultancy services for gas boards. The Eastern Gas Board were offering a lucrative contract in regard to the building of four depots and IDC was very keen to obtain the business. The defendant was acting for IDC in the matter and the Eastern Gas Board made it clear to the defendant that IDC would not obtain the contract because the officers of the Eastern Gas Board would not engage a firm of consultants. The defendant realised that he had a good chance of obtaining the contract for himself. He therefore represented to IDC that he was ill and because IDC were of the opinion that the defendant was near to a nervous breakdown, he was allowed to terminate his employment with them on short notice. Shortly afterwards the defendant took steps which resulted in his obtaining the Eastern Gas Board contracts for the four depots for himself. In this case DC sued the defendant for an account of the profits that he would make on the construction of the four depots. *Held* – by Roskill J – that the defendant had acted in breach of duty and must account. The fact that IDC might not have obtained the contract itself was immaterial. *Per* Roskill J:

> 'Therefore it cannot be said that it is anything like certain that the [claimants] would ever have got this contract . . . on the other hand, there was always the possibility of the [claimants] persuading the Eastern Gas Board to change their minds; and ironically enough, it would have been the defendant's duty to try and persuade them to change their minds. It is a curious position under which he should now say that the [claimants] suffered no loss because he would never have succeeded in persuading them to change their minds.'

Comment

The High Court ruled in *Gencor ACP Ltd* v *Dalby* [2000] 2 BCLC 734 that the fact that a fiduciary, such as a director, has made a profit makes him liable to account for it to the company. Whether the company would or would not have obtained the profit is irrelevant.

Regal (Hastings) Ltd *v* Gulliver [1942] 1 All ER 378

The Regal company owned one cinema and wished to buy two others with the object of selling all three together. The Regal company formed a subsidiary so that the subsidiary could buy the cinemas in question but the Regal company could not provide all the capital needed to purchase them and the directors bought some of the shares in the subsidiary themselves thus providing the necessary capital. The subsidiary company acquired the two cinemas and eventually the shares in the Regal company and in the subsidiary were sold at a profit. The new controllers of the Regal company then caused it to bring an action to recover the profit made. It was *held* by the House of Lords that the directors must account to the Regal company for the profit on the grounds that it was only through the knowledge and opportunity they gained as directors of that company that they were able to obtain the shares and consequently to make the profit. In particular, the House of Lords stated that directors were liable to account to the company once it was established:

(*a*) that what the directors did was so related to the affairs of the company that it could properly be said to have been done in the course of their management and in utilisation of their opportunities and special knowledge as directors; and
(*b*) that what they did resulted in a profit to themselves.

Comment

(i) This same question was considered by the House of Lords in *Boardman* v *Phipps* [1967] 2 AC 46 where the *Regal* case was followed. It is generally felt that the fiduciary duty to account which was placed on the directors in these two cases is rather high. In the *Regal* case the directors did not have a majority of shares in the company. It would have been possible for them to obtain ratification of their acts by the company in general meeting. Furthermore, it was always conceded that they had acted in good faith and in full belief in the legality of their action, so that it had not occurred to them to obtain the approval of a general meeting. It is also true to say that the directors had not deprived the company of any of its property. The shares in the subsidiary were bought with their own money and those shares had never been the company's property on the facts as the court found them. It would seem that the mere possession of information which results from the holding of office as a director is sufficient to raise the duty to account.

(ii) A further case in point is *Re Bhullar Bros Ltd* [2003] All ER (D) 445 (Mar). The company was a family company running a grocery business from several properties. It also owned investment properties. The two families involved fell out. They decided not to buy any more investment properties and to divide the assets of the company between them. Negotiations came to nothing and one of the families asked the court to order the sale of the shares held by one family to the other family or to the company under s 459 (unfair prejudice). The court refused a buy-out order. However it was discovered that two of the company's directors had, while the company was still trading, bought at an advantageous price two investment properties next to the company's existing investment properties on their own behalf. The Court of Appeal ruled that the directors concerned held the newly acquired properties on a constructive trust for the company. The Court of Appeal affirmed the ruling of the High Court that the properties should be transferred to the company at the price that was paid for them. As the appeal judgment says, whether the company could or would have taken the opportunity to acquire the properties had it been aware of the facts was not to the point. The existence of the opportunity was information that it was relevant for the company to have and the directors concerned were under a fiduciary duty to communicate it to the company.

A director is not accountable for the profits of a competing business which he may be running (*Bell* v *Lever Bros Ltd* [1932] AC 161), unless the articles or his service contract expressly so provide, but he will be accountable if he uses the company's property in that business, or if he uses its trade secrets, or induces the company's customers to deal with him. Furthermore, a director of two or more companies takes the risk of an application under s 459 (unfair prejudice) if he subordinates the interests of one company to those of the other (*Scottish CWS* v *Meyer* [1958] 3 All ER 66). A director is not allowed, either during or after service with a company, to use for his own purposes confidential information entrusted to him by the company (*Baker* v *Gibbons* [1972] 2 All ER 759).

The High Court has ruled that a director who, on leaving his company, persuaded former clients to transfer their advertising business to a new company run by him had acted in breach of his fiduciary duty. The diversion of clients was a misappropriation of the original company's property and the director was liable for profits derived from that property (see *CMS Dolphin Ltd* v *Simonet Ltd* [2001] 2 BCLC 704). The High Court has also ruled that a director who registered the company's name as his own trademark was in breach of a fiduciary duty to the company because the registration was in his own personal interest and in conflict with the interests of the company (see *Ball* v *Eden Project Ltd, Eden Project* v *Ball* [2001] 1 BCLC 313).

It is, of course, possible for a director's service contract to be so drafted as to debar him from running a competing business, allowing the company to seek an injunction if such a business was carried on. It might also justify dismissal if the contract was breached.

A director may keep a personal profit if the company consents, but the consent must be given by the members in general meeting and not by the board, and a resolution in general meeting may be rendered invalid as prejudicial to the minority, if the director concerned controls the voting in general meetings (*Cook* v *Deeks*, 1916, see Chapter 14). Shareholder approval can be given by the unanimous written resolution procedure though in such a case there would be no question of the abuse of minority rights.

However, a director may take advantage of a corporate opportunity on his own account if his company has considered the same proposition and rejected it in good faith.

Peso Silver Mines Ltd (NPL) *v* Cropper (1966) 58 DLR (2d) 1

The board of directors of Peso was approached by a person named Dikson who wanted to sell to Peso 126 prospecting claims near to the company's own property. The board of Peso rejected this proposal after bona fide consideration. However, a syndicate was then formed by Peso's geologist to purchase Dikson's claim. A company called Cross Bow Mines Ltd was incorporated by the syndicate for the purpose. Cropper was a director of Peso and had taken part in the earlier decision of the Peso board and also become a shareholder in Cross Bow Mines. This action was brought claiming that Cropper was accountable to Peso for the Cross Bow shares which he had obtained. *Held* – by the Supreme Court of Canada – that he was not bound to account. On the facts, Cropper and his co-directors had acted in good faith solely in the interest of Peso and with sound business reasons for rejecting the offer. There was no evidence that Cropper had any confidential or other information which he concealed from the board. The court also found that when Cropper was approached to join the syndicate it was not in his capacity as a director of Peso but as an individual member of the public whom the syndicate was seeking to interest as a co-adventurer.

The proper purpose rule

Directors must use their powers for the proper purpose, i.e. for the benefit of the company and not to further their own interests. Consideration has already been given to this rule which is illustrated by the decisions in the *Rolled Steel* case (see Chapter 5), *Clemens* v *Clemens* (see Chapter 14) and *Galloway* v *Hallé Concerts Society* (see Chapter 15) among others.

A further example of improper use of power by directors is to be found in situations where they have issued new shares to persons who were their nominees, e.g. the company's pension trustees, not because the company needed more capital (the proper purpose) but to defeat a genuine takeover bid by another company. The nominees they knew would not accept the bid so that the bidder would not get an adequate majority of shares and so not proceed with the bid, thus keeping the directors in power (see *Hogg* v *Cramphorn* [1966] 3 All ER 420). There is, of course, statutory protection in this area in that the directors require the authority of the members to allot shares, and there are also pre-emption rights given to existing shareholders unless the shareholders have disapplied them. Nevertheless, cases such as *Hogg* have a continuing relevance since in private companies these rights may be disapplied by the articles. In such a situation, the case law would have to be used to render the allotment of shares to the nominees invalid.

A further 'poison pill' device was before the High Court in the following case.

Criterion Properties plc *v* Stratford UK Properties LLC [2002] 2 BCLC 151

The managing director of the claimant company made an agreement with a substantial shareholder that required the company to buy out the shareholder at a high price should there be a change of control or composition of the board of directors of the company. The managing director was later removed from office and the company asked the court to set aside the agreement because it was entered into for an improper purpose. The High Court ruled that the agreement, which was intended to put off an unwelcome bidder, in a predatory takeover, had been made for an improper purpose. The damage that would be caused to the company by making the substantial shareholder buy-out would be greater than any harm likely to be inflicted on it by an acquisition. The agreement was not a proper exercise of a director's powers and could not be enforced against the company.

Comment

A 'poison pill' is North American jargon for a legal device of any form put in place by the management of a company, that feels vunerable to predatory acquisition, designed as a defence mechanism to eliminate or reduce that risk. Other expressions such as 'shark repellant' are also used.

Limitation of actions

A claim for breach of fiduciary duty is equitable in nature and such a claim does not become statute barred by the Limitation Act 1980. There is no time limit on such claims (see *J J Harrison (Properties) Ltd* v *Harrison* [2001] 1 All ER (D) 160). Common law claims for negligence (breach of duty of skill and care, see below) are barred as a general rule after six years.

DUTIES OF SKILL AND CARE

In addition to his fiduciary duties, a director also owes a duty of care to the company at common law not to act negligently in managing its affairs. The standard is that of a reasonable man in looking after his own affairs, and it might fairly be said that the earlier cases show that the duty is not a high one.

Re City Equitable Fire Insurance Co [1925] Ch 407

In this case the chairman of the company committed frauds by purporting to buy Treasury Bonds just before the end of the accounting period and selling them just after the audit. By this method a debt due to the company from a firm in which the chairman had an interest was considerably reduced on the balance sheet by increasing the gilt-edged securities shown as assets. With regard to the duty of auditors it was *held* that they might have been negligent in that they had not asked for the production of the Treasury Bonds but appeared to have trusted the chairman. However, they were held not liable mainly because this was one item in a very large audit. The case does, however, show a movement towards a situation in which the auditors cannot necessarily implicitly trust the company's officers. The case is also concerned with the duties of directors in that it appeared that the directors of this insurance company had left the management of its affairs almost entirely to the chairman and it was perhaps because of this that he had more easily been able to perpetrate his frauds. In the course of his judgment Romer J laid down the following duties of care and skill required of directors, and the general view is that these are not unduly burdensome:

'. . . (1) A director need not exhibit in the performance of his duties a greater degree of skill than may reasonably be expected from a person of his knowledge and experience. A director of a life insurance company, for instance, does not guarantee that he has the skill of an actuary or of a physician . . . (2) A director is not bound to give continuous attention to the affairs of his company. His duties are of an intermittent nature to be performed at periodical board meetings . . . He is not, however, bound to attend all such meetings though he ought to attend whenever, in the circumstances, he is reasonably able to do so. (3) In respect of all duties that, having regard to the exigencies of business, and the articles of association, may properly be left to some other official, a director is, in the absence of grounds for suspicion, justified in trusting that official to perform such duties honestly.'

Comment

A classic illustration of the above principles is to be found in the earlier *Marquis of Bute's Case* [1892] 2 Ch 100 where the Marquis was made president of the Cardiff Savings Bank at six months old by inheriting the office from his father. He attended one board meeting in 38 years and was held by Stirling J not liable for certain irregularities in the lending operations of the bank.

However, in modern times when the directors of companies are often experts in certain fields, e.g. accounting, finance or engineering, a higher standard of competence may now be expected of them in their own sphere. Certainly directors employed by companies in a professional capacity, i.e. executive directors, have a higher objective standard of care to comply with (see *Lister v Romford Ice and Cold Storage Co* [1957] 1 All ER 125), and so have non-executive directors who are qualified or experienced in a relevant discipline.

Dorchester Finance Co Ltd *v* Stebbing [1989] BCLC 498

On 22 July 1977 Foster J dealt, in the Chancery Division, with this case which concerned the duties of skill and care of company directors. The decision was not initially reported, which is unfortunate since it seems to be the first decision in this area of the law since *Re City Equitable Fire Insurance Co Ltd*. The case concerned a moneylending company, Dorchester Finance, which at all material times had three directors. Only one, S, was involved in the affairs of the company on a full-time basis. No board meetings were held and P and H, the other directors, made only rare visits to the company's premises. S and P were qualified accountants and H had considerable accountancy experience, though he was in fact unqualified. It appeared that S caused the company to make loans to other persons and companies with whom he had some connection or dealing, and that he was able to achieve this, in part at least, because P and H signed cheques on the company's account in blank at his request. The loans did not comply with the Moneylenders Acts and adequate securities were not taken so that the loans could not be recovered by the company which then brought an action against the three directors for alleged negligence and misappropriation of the company's property. Foster J held that all three directors were liable to damages. S, who was an executive director, was held to have been grossly negligent and P and H were also held to have failed to exhibit the necessary skill and care in the performance of their duties as non-executive directors, even though the evidence showed that they had acted in good faith throughout. The decision is of particular importance in regard to P and H because the judge appears to have applied a higher standard for non-executive directors than that laid down in the *Re City Equitable* case. In particular, the judge rejected any defence based upon non-feasance, i.e. the omission of an act which a person is bound by law to do. Contrary to *Re City Equitable*, therefore, it would seem from this case to be unreasonable for a non-executive director not to attend board meetings or to show any interest in the company's affairs and merely rely on management, or, according to the judge, on the competence and diligence of the company's auditors.

Comment

It is not possible to say with certainty whether this decision affects the liability of non-executive directors who are not qualified or experienced in a discipline relevant to company administration. It was obviously of importance that P and H were experienced accountants and one would have expected a more objective and higher standard to be applied to such persons, even in their capacity as non-executive directors. The matter is really one which should be dealt with by legislation but there is nothing which is relevant to this problem in the Companies Act 1985. However, it is worth noting that Foster J did not make any distinction between executive and non-executive directors, stating that their duties were the same.

The UK standard of care is also being derived from the law relating to wrongful trading by directors. In particular, s 214 of the Insolvency Act 1986 (see further Chapter 18) provides for personal liability for directors in such amount as the court may decide in an insolvent liquidation as a contribution to the company's debts. The section is based on negligence and the standard is objective. The qualified/experienced (or talented) director is judged by the higher standard he ought to have but other directors are required to reach a level of competence to an objective standard. The court will consider current practice.

Of course, s 214 can only be applied specifically when the company is in insolvent liquidation but the standard required by the section has been cited particularly in *Norman* v *Theodore Goddard* [1992] BCLC 1028 and *Re D'Jan of London* [1994] 1 BLCL 561 as being an accurate statement of a director's duty at common law which could be applied more widely than in wrongful trading; in the *D'Jan* case, for example, to make a director, who failed to read but signed an insurance proposal, which contained inaccurate information and which was repudiated by the insurance company, potentially liable in negligence. Lord Justice Hoffman accepted that a director's duty at common law is the same as that set out in s 214.

Section 13 of the Supply of Goods and Services Act 1982 imposes an implied contractual term that a supplier of a service acting in the course of business will carry out that service with reasonable care. SI 1982/1771 provides that s 13 shall not apply to the services rendered by a company director to his company. It is evidently thought to be enough that they have to act in good faith, carry out fiduciary duties and meet the common law standard of reasonable skill and care.

Directors' negligence: injury to outsiders

As regards the duty of directors not to act negligently so as to injure outsiders, the following case is relevant.

Thomas Saunders Partnership *v* Harvey [1989] 30 Con LR 103

The claimants were architects who were retained on a project to refit office premises, one requirement being for raised access flooring. The defendant was a director of a subcontracting flooring company. He was asked whether the flooring his company offered conformed to the relevant specifications. He confirmed in writing that it did. In fact it did not and the architects were sued by the end users for £75,000, the claim succeeding. They sought an indemnity from the defendant, his company having gone into liquidation. The claim, part of which was based on negligence, succeeded even though the written confirmation had been given on behalf of and in the name of the company. The defendant was a specialist in the field and had assumed a duty of care when making the statement. He was liable in negligence. The judge did not see why the cloak of incorporation should affect liability for individual negligence.

Comment

(i) The decision has implications for companies whose products or services depend to a considerable extent on the skills and expertise of individual directors. In particular, firms of accountants who are transferring from the partnership regime to the limited company regime may not find that this affects their personal liability for negligence.

(ii) Much depends upon the facts of the case and in *Williams* v *Natural Life Health Foods Ltd* [1998] *The Times*, 1 May, the House of Lords decided that a managing director was not liable for a negligent statement as to the profits likely to be made by the claimant under a franchise agreement. He made the statement on behalf of the company as its agent. Their Lordships said that in order for the MD to be liable the claimant must show that he could reasonably rely on an assumption of personal liability by the MD so that a special relationship was created between the claimant and the MD. The claimant had not, they said, established such a relationship. In particular, he did not know the MD and had no significant pre-contractual dealings with him. Furthermore, there had been no conduct by the MD which would have suggested to the claimant that the MD was accepting liability nor did the evidence show that the claimant believed he was. Nevertheless, if the special relationship can be established the court will in effect go behind the corporate structure and find liability in those who are effectively in charge of the company. This, of course, gets around limited liability and is particularly useful where the company is insolvent.

(iii) As the above materials show directors cannot be held personally liable for negligent misstatements unless a special relationship can be established between themselves and the claimant. However directors may be personally liable for fraudulent misstatements (the tort of deceit) irrespective of whether a special relationship is found to exist (see *Standard Chartered Bank* v *Pakistan National Shipping Co (No 2)* [2003] 1 All ER 173).

The criminal standard of proof applies to civil claims for fraud. i.e. proof beyond a reasonable doubt so that it is notoriously difficult to prove. It follows that it remains difficult to impose personal liability upon directors whether in respect of negligent or fraudulent misstatements.

Directors' duties and group companies

Where a person is a director of a number of companies that are within the same group duties are owed to each company within the group individually (see *Re Pantone 485 Ltd, Miller* v *Bain* [2002] 1 BCLC 266).

Reducing the risk of claims

What action can directors take to reduce the risk of claims for damage to the company following 'bad' business decisions? The following steps should be taken where it is thought that, although the transaction is in general terms for the benefit of the company, there are some risks:

- take all proper advice which it is thought necessary;
- document fully and clearly the reasons for the various decisions made;
- enshrine these in the board minutes or other written document; and
- in difficult cases consult the shareholders and ask them to formally approve the decisions by ordinary (or written) resolution. Ratification by the shareholders should protect the directors from the risk of subsequent proceedings by the company against them. Directors/shareholders may vote and give this ratification unless, for example, they are seeking to approve their own fraud.

If the above steps are taken, the directors could hardly be regarded as in breach of their management duties and so could ratify the action as shareholders even if they held a majority of the membership votes (*North West Transportation Co* v *Beatty* (1887) 12 App Cas 589).

DUTIES TO EMPLOYEES

Although in the past the duty of the directors to act for the benefit of the company has meant for the benefit of the shareholders of the company and not others, s 309 of the 1985 Act states that the matters to which the directors of a company are to have regard in the performance of their functions shall include the interests of the company's employees in general as well as the interests of its members. However, this duty is owed by the directors 'to the company (and the company alone) and is enforceable in the same way as any other fiduciary duty owed to a company by its directors'.

It would, for example, be within the provision for the directors so to arrange the company's business as to save jobs, provided the company's interests were also served in a reasonable fashion. It would not be within it for the directors to carry on the company's business at a loss and put it at risk of liquidation in order to save jobs. There must be a balance of interests but the interests of the employees must be considered.

The provisions cannot be enforced by employees unless they are also shareholders and even then a shareholder will have to bring himself within one of the exceptions to *Foss* v *Harbottle* (see Chapter 14). In normal circumstances a shareholder should be able to do this on the grounds that if the directors are ignoring the employee provisions they are doing an act contrary to law, i.e. an act contrary to the Companies Act 1985. However, unless there is damage to the company the most which a shareholder would be entitled to would be a declaration that the directors had failed to consider the interests of the employees in breach of the Act.

While accepting that one cannot predict how the courts will interpret these provisions it does appear to be a declaration of good intent and little more. It is unlikely that the company will take action to enforce the duty. However, if directors do acts favourable to the employees in balance with the rights of shareholders, they are not, at least, now breaking the law, which they would have been before the passing of these provisions when the duties were to shareholders only.

The 1985 Act also provides that the powers of a company are deemed to include, if they do not otherwise do so, the power to make provisions for its own or a subsidiary's employees or former employees when the company itself or that subsidiary:

(*a*) ceases to carry on the whole or any part of its undertaking; or
(*b*) transfers the whole or any part of its undertaking.

The Act specifically states that the exercise of that power need not be in the best interests of the company.

This provision therefore reverses the decision in *Parke* v *Daily News Ltd* [1962] Ch 927. Briefly, the facts of that case were that the defendant company had sold the major part of its business and proposed to use the proceeds to make payments to employees by way of redundancy pay before such payments were required by law. However, the Court held that such payments were not for the benefit of the company, but rather for the benefit of the employees, and therefore the company had no power to make the payments.

Where a company has power to make provision for its employees only by reason of the 1985 Act then the exercise of the power must normally be approved by an ordinary (or written) resolution. However, this does not apply if the memorandum or the articles contain a provision whereby the power can be exercised by a directors' resolution or require its sanction by a resolution other than an ordinary resolution of the company in general meeting, e.g. a special resolution.

The resolution can be implemented by a liquidator even though it was passed before the winding-up (Insolvency Act 1986, s 187). Furthermore, the power may be exercised by the liquidator if the following conditions are complied with:

(*a*) the company's liabilities have been fully satisfied;
(*b*) provision has been set aside for the costs of the winding-up;
(*c*) the exercise of the power has been approved either by such a resolution of the company as is required by the company's constitution or, if there is no such requirement, by an ordinary (or written) resolution of the members; and
(*d*) any other relevant requirements of the memorandum or the articles have been complied with.

It should be noted that if any payment is made before the commencement of a winding-up, then it must be made out of profits available for dividend as defined in the Companies Act 1985. In any other situation it must be made out of those assets of the company that are available to its members on its winding-up. In other words a payment cannot be made in order to prejudice creditors.

In connection with the power of the liquidator to implement the above provisions, it should be noted that s 167 of the Insolvency Act 1986 applies so that in a compulsory winding-up the liquidator exercises this power like all his others subject to the control of the court, and any creditor or contributory of the company may apply to the court with respect to the liquidator's exercise or proposed exercise of these powers if he does not agree with the way in which things are being done. In a voluntary winding-up the liquidator may make an application to the court for directions under s 112 of the 1986 Act if he is in any doubt as to whether he should exercise the above powers.

Since a company employer is bound in any case today to make basic redundancy payments a common application of the above provisions would be where the company intends to make redundancy payments, on a transfer of its business, which are in excess of the basic statutory requirements.

Before leaving the topic of duty to employees it should be noted that the directors must see to it that the company as an employer complies with the requirements of employment law generally.

DUTIES OF DIRECTORS TO SHAREHOLDERS

The directors do not owe, in general, any contractual or fiduciary duties to members of their company (*Percival* v *Wright*, 1902, see below). However, as we have seen, where there is a bid situation the City Panel on Takeovers and Mergers would be concerned and the Stock Exchange is beginning to look critically at the sort of insider dealing which took place in *Percival* v *Wright*, 1902, at least where a listed company is concerned, and has introduced a code of dealing for directors. The rules which the City Panel has laid down do not, of course, have the force of law. However, the Panel can issue and publish a reprimand for insider dealing in the shares of a company prior to its takeover and this could have an adverse effect upon the career, particularly of a professional person (see Chapter 22).

The Stock Exchange, in consultation with the CBI, published a Model Code for Securities Transactions, to give guidance as to when it is proper for directors of listed companies to deal in the securities of the company. This Code received widespread acceptance and became part of the Listing Agreement. The main principles of the Code have already been considered (see Chapter 12).

Percival *v* Wright [1902] 2 Ch 421

The claimant wished to sell shares in the company and wrote to the secretary asking if he knew of anyone willing to buy. After negotiations, the chairman of the board of directors arranged the purchase of 253 shares, 85 for himself and 84 for each of his fellow directors at a price based on the claimant's valuation of £12 10s per share. The transfers were approved by the board and the transactions completed. The claimant subsequently discovered that prior to and during the negotiations for the sale, a Mr Holden was also negotiating with the board for the purchase of the company for resale to a new company, and was offering various prices for shares, all of which exceeded £12 10s per share. No firm offer was ever made, and the negotiations ultimately proved abortive, and the court was not satisfied that the board ever intended to sell. The claimant brought this action against the directors asking for the sale of his shares to be set aside for non-disclosure. *Held* – by Swinfen Eady J – the directors are not trustees for the individual shareholders and may purchase their shares without disclosing pending negotiations for the sale of the company. A contrary view would mean that they could not buy or sell shares without disclosing negotiations, a premature disclosure of which might well be against the best interests of the company. There was no unfair dealing since the shareholders in fact approached the directors and named their own price.

Comment

(i) The Criminal Justice Act 1993 would not seem to affect this decision since it does not apply its insider dealing provisions to private dealings in shares but only to dealings on a recognised stock exchange. In any case, the Act gives no civil claim but merely contains criminal sanctions.

(ii) It should not be assumed that an obligation of trust and good faith may not arise if the circumstances require it. In *Platt* v *Platt* [1999] 2 BCLC 745 the High Court ruled that although the relationship between a company director and the shareholders of the company does not of itself give rise to fiduciary duties, special circumstances may require the imposition of such a duty. Three brothers – Colin, Denis and Keith Platt – were shareholders in an Essex company holding a BMW dealership. Keith ran the business and held ordinary shares. Colin and Dennis, the claimants, did not work in the business and held preference shares. The company did badly in the recession of the early 1990s. By 1992 Keith was the only brother in touch with BMW and the only director of the company. Keith misled his brothers by telling them that BMW was about to withdraw the franchise and was urging him to sell. As a result, Colin and Denis transferred their preference shares to Keith for £1. These transfers were said to be necessary to enable the business to be sold. Subsequently profitable trading resumed and the business was not sold. Later BMW terminated the franchise and the business was sold leaving net profits after all expenses of some £770,000. Colin and Denis, who could not participate in those profits, claimed damages for misrepresentation and breach of fiduciary duty by Keith.

In particular, the court accepted the existence of a fiduciary duty in the circumstances. The interpretation of *Percival* v *Wright* [1902] 2 Ch 421 as deciding that directors owe no fiduciary duties to shareholders was not followed on the ground that the *Percival* case had been interpreted too widely. Such a wide interpretation did not follow from the underlying facts in *Percival*.

(iii) In *Peskin* v *Anderson* [2001] 1 BCLC 372 the Court of Appeal affirmed that, in the absence of a special relationship, directors do not owe a duty to individual shareholders to keep them constantly informed of all matters that might affect their position. Mr Peskin claimed damages against the directors of the RAC because he resigned his membership before its demutualisation and failed to get the consequent cash benefit. The directors had not disclosed from the beginning the negotiations about and proposals for the demutualisation and the Court of Appeal ruled that they were not required to do so. They had not been directed by the members to demutualise and were not therefore negotiating on their behalf. This was a sensible decision because in such matters the board must be left to formulate proposals which may at some stage be put to the members but not as soon as the idea occurs and is moved forward.

Directors may become agents of the members for a particular transaction, in which case the situation of agency gives rise to fiduciary duties.

Allen *v* Hyatt (1914) 30 TLR 444

In this case the directors induced the shareholders to give them options for the purchase of their shares so that the directors might negotiate a sale of the shares to another company. The directors used the options to purchase the shares themselves and then resold them at a profit to the other company. It was *held* by the Privy Council that the directors had made themselves agents for the shareholders and must consequently account for the profit which they had obtained.

Comment

There are disadvantages in this agency arrangement. It was held by the House of Lords in *Briess* v *Woolley* [1954] 1 All ER 909 that where shareholders employ the directors to negotiate a sale of their shares, the shareholders will be vicariously liable in damages to the purchaser if the directors fraudulently misrepresent the state of the company's affairs to the purchaser of the shares.

In addition, there appears to be a duty to shareholders in regard to the advice, if any, given by directors to those shareholders in regard to the acquisition or rejection of a takeover bid. Company legislation does not deal with this. However, in *Gething* v *Kilner* [1972] 1 All ER 1166, it was said that in a takeover the directors of the 'victim' company owe a duty to their shareholders to be honest and not to mislead as by suppressing, for instance, professional advice recommending rejection, and that the court might grant an injunction where this had happened, to prevent the bid going ahead.

As regards damage caused by the directors as a result of negligent mismanagement, again, there would appear to be no duty owed to shareholders individually. Obviously their shares could fall in value but the Court of Appeal said in *Prudential* v *Newman Industries* (*No* 2) [1982] 1 All ER 354 that this was not a personal loss but merely a reflection of the company's loss. A shareholder's right is that of participating in the company as by attending meetings and so on. These rights are not affected by a fall in the value of the shares.

DUTIES TO CREDITORS

In a solvent company the shareholders are entitled, as a general body, to be regarded as 'the company' when questions of the duty of directors arise. However, where a company is insolvent the interests of the creditors intrude. They have power, through insolvency procedures, to control the company's assets which are, in a practical sense, their assets and not the shareholders' assets.

Liquidator of West Mercia Safetywear Ltd *v* Dodd [1988] BCLC 250

Mr A J Dodd was a director of two companies, West Mercia and A J Dodd Ltd. The bank account of West Mercia was in credit while that of A J Dodd Ltd was considerably overdrawn. Both companies eventually went into insolvent liquidation and it then emerged that Mr Dodd had paid away £4,000 of West Mercia's money to discharge a debt which it owed to A J Dodd Ltd at a time when both companies were proceeding towards liquidation and the liquidator had instructed the directors not to operate either bank account. The advantage to Mr Dodd was that he had personally guaranteed the overdraft of A J Dodd Ltd and the payment reduced his liability on the guarantee. The Court of Appeal ordered Mr Dodd personally to repay the money to the liquidator of West Mercia on the basis that he was in breach of his duty to the creditors of West Mercia.

Comment

A further example of a breach of duty to creditors and the company is to be found in the ruling of the Court of Appeal in *MacPherson* v *European Strategic Bureau Ltd* [2000] *The Times*, 5 September. In that case three persons were members of the company. The relationship between them broke down and the company was not a success. The director/shareholders made an agreement under which two of them were to leave the company under a contract that repaid money owed to them being loans to finance the company and the profit from certain contracts of the company. All of this was expressed to be for payment of consultancy services to the company. The company later went to court to challenge the validity of the contracts. The Court of Appeal eventually ruled:

- that the contractual arrangement though supported by consideration in terms of the consultancy was not binding on the company because it was not for its benefit. It amounted to an informal distribution of assets as on a winding-up without making provision for all the company's creditors. It was a breach of the directors' duties and outside the powers of the company;
- although the matter did not arise because the contractual arrangements were not binding on the company, they were basically an infringement of the distribution rules of the 1985 Act since they were not distributions of profit alone but also distributions of the company's assets, which was permitted by law only in a winding-up (see s 263(2)(d)), but, being *remuneration* not *dividend*, they were valid;
- although it was not necessary in the circumstances to reach a definitive view, the arrangements appeared to constitute unlawful assistance for the purchase of shares since it was clearly envisaged that the departing shareholders would transfer their shares to the remaining shareholder with a material reduction in the net assets of the company.

DUTIES OF DIRECTORS TO OTHER OUTSIDERS

Again, there is no *contractual* or *fiduciary duty* (as distinct from a duty in negligence) to outsiders, and the directors are not liable if the company breaks its contracts. However, where the directors make a contract with an outsider on behalf of the company the directors may be liable, as other agents are, for breach of warranty of authority. The basis of this action is that an agent warrants to the third party that his principal has the capacity to make the contract and that he, the agent, is authorised to make it.

In the past actions for breach of warranty of authority against directors have been successful, e.g. in *Weeks* v *Propert* (1873) LR 8 CP 427 where the company borrowed money in excess of its borrowing powers so that the loan was *ultra vires*.

It will be noted, however, that in view of the provisions of s 35 it is most unlikely that a transaction will not bind the company and the action for breach of warranty against directors is, subject to judicial interpretation of s 35, likely largely to disappear from the law.

It might be used where the directors have made an *ultra vires* contract with a connected person which the members did not ratify. Such a contract would not bind the company and the connected person might bring a claim for breach of warranty against the directors (see further Chapter 3).

EFFECTS OF BREACH OF DUTY

1 Liability – extent of

A director cannot be made liable for the acts of co-directors if he has not taken part in such acts and he had no knowledge of them and the circumstances were not such as ought to have aroused his suspicion. The fact that he does not attend all board meetings will not in itself impose liability but habitual absence may do so and the duty may be higher for the executive directors and qualified or experienced non-executive directors (see the *Dorchester Finance* case in this chapter).

A director who is involved in a breach along with others is jointly and severally liable with them and can be required to make good the whole loss with a contribution from his co-directors. There would be no contribution, of course, where money was misappropriated for his sole benefit.

As we have seen, the company can make a director account for any secret profit and a breach will usually entitle the company to avoid any contract it may have made with him. Property taken from the company can be recovered from the director if he still has it or from third parties to whom he may have transferred it unless they have taken the property in good faith and for value.

The court may also grant an injunction where a director's breach of duty is continuing or merely threatened.

2 The company may ratify the breach

The company may by ordinary (or written) resolution waive a breach of duty by a director. Thus in *Bamford* v *Bamford* [1969] 2 WLR 1107 the directors allotted shares to a company which distributed their products. The object was to fight off a takeover bid because the distributors had agreed not to accept the bid. This was an improper exercise of the directors' powers but the allotment was good because the members (excluding the distributors' shares) had passed an ordinary resolution ratifying what the directors had done.

3 Company indemnity

By reason of the provisions of s 310 of the CA the ability of the company to indemnify directors and managers and auditors in regard to claims made against them was limited, indemnity could be given in these cases where a criminal or civil claim was successfully defended so that the person concerned had to bear his or her costs until the conclusion of the proceedings. Section 310 was amended to allow the company to purchase and maintain liability insurance for the above mentioned persons, in regard to claims by the company.

The above provisions are relaxed by the Companies (Audit, Investigations and Community Enterprise) Act 2004 and when the 2004 Act provisions are in force scheduled for April 2005) the position will be as set out below articles notwithstanding.

- *Section 310 will remain (as amended)* forbidding indemnities for auditors in civil and criminal matters unless judgment is given in their favour or they are acquitted. Insurance can be purchased and maintained by the company for its auditors for company claims.

- *for liabilities in connection with claims brought by third parties* both legal costs as they are incurred and judgment costs will be allowed to be paid by the company even if the judgment goes against the director. The only exclusions will be for criminal fines, fines by regulators and the legal costs of unsuccessful criminal proceedings. This means for example that a director could be indemnified against the costs of legal proceedings against him or her by the Financial Services Authority in regard to a breach of the Listing Rules governing the listing of shares on the Stock Exchange. However no indemnity could be given in regard to a civil fine imposed by the FSA if he were found guilty.

These provisions are set out in new sections 309A to 309C of the CA 1985 as inserted by the 2004 Act.

- *companies will be allowed to pay a director's defence costs as they are incurred even where the claim is brought by the company.*

The indemnity for costs in relation to company claims is however more limited than in third party claims because the director will still be liable to pay any damages awarded to the company and also repay the defence costs to the company if the company's claim succeeds.

The above provisions are contained in new section 337A of the CA 1985 as inserted by the 2004 Act.

- *the prohibition on companies indemnifying their company secretaries and managers* is removed altogether.

All indemnities must be disclosed in the directors' annual report and indemnity agreements must be available for inspection by shareholders.

As regards auditors the government has decided against changing the current position. It has ruled out allowing auditors to agree to a cap on their liability but has agreed to examine proposals for allowing auditors to limit their liability by agreeing to be liable for a set proportion only of a claimant's losses.

Section 727 applications

The company cannot excuse a director from liability though it may provide an indemnity where the law permits. However the court can grant relief from liability under s 727 CA 1985 (see below) where the director is considered to have acted 'honestly and reasonably.' The company may indemnify a director in regard to s 727 applications but only if the court does grant relief.

The provisions of s 310 were considered in *Burgoine* v *London Borough of Waltham Forest* [1997] 2 BCLC 612 where the High Court decided that the restriction on indemnities in regard to directors and other officers applies only to indemnities given by the company. It does not make invalid insurance taken out by a director himself in respect of possible liability.

4 Relief by the court

The 1985 Act gives the court power to grant relief to a director who has acted honestly and reasonably and who ought, in all the circumstances, to be excused.

In Re Duomatic [1969] 1 All ER 161

The share capital of the company was made up of 100 £1 ordinary shares and 50,000 £1 non-voting preference shares. At one time E, H and T held all the ordinary shares between them and in addition were directors of the company. E and T did not consider that H was a good director. Although they could have voted him off the board, they decided instead to pay him £4,000 to leave the company perhaps largely because he was threatening to sue the company and generally to cause trouble if he was removed against his will. On payment of the £4,000 H left transferring his shares to E. No disclosure of the payment of the £4,000 was made in the company's accounts.

It was also the practice for each director to draw remuneration as required and for the members to approve these drawings at the end of the year when the accounts were drawn up. The amounts drawn were as follows:

In period A (E, T and H sole directors and ordinary shareholders)	£10,151 paid to E £5,510 paid to H.
In period B (E and T sole directors and ordinary shareholders)	£9,000 paid to E but no final accounts agreed.
In period C (when additional persons had become shareholders)	E informally agreed to limit his drawings to £60 per week but in fact drew approximately £100 per week.

The company then went into voluntary liquidation and the liquidator began proceedings against E, H and T for:

(*a*) repayment of the sums paid to E and H as salaries on the ground that these had never been approved in general meeting;
(*b*) repayment of the £4,000 paid to H for loss of office; and
(*c*) declarations that E and T had been guilty of misfeasance.

Held – by Buckley J – that:

(i) repayment of the sums of £10,151 and £5,510 could not be ordered since they had been made with the approval of all the shareholders;
(ii) although E had not obtained the approval of all the shareholders to the payment of the £9,000, final accounts not having been agreed, in the circumstances and in view of the general practice E ought to be excused repayment of the £9,000;
(iii) since there had been no disclosure to the preference shareholders of the payment of £4,000 compensation to H as required by company legislation, E and T had misapplied the company's funds and were jointly and severally liable to repay the sums. Furthermore, H held the money on trust for the company and if necessary could be required to repay it. E and T had not acted reasonably in this matter and could not be excused.

DIRECTORS AND POLITICAL DONATIONS

The Political Parties, Elections and Referendums Act 2000 applies. Its main purpose is to make provision about the registration and finances of political parties. However, of importance to business are the provisions of ss 139 and 140 which control the making of political donations by companies. The purpose of these sections is to require directors of companies to seek the approval of the company in general meeting to the making of donations to political parties or organisations or to the incurring of expenditure for political purposes. At present the making of political donations and expenditure on other political purposes is left to the general discretion of the directors and management of the company. Detailed arrangements will continue to lie with the directors, but it will be unlawful to take such action unless it is approved in advance by the shareholders in general meeting.

The provisions also cover company donations to political parties in other member states of the European Union. If the directors make donations, etc. without complying with the Act, the company can recover the amounts involved from them and in this regard there are provisions relating to shareholders' actions on behalf of the company to facilitate recovery. Shareholders can seek an indemnity for costs from the company.

THE STOCK EXCHANGE LISTING RULES – A COMBINED CODE

The London Stock Exchange has produced a combined code of corporate governance for listed companies. This is now part of the Listing Rules. Companies are required under the new rules to disclose how they have applied the principles and complied with the detailed provisions of the combined code in their annual report and accounts in respect of accounting periods ending on or after 31 December 1998. The code combines the principles laid down by the Cadbury Report and the Reports of the Greenbury and Hampel committees.

Developments in connection with the Combined Code are considered in Chapter 16.

GRADED QUESTIONS

Essay mode

1 'The rule of equity which insists on those who by use of fiduciary position make a profit, being liable to account for that profit, in no way depends on fraud . . . The profiteer, however honest and well-intentioned, cannot escape the risk of being called upon to account.' *Per* Lord Russell of Killowen in *Regal (Hastings) Ltd* v *Gulliver*.

Comment.

(*University of Plymouth*)

2 (*a*) Give an account of the extent to which the common law fiduciary duties of company directors have been added to by statutory provisions.

(*b*) Henry is a non-executive director of Dreghorn plc. He also runs his own management consultancy business, Manpower & Co. Dreghorn is undergoing a process of internal restructuring. Without knowing of Henry's involvement with Manpower, one of the other directors proposes to the board of directors that Manpower & Co be engaged by the company to advise on recruitment of key staff. Henry, who happens to sit on the

Staff Affairs Committee of the Board of Directors along with two other directors, mentions his connection with Manpower & Co at a meeting of that committee, but it is not minuted and is never mentioned again. The Board resolves to contract with Manpower & Co. Some months later, Henry's connection with Manpower comes to light.

Advise Henry as to his legal position.

(Napier University)

3 A managing director is usually appointed by the other directors and his powers and duties will depend on his contract of service with the company.

(*a*) Explain and illustrate whether a director who has not been appointed as a managing director can bind the company as if he were managing director.

AND

(*b*) Explain the degree of skill and care which the law requires of a company director.

(Glasgow Caledonian University)

4 A director is in a fiduciary relationship with his company. Explain the meaning and effect of this statement with reference to decided cases.

(The Institute of Company Accountants)

5 (*a*) What controls are there on the provision by a public company of loans to its directors and on other financial dealings with them?

(*b*) Eric, Frank and George are the directors of Happy Ltd. At a recent board meeting, Eric proposed that £50,000 be paid to Frank in recognition of his services in opening new trading opportunities for the company. The money has been paid to Frank although no vote was ever taken on the motion. George was away on holiday at the time of the meeting. Happy Ltd now wish to recover the £50,000 but Frank is insolvent. Can they recover it from either Eric or George?

(The Institute of Chartered Secretaries and Administrators)

6 You have recently been appointed as company secretary to a large public company with a Stock Exchange listing for its securities. The board of directors has asked you for advice on certain matters relating to their duties as directors.

You are required to advise the board of directors on the legal aspects of the following three matters.

(*a*) The restrictions which exist upon the freedom of directors to issue company shares.

(*b*) The problems directors might encounter when they deal in the company's securities for their own personal gain.

(*c*) The restrictions which control the lending of funds by the company to directors to meet their business expenses.

(The Chartered Institute of Management Accountants)

7 Landrut plc is a property company. Its principal activity is buying land, building private houses and selling those houses directly to the public.

Six directors form the board. The three executive directors are Jack, a solicitor, in charge of the legal department; Jeremy, a quantity surveyor, responsible for land buying; Philip, the third executive director, is in charge of advertising, marketing and house sales. The three non-executive directors are Joe (who founded the company 30 years ago with his brother Jim), Helen (Jim's widow) and Sam (a retired accountant). Joe is chairman of the board.

The following situations have arisen:

(i) The company recently purchased a small rectangular piece of building land for £500,000. Although the land was surrounded on three sides by existing development, it appeared on visual inspection to have access to the highway on the fourth. Jack dealt with the legal work necessary to complete the purchase. It now appears that a routine inspection of the title deeds would have revealed that a two-metre strip of land runs the length of the fourth side preventing access to the highway and making development impossible. The owner of this strip of land is willing to sell at a price of £100,000. Consider the liability to the company of Jeremy and Jack.

(ii) The company developed and sold a small site of town houses. The houses were marketed and quickly sold at £40,000 each. It is now clear that the houses were undervalued and would have easily sold at £45,000. While the company did not make a loss on the development, its profit was only marginal rather than substantial. Consider the liability to the company of Philip and Sam.

(iii) Jeremy asks the board to consider purchasing two building sites: Toddmoor for £750,000 and Rawsum for £500,000. After full discussion, the board decides to proceed with the purchase of Toddmoor and reject Rawsum. Joe later decides to buy Rawsum personally. He does so and immediately resells the site for £600,000. Sam and Helen who remain silent throughout the discussion are also the only directors and shareholders of a small land company, Helsam Ltd, which is concurrently negotiating for the purchase of Toddmoor. Helsam Ltd subsequently acquires Toddmoor. Consider the liability to the company of Joe, Sam and Helen.

(The Association of Chartered Certified Accountants)

'The matters to which the directors of a company are to have regard in the performance of their functions include the interests of the company's employees in general as well as the interests of its members' (Companies Act 1935, s 309(1)).

What is the effect of this provision and how may it be enforced?

(The Institute of Chartered Accountants in England and Wales)

Objective mode

Four alternative answers are given. Select ONE only. Circle the answer which you consider to be correct. Check your answers by referring back to the information given in the chapter and against the answers at the back of the book.

1 Mike has a service contract with Trent plc for a fixed term of ten years which cannot be terminated by notice. The contract has not been considered in general meeting. What is the legal position?

A The contract is valid.

B The contract is void and the company can terminate it at any time by giving such notice as the company in general meeting may decide.

C The contract is void and the company can terminate it at any time by the giving of reasonable notice.

D The contract is void and the company can terminate it by giving six months' notice.

2 Joe is a director of Slow Ltd and has just unsuccessfully defended an action brought against him by a third party in regard to the affairs of Slow Ltd. Can Joe be indemnified in respect of the legal and judgment costs he incurred from the assets of Slow Ltd?

A The company cannot indemnify Joe without the approval of the members.
B The company cannot indemnify Joe in any circumstances.
C The company can indemnify Joe if the court approves.
D The company can indemnify Joe and the approval of neither the members nor the court is required.

3 Morgan is in breach of his fiduciary duty to the company. How may he be exempted from liability given that the breach is not a fraud on the minority?

A By a written or an ordinary resolution of the members.
B By a provision in the company's articles.
C By a provision in the company's memorandum.
D By a resolution of the board of directors.

4 Mostyn, who is a director of Test Ltd, has caused the company loss by negligent mismanagement. The company wishes to sue Mostyn but the articles of Test exempt the directors from liability for negligence in the course of their duties. What is the legal position given that Mostyn has left the board?

A The company cannot claim since Mostyn is no longer a director.
B The company can make a claim since the article is void and of no effect.
C The company cannot claim because the articles are binding.
D The company can claim if the court makes an order overriding the articles.

5 The register of directors and secretaries must, so far as directors are concerned, give particulars in regard to each director of other directorships currently held and those which have been held in the previous:

A three years.
B two years.
C fifteen years.
D five years.

6 Dee Ltd has net assets of £650,000. It intends to enter into a transaction with one of its directors involving a non-cash asset. At which of the following figures of non-cash asset value will it be necessary to attain member approval?

A £100,000.
B £2,000.
C £65,000.
D £6,500.

Answers to questions set in objective mode appear on p 577.

18

VACATION OF OFFICE, DISQUALIFICATION AND PERSONAL LIABILITY

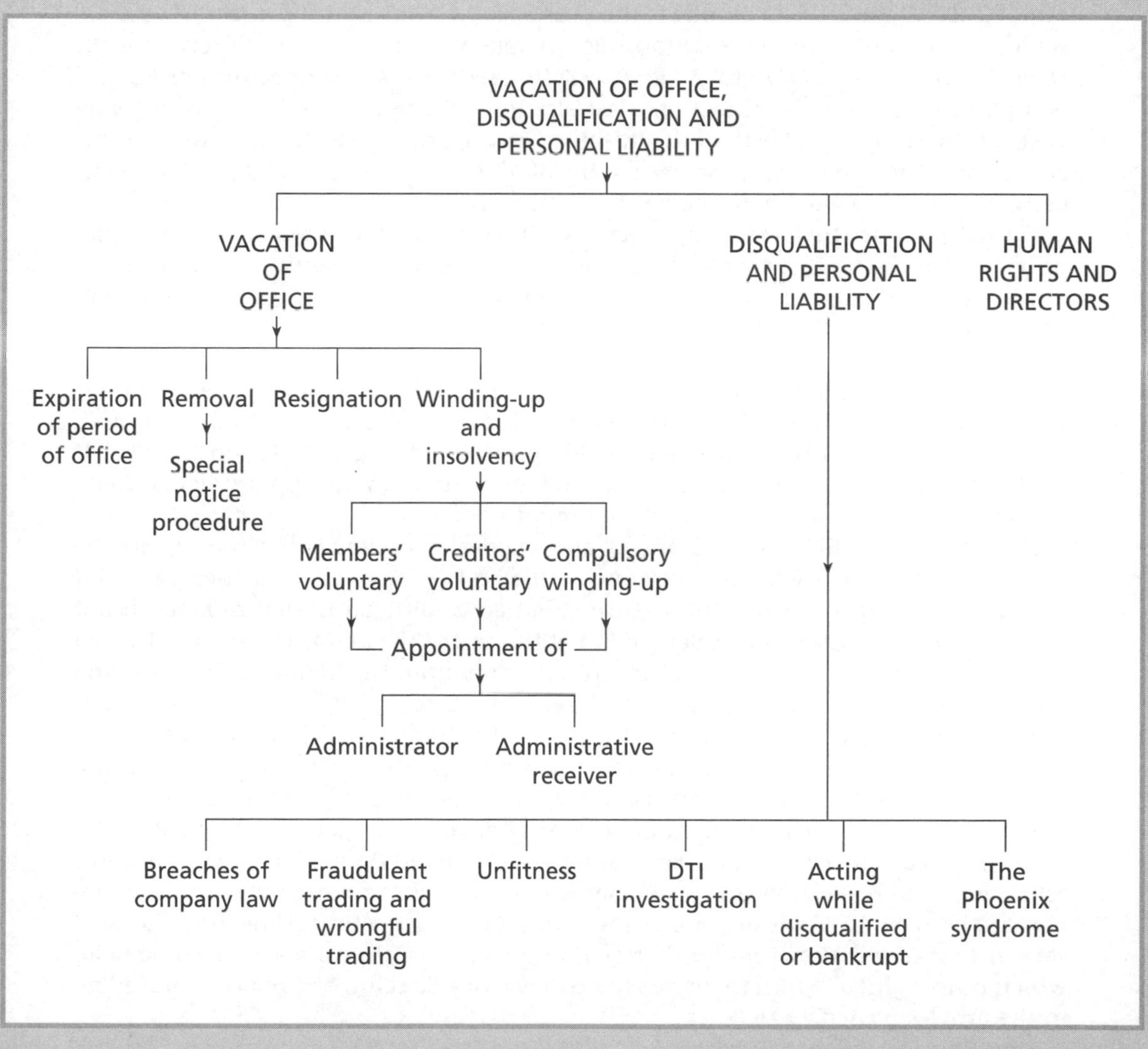

 director may vacate office for a variety of reasons.

EXPIRATION OF THE PERIOD OF OFFICE

The articles usually provide what the period of office shall be. *Table A* provides that at the first annual general meeting all the directors shall retire from office, and at the annual general meeting in every subsequent year one-third shall retire, or if their number is not three or a multiple of three, then the number nearest to one-third shall retire from office. If the company has only two directors one of them will retire every year if *Table* A applies because one is the nearest to two-thirds of the directors who are subject to the retirement by rotation rules. A sole director must retire every year (*Re David Moseley & Sons Ltd* [1939] 2 All ER 791) (but see below). The directors retiring will be those longest in office since their last election. Difficulties may arise in the early years of the company's life if all the directors were appointed at the same time. If this is the case, those retiring must, by reason of *Table A*, be ascertained by agreement between the board and on agreement failing, by drawing lots.

Table A provides that a retiring director shall be eligible for re-election, and further provides that if the office vacated by a director *on retirement by rotation* is not filled, the retiring director shall, if he still offers himself for re-election, be deemed re-elected, unless the meeting expressly resolves not to fill the vacancy or unless the resolution for the re-election of such director has been put to the meeting and lost.

A director who is due to retire by rotation at, e.g., the 2005 AGM but reaches the age of 70 in 2004, prior to the AGM in that year, will vacate office at the AGM in 2004 and, if re-elected, will fall to be included in the directors retiring by rotation in 2005. If re-elected this time, it will be until he next retires by rotation. All appointments would be by the special notice or written resolution procedure.

The board may fill casual vacancies and appoint additional directors up to the maximum in the articles. These persons must stand for re-election at the next AGM and do not count in the one-third retiring, but are additional to that number. If not re-elected, they vacate office under *Table A* at the end of the AGM. There is no deemed re-election as is the case with directors retiring by rotation. Furthermore, the managing director and directors holding any other executive office, e.g. finance director, do not retire by rotation. They are subject to the terms of their contracts but cannot be either managing director or executive director unless also directors. Therefore, they cannot continue in post if they are removed as directors by the members under s 303 or under a provision in the articles. They would normally have a claim for breach of contract.

Since the current *Table A* and previous ones make the AGM the lynchpin of director retirement and re-election, a private company which has dispensed with the requirement to hold an AGM will under existing *Tables A* not have retiring directors. They will stay in post unless they voluntarily resign or a member calls for an AGM to be held, which is his right, at which to discuss the removal of a director, or a removal procedure in the articles is used.

Alternatively, companies wishing to dispense with the AGM requirement but still wanting retirement by rotation would have to insert an article under which retirement by rotation was triggered in some other way, e.g. by a date, such as, say, one-third to retire on 31 March each year.

REMOVAL – UNDER STATUTE

A company may by *ordinary resolution* in general meeting remove a director before the expiration of his period of office regardless of the way in which he was appointed and notwithstanding anything in its articles or in any agreement with him (s 303), though weighted voting rights may render the section ineffective. The unanimous written resolution procedure is not available for this purpose because the director has a right to put his case against removal to the meeting (see below).

Bushell *v* Faith [1969] 1 All ER 1002

Mrs Bushell, Mr Faith and their sister, Dr Bayne, each owned 100 shares in a family company which had an issued share capital of 300 fully-paid shares of £1 each. The company had adopted *Table A* for its articles of association but a special Art 9 provided that, in the event of a resolution being proposed at a general meeting for the removal of a director, any shares held by that director should carry three votes per share.

Mr Faith's conduct as a director displeased his sisters and they requisitioned a general meeting at which an ordinary resolution was passed on a show of hands to remove him. Mr Faith demanded a poll, contending that, in accordance with Art 9, his 100 shares carried 300 votes and that therefore the resolution had been defeated by 300 votes to 200.

Mrs Bushell then claimed a declaration by the court that the resolution had been validly passed and an injunction restraining her brother from acting as a director. Ungoed-Thomas J, at first instance, granted the injunction *holding* that Art 9 was invalid because it infringed what is now s 303 and that therefore the resolution removing Mr Faith had been duly passed. The Court of Appeal did not agree with the decision at first instance and allowed Mr Faith's appeal. In particular, Russell LJ stated that a provision as to voting rights in the articles which has the effect of making a special resolution to alter the articles incapable of being passed if a particular shareholder or group of shareholders exercise his or their voting rights against it is not a provision depriving the company of the power to alter its articles or any of them by special resolution, and so does not contravene what is now s 9 and is valid. However, an article providing that no alteration shall be made in the articles without the consent of a particular person would be contrary to s 9 and so would be invalid.

Mrs Bushell's appeal to the House of Lords ([1970] 1 All ER 53) was also dismissed, their Lordships *holding* that the provisions of what is now s 303 did not prevent companies from attaching special voting rights to certain shares for certain occasions, e.g. to directors' shares on a resolution at a general meeting for the removal of a director.

Comment

In the House of Lords, Lord Reid pointed to what is now *Reg* 2 of *Table A* as justifying the weighted voting provisions. *Table A, Reg* 2 provides 'any share may be issued with such rights or restrictions as the company may by ordinary resolution determine'. This to Lord Reid indicated that there was no reason why shares should not have weighted voting rights if the company wished that to be the position.

Special notice of 28 days to the company is required of the intention to move the resolution. If the company calls a meeting for a date, say, 26 days after receipt of the special notice to foil the attempt to remove, the notice is nevertheless regarded as valid under s 379(3). Under s 379, the meeting at which the resolution to remove is to be considered must be called with at least 21 days' notice. It is not necessary that the person who served the special notice should propose the resolution. This could be done, e.g., by another member.

REMOVAL UNDER THE ARTICLES

This power is in addition to any other means of removal that may be provided in the articles, e.g. a power under which certain of the directors may remove others (*Bersel Manufacturing Co Ltd* v *Berry*, 1968, see below). Thus shareholders who wish to remove a director have a choice: either they can proceed under s 303 or under a provision, if any, in the articles, and if the articles make removal more difficult, as where they require a special resolution, then s 303 will be used. On the other hand, where the articles allow the directors themselves to carry out the removal, as in *Bersel Manufacturing Co Ltd* v *Berry*, 1968 (see below), then, of course, it would be easier to do it through the power vested in the board, first because the articles do not require a members' resolution to effect the removal but perhaps just a letter signed by the company's chairman and secretary and, second, because the article is unlikely to give the director being removed rights of representation as s 303 does.

A quite common use of a clause in the articles setting out a means of removal of directors is to be found in the articles of subsidiary companies where a removal clause allows the holding company to remove the directors of the subsidiary, something which cannot be achieved under s 303 where removal must be by the members of the company of which the person removed is a director.

Bersel Manufacturing Co Ltd *v* Berry [1968] 2 All ER 552

Berry and his wife were the first directors of a private company and were appointed permanent life directors by Art 11 of the company's articles of association. In addition, Art 16(H) provided that 'The permanent life directors shall have power to terminate forthwith the directorship of any of the ordinary directors by notice in writing.' Mr Berry's wife died in 1962. The question before the court in this case was whether or not the power given in Art 16(H) could only be exercised during the joint lives of Mr Berry and his wife and ceased to be exercisable when she died. *Held* – by the House of Lords – that the power was not vested in the permanent life directors as recipients of a joint confidence but for the securing of their joint interests, and the principle that a bare power could not be exercised by the survivor of joint holders did not apply. Furthermore, the principle that a power annexed to an office passed to successive holders of the office was not conclusive since the office in question died with the death of the survivor of the two occupants of the power. Therefore, on a true construction of the articles the power conferred by Art 16(H) remained exercisable by Mr Berry after the death of his wife. In these circumstances it was possible for Mr Berry to terminate the directorship of any of the ordinary directors by a notice in writing.

Comment

The power to remove a director in the articles is effective even if the directors who exercise the power have acted with ulterior motives as in *Lee* v *Chou Wen Hsian* [1984] 1 WLR 1202 where a director who was asking for information about the company's dealings and not receiving all the information he wanted asked the secretary to convene a board meeting but was removed by the other directors two days before the meeting under a power in the articles. A removal under s 303 would seem to be effective in a similar situation.

STATUTORY REMOVAL – RESTRICTIONS

If the s 303 procedure is followed the director concerned is allowed to put his case to the members by the circulation of his representations with the notice of the meeting, or if his representations are received too late for this, they are to be read out at the meeting. The company is required under s 304 to send a copy of the special notice to the director concerned forthwith.

The vacancy so created may be filled at the meeting, or if not so filled, may be filled as a casual vacancy and any person appointed in the place of a director removed under s 303 shall be deemed to hold office for as long as the director removed would have held it, and to retire when he would have retired.

Nothing in s 303 is to deprive a director so removed of any action he may have for dismissal, as where he has a contract outside the articles appointing him for a specified period which has not expired.

At first sight s 303 appears to give any member of a company who is not satisfied with the way in which a director is carrying out his duties the right to ask the members as a whole to consider passing an ordinary resolution in general meeting to remove him.

Let us suppose, as would be usual, that X, a member of the company, chooses the annual general meeting for this purpose. Let us further suppose that he serves special notice on the company secretary in the proper manner of his intention to propose a resolution to remove the director or directors concerned. Are the directors obliged to place that resolution on the agenda and take it at the annual general meeting? According to the decision of Slade J in *Pedley* v *Inland Waterways Association Ltd* [1977] 1 All ER 209, the answer is no, unless, that is, X or persons joining with him satisfy the requirements of s 376.

This section provides that members representing not less than one-twentieth of the total voting rights of all members or 100 or more members holding shares in the company on which there has been paid up an average of not less than £100 per member can, by making a written requisition to the company, compel the company in effect to put a particular item of business up at the annual general meeting.

Therefore, if a particular member or members cannot satisfy, e.g., the one-twentieth voting rights provision, then the directors are not obliged to raise the question of the removal of one or more of their number at the annual general meeting. Thus it would seem that the rights given by s 303, and indeed s 386 (power to remove auditors), are much more restricted than might hitherto have been thought. It is impossible to use these sections unless the member or members concerned can satisfy the requirements of s 376 at least so far as the annual general meeting is concerned.

Although the *Pedley* case dealt only with matters regarding the removal of a director at the annual general meeting it would seem that an individual member is in a similar position if he wishes to remove a director between annual general meetings. Unless the board is willing to call an extraordinary general meeting, he or members joining with him will have to do so. This can be done under s 368, but only by members holding not less than one-tenth of such of the company's paid-up capital as carries voting rights at the general meetings of the company.

RESIGNATION

A resignation need not be in writing; thus an oral resignation at a board meeting is effective. Once resignation has been made it cannot be withdrawn except with the consent of those persons who are entitled to appoint new directors.

WINDING-UP

The position is as follows:

(*a*) *In a members' voluntary winding-up*. Here the company is necessarily solvent and the directors' powers cease only on the appointment of a liquidator, not when the resolution to wind up is passed. However, the members or the liquidator may sanction the continuance of the directors' powers (Insolvency Act 1986, s 91). The directors may decide to resign, but if they do not their powers remain in suspense until they would have retired by rotation and obviously they cannot be re-elected (*Re Zinotty Properties Ltd* [1984] 3 All ER 754). Executive directors may claim redundancy or unfair dismissal as the case may be under the usual employment law rules. There could also be a claim for wrongful dismissal at common law.

(*b*) *In a creditors' voluntary winding-up*. Here the company is necessarily insolvent. The directors' powers cease on the appointment of a liquidator. They may resign but if not they vacate office as in (*a*) above. The position of executive directors is also as in (*a*) above.

If a resolution for a creditors' voluntary winding-up is passed without a liquidator being appointed, the directors' powers are limited under s 114 of the Insolvency Act 1986, e.g. to the disposal of perishable goods (see further Chapter 26).

Although the directors' powers cease on the appointment of a liquidator, the liquidation committee or, if none, the creditors can approve the continuance of the directors' powers in whole or in part (s 103 of the 1986 Act). To do so would be rare.

(*c*) *In a compulsory winding-up*. The directors' powers cease on the making of a winding-up order or on the earlier appointment of a provisional liquidator. There is no mechanism whereby the directors' powers can be continued. The position of executive directors is as in (*a*) above.

APPOINTMENT OF ADMINISTRATOR/ ADMINISTRATIVE RECEIVER

A major change effected by the Enterprise Act 2002 is to restrict the right of a creditor with a full package of securities that includes a floating charge to appoint an administrative receiver. There are a number of exceptions to the prohibition under which the holder of a floating charge entered into after 15 September 2003 will retain the power to make such an appointment. These will be dealt with in Chapter 24. However it should be borne in mind that many lenders, particularly banks, hold floating charges entered into before the above date and may appoint administrative receivers as before. Thus for some time to come the law relating to administrative receivers will be relevant in business. For this reason the following materials have been retained at least for this edition.

On the appointment of an administrative receiver the powers of the directors effectively cease. They are not dismissed, however, though the administrative receiver is entitled to continue the company's business and realise its property without interference by the board (*Gomba Holdings UK Ltd* v *Homan* [1986] 3 All ER 94). There may be rather special situations in which the court will allow the directors to exercise their powers, as the following case shows.

Newhart Developments Ltd *v* Co-operative Commercial Bank Ltd
[1978] 2 All ER 896

A scheme for housing development in North Wales was to be carried out by a company formed specially for the purpose and jointly owned by Newhart Developments Ltd (Newhart) and the Co-operative Commercial Bank Ltd (the bank), finance being provided by the bank. The scheme got into difficulties and the bank appointed a receiver of Newhart under the provisions of a debenture in common form. In particular, clause 2(c) provided that the company should not deal with its books or other debts or securities for money otherwise than by getting in and realising the same in the ordinary course of business. Clause 5 provided that the receiver should have power to take possession and collect and get in the property charged by the debenture and for that purpose to take any proceedings in the name of the company or otherwise. Newhart took the view that they might have a claim against the bank for breach of contract arising from the development scheme. They issued a writ (claim form) and the bank applied to the court to have it set aside because it had been issued by the directors of Newhart without the receiver's consent. The bank's application was successful in the High Court but Newhart appealed to the Court of Appeal which allowed the appeal thus enabling Newhart's claim to proceed to trial.

Shaw LJ said that the function of a receiver was to protect the interests of debenture holders; he was not like a liquidator whose function was to wind the company up. During a liquidation directors were divested of their powers but not so in a receivership. The fact that a receiver had been appointed did not prevent the directors of the company concerned from exercising their powers as the governing body of the company provided that their acts did not threaten the assets which were subject to the debenture holders' charge. In this case the receiver was put into a curious and unenviable position because the action by Newhart was against the bank which had appointed him. Nevertheless, where a receiver had in his discretion chosen to ignore an asset, such as a right of action, there was nothing in law to prevent the directors pursuing it in the company's name. A company might have creditors other than the debenture holders and those creditors were entitled to expect the directors to bring an action which, if successful, might provide a fund out of which to pay them. If the claim succeeded, the receiver would have an interest in the disposition of any money received, but if he decided not to pursue a claim of this kind, the directors could do so provided that nothing in the course of proceedings would influence the security of the debenture holders.

Under the Insolvency Act 1986 the directors have an obligation to co-operate with an administrative receiver, under the penalty of prosecution and a fine if they do not. Continued refusal can result in a fine on a daily basis.

Directors' powers are suspended during an administration. They must give way to the administrator and in addition the administrator may remove them from office and appoint new directors. However, they are not dismissed merely by the appointment of an administrator and retain some residual powers on the lines of the *Newhart* case. They retain their CA 1985 duties in regard to the keeping of records. An administrator has no statutory obligations in this regard.

DISQUALIFICATION – GENERALLY

A director may become disqualified, and if so he automatically vacates office. The following are the reasons for disqualification:

(a) Under a provision in the articles. *Table A* provides that the office of director shall be vacated if the director:

(i) ceases to be a director by virtue of any provision of the Act, e.g. removal under s 303; or becomes prohibited by law from being a director, e.g. is disqualified by the court; *or*

(ii) becomes bankrupt or makes any arrangement or compositions with his creditors generally; *or*

(iii) becomes of unsound mind; *or*

(iv) resigns his office by notice to the company; *or*

(v) has for more than six months been absent without permission of the directors from meetings of the directors held during that period *and* the directors resolve that his office shall be vacated. Under *Table A* one counts from the last meeting he attended and not the first meeting that he missed. It should be noted also that this provision covers involuntary absence, as where the director is ill.

The articles may be altered to provide additional reasons for disqualification (*Shuttleworth* v *Cox Bros*, 1927, see Chapter 4), though an express contract is not affected by alterations in the articles and the director may bring an action for wrongful dismissal (*Southern Foundries* v *Shirlaw*, 1940, see Chapter 4).

A more current example would be where the company is involved in financial services and a director loses a licence or permission to act from a regulatory body such as the Financial Services Authority.

(b) Share qualifications. The office of director is vacated if the director does not within two months from the date of his appointment, or within such shorter time as may be fixed by the articles, obtain his qualification shares, or if after the expiration of that time he ceases at any time to hold his qualification where a qualification is required.

(*c*) ***Age limit***. A director may become disqualified if his age exceeds the limit laid down by the 1985 Act or by the articles. This matter has already been dealt with in Chapter 15.

(*d*) ***Bankruptcy***. Where a director is disqualified because of bankruptcy he does not automatically vacate office unless the articles provide as does *Table A*.

DISQUALIFICATION BY THE COURT AND PERSONAL LIABILITY

This section is based mainly on the provisions of the Company Directors Disqualification Act 1986 and section references are to that Act unless otherwise indicated.

DISQUALIFICATION ONLY

The following headings and their supporting paragraphs deal with areas where directors may be disqualified but personal liability for the company's debts is not involved.

Disqualification on conviction of an indictable offence (s 2)

The offence must be in connection with the promotion, formation, or management or liquidation of a company or with the receivership or management of a company's property. Disqualification is possible even though the indictable offence was tried summarily before magistrates rather than by a jury in the Crown Court.

The court which convicts the offender can make the disqualification order. There is no minimum period of disqualification. The maximum is five years in a magistrates' court and 15 years in a Crown or other court. There are no provisions relating to personal liability.

An example is *R* v *Corbin* [1984] Crim LR 302. C set up in business selling yachts through three companies. He obtained money and property by fraud, e.g. he obtained money from two finance companies to buy yachts by falsely representing that a deposit had been paid on them and took a part-payment for a yacht from a customer but the yacht never materialised. He was sentenced to two and a half years' imprisonment and disqualified from acting as a director for five years.

It should also be noted that there have been disqualifications in more recent times where a director has been tried and convicted of an indictable offence under the Health and Safety at Work Act 1974, for an infringement of health or safety requirements, which is a management offence within s 2.

Disqualification for persistent breach of company law (ss 3 and 5)

A person may be disqualified following persistent default under company legislation, e.g. in filing returns, accounts and other documents with the Registrar.

Persistent default is conclusively proved by three convictions (whether or not on the same occasion) within a period of five years.

There is no minimum period, but the maximum, whether in a magistrates' or other court, is five years. There are no provisions relating to personal liability.

Disqualification following the crime of fraudulent trading (s 4)

The court may make a disqualification order following an offence under s 458 of the Companies Act 1985 (crime of fraudulent trading). There is no minimum period but the maximum is 15 years. There are no provisions for personal liability.

Disqualification for unfitness (ss 6, 7, 9 and Sch 1)

The court *must* disqualify a director (including a shadow director) on the application of the DTI through the medium of the Trade Secretary or the Official Receiver if the company concerned has become insolvent while the person concerned was a director (or subsequently) *and* his conduct makes him unfit to be concerned in the management of a company. Insolvency arises under the Act from insolvent liquidation or the making of an administration order or the appointment of an administrative receiver.

Liquidators, administrators and administrative receivers must report alleged unfitness to the DTI.

The minimum period of disqualification is two years and the maximum is 15 years. There is a time limit of two years from the date on which the company became insolvent, e.g. the date when the company went into insolvent liquidation, during which an application must be made, although the court can allow a later application.

The first check on the suitability of disqualification proceedings under these sections is the DTI. The DTI may, not must, apply for disqualification. The second check is with the court which must be satisfied as to unfitness. Schedule 1 sets out matters to be taken into account when determining unfitness.

The schedule, which is long, reflects the experience of the government's insolvency service and the comments and experience of practitioners. It is concerned with the way in which the directors have managed the company. It includes matters usually found when a company has been badly managed by incompetent directors, e.g. failure to keep accounting records and failure to send the annual return and to keep necessary registers.

Schedule 1 is split into: Part I, matters applicable in all cases; and Part II, matters applicable where the company has become insolvent. This is to take care of disqualification after inspection (see below) where the company need not be insolvent.

There are no provisions relating to personal liability for the debts of the company.

The case law indicates that unfitness has become divided into three main areas, i.e. (1) commercial immorality; (2) recklessness in management; and (3) gross incompetence.

Disqualification following DTI investigation (s 8)

If it appears to the Trade Secretary: (*a*) from a report made by inspectors under s 437 of the Companies Act 1985 (provision for inspectors to make interim and final reports) or (*b*) from information or documents obtained under s 447 (power to require production of documents) or s 448 (regarding entry and search of premises) of the 1985 Act that (*c*) it is in the public interest that a disqualification order should be made against a person who is or has been a director or shadow director of any company, then (*d*) the Trade Secretary may apply to the court for such an order. *The company need not be insolvent.* The court must be satisfied that the particular director's conduct makes him unfit to manage a company and Sch 1 applies.

There is no minimum period of disqualification. The maximum is 15 years. There are no provisions in s 8 relating to personal liability of directors.

Disqualification: some illustrative case law

The following cases in which the courts have interpreted the various sections of the Company Directors Disqualification Act 1986 are included in order to enable the student to give examples of the application of the Act in the business context.

Nationality, residence and domicile

The High Court decided in *Re Seagull Manufacturing Co* (*No 2*) [1994] 2 All ER 767 that a disqualification order may be made against a director regardless of his or her nationality and current residence and domicile. Furthermore, the conduct leading to the disqualification need not have occurred within the jurisdiction. In other words, you can run an English company badly from abroad. The director concerned was a British subject but at all material times he was resident and domiciled in the Channel Islands. Nevertheless, he could be disqualified under s 6 for unfitness. The relevant legislation contained no express jurisdiction requirement or territorial distinction.

Director/Secretaries

The High Court also decided in *Re Pamstock Ltd* [1994] 1 BCLC 716 that a director who was also the secretary of the company could be disqualified as much for failure to perform his duties as secretary as those of a director. The company had two directors and one was also the company secretary. It traded beyond the point at which it should have ceased to do so and went into insolvent liquidation. The judge said that as the company secretary one of the directors had failed to ensure that accounts and returns were filed on time and that an adequate system of management was put in place. These were serious defaults which must be taken into account when dealing with the period of disqualification. This implies that it was the director's failure to carry out his duties as a secretary that was at the root of his disqualification for two years. There is, of course, no power to disqualify a company secretary from acting as such.

Inactive directors

It is also worth noting that it is not a defence to an application for a disqualification order that the director concerned was not an active participant in the business of the company. Thus in *Re Park House Properties Ltd* [1997] 2 BCLC 530 the High Court disqualified three directors as unfit by reason of irresponsible trading leading to insolvency even though they were inactive in the running of the business. The company was run by a husband but his wife, son and daughter were also directors and shareholders but played no part in the running of the business and did not receive a salary or fees. Having disqualified the husband for four years, Neuberger J disqualified the other three directors for two years in each case, saying that a director has legal duties and could not escape liability by saying that he or she knew nothing about what was going on.

Conduct in collateral companies

The Court of Appeal has decided that in order to satisfy the requirements of s 6(1)(b) of the Company Directors Disqualification Act 1986 the director concerned must be a director of the lead company which must be insolvent. However, his conduct in relation to other companies of which he is or has been a director may be taken into account. This conduct does not have to be the same or similar to that in regard to the lead company, and the collateral companies do not have to be insolvent, although the lead company must be. See *Secretary of State for Trade and Industry* v *Ivens* [1997] BCLC 334.

Failure to keep proper accounting records and improper retention of monies due to the Inland Revenue, Customs and Excise and National Insurance Contributions

The following case covers the above points and others and to that extent is probably one of the most seminal cases on disqualification for unfitness.

Re Firedart Ltd, Official Receiver *v* Fairall [1994] 2 BCLC 340

Mr Alan John Fairall was a director of Firedart which was an advertising agency. It began trading in 1984 and went into insolvent liquidation in 1988. The Official Receiver as liquidator applied to the court under s 6 of the Company Directors Disqualification Act 1986 (Unfit Directors) for Mr Fairall to be disqualified as a director. The main allegations against Mr Fairall were:

- failure to maintain accounting records as required by s 221 of the Companies Act 1985;
- trading through the company while it was insolvent;
- the receipt of remuneration and benefits in kind which exceeded the level which the company could be expected to bear; and
- improper retention of monies due to the Inland Revenue, Customs and Excise and what is now the Contributions Agency (NIC contributions).

In disqualifying Mr Fairall for six years Mrs Justice Arden stated how essential it was for officers of a company to ensure that proper accounting records are maintained. She said:

> 'When directors do not maintain accounting records in accordance with the very specific requirements of s 221 of the Companies Act 1985 they cannot know their company's financial position with accuracy. There is, therefore, a risk that the situation is much worse than they know and that creditors will suffer in consequence. Directors who permit this situation to arise must expect the conclusion to be drawn in an appropriate case that they are in consequence not fit to be concerned in the management of a company.'

Also raised was the responsibility for maintenance of accounting records. On this the judge said:

> 'Mr Fairall states that the company's accountants maintained its accounting records from 31 January 1987. The accountants however say that they were not responsible for writing

up the books prior to August 1987. However that may be I accept the submission on behalf of the Official Receiver that it was Mr Fairall who was responsible for providing information to the accountants to enable the accounting records to be maintained accurately and up to date. I further find that he did not provide all the necessary information and explanations, that there is no excuse for his failure to do so and that therefore he is responsible for the deficiencies in the accounting records even after the firm of accountants had been instructed to carry out the bookkeeping function for the company. According to Terence Anthony Price, a partner in or proprietor of Firedart's accountants, the flow of information from Mr Fairall was "spasmodic" and Mr Fairall was always too busy to provide any necessary explanations. I accept this evidence.'

Comment

(i) It is of interest that the court affirmed that it is the duty of the directors to keep and supply accounting information and that the duty cannot be avoided merely by employing accountants.

(ii) The necessity for directors to make use of and understand the company's accounts was also stressed in *Re Continental Assurance Co of London plc* [1996] 28 LS Gaz 29. The High Court disqualified a corporate financier from acting as a director for three years because in his role as a non-executive director he failed to read the company's accounts (which he would have understood) and so did not discover illegal loans made to acquire the company's own shares constituting illegal finanacial assistance contrary to s 151 of the Companies Act 1985.

(iii) The disqualification regime is important to lawyers and accountants engaged in insolvency practice. For those in business as directors the cases represent a 'warning order' as to what to avoid to prevent disqualification. For professionals in general and audit practice they are less important in that they will normally have resigned some time before insolvency proceedings take place. A wise professional will not stay long with a board that fails to keep accounting records and file accounts!

Pleas in mitigation

As regards pleas in mitigation by directors in connection with disqualification case law indicates that the following might be successful:

- reliance on professional directors; thus where a board contains say a qualified accountant the others being business amateurs, the court may excuse them while disqualifying the accountant though the court will not in any case excuse sheer incompetence;
- the effect on employees may be relevant in the sense that it will be difficult to run the company if the director is disqualified so that jobs may be lost.

Directors' undertakings not to act

It was held by the High Court in *Re Blackspur Group plc* [1997] 1 WLR 710 that an undertaking by a director not to act as such or in the management of a company was not acceptable to the court except possibly in exceptional circumstances. The court would not, therefore, prevent the Secretary of State proceeding with an application for disqualification merely because the director concerned had given such an undertaking. A statutory amendment would be required to allow the court to accept such an undertaking on a general basis. However, the High Court did say that it would be desirable to amend the relevant legislation in order to give an undertaking the same status and effect as an order under the 1986 Act. In *Secretary of State for Trade and Industry* v *Cleland* [1997] 1 BCLC 437 the High Court did grant a stay of disqualification proceedings in return for an undertaking from a director that he would not work as a director in the future. There were special circumstances in that the director was 60 years of age and in poor health. Additionally, the Secretary of State's action was out of time and the DTI were asking for an extension of time. The action failed.

Insolvency Act 2000

The relevant legislation was amended by s 6 of the Insolvency Act 2000. This allows the Secretary of State for Trade and Industry to accept from a director he considers unfit a consent to a period of disqualification without the need for court involvement. The director's undertaking suffices. The relevant periods of disqualification are as for those in court proceedings. The director concerned may subsequently apply to the court to vary the undertaking he has given. The Secretary of State is entitled to make acceptance of the undertaking conditional on there being a statement giving the basis on which the director admits he is unfit to be concerned in the management of a company (*In re Blackspur Group plc* (*No 3*) [2001] *The Times*, 5 July). The reasons for unsuitability will normally emanate from the insolvency practitioner concerned who has recommended the disqualification.

The decision in *Re Blackspur Group plc*, 1997 (above) is largely overtaken by the Act of 2000, as is *Cleland* since the normal procedure now would be to give an undertaking to the Secretary of State not the court. The material is retained as explanatory of the use of Insolvency Act 2000 procedure.

DISQUALIFICATION AND PERSONAL LIABILITY

Disqualification and personal liability for fraudulent and wrongful trading (s 10)

The court may disqualify a director who has participated in fraudulent trading under s 213 of the Insolvency Act 1986 (IA 1986), or wrongful trading under s 214, IA 1986. There is no minimum period, the maximum being 15 years.

Fraudulent trading

The crime of fraudulent trading in s 458, CA 1985 is now separated from the personal liability section, which is in s 213, IA 1986. Criminal liability can arise whether the company is in liquidation or not. Civil liability arises only if the company is wound up.

In the case of fraudulent trading and wrongful trading (see below) only the liquidator may apply to the court for a declaration of civil liability, but all persons, knowingly parties (including the directors), may have civil liability under s 213, IA 1986: for example, a creditor or accountant or auditor of the company may be held liable if he has participated. Only directors and shadow directors are liable under s 214, IA 1986 for wrongful trading. There is thus no danger of auditors, bankers or other advisers who are merely mounting a rescue campaign for the company becoming involved under s 214, IA 1986 unless they participate in management more than is necessary to carry out their functions, when they might be regarded as shadow directors.

Since it is necessary to prove fraud under s 213, IA 1986, which is not an easy matter, whereas only proof of negligence is required under s 214, IA 1986, it would appear that s 214, which sets out the requirements for wrongful trading, will clearly become the main section for directors' personal liability.

There is no need for participation in the company's management or business. Liability for fraudulent trading and to contribute to the company's assets may be incurred by a creditor who accepts payment of his debt out of money that he knows has been obtained by the fraud of the directors (see *Morris* v *Banque Arabe et Internationale D'Investissement SA* (*No 2*) [2000] *The Times*, 26 October).

It is important to note that s 213 IA 1986 requires that the business has been carried on to defraud *creditors*. The fact that only one creditor has been defrauded does not satisfy the definition of fraudulent trading ruled the Court of Appeal in *Morphites* v *Bernasconi* [2003] 2 BCLC 53. In that case it was only the company's landlord that was defrauded in regard to payment of rent.

Wrongful trading generally

Section 214, IA 1986 sets out the requirements for wrongful trading. They are: (a) that the company has gone into insolvent liquidation; (b) that at some time before the commencement of the winding-up the person concerned knew or ought to have concluded that there was no reasonable prospect that the company would avoid going into insolvent liquidation; and (c) that the person concerned was a director or shadow director of the company at that time. The court cannot make a declaration of civil liability where the time mentioned in (b) above was before 28 April 1986.

If the requirements, (a) to (c) above, are satisfied the court may, on the application of the liquidator, declare the person concerned liable to make such contribution (if any) to the company's assets as the court thinks proper (see below).

The court will not make a declaration if satisfied that the person concerned took every step that he ought to have taken, with a view to minimising the potential loss to the creditors.

The section is concerned with liability for negligence and the court is required to take into account not only the director's own knowledge, skill and experience, but also the skill and experience that can be expected from a reasonably diligent director. The test is objective and not subjective. Thus a director may be liable even if he does his best if he falls below the standard of the reasonably diligent director. The court will have to consider current practice.

In Re Produce Marketing Consortium Ltd [1989] 3 All ER I

The liquidator of Produce Marketing had asked the court for an order that Eric Peter David and Ronald William Murphy, who were directors of the company, should contribute to the company assets in his hands.

This followed a finding by the court that the two directors concerned were liable for wrongful trading on the basis that they had pressed on with their insolvent company's business in the unrealistic – but not fraudulent or dishonest – hope that it would eventually trade out of its difficulties.

Mr Justice Knox said the fact that wrongful trading was not based on fraud was not a reason for giving a nominal or low figure of contribution. Having taken into account all the surrounding circumstances – that the case was one of failure to appreciate what should have been clear rather than a dishonest course of wrongdoing, that there had been occasions when positive untruths were told, that a solemn warning from the company's auditors in February 1987 that it was insolvent was ignored – a contribution of £75,000 plus interest was an appropriate contribution for the directors to make. Mr David and Mr Murphy were jointly and severally liable for the payment of this sum and, in addition, they were liable for the costs of the case.

Comment

(i) This was the first case to deal with compensation to the company for wrongful trading. It was a significant breakthrough for creditors, since the assets available to them in the winding-up may be considerably increased by a personal contribution from directors if, of course, they can pay it.

It does give a warning order to directors to take professional advice at the earliest possible date, since this could be much cheaper than having to face the possibility of making contributions of considerable amounts to the company's assets in the event of a winding-up.

(ii) In an earlier decision, *Halls* v *David and Another* [1989] *The Times*, 18 February, the court had decided that its power to forgive directors who had acted honestly and reasonably (see Chapter 17) was not available in regard to wrongful trading.

The amount payable

In cases of wrongful trading the court may declare that the director(s) concerned should make a personal contribution to the company's assets if the liquidator of the company makes an application. The amount of the contribution depends on the facts in each particular case and the court is given a wide discretion. However, the general approach is that the directors' personal contributions should be the amount by which the company's assets have been depleted by their conduct. As we have seen, the court can also make a disqualification order. *However, if the court does not make a declaration regarding personal liability, it cannot make a disqualification order.*

Time limits

Section 214 does not straightforwardly contain any time limit on the liquidator's ability to bring such proceedings. The Court of Appeal has decided that it is six years from the cause of action, i.e. the time at which the relevant ingredients of wrongful trading could have been established on the basis of the evidence.

Moore *v* Gadd [1997] 8 LSG 27

The liquidators of Farmizer (Products) Ltd brought proceedings under s 214 of the Insolvency Act 1986 against Mr Richard Gadd and Mrs Ada Gadd, the directors of the company, for a declaration that they knew or ought to have concluded that there was no reasonable prospect that the company would avoid going into insolvent liquidation and that they should make a contribution to the assets of the company. The proceedings were brought more than six years after the cause of action, i.e. the time when the relevant ingredients of wrongful trading could have been established on the basis of the evidence. Counsel for the liquidators contended that the section did carry a limitation period and, indeed, it does contain almost at the beginning, the phrase 'if in the course of winding-up'. Therefore, it was contended that so long as the company was in the course of winding-up, which it was, the liquidators could ask the court for the declaration. The Court of Appeal did not accept this contention on the basis that limitation periods are normally specific and the expression 'in the course of winding-up' was markedly dissimilar to any other prescribed period of limitation. The Court of Appeal went on to conclude that s 214 proceedings were proceedings for the recovery of a sum of money which the court declared the delinquent director(s) liable to contribute to the assets of the company. This fell within s 9(1) of the Limitation Act 1980 which applies to proceedings to 'recover any sum recoverable by virtue of any enactment' (in this case the Insolvency Act 1986). The six-year limitation provision of s 9(1) of the 1980 Act applied and therefore the liquidators' proceedings was struck out as time barred.

Comment

It should be noted that this case has no effect on the absence of time limits in cases of disqualification for unfitness already considered.

The 'every step' defence

Directors may have a defence against personal liability for wrongful trading if they can show that they took 'every step' that a reasonably diligent person would have taken to minimise the potential loss to creditors, once they knew (or ought to have known) that the company was unlikely to avoid going into insolvent liquidation. If the directors can establish such a defence, the court cannot make an order against them.

It may be difficult to satisfy the court that a particular director took 'every step' or even most of the steps and the court will have to take a view of conduct in all the circumstances of the case. Taking every step may well involve immediate cessation of trading or, if the business can be sold, it could mean the appointment of an administrator who will keep the company going until it is sold. Certainly directors of companies which are in danger of insolvent liquidation should take competent professional advice at the earliest possible opportunity.

Abilities of a director

As we have seen, wrongful trading is concerned with liability for negligent mismanagement, not dishonesty, though a dishonest person will, in most, if not every, case have been guilty also of negligent mismanagement. The court has to assess what steps a director took (or ought to have taken) when considering whether to apply the relief from liability. The court must take into account the director's conduct by the standard of a reasonably diligent person who has the following abilities.

(*a*) General ability, i.e. the general knowledge, skill and experience that can reasonably be expected of a person carrying out the same functions as the director. This is the lowest standard allowed. Nevertheless, general incompetence will not be sanctioned. Thus directors may be liable even if they have done their best if their best was not good enough for the office they held. Furthermore, it is no defence for directors to say that in fact they did not carry out any functions such as attending board meetings because they will be judged by the functions of the office with which they have been entrusted. The general knowledge, skill and experience to be expected for a director of a small company with limited operations will be less than for the directors of bigger and more sophisticated organisations, although the courts have already decided that there are basic minimum standards to be applied to everyone.

(*b*) Actual ability, i.e. the standard of a reasonably diligent person with the general knowledge, skill and experience that the director actually has. In this case the actual ability of the director will be assessed. This introduces a higher standard for talented and professionally qualified or experienced directors. However, the reverse will not apply and directors with less than average ability will be judged by the general standard even if they are personally below it.

In summary, talented directors are judged by their own standards while incompetent directors are judged by the standard of reasonably competent directors. The court will consider current standards of business practice.

Wrongful trading: profitable but undercapitalised companies

When discussing the matter of a director's knowledge at a particular time of the company's insolvency and yet continuing to trade it is important to note the decision of the Court of Appeal in *Secretary of State for Trade and Industry* v *Creegan* [2002] 1 BCLC 99. It deals essentially with what is meant by insolvency for this purpose. There are two forms of insolvency. One is balance sheet insolvency, i.e. the company's liabilities exceed its assets. The second is cash flow insolvency, i.e. where the company does not have sufficient funds coming in to pay its creditors as they fall due. The Court of Appeal made clear in the above case that both tests of insolvency must be satisfied and the director must know or ought to know that these tests are not satisfied and yet continue to trade. Therefore a company that is undercapitalised but has at the particular time no cash flow problem can continue trading without the directors being under threat of wrongful trading proceedings even though the situation may not be desirable in general business terms.

Action by directors

There are several actions which directors can take to avoid disqualification and personal liability if an insolvency were to ensue:

(*a*) Make sure that the board has up-to-date and adequate financial information. A mitigating factor for the court in deciding whether to disqualify directors or find them personally liable is whether the board has considered regular budgets and whether forecasts were produced carefully, even if they turned out to be inaccurate.

(*b*) Seek professional accounting advice if there are any doubts about the financial position of the company. If things have gone too far, an insolvency practitioner should be asked to give advice on alternative insolvency procedures. If there is still hope for the company, an administration order might be the solution so that ultimately there may be no need for liquidation. The most common applicants for administration orders are directors who hope that the appointment of an administrator may save their companies.

(*c*) Early warnings from the company's auditors must be heeded. Directors have generally found greater difficulty when asking the court for relief if they have not acted upon warnings from the company's auditors about the financial state of the company.

(*d*) Any difficulties should be discussed fully at frequent board meetings and the board should try to act unanimously. If one or two directors wish to stop trading but are overruled by the majority who wish to carry on, then the majority may have difficulty later on in justifying their decision to continue trading.

(*e*) The proceedings of board meetings should be minuted properly. Although board minutes are not normally conclusive, they can be good evidence that a board exercised its functions properly.

(*f*) Resignation from the board is not usually an adequate response to a problem within the company because a director must take 'every step' to protect creditors. A director who feels, however, that the rest of the board is inadvisedly but implacably determined to continue trading in spite of insolvency or impending insolvency might usefully write to the board giving his view. If this produces no change and he resigns, the court might well accept that resignation was the only course open to him. However, the High Court has decided that a director of an insolvent company whose recommendations regarding necessary economies had been disregarded by the controlling directors was not necessarily to be treated as unfit to be concerned in the management of a company under s 6(1)(b) of the Company Directors Disqualification Act 1986 simply because he failed to resign from the board.

Re a Company (No 004803 of 1996) [1996] *The Times*, 2 December

Mr Taylor was employed as a bookkeeper of a company at an annual salary of £8,000 and was also a director and 10 per cent shareholder of the company. As a result of a letter from the company's bankers in October 1991, Mr Taylor had made recommendations to the company for specific economies which would have given it a reasonable chance of trading out of its difficulties. However, the other directors had refused to implement these recommendations. In September 1993 the company went into voluntary liquidation with a deficiency in excess of £100,000. The Secretary of State had argued that Mr Taylor ought to have resigned his directorship by the end of 1992 and, in failing to do so, he should be treated as unfit to be concerned in the management of a company under s 6(1)(b) of the Company Directors Disqualification Act 1986. The district judge did not agree, though he thought that perhaps Mr Taylor would have been wiser to resign since by continuing to act as a director of an insolvent company he had exposed himself to potential liability under s 214 of the Insolvency Act 1986 (wrongful trading). However, Mr Justice Chadwick said that the district judge, against whose decision the DTI appealed, had properly considered the question of Mr Taylor's personal responsibility. He had seen and heard both Mr Taylor and the company's auditor. A director who protested against further trading, because he thought that there was no reasonable prospect of avoiding insolvency, was entitled to remain on the board using his influence to try to bring trading to an end. It was necessary to consider the purpose of a director remaining in that capacity. If it could be shown that the only reason why he remained a director was to draw his fee or preserve his status, then a court might think he lacked an appreciation of a director's duties and was unfit to be concerned in a company's management. In this case the district judge in the lower court had not found Mr Taylor lacking in this way and therefore the original decision was upheld. Mr Taylor was not disqualified.

(*g*) The court is bound to look more favourably on directors who have acted honestly and have not tried to benefit themselves at the expense of creditors. The court is also likely to take into account the willingness of directors to make a financial commitment to the company. The court will also consider relevant personal circumstances, such as matrimonial difficulties or more general factors such as recession.

Creditors

If a company becomes insolvent these days, its creditors have a better chance than ever of gaining access to the private assets of the directors in order to increase the amount which they are likely to receive. At the various creditors' meetings, which must be held in insolvent liquidation, creditors can impress upon the liquidator their wish to pursue the recovery of money from the directors personally. Any cash received will be available for distribution to the creditors and improve their position in terms of the dividend which the liquidator can pay.

Disqualification in other capacities (s 1)

It is worth noting that the Company Directors Disqualification Act 1986 provides that when making a disqualification order the court can disqualify a person not only from acting as a director but also from acting as a liquidator or administrator of a company, or from acting as administrative receiver, or from being concerned in any way directly or indirectly in the promotion, formation or management of a company. The legislation could, therefore, bear very hard on accountant/directors who could be disqualified not only from membership of the board but also from certain of their professional activities.

In this connection the Insolvency Act 2000 amended s 1 of the CDDA 1986 by providing that an individual who is the subject of a disqualification order or undertaking cannot obtain leave of the court to act as an insolvency practitioner. He may ask the court for leave to act as a director.

Competition violation: disqualification of directors

The Enterprise Act 2002 applies and inserts new provisions into s 9 of the CDDA 1986. A competition violation involves engaging in conduct that infringes any of the following:

- Chapter 1 of the Competition Act 1998 (agreements preventing, restricting or distorting competition, e.g. restricting retail outlets for goods);
- Chapter II of the 1998 Act (abuse of a dominant position, e.g. monopoly trading); and
- Articles 81 and 82 of the EU Treaty that carry similar prohibitions.

The Office of Fair Trading makes application to the court for a disqualification order.

Register of disqualification orders

This register is kept by the Registrar of Companies. The public can inspect the register and see the names of those currently disqualified from acting as directors. Obviously the name is removed at the end of the period of disqualification.

PERSONAL LIABILITY ONLY

Acting while disqualified or a bankrupt

By reason of s 15 a person who is disqualified and/or an undischarged bankrupt who becomes involved in the management of a company is jointly and severally liable with the company and any other person who is liable for the company's debts under s 15 or under some other section for such debts and other liabilities of the company as are incurred while the person concerned was involved in management.

In order to prevent disqualified persons and undischarged bankrupts from running a company through nominee managers, s 15 provides that anyone who acts or is willing to act (without leave from the court) on instructions given by a person whom he knows, at the time of acting or being willing to act, to be in either or both of the above categories, is also jointly and severally liable for debts and other liabilities incurred while he was acting or willing to act.

The Phoenix syndrome (IA 1986, s 216)

The purpose of this section is to prevent a practice under which company directors may contrive to mislead the public by utilising a company name which is the same as or similar to one of a failed company of which they also were directors in order to conduct a virtually identical business.

The provisions used to prevent this forbid a director or shadow director of the failed company from being a director or shadow director of a company with the same or similar name and business to the failed company for five years. If they infringe the above rules, they commit a criminal offence and under s 217 of the IA 1986 are personally liable jointly and severally for the debts of the second company during the period for which they managed it. If they manage through nominees who are aware of the circumstances, the nominees are also jointly and severally liable with the directors and shadow directors.

The court can, as in *Penrose* v *Official Receiver* [1996] 2 All ER 96, give exemption from the above requirements and the business and its name can be sold by an insolvency practitioner and run by a new management. There is no objection to this.

Disqualification: can violation of s 216 be taken into account?

The High Court has ruled that when deciding whether to disqualify a director for unfitness under s 6 of the CDDA 1986 the court may take into account the unauthorised use of a liquidated company's name even though breach of s 216 does not appear in Sch 1 of the CDDA 1986. Schedule 1 was not exhaustive in terms of what the court could take into account (*In re Migration Services International Ltd* [2000] 1 BCLC 666).

Directors and National Insurance contributions

The Social Security Act 1998 contains two new powers to deal with problems caused by unscrupulous directors who fail to pay employees' National Insurance contributions, as follows: those found guilty of the new criminal offence could be imprisoned for up to seven years, or the NIC debt can be transferred to the fraudulent or negligent directors as a personal debt. (See s 64 of the Social Security Act 1998, inserting ss 121C and 121D into the Social Security and Administration Act 1982.)

Liability as a signatory, s 349

Reference has already been made in Chapter 3 to the acquisition of personal liability where, for example, a director signs a cheque on which the company's name is not fully and properly stated.

Leave to act while disqualified

Section 17 of the CDDA 1986 gives the court power to grant leave to directors to act while disqualified. In *Re Westmid Services Ltd, Secretary of State for Trade and Industry* v *Griffiths* [1998] 2 All ER 124 the Court of Appeal gave guidance as to the exercise of the court's discretion under s 17. This includes:

- the age and state of health of the director;
- the length of time he has been disqualified;
- whether the offence was admitted;
- the general conduct before and after the offence;
- the periods of disqualification of the co-directors;
- the responsibilities that the disqualified director wishes to take on.

It can also be helpful to a submission to the court for leave to act if a professional such as a qualified accountant has joined or will join the board. A helpful case in ascertaining the attitude of the court in the matter of granting or refusing leave appears below.

Re China Jazz Worldwide plc [2003] All ER (D) 66 (Jun)

The director concerned had been disqualified for five years for unfitness in regard to his directorship of China Jazz. He was a part-time director and had been for less than two years. There was no remuneration. He was also employed as a director of four companies in the FM Group but could not carry on in view of the disqualification. His duties in China Jazz had been undertaken in his spare time. It was accepted that he had acted throughout with honesty and not for personal gain. He asked the High Court to grant him leave to continue acting as a director of the FM Group companies and to have an involvement in the management of other companies. His application was granted. The judge referred to relevant circumstances as follows:

- he had not been disqualified for *more* than five years. If he had it would have been unlikely that leave would have been granted;
- he had acted honestly. Leave will not normally be granted otherwise;
- the FM Group had procedures in place to ensure proper accountability. Leave is unlikely to be granted otherwise;
- there was evidence that the companies needed the services of the director and that he needed to continue his career. Although there is case law suggesting that these matters are not a requirement of granting leave *China Jazz* affirms that they are important and should be included in an application for leave in appropriate circumstances.

Comment

Those who have given disqualification undertakings can also apply to the court to cancel or reduce the period of disqualification. Presumably the above principles will guide the court in these applications.

HUMAN RIGHTS AND DIRECTORS

The Human Rights Act 1998 came into force on 2 October 2000. It incorporates the European Convention on Human Rights into UK law. The major impact is to allow human rights issues to be brought before UK courts as distinct from a former requirement to take them to the European Court of Human Rights (ECHR) in Strasbourg. Importantly, UK courts are required to interpret legislation in a way that is compatible with Convention rights. The likely effect upon proceedings against directors is set out below.

Public authority

The 1998 Act makes it unlawful for a public authority to conduct its affairs in a way that is incompatible with a Convention right. The expression 'public authority' is defined widely and includes government departments and regulators such as the Financial Services Authority as well as courts and tribunals within the UK. The activities of these bodies insofar as they affect directors will provide the major impact in this area.

Right to a fair trial (Art 6)

Article 6 of the Convention gives a right to access to justice and a fair trial in civil and criminal matters by an independent and impartial tribunal within a reasonable time. Impact on directors here will certainly take the form of protection against self-incrimination. In *Saunders* v *UK* (1997) 23 EHRR 313 the European Court of Human Rights held that protection against self-incrimination was at the heart of fair procedure. Mr Saunders had been compelled to give DTI inspectors information regarding the takeover by Guinness, of which he was a director, of the Distillers Company. There were, among other things, allegations of market abuse in the form of loans to individuals to buy Guinness shares so as to increase the market price and make them more attractive to the shareholders of Distillers. When criminal proceedings were later brought against Mr Saunders, the prosecution sought to bring in the information as evidence but the ECHR decided that this would be contrary to Art 6.

It can be seen from the *Saunders* case that Art 6 extends to cover the use of statements made by the Financial Services Authority and the Serious Fraud Office acting under statutory powers, such as the Financial Services and Markets Act 2000. However, Art 6 does not apply where the DTI investigation is not 'adjudicative' in the sense that it reaches conclusions as to liability. Thus in *Fayed* v *UK* [1994] *The Times*, 11 October, a report by DTI inspectors into the takeover of the House of Fraser by the Fayed brothers stated that they lied about their origins, but the European Court of Human Rights held that the report was not unlawful under Art 6 because it was investigative rather than adjudicative, or administrative rather than judicial, and in any case the limits of acceptable criticism of business people involved in the affairs of large companies were wider than in cases involving private persons.

Article 6 also prohibits undue delay in investigating and determining proceedings. Thus in *EDC* v *UK* [1998] BCC 370 the ECHR ruled that disqualification proceedings that had taken five years to conclude infringed Art 6 on the ground of unacceptable delay. In this context it is worth noting that Art 6 may apply to DTI investigations which also take many years to conclude.

The employment dimension

Employment law is thought by many to be the area of law where the 1998 Act will have most impact. Directors should be aware of these ramifications as managers of staff. The most significant rights of the Convention that are likely to be involved are in the following areas:

Prohibition of discrimination (Art 14)

The Convention may have the effect of widening the scope of discrimination in relation to sexual orientation, religion, age and sexual identity.

Right to respect for private and family life (Art 8)

This area will, it seems, have the greatest impact on the employer/employee relationship, involving access to medical records and employee surveillance.

Right to freedom of thought, conscience and religion (Art 9)

This may mean that employers will have to allow employees to hold controversial religious or political beliefs and to have time off for religious purposes. Such rights, however, are subject to the employment contract which, if freely negotiated, may exclude time off, as in *Stedman* v *UK* (1997) 23 EHRR CD 168 where the ECHR rejected a claim by a Christian required to work on Sunday on the grounds that she had signed a contract requiring her to work on that day.

Right to freedom of expression (Art 10)

Employers will be able to insist that confidential information about the business is not disclosed though 'whistleblowers' will be protected. It seems also that the employer will be allowed to place reasonable restrictions on the clothes worn by and hairstyles of employees as part of a dress code.

GRADED QUESTIONS

Essay mode

1 Melchester FC Ltd was incorporated by Albert Arkwright and Bertie Boozer in 1950. The company was set up to take over the running of Melchester FC, a Lancashire football club, who were founder members of the Football League. Arkwright, at the age of 70, is still a director and shareholder of the company. Bertie has since died with his shares passing on to his family who have recently sold out to Loadsamoney and two associates, all three becoming directors of the company.

Arkwright is deeply passionate about football and in particular has a strong affection for Melchester FC, having spent a great deal of his childhood and adult life associated with the club. Loadsamoney has expansionist plans for the club and is considering ways of merging Melchester FC with Ambridge United, a rival team, and also to start up a professional basketball team, both of which will require a heavy investment.

Arkwright objects to Loadsamoney's plans but finds himself outvoted on the board. Loadsamoney considers that Arkwright can no longer serve a useful purpose. He decides to remove him as director by securing an ordinary resolution at the next general meeting. Despite his removal, Arkwright is still able to raise objections as a shareholder. His objections, however, go unheard and he receives minimal co-operation from the board in response to his requests for information on the company's plans. Loadsamoney, annoyed with Arkwright's interference, decides to make an offer to Arkwright to buy out his shareholding at a price fixed by the board. Arkwright declines Loadsamoney's offer, but finds himself faced with a proposal, at an extraordinary meeting of the company, that the company's articles be changed so that any member can be requested by the board to transfer their shares to a nominated person at a fair value.

Advise Arkwright.

(*University of Greenwich*)

2 'The combined effect of the Insolvency Act 1986 and the Company Directors Disqualification Act 1986 is to give a clear signal to directors that to allow their companies to continue trading and to incur debts at a time when the position is hopeless is both a costly and foolhardy thing to do. In particular, the temptation to use money owed to the Crown to keep their companies afloat must be avoided at all costs.'

Discuss.

(*The Institute of Chartered Secretaries and Administrators*)

3 D was appointed director and managing director of X Ltd. The terms of his service contract provided that he should hold office for eight years and this term was also stated in the articles of association of X Ltd. The other directors of the company decided that D should be removed from his directorship and managing directorship. They placed a resolution before the shareholders in general meeting that D be removed from office and it was duly passed. D was at that meeting and made a statement that he intended to take legal advice for he was certain that he could not be removed in breach of the articles of association and of his service contract. The directors of X Ltd have asked your advice.

You are required to draft a statement for the board of directors explaining whether the shareholders had the authority to pass the resolution and suggesting what legal redress D might have.

(*The Chartered Institute of Management Accountants*)

4 Mini-mo Ltd is a registered company whose main activity is the production of animal feedstuffs. The company has an authorised fully issued share capital of 10,000 £1 shares. The three directors, George, Sheila and Robert, each hold 1,000 shares and the remaining shareholders Emily and Maurice hold 5,200 and 1,800 shares respectively. The articles provide that in the event of a resolution being proposed at a general meeting for the removal of a director any shares held by that director should carry three votes per share. Maurice is a director of another company, Plucko Ltd, whose main activity is also the production of animal feedstuffs. The directors wish to alter the articles of the company to give them power to require any member who engages in any competing business to transfer his shares at a fair value to the directors' nominees. Emily agrees to support the proposed alteration.

(*a*) Advise the directors on the statutory procedures which must be observed to effect the change in the articles.

The articles are altered accordingly. Emily is then surprised to find that the three directors have appropriated and allocated Maurice's shares equally between themselves. She decides to take action to remove George, Sheila and Robert as directors.

(*b*) Advise Maurice as to whether he can successfully challenge the alteration to the articles.
(*c*) Advise Emily on (i) the procedures she must follow if she wishes to remove the directors from office and (ii) her chances of success.

(*The Association of Chartered Certified Accountants*)

5 Harold was appointed managing director of Aire Ltd with a service contract for a term of four years.

A group of shareholders is dissatisfied with Harold's conduct of the company's affairs and wishes to remove him from office.

Advise the shareholders.

(*The Institute of Chartered Accountants in England and Wales*)

6 The following situations have arisen in the affairs of Harbottle Ltd:

(*a*) The company's managing director and founder member wishes to retire and move permanently to the south of France. For this purpose he needs capital. He owns 900,000 shares in the company which he needs to dispose of. Other members of the company are willing and able to purchase between them 600,000 of his shares. There is no other way of purchasing his remaining 300,000 shares without resorting to the company's capital. The directors propose to use the company's capital to purchase the shares.
(*b*) The company has a class of preference shares entitled to 8 per cent cumulative dividend. Dividends have not been declared for the last four years as the company has not been making significant profits. This year the company has made substantial profits large enough to pay the arrears of dividend. The directors propose to transfer the profits to reserve.
(*c*) The company owns a luxury villa in the south of France. Because of the property boom the villa has trebled in price. The directors of the company, however, resolve to sell the villa to the managing director's wife at its original price.

Discuss the legal validity of the above transactions.

(*University of Plymouth*)

7 'A modern company secretary is not a mere clerk but an officer of the company with extensive duties and responsibilities and he has ostensible authority to sign contracts in connection with the administration side of a company's affairs.'

Discuss this statement.

(*The Institute of Company Accountants*)

Objective mode

Four alternative answers are given. Select ONE only. Circle the answer which you consider to be correct. Check your answers by referring back to the information given in the chapter and against the answers at the back of the book.

1 A director can be removed at a general meeting of his company. What kind of resolution is required?

A An ordinary resolution following special notice to the company.
B An ordinary resolution.
C A special resolution following special notice to the company.
D A special resolution.

2 The following directors of Julius Ltd have been disqualified for two years following their misconduct while directors of the company – Jane, Harry, Mary and James. Jane is now working as a secretary with Julius Ltd; Harry has taken a management consultancy appointment with Archer Ltd; Mary has formed a new company in a different kind of business; and James has returned to his accountancy practice and has recently accepted an appointment as an administrative receiver. Which one of them is complying with the disqualification order?

A James.
B Mary.
C Harry.
D Jane.

3 The court is about to disqualify the directors of Blue Ltd for unfitness. How long may the order last?

A A maximum of 15 years with no minimum.
B A minimum of two years with a maximum of 15 years.
C A minimum of two years with a maximum of five years.
D A minimum of five years with a maximum of 15 years.

4 Unless the articles of a company carry a contrary provision directors must retire from office:

A every five years but may be re-elected any number of times.
B every three years with re-election any number of times.
C every three years with re-election only three more times.
D every five years with re-election only three more times.

5 Harry has been found guilty of persistent default in sending various documents and returns to the Registrar. What is the maximum period for which he may be disqualified?

A Five years.
B Ten years.
C Three years.
D Fifteen years.

6 Joe has been found guilty of wrongful trading. What is the maximum period for which he can be disqualified?

A Fifteen years.
B Five years.
C Ten years.
D Three years.

Answers to questions set in objective mode appear on p 577.

19

MEETINGS AND RESOLUTIONS

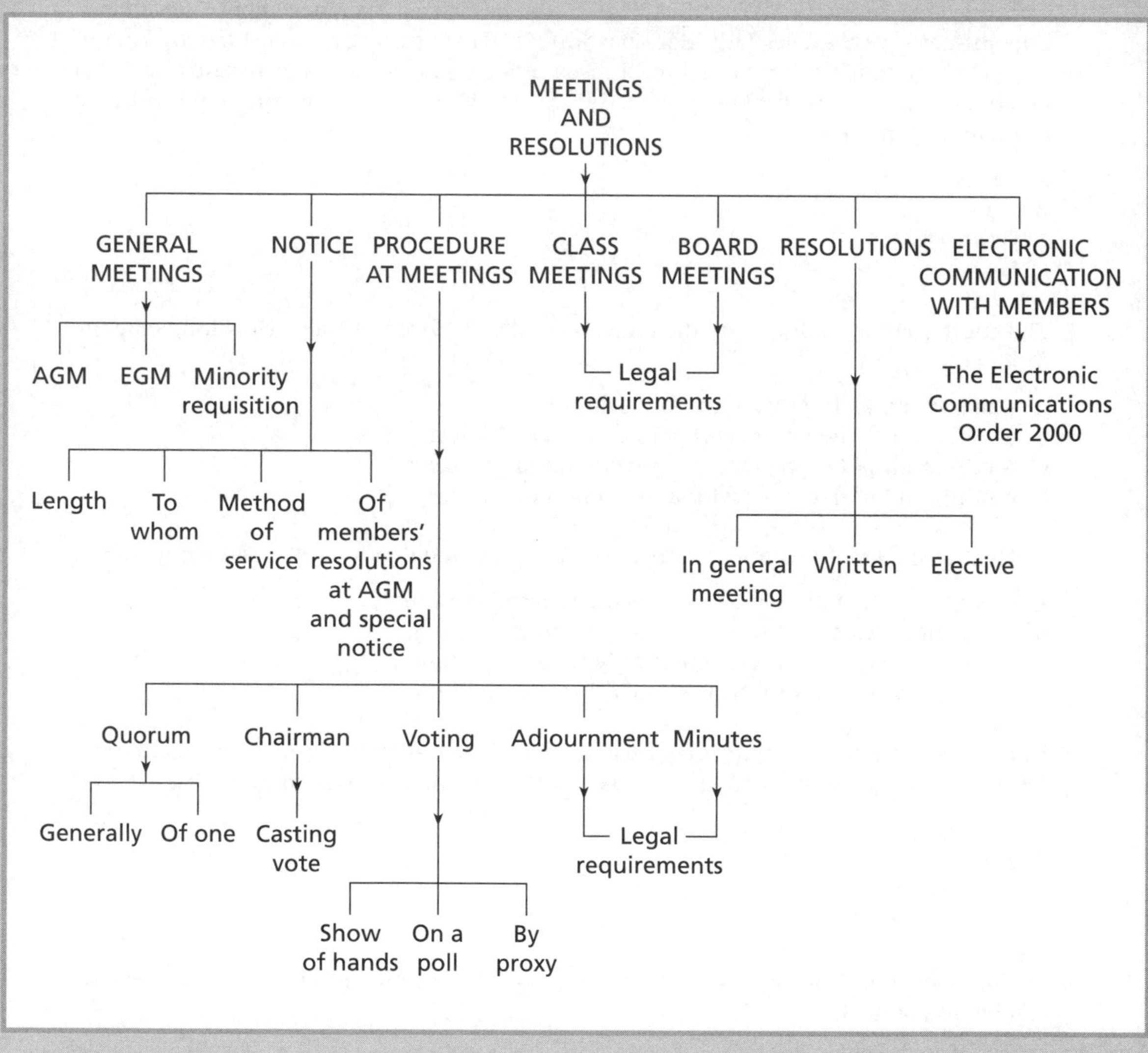

A company is compelled by law to hold certain general meetings of shareholders, i.e. annual general meetings and in exceptional cases extraordinary general meetings. The articles of a company provide for the holding of general meetings, the relevant provisions of *Table A* being in *Regs* 36 and 37. All section references in this chapter are to the Companies Act 1985 unless otherwise indicated.

Once the principles of meetings and resolutions in terms of paper communication have been grasped, the reader will find it necessary to refer to the material relating to the introduction of new technology in terms of changes to the law to allow electronic communication with shareholders (see page 115).

GENERAL MEETINGS OF THE COMPANY

1 Annual general meeting

Subject to certain exceptions applying to private companies (see below) every company must, under s 366, in each year hold a general meeting as its annual general meeting, in addition to any other meetings in that year, and must specify the meeting as such in the notices calling it. Not more than 15 months must elapse between the date of one annual general meeting and the next, but so long as a company holds its first annual general meeting within 18 months of its incorporation it need not hold it in the year of its incorporation or in the following year. Thus a company incorporated between July and December 2004 need not hold its first annual general meeting until the year 2006.

If default is made in calling an annual general meeting, the Department of Trade and Industry may, on the application of any member of the company, call or direct the calling of an annual general meeting of the company, and may give directions as to the conduct of it, and may direct that one member present in person or by proxy shall constitute a valid meeting. Such a provision is useful where a company has only one member willing to attend and yet a meeting is required to decide certain issues.

There is no statutory provision which deals with the business which may be conducted at the annual general meeting and *Table A* contains no such provision. Items of business such as a declaration of dividend must therefore appear in the notice of the meeting. Earlier *Tables A*, such as Art 52 of *Table A* to the CA 1948, stated that the ordinary business of the annual general meeting was the declaration of a dividend, the consideration of the accounts, balance sheets and the reports of the directors and auditors, the election of directors in place of those retiring, and the appointment of and the fixing of the remuneration of the auditors. Where a company has such an article, no notice need be given of the intention to raise the above items. Other business was special business and required notice. Since *Table A* to the CA 1985 makes no reference to ordinary and special business notice must be given of the matters which it is intended to raise at the meeting by companies which have adopted that *Table A*. It is no longer necessary to read the auditors' report at the meeting, but auditors may choose to read out only highlights, provided they make it clear that they are not reading the full report.

A matter that may be overlooked arises as a result of the provisions of Sch 13, Pt IV para 29 which states that the register of directors' interests must be produced at the commencement of the meeting and remain open and accessible during the continuance of the AGM to any person attending the meeting.

The meeting is a safeguard for the shareholders in that it provides them with an opportunity of questioning the directors on the accounts and reports, which are usually, but not necessarily, presented to the AGM (see further Chapter 21), and on general matters. Moreover, it is a meeting which must be held whether the directors wish it or not, unless in a private company an elective resolution has been passed to dispense with the need to hold it.

Electronic communication

Although it is not necessary to lay the annual report and accounts before an AGM they are in practice often so laid and it may be convenient to consider here the rules relating to electronic communication with shareholders (see pages 115 and 433).

Reform

The government White Paper *Modernising Company Law* sets out proposals for the holding of the AGM. As regards private companies the proposal is to remove the requirement for these companies to hold an AGM unless members opt by ordinary resolution to hold them. This is the opposite of existing law under which a private company is required to hold an AGM unless its members decide unanimously by elective resolution to dispense with the requirement.

2 Extraordinary general meetings

Meetings of the members other than the annual general meeting are called extraordinary general meetings, and may be convened when the directors think fit. However, a percentage of the members have the right to convene an extraordinary general meeting and the procedure is outlined below. The court has power under s 371 to call a general meeting if it is impractical to call one in the usual way, and the court may direct that one member of the company present in person or by proxy shall be deemed to constitute a valid meeting.

An example of the use of s 371 is to be found in the following case.

Re British Union for the Abolition of Vivisection [1995] *The Times*, 3 March

It appeared that in 1994 an EGM had been so disrupted that a near riot had broken out as a result of animosity between opposing factions within the Union and no business had been done. The Union's articles stated that no votes by proxy were allowed at AGMs or EGMs, but the committee members of the Union wished to change that provision, allowing proxies so that it would be possible for members to vote without actually attending the meeting. The committee members asked the court to direct them to hold an EGM at which only the 13 committee members would be present, i.e. 13 out of 9,000 members. The change to proxy voting could then be resolved upon at the meeting. The court made the necessary direction under s 371. It was clearly not practical to hold a meeting in the normal way or, in fact, at all.

Comment

(i) It may seem that the case is likely to apply in rather special and isolated situations but it could be useful as a precedent where, in a private family company, opposing factions within the family were making it difficult to do business. However, it should be borne in mind that the courts are unlikely to use the section to suppress genuine and orderly debate.

(ii) Section 371 is not available to sort out disputes between shareholders simply because they have equal shareholdings. It is available for quorum disputes as where A and B are the only shareholders in Boxo Ltd and, say, A will not attend general meetings so that there is no quorum and business cannot proceed. In such a case the court can, under s 371, authorise a valid meeting with only B present. However, if the problem is deadlock as where A and B each own 50 per cent of the voting shares and business cannot proceed because A votes one way and B another, s 371 is not available to enable the court to make an order allowing B to outvote A or vice versa (see *Ross* v *Telford* [1998] 1 BCLC 82). Such a deadlock will, unless it can be resolved by agreement between the parties, generally result in the liquidation of the company.

(iii) The decision in *Ross* may be contrasted with *Re Whitchurch Insurance Consultants Ltd* [1993] BCLC 1359 where the shareholdings were unequal. The issued capital was 1,000 shares, of which the husband held 666 and the wife 334. Their personal and business relationship had broken down. The wife would not attend board and general meetings so that there was no quorum and the husband could not remove his wife from the board. The court ordered that a general meeting be held without the wife because otherwise a minority shareholder would prevent the majority shareholder from exercising majority power.

In addition, an auditor has the right to requisition a meeting on his resignation (see Chapter 21), and a meeting must be called by a plc if there is a serious loss of capital (see Chapter 7).

Convening of general meetings

General meetings are normally convened by the board of directors, though, as noted above, the court and the DTI have power to do so in certain circumstances.

The company secretary or other executive has no power to call general meetings unless the board ratifies his act of doing so (*Re State of Wyoming Syndicate* [1901] 2 Ch 431).

As regards the time and place at which the meeting is to be held, this is in general terms a matter for the directors. However, it must be reasonably convenient for the members to attend and this probably prevents general meetings being held overseas. In addition, the directors must act in good faith when they call a meeting. Thus, in *Cannon* v *Trask* (1875) LR 20 Eq 669 the directors called the annual general meeting at an earlier date than was usual for the company to hold it in order to ensure that transfers of shares to certain persons who opposed the board would not be registered in time so that they would be unable to vote. An action for an injunction to stop the meeting succeeded. It should also be noted that once the directors have called the meeting they cannot postpone it and the meeting may be held even though the directors try to postpone or cancel it (*Smith* v *Paringa Mines Ltd* [1906] 2 Ch 193). With the consent of the majority of those present and voting it could, however, once held, be adjourned.

Rights of minorities to requisition extraordinary general meetings

The articles of a company usually provide that, apart from annual general meetings, meetings of the company can be convened by the directors whenever they think fit. The directors are, therefore, seldom under any obligation to call general meetings at which minority grievances can be put forward. However, under s 368 members holding not less than one-tenth of such of the company's paid-up capital as carries voting rights at the general meetings of the company can requisition a meeting. Thus, where a company has 200,000 £1 A ordinary shares, 50p paid, and (say) 50,000 B ordinary shares of £1 each, fully paid, and all the shares carry voting rights, the requisitionists must have paid up on their shares, whether A or B ordinary, one-tenth of £150,000, i.e. £15,000. Where the company does not have a share capital, members of the company representing not less than one-tenth of the total voting rights of all the members having a right to vote at general meetings of the company may make a requisition.

The requisitionists must deposit at the company's registered office a signed requisition stating the objects for which they wish a meeting of the company to be held. The directors must then convene an *extraordinary general meeting*, and if they have not done so within 21 days after the deposit of the requisition, the requisitionists, or any of them representing more than one-half of their total voting rights, may themselves convene the meeting so long as they do so within three months of the requisition. The requisitionists can recover reasonable expenses so incurred from the company, and the company may in turn recover these from the fees of the defaulting directors.

To ensure that the directors do not call the meeting for a date so far in the future as to frustrate the minority's aims the Act provides that the directors are deemed not to have duly convened the meeting if they call it for a date more than 28 days after the notice convening it. If they infringe this rule, the requisitionists' power to call the meeting arises.

The company's articles cannot deprive the members of the right to requisition a meeting although they can provide that a *smaller number* of persons may requisition, e.g. one-twentieth. An article would not be effective if it required a larger number than one-tenth.

It should be noted that s 368 uses the plural expression 'members' throughout so that the section basically requires two or more members holding the one-tenth share or voting requirement. One member would not suffice even though he held the one-tenth requirement. This requirement is presumably to ensure that there will be a quorum at the requisitioned meeting.

In fact, the case of *Morgan* v *Morgan Insurance Brokers Ltd* [1993] BCC 145 proceeded on this basis. Briefly, Mr Morgan wanted to requisition an EGM and had 77 per cent of the shares. To mount his requisition he wanted to transfer one of his shares to his daughter so that there would be two requisitionists. The other directors blocked the transfer under powers in the articles. Nevertheless, Mr Justice Millett proceeded on the basis that two requisitionists were required. There are those lawyers who may say that under the Interpretation Act of 1978 the plural includes the singular and vice versa unless there is a contrary intention and surely there is a contrary intention because unless there are at least two persons as requisitionists there may well not be a quorum at the meeting when it is held. Section 371 (see above) allows one member to ask the court to call a meeting and says so but there is no quorum problem here because the court when calling a meeting can fix the quorum even at one if it wishes.

It is important to note that if the requisitionists wish to put resolutions to the meeting, they must be clear and capable of being voted on. It is not enough that they state broad objects. For example, it is not enough for the requisitionists to state in their request for an EGM that the meeting will be asked 'to elect a new board of directors'. Such a resolution would be ineffective in the absence of details as to which persons are to be elected and what is to be the exact size of the new board or which members of the old board are to be removed. Unless resolutions are clear and would be effective if voted on, the directors are not obliged to call the EGM (see *Rose* v *McGivern* [1998] 2 BCLC 593).

Members' requisition: a fax will do

The High Court has considered and approved the use of a fax to request the directors of a company to convene an EGM under s 368.

PNC Telecom plc *v* Thomas [2003] BCC 202

Following service of a notice on a company by fax under s 368 of CA 1985 the company applied to the court for relief on the basis that the requisition by fax was not a proper *deposit* at the registered office as s 368 requires. The deposit, contended the company, had to be by hand or by post. The court dismissed the application and referred to the Companies Act 1985 (Electronic Communications) Order 2000 that specifically allows electronic communications to be accepted as well as communication by post. In addition the fax had been in use for a long time and no one had been disadvantaged or misled by the transmission. There was no reason why such a transmission should not be regarded as a valid deposit under s 368.

Other minority rights to call general meetings

Under the 1985 Act two or more members holding not less than one-tenth of the issued share capital of the company, or if there is no issued share capital, not less than 5 per cent in number of the members, may call a meeting, *but the section has effect only in so far as the company's articles do not provide to the contrary*. Its main purpose is to allow members to call general meetings where there are no directors, or not enough to form a quorum, and *Table A* confines its exercise to that sort of situation. The relevant part of *Table A* provides: 'If there are not within the United Kingdom sufficient directors to call a general meeting, any director or any member of the company may call a general meeting.'

Under *Table A*, therefore, it is easier to call a general meeting than it is under the Act and in a *Table A* company the *Table A* provisions would be used, if the problem was insufficient directors to form a quorum.

NOTICE OF MEETINGS

Regulations relating to notice of meetings are usually laid down in the company's articles and these must be referred to, although there are certain statutory provisions with regard to notice which must not be overlooked.

Length of notice

The company's articles must be followed, but s 369 provides that any provision in the company's articles is void if it provides for the calling of a meeting of the company (other than an adjourned meeting) by a shorter notice than:

(*a*) in the case of the annual general meeting or a meeting to pass a special resolution (or under *Table A* a meeting called for the passing of a resolution appointing a person as a director) not less than 21 days' notice in writing; and

(*b*) in the case of a meeting other than an annual general meeting, or a meeting for the passing of a special resolution, 14 days' notice in writing, or in the case of an unlimited company, seven days' notice in writing.

Where the company's articles do not make provision, the above periods apply.

The Combined Code that applies to public limited companies but is an indicator of good practice in all companies generally recommends 20 working days for AGM notice and papers.

Short notice

It should be noted that a meeting of a company, if called by a shorter period of notice than that prescribed in the Act or by the company's articles, shall be deemed *validly called if*:

(*a*) in the case of the annual general meeting, *all the members entitled to attend and vote* thereat *agree*; and

(*b*) in the case of any other meeting, *it is agreed by a majority in number* of the members having a right to attend and vote at the meeting, being a majority together *holding not less than 95 per cent in nominal value of the shares* giving a right to attend and vote at the meeting; *or* in the case of a company not having a share capital, a majority representing *95 per cent of the total voting rights* at the meeting. Private companies may by an elective resolution provide that the percentage be reduced from *95 per cent* to a minimum of *90 per cent.*

Since in both (*a*) and (*b*) above *all* the members of the company with voting rights would have to be in attendance the concession is in practice confined to meetings of private companies. Furthermore, it was held in *Re Pearce Duff Co Ltd* [1960] 3 All ER 222 that the mere fact that all the members are present at the meeting and pass a particular resolution, either unanimously or by a majority holding 95 per cent of the voting rights, does not imply consent to short notice and anyone who voted for a resolution in these circumstances can later challenge it. In practice a document setting out the agreement of the members to short notice should be signed by members at the meeting if all are present or, if not, consent can be given by means of a number of documents sent out to members and returned by post. There would appear to be no reason why this should not be done after a meeting called by inadequate notice has taken place.

The days of notice must be 'clear days', i.e. exclusive of the day of service and the day of the meeting.

Persons to whom notice must be given

The 1985 Act does not make any provision in this regard and it depends upon the class rights of the shareholders or on the articles. *Table A* provides that notice of general meetings shall be given to all the members, to all persons entitled to a share in consequence of the death or bankruptcy of a member, and to the directors and auditors. Notice of every general meeting must be given to the auditors, and if notice of a meeting is not given to every person entitled to notice, the proceedings and any resolution passed at the meeting will be invalid.

Young *v* Ladies Imperial Club [1920] 2 KB 523

Mrs Young, who was a member of the club, was expelled by a resolution passed by the appropriate committee. The Duchess of Abercorn, who was a member of the committee, was not sent a notice of the meeting, it being understood that she would not be able to attend. In fact, she had previously informed the chairman that she would not be able to attend. Nevertheless, in this action which was concerned with the validity of the expulsion, it was *held* – by the Court of Appeal – that the failure to send a notice to the Duchess invalidated the proceedings of the committee and rendered the expulsion void. *Per* Scrutton LJ:

> 'Every member of the committee ought, in my view, to be summoned to every meeting of the committee except in a case where summoning can have no possible result, as where the member is at such a distance that the summons cannot effectively reach the member in time to allow him or her to communicate with the committee. Extreme illness may be another ground, though I should myself require the illness to be extremely serious, because a member of the committee receiving a notice to attend may either write to ask for an adjournment of the meeting or express his views in writing to the committee, and I should require the illness to be such as to prevent that form of action being taken on receiving notice of such a meeting.'

However, under *Table A* the *accidental omission to give notice* of a meeting, or the non-receipt of notice of a meeting by any person entitled to receive notice, *does not invalidate the proceedings at that meeting* and any resolutions passed.

Re West Canadian Collieries Ltd [1962] Ch 370

The company failed to give notice of a meeting to certain of its members because their plates were inadvertently left out of an addressograph machine which was being used to prepare the envelopes in which the notices were sent. The proceedings of the meeting were not invalidated, it being *held* in the High Court to be an accidental omission within an article of the company similar to *Table A*.

Musselwhite *v* C H Musselwhite & Sons Ltd [1962] Ch 964

The company failed to give notice of a general meeting to certain persons who had sold their shares but had not been paid and remained on the register of members. The directors believed that the mere fact of entering into a contract of sale had made them cease to be members. *Held* – in the High Court – the proceedings of the general meeting were invalidated since the error was one of law and not an accidental omission within an article of the company similar to *Table A*.

In the absence of a provision to the contrary in the articles, preference shareholders without the power to vote have no right to be summoned to general meetings (*Re Mackenzie & Co Ltd* [1916] 2 Ch 450). Where the company has share warrants, some arrangements will have to be made to advertise the meeting if the holders of the warrants have any right to attend under the articles.

Section 369 sets out, as we have seen, certain minimum periods of notice for general meetings. This makes it impossible and therefore unnecessary to send notice to persons becoming members after the notice is sent out. Such persons, do, however, have the right to attend and vote at the meeting or appoint a proxy and if this causes difficulty legal advice should be sought on the drafting of an article which states expressly that notice need not be sent to such persons and also that they cannot attend and vote at the meeting.

Method of service

With regard to service of notice, the matter is again one for the articles, and a company is not compelled to post a notice to its members; it might, for example, use an advertisement or even a notice board. However, *Table A* provides for service of notice and this sort of procedure is generally followed. These provisions are as follows:

(i) A notice may be given by the company to any member or his representative either personally or by sending it by post to his registered address.
(ii) A notice may be given to *joint holders* by giving notice to the first joint holder named in the register of members.

The minimum number of days which must intervene between the day of posting the notice and the day of the meeting is not affected by the length of time which it takes for the Post Office to deliver the notice. The articles must, of course, be looked at but under *Reg* 115 of *Table A* service of a notice of meeting is deemed to have been effected 48 hours after posting. Thus under *Table A* an annual general meeting due to be held on 25 March would be validly convened by notices sent on 1 March whether by first or second class mail. It will be recalled that days of notice must be 'clear days'.

However, such a provision will not always be applied. In *Bradman* v *Trinity Estates plc* [1989] BCLC 757, the High Court refused to accept deemed delivery of notices posted to shareholders outside London during a postal dispute. Those who attended the meeting were members with London addresses who received their notices by courier. Mr Bradman, a shareholder, asked for and obtained an injunction to prevent the company from acting on a resolution passed at the meeting.

If the letter containing the notice has clearly not been delivered, as where it is returned to the company, notice would under *Table A*, *Reg* 115 still be regarded as having been given. Evidence of proper posting is, under that regulation, 'conclusive' evidence that notice was given and this cannot be rebutted as is the case with all evidence which is regarded as conclusive. Other articles may not carry a provision regarding the conclusive nature of receipt of notice and evidence of non-delivery would prevent the deeming provisions from applying. These points were decided in *Re Thundercrest* [1994] *The Times*, 2 August.

Contents of notice

The articles generally specify what the notice must contain, but *Table A* provides that it must specify the time and place of the meeting, and the general nature of the business to be transacted.

If the meeting is the annual general meeting, the notice must under s 366 say so. If it is convened to pass a special or extraordinary resolution, it must say so and the resolution(s) must be set out verbatim (*McConnell* v *Prill* [1916] 2 Ch 57), as must ordinary resolutions of which special notice is required and resolutions put on the agenda of the annual general meeting by shareholders (see below). In addition, the notice must be adequate to enable members to judge whether they should attend the meeting to protect their interests. Thus in *McConnell* v *Prill* [1916] 2 Ch 57 a notice of a meeting called to increase the nominal capital of the company did not say by how much. It was held that the notice was invalid because the eventual issue of the new shares (and there were no pre-emption rights then) could affect the rights of existing shareholders and they were therefore entitled to know by how much the nominal capital was to be increased.

Under s 372 the notice must clearly state the right of a member to appoint a proxy.

Notice of members' resolutions at the AGM

Members representing not less than one-twentieth of the total voting rights of all the members, or 100 or more members holding shares in the company on which there has been paid up an average sum of not less than £100 per member, can, under s 376, by making a written requisition to the company, *compel the company*:

(*a*) to give to members who are entitled to receive notice of the next annual general meeting, *notice of any resolution* which may be properly moved and which they intend to move at that meeting; *and*

(*b*) to circulate to members who are entitled to have notice of any general meeting sent to them, any *statement* of not more than 1,000 words with respect to the matter referred to in any proposed resolution or the business to be dealt with at the meeting.

The amount which has been paid up on the shares is not material so, assuming that a company has 300,000 £1 ordinary shares 50p paid and 100,000 £1 preference shares fully paid all with voting rights, then the requisition could be made by the holders of 80,000 shares. If made by 100 requisitionists, then the amount paid up on their shares if added together would have to come to at least £10,000.

The requisition must be *signed* by the requisitionists, and must under s 377 be *deposited* at the registered office of the company:

(i) if the requisition requires notice of a resolution, *not less than six weeks* before the meeting; and

(ii) if no resolution is required, as in (b) above, *not less than one week* before the meeting.

There must under s 377 be tendered with the requisition a sum reasonably adequate to meet the company's expenses in giving effect to the requisition, otherwise the company is not bound to act upon it.

The company is not bound by the above provisions if, on application to the court by the company or any person affected, the court is satisfied that they are being abused in order to secure needless publicity for defamatory or abusive matter. If the company calls an annual general meeting less than six weeks after the deposit of the requisition, the section is nevertheless deemed to have been complied with. This is to prevent the directors defeating the provision as to notice by calling an annual general meeting before the notice has run its course.

The above procedures are confined to resolutions to be proposed at the AGM.

Special notice

An ordinary resolution of which *special notice* has been given is required in the following cases:

(*a*) under s 303, to remove a director before the expiration of his period of office, regardless of any provision in the articles or in any agreement with him. If it is intended to *replace* the director if he is removed, special notice must be given of that also. The section does not prevent companies from attaching special voting rights to certain shares on this occasion (*Bushell* v *Faith*, 1969, see Chapter 18);

(*b*) under s 293, to appoint or reappoint a director who is over the age limit laid down by the Act or the company's articles. The age limit in the Act is 70 years;

(*c*) under s 388, appointing as auditor a person other than a retiring auditor; *or*

(*d*) filling a casual vacancy in the office of an auditor; *or*

(*e*) reappointing as auditor a retiring auditor who was appointed by the directors to fill a casual vacancy; *or*

(*f*) removing an auditor before the expiration of his term of office.

Under s 379, where special notice is required, the resolution is not effective unless notice of the intention to move it has been given to the company not less than 28 days before the meeting at which it is to be moved. The notice should be posted or delivered to the registered office of the company. The company must give its members notice of any such resolution at the same time and in the same manner as it gives notice of the meeting or, if this is not possible, must give them notice of it either by advertisement in a newspaper having an appropriate circulation or by any other method allowed by the articles, *not less than* 21 *days before the meeting*. If a meeting is called for a date 28 days or less after the notice has been given, the notice, though not given in time under the section, shall be deemed to have been properly given.

The above provision is designed to protect shareholders who give notice, e.g. to remove a director or auditor, in case the board calls the meeting of members deliberately at less than 28 days so as to frustrate the removal of the director or auditor.

Where a director gives the special notice it seems it must be acted upon by the board. However, where a shareholder who is not a director gives it, the directors are not, it would appear, bound to comply with it unless it is linked with a requisition under s 376 (if removal of a director is to be at the AGM) or under s 368 (if removal is to be at an EGM) (see further *Pedley* v *Inland Waterways Association Ltd*, 1977, Chapter 18).

PROCEDURE AT MEETINGS – LEGAL ASPECTS

A consideration of the legal, as distinct from the company secretarial, aspects of procedure once the meeting has been convened involves a discussion of the matter of quorum, voting, proxies, the position of the chairman and the recording of minutes.

Quorum: generally

The concept of quorum relates to the minimum number of persons suitably qualified who must be present at a meeting in order that business may be validly transacted.

If the articles do not lay down the quorum required for general meetings, s 370 provides that in the case of both public and private companies two members *personally* present shall be a quorum.

Therefore, as a general rule and in the absence of a provision in the articles at least two members *present in person* are required to constitute a meeting. The position in regard to single-member companies has already been considered in Chapter 1 but the quorum there is one member present in person or by proxy.

Sharp *v* Dawes (1876) 2 QBD 26

The Great Caradon Mine was run by a mining company in Cornwall and was carried on on the cost-book system, being controlled by the Stannaries Act 1869. The company had offices in London, and on 22 December 1874 notice of a general meeting was properly given. The meeting was held, but only the secretary, Sharp, and one shareholder, a Mr Silversides who held 25 shares, attended. Nevertheless, the business of the meeting was conducted with Silversides in the chair. Amongst other things, a call on shares was made and the defendant refused to pay it. He was sued by the secretary, Sharp, who brought the action on behalf of the company, and his defence was that calls had to be made at a meeting and there had been no meeting on this occasion. *Held* – by the Court of Appeal – the call was invalid. According to the ordinary use of the English language, a meeting could not be constituted by one shareholder.

In Re London Flats Ltd [1969] 2 All ER 744

The company was in liquidation and a meeting was called under what is now the Insolvency Act 1986 to appoint a successor to the liquidator who had died. At the meeting X, one of the only two shareholders, proposed that he be appointed liquidator and put forward an amendment to the resolution before the meeting which substituted his own name in the resolution for the person named therein who was a chartered accountant. The other shareholder, Y, left the meeting saying, 'I withdraw from the meeting, you now have no quorum.' The meeting continued and the amended resolution was put to the vote. There being one vote in favour and none against, X as chairman declared the amendment carried, thus making himself liquidator. Y made application to the court for the removal of X and the appointment of a liquidator by the court on the ground that the appointment of X was invalid, the meeting having consisted of only one shareholder. *Held* – by Plowman J – that the appointment of X was invalid. The matter was then referred to chambers for the appointment of an independent liquidator. An accountant unconnected with the parties was appointed.

The articles may provide that presence by proxy is enough. For example, *Table A* provides that in both public and private companies two members present in person or by proxy shall be a quorum. Thus, under the regulation, one member holding a proxy for another, or two persons holding proxies for members, could validly pass resolutions in general meeting. The persons who are to be counted in the quorum must be able to vote; mere presence is not enough. Thus a quorum cannot be constituted by persons who are merely in a position to seek membership, e.g. executors. If executors wish to vote, their names must be entered on the register as members. Then they can count towards the quorum.

Quorum of one

Where an annual general meeting is called by the Department of Trade and Industry or where an annual general meeting or other general meeting is called by the court, the Department or the court, as the case may be, may decide upon the quorum which may even be one member present in person or by proxy.

Re El Sombrero Ltd [1958] 3 All ER 1

The applicant in this case held 90 per cent of the shares of the company which was a private company. The company's two directors held 5 per cent of the shares each. The company's articles provided that the quorum for general meetings was two persons present in person or by proxy, and if within half an hour from the time appointed for holding a meeting a quorum was not present, the meeting, if convened on the requisition of the members, was deemed dissolved. On 11 March 1958, the applicant requisitioned an extraordinary general meeting to pass a resolution removing the two directors and appointing others in their place. The directors did not comply with the requisition, so the applicant himself convened an extraordinary general meeting for 21 April 1958. The two directors deliberately failed to attend, and since no quorum was present, the meeting was dissolved. The applicant took out a summons asking for a meeting to be called by the court to pass a resolution removing the two directors, and for a direction that one member of the company should be deemed to constitute a quorum at such meeting. The application was opposed by the directors. *Held* – by the High Court – since in practice a meeting of the company could not be convened under the articles, the court had a jurisdiction to order a meeting to be held, and for one member to constitute a quorum, and such an order was made. The applicant was entitled to enforce his statutory right to remove the directors by ordinary resolution, and the directors had refused to perform their statutory duty to call a meeting for the sole reason that, if a meeting was held, they would cease to be directors.

Comment

This case was followed in *Re HR Paul & Son* [1973] *The Times*, 17 November, where Brightman J ordered a general meeting to take place with a quorum of one where a 90 per cent shareholder could not get alterations in the articles because the minority had refused to attend general meetings. In cases such as this it is often impossible for the major shareholder to transfer a few shares to a nominee in order to make a quorum, either because there are pre-emption provisions in the articles or the remaining members are also directors who have a majority on the board and refuse to register the necessary transfers.

Section 125 is concerned with the matter of quorum at class meetings, fixing it at two persons holding or representing by proxy at least one-third in nominal value of the issued share capital of the class in question. At an adjourned class meeting the required quorum is one person holding shares of the class in question or his proxy. In addition, in *East* v *Bennet Bros Ltd* [1911] 1 Ch 163 it was held by Warrington J that *one* member who held *all* the shares of a class constituted a valid class meeting.

The position in single-member private companies has already been considered.

Quorum of one: committees of directors

Table A, Reg 72 authorises delegation by the board to one director acting as a committee of the board. The court accepted in *Re Taurine Co* (1883) 25 ChD 118 that under a similar provision in articles a director meeting alone constituted a valid meeting of the committee.

Effect of no quorum

Unless there is a quorum present, the meeting is null and void, but the articles must be looked at in order to ascertain whether a quorum is required throughout the meeting or only at the beginning. *Table A* provides that a quorum is required throughout the meeting but if the articles are silent on this particular point the better view is that a quorum need only be present at the beginning and need not be present throughout, though no valid resolutions can be passed if the number of persons present falls to one (*In Re London Flats Ltd*, 1969, but see above).

Table A provides that if within half an hour from the time appointed for the meeting a quorum is not present, the meeting shall stand adjourned to the same day in the next week at the same time and place, or to such other day and at such time and place as the directors may determine. The same provision applies if there ceases to be a quorum during the course of the meeting. There must be a quorum of two at the adjourned meeting or it is similarly adjourned until there is. Ultimately application to the DTI or the court would be necessary.

CHAIRMAN

It is his duty to preserve order, to call on members to speak, to decide points of order, such as the acceptability of amendments, and to take the vote after a proper discussion in order to ascertain the sense of the meeting. However, he is not bound to hear everyone. He must be fair to the minority but as Lindley MR said in *Wall* v *London Northern & Assets Corporation* [1898] 2 Ch 469, the majority can say: 'We have heard enough. We are not bound to listen until everybody is tired of talking and has sat down . . .' Under s 370 the members present at the meeting may elect one of their number as chairman unless the articles otherwise provide.

Table A provides that the chairman (if any) of the board of directors shall preside as chairman at every general meeting of the company, or if there is no such chairman, or if he is not present within 15 minutes after the time appointed for the holding of the meeting, or if he will not act, the directors present shall elect one of their number to be chairman of the meeting, and if there is only one director present and willing to act he shall be chairman.

If no director is present, or no director present is willing to act within 15 minutes after the time appointed for holding the meeting, the members present must choose one of their number to be chairman of the meeting.

VOTING

Unless the articles provide to the contrary, voting is by show of hands only. Articles usually allow an initial vote by show of hands, particularly for routine matters, and each member has only one vote, regardless of his shareholding. Under s 372 there cannot be any voting in respect of proxies held, unless the articles provide, and *Table A* does not allow proxy votes on a vote by show of hands. On controversial issues it is usual to demand a poll on which members can vote according to the number of shares they hold and proxy votes can be used. *Table A* allows a poll to be demanded before a vote on a show of hands is taken. The provisions of *Table A* state that in the case of joint holders the person whose name appears first in the register of members shall be allowed to cast the vote in respect of the shares, and no member shall be entitled to vote at any general meeting unless all moneys presently payable by him in respect of the shares have been paid. *Table A* also provides that objections to the qualification of a voter can only be raised at the meeting at which the vote is tendered. Objections are to be referred to the chairman of the meeting whose decision is final and conclusive.

It should also be noted that a shareholder, even if he is a director, can vote on a matter in which he has a personal interest subject to the rules relating to prejudice of minorities (see Chapter 14). Furthermore, a bankrupt shareholder may vote and give proxies if his name is still on the register, though he must do so in accordance with the wishes of the trustee (*Morgan* v *Gray* [1953] Ch 83).

If no poll is demanded, the vote on the show of hands as declared by the chairman and recorded in the minutes is the decision of the meeting and under *Table A* his declaration is *conclusive*, without proof of the number of votes cast for or against the resolution, unless there is an obvious error, as where the chairman states: 'There being a majority of 51 per cent on the show of hands, I hereby declare that the special resolution to alter the articles has been passed.' The chairman's declaration would not be conclusive either if he had improperly refused a poll.

The articles may set out the provisions governing the demand for a poll, but s 373 lays down that such provisions in the company's articles shall be *void* in certain circumstances:

(*a*) *They must not exclude* the right to demand a poll at a general meeting on any question other than the election of the chairman or the adjournment of the meeting.

(*b*) *They must not try* to stifle a demand for a poll if it is made by:

- (i) *not less than five members* having the right to vote at the meeting; *or*
- (ii) *a member or members representing not less than one-tenth of the total voting rights of all the members* having the right to vote at the meeting; *or*
- (iii) *a member or members holding shares* in the company which confer a right to vote at the meeting and *on which an aggregate sum has been paid up equal to not less than one-tenth of the total sum paid up on all such shares*. For example, if the share capital of the company was 10,000 shares of £1 each with 50p per share paid, the company would have received £5,000 from the shareholders and those wishing to demand a poll under this head would have had together to have paid up £500.

Thus the articles cannot prevent a fairly sizeable group of members from demanding a poll, and under s 373 the holder of a proxy can join in demanding a poll. Thus a proxy for five members could in effect demand a poll on his own.

Table A contains provisions similar to those of the Act but also provides that the chairman can demand a poll, and indeed it would be his duty to do this if he felt it necessary to ascertain the sense of the meeting. It also ensures that the board can exercise its full voting rights. *Table A* also provides that two members present in person or by proxy can demand a poll, and no provision in the special articles can increase this number beyond five, as we have already seen.

Unfortunately for the cause of greater democracy in companies, it appears that some chairmen of UK companies are not exercising this power to call for a poll even though they and the board know that the proxy votes are against a particular resolution. They are allowing these matters to be carried by a vote of a show of hands from those present and voting at the meeting. Unfortunately this procedure is legal in that proxy votes are not taken into account unless a poll is demanded. Obviously it is possible for the appropriate number of members to demand a poll but, in all probability, they will be unaware of the proxy state. The fact that it appears that chairmen of UK companies are adopting the vote on a show of hands (see Pensions & Investment Research Consultants' *Proxy Voting Trends 1999*) emphasises the need for the introduction of postal voting, pending perhaps electronic arrangements.

Taking the poll

A poll, if demanded, is usually taken straight away, the result being announced at the end of the meeting, but the articles may allow the poll to be taken at a later date. *Table A* provides that on any issue, other than the election of a chairman or on the adjournment of the meeting, a poll may be taken at such time not being more than 30 days after the poll is demanded, as is directed by the chairman who then proceeds to the next business.

Persons not actually present at the first meeting may vote on the subsequent poll. Under *Table A* in the case of a poll taken more than 48 hours after it is demanded, the proxies must be deposited after the poll has been demanded and not less than 24 hours before the time appointed for the taking of the poll. Where the poll is not taken forthwith but is taken not more than 48 hours after it was demanded, proxies must be delivered at the meeting at which the poll was demanded to the chairman or to the secretary or to any director and an instrument of proxy which is not deposited or delivered in a manner so permitted is invalid.

Even where a poll is taken immediately, the result may not be declared until a future date, because of the problems involved in checking the votes and the right of the members to cast them. Postal votes are not acceptable. Under s 374, where a proxy holder is acting for several principals, he need not use all the votes in the same way on a poll. This enables him to vote in the way each principal directs.

Chairman's casting vote

The chairman of the meeting has no casting vote unless the articles so provide. *Table A* provides that in the case of an equality of votes, whether on a show of hands or on a poll, the chairman of the meeting shall be entitled to a second or casting vote in addition to any other vote he may have.

The chairman is not bound to exercise this casting vote and may declare that the resolution has not been passed or exercise the casting vote for or against it. He ought normally to vote against it so that it is clearly lost because since those who want the resolution passed and those who want it to fail are equal in number it would not be fair to pass the resolution in the face of such opposition. The most common use of a casting vote is by a chairman on a show of hands, in favour of the resolution, where he knows that there are a lot of proxies in favour of the resolution.

PROXIES

Under s 372 every member of a company having a share capital and entitled to vote at a meeting may appoint a proxy, and the person appointed need not be a member of the company. However, the proxy should have full legal capacity and the appointment of a minor is probably void; certainly the Insolvency Rules 1986 (SI 1986/1925) exclude minors as proxies in meetings concerned with winding-up (see rule 8.1(3)). In addition, the notice of the meeting must make it clear that proxies can be appointed and failure to do this results in default fines on directors and the secretary but even so the meeting is valid. In public companies a member may appoint two or more proxies, but in a private company only one unless the articles provide to the contrary. *Table A* allows two or more in both public and private companies.

The Electronic Communications Order 2000 modifies s 372 so that provided *Table A* or the company's special articles are complied with in general the appointment of a proxy may be notified to the company at an address designated for the purpose. The Order modifies *Table A* and special articles accordingly (see further pages 115 and 433).

The expression 'proxy' also refers to the document by which the voting agent is appointed. The articles frequently set out the form of a proxy but a written appointment in reasonable form will suffice (*Isaacs* v *Chapman* (1916) 32 TLR 237). Furthermore, minor errors which do not seriously mislead will not make a proxy invalid. Thus in *Oliver* v *Dalgleish* [1963] 3 All ER 330 a proxy form gave the correct date of the meeting but said it was the annual general meeting and not an extraordinary general meeting as it in fact was. It was held by the High Court that the proxy was nevertheless valid.

Table A provides for two-way proxies, as distinct from appointing a person to exercise the vote, under which a member can indicate whether he wishes to vote for or against a particular resolution. The articles of association must not forbid two-way proxies if the Stock Exchange is to give a listing or the shares are to be dealt in on the AIM. It is uncertain whether the company is bound by a two-way proxy as regards the choice of vote but the better view is that it is bound so that if a proxy tried to cast his votes differently from the way in which the member had indicated the company ought not to accept the change (*Oliver* v *Dalgleish* [1963] 3 All ER 330).

The board may circulate proxy forms in favour of the board to members and meet the expense from the company's funds (*Peel* v *L & NW Railway* [1907] 1 Ch 5). However, these forms must be sent to all members entitled to attend and vote. This provision prevents the directors merely soliciting the votes of those who are likely to vote in favour of the board's proposals. In addition, the directors may also send circulars with the notice of the meeting putting forward their views on various resolutions and pay for the circularisation out of the company's funds (*Peel* v *L & NW Railway* [1907] 1 Ch 5). However, the circular must be issued in good faith to inform the members of the issues involved and must not be unduly biased in favour of the directors' views.

The right to appoint a proxy would be useless if it had to be made many weeks before the meeting. So, whatever the articles may provide, a proxy is valid if lodged not later than 48 hours before the meeting. If the articles do have an earlier requirement, it is void and it appears that the company cannot then require any period of lodgement at all so that if the proxy turns up at the meeting with his form and votes his vote must be accepted.

The law relating to faxed proxies is unclear. The court may not regard a fax as 'executed' (signed) by the member as *Table A, Reg* 60 requires, and perhaps also as not 'deposited with the company' as *Reg* 62 requires. Also the proxy remains with the member and the company does not get 'deposit' of it but only a 'copy' of it (but see *PNC Telecom plc* v *Thomas* [2003] BCC 202 that seems to support the view that a fax will be 'deposited' as the law requires). However, in the last analysis it is up to the chairman of the meeting to decide whether or not to accept a proxy, and he would be wise to accept a faxed proxy rather than risk a challenge in the courts as to the validity of the meeting brought by the shareholder whose faxed proxy was rejected.

It is worth noting that the acceptance of a faxed proxy is reinforced by the decision of the High Court in *Re a Debtor (No 2021 of 1995), ex parte IRC* v *Debtor* [1996] 2 All ER 345 where Laddie J held that a faxed proxy form was signed for the purposes of a creditors' meeting in a proposed voluntary arrangement and under r 8.2(3) of the Insolvency Rules of 1986 if it bore upon it some distinctive or personal marking which had been placed there by or with the authority of the creditor. When a creditor faxed a proxy form to the chairman of a creditors' meeting he transmitted the contents of the form and the signature applied to it. The receiving fax was instructed by the transmitting creditor to reproduce his signature on the proxy form which was itself being created at the receiving station. It followed that the received fax was a proxy form signed by the principal. The judge did, however, make clear that his decision was on the Insolvency Rules and that different considerations may apply to faxed documents in relation to other legislation. There is at present no case law relating to meetings held under the Companies Act 1985. To avoid any doubt, special articles could be drafted so as to specifically allow faxed proxy forms to be accepted. Obviously, faxed proxies are acceptable where the company has set up electronic communication systems with the consent of the relevant member(s) (see further page 418).

As regards revocation of a proxy, since the proxy is merely an agent of the member this can be done expressly by telling the proxy not to vote or by the member exercising his right to vote in person, in which case his personal vote will override that of the proxy if the latter votes (*Cousins* v *International Brick Co Ltd* [1931] 2 Ch 90). There is also automatic revocation of a proxy if the member who made the appointment dies or becomes bankrupt or of unsound mind. It should be noted that revocation is impossible if the proxy has an interest. Thus where *L* lends money to *B* and takes *B*'s share certificates in X Ltd as security but is not registered it may be part of the agreement that *L* should always be appointed *B*'s proxy at meetings of X Ltd. If so, the appointment of *L* as proxy is irrevocable until the loan is repaid.

All that is said in the above paragraph is subject to the articles of the company concerned (*Spiller* v *Mayo (Rhodesia) Development Co (1908) Ltd* [1926] WN 78). *Table A* provides that a vote given or poll demanded by a proxy or by the duly authorised representative of a corporation shall be valid notwithstanding the previous determination of the authority of the person voting or demanding a poll unless notice of the determination was received by the company at the office or at such other place at which the instrument of proxy was duly deposited before the commencement of the meeting or adjourned meeting at which the vote is given or the poll demanded or (in the case of a poll taken otherwise than on the same day as the meeting or adjourned meeting) the time appointed for taking the poll. Thus under *Table A* the acts and votes of a proxy are valid *unless the company knows* of any revocation.

Corporate representatives

Where a company is a member of another company, the member company is entitled under s 375 to appoint by resolution of its directors a representative to attend meetings. If the member company is in liquidation, the liquidator may also make the appointment (*Hillman* v *Crystal Bowl Amusements* [1973] 1 All ER 379). The representative is not a proxy and has the full rights of a member; thus he always counts towards the quorum, can move resolutions and amendments, can speak, even if the company is a public one, and can always vote on a show of hands. It is of some advantage to a company to appoint a representative, though if the meeting is not controversial a proxy will do just as well.

It is the view of the DTI that a company representative cannot himself appoint a proxy and there would not seem to be any legal provision which does.

Only one person can be appointed to represent the company. Thus where the company requiring representation is a nominee company holding shares for a number of persons with different interests, it should appoint proxies for the different holdings if each person requires someone to attend the meeting to represent his interest. More than one proxy can be appointed by a shareholder under *Table A*.

Lastly, under s 372 a proxy may speak at meetings of private companies but not at those of plcs.

Proxies in guarantee companies

In the case of a company limited by guarantee without a share capital unless the articles otherwise provide each member has one vote at a general meeting (s 370(1) and (6)) but is not entitled to appoint a proxy to represent him (s 372(2)).

ADJOURNMENT OF THE MEETING

A meeting may be adjourned for various reasons, e.g. where the business cannot be completed on that day, or where there is no quorum. The adjourned meeting is deemed to be a resumption of the original meeting and the articles may provide as to the amount of notice required for it, but no business may be transacted at an adjourned meeting except that which was left unfinished at the original meeting.

Where a resolution is passed at an adjourned meeting of the company, or at a class meeting or a meeting of the directors, the resolution shall be deemed for all purposes to have been passed on the date when it was in fact passed and not at the date of the earlier meeting. The section is thus important in deciding on what date to file a resolution which has to be filed within so many days of its being passed.

The articles usually determine who shall decide to adjourn, whether the members or the chairman. A chairman must not adjourn frivolously, and if he does so the members may elect a new chairman and proceed with the meeting. *Table A* provides that the chairman may (and *shall* if so directed by the meeting), with the consent of the meeting, adjourn the meeting from time to time and from place to place.

The chairman can, of course, adjourn under the common law without any resolution of the members where there is disorder at the meeting. However, he must exercise the power properly. Thus, if he adjourns the meeting immediately upon the outbreak of disorder without waiting to see whether it will subside, the adjournment will be invalid and the meeting may continue (*John* v *Rees* [1969] 2 All ER 274).

Another example of an invalid adjournment is to be found in *Byng* v *London Life Association Ltd* [1988] *The Times*, 22 December. A meeting of London Life was called to be held at the Barbican Centre in London. The main meeting place was not large enough to hold all those who wished to attend and the audio-visual linking system in the overflow rooms had broken down. The chairman adjourned the meeting without the consent of the meeting as London Life's articles required. His adjournment was challenged by Mr Byng, a shareholder, because the members had not consented. However, the Court of Appeal held that even so the chairman could use his common law right to adjourn in the difficult circumstances of the case. However, he had not exercised it reasonably. He had adjourned the meeting only until the afternoon of the same day at the Café Royal. He must have known that many people who had tried to attend the meeting at the Barbican would be unable to attend at the Café Royal in the afternoon at such short notice. Accordingly resolutions passed at the Café Royal by the much diminished number of people who did attend were invalid. Incidentally the court also held that a meeting may be validly held even though not everyone is in the same room, as where some are using audio-visual equipment in overflow rooms.

MINUTES

Under s 382 every company must keep minutes of all proceedings of general and directors' meetings, whether they be meetings of the full board or a committee of the board, and enter these into a minute book. If a minute is signed by the chairman of the meeting or of the next succeeding meeting, the minutes are prima facie evidence of the proceedings. This means that although there is a presumption that all the proceedings were in order and that all appointments of directors, managers or liquidators are deemed to be valid, evidence can be brought to contradict the minutes. Thus in *Re Fireproof Doors* [1916] 2 Ch 142 a contract to indemnify directors was held binding though not recorded in the minutes. On the other hand, if the articles provide that minutes duly signed by the chairman are *conclusive* evidence, they cannot be contradicted. Thus in *Kerr* v *Mottram* [1940] Ch 657 the claimant said that a contract to sell him preference and ordinary shares had been agreed at a meeting. There was no record in the minutes and since the articles of the company said that the minutes were conclusive evidence the court would not admit evidence as to the existence of the contract.

Under s 383 the minute books are to be kept at the registered office of the company, and the minutes of general meetings are open to the inspection of members free of charge. Copies or extracts from the minutes must be supplied and a charge may be made. The copy must be given within seven days of the request. The auditor of the company has a right of inspection at all times. Minute books may be kept on a loose-leaf system so long as there are adequate precautions to prevent fraud. However, it seems that some sort of visual record is required and the 1985 Act would not appear to envisage tapes being used.

Many companies keep their statutory registers on computer using one of the software packages available and this is permitted by s 722. The difficulty with keeping minutes in this way is that if they are kept in a form other than hard copy their value as evidence is reduced. Until the law on the acceptance of electronic signatures is made clear, signed hard copy minute books should be retained.

We have already referred in Chapter 1 to the need in one-member companies for the member to supply the company with a written record of decisions made at general meetings unless they are by written resolution.

CLASS MEETINGS

Class meetings may be held in respect of shareholders and debenture holders. The articles must be looked at for the provisions relating to the class meetings of *shareholders*; in the case of *debenture holders*, provisions are usually found in the trust deed under which they are issued. The only statutory provisions relating to class meetings of members are as follows:

(i) *Proxies*. The provisions regarding appointment of proxies apply to class meetings.
(ii) *Representation of corporations*. The provisions under which a corporation may be represented at meetings by a representative apply also to class meetings.
(iii) *Resolutions passed at adjourned meetings*. The provisions under which a resolution passed at an adjourned meeting shall be deemed for all purposes to have been passed on the date when it was in fact passed and not an earlier date apply also to class meetings.
(iv) The necessary quorum at a class meeting is at least two persons holding or representing by proxy one-third of the issued shares of the class, and any holder of the shares of the class present in person or by proxy may demand a poll. At an adjourned class meeting, the required quorum is one person holding shares of the class in question or his proxy. At any class meeting, any holder of the shares of the class in question may demand a poll, whether he is present in person or by proxy.

COMPANY MEETINGS AND THE DISABLED

The Disability Discrimination Act 1995 places a duty on those who provide goods, facilities and services not to discriminate against disabled people. The Act applies to any person, organisation or entity which is concerned with the provision in the UK of goods, facilities or services *to the public or a section of the public*. The Act will therefore apply, it would seem, if a company meeting can be described as a meeting involving the public. In the case of a plc which is also listed, the AGM would seem to be a public meeting and consideration would have to be given, for example, to access for the disabled and the provision of reports and accounts in Braille, together with systems designed to enable the deaf to participate in the meeting. However, since in this connection private companies provide the overwhelming majority of corporate structures in the UK (many with five or fewer members), it is unlikely that the Act would apply in this context. Of course, it does a company no harm to give proper consideration to its disabled members, if any.

BOARD MEETINGS

The powers of the directors must be exercised collectively at a board meeting and not individually, though an informal agreement made by them all will bind the company. This is envisaged by *Table A* which provides that a resolution in writing signed by all the directors entitled to receive notice of a meeting of directors or of a committee of directors shall be as valid and effectual as if it had been passed at a meeting of directors or (as the case may be) a committee of directors duly convened and held and may consist of several documents in the like form each signed by one or more directors; but a resolution signed by an alternate director need not also be signed by his appointor and if it is signed by a director who has appointed an alternate director, it need not be signed by the alternate director in that capacity.

A meeting of the board can be called by any director unless the articles otherwise provide. *Table A* provides that a director may, and the secretary shall at the request of a director, summon a meeting of the board.

Notice of board meetings

Notice of a board meeting should normally be given to all the directors and the time must be reasonable. This may be a matter of days, hours, or even minutes, depending on the circumstances. It has been held that three hours' notice to directors who had other business to attend to was insufficient, even though their places of business and the place where the board meeting was to be held were all in the City of London (*Re Homer District Consolidated Gold Mines Ltd, ex parte Smith* (1888) 39 Ch D 546). On the other hand, five minutes' notice to a director was held sufficient where neither distance nor other engagements prevented him from attending (*Browne* v *La Trinidad* (1887) 37 Ch D 1). Notice of a board meeting need not be given to a director whose whereabouts are unknown because, for example, he is travelling, and *Table A* provides that notice need not be sent to a director who is for the time being absent from the United Kingdom, e.g. where he is absent on business; but unless the articles are in the form of *Table A*, notice must be given to all directors if their whereabouts are known.

The effect of failure to give proper notice is uncertain, but it is the better view that it does not render resolutions passed at the meeting void. The law is not entirely clear, but in *Re Homer, etc.* (above) it was held that all resolutions passed at the meeting were void, whereas in *Browne* v *La Trinidad* (above) it was held that failure to give proper notice to a director merely entitles him to require that a second meeting be held if he does not attend the first. If he does not require a second meeting to be held within a reasonable time, then he waives his right to ask for it and the resolutions passed at the first meeting are then valid. The notice need only specify when and where the meeting is to be held. It is not necessary to set out the business to be transacted but in practice it is usual to do so.

Quorum

This is normally fixed by the articles, and *Table A* provides that the quorum shall be fixed by the directors and unless so fixed shall be two. A private company may have only one director, and if this is intended to be so in practice the articles should provide for a quorum of one. Alternatively, the sole director could presumably fix the quorum at one and minute the decision.

A person who holds office only as an alternate director shall, if his appointor is not present, be counted in the quorum. This does not, of course, apply to a private company with only one director. Certainly no business can be validly transacted without a quorum, and the quorum must if the articles so require (*Re Greymouth Point Elizabeth Rail & Coal Co Ltd* [1904] 1 Ch 32) consist of directors who are not personally interested in the business which is before the meeting, although in such a case interested directors are entitled to notice of the meeting and may attend and speak but not vote.

As regards personal interest, *Table A* provides as follows. A director shall not vote at a meeting of directors or of a committee of directors on any resolution concerning a matter in which he has, directly or indirectly, an interest or duty which is material and which conflicts, or may conflict, with the interest of the company unless his interest or duty arises only because the case falls within one or more of the following areas:

(*a*) the resolution relates to the giving to him of a guarantee, security, or indemnity in respect of money lent to, or an obligation by him for the benefit of, the company or any of its subsidiaries;
(*b*) the resolution relates to the giving to a third party of a guarantee, security or indemnity in respect of an obligation of the company or any of its subsidiaries for which the director has assumed responsibility in whole or part and whether alone or jointly with others under a guarantee or indemnity or by the giving of security;
(*c*) his interest arises by reason of his subscribing or agreeing to subscribe for any shares, debentures, or other securities of the company or any of its subsidiaries, or by reason of his being, or intending to become, a participant in the underwriting or sub-underwriting of an offer of any such shares, debentures or other securities by the company or any of its subsidiaries for subscription, purchase or exchange;
(*d*) the resolution relates in any way to a retirement benefit scheme which has been approved, or is conditional upon approval, by the Board of Inland Revenue for taxation purposes.

For the purposes of *Table A* an interest of a person who is, for any purpose of the Companies Act, connected with a director shall be treated as an interest of the director and in relation to an alternate director, an interest of his appointor shall be treated as an interest of the alternate director in addition to his own interests. A director shall not be counted in the quorum present at a meeting in relation to a resolution on which he is not entitled to vote. A director may vote on the appointment of a fellow director to an office of profit under the company, but not on his own appointment. The company may by ordinary resolution suspend or relax to any extent, either generally or in respect of any particular matter, any provision of the articles prohibiting a director from voting at a meeting of directors or of a committee of directors. If the company is to have a listing on the Stock Exchange, the rules of the Stock Exchange require that the company's articles follow the above provisions of *Table A* in terms of directors' interests, otherwise a listing will not be granted.

Voting at board meetings

The voting at board meetings is usually governed by the articles and is normally one vote per director, but *Table A* provides, as we have seen, that directors with a personal interest in the business before the meeting are not allowed to vote. A majority of one will carry a resolution, though an equality of votes means that the resolution is lost, unless the position is resolved by the use of the chairman's *casting vote* if he is given one under the articles. *Table A* gives the directors power to appoint a chairman to preside at board meetings and give him a casting vote.

Minutes

Every company must keep minutes of all proceedings at directors' meetings, and where there are managers all proceedings at meetings of managers must be entered in books kept for that purpose. When the minutes are signed by the chairman of the meeting, or by the chairman of the next succeeding meeting, they are prima facie evidence of the proceedings. The members have no general right to inspect the minutes of directors' meetings (*R* v *Merchant Tailors Co* (1831) 2 B & Ad 115), but the directors have.

Meetings by telephone

As we have seen, *Table A* allows written resolutions of directors to be as effective as resolutions passed in a board meeting. Therefore, *Table A* does not require a 'face to face' meeting either in the 1985 version or the 1948 version (see Part I, Art 106 – plcs and Part II, Arts 1 and 5 – private companies).

Thus if the relevant provisions were altered to allow valid decisions to be taken by telephone, either by the chairman obtaining the agreement of the majority of the board having contacted them all by telephone or by means of a 'conference' call, there would be no need for a meeting of the board. Impersonation of a director could arise but should not in general be a serious problem. A record equivalent to minutes would have to be kept. As regards general meetings of members, this does not have the same impact for change in the articles as in the case of board meetings. In view of the written resolution procedure and the infrequency of general meetings compared with board meetings, there is obviously less point in such a change. After all, a unanimous written resolution is effective as soon as the last member has signed his copy and a telephone call to each member to ascertain this means that the business which was the subject matter of the resolution can be proceeded with. There is no need to wait until the separate copies are returned (though they must be) and collated in one place. The conduct of business by Internet exchanges is undesirable because there is, as yet, no guarantee of security in this medium.

RESOLUTIONS – GENERALLY

Resolutions passed at meetings are of three kinds: (1) special, (2) extraordinary and (3) ordinary. The type of resolution will depend upon the articles and is based on the nature of the business transacted; it has no necessary connection with the type of meeting. Thus all the above resolutions can be passed at any general meeting.

In addition, under *Table A*, a resolution in writing signed by or on behalf of all the members for the time being entitled to receive notice of, and to attend and vote at, general meetings is as valid and effective as if it had been passed at a general meeting of the company duly convened and held, and may consist of several instruments in the same form each executed by or on behalf of one or more members. The provisions apply to public and private companies and to ordinary, extraordinary and special resolutions, though in practice written resolutions are not likely to be a viable proposition in public companies.

The provisions of *Table A* are given express authority in the Companies Act 1985 (as amended by the Companies Act 1989) but only in the case of private companies. Public companies may rely on *Table A* if they have adopted it, or that part of it, or have a similar article of their own. Written resolutions must comply with the rules regarding the filing of resolutions with the Registrar (see below).

1 Special resolutions

A special resolution is one passed by a majority of not less than three-quarters of such members as are entitled to and do vote in person, or, where proxies are allowed, by proxy, at a general meeting of which *not less than 21 days' notice* specifying the intention to propose the resolution as a special resolution has been duly given.

As we have seen, a resolution may be proposed and passed as a special resolution at a meeting of which less than 21 days' notice has been given if it is agreed by a majority in number of the members having the right to attend and vote at any meeting, being a majority holding not less than 95 per cent in nominal value of the shares giving that right, or in the case of a company not having a share capital, a majority together representing 95 per cent of the total voting rights at the meeting of all members.

The following matters must be carried out by special resolution and the memorandum and articles cannot provide to the contrary:

(i) alteration of the objects;
(ii) alteration of the articles;
(iii) the changing of the company's name;
(iv) the reduction of the company's share capital;
(v) the creation of reserve capital;
(vi) rendering the liability of the directors unlimited;
(vii) a resolution that the company be wound up by the court;
(viii) a resolution to wind up the company voluntarily;
(ix) a merger or reconstruction, e.g. the authorising of the liquidator in the voluntary winding-up of the company to sell the company's assets for shares in another company (see further Chapter 22);
(x) to authorise an off-market purchase of own shares;
(xi) in private companies, to authorise the provision of financial assistance for the purchase of own shares.

2 Extraordinary resolutions

A resolution is an extraordinary resolution when it has been passed by a majority of not less than *three-quarters* of the members who are entitled to and do vote, in person or by proxy, at a general meeting of which notice specifying the intention to propose the resolution as an extraordinary resolution has been duly given.

There are no provisions as to notice and so, if such a resolution were to be passed at the AGM, 21 days' notice would be required, and at an EGM 14 days' notice would suffice or seven days in the case of unlimited companies. The short notice procedure could be applied.

An *extraordinary resolution* may be required by the articles for any business specified therein, but *must be used*:

(i) to wind up the company voluntarily when it cannot pay its debts; and
(ii) to authorise the liquidator to compromise or make an arrangement with creditors or contributories in a members' voluntary winding-up (see further Chapter 25).

3 Ordinary resolutions

An ordinary resolution is used where the articles so provide. Such a resolution is not defined by the Act, though notice must be given of the intention to pass such a resolution, and there must be more members voting for the resolution than against it. The majority is not a majority of the members of the company, but only a majority of those who attend and vote.

Whenever in company legislation the 'approval of the members' is required, an ordinary resolution is enough unless some other resolution is specified.

No specific period of notice is required unless it is an ordinary resolution after special notice (see page 428). Otherwise it depends upon the meeting at which the resolution is to be passed (if not passed as a written resolution), i.e. AGM 21 clear days; EGM 14 clear days with the option of applying the short notice rules.

Seconding resolutions

The chairman can put any resolution to the meeting without its being seconded though not if the articles forbid it (*Re Horbury Bridge Coal, Iron & Wagon Co* (1879) 11 Ch D 109). Whether a resolution requires a seconder and whether that seconder must be a member depends upon the articles. *Table A* does not require a seconder at all so that the motion or resolution could be put to the meeting after proposal and no seconder is required at common law (see *Re Horbury Bridge Coal, Iron & Wagon Co*, 1879, above).

Registration of resolutions

Special and extraordinary resolutions must be registered with the Registrar of Companies. This is achieved under s 380 by sending a printed copy of the resolution to the Registrar within 15 days after its passing. It is not necessary to send a *printed* copy of the resolution to the Registrar if instead the company forwards a copy in some other form approved by him. A copy of each such resolution must also be embodied in or attached to every copy of the articles of association issued after the passing of the resolution. Documents registered must be suitable for microfilming.

Where, as will often be the case, a special resolution alters the company's memorandum or articles, the Registrar must advertise the filing of the resolution effecting the alteration in the *London Gazette*. The alteration is not effective against other persons who at the material time are unaware of it having been made until the advertisement is published. 'Other persons' in this context would appear to mean persons other than the company and therefore includes shareholders and directors as well as outsiders. As regards the material time, this appears to mean the time when a transaction was entered into. In addition, when an alteration is made in the memorandum or articles (except in the case of a special or written resolution altering the objects), a printed copy of the whole memorandum or articles as amended must be delivered to the Registrar with the resolution. This helps when looking through a company's file at the Registry because there is no need to check back to the original memorandum and articles in order to see the overall effect of subsequent alterations.

An ordinary resolution need not be registered except where it has been used to increase the authorised capital when it must be filed with the Registrar within 15 days or to consolidate or subdivide shares, or to convert shares into stock or reconvert stock into shares. In this case notice of the resolution must be filed with the Registrar *within one month* after the change in capital has been made. In addition an ordinary resolution to give, vary, revoke or renew, whether in the articles or otherwise, the authority of directors to allot shares and an ordinary resolution giving authority for a market purchase of the company's shares must be registered within 15 days.

It has already been noted (see Chapter 10) that if shares in a public company are forfeited or surrendered to the company, the company must see to it that the shares are disposed of and if this has not been done within three years it must cancel the shares. If the result of this is that the company's issued share capital is brought below the authorised minimum, the company will have to apply for re-registration as a private company, and a resolution of the directors is sufficient to change the company's memorandum of association to prepare it for re-registration. That resolution of the directors is registrable with the Registrar within 15 days of its being passed.

The Electronic Communications Order 2000 enables the Registrar to direct that any document required to be delivered to him under the Companies Act 1985 or the Insolvency Act 1986 may be delivered electronically in a manner decided by him (see further pages 115 and 433).

ORDINARY RESOLUTIONS REQUIRING SPECIAL NOTICE

An ordinary resolution of which *special notice* has been given is required in the following cases:

(*a*) to remove a director before the expiration of his period of office, regardless of any provision in the articles or in any agreement with him; and to appoint another director in his place if this is intended. The section does not prevent companies from attaching special voting rights to certain shares on this occasion (*Bushell* v *Faith*, 1969, see Chapter 18);

(*b*) to appoint or reappoint a director who is over the age limit laid down by the Act or the company's articles. The age limit in the Act is 70 years;

(*c*) appointing as auditor a person other than a retiring auditor; *or*

(*d*) filling a casual vacancy in the office of an auditor; *or*

(*e*) reappointing as auditor a retiring auditor who was appointed by the directors to fill a casual vacancy; *or*

(*f*) removing an auditor before the expiration of his term of office.

Where special notice is required, the resolution shall not be effective unless notice of the intention to move it has been given to the company not less than *28 days* before the meeting at which it is to be moved. The notice should be posted or delivered to the registered office of the company. The company must give its members notice of any such resolution at the same time and in the same manner as it gives notice of the meeting or, if this is not possible, must give them notice of it either by advertisement in a newspaper having an appropriate circulation or by any other method allowed by the articles, *not less than 21 days before the meeting*. If a meeting is called for a date 28 days or less after the notice has been given, the notice, though not given in time under the section, shall be deemed to have been properly given.

It should be noted that the actual resolution need not be moved at the meeting by the same member who served the special notice.

AMENDMENTS

As regards amendments to resolutions, which must be set out verbatim, such as special and extraordinary resolutions, it is often suggested that no amendment is possible since the Act requires *notice* of the resolution and some say, by implication, of any amendment, because if the resolution is changed by an amendment then proper notice has not been given of that part of it which was amended. It is generally believed that this view is too strict, and indeed in *Re Moorgate Mercantile Holdings* [1980] 1 All ER 40 Mr Justice Slade decided that such a resolution could depart in some respects from the text of the resolution set out in the notice, e.g. on account of correction of grammatical or clerical errors, or the use of more formal language. However, apart from alterations of form of this kind, there must be no alterations of substance; otherwise only where all the members (in the case of an AGM) or a majority in number and 95 per cent in value of members (in the case of any other meeting) have waived their rights to notice, could a special resolution be validly passed. The judge also decided that in the case of notice of intention to propose a special resolution nothing is achieved by the addition of such words as 'with such amendments and alterations as shall be determined on at the general meeting'.

The facts of the case were that the company wished to reduce its share premium account on the grounds that it had been lost in the course of trade. The share premium account to be cancelled was stated in the notice to be £1,356,900.48p. That figure included the sum of £321.17 which had been credited to the share premium account under an issue of shares made on the acquisition of the outstanding minority interest in a subsidiary. This share premium could not be regarded as lost. At the meeting the chairman proposed to amend the special resolution and, although not all the members of the company were present, a special resolution was passed in the following form: 'That the share premium account of the company amounting to £1,356,900.48p be reduced to £321.17p'. The court was then asked to agree to the reduction and the judge refused to do so on the grounds that the special resolution had not been validly passed.

Subject to what has been said above, once a resolution has been moved and, if the articles require, seconded, any member may speak and move amendments. No notice of the amendments is required unless the amendment effects a substantial change in the original resolution, i.e. is the change such that a reasonable man who had decided to absent himself from the meeting would have decided to come if he had received notice of the amended resolution? This is a decision which the chairman must take and hope that if his decision is questioned in court the judge will agree with him. For example, in *Re Teede and Bishop Ltd* (1901) 70 LJ Ch 409 it was held that at a meeting to resolve that *A* Ltd should be sold to *B* Ltd and then that *A* Ltd should be wound up, it was not in order to accept an amendment that *A* Ltd be wound up without the sale to *B* Ltd unless notice had been given of it.

Amendments must be put to the vote before the resolution is voted upon. Improper refusal by the chairman to put an amendment renders the main resolution void (*Henderson* v *Bank of Australasia* (1890) 45 Ch D 330). Proxies cannot move resolutions or amendments or speak unless the company is a private one when a proxy may address the meeting.

Resolutions and the 'Duomatic principle' of unanimous consent

Where all the shareholders of a company assent to a matter that could be brought into effect by a resolution in general meeting the unanimous consent of the shareholders without a formal meeting is enough. This is called the 'Duomatic principle' from the case in which it was most famously canvassed, i.e. *Re Duomatic* [1969] 1 All ER 161. Alterations in the articles can be achieved in this way and in this connection the Duomatic principle has been applied to changes in shareholders' agreements that are often used in private companies to supplement the articles in confidential areas of governance (see *Euro Brokers Holdings Ltd* v *Monecor (London) Ltd* [2003] 1 BCLC 506).

WRITTEN RESOLUTIONS OF PRIVATE COMPANIES

As part of the deregulation of private companies, the Companies Act 1985, as amended by the Companies Act 1989, provides for written resolutions which can be passed by the members of a private company without the need to call or hold a meeting. The 1985 Act now provides that anything which can be done by a private company by a resolution in general meeting or in a class meeting – as where a class of shareholders is being asked to vary their rights and they are unanimous in wishing to approve the variation (in the absence of unanimity there would have to be a class meeting) – can be done without a meeting, and without any previous notice being required, by a resolution signed by or on behalf of *all* the members of the company who at that date of the resolution were entitled to attend and vote at meetings of the company. The signatures need not be on a single document so that the resolution may, e.g., be typed on separate sheets of paper and circulated to the members for signature. The date of the resolution is the date on which it is signed by, or on behalf of, the last member to sign.

There are some cases where the written resolution procedure cannot be used, e.g. the removal of a director or auditor by ordinary resolution after special notice to the company. The ordinary resolution must be passed at a meeting of the company because the director or auditor concerned is allowed to make representations as to why he should not be removed, either in writing with the notice of the meeting, or orally at the meeting.

The company is required to keep a record of written resolutions and the signatures of those members who signed them in a record book which is, in effect, a substitute for what would, in the case of a meeting, be the minutes.

Written resolutions: special adaptations

Schedule 15A of the CA 1985 contains special adaptations to the written resolution procedure in certain circumstances, e.g. where documents have to be available at the meeting at which the resolution is passed, if that method were followed instead of a written procedure where there is no meeting, as in approval of a director's service contract exceeding five years, where the contract must be supplied to members before or at the time of signing the resolution instead of being available at the meeting where a non-written resolution is passed.

Filing of written resolutions

There is no general need to file a written resolution with the Registrar unless it takes effect, e.g., as a special or elective resolution or an ordinary resolution increasing authorised share capital. Even where a written resolution does have to be filed, there is no requirement to file the original. A copy can be filed and the signed copy kept in the minute book. In connection with the filing of written resolutions, Companies House states that it has received copies of 'written special resolutions'. There is, of course, no such thing. There are written resolutions *which take effect as special resolutions*. It would be a better approach to indicate on the filed copy and minute copy of the resolution that it took effect as a special resolution.

Involvement of auditors

The Deregulation (Resolutions of Private Companies) Order 1996 deals with the involvement of the company's auditors (if any) in the written resolution procedure as follows:

- Article 3 repeals the pre-existing provisions of the CA 1985, i.e. ss 381B and 390(2), and substitutes a new s 381B (duty to notify auditors of proposed written resolutions). The new section imposes a duty on the directors and secretary of a company to send the company's auditors (if any) a copy of, or otherwise inform them of the contents of, any written resolution proposed under s 381A (written resolutions of private companies) at or before the time that resolution is supplied to a member for signature. Breach of the duty will result in a criminal offence but will not affect the validity of any resolution passed under s 381A.

  As regards the criminal offence, it is a defence for the accused to prove:

  (*a*) that the circumstances were such that it was not practicable for him to comply with the requirements; or

  (*b*) that he believed on reasonable grounds that a copy of the resolution had been sent to the company's auditors or that they had otherwise been informed of its contents.

- Since s 381B is repealed, the auditors have no right to require the company to call a meeting rather than use the written resolution procedure, nor need the company wait for seven days to see whether the auditors state whether the resolution does or does not concern them as auditors.

So far as the auditors are concerned, the regulations operate merely to give them information as to resolutions being passed by the company bearing in mind that had the company passed the resolution at a general meeting the auditors would have received notice of it and have been entitled to attend and be heard on any part of the business which concerns them as auditors (s 390(1)). If the result of the resolution is that the auditor leaves office, bearing in mind that an auditor cannot be removed before his period of office expires by a written resolution anyway – although he might not be reappointed at the end of that period by such a resolution – the auditor will be alerted to make a statement under s 394.

Additionally, Art 4 amends s 381C(1) to make it clear that the statutory written resolution procedure under s 381A may be used notwithstanding any provision in the company's memorandum or articles but does not prevent the use of any power conferred by such a provision instead.

It seems likely that a court would take the view, at least in regard to dormant and audit-exempt companies, that since the law allows them to exist and/or operate without auditors, they may pass written resolutions without complying with s 381B (rights of auditors in relation to written resolutions) – since it is impossible for them to do so and this impossibility is recognised by and is within the law.

It has already been noted as appropriate in the various chapters of this text that where written resolutions are used procedural changes may be required in terms that documents which must be available for inspection by members at a meeting have instead to be circulated with the copy of the written resolution. *Table A* extends the power to have written resolutions to public companies while the CA 1985 confines the procedure to private companies.

ELECTIVE RESOLUTIONS OF PRIVATE COMPANIES

Private companies, whether limited or unlimited, are allowed to pass elective resolutions to dispense with the following formalities and requirements:

(*a*) the holding of the annual general meeting, but any member may require an AGM to be held in any particular year. An elective resolution is ineffective to exempt from the need to hold an AGM where the statutory date for holding it has passed (AGM to be held in each year and not more than 15 months from the last one). Section 366A(2) states that an election does not affect any liability already incurred by reason of default in holding an AGM;

(*b*) the laying of accounts and reports before the company in general meeting, but any member, or the auditors, may require them to be laid in any particular year. Care should be taken where, say, accounts to 31 December 2004 are to be laid before an AGM in, say, April 2005. An elective resolution passed in, say, February 2005 would not do away with the need to lay the 2004 accounts before the AGM (or other general meeting) *because the exemption applies only to financial statements for the year in which the elective resolution was passed.* Thus in the above situation the elective resolution should be passed before the end of the financial year, i.e. before 31 December 2004;

(*c*) the percentage of shares required to be held by persons agreeing to an extraordinary general meeting being held at short notice may be reduced from 95 per cent down to not less than 90 per cent;

(*d*) the period for which a general meeting may authorise the directors to allot shares may exceed the usual limit of five years;

(*e*) the requirement to appoint auditors annually. An election to dispense with the annual appointment of auditors will have to be made before the time for appointing auditors for the relevant year has expired.

As we have seen, the resolution required to achieve the opting out is called an elective resolution and it can be passed at a meeting of the company. Such a resolution is not effective unless:

(i) at least 21 days' notice in writing is given of the meeting at which it is to be proposed, the terms of the resolution and the fact that it is an elective resolution being stated; shorter notice is available if *all* members agree; and
(ii) the resolution is agreed to at the meeting, in person or by proxy, by all the members entitled to attend and vote at the meeting.

Under the Deregulation (Resolutions of Private Companies) Order 1996 less than 21 days' notice may be given of a meeting at which an elective resolution is to be proposed, provided that all the members entitled to attend the meeting and vote agree to short notice.

An elective resolution may be revoked by an ordinary resolution of the company and an elective resolution ceases to have effect if the company is re-registered as a public company. A written resolution may be used as an elective resolution.

An elective resolution and any revoking resolution must under s 380 be filed at Companies House within 15 days of passing and, as we have seen, takes effect notwithstanding any contrary provision in the company's articles.

MEETINGS OF SINGLE-MEMBER COMPANIES

The amendments of the law relating to meetings to accommodate the single-member company have already been considered in Chapter 1.

ELECTRONIC COMMUNICATIONS – PRACTICE ASPECTS

The passing of the Electronic Communications Act 2000 enabled the government to use delegated legislation to legislate to allow companies to communicate with their shareholders electronically. The relevant order was passed and is entitled The Companies Act 1985 (Electronic Communications) Order 2000 (Electronic Communications Order 2000).

Those wishing to use electronic communication with members will have to translate the provisions of the Electronic Communications Order 2000, referred to above, into practical changes in procedures within the company. The main areas for review are set out below.

Articles of association

The order amends the provisions of the CA 1985 that prevented or hindered the use of electronic communication. *Table A* to the CA 1985 (SI 1985/805) is also amended by the order which inserts new provisions for the use of electronic communications in the following areas:

- to appoint proxies;
- to give notice; and
- to amend the 'deemed service' provisions, i.e. when an electronic communication shall be regarded as received.

Companies do not have to amend their articles before using electronic communications. If the company does not have specific provisions in its articles providing for electronic communication, the order states that the amended provisions of *Table A* will apply. Thus no alteration is required where the company has adopted *Table A* and special articles need not be changed. However, if a particular company wishes to change its articles so that they correctly reflect the underlying legal position, the amendments to *Table A* set out in the Electronic Communications Order 2000 provide a useful guide, and so does the guidance issued by the Institute of Chartered Secretaries and Administrators (copies of the guidance can be obtained from the ICSA, 16 Park Crescent, London W1B 1AH, priced £10 per copy).

If articles are amended, legal advice should be taken since changes in one clause may have unforeseen effects on other clauses and it is not possible to provide definitive guidance on the amendments that every company will need to make.

Inviting shareholders to use electronic communications

Any communication to shareholders regarding the company's intended use of electronic communication should be prefaced by a statement that its use is entirely voluntary and that shareholders cannot be compelled to make use of the facility. Other matters that must be set out in the communication to shareholders are:

Consent

Shareholders should be asked to return a registration slip if they consent to and wish the receipt of the relevant communications by electronic means. In general terms, this will require the shareholder to provide an e-mail address or, say, a fax address through which communication may be made. It is essential that the offer to use electronic communication should not discriminate between shareholders of the same class or between classes. The facility should be made available to all shareholders on equal terms and in such a way as to make it as easy as possible for shareholders to participate. The option to receive relevant materials in hard copy should be retained. The invitation should be extended to all new shareholders and repeated, for example, with the notice of the AGM each year where some shareholders have not taken up the electronic option. If the company has a Website, the availablity of the electronic facility should be posted on it all year round.

Where communication is by Website, there should be a statement on the Website to the effect that the various communications do not constitute an offer or invitation to invest in the company's shares or other securities. Private companies are not permitted to make public offers and it is essential to indicate that, e.g., share information sent to members is not to be construed as a general offer to the public.

Proxy forms: availability

There are three options as follows:

- send out a printed form of proxy to each member, as is current practice, but invite members to fax the completed form to a stated fax number or to telephone the company secretary (or Registrar) to register the relevant appointment by telephone;
- send a hard copy to members other than those whose e-mail addresses are registered. Those who have registered e-mail addresses could be sent a form of proxy by e-mail, or sent an e-mail stating that a form of proxy is available on the Website;
- send a hard copy to all members with a notification that an online form is available for completion on the Website.

Proxies: return of

The following points are relevant:

- the proxy form must state clearly the methods that may be used to return it and the 'address' for each method;
- it should be made clear that appointments can only be made on the company's form so that a member cannot merely send an e-mail to the company stating, for example, that he wishes to appoint the chairman as his proxy;
- the company could use online forms of proxy that can be completed and submitted electronically.

Proxy form: contents

The ICSA's *Best Practice Guide* recommends that electronic proxy forms contain:

- clear instructions regarding the address to which the proxy form should be returned;
- a warning that electronically lodged proxies will be valid only if lodged at the address that the company has supplied; and
- if applicable, a notice that proxy appointments may, subject to a specified verification procedure, be made by telephone. A telephone option does not have to be made available.

Proxies: evidence of receipt

The ICSA's guide does not recommend that companies establish systems for automatically acknowledging receipt of an electronically communicated proxy. It does, however, recommend that a receipt be provided where a shareholder specifically requests this. There is also a suggestion that in the case of online proxies the member might be able to log on to a secure section of the Website to check that the proxy form has been received and to check its details.

Proxies: security

There is no requirement in the CA 1985 (as amended by the order) for a form of proxy to be signed. The articles need not require a signature either. There are ways of signing electronically the most secure being through encryption technology, and some firms already offering electronic signature services may move into a service specifically for shareholder communication with companies. However, the guidance suggests that each shareholder should be allocated a distinctive personal identifier which can be quoted on faxed or e-mailed proxy forms that could be matched against the share register in order to ascertain any duplication.

Website publication

Consideration has already been given to the problem of securities advertisement and how to prevent it. The ICSA guidance also recommends, in particular, that the auditors be asked at an early stage to give clearance for audited information to be put on the Website including, in particular, the precise form of the auditors' report. The company should also establish systems to ensure that Website information has not been tampered with and to ensure that the home page of the statutory section of the Website indicates the time and date when the contents were last verified. Finally, no price-sensitive information about the company should appear on the Website until it is in the public domain.

GRADED QUESTIONS

Essay mode

1 (*a*) Explain how and in what circumstances a general meeting of a company will be called.

AND

(*b*) Explain what minimum period of notice must be given to call an extraordinary general meeting and whether and how such period may be shortened/lengthened.

AND

(*c*) Explain how many members must be present for a quorum at a general meeting of a company and whether and how the quorum may fall below the required minimum.

(*Glasgow Caledonian University*)

2 (*a*) What members' meetings are held by registered companies?

(*b*) Name and define the different kinds of resolution which may be passed by such companies in general meeting. In the case of each kind of resolution give one example of business for which such a resolution is necessary.

(*The Institute of Company Accountants*)

3 You are required to explain the following issues relating to company meetings.

(*a*) What is an extraordinary resolution and when is such a resolution required under the Companies Act 1985?
(*b*) What is proxy voting? State whether such voting is always possible at company meetings.
(*c*) What is a poll vote and who may demand such a vote?
(*d*) What is special business? Identify two matters which would be included under such business.
(*e*) What is a requisitioned circular? Who may demand it and who bears the cost?

(*The Chartered Institute of Management Accountants*)

4 Maurice, a shareholder of Traders plc, has informed the company secretary that he intends to propose a resolution at the forthcoming annual general meeting that the company should discontinue its business activities in a particular overseas country.

The directors have instructed the secretary not to include the proposed resolution on the agenda for the meeting.

Advise Maurice.

(The Institute of Chartered Accountants in England and Wales)

5 Directors owe their company a duty to exercise their powers only for a 'proper purpose'. Explain what is meant by 'proper purpose' and discuss the nature and scope of this duty. Illustrate your answer with references to decided cases, particularly those dealing with the power to issue shares.

(The Association of Chartered Certified Accountants)

6 XY Bank plc is the subject of a takeover bid by Able Securities plc. In order to frustrate the takeover bid, the board of directors take the following action:

(*a*) they allot one million unissued shares to Lionel who will vote against the takeover bid by Able Securities plc. Lionel does not have enough money to pay for the shares but secures a loan from XY Bank plc to cover the payment;
(*b*) they make a payment of £1 million to Computer Security Services Ltd as an advance payment on a contract that has been negotiated between the two companies. Computer Security Services Ltd is informed by the directors that it should buy shares in XY Bank plc if it wants to make a quick profit and keep the contract. Computer Security Services Ltd buy £1 million of shares in XY Bank plc;
(*c*) they decide that XY Bank plc should buy its own shares as a good investment and £10 million of shares are purchased.

The shares rise in value and all purchasing parties make a profit. The takeover bid is frustrated.

Advise the directors as to the legality of their actions and of any proceedings that could be brought against them or the company.

(University of Central Lancashire)

Objective mode

Four alternative answers are given. Select ONE only. Circle the answer which you consider to be correct. Check your answers by referring back to the information given in the chapter and against the answers at the back of the book.

1 In what circumstance may the members of a company who have requisitioned an EGM call the meeting themselves?

A If the directors do not call a meeting to be held within 21 days of the deposit of the requisition.
B If the directors do not within 21 days from the date of the deposit of the requisition call a meeting for a date not more than 28 days after the notice calling the meeting.
C If the directors take action to call a meeting within 21 days but the date of the meeting is set at a date more than three months from the date of the deposit of the requisition.
D If the directors fail to call a meeting to take place within 28 days of the date of the deposit of the requisition.

2 Felicity is a member of Wash plc. She has appointed Thomas as her proxy for the next AGM. Thomas will be able:

A to vote on a show of hands and speak at the meeting.
B to vote on a show of hands but not speak at the meeting.
C to vote but only on a poll and speak at the meeting.
D to vote only on a poll but not speak at the meeting.

3 Cunnane Ltd was incorporated on 1 February 2004. What is the latest date on which it must hold its first AGM?

A 31 July 2005.
B 31 December 2005.
C 31 March 2006.
D 31 December 2006.

4 Thames Ltd wishes to pass a special resolution of the members to change the articles. What length of notice is required, and how many of the company's members present and voting in person or by proxy are needed to pass the resolution?

A 21 days' notice and over 50 per cent.
B 28 days' notice and over 50 per cent.
C 21 days' notice and 75 per cent.
D 28 days' notice and 75 per cent.

5 What is the minimum period of notice which must be given to the members of a limited company who are entitled to be present and vote in person or by proxy at an EGM to pass an ordinary resolution?

A 28 days.
B 21 days.
C 14 days.
D 7 days.

6 What quorum is required for a general meeting of a multi-member registered company?

A Two persons who are either members or proxies for members.
B Three persons who are members or proxies for members.
C Two persons who are members.
D Three persons who are members.

Answers to questions set in objective mode appear on p 577.

20

DEBENTURES AND CHARGES

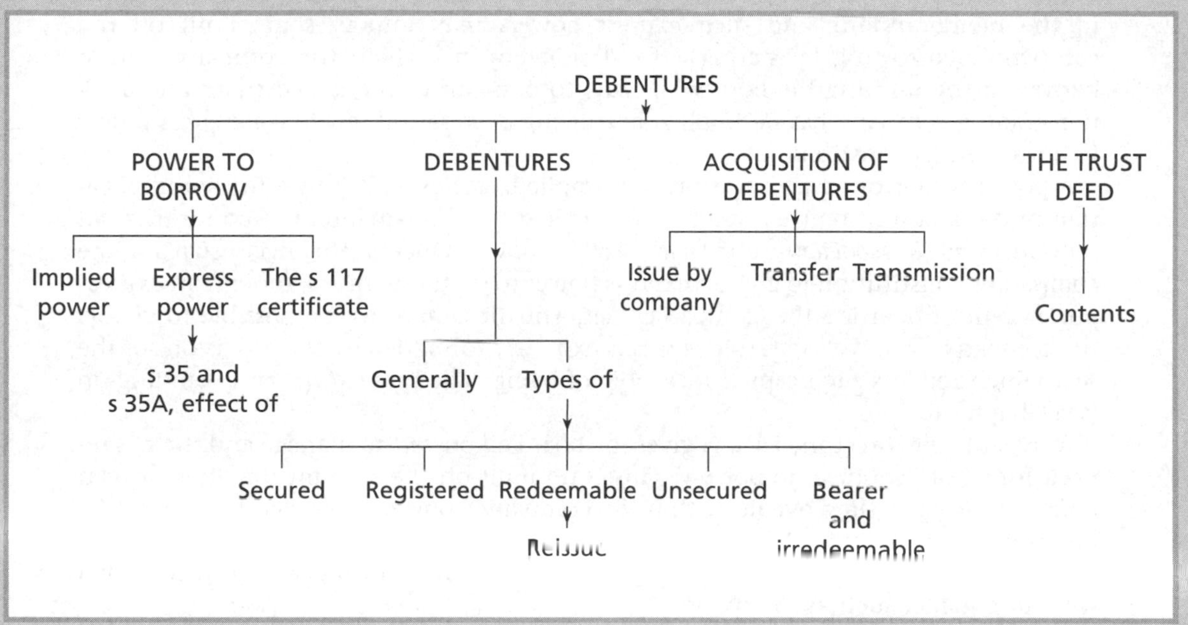

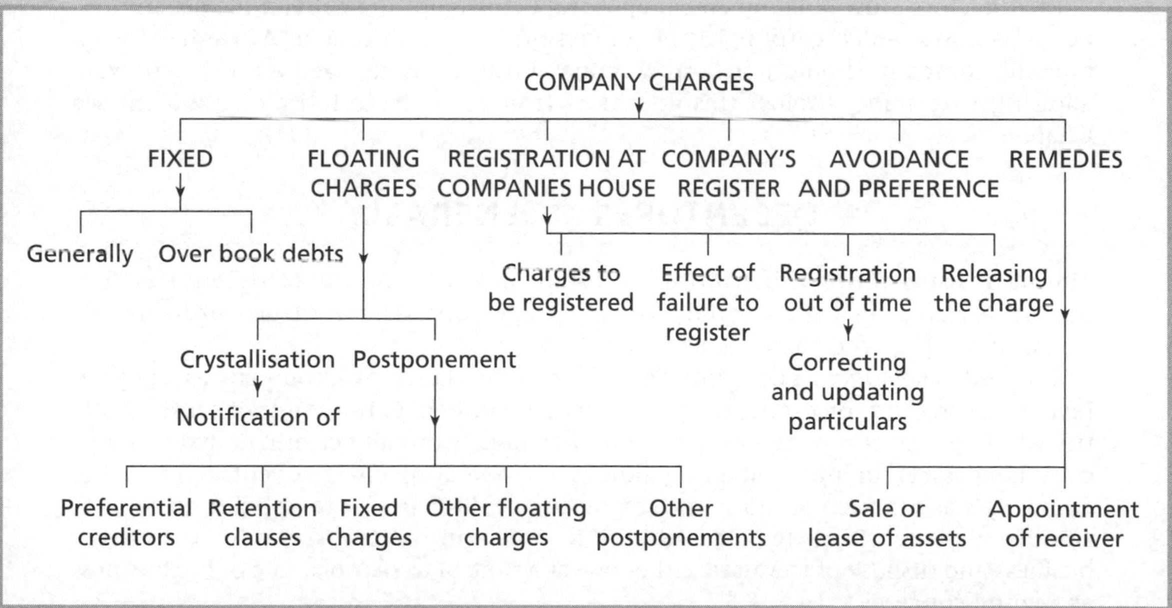

In this chapter we shall be concerned with a company's loan capital and the means of securing loans by charging the company's assets.

POWER TO BORROW

A trading company has implied power to borrow (*General Auction Estate and Monetary Co* v *Smith* [1891] 3 Ch 432). Nevertheless, it is usual for an express power to be given in the memorandum, and such express powers may impose some limit on the company's borrowing by stating a fixed sum beyond which the company cannot borrow, or by limiting the borrowing, say, to one-half of the issued share capital. A non-trading company has no implied borrowing powers and must take express power to borrow in its constitution.

A power to borrow, whether express or implied, carries with it by a further implication of law a power to give a security for the loan and to pay interest upon it (*General Auction Estate & Monetary Co* v *Smith*, 1891, above). Once again, it is usual for the company's constitution to give an express power to do these things, though an express power cannot override the Companies Act. Thus it would not be possible to charge the company's reserve capital since this is expressly forbidden by the provisions of the Act, which renders such capital incapable of being called up except on a winding-up (see Chapter 6).

As regards the directors, *Table A* gives the board all powers to manage and there is no need for a *specific* power to borrow. This is no limit on the amount the directors can borrow so long as they remain within the company's power. However, in view of the provisions of s 35 and s 35A (see Chapter 3), borrowing by the directors beyond the provisions of the company's constitution is much less likely to affect a contract of loan with an outsider such as a bank.

The directors must obtain member approval before allotting convertible debentures, i.e. debentures which carry rights of conversion into share capital. As we have seen, a public company should not borrow money until it has received a s 117 certificate allowing it to trade, though this does not affect the enforceability of the loan (see Chapter 1).

DEBENTURES – GENERALLY

The most usual form of borrowing by companies is by means of debentures. The debenture also gives a charge on the company's property. The word 'debenture' has its origin in a Latin word for 'owing'.

As regards a definition, a debenture is a document executed by a company as a deed in favour of a creditor, providing the creditor with security over the whole or substantially the whole of the company's assets and undertaking, normally creating a fixed charge over fixed assets such as land and buildings and a floating charge over the rest of the company's assets such as stock and giving the creditor power to appoint an administrative receiver with extensive authority to collect in the assets, run the company's business and dispose of the assets either one at a time or as part of a sale of the business as a going concern.

Debenture holders are creditors (but see p 445 for the position under a trust deed) and not members of the company, and are entitled to interest on their debentures whether the company earns profits or not. Holders are provided with a safe if limited income, and debentures appeal to a cautious investor.

Debentures may also be *convertible* which means that they are issued with an option, tenable for a certain period of time, to exchange them for shares in the company. Debentures can be issued at a discount without restriction, but the issue of convertible debentures must not be allowed to operate as a device to issue shares at a discount as would be the case if a debenture for £100, issued at £90, were later to be exchanged for 100 shares of nominal value of £1 each. This would in effect be an issue of shares at a discount which is forbidden by the Act.

TYPES OF DEBENTURES

Debentures may be issued in a series, e.g. where there is a public offer, or alternatively they may be issued singly, e.g. to secure a bank loan or overdraft. They may also be issued in respect of either an existing debt or a fresh loan.

In the case of a public offer the admission of debentures to listing must comply with Part VI of the Financial Services and Markets Act 2000 while a public offer of unlisted debentures must be carried out under the Public Offers of Securities Regulations 1995. These matters are considered in Chapter 9.

Where debentures are issued in a series, it is usual to provide expressly that they are to rank *pari passu*, i.e. equally. This is essential because loans rank for priority according to the time they are made, and if such an express provision were not made, the debentures in the series would rank for priority of payment and security according to the date of issue, and if all were issued on the same day, they would rank in numerical order.

Gartside *v* Silkstone and Dodworth Coal and Iron Co Ltd (1882) 21 Ch D 762

The company issued 150 debentures of £100 each on the same day. They were issued in two lots, one lot being numbered 501–600 and the second lot 601–650. Each of the debentures contained a provision that it was to rank *pari passu* with the others, but the first group referred to the amount of £10,000 and the second to £5,000, this being the only difference in the respective provisions. Nevertheless, this suggested that they were independent issues. The company was in liquidation and the question of priority arose. When two deeds are executed on the same day, the court must inquire which of them was executed first, but if there is anything in the deeds to show such an intention, they may take effect *pari passu*. *Held* – by the High Court – the company could, therefore, choose to give security in the form of a second floating charge of the kind outlined, and this was valid and did rank equally with the first charge because they were expressed to be *pari passu*.

Where debentures rank *pari passu*, there can be no action at law brought by an individual debenture holder merely in respect of his own rights, and any such action brought by him is deemed to be a representative action on behalf of all the debenture holders of the series.

Debenture stock may be issued so long as the stock is fully paid, and this affects transfer. A debenture must be transferred as a whole unit whereas debenture stock can be transferred in part, though the articles or the terms of issue usually fix a minimum amount which can be transferred, e.g. £1.

Debentures are usually *secured, registered* and *redeemable,* though they may be unsecured, unregistered (i.e. bearer debentures) and irredeemable.

Secured debentures

These are normally secured by a charge on the company's assets, either by a provision to that effect in the debenture itself, or by the terms of the trust deed drawn up in connection with the issue. Sometimes a provision appears in both documents.

Registered debentures

These are recorded in the register of debenture holders. Such debentures are transferable in accordance with the provisions of the terms of issue, but transfer is usually effected by an instrument in writing in a way similar to that of shares. The transferee of a debenture takes it subject to equities, and this includes claims which the company has against the transferor. However, the company's claims are normally excluded by the terms of issue of the debentures, these terms usually stating that the money secured by the debentures will be paid without regard to any equities between the company and previous holders.

Re Goy & Co Ltd, Farmer *v* Goy & Co Ltd [1900] 2 Ch 149

In a voluntary winding-up of the company W H Doggett had been appointed liquidator and also receiver. At this point, Chandler, a former director, transferred £600 of debentures to G D Robey by way of security for a loan. The conditions of the debentures provided that on complying with certain formalities, the principal and interest secured by the debentures would be paid without regard to any equities between the company and the original or intermediate holder. After Robey had taken the transfer, it was discovered that Chandler had been guilty of misfeasance and he was ordered by the court to pay £300 to the liquidator. Robey, who had no notice of this cross-claim, sent his transfer to the liquidator, for registration. The liquidator declined to register it, and claimed the right to deduct the £300 owed by Chandler. *Held* – by the High Court – the right to transfer and have the transfer registered was not affected by the winding-up or by the court order against Chandler, and Robey was entitled to have the debentures registered without deduction.

It should also be noted that when a company sets up a register of debenture holders, the 1985 Act provisions relating to no notice of trust do not apply to it, and the company would be bound by any notice of trust or other equity over the debentures. It is, therefore, usual to provide in the terms of issue that the company shall not be bound to recognise anyone other than the registered holder.

Redeemable debentures

Debentures are usually redeemable, and the company may provide a fund for their redemption. The annual amount so provided must be charged whether profits are made or not, though in some cases the terms of issue may stipulate that the fund shall be provided only out of profits, if made.

Debentures may be redeemed in the following ways:

(*a*) *By drawings by lot*, either at the company's option or at fixed intervals.
(*b*) *By the company buying them in the market*, and if the debentures are bought in the market at a discount, the consequent profit to the company is a realised profit available for dividend unless the articles otherwise provide.
(*c*) *By the company redeeming them either out of a fund or possibly by a fresh issue of debentures*. A fresh issue is useful to the company where rates of interest have fallen, because the old debentures can be redeemed and the money reborrowed by the fresh issue at lower rates of interest. Where redemption is by a fresh issue, it is usual to allow the existing debenture holders to exchange the old debentures for the new ones if they so wish.

The company will redeem at a fixed future date, but usually has an option to redeem on or after a given earlier date, and this allows the company to choose the most convenient time for redemption.

Redemption may be at the issue price or at a higher price, and debentures may be issued at (say) 80 and redeemed at 100, or issued at 100 and redeemed at 110, thus giving the debenture holders a capital gain in addition to the interest payments made.

Reissue

The 1985 Act allows the company to reissue debentures which it has redeemed unless the company has resolved that the debentures shall not be reissued, or unless there are provisions in the articles or terms of issue of the original debentures that they shall not be reissued. A person to whom debentures are reissued has the same priorities as had the original debenture holder.

The articles and/or the trust deed under which the debentures are issued invariably forbid reissue, and if there was a reissue in that situation the purchasers of the reissued debentures would be deferred to other persons holding debentures at that time.

Where a company has issued debentures to secure advances made from time to time on a current account such as a bank overdraft, the debenture shall not be considered redeemed by reason only of the account ceasing to be at a certain point in debit so long as the debentures are still deposited with the person making the advances. They are a valid security for fresh advances.

Unsecured debentures

Such a debenture is no more than an unsecured promise by the company to repay the loan. The holder can, of course, sue the company on that promise, but is only an ordinary creditor in a winding-up, although, since he is a creditor, he can petition the court for a winding-up.

Bearer debentures

These are negotiable instruments and are transferable free from equities by mere delivery and it is not necessary to give the company notice of transfer.

Interest is paid by means of coupons attached to the debenture, these coupons being in effect an instruction to the company's banker to pay the bearer of the coupon a stated sum on presentment to the bank after a certain date. The company can communicate with the holders of bearer debentures only by advertisement, and it is often provided that the holders of such debentures may exchange them for registered debentures.

Irredeemable debentures

A debenture which is issued with no fixed date of redemption is an irredeemable debenture, though such debentures are redeemable on a winding-up, and the liquidator is empowered to discharge them. In addition, irredeemable debentures always empower the debenture holders to enforce their security should the company, for example, fail to pay interest on the loan and such enforcement will result in the payment of the debenture debt. The 1985 Act provides that such debentures may be issued, and this provision is necessary because otherwise the general rule of equity, that redemption of a mortgage cannot be postponed for too long a time, would apply. The result is that a company can create long mortgages over its land and other property by means of debentures, whether irredeemable or for a long contractual period prior to redemption.

Knightsbridge Estates Trust Ltd *v* Byrne [1940] AC 613

The claimants owned a large freehold estate close to Knightsbridge. This estate was mortgaged to a Friendly Society for a sum of money which, together with interest, was to be repaid over a period of 40 years in 80 half-yearly instalments. The company wished to redeem the mortgage before the expiration of the term, because it was possible for it to borrow elsewhere at a lower rate of interest. *Held* – by the House of Lords – the company was not entitled to redeem the mortgage before the end of the 40 years because the effect of what is now the Companies Act 1985 was to remove the application of the equitable doctrine of no postponement of the right of redemption from mortgages given by companies. Therefore, Knightsbridge was not entitled to redeem the mortgage except by the half-yearly instalments as agreed.

A debenture with no fixed date for redemption, but which gives the company the right to repay it at its option, is properly called a *perpetual* and not an irredeemable debenture.

ACQUISITION OF DEBENTURES

Debentures may be acquired either from the company itself or by transfer or transmission.

Issue by the company

A company may issue debentures either individually or in a series. The provisions of the 1985 Act forbidding the allotment of shares at a discount do not apply to debentures, and accordingly they may be allotted at par, at a discount, or at a premium, unless this is forbidden by the company's articles. However, if debentures are issued at a discount together with a right to exchange them for shares at par value, the debentures are good but the right to exchange is void (*Mosely* v *Koffyfontein Mines Ltd* [1904] 2 Ch 108). The share premium provisions do not apply to an issue of debentures and so if they are issued at a premium there is no need to open the equivalent of a share premium account.

If a person agrees to take a debenture from the company in return for a loan, the contract may be enforced by both the lender and the company by *specific performance*. The 1985 Act gives this right because, in the absence of such statutory provision, equity would not specifically enforce a loan.

A private company cannot offer securities including debentures to the public.

The company must have certificates ready within two months after allotment or transfer, unless the terms of issue otherwise provide. (But note the position on transfer through the Stock Exchange system – see Chapter 11.)

Transfer

Registered debentures are transferable in accordance with the method laid down in the terms of issue, usually a stock transfer form as for shares. The company cannot refuse to register a properly stamped transfer, provided the terms of issue allow transfers and contain no restrictions, but a proper instrument of transfer must be produced to the company except, e.g., in cases of transmission. Where the company refuses to register a transfer, it must send a notice to this effect to the transferee within two months of the transfer being lodged.

Certification by the company of an instrument of transfer has the same effect in the case of debentures as it has in the case of shares, i.e. it is a representation that documents have been produced to the company which show a prima facie title in the transferors.

In the case of bearer debentures, transfer is by mere delivery and the company is not involved.

Transmission

As in the case of shares, debentures pass by operation of law (*a*) to the holder's personal representatives on *death*, and (*b*) to the holder's trustee on *bankruptcy*, and the rights of such persons are similar to their rights when shares pass by operation of law (see Chapter 11).

THE TRUST DEED

When debentures are offered for public subscription, the company enters into a trust deed with trustees, being a trust corporation such as an insurance company. The charge securing the debentures is made in favour of the trustees who hold it on trust for the debenture stock holders. The trustees are usually appointed and paid by the company to act on behalf of the debenture stock holders.

Debenture stock holders, unlike debenture holders, are not creditors of the company. Thus in *Re Dunderland Iron Ore Co Ltd* [1909] 1 Ch 446 it was held that the holder of debenture stock secured by a trust deed could not present a petition to wind up the company since he was not a creditor. The trustees are the creditors for the whole debenture debt, and the stock holder is an equitable beneficiary of the trust on which they hold that debt. Consequently, his remedies are against the trustees, but by suing them, on behalf of himself and the other debenture holders, to compel them to exercise their remedies against the company, he can indirectly enforce the same remedies against the company as the holder of a single debenture can enforce directly.

The creation of a trust deed has the following advantages:

(*a*) *It enables a legal or equitable mortgage on specific assets of the company to be created.* The deeds of property can be held by the trustees, and where there is a legal mortgage the legal estate can be vested in them. It could not be vested in hundreds or possibly thousands of debenture holders because, since the property legislation of 1925, the legal estate in land cannot be vested in more than four persons.

(*b*) *There is also the matter of priorities.* A mortgage, in general terms, ranks in the order of its creation, so without a trust deed, in an issue to the public, the holder of the first certificate to be issued would rank in front of the second and so on. Holder number one would be entitled to payment from the company's assets *in full* before the second certificate holder got anything. Certificate holder, say, 1,000 might get nothing if the company's assets were insufficient. Under the trust deed the trustees have the charge and can, e.g., sell the company's assets and distribute the proceeds equally so that all the stockholders get the same amount even if it is not a payment in full. Distribution is *pari passu*, which is a term commonly used of this procedure.

(*c*) *The interests of the debenture holders are better safeguarded* by the employment of a professional trust corporation, or by a small number of expert trustees, than they would be if left to the debenture holders themselves. The latter are often widely dispersed and often lack the knowledge required to safeguard their interests properly.

Trustees usually have the power to call meetings of the debenture holders to inform them of matters of particular concern to them.

(*d*) *The trust deed usually gives the trustees power to sell the property charged* without the aid of the court, and to appoint an administrative receiver should the company default, for example, in the payment of interest or repayment of the principal sums borrowed.

(*e*) *The trust deed usually gives the trustees power to see that the security is properly maintained and repaired and insured.*

Where debentures are issued under a trust deed, the debentures themselves refer to the deed and thereby incorporate its terms.

Contents of the trust deed

The main clauses of a trust deed are as follows:

(*a*) *The nature of the security*. Details of the assets charged are given, and it sets out the powers of the trustees to deal with them on default by the company and on a winding-up.

(*b*) *The nature of the charge*. The deed will state whether the charge is a fixed or a floating charge. Usually there is a combination of both, i.e. a fixed charge on certain of the company's assets and a floating charge on the rest. There will also be a provision relating to the company's power to create other charges ranking equally with, or in priority to, the present charge.

(*c*) *The kind of debentures to be issued*. This clause will state whether the debentures are to be registered or bearer, or whether debenture stock is to be issued; and if stock, the minimum amount which can be transferred.

(*d*) *The method of redemption*. The clause will state whether there is to be an ordinary redemption by the company, or whether redemption is to be made by drawings or in the market, and when the redemption is to take place. This clause will also give details of any fund which the company proposes to set up to provide for the redemption of the debentures.

A copy of any trust deed for securing any issue of debentures must be forwarded to every holder of any such debentures on payment of a fee.

The 1985 Act prevents a trust deed from exempting the trustees from liability for breach of trust on grounds of negligence. It can, however, permit subsequent release from such liability by a majority of not less than three-quarters in value of the debenture holders present and voting at a meeting summoned for the purpose.

COMPANY CHARGES

Before looking at the law relating to company charges perhaps a brief look at attempts at reform should be made. There have been a number of consultation documents from the government and the Law Commission has looked at reform. However, the only attempt at statutory reform was the Companies Act 1989 which inserted sections into the Companies Act 1985. Previous editions of this text have included the unimplemented provisions of the 1989 Act. However, they do not appear in this edition because it is now obvious that although these laws remain on the statute book they will never be implemented so that a knowledge of them is of no value to those who seek to become involved in the corporate sector.

Debentures may be secured by a fixed or by a floating charge, or by a combination of both types of charge. The expression 'mortgage debenture' normally denotes a debenture secured by a fixed charge.

Fixed (or specific) charge

Such a charge usually takes the form of a legal mortgage over specified assets of the company, e.g. its land and buildings and fixed plant. The mortgage is usually created by a charge by deed expressed to be by way of legal mortgage under s 85(1) of the Law of Property Act 1925. The major disadvantage from the company's point of view is that it cannot dispose of the asset or assets subject to the charge without the consent of the debenture holder. However, there is a major advantage for the directors in a fixed charge because they will almost always have personally guaranteed the company's overdraft, and in an insolvency it is important to them that the bank gets as much as possible from the debenture securing the overdraft so that their liability is extinguished or reduced. In this connection it is worth noting that a fixed charge is not postponed to preferential creditors and other creditors as is a floating charge, and the bank will get more from the security on realisation. This will not apply if the fixed charge is, by agreement between lenders, to rank behind a floating charge, in which case the second ranking fixed charge is subject to the floating charge and ranks after it *and the claims of the preferential debts, e.g. wages and salaries, upon it* (see *Re Portbase (Clothing) Ltd, Mond* v *Taylor* [1993] 3 All ER 829).

Where the company has no land, buildings or fixed plant, a bank can be asked to take a fixed charge over book debts.

The words used by the parties are not conclusive. If the court finds on the facts that the charge is a floating charge, it will not be persuaded that the charge is a fixed charge merely because the parties have said that it is (*Re ASRS Establishment Ltd* [1999] *The Times*, 17 November).

Floating charge

This is a charge which is not attached to any particular asset(s) identified when the charge is made. Instead it attaches to the company's assets as they then are, if and when the charge crystallises. The company is in the meantime free to dispose of its assets, and any new assets which the company may acquire are available to the debenture holder should the charge crystallise. Because such a charge does not fix at the time of its creation upon any particular asset it is equitable by nature, and this is relevant when considering the question of priority of charges when more than one has been created over the assets of the company.

Fixed charges over book debts

The advantage to the directors, and to the bank as debenture holder, of such a charge has already been considered. However, since a charge over book debts is over after-acquired property, the legal position was not absolutely settled, though it had been held in England that such a charge was valid (see *Siebe Gorman & Co Ltd* v *Barclays Bank Ltd* [1979] 2 Lloyd's Rep 142), and this decision was affirmed by the Irish Supreme Court in *Re Keenan Bros Ltd* [1985] 1 RLM 641, and again by the English Court of Appeal in *Re New Bullas Trading Ltd* [1994] 1 BCLC 485.

There are procedures to be set up by the bank in order to safeguard its position as a fixed charge holder but these are not considered here because they are a matter for the bank's legal advisers. Those advising the company can only suggest the fixed charge and point out to the directors its advantage to them in terms of their guarantees to the bank.

It is, however, of interest to note that the High Court has held that the terms of a debenture which contained provisions for a lending bank to have control of the borrowing company's book debts and other debts over which it had taken a specific charge, were essential to protect the validity of such a charge. Although the terms restricted the company's commercial use of its book and other debts, they were not anti-competitive, nor contrary to Arts 81 and 82 of the Treaty of Rome *(Oakdale (Richmond) Ltd* v *National Westminster Bank plc* [1997] 1 BCLC 63).

A major difficulty arose in connection with fixed charges over book debts following the ruling of the Privy Council in *Agnew* v *Inland Revenue* [2001] All ER (D) 21 (the *Brumark* case).

This ruling came out of an appeal from New Zealand and represented the usual sort of challenge to the fixed charge. If it is a fixed charge it will as we have noted rank before the preferential creditors. The Inland Revenue is now no longer a preferential creditor but ranks with the unsecured trade creditors but the Revenue often tried to attack the fixed charge over book debts hoping that it would be regarded as a floating charge which is postponed to preferential creditors.

The difficulty with *Brumark* was that the Privy Council ruled that the lender must have systems in place to exercise control over the book debts both collected and uncollected. In *Brumark* the charge left the company free to collect and use the book debts in the ordinary course of its business. This in the view of the Privy Council made the charge floating not fixed by reason of the lender's lack of sufficient control.

The *Brumark* decision was of course only persuasive as are decisions of the Privy Council but it added a new strand worrying to business because businessmen and women had always understood that if a debenture took a fixed charge over book debts under what was known as the *Siebe Gorman* formula the court would treat it as a fixed charge. The *Siebe Gorman* charge merely:

- prohibits the borrower from disposing (as by sale) of its book debts before collection; and
- requires the proceeds of the book debts to be paid into an account with the lending bank. **It does not prevent use of the proceeds by the company in its business.**

In the latest case in the saga, *In re Spectrum Plus Ltd (in liquidation)* [2004] NLJR 890, the Court of Appeal refused to follow *Brumark* and restored the *Siebe Gorman* formula to validity. Why? Well, as the Master of the Rolls pointed out, for 25 years parties have used the *Siebe Gorman* form of debenture on the understanding that its meaning and effect were those held by the judge in the High Court in that case, i.e. that a fixed charge was created. That form of debenture had therefore acquired *by customary usage* the meaning and effect attributed to it as creating a fixed charge. The ruling put the bank as lender before the preferential creditors. We have yet to hear from the House of Lords on the matter.

CRYSTALLISATION OF FLOATING CHARGES

A floating charge crystallises:

(*a*) In the circumstances specified in the debenture. This means that crystallisation can take place by agreement between the parties and the particular debenture must be looked at. However, most usually where the loan is repayable on demand, as in the case of an overdraft, the charge will crystallise automatically when the bank calls in the overdraft which the company cannot pay. The bank may then appoint an administrative receiver. However, the High Court has decided that where a bank has lent a company money that is repayable on demand with a security over the company's assets, the timing of the bank's appointment of an administrative receiver is governed, where the company has the means to repay by the time it needs to set the mechanics of repayment in motion. If the company has made it clear that it cannot pay, the bank may make the appointment straightaway as could any other secured creditor (see *Sheppard and Cooper Ltd* v *TSB Bank plc* [1996] 2 All ER 654). Other circumstances specified include failure of the company to pay interest or the principal sum when due as agreed. These may also result in automatic crystallisation. In some cases the charge may be stipulated to crystallise when the company exceeds a specified borrowing limit.

(*b*) Automatic crystallisation occurs on the appointment of a receiver under a fixed charge or an administrative receiver under a fixed/floating charge, or if the company commences to wind up and on cessation of its business (*Re Woodroffes* (*Musical Instruments*) [1985] 2 All ER 908).

Once a floating charge crystallises, the assets subject to the charge pass into the eventual control of the receiver and pass out of the control of the company immediately. Any disposition of those assets by the company after the charge crystallises means that the purchaser from the company takes the assets subject to the charge, i.e. the right of the debenture holder to proceed against them to satisfy the debt.

Note. The appointment of administrative receivers is now much restricted (see page 535).

POSTPONEMENT OF FLOATING CHARGES

A person who lends money on the security of a fixed charge over the company's property is always entitled to repayment of his loan from the proceeds of sale of the mortgaged property before any other creditor, except a creditor with a prior fixed charge. A person who takes a floating charge is not so secure. There are cases in which his receiver will have to yield priority to other classes of creditors. The detailed law in this area is not considered because it is relevant only in an insolvency and is therefore more within the specialist province of the insolvency practitioner. It is not likely to be examined in detail in a general paper on company law. However, an outline of the position is given below.

Preferential creditors

Once a floating charge has crystallised the owner of the charge, e.g. the bank, is entitled to repayment of the loan out of the assets to which the charge has attached before the company's unsecured creditors. However, there is one statutory exception to this, which is that when a floating charge crystallises the claims which would be preferential in a winding-up rank in front of the debenture holder in respect of realisation of assets under the floating charge. The debenture debt is postponed only to preferential payments accrued at the date of the appointment of an administrator and not to those which accrue subsequently. Schedule 6 of the Insolvency Act 1986, as amended by the Enterprise Act 2002 applies, and there are no provisions for payment of interest on these debts until payment. Schedule 6 should be referred to if necessary for further detail, but the main preferential debts are as follows:

(*a*) wages or salaries of employees due within four months before the relevant date, up to a maximum of £800 for each employee. The fees of non-executive directors are not preferential, though executive directors will normally be regarded as employees (see further Chapter 15) to the extent of the remuneration paid to them in respect of their duties as executives, except where they are also controlling shareholders (see e.g. *Buchan* v *Secretary of State for Employment* (1997) 565 IRLB 2). A practice has developed of regarding the £800 as a gross sum, thus reducing the amount payable to the relevant preferential creditor. The legislation does not specify net or gross;

(*b*) all accrued holiday remuneration of employees;

(*c*) unpaid pension contributions for a maximum of four months before the relevant date.

It should be noted that if a bank has provided funds to pay wages and salaries *before* the administration that debt becomes preferential under the rule of subrogation. The justification for the subrogation principle which is contained in Sch 6, para 11 to the 1986 Act is that the protection it offers to banks and other lenders may encourage them to advance further money for the payment of wages at a critical time in the debtor company's affairs so as to enable it to continue trading and possibly avoid insolvency leading to the appointment of an administrator or liquidator.

The main advantage of being a secured or preferential creditor in an administration (administrative receiverships being largely abolished under Enterprise Act 2002 amendments to the Insolvency Act 1986) is that the administrator's proposals for achieving the purposes of the administration must preserve the rights of the preferential creditors to prior payment of their debts. The priority of secured creditors such as floating chargeholders in terms of payment must also be preserved though in this case payment is subject to a ring-fenced fund for payment of unsecured creditors of a percentage that shall not be distributed to floating chargeholders. These matters are further considered in the chapters on corporate insolvency.

Protection of employees

Under ss 167–170 of the Employment Rights Act 1996 (as amended), an employee who loses his job when his employer becomes insolvent can claim through the National Insurance Fund certain payments which are owed to him rather than relying on the preferential payments procedure. The administrative receiver will normally calculate what is due and obtain authorisation through the Department of Trade and Industry. In so far as any part of this payment is preferential, the rights and remedies of the employee concerned are transferred to the Department of Trade and Industry, which becomes preferential in respect of them. Major debts covered are:

(*a*) arrears of pay for a period not exceeding eight weeks up to a maximum of £270 per week;

(*b*) pay in respect of holidays taken and accrued holiday pay up to £270 per week up to a limit of six weeks in the last 12 months of employment;

(*c*) payments in lieu of notice at a rate not exceeding £270 per week up to the statutory minimum entitlement of a particular employee under the Employment Rights Act 1996;

(*d*) any payment outstanding in regard to an award by an employment tribunal of compensation for unfair dismissal, limited to the amount of the basic award;

(*e*) reimbursement of the whole or part of any fee or premium paid by an apprentice or articled clerk;

(*f*) certain unpaid contributions to an occupational or a personal pension scheme. The amount of £270 refers throughout to the employee's gross wage.

There is a provision in s 167 of the Employment Rights Act 1996 for the Department of Trade and Industry to make payments relating to redundancy direct to the employee where the employer is insolvent. The Department will normally claim against the employer, but such a claim is unsecured and does not concern the receiver in terms of preferential payments. There is no qualifying period of employment for claimants on the National Insurance Fund, though, of course, certain periods of employment will have been necessary before an award for unfair dismissal and redundancy would be made.

The Employment Appeal Tribunal has decided that in the above situation the statutory insolvency provisions apply including the right to set-off. Thus if the employee owes money to the employer, this must be set off against the payment and only the balance paid to the employee (see *Secretary of State for Employment* v *Wilson* (1996) 550 IRLB 5 – decided when the Employment Secretary was responsible for these payments).

Employees working outside the UK: who pays?

Where within the EU an employee works in the UK for an Irish company which is wound up in Ireland, the DTI is responsible for the insolvency payments described above (see *Everson* v *Secretary of State for Trade and Industry* [2000] All ER (EC) 29). The case is to the effect that the country in which the claimant works is the payee. This may depend, however, on the number of employees employed in the country alleged to be liable to pay. Where there is only an insignificant number of employees, the country in which the employing company is being wound up may be liable instead (see the *Danmarks/Bosbaek Case* [1998] All ER (EC) 112 where only one employee was involved). In *Everson* the Irish company had a registered branch at Avonmouth employing over 200 people. The above rulings are from the European Court, UK law being silent on the matter.

Retention of title clauses

These clauses have as their purpose the retention of the seller's ownership in goods supplied until the buyer has paid for them, even though the buyer is given possession of the goods and may resell them or use them in the manufacture of other goods which will be resold. These clauses may also extend to the proceeds of sale.

If the clause is valid and if the purchasing company goes into an administrative receivership (where this is still possible) or liquidation, then the seller may try to recover the goods which the purchasing company still has in stock, and sometimes even the proceeds of resale by the purchasing company, on the basis that the purchaser is a mere *bailee* of the goods and not the owner, the seller being the owner and bailor.

In an administration a valid retention clause is subject to a stay on creditors' remedies under Insolvency Act 1986 Sch B1 so the creditors' rights under the clause cannot generally be enforced and the administrator may dispose of the retained property free of the proprietory interest of creditors with the consent of the court.

The Romalpa *case*

The decision in *Aluminium Industrie Vaassen BV* v *Romalpa Aluminium* [1976] 2 All ER 552 was the first UK decision to alert the accountancy and legal professions to the problems which these clauses might cause in insolvency practice. The claimants in that case were successful in recovering aluminium foil supplied under a retention clause, together with the proceeds of resale of the foil which the clause also covered.

It should, however, be noted that any interest which the seller may claim in the proceeds of resale will, in view of more recent case law, be regarded by the courts as a charge on book debts which will be void under s 395 if not registered at Companies House. The relevant authorities are *Modelboard Ltd* v *Outer Box Ltd (in liquidation)* [1993] BCLC 623 and *Compaq Computers Ltd* v *Abercorn Group Ltd (t/a Osiris)* [1993] BCLC 603.

It does not matter what the seller's retention clause says, e.g. proceeds to be held 'on trust', the buyer acts as 'agent' of the seller, and so on. The courts have in recent times looked beyond the language to the reality and regarded the relationship as that of debtor (buyer) and creditor (seller), which is not an equitable fiduciary relationship, so that the equitable remedy of tracing is not available and recovery of the proceeds of sale is not possible without the creation and registration of a charge over what are, in effect, book debts. Those in equitable relationships, such as trustee and beneficiary, can trace trust property without the need for registration.

The recovery of the proceeds in *Romalpa* has been looked on in more recent times as not significant since the receiver in that case conceded the proceeds and did not contest their recovery, so the court did not have to rule on the matter.

Subsequent cases

Since the decision in the *Romalpa* case the courts have, broadly speaking, had to deal with two main types of actions, as follows:

(i) Those cases where the supplier has been solely concerned to implement that part of his retention clause to retain title over goods supplied under a contract of sale where the goods have not been changed or added to in a process of manufacture, as was the situation in *Romalpa*. These actions will probably succeed and insolvency practitioners will normally release the stock to the supplier provided the goods can be identified with invoices unpaid. Otherwise the insolvency practitioner faces an action in conversion by the supplier. However, should the insolvency practitioner believe that either the clause has not been properly communicated and is therefore not part of the contract of sale (see below), or that the goods have not been properly identified, he cannot be prevented from selling them as part of the realisation of assets. It is clear from the decision of the House of Lords in *American Cyanamid Co* v *Ethicon* [1975] AC 396 that an application for an injunction to prevent sale will fail because the supplier has an alternative claim for damages in conversion, if his contention that the retention clause is enforceable is correct.

(ii) Those cases in which the supplier is trying to use a retention clause to cover goods supplied to be used in manufacture, as in *Borden (UK) Ltd* v *Scottish Timber Products Ltd* [1979] 3 All ER 961 (seller's resin used in making chip board and mixed with the company's material). In these cases the supplier may well have difficulty in recovering even those goods in stock and not yet used by the purchaser in the manufacturing process, because it is difficult to construe a bailment where the purchaser can use the goods in manufacture. This must give the company some sort of ownership of them. Without the relationship of bailment, there can be no recovery of the goods.

Where the goods have been mixed with the purchaser's goods, or where the purchaser's workforce has added value by skill and effort, the clause will not work unless the retention clause is registered at Companies House as a charge over the purchasing company's assets. Such a charge is in fact registrable under the CA 1985. An example is provided by *Re Peachdart Ltd* [1983] 3 All ER 204, where the seller's leather was converted into handbags by the skill of the purchaser's workforce and the purchaser supplied handles and other decoration. The stock of leather was not recoverable, nor were the finished handbags or work in progress, even though the retention clause purported to extend to finished products and work in progress.

Other points to be borne in mind regarding retention clauses are:

(*a*) the need to ensure that the clause has become part of the contract of sale. It is not enough to include the clause on an invoice, because the contract has already been made by the time the invoice is issued and new terms cannot be introduced unless there have been previous dealings, including retention clauses, which can be incorporated;

(*b*) the need to identify the goods which it is sought to recover. Where goods have been supplied over a period of time it is essential to be able, e.g. by serial numbers on the goods and unpaid invoices, to identify which goods have not been paid for.

Fixed charges

A fixed charge, whether legal or equitable and whenever created, takes priority over the equitable floating charge on the asset(s) concerned. The only exception is where the floating charge expressly prohibits the creation of charges in priority to the floating charge (called a negative pledge clause) and the person taking the fixed charge knew this to be so. At the present time this has to be actual knowledge, because registration of the charge at Companies House gives only constructive notice of the charge but not its particulars (see *Wilson* v *Kelland* [1910] 2 Ch 306). However, s 416 of the CA 1985 (which has not yet been implemented) provides that registration of the charge gives constructive notice also of its contents or particulars. The effect would be that the negative pledge clause would be constructively communicated and *Wilson* overruled.

There may be agreement between lenders that a particular floating charge shall rank in front of a particular fixed charge. Where this is so the first ranking floating charge remains subject to preferential debts and the second ranking fixed charge is subject to the prior ranking floating charge and the calls of the preferential debts on it (*Re Portbase (Clothing) Ltd, Mond* v *Taylor* [1993] 3 All ER 829).

Other floating charges

If a company is to have power to create a second floating charge over its undertaking ranking before the first, the debenture securing the first charge must so provide. Otherwise floating charges rank for priority in the order in which they were created.

In this connection, it is worth noting that in *H & K Medway Ltd, Mackay* v *IRC* [1997] 2 All ER 321 the High Court decided that if a company grants two floating charges over its assets in favour of two different debenture holders and the second ranking debenture holder appoints a receiver first, the preferential creditors of the first ranking debenture holder are entitled to be paid before the first ranking debenture holder even though that debenture holder is not the person appointing the receiver.

Garnishee orders (now called Third Party debt claims for procedural purposes)

A garnishee order nisi may be issued on behalf of a judgment creditor as a method of enforcing judgment. It may attach to debts owed to the judgment debtor by others. Service of a garnishee order nisi operates as an equitable charge on the debt preventing the debt from being paid to anybody except the judgment creditor. However, the judgment debtor's funds in the hands of a third party, e.g. a bank, cannot in law be actually paid over to the judgment creditor until the garnishee order is made absolute. Between order nisi and absolute the judgment debtor may bring evidence to the court as to why the funds should not be paid over to the judgment creditor, which will normally be difficult since the creditor has gone to judgment. If the funds are paid over while the order has not been made absolute, the third party, e.g. a bank, must replace the funds of the judgment debtor even though a debt of the judgment debtor has, in effect, been paid because the bank has no authority to make the payment (see *Crantrave Ltd (in Liquidation)* v *Lloyds Bank plc* [2000] 3 WLR 877, CA where a liquidator recovered a sum of money paid by the company's bankers to the judgment creditor at a time when the relevant garnishee order was not absolute).

Other postponements

Judgment creditors may, in certain circumstances, be able to retain the proceeds of sale of the company's goods taken in execution by bailiffs. Finance companies may be able to recover goods which the company has taken on hire-purchase.

However, in the case of an administration which will be the normal insolvency procedure followed by holders of floating charges now that administrative receivership is restricted to special cases that will be considered in the chapters on corporate insolvency, a moratorium prevents execution by judgment creditors who have not actually taken property and sold it through the bailiff system. A finance company would be prevented by the moratorium from recovering goods on hire-purchase and the administrator can ask the court for an order to sell the goods provided the proceeds are applied to paying the sums payable under the hire-purchase agreement plus any additional sum to make the proceeds up to market value where the sale has been below market value. This is to assist the administrator to rescue the company by selling it as a going concern without having to ask permission of owners of goods such as finance companies to sell them.

As regards landlords who may seek to enforce non-monetary remedies to deal with any liabilities outstanding under the company's lease, para 43(4) of Sch B1 to the Insolvency Act 1986 prevents a landlord or other person to whom rent is payable from exercising any right of forfeiture except with the leave of the court or the consent of the administrator.

VALIDITY OF CHARGES

Consideration will now be given to how a charge may be made invalid by failure to register particulars of it, or where it is a floating charge by avoidance under the Insolvency Act 1986 or because the charge is regarded under the same Act as a preference.

REGISTRATION OF CHARGES

The 1985 Act provides for the registration of certain charges created by companies over their assets. Accordingly, the secured debenture given typically to a bank to secure an overdraft must be registered at Companies House. Sections 395 and 396 apply.

Charges to be registered

These are as follows:

1 A charge on land or any interest therein belonging to the company and wherever situate, other than a charge on rent payable by another in respect of the land.
2 A charge on the company's goods where the company is to retain possession of the goods. If the lender takes possession of the goods, as in a pawn or pledge, or takes a document of title to them so that the borrower cannot dispose of them effectively, the charge need not be registered.
3 Charges on the following intangible movable property of the company:

(*a*) goodwill;
(*b*) intellectual property – this covers any patent, trade mark, service mark, registered design, copyright or design right, or any licence under or in respect of any such right. In the case of a trade mark the charge is ineffective unless the charge is also registered at the Trade Mark Registry under s 25 of the Trade Marks Act 1994. This is just as important as registration at Companies House;
(*c*) book debts, whether originally owing to the company or assigned to it;
(*d*) uncalled share capital of a company or calls made but not paid;
(*e*) charges for securing an issue of debentures;
(*f*) floating charges on the whole or part of the company's property.

It should be noted that (*e*) and (*f*) above are 'sweep-up' provisions, and (*e*) above would cover an investment company whose only assets were shares and debentures of other companies. Such a company would have to register a charge over those assets to secure a debenture even though the securities which are its assets are not included specifically under other headings.

So far as (*f*) above is concerned, this would cover a floating charge which was not part of the issue of a debenture, and so a charge over mixed goods by means of a retention clause would be registrable under this head.

Contractual liens

The High Court has decided that a contractual possessory lien, i.e. the right to retain another's property until he has met a debt due in respect of that property coupled with an eventual right of sale of the relevant property, does not amount to a charge that requires registration under the CA 1985 (*Re Hamlet International plc: Re Jeffrey Rogers (Imports) Ltd* [1998] 95 (16) LSG 24).

Thus A sells goods to B and takes a contractual possessory lien over the goods until B pays for them. There is also a power for A to sell the goods if B fails to pay. B goes into administration as in the *Hamlet* case. The administrator of B claims the goods regarding the lien as a type of floating charge which is void against the administrator because it is unregistered. In this case the lien (which is not a charge) is valid since registration is not required of such an arrangement. A keeps the goods and does not have to deliver them into an insolvent company's assets and take the very great risk of receiving payment. If A has delivered the goods to B, then, of course, the lien being possessory is lost and the administrator may deal with the goods.

Charges by banks over customer deposits

It was held by the House of Lords in *Re Bank of Credit and Commerce International SA (No 8)* [1997] 4 All ER 568 that a bank could take a charge over its customers' deposits, thus doubting and refusing to follow the decision in *Re Charge Card Services Ltd* [1986] 3 All ER 289 which had regarded this as a 'conceptual impossibility'. The decision was because a deposit with a bank was a debt owed by the bank to the customer concerned, and as such was an asset in the customer's hands which could be charged by him to anyone. The case is of significance to banks since it extends their options in taking security over third party deposits. Banks may be enabled in future to use deposits of subsidiary companies as assets to be set off against loans made to parent companies. Until this decision banks have had to rely on special contractual arrangements which have not always survived the liquidation process. The decision in *BCCI (No 8)* raises the question of whether charge-backs should be registered. The House of Lords left this matter open but given that a charge is void unless registered the safest course would be to submit the charge for registration as an equitable floating charge.

Registration at Companies House

Section 398 states that it is the duty of the company to deliver particulars of a charge within 21 days of its creation. Section 414 also applies, and in general the date of creation of the charge is when the instrument involved is signed on behalf of the company. The delivery of particulars can be made by 'any person interested in the charge' such as the lender, and the document creating the charge must also be filed. It is an offence for a company and every officer in default to fail to deliver particulars of a charge within the specified time.

Re Advantage Healthcare (T10) Ltd [1999] All ER (D) 1294

In this case the High Court held that although in the normal course the applicant for registration of a charge is required to include correctly the company's number, that number is not a particular of the charge to be registered. Thus failure to give the correct number does not constitute a breach of s 395 of the 1985 Act and the registration is valid.

Comment

The inclusion of the wrong company number, if not detected and changed, does, of course, affect those who search the register for the chargor. Presumably such cases are rare. The High Court was appraised of this problem hut nevertheless found the charge valid.

The lender will usually take responsibility for the registration process because of the protection it obtains: firstly because the charge is registered and therefore not void, and secondly because registration establishes priority since charges registered earlier have priority over those registered later.

The Registrar will, under s 418, check the particulars and issue a certificate of registration which is currently conclusive evidence that the requirements of registration have been satisfied.

Effect of non-registration

If a charge is not registered as required by the 1985 Act, it is void as against a liquidator or an administrator and any creditor of the company. Thus the holder of the charge becomes an unsecured creditor on a winding-up. However, the charge is not void against the company while it is a going concern and can be enforced, e.g., by a sale of the assets charged. Such a sale cannot be set aside in the event that a liquidation takes place afterwards. In addition, when the charge becomes void, all sums including any interest payable become payable immediately on demand.

It will be noted that under the 1985 Act an unregistered charge is not void where exceptionally there is an administrative receivership.

However, the charge is void against a company when it is in administration or liquidation. Although s 395 refers to an unregistered charge being void 'against the liquidator or administrator', this means only that the relevant insolvency practitioner can employ the assets in the process of liquidation or administration for insolvency purposes. Yet if a person holding an unregistered charge removes the property charged then unless the provisions of s 395 can be construed as making the charge void also against the company, a liquidator or administrator cannot sue for damages for conversion in a personal capacity because the asset is not his. Assets do not vest into the ownership of insolvency practitioners and ownership is essential in most cases for a successful action in conversion. If the charge is also void against the company then the insolvency practitioner can bring a claim in conversion on behalf of the company, as the administrator did successfully in *Smith (Administrator of Coslett (Contractors) Ltd)* v *Bridgend County Borough Council* [2001] UKHL 58, [2002] 1 All ER 292 where the House of Lords decided that s 395 must be regarded at least in an insolvency as making an unregistered charge void also against the company.

Registration out of time

It is necessary to ask the court to allow registration out of time. A usual condition imposed by the court is that late registration is to be allowed but 'without prejudice to the rights of any parties acquired prior to the time when the charge was registered'. In effect, then, the charge ranks for priority from the date of its late registration.

Registration out of time and insolvency

Except in very exceptional circumstances the court will not grant late registration where a liquidation has commenced. The court is also reluctant to give permission where liquidation is imminent (*Re Ashpurton Estates Ltd* [1982] 3 All ER 665). However, late registration was allowed in *Barclays Bank* v *Stuart London Ltd* [2001] 2 BCLC 316 where the order provided in effect that if winding-up commenced before the end of the extension time the liquidator could set it aside on application to the court thus reducing the holder of the charge to an unsecured creditor.

Releasing the charge: Companies House

Under s 419 and on application being made to him by the company that the charge has been released or redeemed the Registrar will enter a memorandum of satisfaction on the register.

Releasing the charge: act of parties

A security over property may be released by act of parties. An example is provided by *Western Intelligence Ltd* v *KDO Label Printing Machines Ltd* [1998] BCC 472 where the High Court hold that when goods were transferred with the consent of the bank from a company in financial difficulties to a new company controlled by the same directors, the goods were released from a debenture granted by the original company to the bank.

COMPANY'S REGISTER

Section 407 provides that every company shall keep at its registered office a register of charges and enter in the register all charges affecting the property of the company. The company must enter in the register a short description of the property charged, the amount of the charge and the names of the persons entitled to the charge, except in the case of securities to bearer.

The company must also keep at its registered office a copy of every instrument creating a charge, whether requiring registration under the Act or not. The documents and register must be kept open to the inspection of members and creditors free of charge and to other persons on payment of a fee.

As regards failure to register a charge in the company's register, there is a default fine on any officer of the company who is in default as well as upon the company itself, but the charge is still valid. In other words, it is only failure to register at Companies House which affects the validity of the charge.

The company must keep a register of debenture holders but only if the terms of issue of the debentures require it. The register, if it exists, must be kept at the registered office or the place where it is made up so long as it is within the country in which the company is registered. The register may be inspected free of charge by those who are registered holders of debentures and, in addition, shareholders in the company, and by other persons on payment of a fee. Members, registered holders of debentures and other persons may acquire a copy of the register on payment of a fee. The register of directors' interests must show their debenture holdings also. This register is dealt with more fully in Chapter 13.

Because a power of inspection exists a company must maintain the register even though there are no entries in it if only to indicate that this is so.

AVOIDANCE OF FLOATING CHARGES

Under s 245 of the Insolvency Act 1986, a floating charge created by a company within one year before the commencement of its winding-up or the making of an administration order is void as a security for any debt other than cash paid or goods supplied to the company in consideration of the charge at the time the charge was created or subsequently, with interest, if any, thereon as agreed. The above provisions do not apply if the company was solvent immediately after the creation of the charge.

It was held in *Power* v *Sharp Investments Ltd* [1993] BCC 609 that no moneys paid to the company *before* the execution of the debenture would qualify for the invalidity exemption in s 245 unless the interval between the payment and execution of the debenture was minimal and could be regarded as contemporaneous.

If the person in whose favour the charge was created was connected with the company, e.g. a director or shadow director (see further Chapter 16), the period is two years, and the charge is void even though the connected person gave consideration at the time or subsequently, and even though the company was solvent immediately after the charge was given.

The purpose of the section is to prevent a company which is unable to pay its debts from, in effect, preferring one of its unsecured creditors to the others by giving him a floating charge on its assets. There is no objection to the creation of a floating charge where the company actually receives funds or goods at the time or afterwards because these may assist it to carry on business, and indeed avoid winding-up or administration. The charge only extends to the value of the funds or goods supplied after it was given and does not secure the existing debt to the unsecured creditor. As regards goods supplied, the charge extends only to the price which could reasonably have been obtained for them in the ordinary course of business at the time when they were supplied. The security would not extend to the whole of the value of goods supplied at an artificially high price.

Practical points arising

(i) Most importantly, a floating charge is valid as a security for loans made after the date it was created if the lender promised to make such loans (covenanted loans), and even if the lender did not (uncovenanted loans) (*Re Yeovil Glove Co Ltd* (1965), see below). Consequently, advances made to an insolvent company by its bank on an overdraft facility during the year before it is wound up are validly secured in the winding-up (or administration if relevant) by a floating charge given before the advances were made. The debenture creating the charge must expressly cover covenanted and uncovenanted loans, i.e. agreed loans and other loans not agreed at the time.

Re Yeovil Glove Co Ltd [1965] Ch 148

The company was in liquidation and had an overdraft of £67,000 with the National Provincial Bank Ltd. The overdraft was secured by a floating charge given less than

12 months prior to winding-up at a time when the company was insolvent. The charge was therefore void under what is now s 245 of the Insolvency Act 1986. However, the company had paid in some £111,000 and the bank had paid cheques out to the amount of some £110,000. The Court of Appeal held that under *Clayton's Case* (1816) 1 Mer 572, under which the earliest payments into an account are set off against the earliest payments out and vice versa, the overdraft, which was not validly secured, had been paid off and the floating charge attached to the money drawn out because the company had received consideration for this. It did not matter that the floating charge did not require the bank to make further advances. It did, however, expressly secure uncovenanted loans.

Comment

The Cork Committee said that this case defeated the object of what is now s 245. They thought it should be repealed by statute so that for the purposes of s 245 payments into the account should be treated as discharging debit items incurred after the creating of the floating charge before those incurred before it (see Cmnd 8558, para 1562).

(ii) The period of one (or two) year(s) from the creation of the floating charge is calculated from the date when the instrument imposing the charge is executed and not from the date of the issue of the debenture which may be later.

(iii) If an unsecured creditor takes a new loan to the company on the security of a floating charge on the understanding that the loan will be applied immediately in paying off his existing unsecured debt, the floating charge will normally be invalid unless the company is solvent immediately after the charge is given (*Re Destone Fabrics Ltd* [1941] 1 All ER 545).

(iv) Floating charges are invalidated only if the company is wound up or goes into administration, and so if before either of those events it redeems a floating charge which would have been invalid in those situations, the liquidator or administrator cannot require the owner of the charge to repay what he has received (*Re Parkes Garage (Swadlincote) Ltd* [1929] 1 Ch 139). However, if the redemption takes place within six months (two years if the debenture holder is a connected person) before the winding-up or administration it may be a preference of the debenture holder, in which case the relevant insolvency practitioner can recover the amount paid to the debenture holder under s 239 of the Insolvency Act 1986 (see below).

The s 245 avoidance provisions do not apply to fixed charges, but the preference provisions of s 239 do (see below).

PREFERENCE

A liquidator or an administrator may avoid a fixed or floating charge as a preference under s 239 of the Insolvency Act 1986 if:

(*a*) in giving the charge the company was influenced by a desire to better the position of a creditor or surety. Thus, to give a charge to a lender where the directors had personally guaranteed the loan would be a preference (see *Re Kushler* [1943] 2 All ER 22). However, the giving of a charge to an unsecured creditor about to levy execution on the company's goods may very well not be, because it would be given to preserve the company's assets at market value, bearing in mind that sheriff sales are often at throwaway prices;

(*b*) the company was insolvent when the charge was given; and

(*c*) the charge was given within the six months preceding the commencement of the winding-up or administration.

Where the creditor preferred is a connected person, e.g. a director or shadow director, the time period is two years and (a) above is presumed.

In this connection, the High Court decided in *Weisgard* v *Pilkington* [1996] CLY 3488 that a company's transfer by lease of certain of its assets (six flats) to two of its directors before it went into insolvent liquidation – ostensibly in discharge of a debt the company owed them – was a preference to connected persons so that the transfer must be reversed and the flats returned to the company. The directors had not displaced the presumption under s 239 that the transfers constituted a preference to connected persons. The transfers had put the directors in a better position than they would have been in given an insolvent liquidation. This was so even in regard to two of the flats which were charged to a bank to secure an overdraft since the charge operated to reduce the directors' liabilities as guarantors of that overdraft.

REMEDIES OF SECURED DEBENTURE HOLDERS

Where the debentures are secured on the assets of the company the following main remedies are available:

(*a*) the property charged may be sold or leased;

(*b*) a receiver may be appointed to take possession of the property.

Where the debenture is secured by a fixed charge, these remedies are available under s 101 of the Law of Property Act 1925. However, since a floating charge may not be covered by s 101 (see *Blaker* v *Herts & Essex Waterworks* (1889) 41 Ch D 399 under earlier similar legislation), the remedies are invariably given in the debenture.

After sale of the assets in a receivership any surplus, after paying off the debenture holders and the cost of realisation and receivers' costs and charges, belongs to the company.

ENVIRONMENT ACT 1995

Amendments made to the above Act at Report Stage resolved a particular difficulty foreseen by insolvency practitioners and those who appointed them which related to the liability for cleaning up contaminated land in the sense that they might be regarded as 'owners' of such land where they had taken charge of the assets of an insolvent company that owned the land. The amendments protect insolvency practitioners and official receivers who do not act unreasonably in respect of contaminated land. Lenders are not specifically protected but so long as they do not take possession of the land themselves they are not liable as 'owners' (see Environment Act 1995, s 57).

GRADED QUESTIONS

Essay mode

1 Richard is the founder, managing director and controlling shareholder of RST Ltd. For some years Richard kept the company afloat by making a number of unsecured loans to it. At the last tally the company owed him £20,000, and yet needed a further loan of £5,000. Richard is willing to advance the money, but realising that the company is very likely to go into liquidation, and with a view to salvaging something for himself from the company's assets, causes the company to execute in his favour a deed of debenture secured by a floating charge over all the assets of the company. The floating charge is stated to secure not only the £5,000 paid to the company at the time the charge was executed but also the £20,000 outstanding debt owed him by the company.

The company goes into insolvent winding-up three months after the floating charge is executed. Its assets are estimated at a little over £25,000, and its unsecured debts add up to £20,000.

Discuss the competing claims of Richard, who is a secured creditor, and the company's unsecured creditors.

(*University of Plymouth*)

2 In January 2003 Jones made an unsecured loan of £3,000 to a company of which he was a director. In January 2005 the directors resolved that in consideration of a further loan of £2,000 Jones should be issued with a debenture for £5,000, secured by a floating charge on the assets and undertaking of the company. Jones made this further loan and the debenture was issued. The company was wound up four months later.

Advise the liquidator as to the points to bear in mind regarding this transaction. Would your answer be different if the debenture had been secured by a fixed charge on the company's factory?

(*The Institute of Company Accountants*)

3 Compare and contrast equity shares and debentures as alternative forms of investment, explaining also the difference between fixed and floating charges.

(*Kingston University*)

4 'A person who lends on the security of a specific mortgage of a company's property is always entitled to repayment on his loan out of the proceeds of sale of the mortgaged property before any other creditor. A person who takes a floating charge is not in as secure a position.' *Pennington.*

Why is the holder of a floating charge in a less favourable position?

(*The Institute of Chartered Accountants in England and Wales*)

5 (*a*) What are the statutory requirements in respect of calling an annual general meeting? What is the usual business at an annual general meeting of a company?

(*b*) What is an extraordinary general meeting? When must the directors call such a meeting? What consequences may follow the directors' failure to call such a meeting?

(*c*) The directors of Fireworks Ltd, a company whose articles are regulated by *Table A*, wish to give effect to the following matters:

(i) to change the company's name to Chatterbox Ltd,
(ii) to increase the company's share capital to £30,000.

Explain to the directors the requirements of the Companies Act 1985 in relation to both the calling of a meeting and the passing of resolutions to give effect to these proposals.

(*The Association of Chartered Certified Accountants*)

6 (*a*) Distinguish between (i) ordinary, (ii) special and (iii) extraordinary resolutions. Indicate, in particular, the length of notices and matters in respect of which each resolution is required.

AND

(*b*) Fred is a managing director of Pine Wood Ltd. He also owns 25 per cent of the company's ordinary shares which carry voting rights. It has just been discovered by the other directors that Fred is acting as a consultant to another company which is in direct competition with Pine Wood Ltd. The other directors wish to propose an alteration of articles to restrict Fred's powers.

Advise the directors on whether and how they may alter the articles.

(*Glasgow Caledonian University*)

Objective mode

Four alternative answers are given. Select ONE only. Circle the answer which you consider to be correct. Check your answers by referring back to the information given in the chapter and against the answers at the back of the book.

1 Ouse Ltd has borrowed £10,000 from the Barchester Bank which is secured by an equitable charge over the company's freehold land. The charge, which states that it will rank in front of subsequent charges including fixed charges, has been registered. Later on Ouse granted a fixed charge over the freehold land to Onslow who had made it a loan. Onslow has not examined the Register of Charges at Companies House and has no other knowledge of the bank's equitable charge. Which charge has priority?

A The equitable charge taken by the bank because the first in time prevails.
B The equitable charge taken by the bank since registration is equivalent to notice of the contents of the charge.
C Onslow's legal charge because legal charges take priority to equitable charges.
D Onslow's legal charge since he had no notice of the equitable charge.

2 Thames Ltd is insolvent and is being wound up. The bank has a floating charge over its assets in regard to an overdraft which has not been registered. What is the effect of this?

A The charge is void against the liquidator and the bank proves as an ordinary creditor.
B The debt is void as against the liquidator and the bank will get nothing.
C The charge is voidable by the liquidator if the company was insolvent when the charge was created.
D The charge is void against subsequent secured creditors and the bank loses its priority accordingly.

3 Tees Ltd has issued a debenture in regard to a loan which will only be repaid if the company is wound up. What is such a debenture called?

A Redeemable.
B Bearer.
C Unsecured.
D Irredeemable.

4 Tay Ltd has assets of £10,000. Its trade creditors are worth £20,000 and it has an unsecured overdraft with the Barchester Bank of £20,000. Tay wants to increase the overdraft facility to £30,000. The bank has agreed and has been given a floating charge over Tay's assets to secure the overdraft. Tay Ltd is now in liquidation. Given that the overdraft is repayable on demand, how much is the bank entitled to as a secured creditor?

A £30,000.
B £20,000.
C Nothing.
D £10,000.

5 Within how many days of its creation must a charge over the assets of a company be registered?

A 12 days.
B 21 days.
C 15 days.
D 14 days.

6 The Barchester Bank has just taken a floating charge over the assets of Derwent Ltd, a manufacturing company. Who can be appointed by the bank to safeguard its security should circumstances require this?

A The trustee for the debenture holder.
B The Official Receiver.
C An administrator.
D An administrative receiver.

Answers to questions in objective mode appear on p 577.

21

ACCOUNTS AND AUDIT

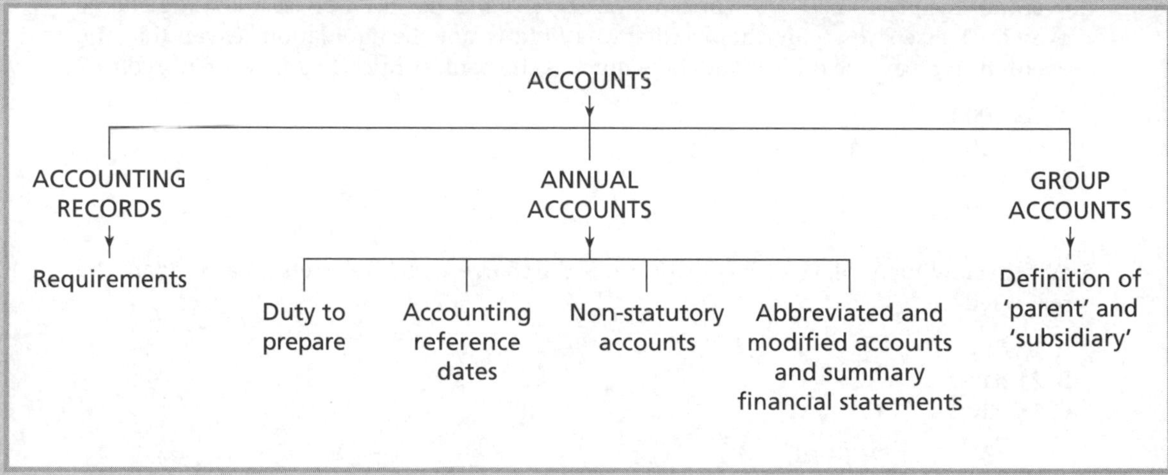

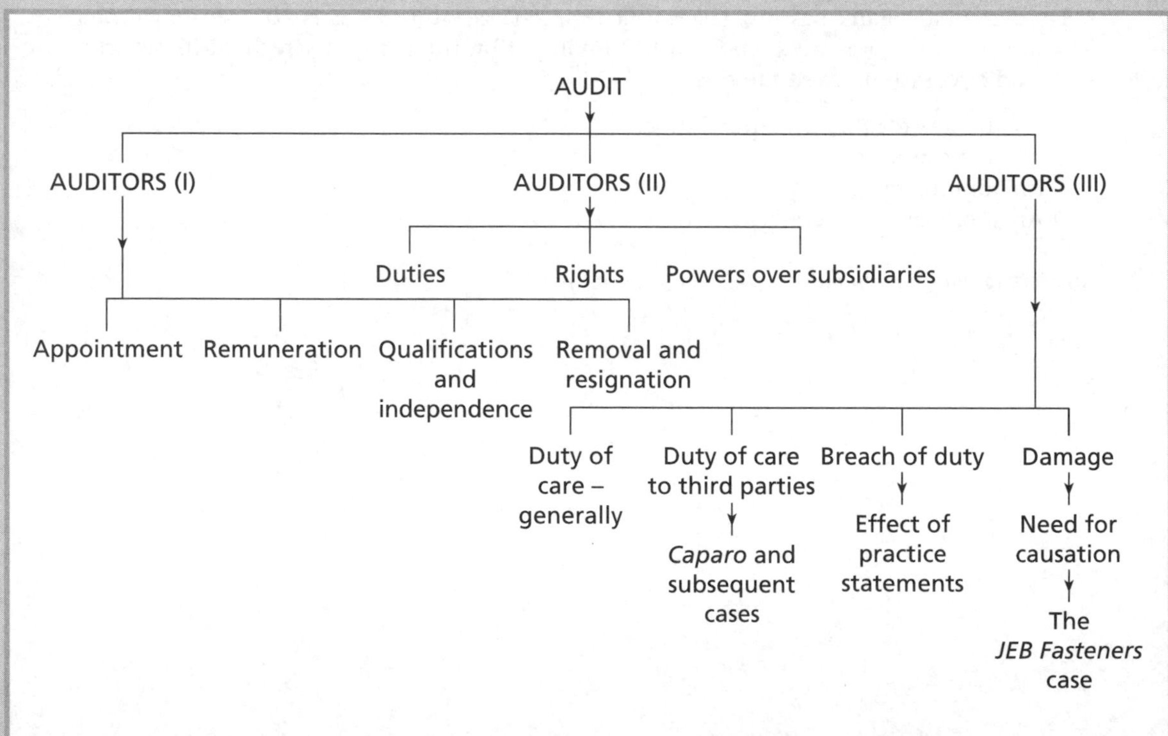

In this chapter we shall consider the main underlying principle of company law in regard to a company's accounts, which is to achieve disclosure of a company's financial affairs for the benefit of those who have invested in it and those who do business with it. The purpose of an audit by independent accountants is to add credibility to the financial statements forming part of the annual accounts and to ensure that they comply with regulations and give a true and fair view though small companies may take exemption from audit.

The keeping of accounts, the audit and filing with the Registrar are the price which the members and directors of a limited company must pay for limited liability. As we have seen, a free-standing unlimited company does not have to file accounts though its directors have a duty to see that annual accounts are prepared and audited (see further Chapter 1).

Only matters of company law have been included. No attempt has been made to give a comprehensive survey of the subject matter of accounting and auditing.

However, it is worth noting that there is no definition of 'true and fair' in company legislation though it is a fundamental requirement of the Companies Act 1985 that the accounts should give a true and fair view of the company's financial affairs. The matter is governed by accounting standards issued by an independent Accounting Standards Board which is assisted by an Urgent Issues Task Force. The Board issues Statements of Standard Accounting Practice and Financial Reporting Standards which provide a framework for consistent and logical accounting interpretation. These standards have no direct legal effect but a court will normally require that they be complied with to meet the true and fair requirement.

ACCOUNTING RECORDS

Under s 221, the directors of a company must keep accounting records sufficient to show and explain the company's transactions. They must disclose with reasonable accuracy, *at any time* throughout the financial year, the financial position of the company *at that time*. They must also enable a balance sheet and profit and loss account to be prepared to give a true and fair view of the company's state of affairs and profit and loss. They must contain (a) entries from day to day of all sums of money received and expended with details of transactions, and (b) a record of assets and liabilities.

Additionally, a company dealing in goods must keep statements of stock held at the end of the financial year, and of stocktaking from which the year-end statement is made up and of all goods sold and purchased, other than retail trade transactions, showing goods, buyers and sellers, so as to allow identification.

Under s 222 accounting records must be open for inspection by the officers of the company at all times and kept for six years (public company) and three years (private company).

As regards statements of work in progress, the Act does not specifically require these to be kept, on the grounds that many small companies have little or no work in progress and those for whom it is significant will have to keep statements as part of the general requirement to keep records sufficient to disclose the financial position of the company and to enable accounts to be prepared.

Under s 221 failure to keep accounting records as required is an offence for which officers of the company in default are liable. The offence is punishable with a maximum of two years' imprisonment and/or a fine.

Company legislation does not deal specifically with the legality of keeping accounting records on computer but such records are generally regarded as complying with the law. In particular, s 723 provides '. . . that the power conferred on a company by s 722(1) to keep a register *or other record* by recording the matters in question otherwise than by making entries in bound books includes power to keep the register *or other record* by recording the matters in question otherwise than in legible form so long as the recording is capable of being reproduced in legible form'. The words in italics would seem to apply to any record and not merely the company's registers.

ANNUAL ACCOUNTS

The term 'annual accounts' is commonly used in business and is now in fact an expression used in company legislation. For legal purposes it can be taken to mean the year end balance sheet together with the related profit and loss account and directors' and auditors' reports.

Duty to prepare accounts

Directors must prepare accounts based on an *accounting reference period*. This begins on the day after the date to which the last accounts were prepared, e.g. if 31 December, 1 January, and ends on the last day of the company's normal financial year, called the *accounting reference date*, though the directors may, in their discretion, move the reference date to seven days before or after the last day of the company's normal financial year.

Under s 241 the accounts, which need not be printed, and the auditors' and directors' reports must be laid before a general meeting and, under s 244, except for certain unlimited companies which are exempt, filed with the Registrar within seven months of the reference date (public companies) or ten months (private companies). The Department of Trade and Industry may extend these periods if there are special reasons, e.g. in the smaller company, illness of a sole director.

Under s 242 non-compliance with the requirement to lay before a general meeting and file with the Registrar can result in conviction of the directors. It is a defence to have taken reasonable steps to comply.

Under s 242A, failure to comply with the requirement to file accounts with the Registrar makes the *company* liable for penalties which are recoverable by the Department of Trade in civil proceedings. There is no defence for the company.

The penalties are as follows:

Delay in filing accounts	*Private company*	*Public company*
Up to 3 months late	£100	£500
Up to 6 months late	£250	£1,000
Up to 12 months late	£500	£2,000
Over 12 months late	£1,000	£5,000

Additionally, under s 242, if there is failure to comply with the filing requirements, a member or creditor or the Registrar may serve a notice on the directors asking for compliance and if the directors do not comply within 14 days after service of the notice the above-named persons may ask the court for an order directing compliance, the costs being borne by the directors.

There is a specific requirement in the 1985 Act for the annual accounts to be approved by the board of directors and for the balance sheet to be signed by at least one director. The sole signature of the company secretary is not enough.

In addition, as we have seen, a private company may, by elective resolution, opt out of the requirement to lay its accounts and reports before a general meeting.

Accounting reference dates: change of, and first

Sections 224 and 225 apply and at any time during the course of an accounting reference period a company may give notice to the Registrar specifying a new accounting reference date lengthening the current and subsequent accounting reference periods of the company.

The Companies Act 1985 (Miscellaneous Accounting Amendments) Regulations 1996 (SI 1996/189) provide some relaxation in terms of when a company can change its current accounting reference period. Before the regulations, a company could only change its current accounting reference period where the period for laying those accounts had not expired, the company was a subsidiary or parent of another company and the new date coincided with that other company's accounting reference date. Now it can change its current (or previous) accounting reference period so long as the period for laying those accounts has not expired. The restrictions where the period is to be extended more than once in five years (see below) continue. There is no need for a resolution of the members but merely a board resolution and minute.

The notice to the Registrar must state whether the new period is longer or shorter than the current period. Extension is not possible if the current period plus the extension is more than 18 months. Unless the DTI otherwise directs, extensions are not allowed more than once in five years unless to coincide dates within a group. These restrictions do not apply where the period is shortened. A subsidiary company can extend its ARD more than once in five years on the grounds that it is bringing its ARD into line with a foreign parent company, provided the parent company is incorporated within the European Economic Area.

Finally, for a newly incorporated company formerly its accounting reference period ended on the last day of the month in which the anniversary of its incorporation fell unless it gave notice to the Registrar of a different date within nine months of its incorporation. The latter alternative has now been dropped for companies incorporated on or after 1 April 1996 and the anniversary rule applies. Nevertheless, it is still possible to change that date by electing to have a shorter first accounting period.

Non-statutory accounts

This is an expression introduced into the 1985 Act as s 240 by the Companies Act 1989. The effect of it is that if any part of the full accounts, e.g. the directors' or auditors' report, is left out of a published version this version, though not in any other way abridged, will be regarded as non-statutory and must carry an appropriate statement as to its status.

Abbreviated or modified accounts of certain companies and groups

We have already considered in Chapter 1 the provisions under which certain companies and groups may file abbreviated or modified accounts (see further Chapter 1).

Summary financial statements

Listed companies are allowed to send summary financial statements to shareholders rather than the full accounts. However, copies of the full accounts must be sent to all shareholders who inform the company that they wish to receive them. The content of the summary financial statement and the way in which shareholders indicate that they wish to receive full accounts are laid down in regulations. These provisions now extend to holders of listed debentures.

GROUP ACCOUNTS

If a company has subsidiaries, group accounts showing the state of affairs and profit or loss of the company and the subsidiaries must be laid before the company at the general meeting at which the company's own balance sheet and profit and loss account are laid.

However, there are some exceptions, e.g. *group accounts are not required* if the company is, at the end of its financial year, the wholly-owned subsidiary of another body corporate incorporated in Great Britain, and also where the business of the subsidiary is very different from that of the parent company.

Any director who fails to take all reasonable steps to secure compliance with the statutory requirements regarding the accounts is liable to imprisonment and/or a fine. However, it is a defence for a director to prove that he took all reasonable steps for securing compliance with the requirements of the Companies Act.

It is of interest to note that as a result of amendments introduced by the Companies Act 1989, non-group accounts are referred to as 'individual accounts' clearly to distinguish them from group accounts.

Definition of 'parent' and 'subsidiary'

A major contribution of the Companies Act 1989 was to insert provisions into the 1985 Act to implement the EC Seventh Company Law Directive. This widens the definition of the parent–subsidiary relationship to include tests based on control and dominant influence as well as the more traditional tests such as holding a majority of equity share capital. This will bring many of the so-called 'off-balance sheet vehicles' back within consolidation. Such vehicles were often used to borrow money but since they were not consolidated it kept, what was in effect, group borrowing out of the group accounts thus improving the group's apparent debt/equity share capital ratio. This undermined the value of group accounts.

An undertaking A will be regarded as a parent to another B if:

(*a*) it holds a majority of the voting rights in B; *or*
(*b*) it is a member of B and has the right to appoint or remove the majority of its board of directors; *or*

(*c*) it has the right to direct the operating and financial policies of B under its memorandum or articles, or by reason of a written control contract; *or*

(*d*) it is a member of B and controls, alone, under an agreement with other members, a majority of the voting rights in B; *or*

(*e*) it has a participating interest in B and actually exercises a dominant influence over B, or if A and B are managed on a unified basis. A participating interest is presumed when A holds 20 per cent of B's shares.

Any of the above relationships may be traced through intermediate subsidiaries so that if the above relationship is established between A and B, and C is in one or other of the above relationships with B, then C is also in that relationship with A.

As an example of the influence of practice statements, it should be noted that Financial Reporting Standard 2 issued by the Accounting Standards Board tightens up the above rules by a general principle which states that subsidiaries should be consolidated even if their businesses are very different from that of the parent company, even though the 1985 Act says, as we have seen, that such subsidiaries need not be consolidated.

Directors' report

The statutory contents of the directors' report which is made annually to the members with the accounts appear in Sch 7 to the Companies Act 1985.

An illustration of the contents of the directors' report for a small company appears in Figure 21.1.

Payment practice

Regulations entitled the Companies Act 1985 (Directors' Report) (Statement of Payment Practice) Regulations 1997 amend s 234 of CA 1985 (duty to prepare directors' report) and Part VI of Sch 7 to CA 1985 (matters to be dealt with in directors' report). The new provisions require that the directors' report of public companies and large private companies, i.e. those which do not qualify as medium or small and which are subsidiaries of a public company, must contain a statement of the company's policy and practice on payment of its suppliers. The directors' report must state the figure expressed in days, which bears the same proportion to the number of days in the year as the amount owed to trade creditors at the year end bears to the amounts invoiced by suppliers during the year.

The test, which gives only a guideline, could appear as follows:

$$\frac{\text{Amount owed to trade creditors at year end}}{\text{Amount invoiced by suppliers during the year}} \quad \frac{2{,}500}{20{,}000} \times 365 = 46$$

AUDITORS

An audit is a process which is concerned to establish and confirm confidence in the accounting information yielded by the company's records and systems so that an opinion may be given upon the accounts which have been prepared by the company from those records and systems. The audit is carried out primarily for the shareholders

Report of the directors – Boxo Limited

The directors present their report with the audited accounts of the company for the year ended 31 March 2XXX.

PRINCIPAL ACTIVITY
The principal activity of the company in the year under review was that of the distribution of car components.

REVIEW OF BUSINESS
The results for the year together with the financial position of the company and recommended transfer to reserves are shown in the accounts annexed to this report. During the year the volume of business has remained substantially the same. The directors hope that a modest upturn in the national economy will result in an increase in business for the company in the next financial year.

DIVIDENDS
No interim dividends were paid during the year ended 31 March 2XXX. The directors recommend final dividends as follows:

£1 Ordinary shares 10p per share

The total dividends for the year ended 31 March 2XXX will be £8,000.

SHARE PURCHASE
On 20 December 2XXX the company purchased 4,000 ordinary shares from one of the original members who left the country in order to work abroad. Consideration of £XX,XXX was paid for the shares that represented 5 per cent of the issued ordinary shares.

DIRECTORS
The directors of the company in office during the year and their beneficial interests in the issued share capital were:

Name	*Ordinary shares (this will be at year end)*	*Ordinary shares (this will be at the beginning of the year)*
A. White	5,000	5,000
B. Brown	5,000	5,000
G. Green	5,000	5,000

EURO
The directors do not believe that the introduction of the euro will have a significant impact on the company.

AUDITORS
In accordance with section 386 of the Companies Act 1985, the company has passed an elective reolution to retain Bloggs, Snooks and Twitchet as auditors without the need for annual re-election. Bloggs, Snooks and Twitchet have indicated their willingness to continue in office.

ON BEHALF OF THE BOARD

A. White – Director ______________________

Dated XX August XXXX

Figure 21.1 Directors' report for a small company

Note: (i) The above report assumes that the company has not taken advantage of the exemptions in s 246(4), e.g. a small company need not include a Review of Business. Public limited companies and large private companies are required to include more than the above (see Sch 7, CA 1985). (ii) For the avoidance of doubt a small company that has taken the audit exemption need not comply with the Companies (Audit, Investigations and Community Enterprise) Act 2004 and include a statement in the directors' report that so far as each director is aware there is no relevant information of which the company's auditors are unaware (see further page 477).

as a check upon the directors' stewardship, but it is obviously also of benefit to creditors and potential investors. The statute law relating to auditors in terms of their appointment, rights, remuneration, removal and resignation are to be found in ss 384 to 394A of the 1985 Act.

Companies are required to appoint auditors unless they can be classified as dormant or are small companies which are audit-exempt (see further Chapter 1).

Appointment of auditors

At each general meeting at which accounts in respect of an accounting reference period are laid the members must appoint auditors who will hold office until the conclusion of the next general meeting at which accounts in respect of an accounting reference period are laid. If no appointment is made, the Department of Trade and Industry must be told within one week, whereupon the Department may make an appointment.

As regards the first auditors, they may be appointed by the directors to hold office until the conclusion of a general meeting at which accounts are laid. If the directors fail to make an appointment the company in general meeting may appoint. As regards casual vacancies, these may be filled by the directors or by the members in general meeting.

As we have seen, private companies may by elective resolution opt out of the annual appointment of auditors, the relationship lasting until either party wishes to terminate it: the auditor by resignation; the company by appointing another auditor in place of the existing one.

Remuneration

The remuneration of the auditors is fixed by the company in general meeting or in such way as the company in general meeting may determine, e.g. the company may and usually does delegate the fixing of remuneration to the directors.

Where the auditor is appointed by the directors or the Department of Trade and Industry, his remuneration is fixed by the directors or the Department as the case may be. Remuneration for non-audit work is disclosed in the auditors' report or accounts.

Non-audit services

The Companies (Audit etc.) Act 2004 enables the Secretary of State to make regulations requiring companies to publish more detailed information in regard to the non-audit services that they purchase from their auditors. The supply of these services can be more lucrative to the auditors than the audit fee and can threaten their independence in the audit function because they do not wish to lose the income. Non-audit services most commonly found are taxation advice, valuations, actuarial services, IT services and litigation support in terms, e.g., of quantifying damages that should be claimed from a particular loss situation.

Qualifications and independence

Only those persons recognised as qualified by the Chartered Institutes of England and Wales, Scotland, and Ireland, the Association of Chartered Certified Accountants and the Association of Authorised Public Accountants, and persons with oversea and other qualifications recognised by the Department of Trade and Industry, may act as auditors. Following the implementation of the EC Eighth Directive, the profession of auditing has been brought more directly under statutory control and the accounts of companies must be audited by a 'registered auditor' which status will usually be held through membership of the above-mentioned professional bodies.

They have become supervisory bodies and must ensure that those of their members who wish to be auditors are fit and proper persons and are subject to adequate rules on professional integrity, independence and technical standards. The supervisory body must be able to monitor and enforce compliance with the rules and must be able to investigate effectively complaints against members. The Secretary of State may moderate examinations and the designation 'registered auditor' must be restricted to persons who have completed at least three years of practical training, of which a substantial part was spent being trained on company audit work.

The Secretary of State may require a second audit where an audit has been carried out by a person who was, for any part of the period, ineligible. Alternatively, he may retain an eligible person to review the first audit and report as to whether a second audit is needed.

The Companies (Audit etc.) Act 2004 enables the Secretary of State to delegate to an independent body, the Professional Oversight Board for Accountancy (POBA), power to authorise recognised supervisory bodies. The POBA will for the future organise independent arrangements for:

- establishing auditing standards regarding professional integrity and independence and technical standards;
- monitoring audits of listed companies and others where financial condition is of importance; and
- investigation into and the taking of action in regard to public interest cases.

There will be a levy on business to fund these activities.

The following persons cannot be appointed as auditors to a company even though they are authorised:

(*a*) An officer or servant of the company. Although an auditor is an officer of the company for some purposes, the provision means officer other than the auditor for the time being.

(*b*) A person who is employed by or is the partner of an officer or servant of the company. 'Officer' includes a director, manager or secretary.

(*c*) Officers and servants of the company's holding or subsidiary companies and their employees or partners.

(*d*) A person is ineligible for appointment if there exists between him or any associate of his and the company, or any parent or subsidiary company, a 'connection' of such description as may be defined by regulations. A 'connection' includes cases where the company to be audited is owned or controlled by a member of the auditor's family and cases where the auditor has a financial interest in the client company. The word 'associate' is defined as covering, e.g., the auditor's spouse and minor children and so their 'connections' are in effect his and would bar him from being auditor if they existed.

A body corporate may now be an auditor and the Companies Act 1989 inserted provisions into the 1985 Act under which accounting firms may become limited companies, even with outside shareholders, provided that qualified persons control the company and the board.

Removal and other special notice requirements

The members of a company may remove the auditors before the expiration of their office and if this is done the Registrar must be informed within 14 days of removal. As regards procedure, special notice of 28 days is required for an ordinary resolution at a general meeting:

(*a*) appointing as auditor a person other than a retiring auditor; *or*
(*b*) filling a casual vacancy in the office of an auditor; *or*
(*c*) reappointing as auditor a retiring auditor who was appointed by the directors to fill a casual vacancy; *or*
(*d*) removing an auditor before the expiration of his term of office.

In cases (*a*) and (*d*) above, the auditor may make representations in writing to the company and require the notification of these representations to the members of the company. Failing such notification, he may require that the representations be read out at the meeting and in any case he has the right to be heard orally at the meeting. If the court is satisfied, on the application of the company or any other person who claims to be aggrieved, that these rights are being used to secure needless publicity for defamatory matter, the representations need not be sent out or read out at the meeting.

Resignation

An auditor of a company may resign his office at any time by depositing at the registered office of the company a notice in writing to that effect. The date of his resignation is the date of the notice or such later date as may be specified in the notice. The notice of resignation must contain a statement either:

(*a*) to the effect that there are no circumstances connected with his resignation which he considers should be brought to the notice of the members or debenture holders of the company; *or*
(*b*) a statement of such circumstances.

On receiving the auditor's notice of resignation, the company must send a copy of it to the Registrar. In addition, if the notice contains a statement of circumstances connected with his resignation, a copy must be sent to every person entitled to receive a copy of the accounts.

If the notice contains a statement of circumstances connected with his resignation, the auditor has the following additional rights:

(*a*) to require the directors to call an extraordinary general meeting to receive and consider his explanation of those circumstances; and
(*b*) to request the company to circulate a statement of the circumstances to the members before:
   (i) the holding of the meeting requisitioned by him; *or*
   (ii) the meeting at which his office would otherwise have expired; *or*
   (iii) a meeting where it is proposed to fill the vacancy by his resignation.

If the statement is received too late for circulation, the auditor may demand that it should be read out at such a meeting. The statement need not be circulated or read out if the court holds that the statement was made to secure needless publicity of defamatory matter.

A resigning auditor is entitled to attend a meeting at which it is proposed to fill the vacancy and to be heard on such business as concerns the audit function as is an auditor who has been removed.

It should be noted that under provisions inserted into the 1985 Act by the Companies Act 1989, the statement connected with circumstances to be brought to the attention of members on resignation must now be made whenever an auditor ceases to hold office, e.g. if he is removed or not reappointed.

DUTIES OF AUDITORS

An auditor has *two main duties*: (1) *to audit* the accounts of the company; and (2) *to report* to the members of the company on the accounts, i.e. on every balance sheet and profit and loss account and all group accounts, if any, laid before the company in general meeting during his tenure of office. The auditor's report must be open to inspection by any member.

As regards the role of the auditor *in combating corporate fraud*, expectations which the public and some in business have of the auditor often go beyond their role as auditors. Although the term 'fraud' is often met with, there is in fact no crime of that name and if auditors are to be responsible for exposing it or reporting on it, then there must first be legislation to define what it is they are to report upon. There are some specific reporting duties in the field of money laundering in connection with drugs or terrorism set out in the Criminal Justice Act 1993. Reporting duties also exist in areas where organisations take deposits of the public's money, e.g. banking, insurance and investment funds, and, in particular, there is a duty on the auditors to a pension scheme to report to the Occupational Pensions Regulatory Authority if they have reasonable grounds to believe that any duty imposed upon the scheme trustees, the employer or any professional adviser is not being complied with and is of material significance. Sections 47 and 48 of the Pensions Act 1995 contain these 'whistleblowing' provisions.

In this connection, workers are protected in terms of whistleblowing on matters arising during their employment by the Public Interest Disclosure Act 1998. In relation to this and to the receipt of information in this way generally, the Institute of Chartered Accountants in England and Wales has issued a discussion paper, i.e. TECH 5/98, *Receipt of Information in Confidence by Auditors* (and see below).

RIGHTS OF AUDITORS

The auditors are given wide statutory rights and powers to enable them to obtain whatever information they require for the purposes of their audit. In particular:

(*a*) they have a right of access at all times to the books, accounts and vouchers of the company and are entitled to require from the officers of the company such information and explanation as they think necessary for the performance of their duties as auditors;

(*b*) it is a criminal offence for any officer of a company knowingly or recklessly to make a statement which is misleading, false or deceptive in a material particular;

(*c*) they have a right to receive notices of and other communications relating to general meetings and to attend them. They also have a right to be heard at any general meeting which they attend on any part of the business which concerns them as auditors;

(*d*) they also had a right to receive copies of written resolutions of private companies and, if the resolution affected them as auditors, to require the company to convene a general (or class) meeting to consider it. This provision has now been reviewed (see further Chapter 19).

POWERS OF AUDITORS IN RELATION TO SUBSIDIARIES

The auditor of a subsidiary incorporated in Great Britain is required to give the auditors of the holding company such information and explanation as they may reasonably require for the purposes of their duties as auditors of the holding company (s 389A (3)).

The Consultative Committee of Accounting Bodies asked for this provision because although in practice there is often consultation between the auditors of a holding company and subsidiaries, the section is useful if good practice breaks down.

INFORMATION AND THE COMPANIES (AUDIT, INVESTIGATIONS AND COMMUNITY ENTERPRISE) ACT 2004

This Act entitles an auditor to require information from employees and to that extent widens the auditor's sources of information. The right applies to subsidiary companies including those that are non-GB where the parent company carries the responsibility for obtaining the information.

In addition it is a criminal offence to fail to provide information or explanations required by the auditor.

The 2004 Act also requires the directors' report to state that so far as *each* director is aware there is no relevant information of which the company's auditors are unaware and that each director has taken all the steps that he ought to have taken as a director in order to make himself aware of any relevant audit information and to ensure that the company's auditors were aware of it.

'Relevant audit information' is defined as information needed by the company's auditors in connection with the preparation of their report.

It is a criminal offence if a false statement is made applying to each director who knew or was reckless as to the existence of undisclosed information. It does not seem possible for the directors to make a qualified report.

DUTY OF CARE OF THE AUDITOR

When carrying out their duties auditors must exercise skill and care and the degree of skill and care to be shown in particular in relation to the depth of the investigation and the sorts of check to be made is to be found in judicial decisions. The relevant case law is summarised below:

(*a*) It is not their duty to see that the business is being run efficiently or profitably or to advise on the conduct of the business. The auditors' concern is to ascertain the true financial position of the company at the time of the audit. However, an auditor is not an insurer and does not guarantee that the accounting records show the true state of the company's affairs. Nevertheless, he must be honest and not certify what he does not believe to be true and must take reasonable care and skill before he believes that what he certifies is true.

Re London and General Bank [1895] 2 Ch 166

The greater part of the capital of the bank, which was being wound up, had for some years been advanced to four of the 'Balfour' companies and a few special customers on securities which were insufficient and difficult of realisation. The auditors drew attention to the situation in a confidential report to the directors, stressing its gravity, and ending by saying – 'We cannot conclude without expressing our opinion unhesitatingly that no dividend should be paid this year.' The chairman, Mr Balfour, persuaded the auditors to strike this sentence out before the report was officially laid before the board of directors. The certificate signed by the auditors and laid before the shareholders at the annual general meeting stated that 'the value of the assets as shown on the balance sheet is dependent on realisation'. As originally drawn, it also said – 'And on this point we have reported specifically to the board.' But again Mr Balfour persuaded them to withdraw this statement by promising to mention this in his speech to the shareholders which he did without drawing special attention to it. The directors declared a dividend of 7 per cent. *Held* – by the Court of Appeal, affirming the decision of Vaughan Williams J – that the auditors had been guilty of misfeasance, and were liable to make good the amount of dividend paid. It is the duty of an auditor to consider and report to the shareholders, whether the balance sheet exhibits a correct view of the state of the company's affairs, and the true financial position at the time of the audit. He must take reasonable care to see that his certification is true, and must place the necessary information before the shareholders and not merely indicate the means of acquiring it. In the course of his judgment Lindley LJ said:

> 'An auditor . . . is not an insurer; he does not guarantee that the books correctly show the true position of the company's affairs; he does not even guarantee that his balance sheet is accurate according to the books of the company . . . but, he must be honest, i.e. he must not certify what he does not believe to be true, and he must use reasonable care and skill before he believes that what he certifies is true. What is reasonable care in any particular case must depend upon the circumstances of the case.'

Theobald, the auditor, stated the true position to the directors, and if he had done the same to the shareholders, his duty would have been discharged.

(*b*) As we have seen, there is no statutory duty upon an auditor to detect fraud but if suspicions are aroused the auditor has a duty to investigate matters. A standard issued by the Auditing Practices Board (SAS 110) states that an auditor's prime duty is to ensure that the company's accounts give a true and fair view of its position and not to detect fraud. Nevertheless, says the standard, material fraud can distort a company's accounts and auditors should be alert to the possibility of its existence. Other guidelines issued by the APB state that auditors may be barred from auditing financial services companies if they detect fraud and fail to report on it to the relevant regulator, e.g. the Financial Services Authority.

(*c*) An auditor may have to value shares and in this connection it should be noted that if on the facts of the case the court takes the view that the auditor was employed in the capacity of arbitrator rather than expert there is no liability in negligence. However, in most cases the auditor will be regarded as valuing as an expert because the parties are seldom in dispute with regard to the value of the shares and are simply seeking a professional valuation. Where the auditor values as an expert he will be liable in negligence under the rule in *Hedley Byrne & Co* v *Heller & Partners* [1963] 2 All ER 575 if he reaches a valuation without the exercise of proper skill and care. In addition, the auditors' valuation of shares is generally binding on the parties even if it is wrong. The courts are reluctant to set aside a professional valuation in the absence of fraud, or collusion (*Baber* v *Kenwood Manufacturing Co* [1978] 1 Lloyd's Rep 175), and this makes the remedy against the auditors more attractive provided, of course, negligence can be established.

(*d*) The auditor should be familiar with the company's constitution, i.e. its memorandum and articles (*Re Republic of Bolivia Exploration Syndicate Ltd* [1914] 1 Ch 139) and must, of course, check and verify the company's accounts (*Leeds Estate, Building and Investment Co* v *Shepherd* (1887) 36 Ch D 787).

(*e*) The auditor is not under a duty to take stock and can accept as honest any statements made by the company's officers and servants so long as he acts reasonably in so doing and the circumstances are not suspicious (*Re Kingston Cotton Mill Co* (1896), below). In other words, he must act as a reasonably careful and competent auditor would.

Re Kingston Cotton Mill Co [1896] 2 Ch 279

The directors of a company were enabled to pay dividends out of capital because the stock in trade of the company was overstated for several years. The auditors had not required the production of the stock records but had accepted the certificate of the company's manager regarding the value of the stock. *Held* – by the Court of Appeal – the auditors were not liable. It was stated that an auditor is 'a watchdog not a bloodhound'. He can assume that the company's servants are honest and can rely upon statements they make unless there are suspicious circumstances which would give reason for distrust. *Per* Lopes LJ:

> 'It is the duty of an auditor to bring to bear on the work he has to perform that skill, care and caution which a reasonably competent, careful and cautious auditor would use. What is reasonable skill, care and caution must depend on the particular circumstances of each case. An auditor is not bound to be a detective, or, as was said, to approach his work with suspicion, or with a foregone conclusion that there is something wrong. He is a watchdog, but not a bloodhound. He is justified in believing tried servants of the company in whom confidence is placed by the company. He is entitled to assume that they are honest and to rely upon their representations, provided he uses reasonable care. If there is anything calculated to excite suspicion, he should probe it to the bottom; but in

the absence of anything of that kind he is only bound to be reasonably cautious and careful. . . . It is not the duty of an auditor to take stock; he is not a stock expert; there are many matters on which he must rely on the honesty and accuracy of others.'

Comment

The rule laid down in the above case has been modified by subsequent cases. In *Westminster Road Construction and Engineering Company Ltd* (1932) unreported, a company paid dividend out of profits which were overstated by reason of the overvaluation of work in progress. This figure was supplied by the manager and secretary and it was held that the auditor was liable to repay the money paid out as dividend because he had accepted the certificate given by them without making proper enquiries which would have revealed that the valuation was inflated.

See also *Re City Equitable Fire Insurance Co Ltd*, 1925 (Chapter 17).

It should be borne in mind, however, that the cases relating to the general duty of care of the auditor are rather old and that professional standards have risen since they were decided. Thus, it is now generally accepted that an auditor should not rely on the accuracy and honesty of other persons even in the matter of stocktaking, and that he should carry out a check on at least one or more sample items. The standard of care required of an auditor at the present time was probably more accurately expressed by Lord Denning in *Fomento (Sterling Area) Ltd* v *Selsdon Fountain Pen Co Ltd* [1958] 1 WLR 45 at p 61 where he said:

> 'An auditor is not confined to the mechanics of checking vouchers and making arithmetical computations. He is not to be written off as a professional "adder-upper and subtractor". His vital task is to take care to see that errors are not made, be they errors of computation, or errors of omission or commission, or downright untruths. To perform this task properly he must come to it with an enquiring mind – not suspicious of dishonesty . . . – but suspecting that someone may have made a mistake somewhere and that a check must be made to ensure that there has been none.'

This higher duty of care was to some extent applied in the following case.

Re Thomas Gerrard & Son Ltd [1968] Ch 455

The managing director of the company had falsified the accounts by three methods one of which involved including non-existent stock and altering invoices. The auditors who were put on inquiry by alterations of invoices negligently failed to investigate the matter and gave a falsely favourable picture of the profits of the company as a result of which it declared dividends it would not otherwise have declared which in turn resulted in extra tax being payable. The company was wound up and in misfeasance proceedings under what is now s 212 of the Insolvency Act 1986 against the auditors they claimed that they had not been given enough time to do their work. *Held* – this was no defence and the auditors must repay the dividends, the cost of recovering the extra tax and any of the extra tax not recoverable. In the course of his judgment Pennycuick J made the following points:

(i) if directors do not allow the auditors adequate time to make proper investigations, they must either refuse to make a report at all or qualify it;

(ii) while leaving open the question whether the auditors would have been in breach of duty had the only fraud been falsification of stock, the judge held that once they were on notice of the altered invoices, they had a duty to make an exhaustive inquiry. Having failed to do so, they were liable to the company under what is now s 212 of the Insolvency Act 1986.

AUDITORS' LIABILITY

The liability of auditors can be brought under three headings as set out below.

By statute

As we have seen in *Re Thomas Gerrard* (above) an auditor may be liable in a winding-up for misfeasance or breach of any fiduciary or other duty in relation to the company. Under this provision an order may be made to repay money or to make compensation as the court thinks just.

In contract

An auditor has a contract with the company and if he is in breach of his duty in regard to the work he has agreed to do for the company, which is normally set out in a 'letter of engagement', he can be sued by the company for damages.

In tort

The claim here will normally be in negligence. It is unlikely that a professional person would make statements which he *knew* to be false in order dishonestly to deceive a party, but if he did the claim would be in the tort of deceit.

To succeed in a claim for negligence, the claimant must show that the defendant auditor owed him a duty of care, that the auditor was in breach of that duty, and finally that the breach caused the damage to the claimant.

Duty of care

The duty of care in regard to negligent misstatements by auditors has been considered in a number of cases since the early 1950s. However, the present position has been the subject of comprehensive analysis by the House of Lords in *Caparo Industries plc* v *Dickman* [1990] 1 All ER 568 and by the High Court in *Al Saudi Banque* v *Clarke Pixley* [1989] 3 All ER 361.

From these decisions and important later ones the position would appear to be as follows:

(*a*) Auditors do not owe a duty of care to potential investors in the company, e.g. those who rely on the audited accounts when contemplating a takeover bid. The fact that the accounts and auditors' report might foreseeably come into their hands and be relied on is not enough to create a duty of care. In addition, it was decided in *James McNaughton*

Paper Group v *Hicks Anderson* [1991] 1 All ER 134 that even if an auditor knew that the audited accounts would be used by a bidder as the basis of a bid, he would not be liable if he reasonably believed and was entitled to assume that the bidder would also seek the advice of his own accountant.

(*b*) Auditors do not owe a duty of care to potential investors even if they already hold shares in the company since, although they are shareholders and auditors are under a statutory duty to report to shareholders, the duty of the auditors is to the shareholders as a whole and not to shareholders as individuals.

(*c*) Even where the auditors are aware of the person or persons who will rely upon the accounts, they are not liable unless they also know what the person or persons concerned will use them for, e.g. as the basis for a takeover.

(*d*) Where there is knowledge of user and use, then in that restricted situation the Court of Appeal held in *Morgan Crucible Co plc* v *Hill Samuel Bank Ltd* [1991] 1 All ER 148 that a duty of care would exist in regard to the user. However, even in such a situation the auditor will not be liable if, in the circumstances, he was entitled to assume that the user would also seek the advice of his own accountant and not rely solely on the audited accounts (see the *McNaughton* case, above).

(*e*) A case which appears to widen the liability of auditors beyond misstatements to mere omissions is *Coulthard* v *Neville Russell* [1997] *The Times*, 18 December, where the Court of Appeal held that as a matter of principle auditors have a duty of care to advise that a transaction which the company and its directors intend to carry out might be a breach of the financial assistance provisions of the Companies Act 1985 (see also Chapter 7).

(*f*) In addition, the High Court ruled in *Abbot* v *Strong* [1998] *The Times*, 9 July, that a circular issued by a company to its shareholders in connection with a rights issue and allegedly containing misleading profit forecasts by the directors together with an allegedly negligent letter from the company's accountants and management consultants affirming that the forecast statement was properly compiled and in accordance with the company's accounting policies did not lead to the accountants having a duty of care in negligence to the shareholders who acquired shares in the rights issue so that their attempt to claim against the accountants failed. Mr Justice Ferris ruled that the accountants did not owe a duty of care to the shareholders individually for their alleged loss. The judge proceeded by analogy with the issue of shares under listing particulars or prospectus. In such cases, as we have seen, there is a requirement that any statement by accountants should make clear that it has been given with their consent and that the consent has not been withdrawn. This shows that the accountants *adhere to or are part of* the issue process and, of course, in that situation they can be liable for their misstatements. There was, said the judge, no such statement in this case. Once again, the court has decided that there is no duty of care in those advising companies to the individual shareholders, maintaining the *Caparo* line. There were in fact 200 claimants in this case, so the decision may be based on public policy, bearing in mind the problems of obtaining indemnity insurance.

(*g*) The High Court has ruled that two companies that invested venture capital in a shopfitting company that later went into receivership were entitled to damages from the company's auditors on the basis of negligent misstatements by the auditors in the company's accounts and in letters sent by the auditors to the investing companies. The auditors owed those companies a duty of care (see *Yorkshire Enterprises Ltd* v *Robson Rhodes New Law Online* (1998) 17 June, Transcript Case No 2980610103 approved judgment). A main problem had been that the provision for bad debts was inadequate. The court was saying in summary that if the auditors had carried out the audit work thoroughly, they would have found certain bookkeeping errors and would have made a greater and more appropriate provision for bad debt (or qualified the accounts). In consequence, the auditors were liable in damages. The facts of the case showed that the auditors were aware of the user of their statements and the use to which they would be put.

Breach of duty

An auditor will not be liable if, given a duty of care, he is not in breach of it. An auditor is not likely to be in breach of duty if he follows Auditing Standards and Guidelines, Statements of Standard Accounting Practice and Financial Reporting Standards devised and issued by the profession. If he does that, he will at least have the advantage of the judgment of McNair J in *Bolam* v *Friern Hospital Management Committee* [1957] 2 All ER 118. He said in connection with doctors: 'A doctor is not guilty of negligence if he has acted in accordance with a practice accepted as proper by a responsible body of medical men skilled in that particular art . . . merely because there is a body of opinion who would take a contrary view.' The statement is of course equally applicable to other professions including that of accountant and auditor.

In addition, the explanatory foreword to the profession's Auditing Standards and Guidelines states that 'a court of law may, when considering the adequacy of work of an auditor, take into account any pronouncements or publications which it thinks may be indicative of good practice. Auditing standards and guidelines are likely to be so regarded.'

The importance of professional pronouncements was also stressed in *Lloyd Cheyham* v *Littlejohn* [1987] BCLC 303 where Woolf J remarked that 'while SSAPs are not conclusive so that a departure from their terms necessarily involves a breach of duty of care and they are not rigid rules, they are very strong evidence as to what is the proper standard which should be adopted and unless there is some justification a departure will be regarded as constituting a breach of duty'.

This statement would, of course, apply with equal force to the more recent Financial Reporting Standards.

The effect of the decision in *Bolitho* v *City and Hackney Health Trust* [1997] 4 All ER 771 is considered in Chapter 8 in relation to company distributions and should be referred to again at this point by way of revision.

Damage

It must be shown that the breach caused the damage. Thus in *JEB Fasteners Ltd* v *Marks Bloom & Co* [1983] 1 All ER 583, the accounts of BG Fasteners were prepared by the defendants who were the auditors of BG. Unknown to the auditors, they were handed to the directors of JEB by the directors of BG as part of a takeover discussion. JEB took over BG and then complained through its directors that it had paid too much for BG and that this was the result of relying on the defendants' accounts which, it was alleged, were negligently prepared and showed BG to be a better proposition than it actually was.

In the High Court it was decided that the auditors should have foreseen the use of the accounts by JEB in the takeover and that this was enough to establish the duty of care. This part of the decision cannot now be supported in view of the requirement of *knowledge of use and user* in *Caparo* and subsequent cases. However, the High Court went on to hold that the auditors were not liable because it appeared in evidence that a major motive in taking over BG was to obtain the technical services of its two directors. It was admitted that JEB would have taken over BG anyway, regardless of the accuracy or otherwise of BG's annual accounts. The auditors' alleged negligence did not cause the damage and they were not liable.

Developments in exclusion of liability

The case of *Royal Bank of Scotland plc* v *Bannerman Johnstone Maclay (a firm)* 2003 SLT 181 raised issues in regard to auditors' liability and also their ability to exclude that liability.

The bank lent money to a company APC Ltd on the strength of accounts audited by the defendants. It was alleged by the claimant that the audited accounts were less than adequately informative in terms, e.g., of the going concern factor. The bank had later to appoint a receiver to the company which was insolvent.

The auditors had notice that under overdraft facility letters the bank was entitled to see management accounts and annual audited accounts. However, they contended that the claimant had to prove that as auditors they *intended* the bank to rely on the accounts to make further loans or advances. The auditors said in effect 'when auditing the accounts our only intention was to carry out Companies Act duties to audit the accounts'. The Scottish Court of Session (Outer House) in this case, equally applicable in England and Wales, ruled that the case law did not support a requirement of intention. The compelling effect of the authorities was that knowledge of user and use formed the basis of a duty of care for those making information or advice available. The auditors had the requisite knowledge and therefore owed a duty of care.

The bank had yet to prove that the accounts were prepared negligently. These duty of care cases are decided without proof of the allegations of negligence. A major matter relating to this case was that *the auditors had not disclaimed liability to third parties such as the bank*. In this connection, the Institute of Chartered Accountants in England and Wales has stated that it is clear that auditors assume reponsibility for the contents of the audit report to shareholders as a body under s 235 of the Companies Act 1985. It also states that the absence of a disclaimer may in some cases enable a court to draw an inference that the auditors have assumed responsibility for the audit report to a third party such as the bank in this case. *The ICAEW recommends* that auditors include the following wording in audit reports to clarify their duty of care to third parties by indicating that no such duty is owed.

> This report is made solely to the company's members as a body, in accordance with s 235 of the Companies Act 1985. Our audit work has been undertaken so that we might state to the company's members those matters we are required to state to them in an auditor's report and for no other purpose. To the fullest extent permitted by law, we do not accept or assume responsibility to anyone other than the company and the company's members as a body, for our audit work, for this report, or for the opinions we have formed.

Capping liability

For the larger firms of accountants providing audit services indemnity insurance adequate to cover potential liability is not available. The sums of damages potentially involved are of Armageddon proportions. In consequence the profession continues to lobby the government for a statutory cap on their liability. Failure by the government to respond may result in the larger groups of companies and public authorities being unable to obtain audit services.

GRADED QUESTIONS

Essay mode

1 Detail the provisions of the Companies Act 1985 relating to the qualifications, method of appointment and procedures for the removal of a company auditor.

(The Institute of Company Accountants)

2 (*a*) How may a company remove an auditor from the position he holds before the expiration of the term of his office? What can the auditor do if he is removed?

(*b*) What can a company do if it considers that the auditor has been negligent in his duties to the company?

(*c*) Can an individual shareholder sue an auditor if he carries out his duties negligently?

(The Chartered Institute of Management Accountants)

3 Lagjet Ltd has a fully issued authorised share capital of £40,000 divided into 40,000 ordinary £1 shares; 75p has been paid up on each share. The shares are allocated as follows:

the directors, Constance, Alan and Jack, each hold 6,500 shares;
James holds 9,500 shares;
Alfred and Florence each hold 5,500 shares.

The board wishes to call an extraordinary general meeting to pass the following resolutions:

1 to reduce the company's share capital by extinguishing the liability of shareholders in respect of the unpaid capital on their shares;
2 to appoint a new auditor, Bill, to fill a casual vacancy caused by the sudden death of the auditor appointed at the last annual general meeting.

James, who is owed £5,000 by the company for goods supplied, is opposed to the proposal to reduce the share capital. Alfred and Florence are opposed to the choice of Bill as auditor.

(*a*) Advise the board on the following matters:

(i) the statutory provisions relating to length of notice before such resolutions can be validly presented to an extraordinary general meeting;
(ii) the number of votes which must be secured before the above resolutions can be passed;
(iii) any further action it can take to secure the appointment of Bill as auditor if it fails to obtain the necessary majority at an extraordinary general meeting.

(*b*) In the event of the resolution to reduce the company's share capital being passed, advise:

(i) the board as to any further action it must take to make the reduction effective;

(ii) James who is still determined to prevent the reduction becoming effective until he has obtained repayment of his debt.

(*c*) What possible difference (if any) would it have made if BOTH Florence had not received notice of the meeting due to an error on the part of the company secretary and in consequence had failed to attend the meeting AND Jack had been unable to attend the meeting and had failed to appoint a proxy?

(*The Association of Chartered Certified Accountants*)

4 (*a*) Examine the nature of 'floating charges' as security for moneys lent or credit given to registered companies.

(*b*) Multifix Plc borrowed £1,000,000 from Moneybags giving as security a floating charge over all its undertakings. A clause in the contract provided that the company was not to create any other charges over its assets ranking in priority to or *pari passu* with the floating charge created in favour of Moneybags. Multifix purchased land and several buildings for development and resold most of the properties for substantial profits. A fixed charge was created over the unsold properties valued at £1,500,000 in favour of Finance Limited to secure moneys borrowed from the latter. Multifix has now gone into insolvent liquidation.

Advise the liquidator as to the respective rights of Moneybags and Finance Limited if in the event the assets of the company are insufficient to pay both parties in full.

Would your answer be different if in the contract with Moneybags there was a term to the effect that any attempt by the company to create any other charge over the assets subject to the floating charge, without the consent of Moneybags, would result in the immediate crystallisation of the floating charge?

(*University of Plymouth*)

Objective mode

Four alternative answers are given. Select ONE only. Circle the answer which you consider to be correct. Check your answers by referring back to the information given in the chapter and against the answers at the back of the book.

1 Morgan Ltd has just delivered its accounts to 31 December 2004 to the Registrar. The accounting records for that period must under the Companies Act 1985 be kept until:

A 31 December 2005.
B 31 December 2006.
C 31 December 2007.
D 31 December 2008.

2 Plush plc has prepared its accounts for the financial year ended 31 December 2004. What is the last date by which the accounts must be laid before a general meeting and filed with the Registrar?

A 31 July 2005.
B 31 October 2005.

C 31 December 2005.
D 31 March 2005.

3 The following resolutions may all be moved at a general meeting of a company:

(i) appointing a person as auditor other than a retiring auditor;
(ii) filling a casual vacancy in the office of auditor;
(iii) removing an auditor before the expiration of his term of office.

Which of these resolutions requires the special notice procedure?

A (i).
B (iii).
C (i) and (iii).
D (i), (ii) and (iii).

4 Which one of the following qualifications does a person require in order to seek the designation 'Registered Auditor'?

A A member of the Chartered Institute of Management Accountants.
B A member of the Chartered Institute of Public Finance and Accountancy.
C A member of the Association of Chartered Certified Accountants.
D A member of the Association of Accounting Technicians.

5 There are provisions in the Companies Act 1985 which relate to the appointment of auditors in the following situations:

(i) where the first auditors are to be appointed before the first general meeting at which the company's accounts are laid;
(ii) where there is a casual vacancy in the office of auditor;
(iii) where a general meeting at which accounts were laid did not appoint an auditor.

In which of the above situations have the directors of a company power to appoint auditors?

A (i) only.
B (i) and (ii).
C (i) and (iii).
D (ii) and (iii).

6 The directors of Tomos Ltd want to change their auditors and are putting the relevant resolution before a general meeting. What statutory rights have the auditors got to make representations to the shareholders of Tomos?

A They may speak at the meeting but cannot communicate with the shareholders in writing.
B They may communicate in writing with the shareholders before the meeting but cannot speak at it.
C The auditors may communicate in writing directly with shareholders and speak at the meeting.
D The auditors may communicate in writing through the company with the shareholders before the meeting and can speak at it.

Answers to questions in objective mode appear on p 577.

22

AMALGAMATIONS, RECONSTRUCTIONS AND TAKEOVERS

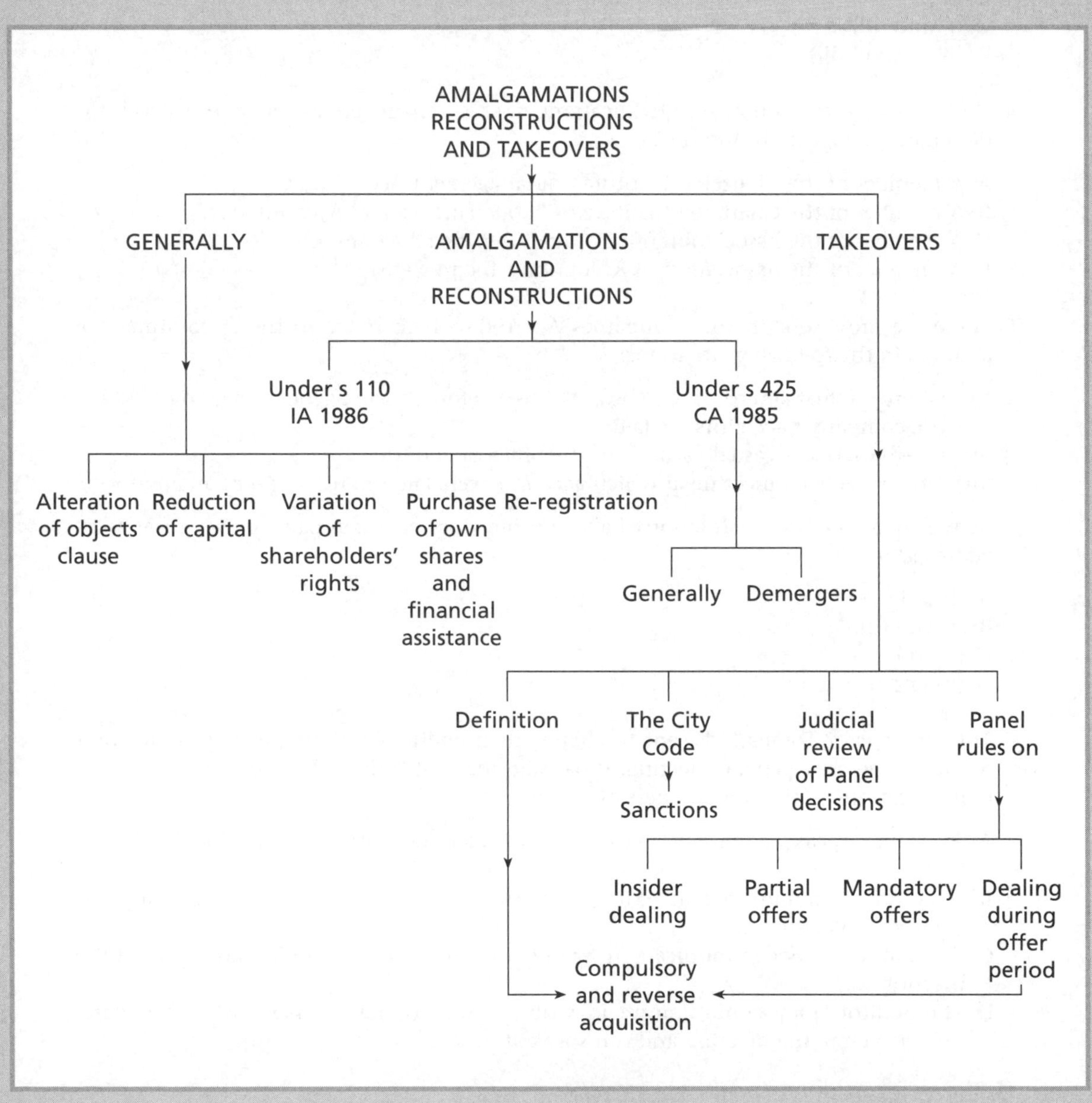

GENERALLY

The ways in which companies can alter their structures are set out below.

Objects clause

We have already considered the procedures under which a company may alter its objects clause to incorporate a new business (see further Chapter 3).

Reduction of capital

If the company merely wishes to reduce its share capital it may do so under the procedures set out in Chapter 7. The reduction requires the passing of a special resolution and the subsequent confirmation of the court.

Variation of shareholders' rights under the memorandum and articles or under the Companies Act

If the company wishes to alter the rights of shareholders, this can be effected by the approval of the variation at class meetings followed by a special resolution of the company. There is, of course, always the possibility that dissentients within the class will apply to the court (see further Chapter 6).

The relevant sections apply only to registered companies and in addition do not enable any variation to be made in the rights of creditors, including debenture holders. Often, however, the trust deed of an issue of debentures will contain a similar variation clause under which the rights of debenture holders can be varied. In such a case, however, the only remedy of dissenting debenture holders is to plead a general fraud on the minority.

Purchase of own shares and financial assistance

As we have seen, the 1985 Act allows the purchase by a company of its own shares (see further Chapter 7), and lays down procedures under which a company may give, in appropriate circumstances, financial assistance for the acquisition of its shares (see further Chapter 7).

Re-registration

It should also be borne in mind that a private limited company may now re-register as unlimited, but only with the consent of all the members, and that an unlimited company may re-register as a private limited company, though with the preservation of the liability of former members (Insolvency Act 1986, s 77).

Other methods of changing corporate structures

In addition to the areas of reconstruction described above, for most of the transactions which a company wishes to enter into, the powers of the board combined with the approval of 51 per cent of the members in general meeting will suffice. Why, then, is it necessary to include in the Companies Act 1985, s 425 and in the Insolvency Act 1986, s 110 provisions to deal with amalgamations and reconstructions?

The reason is that the provisions referred to above do not permit a company to *compel* a shareholder to sell or otherwise dispose of his shares, except as part of a reduction when he is, for example, paid off, or under s 429 in a takeover (see below). Nor do they allow the rights of creditors to be affected or enable the liability of members to be increased without their individual consent. Nor, again, do they provide a means of amalgamating two or more companies or the transfer of the undertaking of one company to another, or the demerger or partition of a company into separate management in another company or companies.

Section 425 of the Companies Act 1985 and s 110 of the Insolvency Act 1986 provide procedures for these kinds of changes to be made in a corporate structure.

In addition, there are some companies which cannot remedy internal problems by the use of the specific procedures referred to above. For example, the provisions allowing variation of shareholders' rights do not apply to companies which do not have a share capital. Therefore, if the rights of members are to be varied, s 425 will be used.

NFU Development Trust Ltd [1973] 1 All ER 135

The company was limited by guarantee without a share capital and had 94,000 members. All members could vote at general meetings and in the event of a winding-up had a right to the surplus assets of the company in such proportions as the directors should determine. The company proposed a scheme of arrangement where in order to reduce the expense of administration in sending out notices and other communications to the 94,000 members, the number of members of the company would be reduced to seven, all the other members being deprived of their membership. At a meeting to consider the scheme 85 per cent of the votes were cast in favour of it. Application was then made to the court to sanction the scheme. *Held* – by Brightman J – that the scheme would not be approved. It was not a compromise or arrangement within the terms of s 425. The rights of members were being expropriated without any compensating advantage and in this sense it could not be said that they were entering into a compromise or arrangement with the company.

Comment

Section 425 had to be used here, albeit unsuccessfully, because the company did not have a share capital, which meant that the usual variation of rights procedure was not available. Brightman J suggested that the solution was that members who were not interested in receiving, e.g., reports and accounts, should be asked to resign.

AMALGAMATIONS AND RECONSTRUCTIONS

The term 'reconstruction' is not defined by company legislation. However, it may be said that in a reconstruction the undertaking of the company concerned is preserved and is carried on *after* reconstruction by substantially the *same people* as it was before.

The contrast with an 'amalgamation' is that while a reconstruction consists of the reorganisation of one company or group, an amalgamation involves two or more companies (e.g. A and B) being brought together under one. That one may be either a new company, C, to absorb both A and B, or one of the companies, say B, may absorb the other, A.

Nevertheless, s 425, which is the major reconstruction section of the 1985 Act, can be used to effect an amalgamation by takeover by one company of another.

The takeover

Section 110 of the Insolvency Act 1986 is useful in obtaining mergers where the boards of the companies concerned are willing for the merger to take place. If they face opposition from members and/or creditors, then s 425 would be the better approach.

In a takeover proper, the board of the company to be acquired, say B, is not willing to co-operate so that the company seeking to acquire is forced to address an offer direct to the shareholders of B. This area of corporate activity is, as we shall see, not entirely covered by the law, control depending upon the extra-legal rules of the Panel on Takeovers and Mergers, though there are now criminal penalties for insider dealing generally and during a takeover, under the Criminal Justice Act 1993.

In an amalgamation or takeover involving A and B where A and B are in a similar line of business or are complementary, as where A makes the goods and B markets them, there is potentially a monopoly. In such a case the Secretary of State for Trade and Industry may, on the recommendation of the Director of Fair Trading, refer the merger to the Competition Commission under the Competition Act 1998. The merger will not then proceed until the Commission agrees that it should.

When a merger has been referred to the Commission, the parties are prohibited, for the duration of the inquiry, from acquiring shares in any of the other parties without the consent of the Secretary of State.

The Secretary of State is permitted to accept legally binding undertakings for part of the merged business to be disposed of, as an alternative to reference to the Commission.

Formerly these undertakings had to involve agreements to dispose of parts of the business. The Competition Act 1998 now provides for the acceptance of a wider range of undertakings, such as agreements for the future conduct of the business.

AMALGAMATION (OR RECONSTRUCTION) UNDER INSOLVENCY ACT 1986, S 110

Section 110 gives a liquidator power to accept shares as consideration for the sale of the property of a company, so that if A is in voluntary liquidation it may empower its liquidator by special resolution to sell its business and assets to B in exchange for B's shares.

The section would be used where there was no real opposition to an *amalgamation* by the members of A and no compromise with creditors was necessary. There are no provisions for variation of creditors' rights. Creditors are still entitled to prove in the liquidation of A.

If, in order to effect a *reconstruction*, the transfer of the undertaking of one company, A, to another, B, is to be associated with the liquidation of A, the scheme may be carried out under s 110 provided no compromises are required. For example, the section may be used to *demerge*, as where the various business activities of one large company, A, are placed under separate management in a number of other companies, B, C and D, and A is wound up. It may also be used to *partition* companies, as where a family company, E, is carrying on various activities and certain members of the family wish to carry on the activities separately through independent companies, F, G and H, and E is to be wound up.

Procedure

This is as follows:

(*a*) The company proposing to be wound up voluntarily will pass a special resolution for winding-up and appoint a liquidator.
(*b*) It will authorise the liquidator by special resolution to transfer the company's assets to a new company in return for shares in the new company. The new company may be one formed for the purpose or it may be an existing company.
(*c*) Such shares will be distributed among the members of the old company.
(*d*) Any member who did not vote in favour of the resolution can express his dissent by serving a written notice on the liquidator within seven days requiring him either:

   (i) to abstain from carrying the scheme into effect, or
   (ii) to purchase his shares at a price to be fixed by agreement or by arbitration, and the company must not be wound up until any such dissentient has been paid off, so that opposition from too many members could be costly.

(*e*) In *Payne* v *The Cork Co Ltd* [1900] 1 Ch 308 it was held that any provision in the articles preventing a member from dissenting was void.
(*f*) If an order for the compulsory winding-up of the company is made within a year, the special resolution authorising the transfer is void unless the leave of the court is given.
(*g*) It should be noted that in the case of a creditor's voluntary winding-up, the consent of the liquidation committee (if any) or the court is necessary. Apart from this there is no provision for a compromise with creditors.

AMALGAMATION (OR RECONSTRUCTION) UNDER S 425

If on a company *reconstruction* any compromise or arrangement is proposed between the company and its members or creditors s 425 must be used. The use of this section is essential for *amalgamation* where rights of members, debenture holders and creditors are to be compromised.

Procedure

This is as follows:

(*a*) The court has to be consulted at the outset and must be asked to direct the holding of meetings of members, creditors and debenture holders to discuss the proposed scheme. At this first stage the court will not exercise its discretion to call the meetings if, having regard to the opposition to the scheme by the holders of the majority of the votes, the meetings will serve no useful purpose. In addition, the court is concerned to see that the meetings are properly constituted. For example, a class meeting of shareholders may not be enough if there are groups within each class with different interests (*Re Hellenic and General Trust Ltd*, 1975; see further Chapter 1). The same problems can exist with creditors who may have different interests, e.g. some may have securities and others not.

However, in *Anglo-American Insurance Ltd* [2001] 1 BCLC 755 the High Court ruled that separate meetings of creditors were not required even though some were short term and some long term or resident in the USA. It appeared that they all had the same substantial rights under the scheme. The problems presented by a challenge to the suitability of the meetings held should not occur unless the company's creditor and/or member structure is significantly diverse. This view is supported by the decision in *Re Hawk Insurance Co Ltd* [2001] All ER (D) 289 (Feb) which is to the effect that unless significant and substantial differences in rights exist all creditors/members are capable of consulting together. The decision prevents unreasonable and oppressive complaints by minority interests but it has also, some say, significantly reduced the consideration and protection of minority concerns.

If the court agrees, the meetings will be summoned and full details of the scheme presented. The scheme may involve a winding-up of the company and a transfer of assets under s 427 (see below) or it may be an internal reconstruction of the kind seen in *NFU Development Trust Ltd*, 1973. In particular, the scheme must disclose the effect of the amalgamation upon directors, especially where it involves the retirement of some of them and payment to them of compensation for loss of office. This must be disclosed in the notices and sanctioned by the members.

Where the rights of debenture holders are affected, a reference to the material interests, if any, of the trustees for the debenture holders must be disclosed as for directors.

(*b*) The scheme must be approved by a majority in number and three-quarters in value of the members, creditors and debenture holders. For example, if a company has 100 members and A has got 901 shares of £1 each, and the other 99 members have one share each, then the rest cannot force a scheme on A. Equally, A plus 49 of the rest cannot force a scheme on the remainder but A plus 50 of the rest can force the scheme on the others. The same rules apply to creditors and debenture holders. The court must then be asked to consent to the scheme as approved. The court will have to be satisfied in particular that creditors are not being prejudiced by the scheme of arrangement proposed by the company; and creditors have not only the right to hold their own meeting before the court hearing, as we have seen, but also to be represented in court on the issue of the court's approval. In practice, the company will make sure at a very early stage that creditors are fully satisfied with the proposed scheme and will not raise objections. Furthermore, the court must be satisfied that there is a genuine 'compromise or arrangement' within the meaning of s 425; this implies some element of accommodation on each side, so that a scheme involving the total surrender of the rights of one side will not be approved (see *NFU Development Trust Ltd*, 1973).

(*c*) If the court approves the scheme it will do so by order and a copy of the court order certified by the Office of the Supreme Court is delivered to the Registrar at which point the scheme becomes binding on all concerned.

Although any member or creditor can ask the court to convene meetings under s 425, provided some compromise or arrangement is proposed, it appears that the court cannot do this unless the company has generated, or at least approves of, the scheme.

Thus in *Re Savoy Hotel Ltd* [1981] 3 All ER 646, Trusthouse Forte had made a bid for the shares of Savoy but could not get acceptance from the major class of voting shareholders. Trusthouse Forte asked the court to convene a meeting of those shareholders under s 425 so that the bid might be discussed with them, and hopefully they might be convinced to accept it. The judge held that he had no power to convene the meeting because the Savoy Company had not generated the scheme, nor did the board or the voting members appear to approve of it.

However, where the board and the majority of the shareholders of the company to be acquired wish to accept the bid a scheme under s 425 is useful, because s 425 only requires a majority in number and 75 per cent in value of the shareholders attending a meeting and voting in favour of the acquisition of their company to bind any dissenting minority, whereas under a normal takeover offer 90 per cent of the shareholders of the victim company must accept the bid before the predator company can compulsorily acquire the rest.

The provisions of s 427

Where a scheme under s 425 involves a winding-up, either to an internally reconstructed new company having the same members, debenture holders and creditors, or to a new or existing company as part of a merger, the court may by order:

(*a*) Transfer assets to the other company.
(*b*) Allot shares or debentures to members and debenture holders of the old company.
(*c*) Allow the old company's actions to be brought in the name of the other company.
(*d*) Dissolve the old company without a winding-up.
(*e*) Provide for dissentients otherwise than outlined in the scheme, e.g. by requiring them to be paid off.

Orders made under s 427 must be filed with the Registrar.

Examples of schemes of internal reconstruction approved by the court under s 425

Where s 425 is used internally, it represents a means by which a company can enter into a compromise or arrangement with its creditors and/or members without going into liquidation. Schedule 4, Part I of the Insolvency Act 1986 allows a compromise with creditors in the context of a winding-up, though Part I of the 1986 Act also provides a procedure for compromise with creditors, even though the company concerned is not in the course of winding-up. These provisions are considered in more detail later.

The court has approved the following types of internal reconstructions under s 425:

(*a*) Debenture holders have given extension of time for the payment of their loan capital.
(*b*) Debenture holders have accepted a cash payment less than the par value of the debentures.
(*c*) Debenture holders have given up their security, thus releasing it to secure further loans.
(*d*) Debenture holders have exchanged their debentures for shares.
(*e*) Creditors have taken cash in part payment of their debt and the balance in shares.

(*f*) Preference shareholders have given up their right to arrears of dividend.
(*g*) To simplify the capital structure of companies within a group, as where H is the holding company of several partly-owned subsidiaries, all of which have old-fashioned complex capital structures comprising many types of shares carrying widely varying rights. The capital structure of the group has been simplified by exchanging all the subsidiary companies' shares held by minority shareholders for ordinary shares or even loan stock in the holding company by means of a scheme of arrangement under s 425.

As (*g*) above shows, reconstruction does not necessarily involve compromising with creditors, nor is it always set in a context of financial difficulty. It is, for example, a technique used for demerging and incentives to dismantle a large group of companies are given, as we have seen, by the Companies Act 1985 in terms of share premium (see Chapter 12).

An example of a demerger attracting share premium relief appears in Figures 22.1 and 22.2. The activities of the companies are indicated, as is the holding of H in each.

(*a*) A allots 1,000 £1 ordinary shares (valued at £6.00 per share) to H.
(*b*) H transfers its 75 per cent holding in B to A.
(*c*) C allots 1,000 £1 ordinary shares (valued at £6.00 per share) to H.
(*d*) H transfers its 65 per cent holding in D to C.
(*e*) H is then wound up, its holdings in A and C being sold, e.g. by a public placing.

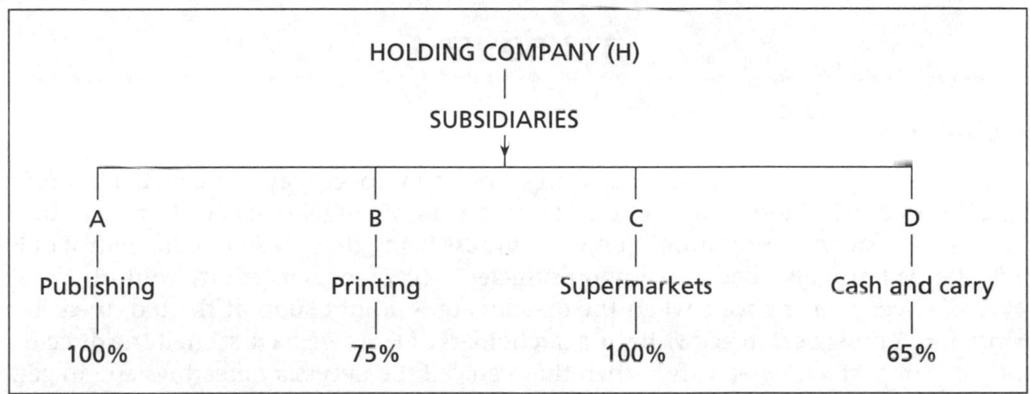

Figure 22.1 Old group structure

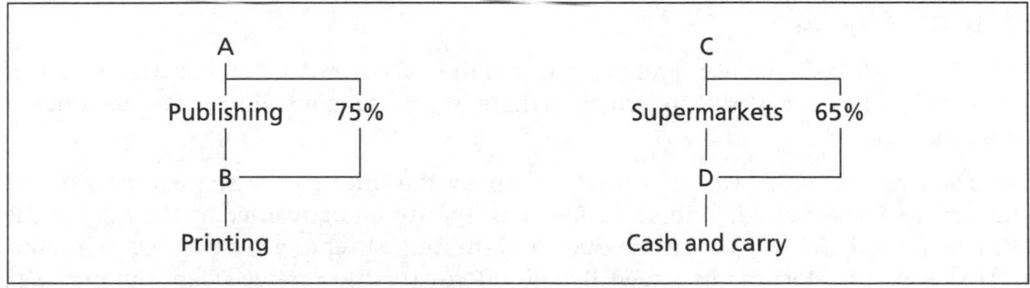

Figure 22.2 New demerged structure

Share premium relief: s 132

A and C need only transfer to share premium the 'minimum premium value'. This is the amount, if any, by which the base values of the shares in B and D exceed the aggregate nominal value of the shares A and C allotted to H.

Base value is the lower of the cost to H of the shares in B and D and the amount at which the shares of B and D were stated immediately prior to the transfer in the accounting records of H.

Example

(i) Shares in B and C cost H £4,000 in each case but stood in the accounting records of H at £3,000: base value £3,000.

(ii) Nominal value of shares allotted by A and C was £1,000, so minimum premium value is £2,000. This goes to a share premium account in the books of A and C, but not the true value of the consideration received from B and D by allotting shares to H. The true value, of course, is the total value of the assets of B and D which could run into many thousands or millions of pounds.

It should be noted that share premium relief under s 132 is available where the consideration for the issue of the shares consists of any *non-cash assets* of the company providing the consideration and not merely of shares in another subsidiary of the holding company (SI 1984/2007).

TAKEOVERS

Definition

On the assumption that A plc is acquiring B plc, a takeover may be defined as an offer to all the shareholders of B or one or more classes of shareholders of B, to buy their shares for cash and/or securities in A, the purpose being that A will obtain control of B. A's offer is normally conditional upon sufficient acceptances to ensure control.

A takeover proper occurs when the directors of B do not support the bid. In such a situation A must deal direct with the shareholders of B. As we have seen, if the directors of B do support a merger with A, then they can call the necessary meetings and in general terms organise an amalgamation by methods set out in s 110 of the Insolvency Act 1986 or s 425 which have already been dealt with.

Why the City Code?

The City Code on Takeovers and Mergers and the Takeover Panel which administers it are required because at the present time there is no legal control in regard to some of the following:

(*a*) *The offer document*, which is used to convey the offer to the shareholders of the company to be acquired, in this case B, is a prospectus and governed by the rules of the Financial Services and Markets Act 2000 and the Stock Exchange Listing requirements.

However, the documents issued by the offeror (or the offeree board, giving, e.g., advice to its members whether or not to accept) are also governed by section J of the

City Code, rules 23–27. The full details are beyond the scope of a book of this nature. However, rule 23 expresses the general standard of care in regard to documents from the offeror and offeree board as follows: 'Shareholders must be given sufficient information and advice to enable them to reach a properly informed decision as to the merits or demerits of an offer. Such information must be available to shareholders early enough to enable them to make a decision in good time. The obligation of the offeror in these respects towards the shareholders of the offeree company is no less than an offeror's obligation towards its own shareholders.' Of major importance is the requirement to give stated financial information about the offeror company (see rule 24.2). This includes, for the last three financial years for which information has been published, turnover, net profit or loss before and after taxation, the charge for tax, extraordinary items, minority interests, the amount absorbed by dividends and earnings and dividends per share.

(*b*) *Partial bids*. In the absence of the City Code there would be nothing to prevent a company making a partial bid in order to achieve control of a company 'on the cheap' as it were. It is not in practice necessary to acquire 50 per cent or more of the voting power of a company in order to control it. The making of partial bids is controlled by the Code and there are provisions under which a mandatory bid must be made for the remainder of the shares of the company to be acquired once a certain number of shares in that company has been obtained. These matters will be considered in more detail later.

(*c*) *Insider dealing*. The Code deals with insider trading in quoted companies and the Takeover Panel can publish reprimands in respect of those who deal inside. These are extra-legal sanctions, the Criminal Justice Act 1993 providing for criminal sanctions. The contribution in this field made by the Financial Services and Markets Act 2000 on market abuse under the control of the Financial Services Authority has already been noted (see Chapter 12).

(*d*) *Misleading profit forecasts*. Directors and other officers of companies do, from time to time, make public statements as to the future profits of companies which are misleading. The Panel has been active in this area in requiring the publication of corrections of misleading statements.

In addition, when a forecast of profit before taxation appears in a document addressed to shareholders, there must be included forecasts of taxation, extraordinary items and minority interests.

(*e*) *Tactics of directors*. The directors of the company to be acquired have in the past used tactics to frustrate the bid and retain control. The Panel takes action on the basis of the Code's general principle 7 which states:

> 'At no time after a bona fide offer has been communicated to the board of the offeree company or after the board of the offeree company has reason to believe that a bona fide offer might be imminent may any action be taken by the board of the offeree company in relation to the affairs of the company, without the approval of the shareholders in general meeting, which could effectively result in any bona fide offer being frustrated or in the shareholders being denied an opportunity to decide on its merits.'

In the past, directors' tactics used to frustrate a bid have often consisted of the issue of additional shares to a company or person(s) who would not accept the bid, without consulting the shareholders of the victim company as to whether this tactic of the directors was acceptable. Obviously general principle 7 would apply to such a situation but now the 1985 Act provides, as we have seen, that the authority of the company is required before the allotment of certain securities by the directors (see Chapter 10). This is reinforced by rule 21 which carries a similar provision regarding the issue of shares but extends to the making of other contracts otherwise than in the ordinary course of business.

However, there are some situations where general principle 7 and rule 21 would be the only sanction, for example where the directors lease off the company's property to put it beyond the control of the bidder so that he does not continue with his bid. If we assume that company B, our victim company, owns the freehold of a large block of flats which a bidder for company B wishes to demolish in order to develop the site, then if the directors of B were to lease out the block of flats for, say, 99 years, thus preventing the bidder, even if he were successful, from demolishing the premises for that period so that he did not proceed with his bid, then such a tactic would, unless approved by ordinary resolution of the members, infringe general principle 7 and rule 21 and the 'proper purpose' rule and could be the basis of a complaint to the Panel and action by it to prevent infringement of the Code.

Has the Code any teeth?

Since the whole of this chapter is based on the acquisition of companies where at least one is a *listed* company, the answer is 'yes'. This is based on the fact that every company which seeks the Stock Exchange as a market for purchase and sale of its securities is required to enter into a 'listing agreement' with the UK Listing Authority (an arm of the Financial Services Authority), which binds the company to observe certain rules and procedures. The ultimate sanction for breach of the agreement is in essence very simple and consists in the deprivation of the facilities of the market. The regulations of the Authority do not have the force of law but it will be readily understood that, with a sanction of the nature mentioned above, there will normally be compliance with the rules of the UK Listing Authority and the City Code, which the UK Listing Authority supports.

In addition, the membership of the Panel covers a wide range of services within the City and therefore a flagrant flouting of the Code could lead to problems in addition to the loss of the Stock Exchange market for purchase and sale of securities. The Code is issued on the authority of the Takeover Panel.

Membership of the Panel

The chairman, deputy chairmen and certain further members of the Panel are appointed by the Governor of the Bank of England. In addition, its membership comprises individuals nominated by the following bodies, all of which are committed to support its activities:

The Association of British Insurers;
The Association of Investment Trust Companies;
The Association of Private Client Investment Managers and Stockbrokers;
The British Bankers' Association;
The Confederation of British Industry;

The Institute of Chartered Accountants in England and Wales;
The London Investment Banking Association (with separate representation for its Corporate Finance Committee and Securities Trading Committee);
The National Association of Pension Funds;
The Investment Management Association;
London Investment Banking Association Securities Trading Committee.

Each of the bodies listed above may also nominate designated alternates.

In addition, the Panel publishes reprimands which may even appear in the professional press. The publication of this sort of information should have some effect upon practitioners for publication leads to knowledge by their colleagues that they have transgressed the ethics of the Code.

In connection with the exercise of its functions, the City Code states in the Introduction section that the Panel operates in accordance with the Human Rights Act 1998.

The system works efficiently. At any time before or during the offer period any party or his adviser can contact any member of the Panel executive and get a speedy ruling – usually within a day. At very short notice an appeal can be made to the Panel itself, the members of which will review the decision of the executive. Further appeals go to the Appeal Committee which comprises a chairman and deputy chairman appointed by the Governor of the Bank of England being persons who have held high judicial office, e.g. a former Lord Justice of Appeal and three members of the Panel who have not previously dealt with the matter under review. It is quite rare in practice for the appeal procedures to be invoked.

Judicial review

In *R* v *Panel on Takeovers* [1987] 1 All ER 564 the Court of Appeal decided that, having regard to the public consequences of non-compliance with the Code, e.g. that a bid by one company for another could be declared invalid if the procedures of the Code were infringed, an application to the High Court to consider a Panel ruling by way of judicial review would be available in an appropriate case. The courts are not, however, anxious to intervene because judicial review of a Panel decision introduces an element of delay which is undesirable in the takeover situation.

All that now remains is to consider some of the major steps in a takeover bid and see how the various rules of the Code affect the position. In addition, we must give special consideration to the duties of directors in takeovers since this is not only the greatest area of practical problems but is also most likely to be required for examination purposes.

In all situations company A is attempting to acquire company B.

Secrecy during negotiations: insider dealing

The relevant provisions, which are set out in rules 2 and 4, are designed to prevent insider dealing and they are *extra-legal* in their operation. The *legal* provisions, under which insider dealing may, in certain circumstances, be a criminal offence punishable by a fine and/or imprisonment, are set out in the Criminal Justice Act 1993 (see Chapter 12).

There are, as we have seen, additional *civil* sanctions for market abuse in the Financial Services and Markets Act 2000 that are administered by the Financial Services Authority.

Rule 2, which is concerned with keeping bids secret before public announcement, states: 'The vital importance of absolute secrecy before an announcement must be emphasised.'

Rule 4, which is concerned with dealings before and during the offer, requires all persons who have confidential price-sensitive information concerning an offer or contemplated offer to treat it as secret and not pass it on to anyone else unless it is necessary to do so, as where it is part of a person's work to pass it on as, e.g., by one member of an audit team to another as part of the audit function.

Additionally, there must not be dealings in securities of the offeree or the offeror company by persons (other than the offeror) who have price-sensitive information prior to the announcement of an approach by a bidder, or an actual bid, or of the termination of negotiations. Dealing is allowed in the shares of the offeror company where the bid will not significantly affect the value of the offeror's shares, which may often be the case. It is the shares of the offeree company which are most likely to be affected by a bid.

If those involved in the negotiations feel that secrecy cannot be maintained, they should ask the Stock Exchange for a temporary halt in dealings.

Failure to comply with rules 2 and 4 may result in a reprimand from the Panel which may be published.

The rules of the Code are now preventive and information suggesting that insider dealing has taken place which might be revealed by dealings on the Stock Exchange would be passed by the Stock Exchange and by the Panel to the Financial Services Authority for investigation.

Offer document and response of offeree board

The rules derive from section J (consisting of rules 23–27) of the City Code. It is worth referring again to the general object of the detailed contents of the offer document and any documents issued by the offeree board which is stated in rule 23 (see page 497).

More important than the contents of the offer document is what an individual shareholder can do if he is misled by the contents of the offer document. While accepting that this branch of the law is not well developed, the judgment of Brightman J in *Gething* v *Kilner* [1972] 1 WLR 337 would seem to justify the following statement:

> 'If an offer document or a recommendation circulated by the directors of the offeree company contains a false or misleading statement made knowingly, or presumably, if such a document omits information known to the persons issuing it which the law or good practice requires it to contain, any shareholder of the class to whom the bid is addressed may apply to the court for an injunction to restrain the offeror from proceeding with the bid or declaring it unconditional.'

Partial offers and mandatory offers

In this connection a knowledge of rule 36 (partial offers) and rule 9 (mandatory offers) is of importance. However, before considering the rules relating to partial offers which can result in a bidder obtaining control of a company 'on the cheap', as it were, the nature of a partial bid should be understood. If we take three shareholders of the target company and their holdings to be Mr A (100 shares), Mr B (50 shares), and Mr C (40 shares), then a 50 per cent partial bid will involve, e.g., an offer to take 50 of A's shares,

25 of B's shares, and 20 of C's. When this sort of bid is being contemplated, rule 36 must be followed. Under the rule the Panel's consent is required for any partial offer.

In addition, the following subrules of rule 36 should be noted.

In the case of an offer which would result in the offeror holding shares carrying less than 30 per cent of the voting rights of a company, consent will normally be granted (rule 36.1).

Any offer which would result in the offeror holding shares carrying 30 per cent or more of the voting rights of a company must normally be conditional, not only on the relevant number of acceptances being received, but also on approval of the offer, normally signified by means of a separate box on the Form of Acceptance and Transfer, being given by shareholders holding 50 per cent of the voting rights not held by the offeror and persons acting in concert with it. This requirement may on occasion be waived if over 50 per cent of all voting rights of the offeree company are held by the shareholder (rule 36.5).

Where an offer is made for a company with more than one class of equity share capital which would result in the offeror holding shares carrying 30 per cent or more of the voting rights, a comparable offer must be made for each class (rule 36.8).

In connection with mandatory offers, the following subrules of rules 2 and 9 should be noted.

Mandatory offers

A mandatory bid must be made unless the Panel gives its consent:

- by a person who acquires whether by a series of transactions over a period of time or not shares which taken together with shares held or acquired by persons acting in concert with him carry 30 per cent or more of the voting rights of the company;
- by a person who together with people acting in concert with him holds not less than 30 per cent but not more than 50 per cent of the voting rights of a company if there is *any increase at all* in the percentage level of that holding.

Previously in such situations a person or a group acting in concert could acquire in any 12-month period additional shares carrying up to 1 per cent of the voting rights without making a general offer for the company. The change was made following criticism of the ability of a person or concert party to achieve control over a period of time without making a formal bid as where the holding was, say, 48 per cent and the 1 per cent acquisitions eventually brought over 50 per cent and thereby basic control.

The second rule is to deal with persons who have made a bid that has failed to achieve control but which has left the bidder with, say, a 35 per cent holding. Although the City Code consists of extra-legal rules, the High Court applied the 30 per cent mandatory bid rule in effect by the decision in *Philip Morris Products Inc* v *Rothmans International Enterprises Ltd (No 2)* [2000] *The Times*, 10 August.

Immediately upon an acquisition of shares which gives rise to an obligation to make an offer under this rule, the offeror shall make an announcement of its offer giving the information required by the Code. The announcement of an offer under this rule should include confirmation by a financial adviser or other appropriate independent party that resources are available to the offeror sufficient to satisfy full acceptance of the offer (rule 2.5(c)).

An important exception to the requirement to make a mandatory bid occurs when there is a rescue operation. If company B is in financial difficulties but company A is willing to invest in the share capital of B in order to save it, then if A takes an issue of shares in B which gives A, say, 35 per cent of the share capital of B, the Panel will consider waiving the mandatory bid requirement for the rest of B's shares.

Except with the consent of the Panel, no nominee of the offeror or persons acting in concert with it shall be appointed to the board of the offeree company, nor shall the offeror and persons acting in concert with it transfer, or exercise the votes attaching to, any shares in the offeree company, until the offer document has been posted (rule 9.7).

The Code defines 'acting in concert' as follows: 'Persons acting in concert comprise persons who, pursuant to an agreement or understanding (whether formal or informal), actively co-operate, through the acquisition by any of them of shares in a company, to obtain or consolidate control of that company.'

Then follows a list of persons who will be presumed to be persons acting in concert with others in the same category unless the contrary is established. These include a company, its parent, subsidiaries, and fellow-subsidiaries, and their associated companies.

For this purpose, ownership or control of 20 per cent or more of the equity share capital of the company will be regarded as a test of associated company status. Other persons presumed to be acting in concert are a company with any of its directors (together with their close relatives and related trusts); a company with any of its pension funds; a person with any investment company, unit trust or other funds whose investments such person manages on a discretionary basis; a financial adviser with his client where the financial adviser has shares in the client company; and finally, directors of a company which is subject to an offer or where the directors have reason to believe a bona fide offer for their company may be imminent.

It should be noted that although an interest of under 30 per cent does not constitute control in the Takeover Panel's eyes, the Office of Fair Trading may take the view that it could constitute a merger giving the Office of Fair Trading power to make a reference to the Competition Commission with a view to preventing the takeover going ahead if it is thought by the Competition Commission to be undesirable in the public interest. The relevant provisions are contained in the Competition Act 1998 and the Enterprise Act 2002.

Compulsory acquisition

Section 429 is a section which can be used but only by a corporate bidder who has made a bid to acquire compulsorily the shares of a small minority who have not accepted the offer. The provisions of the section are as follows:

(*a*) Where A already has not more than 10 per cent of B or no holdings in B at all, then if 90 per cent of B's shareholders, or other shareholders, have accepted the offer within four months A may within two months after the reaching of the 90 per cent threshold serve a notice on dissentients that it intends to acquire their shares. The dissentients have six weeks from the date on which the notice was given to appeal to the court. If there is no appeal or the court does not order otherwise, A acquires the shares.

(*b*) Where A has more than 10 per cent of B, then under s 428 of the 1985 Act three-quarters in number and 90 per cent in value of B's other shareholders must accept within four months of the offer.

The court will seldom interfere if the offer is fair but will not allow the section to be used for improper purposes such as the expulsion of a minority.

Re Bugle Press Ltd [1960] 3 All ER 791

Holders of 90 per cent of the shares in a company formed a new company which made an offer for the shares of the old company. As was to be expected, 90 per cent of the shareholders accepted the offer and the new company then served notice on the holder of the other 10 per cent of the shares stating that it wished to purchase his holding. *Held* – by the Court of Appeal – that in substance the new company was the same as the majority shareholders, and the scheme was in effect an expropriation of the minority interest. 'What the section is directed to is a case where there is a scheme or contract for the acquisition of a company, its amalgamation, re-organisation or the like, and where the offeror is independent of the shareholders in the transferor company, or at least independent of that part or fraction of them from which the 90 per cent is to be derived.' *Per* Evershed MR.

The High Court (affirmed by the Court of Appeal) has ruled that s 429 allows a bidder who holds 90 per cent in value of the shares in the victim following a bid to compulsorily acquire the shares of the remaining members even though they did not receive the offer documents.

In Re Joseph Holt plc Winpar Holdings Ltd *v* Joseph Holt Group plc [2000] 97 (44), LSG 44. Appeal case available at www.lawtel.com, under Case Law-CO100109

In March 2000, Inhoco 1849 plc, now the Joseph Holt Group plc, announced that it was making an offer to acquire all the issued share capital of Joseph Holt plc. The offer document was sent to most of Joseph Holt plc's existing shareholders, and an advertisement was placed in the London edition of the *Financial Times*. The offer document was not sent to shareholders whose addresses were in Australia, Canada, Japan or the USA because complying with the securities laws of those countries was difficult and costly.

By April 2000, Joseph Holt Group plc had received acceptances which, together with the shares it already held, amounted to over 90 per cent in value of Joseph Holt plc.

Notices of compulsory acquisition under s 429(1) were sent to the remaining shareholders. Once notices are sent, the bidder is entitled to, and must, acquire the outstanding shareholdings under s 430(2).

A s 429(1) notice was sent to Winpar Holdings Ltd in Australia. The company objected on the ground that the notice was invalid since it had not received the offer documents.

The High Court ruled (later affirmed by the Court of Appeal) that the offer was to acquire all the shares as required by s 428. The fact that the offer was not communicated to a particular shareholder was not fatal to the offer and the subsequent proceedings under s 429(1). For the compulsory acquisition procedure to apply, it was necessary only that an offer for all the shares was made: it was not necessary that such an offer was received by or known to a particular shareholder. The offer made by Joseph Holt Group related to Winpar's shares, even though Winpar was not aware of it. The offer documentation was a general and not a limited process, and in addition the offer did not exclude the shares of those resident in Australia. The s 429(1) notice to Winpar was therefore valid and the compulsory purchase procedure applied to its shares.

Comment

Transfer of the acquired shares is effected by an instrument of transfer executed on behalf of the shareholder by a person appointed by the offeror (see s 430(6)).

Reverse acquisition

Under s 430A where A has acquired 90 per cent of B but does not intend to buy out the dissentients, then A must, within one month of acquiring 90 per cent, notify the dissentients of that fact. The dissentients then have three months to request A to buy them out and on receipt of such a request A must do so.

Directors' duties in a takeover by general offer

Suppose that in a bid situation the directors bargain for additional payments to themselves, what can the other shareholders do?

Apart from the provisions of the City Code, if the directors of B retire from office 'golden handshakes' are covered by the 1985 Act and such sums are held in trust for those shareholders who sold their shares as a result of the offer, if the payments were not disclosed and approved by ordinary resolution of the members.

If they do not retire, the 1985 Act does not apply and additional payments made to directors are not recoverable. Thus if no change is made in the directorship but, for example, the board are paid £100,000 to persuade them to recommend the offer to the other shareholders, or are paid an increased price for their shares because they hold a large block, it seems there can be no recovery under the Act.

It will be apparent, therefore, that there are situations in which the directors, in connection with a takeover bid, may receive additional payments without being liable to account for them under the statute.

The Code also applies and provides that unless the Panel consents the offeror, or persons acting in concert, may not make arrangements to deal or buy or sell shares of the offeree company during an offer or when one is in contemplation, if those arrangements have attached to them favourable conditions not being extended to all shareholders.

The City Code and the supervision of the Panel should in most cases prevent this occurring in the case of public companies but it could still occur in the case of private ones where in fact some of the worst abuses have occurred in the past. Where a private company is concerned or, in the case of a public company if the Panel is not effective, the most hopeful line, in terms of getting the money back from the directors, is to allege a breach of their fiduciary duties towards the company. The general equitable principle exemplified in *Regal (Hastings) Ltd* v *Gulliver*, 1942 (see Chapter 17) could apply. However, the action is not straightforward because the wrong covered in that case is basically one to the company and payments made to directors to secure favourable recommendation to the shareholders in a bid situation seem merely to be a payment to them in their capacity as directors, no corporate action being involved, though the extra money received is, of course, an undisclosed benefit or profit from office and is recoverable by the company on the basis of a breach of fiduciary duty.

However, it is somewhat futile to allow the company to recover in cases where those who are really wronged are the other shareholders who have sold. The 1985 Act provides that moneys paid as a result of retirement are held on trust for the shareholders but the judge-made equitable rules as seen in the *Regal* case do not necessarily extend to shareholders. However, American courts are ahead of ours and have allowed recovery by the individual shareholders who have suffered, notwithstanding that the basic principle in the case was that a duty to the company had been broken.

Dealings in shares during offer period

Another problem which can arise if the directors have been offered incentives to recommend a bid is that the bid price for the shares may be lower than it should be. Where this is so, the offeror company (A) may, in order to enhance its chances of successful control, purchase shares in B on the market at a price higher than the bid price.

Since it is not desirable to fetter the market in shares, rule 8.1 of the Code provides that dealings in relevant securities by the parties to a takeover and by any associates, for their own account, or the account of discretionary investment clients, must be disclosed daily to the Stock Exchange (Company Announcements Office), the Panel and the press (discretionary) not later than 12 noon on the business day following the date of the transaction. Such disclosures must state the total of all relevant securities of any offeror or the offeree company purchased or sold on any day during the offer period, in the market or otherwise, and the prices paid or received.

In this connection, rule 6.2 provides that if the offeror or persons acting in concert purchase securities during the offer period at above the offer price, then it shall increase its offer to not less than the highest price paid for the securities so acquired. Rule 7.1 provides that an announcement of any such purchase and the consequent increased offer must be made immediately.

The Code provides that a person with a significant commercial interest in the outcome of an offer should not, without the consent of the Panel, deal in the shares of an offeror or an offeree company during an offer period.

Reform

The proposed EC Thirteenth Company Law Directive governing the conduct of takeover bids had continued to make progress through EU institutions. The draft Directive was largely based on the UK Takeover Code; however, the European Parliament rejected the final draft on 4 July 2001. In this connection the Commission set up an expert group to prepare new proposals and it appears that these will be approved. They are unlikely to have a major impact on the Code or the role of the Panel in the UK.

GRADED QUESTIONS

Essay mode

1 In order to raise additional finance Devonia Trust plc, a holding company, intends to make a rights issue. Its subsidiaries have their own classes of share capital with different voting and dividend rights. With a view to simplifying the capital structure of the group it is proposed to exchange all the subsidiary companies' shares held by minority shareholders for ordinary shares in the holding company itself.

Advise Devonia Trust plc as to how its objective could be achieved, the steps necessary to be taken and the implications of any such scheme.

(*University of Plymouth*)

2 Write notes on TWO of the following:

(*a*) promoters;
(*b*) redeemable shares;
(*c*) disqualification of directors;
(*d*) schemes of arrangement.

(*The Institute of Chartered Secretaries and Administrators*)

3 Zed Ltd wish to acquire the undertaking of a company which is in members' voluntary liquidation but still trading. Zed Ltd cannot afford cash for the purchase and suggest they should issue their own shares to the value required. How can this suggestion be implemented?

(*The Institute of Chartered Accountants in England and Wales*)

4 Beefy Farm Ltd was incorporated in 2005. Its articles of association appointed Peter and Richard as directors for life. The objects clause of the company's memorandum of association provided that the company should carry on the business of beef breeding with any other activities reasonably incidental thereto. The objects clause included a power to borrow money and a provision that no object or power should be deemed subsidiary to any other.

In November 2005 Beefy Farm Ltd unexpectedly received what appeared to be an attractive proposition from an Italian company to manufacture their ice cream under licence. The Italian company encouraged them to use the farm's milk in the manufacture. Beefy Farm Ltd borrowed £100,000 from National Bank plc to get started with the new business but subsequently refused to repay it on the ground that the loan was *ultra vires*.

(*a*) Advise National Bank plc on their legal position.

AND

(*b*) How far, if at all, would your answer to (*a*) differ if the bank had a copy of Beefy Farm Ltd's memorandum of association at the time of lending the money?

AND

(*c*) How far, if at all, would your answer to (*a*) differ if Richard alone negotiated the loan agreement and Peter knew nothing about it?

(*Glasgow Caledonian University*)

5 B Ltd held a general meeting including the following alterations to the articles which were duly passed:

(*a*) 'a member shall, upon the request of the board, transfer his shares to a person nominated by the board';
(*b*) 'a director shall vacate office upon the written request of all other directors';
(*c*) 'upon the death of a director his/her shares shall be forthwith registered in the name of his/her spouse or other next of kin notwithstanding any testamentary disposition to the contrary';
(*d*) 'a member wishing to sell his shares shall inform the directors who shall buy them at a fair valuation made by the auditors'.

Henry has been a director for five years and was appointed by the articles. He has no service contract, but the articles appointed him for life. He has been asked to resign under (*b*) above.

John, who holds 1,000 shares, and is also a shareholder in a rival company with which he now trades (having formerly traded with B Ltd), has been requested under (*a*) above to transfer his shares to Alice, the daughter of one of the directors.

Sally is executor of Jim, a deceased director who by his will bequeathed his shares to his daughter Lyn. The board has refused to transfer his shares to Lyn saying they have been registered under (*c*) above in the name of Rebecca, Jim's widow, from whom he had been separated but not divorced for 40 years.

Vera has informed the board that she wishes to sell her shares, but two months have elapsed and the board has taken no action at all.

Advise Henry, John, Sally and Vera of any legal remedies which may be open to them.

(*Kingston University*)

Objective mode

Four alternative answers are given. Select ONE only. Circle the answer which you consider to be correct. Check your answers by referring back to the information given in the chapter and against the answers at the back of the book.

1 Thames plc is in financial difficulties and wants its debenture holders to exchange their debentures for shares in order to get rid of the requirement to pay interest on the debentures. How should Thames proceed?

A Under s 110 of the Insolvency Act 1986.
B Under s 425 of the Companies Act 1985.
C By a reduction of capital.
D By unilaterally altering the terms of issue of the debentures.

2 Developer plc wishes to take over Hotels Ltd in order to develop the sites on which various hotels belonging to Hotels Ltd stand as supermarkets. Developer's bid is likely to be accepted by a majority of Hotels' shareholders. The directors of Hotels Ltd have sold the various hotels to a subsidiary of Hotels Ltd and taken a lease back of them. The lease restricts the use of the various premises to the hotel business. Developer has now withdrawn its bid. What is the position of the directors of Hotels Ltd?

A They are only in breach of the 'proper purpose rule'.
B They are not in breach of any fiduciary duty.
C They are in breach of the 'proper purpose rule' and the City Code.
D They are liable for breach of warranty of authority.

3 Tay plc is to make a bid for shares in Uncle plc. If the bid is successful it will result in Tay holding 20 per cent of the shares in Uncle. What is the position under the City Code?

A The Panel must consent and will normally do so.
B There is no need for the Panel to be involved.
C The Panel must consent and is unlikely to do so.
D The City Code does not allow this sort of bid.

4 Toys plc is in financial difficulties. Cycles plc is prepared to inject new capital into Toys, which when completed will leave Cycles with 35 per cent of the share capital of Toys. What is the position under the City Code?

A Cycles is required to make a bid for the rest of Toys' shares.
B The City Code provides for rescue bids to go through without recourse to the Panel.
C The City Code is not concerned with rescue bids.
D The Panel may in the case of a rescue bid waive the normal requirements for a mandatory bid.

5 Fred, a financier, has made a personal bid for the equity shares of Brick plc. He has acquired 92 per cent of the shares in Brick and intends to compulsorily acquire the rest. What is the legal position?

A Fred will be able compulsorily to acquire the shares under the Companies Act 1985.
B Fred cannot compulsorily acquire the shares under the Companies Act 1985 because he did not get 95 per cent.
C There are no legal provisions which allow compulsory acquisition.
D The compulsory acquisition provisions of the Companies Act 1985 do not apply in this situation.

6 Before incorporation of a company called Alfredo Ltd its promoter, Mostyn, made a contract on behalf of the company. Who will be liable if the contract is not performed by Alfredo Ltd?

A Alfredo Ltd.
B Mostyn.
C The directors of Alfredo Ltd.
D The shareholders of Alfredo Ltd.

Answers to questions in objective mode appear on p 577.

23

CORPORATE INSOLVENCY – COMPANY RESCUE

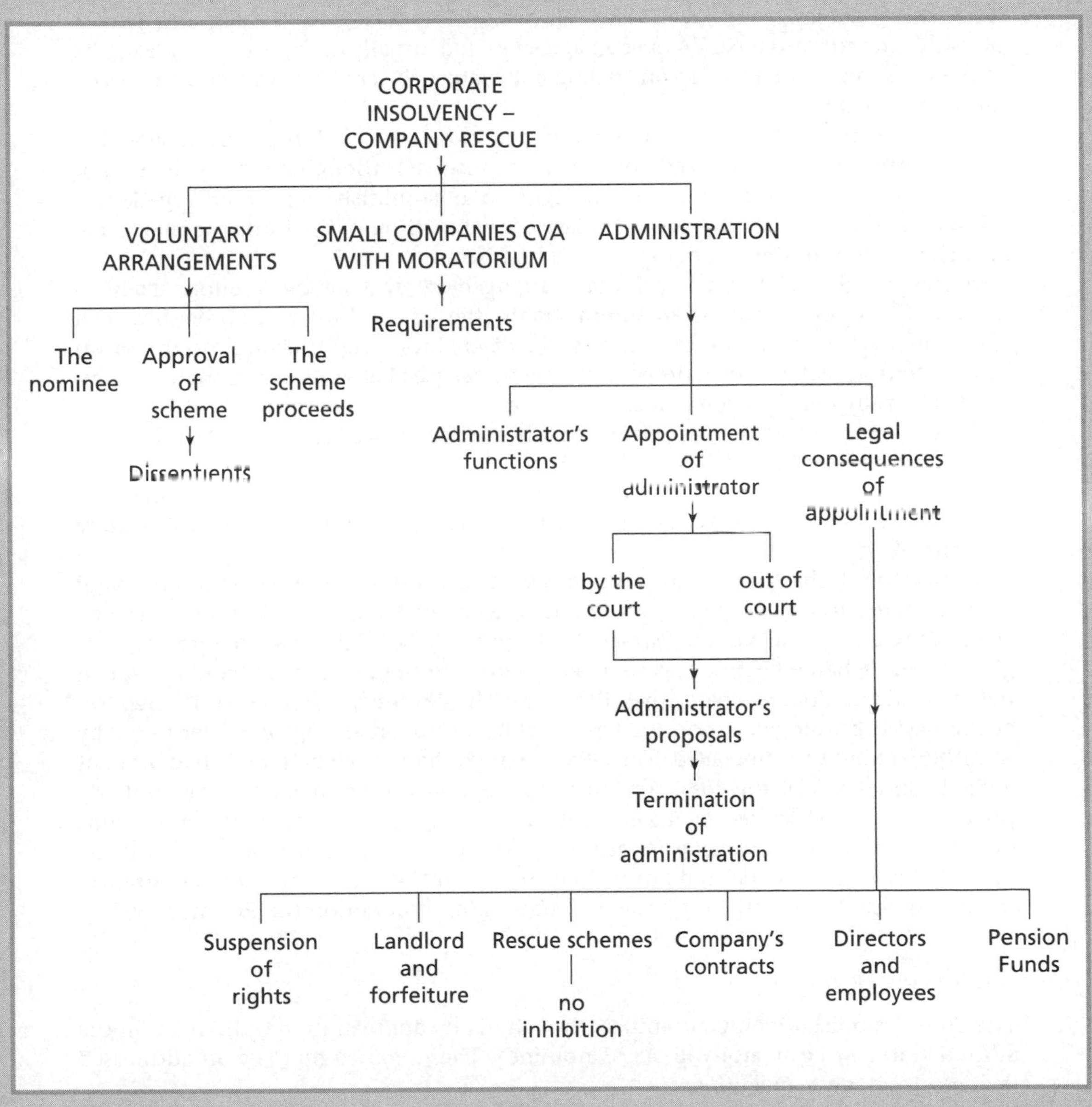

In this chapter we shall consider those aspects of insolvency law which are designed to rescue the company and prevent winding-up.

VOLUNTARY ARRANGEMENTS

Sections 1 to 7 of the Insolvency Act 1986 provide for a type of voluntary arrangement which is concerned to prevent a company from being wound up. In general terms, a CVA is a contract made between the company and its creditors. The contract freezes the existing debts at an agreed date. The company carries on trading and pays a monthly amount into the CVA over an agreed period, usually of three to five years. The CVA allows the company to go on trading but enables the creditors to receive at least a part of their debt.

The company's directors can initiate formal proposals for a voluntary arrangement at any time and the company need not actually be insolvent though it often will be, or at any rate close to it. Once a winding-up begins or an administration order is made (see below), the directors can no longer initiate a scheme, though the initiative may come in such a case from the liquidator or the administrator.

In fact, in general terms a voluntary arrangement will be much more likely to succeed if it is put forward by an administrator after an administration order has been made since as we shall see the suspension of creditors' rights which occurs in an administration will give the administrator/nominee (see below) a better chance to put together a fully considered scheme.

The proposals will be similar to those which must be referred to the court under s 425 of the Companies Act 1985 (see Chapter 22), e.g. creditors agreeing to take, say, 50 pence in the pound. The Insolvency Act 1986 provides a simpler approach than s 425, though that section remains available for major reconstructions for which it is more appropriate.

In this regard, the High Court has approved as a voluntary arrangement a proposal by a company to pay nil pence in the pound to its preferential and other unsecured creditors (see *IRC* v *Adams and Partners Ltd* [1999] 2 BCLC 730). Creditor approval was given to the scheme because it gave a better return to the Bank of Scotland plc which held a fixed and floating charge over the assets. The Revenue, as a preferential creditor, challenged the arrangement on the basis that it was not an arrangement permitted by the 1986 Act but its claim failed. The Revenue might have fared better if it had brought a claim under s 6 of the 1986 Act on the basis that the arrangement was 'unfairly prejudicial' to it. However, such a claim must be brought within 28 days of the results of the creditors' meeting being reported to the court and the Revenue had left it too late for this. The Revenue could only challenge it on the basis that it was an arrangement of a type not permitted by the Act, and on this contention the Revenue failed.

The nominee

The directors must appoint a nominee, though in an administration or liquidation the administrator or liquidator will act as nominee. The nominee must be an authorised licensed insolvency practitioner.

Certain professional bodies recognised by the Secretary of State for Trade and Industry may authorise their members to act as insolvency practitioners. The bodies currently recognised for England and Wales are: The Association of Chartered Certified Accountants, The Insolvency Practitioners Association, The Institute of Chartered Accountants in England and Wales, and The Law Society. Persons not authorised by a professional body may apply to the Secretary of State for Trade and Industry for authorisation. The relevant professional association is the Society of Practitioners in Insolvency.

In this connection, s 4 of the Insolvency Act 2000 authorises persons other than licensed insolvency practitioners to act as nominees or supervisors of company (or individual) voluntary arrangements, provided that such persons are members of bodies that are recognised by the Secretary of State for Trade and Industry. The change seems designed to let in members of bodies such as the Association of Business Recovery Professionals and other turnaround specialists and maybe to provide more competition in the market where there are only some 1,200 IPs at present taking appointments.

The nominee will investigate the scheme and report to the court, within 28 days after he is given notice of the proposed scheme, as to whether the scheme is likely to be viable so that meetings of members and creditors should be called to approve it. If the nominee is already an administrator or liquidator, there is no need to report to the court. Unless the court orders otherwise, where a report is made to it, the nominee will order meetings of creditors and members to be called to consider the proposals for a voluntary arrangement and to approve it.

In order to assist him with his report, he is entitled to a statement of affairs from the directors. Where a nominee is required to report to the court, he must state in his report whether in his opinion the proposed company voluntary arrangement (CVA) has a reasonable prospect of being approved and implemented (Insolvency Act 2000, Sch 2). As we have seen, such a report is not necessary where the nominee is an administrator or liquidator.

Approval of scheme: by members and creditors

Approval requires a simple majority in value of the members voting in person or by proxy (or by written resolution) and a three-quarters majority in value of creditors voting in person or by proxy at a creditors' meeting. Every creditor of the company of whose claim and address the nominee is aware is entitled to attend.

A resolution will fail if at the creditors' meeting more than half in value of the creditors who are not connected with the company, i.e. who are not director creditors or directors' relatives who are creditors, vote against it.

If the meetings approve the arrangement, it becomes binding on all ordinary creditors, but not on preferred or secured creditors, unless they agree, who can pursue their claims against the company.

In *Re Cancol Ltd* [1996] 1 BCLC 100 the High Court decided that a person who was entitled to a future or contingently payable debt such as future payments of rent to fall due under an existing lease was a 'creditor' for the purposes of insolvency legislation and was bound by a company voluntary arrangement approved at a meeting of creditors of which he had notice and at which he was entitled to vote.

The approval of the scheme is reported to the court which may discharge an administration order or a winding-up order.

The decision in *Re Cancol* (1996) is now reinforced by the Insolvency Act 2000 which provides that a CVA will bind all of the company's creditors, including unknown creditors, who are then able to claim from the company only the dividends they would have received if they had come to light after the CVA had been completed. Such creditors may also make an application to the court on the ground that their interests are unfairly prejudiced by the voluntary arrangement that is approved (see Sch 2, paras 6 and 7). Preferential creditors retain their priority, of course, and secured creditors will rely on their security unless they have consented to surrender it to the company and become ordinary creditors when the above provisions of the IA 2000 will apply if, for example, they fail to attend a meeting and vote even where no notice was given.

It is an offence under the IA 2000 for an officer of a company to try to obtain approval of the members or creditors to a proposed CVA by making a false representation or fraudulently doing or failing to do anything (Sch 2, paras 8 and 12). The nominee or supervisor is required under para 10 of Sch 2 to report suspected offences to the Secretary of State. The Secretary of State is granted powers to investigate such suspected offences (para 10).

Dissentients

Dissenting members and creditors may apply to the court to set aside the scheme on the grounds of unfair prejudice or material irregularity. This must be done within 28 days of the nominee reporting the approval of the scheme to the court. The time limit cannot be extended.

The High Court considered the phrase 'material irregularity' in *In re Trident Fashions plc* (2004) *The Times*, 23 April. The application was brought against the company's three joint administrators and the company which employed them. The material irregularity relied on was the failure by one of the administrators to disclose to the meeting the existence of certain offers to purchase the company. It appeared that at the meeting the administrator concerned mentioned only one formal offer without saying that there had been two other offers as well. The judge concluded from this that there had been a relevant irregularity. However, the decision of the Court of Appeal in *Cadbury Schweppes plc* v *Somji* [2001] 1 WLR 615 had to be looked at. It laid down a test in this sort of case which was that if the truth had been told at the meeting it would be likely to have made a material difference to the way in which the creditors would have assessed the terms of the proposed voluntary arrangement: was there a substantial chance that the creditors would not have approved the arrangement? The fact that the meeting might have been adjourned for a few days was not enough. The judge said that in the circumstances it was unlikely that the meeting would have been adjourned but even if it had been adjourned for a few days there was no real prospect that it would have affected the approval of the voluntary arrangement. On the matter of omission of material at the meeting the court could interfere with the arrangement only if the omission was one which no reasonable practitioner would have made. The creditors' application was dismissed.

Approval by creditors only

A decision by the creditors' meeting to approve a proposed CVA will prevail where this conflicts with the decision made by a meeting of the company, subject to the right of a member to challenge this on an application to the court (Insolvency Act 2000 Sch 2 para 5).

If the scheme proceeds

If the scheme proceeds beyond the above stages, the nominee becomes the supervisor and implements the scheme. At any stage in the implementation of the scheme, and as it proceeds, the creditors can challenge the supervisor's decisions in front of the court and, equally, the supervisor may ask the court for directions.

Subsequent liquidation

In *Re Arthur Rathbone Kitchens Ltd* [1997] 2 BCLC 280 the High Court ruled that s 84 of the Insolvency Act 1986 (circumstances in which a company may be wound up voluntarily) allowed members of the company to resolve that the company be wound up voluntarily even though the directors had proposed an approved voluntary arrangement that was still in progress or capable of fulfilment or not, even though this might mean that the members had broken the terms of the arrangement.

Here the decision of the High Court *in Re Brelec Installations Ltd* [2000] *The Times*, 18 April, is of interest. BI had entered into a 'trading out' voluntary arrangement whereby regular payments of a set amount were paid to the supervisors over a fixed period. Some six months later the company failed to pay its debts as they fell due and later went into liquidation. The issue between the supervisors and and liquidator was the monies paid by the company to the supervisors prior to the liquidation. Was it available to the supervisors or the liquidator? The court ruled in favour of the supervisors. It was not appropriate to scrutinise the company's trading to determine when default first occurred so as to pinpoint the date from which payments to the supervisors were to be regarded as held for the benefit of the company rather than for the arrangement. The monies received by the supervisors prior to the liquidation remained subject to the trusts of the voluntary arrangement.

The High Court also ruled in *Re Kudos Glass Ltd* (*in liquidation*) [2001] 1 BCLC 390 that sums held by the supervisor of a creditors' voluntary arrangement are in the event of a compulsory winding-up order made in regard to a non-CVA debt held by the supervisor on trust solely for the CVA creditors. The court ruled that if the petitioner had been the supervisor or a CVA creditor, it would have found that the petitioner had elected to end the scheme and the funds would be transferred to the liquidator.

Small companies: a CVA with a moratorium option

The following provisions of the Insolvency Act 2000 are relevant. Section 1 introduces Sch 1 to the Act, which makes the option of applying for a short moratorium of 28 days available to a small company where its directors intend to put a proposal to the company's creditors for a company voluntary arrangement.

Small companies are not obliged to use this procedure but can proceed under the standard procedure if they wish.

Eligible companies

To be eligible a company must satisfy *two* or more of the conditions for being a small company within s 247(3) of the CA 1985. Certain other companies that are involved in financial markets where the modifications to former law are designed to ensure that financial markets continue to function in the event of the insolvency of one of the participants are also included. Those ineligible are companies that are subject to formal insolvency proceedings, as where a winding-up is in progress, or where in the previous 12 months a moratorium has failed.

Nominee's statement

Directors who want a moratorium must provide information to the nominee as follows:

- a document setting out the terms of the proposed CVA;
- a document giving details of the company's assets, debts and other liabilities, together with any other information that the nominee may request.

Given that the nominee considers that the proposal has a reasonable prospect of success in terms of being approved and implemented and that sufficient funding is available and that meetings of the company and creditors should be held, he must provide the directors with a statement to that effect. In reaching conclusions, the nominee may rely on the information provided by the directors unless he has reason to believe it may be inaccurate.

Documents to be submitted to the court

In order to obtain a moratorium, the directors must file certain documents with the court. These are set out in Sch 1, para 7 and include the terms of the proposed CVA and a statement of the company's affairs.

Duration of moratorium

Schedule 1, para 8 deals with this and provides that the moratorium will come into force when the documents referred to above are filed with the court. The maximum initial moratorium is 28 days. This period can be extended or reduced by order of the Secretary of State. A meeting of the company and creditors held within the initial period may decide to extend the moratorium by up to a further two months. The Secretary of State may by order increase or decrease that period of two months. The moratorium may be brought to an end by a decision of the meetings of creditors and company to approve a CVA. Alternatively, it may be brought to an end:

- by the court;
- by the nominee's withdrawal of his consent to act;
- by a decision of meetings of creditors and the company other than to approve a CVA;
- at the end of the 28-day minimum period if *both* of the first meetings of the company and creditors have not taken place;
- if there is no decision of the above meetings to extend it.

Notification of the beginning of the moratorium

The directors have a duty to inform the nominee that a moratorium has come into force. When a moratorium comes into force and when it ends, the nominee must advertise that fact and notify the Registrar of Companies and the company. When the moratorium comes into force, he must also notify any creditor who has petitioned for a winding-up and, when it ends, any creditor of whose claim he is aware.

Effect of moratorium on creditors

Except for an 'excepted petition', i.e. a petition by the Secretary of State that winding-up is in the public interest under s 124A of the IA 1986, no petition to wind up the company can be commenced nor can any other insolvency proceedings. No steps may be taken to enforce any security over the company's property or repossess any goods in the company's possession under any hire-purchase agreement, nor can any other proceedings, execution or other legal process be commenced or continued, or distraint, e.g. by a landlord, be levied. No meeting of the company may be held or requisitioned without the consent of the nominee or of the court.

Winding-up petitions presented prior to the moratorium are stayed during the period but not 'public policy' petitions which continue unaffected.

Section 127 of the IA 1986 rendering void dispositions of the company's property after presentation of a winding-up petition does not apply.

Securities given during the moratorium

These are unenforceable unless given with reasonable grounds that they would benefit the company.

Company invoices

All invoices and orders and letters where the name of the company appears must give the name of the nominee and state that a moratorium is in force. The officers of the company commit an offence if this provision is breached in the absence of reasonable excuse.

Obtaining credit

During the moratorium the company may not obtain credit to the value of £250 or more without first telling the person giving the credit that a moratorium is in force. This includes payments in advance for the supply of goods and services. There are criminal penalties on the company's officers for breach.

Disposals and payments

While the moratorium is in force the company may only dispose of any of its property or pay a debt that existed at the start of the moratorium if there are reasonable grounds for believing that it will benefit the company and the moratorium committee gives approval. If there is no committee, approval must be given by the nominee. There is nothing to prevent the sale of property in the ordinary course of business as where, for example, a farming supplies company sells a tractor as part of its retail trade. Again, officers of the company commit an offence on breach.

Disposal of charged property

The Schedule allows the disposal by the company during the moratorium of charged property and any goods in its possession under an HP agreement, provided the holder of the security or the owner agrees. The holder of a fixed charge and the owner of goods on HP are entitled to have the proceeds of sale applied to repayment of the loan or debt but the holder of a floating charge retains a charge of equal priority to his original charge over the proceeds of the sale or disposal of the charged property.

Monitoring of company's activities

The Schedule imposes a duty on the nominee to monitor the company's affairs during the moratorium in order to form a judgment as to the viability of a CVA and the company's ability to carry on during the moratorium. The directors have a duty to provide the nominee with information.

Withdrawal of consent to act by nominee

The Schedule provides that a nominee may withdraw his consent to act if:

- he considers that the CVA proposal (or modifications communicated to him) no longer has a reasonable prospect of being approved or implemented; or
- he considers that the company has insufficient funds now and during the moratorium to enable it to continue in business throughout the moratorium; or
- he becomes aware that on the date of filing the company was not eligible for a moratorium; or
- the directors are not providing him with relevant information on request.

On withdrawal of the nominee's consent, the moratorium ends. The above are the only grounds on which the nominee may withdraw his consent and he must give notice to various parties, i.e. the court, the Registrar of Companies, the company and creditors of whom he is aware. He commits an offence by not doing so.

Challenging the nominee's actions

Any creditor, director or member of the company or any other person affected by the moratorium who is not satisfied by any decision or act of the nominee may apply to the court for relief. The court may confirm, reverse or modify any such decision or act and give directions to the nominee or make any order it sees fit either during or after the moratorium.

Where the acts of the nominee have caused the company loss and the company appears not to be taking any action, creditors may apply to the court which, if it thinks that the acts of the nominee were unreasonable, may order the company to make a claim against the nominee or authorise a creditor to do so.

Replacement of the nominee by the court

Where it is, for example, impracticable or inappropriate for the nominee to continue, the court may direct that the nominee be replaced by a qualified person who consents.

Summoning of meetings and their conduct

Schedule 1, paras 27 and 28 deal with this and provide, among other things, that the nominee may call meetings of creditors and of the company whenever he sees fit.

These meetings decide whether or not to approve the proposed CVA with or without modification. These modifications may not affect the rights of secured creditors or preferential creditors unless they consent.

Moratorium committee

In a case where the moratorium is extended, there is provision for the setting up of a moratorium committee to exercise functions conferred on it by the meetings referred to above. The meetings must approve an estimate of the committee expenses.

Members and creditors: conflicting decisions

If the decisions of the members and creditors are conflicting, the decision of the creditors prevails but a member may apply to the court for an order that the members' decision should prevail.

Effect of CVA

The CVA, when approved, binds all creditors of the company including unknown creditors. That includes those creditors who, having followed the insolvency rules, were not served with notice of the relevant meeting(s). Such persons can apply to the court on the grounds of unfair prejudice and the court may, for example, revoke or suspend the approval of the CVA. Otherwise, these creditors are entitled to the dividends payable under the arrangement only. On approval of the CVA, the nominee becomes the supervisor.

Challenge of directors' actions during the moratorium

Any member or creditor can apply to the court for relief on the grounds that the directors are acting in a way unfairly prejudicial to the interests of creditors or members. The court may make an order regulating matters or bring the moratorium to an end. This form of action applies in relation to the acts of directors during the moratorium. The application may be made during or after the moratorium. If made afterwards, the court's order will be to regulate matters and obviously not to bring the moratorium to an end.

Offences by officers of the company

The Schedule provides that if during the 12 months prior to the start of the moratorium an officer of the company has committed certain acts, e.g. fraudulently removed the company's property worth £500 or more or falsified the company's records in relation to its property, he commits an offence, as does an officer who so acts during the moratorium.

It is also an offence for an officer of the company to try to obtain a moratorium or an extension of it by making false statements or fraudulently doing or not doing anything.

Void provisions in floating charge documents

Schedule 1 provides that any provision in a floating charge is invalid if the charge is to crystallise (and therefore become a fixed charge) on the obtaining of, or any action to obtain, a moratorium.

The remainder of the Schedule makes consequential amendments to various parts of the IA 1986, e.g. so that suppliers of gas, water and electricity are not permitted to require a nominee to pay outstanding debts for supply as a condition for supply during the moratorium. There is also a provision that the relevant date for determining preferential claims is the date on which the moratorium comes into force.

Trading with companies that are in a CVA

It is not unusual for creditors to carry on trading with a CVA company. Any new debts will not be covered by the CVA and become, in effect, new liabilities of the CVA company. There are, of course, some concerns about a continuation of trade since, if the company cannot meet its CVA requirements, it will almost certainly be forced into liquidation and the new liabilities, if not paid, may not be met. Set out below are some precautions that a creditor can take in such circumstances:

- where goods are supplied a retention of title clause could be used in the contract of supply to ensure that the seller retains ownership of the goods until they are paid for and if they are still in stock;
- the contract of sale could require cash on delivery;
- an attempt should be made to obtain personal guarantees of the new liabilities from the directors;
- ascertain from the CVA supervisor whether or not the company is up to date with its payments under the CVA;
- it is obviously not wise to carry on trading on the old terms; the terms of trade should be renegotiated.

ADMINISTRATION

Administrator's functions

The functions of an administrator are now contained in Insolvency Act 1986 Sch B1 para 3 (as inserted by Enterprise Act 2002 Pt 10). The administrator now has the function of carrying out a single statutory purpose, i.e.:

- to rescue the company as a going concern;
- if this is not reasonably practicable, to achieve a better result for the company's creditors as a whole than would be likely if the company were wound up (without first being in administration) – an example would be to allow the company to trade on in administration for long enough to complete a large order; or
- if neither of the above is reasonably practicable and the administrator does not unnecessarily harm the interests of the creditors as a whole, realising the company's property to make a distribution to one or more secured or preferential creditors. Nevertheless, even if there are insufficient funds to pay unsecured creditors the administrator must not unnecessarily harm their interests.

Schedule 1 gives an administrator full management powers which are not available to a liquidator. The case of *Re Consumer and Industrial Press Ltd* [1988] BCLC 177, made under previous legislation, gives an example of the second aspect of the single statutory purpose. The company had since 1949 published a magazine. Net liabilities were judged by accountants to be too great to trade out of trouble. The Inland Revenue petitioned for a compulsory winding-up (see p 536) but the directors asked the court to make an administration order which the court did. Administrators were appointed to manage the company so that at least one more issue of the magazine could be published. The court thought that the company might be saved by a voluntary arrangement which an administrator may propose but even if not it would get a better price for the title if publication continued than if it were sold in a liquidation. This would obviously be to the benefit of creditors.

Comment. The expression 'unnecessarily harming' the interests of the creditors as a whole is not defined and its practical effect is not clear. Presumably if the secured creditors wanted an immediate sale of the secured assets (bearing in mind that in the developed future they will not be able to appoint an administrative receiver) but the administrator takes the view that the market is rising giving a better future realisation for the creditors as a whole, would an immediate sale unnecessarily harm the interests of the creditors as a whole? If the administrator had insufficient funds to carry on the administration and so had to sell the assets presumably he would be in the clear. We may see more applications to the court by administrators seeking the court's assistance. The court will, however, be reluctant it seems to interfere with what is, in the end, a business decision (see *T & D Industries plc* [2000] 1 All ER 333: comments made in that case).

Appointment of an administrator by the court

The Enterprise Act 2002 retains with some minor modifications the court route into administration. The court route can be used by the company (by ordinary resolution of the members or a unanimous written resolution), by the directors (by a majority decision at a board meeting or by a unanimous written resolution) or by one or more creditors with no minimum value of debt. A holder of a floating charge must be able to satisfy the requirements of a 'qualifying floating charge'. The most usual applicants for an administration order are the company's directors.

The qualifying floating charge

The requirements are set out in Enterprise Act 2002 Sch 16 which inserts Sch B1 to the IA 1986. Under para 14 of Sch B1:

(i) A qualifying floating charge (QFC) must be created by an instrument that:

- states that para 14 applies to the floating charge;
- purports to empower the holder to appoint an administrator; or
- purports to empower the holder to appoint an administrative receiver.

Note: even those pre-Enterprise Act 2002 floating charges that give power to appoint an administrative receiver will thus give power to apply for an administration order.

(ii) A person will be regarded as holding a qualifying floating charge if he holds one or more debentures of the company secured:

- by a qualifying floating charge that relates to the whole or substantially the whole of the company's property;
- by a number of QFCs that together relate to the whole or substantially the whole of the company's property; or
- by charges (including fixed charges) which together relate to the whole or substantially the whole of the company's property and at least one of which is a QFC.

What is required to satisfy the court in making the order?

The court must be satisfied that the company is, or is likely to become, unable to pay its debts and that the order is reasonably likely to achieve the purpose of administration (see p 518). A qualifying floating charge holder (QFCH) need only show that the charge is enforceable.

The process is initiated by filing a prescribed form of application with the court. There is no requirement for what was known as a 'Rule 2.2 Report' in support of the application. This form of application replaces the former procedure by petition. The matter of the company's insolvency and whether the order, if made, reasonably achieves the purpose of the administration is expressed in a single-page statement from the proposed administrator. This replaces the old Rule 2.2 Report. The application must be served on the holder of any QFC.

If others apply to the court for an order can a QFCH intervene?

A QFCH can intervene and appoint an administrative receiver (if entitled to do so) or administrator or make a request that a person specified by the QFCH be appointed administrator in the application (see IA 1986 Sch B1 para 36). The court may accept or refuse the QFCH's nominee as administrator (see IA 1986 Sch B1 para 36(2)). In practice the court is unlikely to refuse, especially where the QFCH has chosen an insolvency practitioner from one of the large accountancy firms. However, in this connection the High Court ruling in *Re Colt Telecom Ltd* (20 December 2002, unreported), HC is of interest, though not based specifically on the Enterprise Act 2002 provisions. In the case, Jacob J refused to make an administration order because the company was not actually in default to the creditor who was applying to the court. Nevertheless, he went on to say that even if he had had jurisdiction to make the order he would not have done so because the accountant who had made the report to the court in connection with the order was not impartial – he would stand to gain significantly in fees if his report was accepted and he was appointed administrator. Furthermore, there was a potential conflict of interest in that the firm involved had previously given the company tax advice. The judge also stated that the appointment of an administrator who lacked specialised knowledge of the telecoms industry which was possessed by the company's management would 'almost certainly stop the business in its tracks' and would increase its running costs.

Comment. The judge's comments may become highly relevant in regard to challenges to the appointment of administrators under IA 1986 Sch B1 para 36.

Are there any special features in an application to the court by a QFCH?

A QFCH can make an application to the court for an administration order without having to show that the company is, or is likely to become, unable to pay its debts (IA 1986 Sch B1 para 35). The court must, however, be satisfied that the floating charge is a QFC and has become enforceable. The court may also make an administration order on the application of a QFCH, even where the company is in compulsory liquidation so that the administration takes over.

It is also now open for *any* liquidator to make application to the court for the discharge of the liquidation and the appointment of an administrator.

The fact that creditors object to the making of an administration order is not necessarily a bar. In *Structures and Computers Ltd* v *Ansys Inc* (1997) *The Times*, 3 October the High Court held that where it is satisfied that there is a real prospect of an administration order achieving one or more of its purposes, the court has a jurisdiction to make the order under s 8 of the Insolvency Act 1986 despite the fact that it is opposed by more than half of the company's unsecured creditors.

Notice of application for order

Notice of the application must be given to any person entitled to appoint a QFCH who may intervene (see above).

Notification of appointment

An administrator must:

- advertise the court order of his appointment in the *London Gazette* and in a newspaper circulating in the area where the company has its principal place of business; and
- send a copy of the court order to the Registrar of Companies within seven days with the appropriate forms.

The *Gazette* is published by the Stationery Office and these notices are included in the Company Law Official Notifications Supplement to the *Gazette* which is published on microfiche. Copies may be seen at Companies House search rooms and some of the larger public libraries have copies.

Statements in support of an administration order: restriction orders

Under the Insolvency Rules 1986 rule 2.2, a petition for an administration order was supported by a report of an independent person to the effect that the appointment of an administrator for the company is expedient. This report could be inspected by creditors and members of the company concerned under rule 7.31. The report might contain sensitive material and so the court could, under rule 7.31(5), make an order restricting inspection of the whole or part of the report. The same problems may now apply to the shorter statement by the would-be administrator. Application may be made by the Official Receiver or an insolvency practitioner or any other person having an interest. Under a Practice Direction issued in April 2002 (see [2002] 3 All ER 95) the High Court stated that good reason must be shown for a restriction order otherwise it will not be made. The statement lists as appropriate grounds for a restriction order: information about the perceived market for any assets of the company which it is anticipated could be sold in the administration or the period for which it is anticipated that trading of the company would be continued by any administrator and the prospects for such trading.

The business application. This occurs where, for example, the directors of a company are seeking an administration order and have a supporting statement. They may wish to ensure that their legal and other advisers address the matter of a restriction order on matters that the directors think are sensitive at what is after all *a very early stage* in the proceedings.

Appointment of an administrator out of court

Out of court appointments may be made by qualified floating charge holders and by the company or its directors. Ordinary creditors must seek an appointment through the court. The requirements are as follows:

(a) Appointment by a QFCH

A QFCH must give two business days' written notice to any prior QFCH. This notice is not required if the relevant QFCH has consented to the making of the appointment.

This notice of intention to appoint may be filed in court but this is optional.

What must be filed in court following appointment? The QFCH must file in court:

(i) a notice of appointment;
(ii) a statutory declaration by the appointing QFCH that:

- he is a QFCH;
- the floating charge was enforceable when the appointment was made;
- the appointment accords with the requirements of Insolvency Act 1986 Sch B1.

There must also be filed:
(iii) a statement by the administrator that:

- he consents to the appointment;
- the purpose of the administration is reasonably likely to be achieved.

When is the appointment effective? The appointment takes effect once the above filing requirements have been satisfied. In the case of a QFCH, such as a bank, this filing requirement can be achieved out of court hours by fax.

Notification to the administrator. The fact that the court filing requirements set out above have been complied with must be notified by the QFCH as soon as practicable after completion of filing.

Comment. A lender commits a criminal offence if, in the statutory declaration referred to above, it makes a statement that it does not reasonably believe to be true (see IA 1986 Sch B1 para 18(6)).

(b) Appointment by the company or the directors

Where the appointment is to be by the company or by its directors five business days' notice in writing of intention to appoint must be given to:

- persons having the right to appoint an administrative receiver (where an exception applies);
- persons having a right to appoint an administrator under Sch B1 para 14, i.e. a QFCH (IA 1986 Sch B1 para 26).

The notice of intention to appoint must be filed in court along with a statutory declaration by the appointer that:

- the company is likely to become unable to pay its debts;
- the company is not in liquidation;
- the appointment is not prevented because the company has been in administration instigated by the company or its directors, or subject to a moratorium in regard to a

failed company voluntary arrangement in the previous 12 months and that there are no outstanding winding-up petitions in respect of the company and that there is not an administrator or administrative receiver in office.

What else must be filed in court?

- notice of the appointment; and
- a statutory declaration by the appointer that:
  - (*a*) the appointor is entitled to make the appointment;
  - (*b*) the appointment is in accordance with IA 1986 Sch B1;
  - (*c*) the statements in the statutory declaration filed with the notice of intention to appoint are still accurate.
- a statement by the administrator that:
  - (*a*) he consents to the appointment; and
  - (*b*) that the purpose of the administration is reasonably likely to be achieved. In this connection the administrator may rely on information supplied by the directors unless there is reason to doubt its accuracy.

When is the appointment effective? The appointment of the administrator becomes effective when the above-mentioned filing requirements are completed satisfactorily.

Notification to the administrator. The fact that the court filing requirements set out above have been satisfactorily completed must be notified to the administrator as soon as is practicable.

Comment.

(i) Where directors or the company use the out of court route there is a requirement, as we have seen, that notice of intention to appoint an administrator is given to a QFCH. Such a holder then has a period of five business days to appoint its own administrator if it does not consent to the company's or the directors' choice of administrator (IA 1986 Sch B1 paras 14, 26). If the QFCH does not make its own appointment of an administrator the company or the directors can carry on with making their own appointment of an administrator using the out of court route. Nevertheless *an interim moratorium* on action by creditors including action to enforce a security will commence when notice is given by the company or the directors of their intention to appoint an administrator, i.e. earlier than the actual appointment of the administrator (IA 1986 Sch B1 para 44). However, the moratorium will not prevent the appointment of an administrative receiver where one of the exceptions to the general prohibition on these appointments applies.

(ii) The company or the directors cannot make an out of court appointment if a winding-up petition has been filed. A QFCH is not affected and may proceed with an appointment with the petition being suspended (though not dismissed) if an administration is commenced out of court. By contrast, where the court makes an administration order, the court is required to dismiss an outstanding winding-up petition.

Statement of affairs. Following appointment the administrator will request the company's officers and employees (where necessary) to supply a statement of affairs. This must be done within 11 days of the request. It will be appreciated that the statement of affairs is the starting point of the administration as indeed it is of any corporate insolvency procedure although much of the information may be known in outline at least before the appointment of an administrator. The statement gives particulars of the company's assets and liabilities and details of its creditors and although it is basically the responsibility of the company's directors it is often prepared by the company's accountants.

Administrator's proposals

The following paragraphs of IA 1986 Sch B1 (as inserted by Enterprise Act 2002 Sch 16) apply to the administrator, *however appointed.*

1 As soon as is reasonably practicable, and in any case within eight weeks of the company going into administration (not three months as previously), the administrator must make proposals as to how the purpose of the administration is to be achieved. The statement is sent to the Registrar of Companies, the members of the company and all known creditors (para 49).
2 The administrator must call an initial creditors' meeting as soon as is reasonably practicable, and in any case within ten weeks of the company going into administration, to consider the proposals (para 51). The meeting need not be called if the administrator thinks that there is insufficient property to make a distribution to unsecured creditors over and above the ring-fenced asset distribution referred to below (see p 526).
3 If there is a request by creditors whose debts amount to at least 10 per cent of the total debts of the company the administrator must convene a meeting even if the administrator considers that there will be no distribution to unsecured creditors (para 52).
4 Where the meeting is held the creditors will vote on whether to accept the proposals or whether to modify or reject them. A simple majority in value will decide.
5 The relevant times for sending proposals and convening the initial meeting of creditors may be extended by court order or by the consent of all the secured creditors and more than 50 per cent of the unsecured creditors (para 108(2)). It is an offence for an administrator to fail to comply with the above time periods.
6 Secured creditors vote in terms of the value of any shortfall between the debt and the value of the security but the administrator's proposals cannot include action affecting the right of the secured creditors to enforce the security, unless the secured creditor(s) consent (para 73).

Comment. Since the fact of the administration prevents enforcement of the security without the consent of the administrator or the court, this provision will mean that the administrator will need the consent of the secured creditors before putting the proposals to the initial creditors' meeting.

There is no need for secured creditor consent in regard to those proposals (if any) that relate to a company voluntary arrangement under IA 1986 or a scheme of arrangement under CA 1985 (para 73(2)).

As reference to these procedures will show (see p 512) there is secured creditor protection built into both of them.

Powers and duties of the administrator

The powers and duties contained in IA 1986 Sch 1 are retained, as is the power to act as the company's agent (para 69). In addition, an administrator is an officer of the court *whether appointed by the court or out of court* (para 5).

New powers. An administrator may make distributions to secured creditors and preferential creditors and, with the consent of the court, to unsecured creditors (paras 65, 66). This provides a contrast to previous legislation that did not give preference to Crown and employee claims in an administration as was, and is, the case in an administrative receivership and a liquidation. The Crown preference is abolished but employee claims and contributions to an occupational pension scheme will have priority over the claims of a QFCH (para 65(2)).

An administrator retains the right to dispose of property subject to a floating charge as if the charge did not exist. The expenses of the administration rank ahead of the claims of the floating charge holder as regards the proceeds of sale. Other secured assets and property on hire-purchase can be disposed of with the consent of the court (paras 70–72).

Administrator's expenses

These continue to rank in front of the claims of floating charge holders and also have priority over preferential claims. This will relate mainly to employee claims and contributions to an occupational pension fund.

The accountability of an administrator

The accountability of an administrator is as follows:

Creditors and members of the company in administration. These persons can make application to the court where the administrator acts or proposes to act in a way that could unfairly harm their respective interests or where the applicant believes that the administrator is not carrying out relevant functions as efficiently or as quickly as is reasonably practicable (para 74).

Any interested party. These persons can make application to the court where it is alleged that the administrator has misapplied or retained the property of the company or is guilty of misfeasance or in breach of fiduciary duty. So far this aspect of accountability is similar to that under IA 1986 s 212 but now an application can be made while the company is still in an administration instead of waiting until the company has gone into liquidation.

Cessation of an administration

The exit from administration may be achieved in the following ways:

- ***Automatic cessation.*** The appointment of the administrator will come to an end automatically 12 months after the date on which the appointment took effect.
- ***Extension of appointment.*** The period of 12 months can be extended *once only* by a period of up to six months with the consent of the creditors or any number of times by the court on the application of the administrator for such period as the court may determine. Creditor consent means the consent of all the secured creditors and more than 50 per cent in value of the unsecured creditors. Consent may be written or expressed by resolution at a meeting. The above majorities disregard any creditor who does not respond to an invitation to give or withhold consent. The above materials are contained in IA 1986 Sch B1 paras 76–78.

Administration: a timetable of major events

- Seven days after appointment: notice of appointment filed at Companies House.
- Eleven days after administrator's request: company's officers and employees to provide administrator with statement of affairs.
- Eight weeks after appointment: administrator sends proposals to members, creditors and Companies House.
- Ten weeks after appointment: first creditors' meeting held unless not required.
- One year after appointment: automatic end of the appointment of administrator subject to extension.

Termination of administration through notice to Registrar of Companies

If the company is not rescued the exit routes from administration are streamlined by provisions relating to voluntary liquidation and dissolution as follows:

(*a*) *Where funds are available after payment of secured and preferential creditors*. The company can go directly into a creditors' voluntary winding-up. The administrator gives notice to Companies House and the creditors, and files a copy with the court. There is no need to hold a meeting of creditors and the administrator becomes the liquidator unless the creditors put forward a different nomination.

The intention is that these procedures will reduce the number of compulsory liquidations that have followed administration.

(*b*) *If no funds are available for distribution to creditors*. The administrator must, unless the court otherwise orders, give notice to that effect to Companies House. Copies must be sent to creditors and the court. The company will be deemed dissolved after three months from registration of the notice at Companies House, unless an interested person, e.g. a member who believes the company has a good claim for damages against a third party, makes application to the court.

The above provisions are to be found in IA 1986 Sch B1 paras 83–84.

Replacement of administrator

Where a QFCH has used the out of court route, and in the event that there was a prior ranking floating charge holder entitled to make the appointment, then the prior charge holder can apply to the court for the replacement of the administrator by his own nominee for the office (IA 1986 Sch B1 para 96).

Abolition of Crown preference

Enterprise Act 2002 s 251 abolishes the preferential status of Crown debts. These are debts due to the Inland Revenue, Customs and Excise and social security contributions. Employee claims continue to be preferential, as do contributions to an occupational pension fund. IA 1986 Sch 6 is amended accordingly.

Ring-fencing mechanism for unsecured creditors

In order to ensure that the benefit of the abolition of Crown preference does not go solely to floating charge holders the Enterprise Act 2002 sets up a mechanism for ring-fencing assets where there is a floating charge that was created after the 2002 Act provisions came into force. The abolition of Crown debts and the ring-fencing applies to all corporate insolvencies, not merely to administration, though it is convenient to deal with it here. The ring-fence arrangements do not apply where the fund is below a minimum to be prescribed and the insolvency practitioner considers that the costs in distributing it would be disproportionate to the benefits. The provision may also be disapplied by the terms of a company voluntary arrangement or by a scheme of arrangement under CA 1985. The court may also disapply it on the application of the insolvency practitioner if he wishes to take this route.

Ring-fencing: the prescribed percentage

Under the Insolvency (Prescribed Part) Order 2003 the following thresholds apply:

- minimum fund for distribution – £10,000;
- prescribed percentage to be calculated on the basis of a sliding scale as follows: 50 per cent of the first £10,000 of floating charge realisations; 20 per cent of floating charge realisations after that.

Up to a maximum ring-fenced fund of £600,000.

The ring-fencing provisions apply to relevant amounts of the company's 'net property'. Net property is defined in Insolvency Act 1986 s 176A(5) (as inserted by Enterprise Act 2002) as the amount of property which would, but for the ring-fencing provisions, be available for the floating chargeholder. Thus it represents any floating charge realisations.

Important business application

Lenders should check all existing documents to ensure that they cover the new out of court route into administration rather than, e.g., referring merely to administration orders and petitions.

Administrator: legal consequences of appointment

Consideration has been given to the appointment of an administrator both in court and out of court. The following materials deal with the main legal consequences of the appointment together with case law on earlier provisions that carries through to illustrate the law.

Suspension of rights

From the presentation of a petition for an administration order and during the period of the administration:

(i) no resolution to wind up the company may be passed nor may the court make a winding-up order (IA 1986 Sch B1 para 40);
(ii) there can be no enforcement of fixed charges or other security over the company's property except with the consent of the administrator or leave of the court (IA 1986 Sch B1 para 43);
(iii) there can be no recovery of property which the company has under a hire-purchase agreement or leasing arrangement and retention clauses are not enforceable except with the consent of the administrator or the court (IA 1986 Sch B1 para 43);

(iv) no other legal proceedings can be commenced against the company except with the consent of the administrator or leave of the court (IA 1986 Sch B1 para 43).

The Court of Appeal has ruled that the administrator's consent or leave of the court is necessary to commence or continue criminal as well as civil proceedings against a company in administration (see *re Rhondda Waste Disposal Ltd* (*in administration*) [2000] EGCS 25). In this case the Environmental Agency wished to prosecute for failure to comply with one of the conditions of a waste management licence. The court gave leave because the pollution was serious.

Consent or leave is also required even if a civil action is not being brought by a creditor but by a claimant suing for alleged breach of a patent (see *Biosource Technologies Inc* v *Axis Genetics plc* (*in administration*) [2000] 1 BCLC 286).

In regard to (iii) above the High Court ruled in *Razzaq* v *Pala* [1997] 1 WLR 1336 and *Re Lomax Leisure Ltd* [1999] 1 All ER 22 that a landlord's right to forfeit a lease is not in the nature of a security over a company's property in a legal sense. Therefore the moratorium preventing anyone from taking steps to enforce a security over the property of a company while in administration does not bind a landlord. The cases had considerable significance for creditors who initiate an administration, particularly the larger scale administrations where there may be a number of leaseholds among the assets of the company. They have no way of knowing whether the objects of the administration will be achieved since the landlords will be able to frustrate the purpose of the administration by forfeiting leases or by requiring payment of rents for not doing so. Thus placing themselves in a superior position to other creditors since they can achieve payment of arrears of rent or forfeit the lease and market it elsewhere even during the course of the administration.

Landlord's right of forfeiture

IA 1986 Sch B1 para 43(4) prohibits a landlord's right to re-entry by forfeiture of the lease except by leave of the court. Once an administration order has been made or is in force, re-entry by forfeiture continues to be barred except by permission of the administrator or leave of the court.

No inhibition of rescue schemes

In order to prevent the administrator's schemes to save the company or to conduct the company as near as possible as a going concern until liquidation as in *Re Consumer and Industrial Press Ltd* (1988) (see p 518), it is sometimes necessary to deal with persons who have charges or other rights over the property of the company and whose consent is required before the property is sold. A rescue package may very well involve such sales.

In this connection IA 1986 Sch B1 paras 70, 71 provide as follows:

(*a*) Assets subject to a floating charge can be sold by the administrator and the proceeds used in the business. The permission of the chargeholder is not required nor is it necessary for the administrator to obtain the permission of the court. However, the chargeholder has the same priority as he had before over the assets generally as they may be from time to time and this would include the proceeds of sale and other assets which might be purchased with the proceeds because these would be included in the general assets of the company (para 70).

(*b*) Assets held on hire-purchase or subject to a fixed charge can be sold but court approval must be obtained and the proceeds *must* be used to pay off the chargeholder or owner. In addition, and so as to ensure that the administrator gets the market price, IA 1986 Sch B1 para 71 provides that the administrator must make up any difference between the sale price and the market price.

The company's contracts

Following the refusal of administrators to complete a contract entered into by the company before their appointment, the High Court was asked to consider in that context its powers of intervention (see *C E King Ltd* (*in administration*) [2000] 2 BCLC 297).

The judge decided that in general terms it would be inappropriate to make an order requiring the administrators to perform the relevant contract. Administrators were appointed (and expected) to make commercial decisions and where necessary take legal advice. In the end, however, the matter of performing (or not) the company's contracts remains a commercial decision to be taken by the administrators.

Directors and employees

The directors are not dismissed by the appointment of an administrator. However, their powers are suspended and the administrator may remove any director of the company and appoint any person to be a director of it whether to fill a vacancy or as an additional director.

The appointment of an administrator does not operate to dismiss the company's employees. The reason for this is that under IA 1986 Sch B1 para 69 he is said to act as an agent of the company and so there is no change in the personality of the employer. However, an administrator can terminate contracts of employment.

Employees' contracts and Enterprise Act 2002 provisions

The provisions of the Insolvency Act 1986 which were relevant stated, in s 19, that nothing done or omitted to be done within 14 days of appointment (of an administrator and by the administrator) shall be construed as 'adoption' (of employment contracts by the administrator). The position where contracts of employment are adopted by an administrator is that sums outstanding called 'qualifying liabilities', i.e. wages or salaries including sickness and holiday pay and contributions to occupational pension funds incurred after the adoption of an employment contract, are payable in priority to the claims of preferential creditors and holders of floating charges and if, at the end of the administration, there are qualifying liabilities unpaid and there are insufficient funds to pay them and the administrator's remuneration and expenses, the outstanding amount is payable in full before the administrator's remuneration and expenses (see below).

A problem for administrators has been whether failure to act during the first 14 days can be regarded as 'adoption' of employment contracts leading to the above mentioned loss of remuneration and expenses. The matter was raised in the High Court under the old law (see *Antal International Ltd* [2003] EWHC 1339 (Ch), [2003] 2 BCLC 406).

In this case the administrators asked the court for directions on the matter of the alleged adoption of the contracts of a group of French workers. The company, its auditors and the administrators had originally thought the 12 workers were employed by a subsidiary company but it emerged that they were in fact employees of Antal. This was discovered 16 days after the administrators' appointment. Had the contracts been adopted by inactivity in the last two days? The High Court ruled that they had not. Adoption would only occur when the administrators had done something that amounted to choosing to adopt. The mere keeping on of employees did not amount to adoption. Once the administrators became aware of the French employees they took immediate steps to terminate their contracts under French law.

Antal and Enterprise Act 2002 changes

Enterprise Act 2002 inserts new provisions in the 1986 Act as Sch B1. Paragraph 99 of that Schedule applicable to administrations on or after 15 September 2003 states that '*action* taken within the period of 14 days after an administrator's appointment shall not be taken to amount or contribute to the adoption of a [contract of employment]' This seems to cut out all failure to act and is in line with the decision of the House of Lords in *Powdrill* v *Watson* [1995] 2 AC 394 (see below).

The decision in Powdrill v Watson

In *Powdrill* v *Watson* [1995] 2 AC 394 the House of Lords ruled that inaction by the administrators after the 14-day period could not amount to 'adoption' of employment contracts. However, their Lordships did also rule that administrators could not actively retain employees after the 14-day period and avoid liability by sending each employee a letter disclaiming adoption. Such a letter was of no effect. That this was the case was also held by the Court of Appeal and that merely allowing employment to continue after 14 days could amount to adoption. This latter ruling, however, was not acceptable to the House of Lords which ruled that some conduct amounting to an election to adopt an employment contract was required.

The position in case law and under insolvency legislation would appear now to be the same.

Pension funds

The High Court has decided that the duty of an administrator to manage the 'company's affairs' as referred to in Insolvency Act 1986 Sch B1 paras 59, 68; includes the trusteeship of any employees' pension funds where the company had previously been the trustee. Furthermore, the administrator could only be reimbursed those costs out of the pension fund to which the company would have been entitled but could make a claim for any costs or expenses incurred in actually running the scheme as costs of the administration generally and not as a specific charge against the trust fund (see *Polly Peck International plc (in administration)* v *Henry* [1999] 1 BCLC 407). Mr Justice Buckley so ruled when dismissing an application by the administrators of Polly Peck International (PPI) for a new trustee, i.e. the Trustee Corporation Ltd to be appointed as trustee of the two pension funds set up by PPI.

IA 1986 Sch B1 para 68 provides that, where an appointment is made in court, the administration order is an order directing that during the period for which the order is in force, the affairs, business and property of the company shall be managed by a person (the administrator) appointed for the purpose by the court. IA 1986 Sch B1 para 59(c) provides that the administrator of the company may do all such things as may be necessary for the management of the affairs, business and property of the company.

GRADED QUESTIONS

Essay mode

1 The prime intention of the Insolvency Act 1986 with regard to companies is to provide various alternatives to the winding-up of an insolvent company.

Discuss.

(*The Institute of Chartered Secretaries and Administrators*)

2 Corporate entity and limited liability do not always provide complete protection from personal liability for company directors and shareholders.

You are required to discuss the situations where such persons may be personally liable.

(*The Chartered Institute of Management Accountants*)

3 Plym plc is a holding company whose several subsidiaries are all exclusively private companies. The capital structure of the subsidiaries consists of ordinary shares, several classes of preference shares, and debentures. Because of the administrative difficulties caused by the diverse nature of the capital structure of the subsidiaries, the board of directors of Plym plc wish to introduce a simplified system whereby Plym would purchase the minority shares and debentures for cash or in the alternative issue fully paid equity shares in Plym in exchange for the said shares and debentures at an agreed ratio. Preliminary inquiries indicate that there is a substantial minority of members who would neither sell nor exchange their securities for shares in Plym plc.

Advise the directors of Plym plc as to how, if at all, they could achieve their objective in spite of the minority's anticipated refusal to co-operate.

(*University of Plymouth*)

4 Discredit Bank plc is a large merchant bank situated in the City of London. The Chairman and Managing Director of the company is Dan, a high-powered executive who is well-respected in the City. Seven other directors sit on the board, including Maggie, the Finance Director. Dan and Maggie, together with some of the other directors, have a shareholding but they do not represent the majority.

Last year, Dan purchased property on Discredit's behalf from Chivers-Benson plc of whom Dan is a director. The property, which was valued by Chivers-Benson, was bought by Discredit for £400,000. Within two weeks of Discredit buying the property, it was sold to Briac Ltd, a subsidiary company of Chivers-Benson, for £100,000.

Last month Dan was approached by Homestore plc for the financing of new shop development in London. Dan informed Homestore that Discredit was not in a position to provide Homestore with financial backing but that he, himself, could provide the finance through the setting-up of a separate company. He persuades Maggie to assist him in the incorporation of Quick Loan Ltd, which, owing to Dan's influence in the City enabling the finance to be provided to Homestore, makes a profit of £70,000 on the deal. Both Dan's and Maggie's shares in Quick Loan have increased in value.

These activities have come to the attention of TCR plc, a minority shareholder. Dan has become aware of TCR's interest and, in anticipation of TCR raising these activities at the next general meeting, he decides to publish a report, addressed to all shareholders, claiming that all the relevant transactions and decisions involving Discredit were carried out for strict commercial reasons and for the benefit of the company.

Advise TCR, which doubts the accuracy of Dan's statements and considers the report to be misleading, a factor which TCR is convinced is not known to other shareholders who are likely, as far as TCR is concerned, to accept the report's contents.

(*University of Greenwich*)

Objective mode

Four alternative answers are given. Select ONE only. Circle the answer which you consider to be correct. Check your answers by referring back to the information given in the chapter and against the answers at the back of the book.

1 Bloggs Ltd has recently been made the subject of an administration order. John had previously presented a winding-up petition in regard to Bloggs. What will the effect of the administration order be on John's winding-up petition?

A It will be heard by the court.
B It will be dismissed by the court if the administrator applies to it.
C It will be postponed for 12 months.
D It will be automatically dismissed.

2 Which of the following must be given notice of the intention to appoint an administrator out of court by the directors?

A Unsecured creditors and the company.
B Anyone entitled to appoint an administrative receiver.
C Unsecured creditors.
D Anyone entitled to appoint an administrative receiver or an administrator.

3 Who can fill the office of administrator if there is a vacancy?

A The court.
B The creditors.
C Anyone entitled to appoint an administrative receiver.
D Anyone entitled to appoint an administrative receiver provided the court approves of the appointee.

4 An administrator is taken to have adopted contracts of employment within a stated period after his employment. The period is:

A 28 days.
B 15 days.
C 14 days.
D 21 days.

5 A qualifying floating chargeholder is seeking to petition the court for an administration order. Which of the following statements is correct?

A A QFCH cannot petition the court for an order.
B A QFCH can petition but must satisfy the court that the company is unable to pay its debts.
C A QFCH can petition but must satisfy the court that the purposes of an administration can be achieved.
D A QFCH can petition and need only show that the charge is enforceable.

6 Once the court has received a petition for an administration order, when can a liquidator be appointed? He may:

A be appointed if the court consents.
B be appointed if the creditors consent.
C be appointed if the Official Receiver consents.
D not be appointed.

Answers to questions in objective mode appear on p 577.

24

CORPORATE INSOLVENCY – PROCEDURES OTHER THAN RESCUE

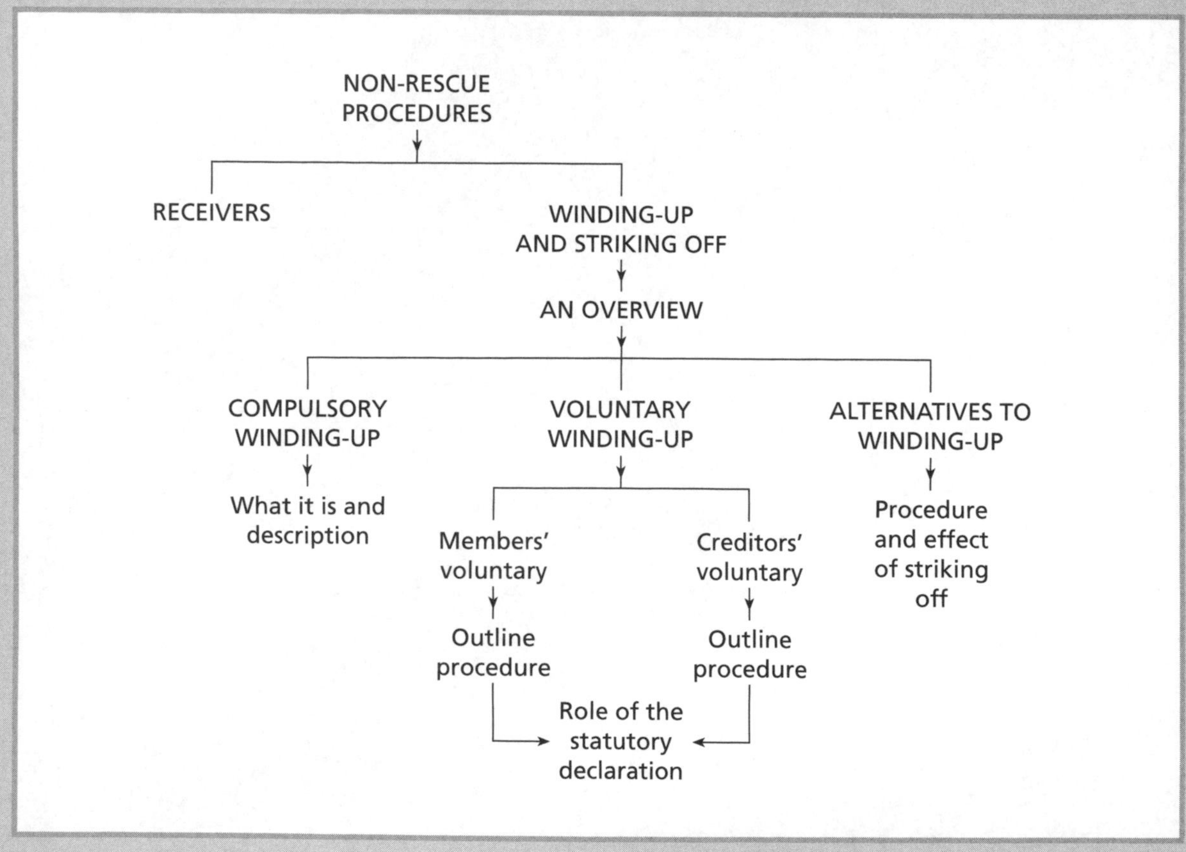

In this chapter we take an overview of corporate insolvency procedures that are not in their major aims concerned to rescue a company from an insolvency situation.

RECEIVERSHIPS

Administrative receivers: demise of

An administrative receiver was the usual appointment of a bank when a company with an overdraft and/or a loan was in financial difficulties. The bank invariably held a floating charge on the company's undertaking and the function of this type of receiver was to undertake such procedures with the company as would pay off the bank. These receivers were not primarily concerned with company rescue as an administrator is. What is more the existence of the office of administrative receiver inhibited the rescue procedures of an administration because if the company or its creditors tried to make an appointment of an administrator the bank, which had to be notified, would often immediately appoint an administrative receiver and this would in law veto the administration.

The Enterprise Act 2002 inserted provisions into the Insolvency Act 1986 that prevent the holder of a floating charge such as a bank from appointing an administrative receiver except in a restricted number of organisations such as some companies involved in financial market operations. These are beyond the scope of this text and are unlikely to be raised in examinations in corporate law at a non-specialist level.

However, it should be recognised that the ban on the appointment of administrative receivers will not be complete for some time since the relevant provisions of the Enterprise Act 2002 did not come into force until September 2003 and banks that had taken floating charges over continuing overdrafts before that date are still able to appoint such practitioners. However, it is most unlikely that an examiner would see the need or the sense in asking questions on the detail of the law relating to administrative receivers. The office is from the student point of view redundant and no more will be said about it in this text.

Receivers

The practice of appointing receivers without management powers by those who have taken fixed charges over corporate property will continue. These practitioners are in no sense managers appointed to deal with the borrowing company's business and pay off the debt. They are appointed merely to sell the charged property to pay the debt or, e.g., to collect income such as rent from the company's tenants (if any) until the debt is paid. They do not have to be authorised insolvency practitioners and the practice is to appoint chartered surveyors to do this work.

WINDING-UP

A company's life can be brought to an end by a process known as *winding-up*. This process is carried through by a *liquidator* whose functions are:

(*a*) to settle the list of contributories;
(*b*) to collect the company's assets;
(*c*) to discharge the company's liabilities to its creditors;
(*d*) to redistribute the surplus (if any) to the contributories according to the rights attaching to their shares of the company's capital.

There are two methods of winding-up:

(i) a compulsory winding-up by the court;
(ii) a voluntary winding-up, which may be either a members' winding-up or a creditors' winding-up.

We shall now proceed to examine the general characteristics of these various types.

COMPULSORY WINDING-UP

A company may be wound up by the court when a number of situations occur – the most common being when the company is unable to pay its debts.

A petition for winding-up may be presented by the company or by the Department of Trade and Industry, but is normally presented by a creditor.

When there is a petition for winding-up, the court is not forced to make an order, but if it does, a liquidator is appointed who realises the assets and pays the creditors, handing over the surplus (if any) to the shareholders. When the company's affairs are fully wound up, the court will make an order dissolving the company. The order is registered with the Registrar of Companies by the liquidator, and the Registrar makes an entry on the Register dissolving the company from the date of the court order.

VOLUNTARY WINDING-UP

A company may be wound up voluntarily:

(*a*) When the period, if any, fixed for the duration of the company by the articles expires, or the event, if any, occurs, on the occurrence of which the articles provide that the company is to be dissolved, and the company in general meeting has passed an *ordinary resolution* requiring the company to be wound up voluntarily. A limitation on a company's duration is in practice very rare.
(*b*) If the company resolves by *special resolution* that the company be wound up voluntarily for any cause whatever.
(*c*) If the company resolves by *extraordinary resolution* to the effect that it cannot by reason of its liabilities continue its business, and that it is advisable to wind up.

When a company has passed a resolution for voluntary winding-up, it must give notice of the resolution by an advertisement in the *Gazette* within 14 days. The voluntary winding-up is deemed to commence at the time of the passing of the resolution.

Declaration of solvency

Where it is proposed to wind up a company voluntarily, the directors, or a majority of them if there are more than two, may at a meeting of the board make a statutory declaration that they have made a full enquiry into the affairs of the company and have formed the opinion that it will be able to pay its debts in full within a stated period of not more than 12 months from the beginning of the winding-up. To be effective, such declaration must be made within the five weeks before the passing of the winding-up resolution or on that date but before the resolution was passed, and must be delivered to the Registrar of Companies for registration, and must embody a statement of the company's assets and liabilities as at the latest practicable date before the making of the declaration, though errors and omissions will not necessarily render the statement invalid. Thus, in *De Courcy* v *Clements* [1971] 1 All ER 681, the statement of the company's assets and liabilities was held to be valid even though it omitted to state that a debt of £45,000 was owed by the company to a third party. Megarry J observed that what is now the Insolvency Act 1986 did not require absolute perfection since, amongst other things, a liquidator who forms the opinion that the company will not be able to pay its debts in full within the period specified in the declaration of solvency must forthwith summon a creditors' meeting and put the matter to them. The creditors can petition for a compulsory winding-up, notwithstanding the voluntary liquidation, and might therefore be regarded as adequately protected. Directors making such a declaration without reasonable grounds are liable to heavy penalties.

The advantage to the company of such a declaration is that the winding-up is then a 'members' voluntary winding-up'. In the absence of such a declaration, it must be a 'creditors' voluntary winding-up'.

Commonly the Revenue (which is no longer a preferential creditor) has not completed its tax assessments on the company and has not therefore been paid. Nevertheless, if funds are available to pay the Revenue when liability (which has been approximated) is ascertained, a members' voluntary winding-up may continue and there is no need to convert to a creditors' voluntary, nor are the directors liable for a false declaration that the company's debts will be paid during the stated period of not longer than 12 months.

MEMBERS' VOLUNTARY WINDING-UP

The company in general meeting, and by ordinary resolution, must appoint one or more liquidators for the purpose of winding up the company and distributing its assets, and may fix the remuneration to be paid to him or them. The appointment may be made at the same meeting at which the resolution for winding-up was passed.

On the appointment of the liquidator all the powers of the directors cease, except in so far as their continuance is sanctioned either by the company in general meeting or by the liquidator. However, a resolution for voluntary winding-up does not automatically dismiss all employees but if the liquidator does not carry on the business, which he may do for beneficial winding-up, e.g. to complete work in progress so that the finished articles may be sold more profitably, then employees are dismissed (*Reigate* v *Union Manufacturing Co* (*Ramsbottom*) [1918] 1 KB 592).

If a liquidator dies, resigns, or otherwise vacates his office, the company may in general meeting and subject to any arrangement with its creditors, fill the vacancy. Such a meeting may be convened by any contributory or, if there were more liquidators than one, by those continuing. However, as a general rule a single shareholder cannot constitute a meeting for the purpose of making a valid appointment of a liquidator (*In Re London Flats Ltd*, 1969, see Chapter 19), except in the case of the single-member company.

Meetings

If the liquidator at any time forms the opinion that the company will be unable to pay its debts in full within the period stated in the statutory declaration, he must forthwith summon a meeting of creditors. When the liquidator calls the meeting of creditors the company is deemed to be in a creditors' voluntary, and that meeting may exercise the same powers as a creditors' meeting at the beginning of a liquidation which is initiated as a creditors' winding-up, including appointing their nominee as liquidator and a liquidation committee.

In any event, if the winding-up continues for more than a year, the liquidator must summon a general meeting of the company at the end of the first year and of each succeeding year, or at the first convenient date within three months from the end of the year, or such longer period as the Department of Trade and Industry may allow. He must lay before the meeting an account of his acts and dealings, and the conduct of the winding-up during the preceding year.

As soon as the affairs of the company are fully wound up, the liquidator must make up an account of the winding-up showing how it has been conducted, and how the property of the company has been disposed of, and then call a general meeting of the company in order to lay the account before it and explain it. The meeting is called by advertisement in the *London Gazette*, specifying the time, place and object of the meeting. The advertisement must be published at least one month before the meeting.

Within one week after the meeting the liquidator must send to the Registrar of Companies a copy of the account, and make a return to him of the holding of the meeting and its date. If no quorum was present at the meeting, the liquidator makes a return to the effect that the meeting was duly summoned and no quorum was present, and this is deemed to constitute compliance. The Registrar must publish in the *London Gazette* notice of the receipt by him of the return of the holding of the meeting.

The Registrar then registers the account and return as to the meeting and three months after such registration the company is deemed to be dissolved. The liquidator or any interested person may apply to the court for the deferment of dissolution and, if the grounds seem adequate, the court may defer the date as it thinks fit. The court may, after the dissolution, make an order declaring the dissolution void, again on the application of the liquidator or any interested person being someone who has a claim against its assets, e.g. a creditor.

In the case of creditors, and others generally, the court cannot order restoration to the Register after two years, but in the case of those wishing to make claims for personal injury against the company, the time can be extended for a longer period up to the maximum time allowed for bringing the claim under the Limitation Act 1980. For example, where the injury was not apparent at the time of an accident the time is three years after the injury did become apparent. Thus if there is an injury to the head which later is seen to have caused blindness, the time would be three years after discovering the blindness; so a company responsible for the initial injury could be restored to the Register, so that a claim could be made against it some years after it had been dissolved. These restoration provisions apply regardless of the method of winding-up. This will enable a person to get a judgment and make a claim on the company, the claim then being, in effect, met by the company's insurers. It is, however, necessary to make the claim against the company before the insurance indemnity is triggered and the above provisions enable this to be done.

Where the liquidator has been obliged to call a meeting of creditors because of insolvency, these procedures are modified and those appropriate to a creditors' voluntary winding-up apply.

CREDITORS' VOLUNTARY WINDING-UP

Where a company proposes to wind up voluntarily and the directors are not in a position to make the statutory declaration of solvency, the company must call a meeting of its creditors not later than the fourteenth day after the members' meeting at which the resolution for voluntary winding-up is to be proposed. Notices of this meeting are to be sent by post to creditors not less than seven days before the day of the creditors' meeting.

The company must advertise a notice of the creditors' meeting once in the *London Gazette* and once at least in two local newspapers circulating in the district where it has its registered office or principal place of business.

The directors must place before the creditors' meeting a full statement of the company's affairs, together with a list of creditors and the estimated amount of their claims, and appoint a director to preside at the meeting. The notice of the meeting must give the name and address of an insolvency practitioner who will give creditors information about the company or state a place where a list of creditors can be inspected.

Appointment of liquidator

The creditors and the company at their respective meetings may nominate a liquidator. If the creditors do not nominate one, the company's nominee becomes the liquidator. If the creditors and the company nominate different persons, the person nominated by the creditors has preference. However, where different persons are nominated, any director, member or creditor of the company may, within seven days after the date on which the nomination was made by the creditors, apply to the court for an order to appoint the company's nominee to act either instead of or in conjunction with the creditors' nominee, or alternatively to appoint some other person.

At the same meeting the creditors may, if they think fit, appoint a liquidation committee to act with the liquidator (see Chapter 25). On the appointment of a liquidator all the powers of the directors cease, except in so far as the liquidation committee, or, if there is no such committee, the creditors sanction their continuance. The position of employees is the same as in a members' voluntary winding-up.

If a vacancy occurs, by death, resignation or otherwise, in the office of liquidator, other than a liquidator appointed by or by the direction of the court, the creditors may fill the vacancy.

Where the winding-up continues for more than a year, the liquidator must summon a general meeting of the company and a meeting of the creditors at the end of the first and each succeeding year, or within three months of that time, and lay before the meetings an account of the conduct of the winding-up during the preceding year. The Department of Trade and Industry may allow modifications to the time limit.

Centrebinding

In the past, when no particular qualifications were required to undertake insolvency work, it was possible for the members in a creditors' voluntary to appoint a liquidator from among a group of unscrupulous persons prepared to participate in fraud. The person appointed would then proceed to dispose of the company assets and dissipate the proceeds often into other enterprises of the directors or their associates. This was done without the holding of a creditors' meeting to affirm the appointment of the liquidator, and by the time the creditors became aware of the liquidation it was too late to do anything about it. The difficulty was that the disposal of the assets by the members' liquidator was quite legal. The court so decided in *Re Centrebind* [1966] 3 All ER 889 and the procedure became known as 'centrebinding'.

The practice has been brought to an end for two reasons as follows:

(*a*) the requirement of qualified insolvency practitioners; *and*
(*b*) because of s 166, which provides that until a meeting of creditors has been called to approve the company's liquidator, that liquidator has power only to take control of the company's property and to sell perishable goods. Any other dispositions of the company's property are invalid.

Final meetings and dissolution

As soon as the affairs of the company are fully wound up, the liquidator makes an account of the winding-up, and calls a general meeting of the company and a meeting of the creditors to lay before them the account and give an explanation of it. This meeting must be advertised in the *London Gazette*, specifying the time and place and object, the advertisement being published one month at least before the meeting.

Within one week after the date of the meeting or, if they are not held on the same date, after the date of the later meeting, the liquidator must send to the Registrar a copy of the account and a return of the holding of the meetings and their dates. If a quorum is not present at either meeting, the return should specify that the meeting was duly summoned and that no quorum was present and this will suffice. As with a members' voluntary liquidation, the Registrar registers the returns and the company is dissolved at the end of three months, subject to the rights of the liquidator or of interested persons to apply for the date to be deferred. The Registrar must cause to be published in the *London Gazette* notice of the receipt by him of the return of the holding of the meeting.

Applications to court

The liquidator or any contributory or creditor may apply to the court to determine any question arising in the winding-up of a company, or to exercise, as respects the enforcing of calls or any other matter, all or any of the powers which the court might exercise if the company were being wound up by the court, and the court may accede to these requests and make such orders as it thinks just. A copy of any such order must be sent forthwith by the company, or otherwise as may be prescribed, to the Registrar of Companies for minuting in his books relating to the company.

Rights of creditors and contributories

Notwithstanding the fact that the company is being wound up voluntarily, a creditor or contributory may still apply to have it wound up by the court, but the court must be satisfied that, in the case of a contributory, the rights of the contributories will be prejudiced by a voluntary winding-up.

ALTERNATIVES TO WINDING-UP

There are two ways in which a company can be dissolved without following winding-up procedures.

Striking off at the instigation of the Registrar: defunct companies

The dissolution here results where the Registrar has a reasonable cause to believe that a company is not carrying on business or is not in operation. This jurisdiction, which has been with us for many years, is currently to be found in s 652 of the 1985 Act. The Registrar may act because, e.g.:

(*a*) he has not received documents from the company which should have been sent to him; or
(*b*) correspondence sent to the company's registered office by the Registrar has been returned undelivered.

The Registrar will enquire if the company is still in business or operation. If he is satisfied that it is not, he will publish a notice in the *London Gazette* of his intention to strike the company off the register. The Company Law Official Notifications Supplement to the *London Gazette* publishes weekly notices in microfiche form. A copy notice is placed on the company's public record.

The Registrar will take into account representations from the company and other interested parties, such as members and creditors, but unless cause to the contrary is shown, the Registrar will strike the company off not less than three months after the date of the notice. The company is, in fact, dissolved on publication of a further notice to that effect in the *Gazette*. It will be seen, therefore, that if the company is to remain in business, it is important for the company to reply promptly to any formal letter of inquiry from the Registrar and to deliver any outstanding documents. Failure to deliver the documents required may result in the directors being prosecuted.

Assets of dissolved company

From the date of dissolution any assets held by a dissolved company will be *bona vacantia* (property without an owner). This means that they belong to the Crown. The main source of enquiry in regard to *bona vacantia* property is the Treasury Solicitor (BV), Queen Anne's Chambers, 28 Broadway, London SW1H 9JS. If the company's registered office is in Lancashire, enquiries should be addressed to the Solicitor to the Duchy of Lancaster, 66 Lincoln's Inn Fields, London WC2A 3LH. Where the registered office is in Cornwall or the Isles of Scilly, enquiries should be made to the Solicitor to the Duchy of Cornwall, 10 Buckingham Gate, London SW1E 6LA.

Applications for striking off

A private company which is not trading but which is sending relevant documents and returns to the Registrar may apply to the Registrar to be struck off the register. The procedure is useful, e.g. for companies formed to pursue what was thought to be a good project but which has failed. Nevertheless, the directors may be in a position to deal with its assets and liabilities and ensure that the company's affairs are brought to a conclusion without the cost of employing an insolvency practitioner as liquidator. Until the company is struck off the register, though, the directors are burdened with duties under the 1985 Act, such as filing accounts and annual returns. Accordingly, the Deregulation and Contracting Out Act 1994, s 13 and Sch 5 introduce new ss 652A–652F into the Companies Act 1985 to provide for the application procedure. These sections were brought into force by the Deregulation and Contracting Out Act 1994 (Commencement No 3) Order 1995.

Application is made by the directors or a majority of them on Form 652a which will be supplied by the Registrar on request. The form is returned to the Registrar and copies must be sent to notifiable parties (see below). In general terms, the company should have concluded its affairs, though even after making application it can conclude its outstanding affairs where necessary or expedient to make or proceed with an application, e.g. paying the costs of running office premises while concluding its affairs and disposing of the office.

It is important to note that in the previous *three months* the company must not have:

- changed its name;
- traded or carried on its business;
- made a disposal for value of property that it held immediately prior to ceasing to trade, for the purpose of disposal for gain in the normal course of business or otherwise carrying on business; or
- engaged in any other activity except for the purposes of making the application, concluding the affairs of the company complying with any statutory requirement or as specified by the Secretary of State by order for the purpose of s 652B(1); furthermore
- any property which has not been transferred out of the company will be regarded as *bona vacantia* (goods without an owner) and will become the property of the Crown. There should therefore be no assets or liabilities at the time of dissolution. The potential liability of the directors to members and creditors remains for 20 years after the dissolution (s 653).

A company cannot apply to be struck off if it is the subject, or proposed subject of:

- any insolvency proceedings such as liquidation and including a situation where a petition has been presented but has not yet been dealt with; or
- a s 425 scheme, i.e. a compromise or arrangement between the company and its creditors or members.

Form 652a should be sent with the requisite fee to the Registrar of Companies.

Notifiable persons

A copy of Form 652a must be sent within seven days of making the application to:

- members;
- creditors;
- employees;
- managers or trustees of an employees' pension fund; and
- any directors who have not signed the Form (see s 652B(6)).

These notifiable persons can object to the court against the striking off for up to 20 years after the publication by the Registrar of the striking off in the *London Gazette*. Such an objection might be raised because a notifiable person was owed money by the company and is taking action in court to recover it or because the conditions for application for striking off have been breached. In addition to persons notifiable under s 652B(6), other interested parties should be informed such as the local authority where there have been planning disputes and health and safety issues. The Inland Revenue and Customs and Excise should be informed of an application to strike off. The Inland Revenue is the main objector in the striking off process and can hold up the procedure for some time. It is better therefore to clear matters with the Revenue and other interested parties before making the application.

Restoration to the register

Companies struck off under s 652 and the new application arrangements can be restored to the register for up to 20 years after dissolution (see above). A court order is necessary and application to the court can be made by interested parties such as creditors, particularly those who did not receive a copy of the company's application for striking off.

An interested party may also sometimes be a person who wishes to bring a personal injury claim against the company. The company will normally have been insured against such claims, but unless a judgment is obtained against the company, the liability of the insurer to meet the claim does not arise. The Secretary of State may also restore a company to the register if he considers this to be in the public interest.

It was thought that interested parties who may apply for restoration to the register must, under s 653, 'feel aggrieved' at the strike off *at the time of strike off*. It followed therefore that a director who had agreed with the board's decision to apply for strike off and who had been instrumental in bringing about the company's dissolution could not successfully ask the court to restore the company to the register (see *Conti* v *Ueberseebank AG* also cited *Conti, Petitioner* [1998] 11 CL 581).

This decision was reversed on appeal (see *Conti* v *Ueberseebank AG* [2000] 4 CL 698) where it was held that a member applying for restoration did not have to show that he had been aggrieved at the date of striking off so long as he could establish *a grievance at the time of his application* to restore the company, such as the possibility of a legal claim.

Outline procedure

Restoration to the register is a matter for the Companies Court, local district registries and county courts that have jurisdiction to wind up companies. The Registrar of Companies must also consent and applications for restoration must be served on him at least ten days before the court hearing. In this connection, it is important to note that it is the normal practice of the Registrar to require delivery of outstanding accounts, annual returns and any other documents in acceptable form before the hearing, before giving his consent to the application. These documents must be delivered to the Registrar at least five working days before the hearing. A member of the company must be joined in the application to give any undertakings required by the Registrar and to be responsible for his costs of the application.

Information is also available on the Companies House website at www.companieshouse.gov.uk.

Delay in application to restore to register

Where there is an application to restore a company to the register so that a claim can be brought against it the claimant should bear in mind that delay in regard to the making of a petition to the court for restoration may mean that the Limitation Act 1980 has applied so that the claim is statute-barred and restoration will not be granted. The period from the company's dissolution until the bringing of the restoration proceedings is taken into account by the court in deciding this issue (see *Whitbread (Hotels) Ltd Petitioners* 2002 SLT 178).

Offences and penalties

The application provisions must not be used to defraud creditors or for any other wrongful purpose. Most offences under the new provisions attract a fine of up to £5,000 on conviction before magistrates and an unlimited fine in the Crown Court. If directors deliberately conceal the application from interested parties, they are liable not only to a fine but up to seven years' imprisonment. There may also be disqualification from being a director, the maximum period being 15 years.

Author's note: *Questions on winding-up can be found at the end of Chapter 25, on p 565.*

25

CORPORATE INSOLVENCY – WINDING-UP IN CONTEXT

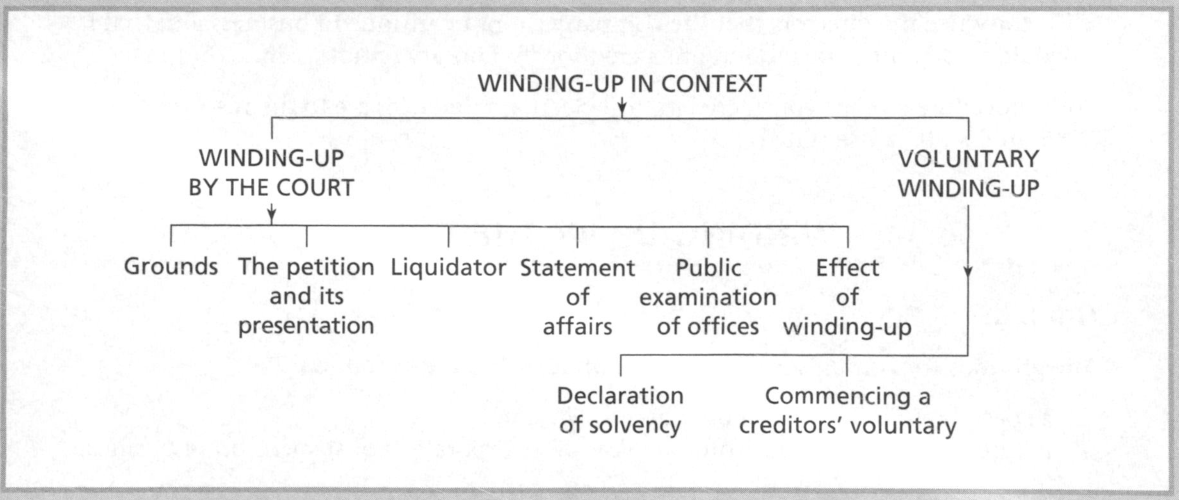

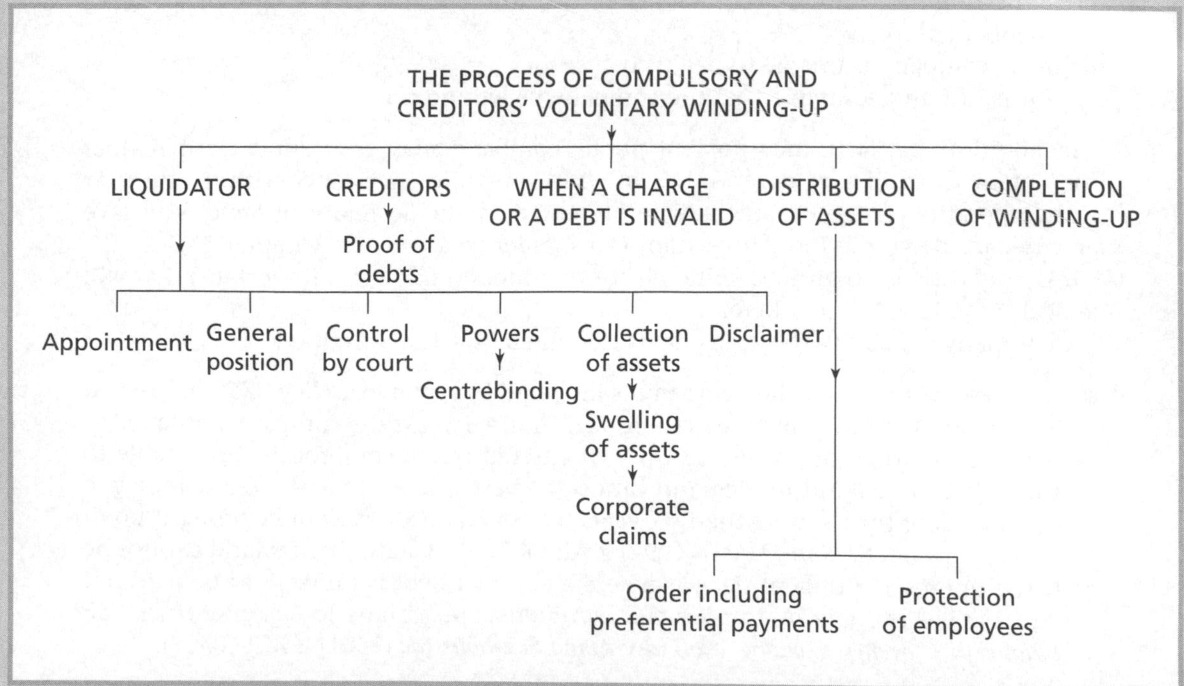

Having outlined the methods of winding-up in terms of a broad overview, we now consider in this chapter the likely course of a winding-up.

Let us assume that we are dealing with a small manufacturing company which has suffered from a recession in trade and is now in difficulties in terms that its creditors are pressing for payment which it cannot make. In addition, let us consider the problem from the point of view of the unsecured or trade creditors who do not wish to appoint an administrator.

Two courses are open to them as follows:

1 To initiate a winding-up by the court. This is slow and expensive.
2 To convince the directors that the company cannot continue in business and that it would be advantageous to initiate a creditors' voluntary winding-up.

Both procedures will be considered in turn. Section references are to the Insolvency Act 1986 unless otherwise stated.

WINDING-UP BY THE COURT

Grounds

The grounds for compulsory winding-up under s 122 are as follows:

(*a*) a special resolution by the members to wind up;
(*b*) failure to start business within one year of incorporation or suspension of business for a whole year;
(*c*) if the number of members falls below two, though not in the case of a single-member company;
(*d*) if the company is unable to pay its debts;
(*e*) if it is just and equitable that the company be wound up.

In addition, a newly incorporated public company may be wound up if it does not obtain a certificate under s 117 of the Companies Act 1985 within one year of incorporation. The petition may be presented by the Secretary of State. We have already considered the more important cases under (*e*) above (see Chapter 14).

It is only the fourth ground (which is the commonest and most important) that will be dealt with in any detail here.

A company's inability to pay its debts is defined by s 123 as follows:

(*a*) If a creditor to whom the company is indebted in a sum *exceeding £750* has served a demand in writing for payment and within three weeks the company has failed to pay the sum due (or given a security or entered into a compromise acceptable to the creditor). A statutory demand cannot be based on a statute-barred debt, e.g. a contract debt that is more than six years old, so an action cannot be brought upon it (*Re a Debtor (No 50A SD/95)* [1997] 2 All ER 789). A statutory demand cannot be based upon a contingent debt as where a contract debt is unlikely to be paid but has not yet become due under the contractual provisions for payment (see *JSF Finance & Currency Exchange Co Ltd* v *Akma Solutions Inc* [2001] 2 BCLC 307).

Note that it is not merely the failure to pay the debt which gives the ground for winding-up. Thus, if a company can satisfy the court that it has a defence to the claim a winding-up order will not be made. In consequence it is advisable for a creditor to sue the company to judgment before serving a demand for payment of the judgment debt, though this is not a legal requirement.

(*b*) If a judgment creditor has tried to enforce his judgment by execution on the company's property and the execution has failed to satisfy the debt.

(*c*) If the court is satisfied that the company is unable to pay its debts. The following case provides an example.

Taylors Industrial Flooring Ltd *v* M & H Plant Hire (Manchester) Ltd
[1990] BCLC 216

M & H supplied plant to Taylors, who were building contractors, in December 1988. M & H invoiced Taylors in mid-January 1989 but by 14 April 1989 the invoice had not been paid, nor had the second invoice which was issued in February 1989. M & H petitioned for the compulsory winding-up of Taylors on 14 April. The Court of Appeal *held* that the petition could proceed. Section 123 was satisfied. Taylors had no grounds to dispute the debt, and the fact that they might not wish to pay it was no defence.

Comment

This is a useful decision in modern times when companies have collapsed so quickly that the wait of three weeks for the statutory demand to trigger has seen the company's assets dissipated.

Petitioners

For our purposes six classes of persons can present a petition as follows:

1 the company itself;
2 the Official Receiver who can present a petition even after the commencement of a voluntary winding-up;
3 the Department of Trade and Industry, following an investigation;
4 a contributory;
5 a creditor;
6 the Trade and Industry Secretary where a public company does not obtain a s 117 (Companies Act 1985) certificate in time.

Only a petition by a contributory or creditor will be considered in any detail here.

(*a*) *Contributory*. The following points should be noted:

(i) A contributory is defined as meaning everyone who is liable to contribute to the assets of the company should it be wound up.

(ii) Although at first sight the term would appear to cover only shareholders whose shares are partly paid, it applies also to holders of fully-paid shares since all members are liable to contribute subject to any limits on their liability provided for by s 74 of the Insolvency Act 1986 (*Re Anglesey Colliery Co* (1886) 1 Ch App 555). The section provides that a person who has fully-paid shares is not liable to contribute but nevertheless he is within the definition of a contributory. So 'contributory' is merely another name for 'member' under s 124.

(iii) Under s 124 a contributory cannot petition unless (*a*) the number of members is reduced below two, but not in the case of a single-member company; or (*b*) he took his shares as an original allottee; or (*c*) by transmission from a deceased shareholder; or (*d*) he had held the shares for six out of the last 18 months. This is presumably a precaution to prevent the purchase of shares with a view to an immediate wrecking operation on the company.

(iv) Finally, a contributory cannot petition unless he has an interest in the process, e.g. it must be likely that there will be surplus assets. Thus, if a company is insolvent, a contributory cannot petition, though he can and has an interest if, because of the potential liability for the company's debts in a multi-member company, the membership is below the statutory minimum of two.

(*b*) *Creditors*. The following points should be noted:

(i) The creditor is the most usual petitioner. A creditor is a person who is owed money by the company and who could enforce his claim by an action in debt.

An unliquidated (or unascertained) claim in contract or tort is not enough. Thus it is better for the creditor petitioner to have the debt made precise as to amount by suing the company to judgment before winding-up. Then on petition the company cannot, by reason of the judgment, deny that it owes the money, or that it is an unliquidated sum.

(ii) The debt owed to the creditor to be *at least* £750. If it is not, he will no doubt find other creditors to make a joint petition with him so that the total debt is at least £750.

The figure of £750 has been adopted by the judiciary from the amount specified in s 123 of the Insolvency Act 1986 though that section does say: 'exceeding £750'.

(iii) Even if the debt on which the petition is based is not disputed, but there are some creditors who think that their best chance of recovering their money lies in the company continuing business, then the court may, in its discretion, refuse a winding-up order. Section 195 gives the court power to have regard to the wishes of the creditors, which in practice usually means the wishes of the majority in value.

Thus, in *Re ABC Coupler & Engineering Ltd* [1961] 1 All ER 354 a judgment creditor for £17,540 petitioned as his debt was not paid. He was opposed by various creditors whose debts were slightly more, namely £18,328. The company had extensive goodwill, orders worth £110,000 and its assets were worth almost £700,000 more than its liabilities. The court found that the wishes of the majority for the company to continue were reasonable.

Presentation of the petition

As soon as a petition is presented, the court may under s 135 take charge of the company's affairs by appointing a provisional liquidator. This is usually the Official Receiver.

It is a somewhat drastic measure to appoint a liquidator before the court has made a winding-up order, but if the company's assets are at risk of being dissipated by the directors it may be done. The role of the Official Receiver as provisional liquidator is to take possession of the assets and accounting records until the hearing of the petition. Normally the directors will also be relieved of the company's cheque books.

Avoiding property dispositions in compulsory winding-up

If a winding-up order is made on a petition for compulsory winding-up the commencement of the winding-up is deemed to be the date of presentation of the petition under what is known as the principle of 'relation back'. If there have been dispositions of the company's property during that period the liquidator may ask the court for an order restoring the property to the company. The directors may have made such dispositions after the petition but before the making of the order. These dispositions are void under s 127 Insolvency Act 1986 whether the recipient of the property is aware of the presentation of the petition or not. Those who are aware of it and wish genuinely to deal with the company should ask the court for a validating order which if given will make the relevant transaction legally enforceable and the property irrecoverable.

Liquidator

Under s 136 the Official Receiver becomes the liquidator of any company ordered to be wound up by the court. Section 136 prescribes the steps to be taken to secure the Official Receiver's replacement as liquidator by an insolvency practitioner. For this purpose he may summon meetings of the company's creditors and members to choose a person to replace him and, under s 141, to decide whether to establish a liquidation committee to supervise the performance by the liquidator of his functions in the winding-up. Alternatively, the Official Receiver may ask the Trade and Industry Secretary to make an appointment of a liquidator. If one-quarter in value of the company's creditors request him at any time to call the meetings of creditors and members referred to above the Official Receiver must do so.

Under s 139, if the members and creditors nominate different persons to be liquidators, the creditors' nominee becomes liquidator. Where a winding-up order follows immediately upon the discharge of an administration order, the court may under s 140 appoint the former administrator to be liquidator.

Statement of affairs

Under s 131, where the court has made a winding-up order or appointed a provisional liquidator, the Official Receiver may require the submission of a statement of affairs of the company giving, e.g., particulars of its assets and liabilities and details of its creditors.

The persons who will most usually be called upon to make the statement are the directors or other officers of the company. However, the 1986 Act empowers the Official Receiver to require other persons connected with the company to produce or assist in the production of the statement, e.g. employees or those employed within the last 12 months.

Investigation by Official Receiver

Section 132 places a duty on the Official Receiver to investigate the affairs of the company and the reasons for its failure and to make such report, if any, to the court as he thinks fit.

Public examination of officers

Under s 133 the court has power on the application of the Official Receiver to require the public examination of persons connected with the company, e.g. its officers or an administrator. Those who without reasonable excuse fail to attend the examination may be arrested and books or papers in their possession seized.

Effect of winding-up

This is as follows:

(*a*) Immediately an order is made all actions for debt against the company are stopped (s 130). Actions in tort, e.g. for personal injury from negligence, continue.

(*b*) The company ceases to carry on business except with a view to a beneficial winding-up. For example, it may be necessary to carry on the company's business for a while in order to realise its assets at a better price, as by completing work in progress, but realisation must not be long delayed.

(*c*) The powers of the directors cease (*Fowler* v *Broads Patent Night Light Co* [1893] 1 Ch 724).

(*d*) Employees are automatically dismissed (*Chapman's Case* (1866) LR 1 Eq 346), though the liquidator may have to re-employ some of them until the winding-up is completed.

EC Regulation on Insolvency Proceedings

The EC Regulation on Insolvency Proceedings came into force on 31 May 2002. It is directly applicable in the UK but a number of amendments were required to UK law to accommodate it. These appear below.

Before the coming into force of the Directive it was possible to wind up a foreign company with assets in the UK in a UK court. Now *the main proceedings* are to be conducted where the company has its centre of main interests. In most cases this will be where the registered office is. Courts of other member states can open proceedings called *territorial proceedings* where the company carries on a non-transitory economic activity with human means or goods. These proceedings are restricted to assets situated in that member state. The proceedings affected are winding-up by the court, voluntary winding-up (with confirmation of the court), administration and voluntary arrangements.

Comment

(i) When an insolvency relates only to a person or entity with all of his or its assets in the same jurisdiction, the Regulation will have no application. In other cases the Regulation effects a most significant change to insolvency practice and merits careful study.

(ii) Although, under the above rules, courts throughout the EU (except Denmark) will be forced to recognise and assist insolvency practitioners from other countries, there are some difficulties, as follows:

- The rules do not apply to the insolvencies of a group of companies. Since this is the most common way in which international businesses are structured where there are operations in different countries, the regulations may not come into effect that often.
- There will also be arguments over whether the company has its 'centre of main operations' in a particular country.
- The provisions do not apply to insolvency practitioners appointed out of court – such as administrative receivers – and although these appointments are to be phased out under the Enterprise Act 2002, that Act does carry provisions under which an administrator may be appointed out of court, e.g. by the directors, and these appointments may not be covered.

The regulations seem to require a court involvement before proceedings are covered.

UK regulations to ensure compatibility

The UK regulations made to ensure the compatibility of the EC Regulation with UK law are: the Insolvency Act 1986 (Amendment) (No 2) Regulations 2002 (SI 2002/1240) and the Insolvency (Amendment) Rules 2002 (SI 2002/1307).

The regulations: an illustration

If the debtor (corporate or individual) has all the business interests in, say, Chester, proceedings will be commenced in the Chester County Court, or the High Court in the case of a corporate debtor with a share capital in excess of £120,000. These will be *main proceedings*. If, however, the debtor has main interests in, say, Paris, with some assets in Chester, the proceedings will be commenced as above but they will be *territorial proceedings* and confined to Chester assets.

The regulations: case law

The High Court has ruled that it could make an administration order against a company incorporated outside the European Union under the above-mentioned Regulations if the centre of the company's main interests was in England (see *In Re Brac Rent-A-Car International Inc* [2003] EWHC 128 (CH), [2003] All ER (D) 98 (Feb)). Certain judgment creditors challenged the jurisdiction of the court on the grounds that the company (which was the petitioner for administration) was incorporated in Delaware and had its registered address in the USA. The court accepted that there was no specific reference to companies outside the EU but since the jurisdiction was defined only in terms of where the petitioner's main interest lay the court had jurisdiction. The company's operations were conducted almost entirely in England and its trading contracts were governed by English law. Its employees worked in England and their contracts were governed by English law.

Comment

(i) It would appear that a UK court will, conversely, be denied its traditional jurisdiction to proceed to total winding-up where the company's centre of interest is not in the UK and be restricted to territorial proceedings confined to local assets.

(ii) Case law is still somewhat confusing on the interpretation to be put on the expression 'centre of main interests'. In the *Brac Rent-a-Car* case the court seems to have laid stress on where the employees were based and where trading took place and operations were put into effect, i.e. England. More recently the High Court has reached a conclusion that would have given the English court jurisdiction because key personnel, e.g. chairman, CEO, chief financial officer and chief operating officer, were based in London. The headquarters function played less of a role in the *Brac Rent-A-Car* case. A future case will hopefully sort out whether high level decision making or lower administration or back office functions are most important (see *King* v *Crown Energy Trading* [2003] EWHC 163 (Comm), [2003] All ER (D) 133 (Feb) which favoured high level decision making).

VOLUNTARY WINDING-UP

This is a more common method of winding-up. If in our situation the directors can be persuaded to take the view that the company has no future and agree it would be best if its existence came to an end, then a voluntary winding-up would be a cheaper method of achieving this purpose.

What sort of voluntary winding-up is applicable?

If we want a members' voluntary winding-up the directors would, as we have seen, have to make a *statutory declaration of solvency*, as it is called, in the five weeks before the special resolution for winding-up was passed, or on that date but before the resolution was passed (s 89). In the declaration they would have to say that in their opinion the company will be able to pay its debts in full plus interest within a stated period of time which must not be longer than 12 months, and a statement of assets and liabilities must be attached. Since the directors and the members control the process in a members' voluntary winding-up, there is a strong temptation for the directors to make a declaration, even if it is not fully justified.

The rate of interest is the rate, if any, in the contract with a creditor, or the interest paid on unpaid judgments under the Judgments Act 1838, which is currently 8 per cent. This rate has been in force since 1 April 1993 (see SI 1993/564). The interest is payable from the commencement of the winding-up until payment and can only be paid if all creditors have been paid the principal sum of their debt in full – in other words, it is payable from surplus assets which would normally belong to shareholders. If the contract provides for interest, this, along with the principal sum, will be proved for in the liquidation in the ordinary way.

False declarations – what are the penalties?

Under s 89, if the declaration is made without reasonable grounds the directors are liable to imprisonment and/or an unlimited fine; *and* if the debts are not in fact paid within the stated period it is *presumed* that the directors did not have reasonable grounds so that they will have to prove that they did, which is not an easy matter.

However, this does not apply to debts which are not fully ascertained. Commonly the Revenue has not completed its assessments and cannot be paid. Nevertheless, if funds are available to pay such debts when ascertained, the members' winding-up continues and there is no need to convert to a creditors', nor are the directors liable for a false declaration.

However, if during a members' voluntary winding-up the liquidator is of the opinion that the company will not be able to pay its ascertained debts although a declaration of solvency has been given, s 95 provides that he must summon a meeting of creditors within 28 days of that opinion and put before it a statement of assets and liabilities.

As from the date when the liquidator calls the meeting of creditors, the company is deemed to be in a creditors' voluntary, and that meeting may exercise the same powers as a creditors' meeting at the beginning of a liquidation which is initiated as a creditors' winding-up, including appointing their nominee as liquidator and a liquidation committee.

If he does not follow this procedure, the liquidator is liable to a fine; and if he does, then the directors are liable to penalties for making a declaration of solvency without reasonable grounds.

The liquidator who has been nominated by the company on the basis that there would be a members' voluntary winding-up can, between the date of summoning the meeting and the meeting taking place, act only with the sanction of the court, except for taking all property under his control to which the company appears entitled. He may also dispose of perishable goods and do all such other things as may be necessary for the protection of the company's assets but no more.

Filing the declaration of solvency

The declaration must be filed with the Registrar before the expiry of the period of 15 days immediately following the date on which the resolution for winding up the company is passed. The company must give the usual 21 days' notice to its members of the extraordinary general meeting to consider the special resolution to wind up voluntarily.

If the statutory declaration is not delivered within the 15-day period, the liquidation remains a members' voluntary liquidation but the company and its officers are liable to a default fine under s 89.

Can we use a members' voluntary winding-up?

Unfortunately, our directors are only too well aware that the company will not be able to pay its debts within 12 months, so we shall have to have a creditors' voluntary winding-up and proceed as follows under s 84:

(*a*) Summon an extraordinary general meeting.
(*b*) Pass an extraordinary resolution that the company cannot by reason of its liabilities continue in business.
(*c*) It is the resolution which marks the start of a voluntary winding-up.
(*d*) The liquidator is appointed by the company if it is a members' voluntary winding-up; in a creditors' voluntary winding-up, though the members may by ordinary

resolution have nominated their choice, the creditors have powers to override and appoint their own nominee, subject to the right of any member or creditor to appeal to the court within seven days.

However, even though the members may appoint their choice of liquidator he has only very limited powers until such time as the creditors have met and confirmed him in office or not. He can take the company's property under his control and dispose of perishable goods and generally protect the company's assets but *no more.*

If the company nominates five persons for what is called the liquidation committee, both in a voluntary winding-up and also in a compulsory winding-up, the creditors can now nominate five more and veto the company's nominees, subject again to a right of appeal to the court.

Purpose of liquidation committee

The purpose of such a committee is to provide a small representative body to help the liquidator. Moreover, if there is a major creditor, who regards the assets of the company as virtually his own, the committee may provide him with a useful safety valve. The liquidator becomes involved in many kinds of businesses but a major creditor, with his knowledge of the trade, can control the committee, and supervise the winding-up, and see that the run-down of the company is carried out to the best advantage. Since a liquidation committee can exercise certain powers, such as, for example, approving payment to any class of creditors, it will save the liquidator the necessity of calling a full meeting of creditors, whose approval would otherwise be necessary.

From now on we will combine consideration of the compulsory and voluntary winding-up process.

THE DUTIES OF A LIQUIDATOR

Appointment

The following points should be noted:

(*a*) If it is a compulsory winding-up, the Official Receiver, who automatically became provisional liquidator on the winding-up order (if not earlier on the presentation of the petition), will commonly continue as the liquidator.

(*b*) In the case of a voluntary winding-up, a person, other than a corporate body or a bankrupt, can be appointed, provided he is a qualified insolvency practitioner (see further Chapter 23). The liquidator is usually an experienced accountant.

(*c*) In a voluntary winding-up, the liquidator will have to notify his appointment to the Registrar of Companies and publish it in the *Gazette*, both within 14 days.

General position of the liquidator

Section 143 states that the functions of the liquidator of a company *which is being wound up by the court* shall be to ensure that the assets of the company are got in, realised and distributed to the company's creditors, and, if there is a surplus, to the persons entitled to it.

Beyond this there is no clear definition of his role; it is a mixture of common law and statutory duties and obligations. He partakes partly of the nature of a trustee, partly of an agent of the company and partly of an officer of the company.

(*a*) *As trustee.* A liquidator is clearly not a trustee in the sense of the Trustee Act 1925, because the property of the company does not automatically vest in him as does trust property in trustees, although the court can make an order so vesting it. However, he takes over the powers of directors who equally, without being trustees, owe fiduciary duties to the company. His duty, like that of the directors, is owed to the company as a whole and not to individual contributories. Also, like a trustee, he cannot, by reason of the Insolvency Rules 1986, buy the company's property without leave of the court, or make a profit out of sales to the company. Moreover, he is in a more vulnerable position than a lay trustee because he is always paid to assume his responsibility and in *Re Home & Colonial Insurance Co* [1929] All ER Rep 231 the court referred to the 'high standard of care and diligence' required from him. 'His only refuge was to apply to the court for guidance in every case of serious doubt or difficulty.'

Furthermore, although it has not been definitely decided, it does not appear that the liquidator can claim the protection of s 61 of the Trustee Act 1925 if he has acted honestly and reasonably and ought to be excused. In *Re Windsor Steam Coal Ltd* [1929] 1 Ch 151 the Court of Appeal held on the facts that the liquidator had not acted reasonably in paying a claim without the directions of the court, but left open the question of whether s 61 was available as a defence.

(*b*) *As agent.* The liquidator can be described as an agent for the company in that he can make contracts on behalf of the company for winding-up purposes.

He has, of course, the paid agent's obligation to bring reasonable skill to his duties. However, he is not a true agent in that he controls the actions of his so-called principal, the company.

(*c*) *As officer.* The liquidator is not named as an officer of the company in the definition section of the 1985 Act, but he is named in s 212 of the Insolvency Act 1986 as a person against whom proceedings may be taken for misfeasance, which will be referred to again later. Neither is it certain that he is entitled to the protection of the Companies Act 1985 whereby the court can relieve any officer who, though negligent or in breach of trust, has acted honestly and reasonably and ought to be relieved. We have already seen an example of this section in operation in *In Re Duomatic* (1969) (see Chapter 17).

Control by the court

Finally, the liquidator is subject to constant control by the court because any person aggrieved by an action or decision of a liquidator in a winding-up may apply to the court. However, it would seem that the court is not anxious to upset his acts. Thus in *Leon* v *York-O-Matic* [1966] 3 All ER 277, where the liquidator was charged by a member of the company with selling assets at an undervalue, the judge said that in the absence of fraud there could not be interference in the day-to-day administration of the liquidator, nor a questioning of the exercise by the liquidator in good faith of his discretion, nor a holding him accountable for an error of judgment.

Powers of liquidator

The following points should be noted:

(*a*) In a compulsory winding-up s 167 provides that something like half of his powers can only be exercised with the approval of the court or of the liquidation committee, e.g. to bring or defend actions, to carry on the business of the company so far as may be necessary for its beneficial winding-up, and to pay any class of creditors in full. Otherwise he can do most acts on his own authority, e.g. sell the company's property or raise money on the security of the company's assets.

(*b*) In a creditors' voluntary winding-up, he can exercise all the powers on his own except three which need the sanction of the court, the liquidation committee or the creditors. These powers are: to pay creditors; to make a compromise with creditors; and to compromise calls and debts (s 165).

(*c*) While the liquidator in a voluntary winding-up has a freedom from supervision by the court which is not available in a compulsory winding-up, he can always get support and guidance by applying to the court on any matter arising out of the winding-up (s 112).

Centrebinding

In the past, when no particular qualifications were required to undertake insolvency work, it was possible for the members in a creditors' voluntary to appoint a liquidator from among a group of unscrupulous persons prepared to participate in fraud. The person appointed would then proceed to dispose of the company assets and dissipate the proceeds often into other enterprises of the directors or their associates. This was done without the holding of a creditors' meeting to affirm the appointment of the liquidator, and by the time the creditors became aware of the liquidation it was too late to do anything about it. The difficulty was that the disposal of the assets by the members' liquidator was quite legal. The court so decided in *Re Centrebind* [1966] 3 All ER 889 and the procedure became known as 'Centrebinding'.

The practice had been brought to an end for two reasons as follows:

(*a*) the requirement of qualified insolvency practitioners; *and*
(*b*) because of s 166, which provides that until a meeting of creditors has been called to approve the company's liquidator, that liquidator has power only to take control of the company's property and to sell perishable goods. Any other dispositions of the company's property are invalid.

Collection of the assets

(*a*) The liquidator will take charge of all assets which can be physically brought under his control, including money in the bank.

(*b*) He will not be able to touch money subject to a trust. Thus in *Re Kayford* [1975] 1 All ER 604 a mail order company in anticipation of liquidation had put customers' deposits for goods which the company might not be able to supply in a special 'Customer Trade Deposit Account' and it was held that these deposits were returnable to the customers and did not come under the control of the liquidator. However, if there are any other assets in the hands, for example, of a sheriff, who is intending to sell the goods as part of a judgment creditor's execution, the liquidator will be able to recover these assets if the process of sale has not been completed before the winding-up commenced.

(*c*) The liquidator will normally in a compulsory winding-up pay all money into the Insolvency Services Account at the Bank of England, but in a voluntary winding-up he need not do so unless he has in his hands assets unclaimed or undistributed for six months.

(*d*) He can bring actions to enforce debts due to the company.

(*e*) He will settle the list of contributories and he can ask the court to exercise its powers under s 237 to order an officer or any person who has previously held office as administrator or liquidator of the company or as an administrative receiver and any trustee for or any banker or agent or officer of the company to hand over any property or money or books, papers or records of the company under his control. Set-off is not allowed to a contributory until all the creditors have been paid in full. In the unlikely event of there being uncalled capital, he can call it up, and will settle the A list of present members and the B list of persons who have been members in the 12 months preceding winding-up. The B list members will only be liable for debts contracted while they were members to the extent that their successors failed to pay the balance due on their shares.

Officers: co-operation with liquidator

It was held by the Court of Appeal Criminal Division in *R* v *McCredie* [2000] BCLC 438 that the company's directors and other officers are required by s 208(1) of the Insolvency Act 1986 to co-operate with the liquidator in terms of the ascertainment and delivery up of the company's property, not merely in a reactive manner but proactively. The requirement to deliver up does not depend on a prior request from the liquidator. It is a continuing and not a once-for-all-time duty. Failure to act in a proactive way can, as this case decides, be a criminal offence under s 208 punishable with imprisonment or a fine.

Swelling the assets

It is the duty of the liquidator, subject to the problems outlined below, to swell the assets by recovering any sums due from the directors or officers of the company. His ability to recover may arise under a number of headings as follows:

(*a*) *Secret profits*. It may be that the directors have made an unauthorised profit out of their position. As we saw in *Regal (Hastings) Ltd* v *Gulliver*, 1942, the directors had helped the parent company out by putting up money for shares in a subsidiary company, but were made to repay to the parent company a profit on those shares when they were sold. Alternatively, the directors may have paid themselves unauthorised salaries which may be recovered. As we have seen, officers of the company can be summoned before the court for examination if they are suspected of having property of the company in their possession.

(*b*) Reference should also be made to the rules relating to wrongful and also fraudulent trading under which the company's officers and others may be personally liable for certain debts of the company (see further Chapter 18).

If the liquidator recovers money under the above heads, it goes into a fund for all the creditors (*Re William C Leitch Ltd* (*No 2*) [1933] Ch 261). In the past if an individual creditor, such as the Revenue, was paid his debt by the directors as a result of his bringing an application for, say, fraudulent trading, then he could keep the money (*Re Cyona Distributors* [1967] 1 All ER 281). This will not arise now because only the liquidator may apply, under the relevant sections.

(*c*) *Power to conduct examinations.* Section 212 allows the court on the application of the Official Receiver, the liquidator, a creditor or a contributory to examine the conduct of any promoter, past or present director, manager, liquidator, administrator, administrative receiver or officer of the company. If it appears that such a person has misapplied or retained or become liable or accountable for any money or property of the company, or been guilty of any misfeasance or breach of trust in relation to the company, the court can order him to repay or restore or to contribute to the assets of the company by way of compensation such a sum as the court thinks just.

Corporate claims in liquidation

Although, in general terms, a liquidator will wish to swell the assets by recovering sums under the headings mentioned above, it should be noted that it is, generally speaking, unwise for a liquidator to enter into litigation for the company. First, because legal aid has been abolished in civil matters (except for family and clinical negligence cases). In addition, the Access to Justice Act 1999 specifically provides in s 6 and Sch 2, para 1 (g) that the new Legal Services Commission shall not fund 'matters of company or partnership law', or under para 1(h) 'other matters arising from the carrying on of a business'. Second, because the Court of Appeal ruled in *Mond* v *Hammond Suddards* [2000] Ch 40 that the cost of an unsuccessful litigation will not be treated as an expense of the liquidation, even though the liquidator had not acted in any way improperly in defending a claim by the company's receiver in regard to title to certain of the company's property. As regards conditional fee arrangements (the no-win no-fee concept), these require security for costs by the litigant or the making of a single premium insurance arrangement which admittedly is recoverable from the defendant (if he has funds) where the action is successful but not otherwise. So costs remain a problem even where the lawyer receives no fee if the claim is lost. 'Lawyer' means the solicitor in the case. Separate arrangements are required with a barrister to take the case in court unless the solicitor is also an advocate. Thus cases that have a good chance of success will continue to be brought if funded by creditors but perhaps rarely otherwise. Litigation funding agreements are dealt with by s 28 of the Access to Justice Act 1999, which inserts a new s 58B into the Courts and Legal Services Act 1990.

The ruling in the *Mond* case was affirmed in *Lewis* v *Inland Revenue Commissioners* [2000] *The Times*, 15 November. The Court of Appeal ruled in that case that a liquidator had no automatic right to recoup litigation costs. A company's liquidator attempting to use the company's realised funds for the purpose of taking proceedings against directors for wrongful trading or the recovery of a preference could not automatically regard the cost as an expense of the liquidation and payable before all other claims under s 115, IA 1986. The liquidator's right to recoup was subject to making an application to the court, under s 112 (voluntary liquidation) or s 156 (compulsory liquidation), for the court to exercise its power under those sections as relevant to dictate a different order of priority of payment in terms of allowing recoupment of litigation costs at the court's discretion.

Comment. The law is obviously anxious to look at each case on its merits. Even where the case is good, litigation is, after all, unpredictable and can be a very quick way to lose the company's funds.

Creditors – proof of debts

The following points should be noted:

1 The liquidator will normally have written to every known creditor on first appointment, sending him a copy of the statement of affairs, and he will advertise in the *Gazette* and a local newspaper (Insolvency Rules 1986) for details of debts to be submitted within a definite period, and he will normally require debts to be verified by affidavit. Then he will examine and decide on every debt, and a rejected creditor can appeal to the court.

2 The admission of debts will depend on whether the company is solvent or not. If the company is solvent, all debts can be proved which could have been enforced against the company if it had not gone into liquidation. However, statute-barred debts are only payable if all the members agree, and future debts are payable subject to a rebate of 5 per cent per annum because they are paid early.

3 If the company is insolvent, the following rules apply and certain debts are non-provable as follows:

(*a*) Claims for unliquidated damages in tort. Damages for breach of contract or trust are provable on an estimate. Thus if a claim can be framed in either contract or tort, as might be the case where injury was caused to a person by the negligence of a company driver, it may be possible to include the claim as one of contract rather than of tort. This is a useful rule for a liquidator because in a compulsory liquidation he does not have to await the outcome of tort proceedings before winding up the company, though, as we have seen, an order can be made by the court restoring it to the Register so that a formal claim may be made against it to trigger its insurance company's duty to indemnify the company against the claim. However, in *Re Islington Metal and Plating Works* [1983] 3 All ER 218, Harman J decided that if a company which started liquidation as insolvent later became solvent, where, as in this case, an action by the liquidator on behalf of the company against its directors for misfeasance might succeed, debts of all descriptions could be proved. In such a situation, once the claims of the undoubted creditors were satisfied and the costs provided for, the tort claimants would be entitled to make claims before distribution of any surplus.

Members' and creditors' voluntaries must be kept open while tort claims are quantified.

(*b*) Debts incurred after notice of a transaction at undervalue or preference (see below), or if the company could not pay its debts as they fell due and had suspended payment of debts.

(*c*) Contingent debts when the value cannot be fairly estimated. In *Re Patent Floor Cloth Co* (1872) 26 LT 467, two persons Dean and Gilbert were employed by the company as travellers for a period of three years on commission. In the first year they made £400 each and then the company was wound up. The court held that an estimate could be made of their entitlement to commission for the purposes of the winding-up but this would have been impossible if there had not been a first year commission on which to base it.

(*d*) Debts barred by the Limitation Act 1980 at the commencement of winding-up are not enforceable, though time stops running on the commencement of the liquidation and if the debt is not statute-barred then it will not become so because of delay in payment arising out of the liquidation.

(*e*) Illegal debts and unenforceable debts are not provable. For example, a debt on a contract for the sale of land which is not in writing as is required by the Law of Property (Miscellaneous Provisions) Act 1989 is not provable. Nor would an illegal debt be provable as where a builder has built premises for a company knowing that there was no planning permission.

If a debt cannot be proved, the creditor gets no dividend and has no rights as a creditor, e.g. to attend and vote at meetings.

There are also certain *deferred debts*. These are provable but no dividend is payable nor is there a right to vote until all provable debts have been paid with interest (see below). The deferred debts are as follows:

(*a*) loans under a written agreement that the lender is to receive a rate of interest varying with the profits of the company, and

(*b*) where the vendor of a business sold to the company is receiving a share of the profits as payment.

Third Parties (Rights Against Insurers) Act 1930

A method of circumventing a liquidation by a creditor is to be found in the above Act, which has been the subject of a Law Commission consultation paper. If a worker is injured by his employer's negligence and the employer is a company that goes into liquidation, the 1930 Act allows the injured worker to make a claim against the company's insurer, thus avoiding a proof in the company's liquidation which might only produce a small payment covering only part of the claim.

However, the claim against the insurer is by no means straightforward since the insurer is only liable to indemnify the company. Therefore, the worker must sue the company to establish its liability before the insurance company is obliged to pay. This may mean an action at law to restore the company to the register if it has been struck off on liquidation and another action against the company to establish its liability. It may then be necessary to bring a legal action against the insurance company if it disputes liability. In a consultation document published in the spring of 1998, the Law Commission suggests legislative changes to enable claims to be dealt with in one set of proceedings. There is as yet no legislation.

Position of secured creditors

As regards secured creditors, a secured creditor must state in his proof that he is a secured creditor and either:

(i) surrender the security and prove for the whole debt as an unsecured creditor; *or*
(ii) value the security and prove for the balance which then remains as an unsecured creditor.

If the creditor values the security and proves for the balance, then the liquidator may (*a*) redeem the security by paying the creditor the amount of the valuation, or (*b*) require the security to be sold by auction to establish its value.

The creditor may at any time after lodging his proof by notice in writing require the liquidator to choose between (*a*) and (*b*) above. The liquidator then has six months from receipt of the notice to make a choice. If he does not make a choice, the creditor owns the security at his valuation and may prove for the balance as an unsecured creditor.

Under s 189 the surplus remaining in any winding-up after payment in full of proved debts is to be applied in the payment of interest to the extent specified on the amount of those debts before it is available for members. The rate of interest payable under the section in respect of any debt is whichever is the greater of:

(*a*) the rate specified in s 17 of the Judgments Act 1838 on the day on which the company went into liquidation (currently 8 per cent per annum (SI 1993/564)); and
(*b*) the rate applicable to that debt apart from the winding-up, e.g. the contract rate of interest, if any.

The court may on the application of the liquidator vary or set aside any extortionate credit transaction between the company and a creditor.

Provisions which may invalidate a charge or debt

There are various provisions, some of which have been considered briefly already, which may invalidate a charge granted by the company or any other disposition it has made or any debt which it has incurred. These are as follows:

(*a*) A charge will be invalid against the liquidator or creditors if it is not registered under the Companies Act 1985 within 21 days with the Registrar. If it is invalid the holder falls to the level of an unsecured creditor.

(*b*) Section 241 enables the court on the application of the liquidator to make orders for restoring the position of the company and its creditors to what it would have been if the company had not entered into a transaction at an undervalue or given a preference to a creditor before the commencement of the winding-up. Preferences within six months from the commencement of winding-up can be set aside. The period is two years if with a connected person, e.g. director. Transactions at undervalue made up to two years before can be set aside whether the recipient was connected with the company or not.

The Act applies to the creation of a charge and to any delivery of goods or the payment of money. A simple example from previous legislation of a preference is *Re Kushler* [1943] 2 All ER 22, where ordinary creditors were ignored but the company paid some £700 into the bank merely to clear the overdraft guaranteed by the directors. Repayment was ordered.

(*c*) As we have seen, by s 245 a floating charge created by a company within the year before the commencement of its winding-up or within two years if given to a connected person, e.g. a director, may be void (see further Chapter 20).

The purpose of this section appears to be similar to a preference to prevent a company, while it is unable to pay its debts, from preferring an unsecured creditor by giving him a floating charge on its assets.

(*d*) It may be necessary to look at the *ultra vires* rule, namely that a company can only carry out transactions permitted by the objects clause in the memorandum of association or any reasonably incidental thereto. An *ultra vires* debt is invalid and the liquidator need not pay it, though the creditor may follow and trace his property into the company's assets.

The Companies Act 1985 will now operate to render most transactions valid. The position under the 1985 Act was considered in Chapter 3.

(*e*) If the liquidator can prove fraudulent trading or wrongful trading against, e.g., a director or officer under the Insolvency Act 1986, which have already been considered, the court may order that person to become personally liable for the debt. (Note also management by disqualified persons, in Chapter 18.)

(*f*) Finally, the liquidator has a very powerful weapon in the right to disclaim given to him by ss 178 and 179. The sections allow him to disclaim property, e.g. stock or shares, unprofitable contracts, property unsaleable or not readily saleable or land burdened with onerous covenants. As regards the latter, an illustration is provided by *Re Nottingham General Cemetery Co* [1955] 2 All ER 504 where contracts between the company and the owners of the grave plots prevented its use for a purpose other than a cemetery. The liquidator can, of course, disclaim such land, and if he does it vests in the Crown subject to the right of any interested party, e.g. a local authority, to ask that the land be vested in him.

The liquidator must disclaim in writing within 12 months (this does not apply if he is the Official Receiver) and if he hesitates, anyone concerned can ask him to decide within 28 days what he will do. If he fails to tell the court within 28 days that he intends to disclaim he will lose his right. The court can assist persons affected by the disclaimer because, although they can no longer prove as creditors in the liquidation, they are entitled to damages. These damages may or may not equal the full amount of the debt. An illustration taken from the law of bankruptcy, which is the same on this point, is set out below.

Re Hooley, ex parte United Ordnance and Engineering Co Ltd [1899] 2 QB 579

Hooley's trustee in bankruptcy disclaimed certain unpaid shares which Hooley held in the company, the shares being of low value. Hooley owed £25,000 under the contract to take the shares. The court assessed the damages payable to the company on the basis of the company's indebtedness. It appeared that the gross amount owed by the company was £16,169. The court deducted from this the cash in hand of £4,000 and directors' fees owing of £1,669, leaving a balance of £10,500. *Held* – this was the measure of damages which the company could prove for in the bankruptcy.

Distribution of assets

The liquidator is now able to distribute the assets. The order laid down for a compulsory winding-up under the Insolvency Rules is usually followed. The order is as follows:

1 First come the costs of the winding-up. In broad terms these cover the costs of getting in the assets, of the petition, of making the statement of affairs, the liquidator's remuneration and the expenses of the committee of inspection.

2 Then come the preferential debts (see Insolvency Act 1986, Sch 6). These debts rank equally between themselves so that if the property of the company is not sufficient to pay them all in full they will have to abate proportionately. The preferential debts are as follows:

(*a*) wages or salaries of employees due within four months next before the relevant date up to a maximum of £800 for each employee;
(*b*) all accrued holiday remuneration of employees;
(*c*) it should be noted that assessed taxes are no longer preferential and also that if a bank has provided funds to pay wages and salaries that debt becomes preferential under the rule of subrogation;
(*d*) contributions to an occupational pension fund.

3 Next come charges secured by a floating charge which take second place to preferential creditors. Fixed chargeholders are not subject to the claims of preferential creditors.

4 These are followed by the unsecured ordinary creditors. It should be noted that secured creditors are paid before the unsecured creditors if the liquidator is allowed to sell the assets charged. This is, however, rare because secured creditors, including both fixed and floating chargeholders, normally appoint a receiver to sell the assets charged, returning any surplus after sale to the liquidator. If there is a shortfall and the proceeds of sale do not cover the debt, the secured creditors prove for the balance as unsecured creditors, as they do if they surrender the security to the liquidator.

In order to ensure that the abolition of the preferential status of Crown debts does not go solely to floating charge holders the Enterprise Act 2002 set up a mechanism for *ring-fencing a percentage of assets for unsecured creditors*. These provisions that apply in all corporate insolvencies have already been detailed in Chapter 23 at page 526 in the materials on administration.

5 Lastly come the deferred debts. These have already been referred to but one could add at this stage sums due to members in their capacity as members, such as dividends declared but not paid.

If there is money left at this stage, the company is solvent and debts such as unliquidated damages in tort will be admitted and paid when quantified by the court.

Finally, any surplus will be distributed among members according to their rights under the articles or the terms of issue of their shares.

Insolvency: protection of employees

Under ss 166–168 of the Employment Rights Act 1996 an employee who loses his job when his employer (in this case a company) becomes insolvent can claim through the National Insurance Fund arrears of wages, holiday pay and certain other payments which are owed to him, rather than rely on the preferential payments procedure.

Any payments made must be authorised by the Secretary of State for Trade and Industry and the legal rights and remedies in respect of the debts covered are transferred to the Secretary of State, so that he can try to recover from the assets of the insolvent employer the costs of any payments made, up to the preferential rights the employees would have had. Major debts covered are as follows:

(*a*) Arrears of wages for a period not exceeding eight weeks up to a rate of £270 per week. The definition of wages includes the same items as are mentioned above.
(*b*) Pay in respect of holidays actually taken, and accrued holiday pay up to a rate of £270 per week, up to a limit of six weeks.
(*c*) Payments in lieu of notice at a rate not exceeding £270 a week, up to the statutory minimum entitlement of a particular employee under the Employment Rights Act 1996.
(*d*) Any payment outstanding in regard to an award by an employment tribunal of compensation for unfair dismissal.
(*e*) Reimbursement of any fee or premium paid by an apprentice or articled clerk.

There is no qualifying period before an employee becomes eligible and virtually all people in employment are entitled.

Completion of winding-up

The final stages of the winding-up are as follows:

(*a*) *Compulsory winding-up*. Once the liquidator has paid off the creditors and distributed the surplus (if any) and summoned a final meeting of the company's creditors, under s 146 he may vacate office and obtain his release. The company is dissolved at the end of three months from the receipt by the Registrar of the liquidator's notice that the final meeting of creditors has been held and that the liquidator has vacated office.

(*b*) *Voluntary winding-up*. In a voluntary winding-up the liquidator will call final meetings of the company and creditors for approval of his accounts. Within a week he will file with the Registrar his accounts and a return of the meetings, and under s 201, two months later the company is dissolved.

Whether it is a compulsory or voluntary liquidation, the court can restore the company to the Register. The law relating to this has already been considered at Chapter 24.

We have now completed a consideration of the two main methods of winding-up. However, it is possible for a company which is in voluntary liquidation to be compulsorily wound up and this is referred to in the next section.

COMPULSORY WINDING-UP BY A COMPANY IN VOLUNTARY LIQUIDATION

The following points should be noted:

(*a*) A voluntary winding-up does not by reason of s 116 bar the right of a creditor or contributory to have the company wound up by the court, though it is necessary to show one of the grounds for a compulsory winding-up. If a creditor applies to the court, the court will take into account the wishes of all the creditors and the majority view would almost certainly prevail.

In the case of contributories, the Act provides that the court must be satisfied that the rights of contributories will be prejudiced by a voluntary winding-up and that a compulsory order would be justified if, e.g., the voluntary winding-up was being conducted in a fraudulent manner or there were suspicious circumstances and a searching investigation was required.

(*b*) Under s 124 the Official Receiver may present a petition but the court will not order winding-up unless it is satisfied that the voluntary winding-up cannot be continued with due regard to the interests of the creditors and contributories. Thus, in *Re Ryder Installations* [1966] 1 All ER 453 the liquidator in a voluntary winding-up had not after eight years called a meeting of creditors and he had five convictions for failing to make the appropriate returns. Here the court ordered a compulsory winding-up by the court.

(*c*) The Secretary of State can also present a petition for a compulsory winding-up after a voluntary winding-up has been started. Thus, in *Lubin, Rosen & Associates* [1975] 1 All ER 577 the Secretary of State for Trade and Industry petitioned because an investigation suggested there had been fraud and the company, formed to build flats in Spain, never had sufficient share capital for its activities. In the event, 198 creditors with claims totalling £540,000 opposed compulsory winding-up. Megarry J held that while such opposition by creditors was a formidable obstacle, the petition of the Secretary of State carried great weight and that when there were circumstances of suspicion it was highly desirable that the winding-up should be by the court with all the safeguards that that provided. Consequently, he ordered a compulsory winding-up.

GRADED QUESTIONS

Essay mode

1 Insolvent Ltd is in compulsory liquidation and its assets are insufficient to meet its liabilities in full.

Advise the liquidator as to what action he should take in respect of the following matters:

(*a*) Three months before the commencement of the winding-up Insolvent Ltd created a floating charge over all its assets to its bank, to secure its overdraft, and this charge was duly registered. Immediately after this the bank allowed the overdraft to be increased by £50,000, which was used in paying wages to company employees.

(*b*) A private individual has put in a claim for an allegedly slanderous statement made by the managing director in the course of his duties.

(*c*) 18 months prior to the winding-up and at a time when the company was solvent a floating charge was created in favour of Grab Ltd which is controlled by a director of Insolvent Ltd.

(*d*) The following debts, *inter alia*, are due from the company:

(i) 12 months' VAT;
(ii) 12 months' corporation tax;
(iii) £20,000 arrears of salary due to 10 employees.

(*e*) A twenty-year lease on a factory which had to be shut down as being unprofitable.

(*University of Plymouth*)

2 Deadloss plc has gone into insolvent winding-up. The petition was presented on 1 April 2005 and the winding-up order was made on 30 May 2005. The liquidator is uncertain as to the priorities and whether the following transactions are binding on him:

(*a*) Deadloss created a floating charge on its undertaking and assets on 1 January 2004 to secure a loan of £500,000 from Financings Ltd. The charge contained a clause restricting Deadloss from creating any further charges ranking in priority or *pari passu* with it. This charge was duly registered within the requisite period.

(*b*) On 1 June 2004 Deadloss created a fixed charge over its land and buildings in favour of Easymoney to secure a loan of £200,000. The charge was not dated and, owing to an oversight, not registered either. The oversight was discovered on 10 July 2004. The secretary of Deadloss promptly filled in the date as 10 July 2004 and had the charge registered, obtaining a certificate of registration from the Registrar of Charges.

(*c*) Deadloss had accumulated a debt of £100,000 with Suppliers Ltd. In order to ensure uninterrupted supplies of raw materials and to prevent an anticipated petition for winding up the company, Deadloss created a floating charge over its assets on 10 January 2005, in favour of Suppliers Ltd. The charge was duly registered within 21 days of execution.

(*d*) The following debts are, among many others, owed by Deadloss:

(i) 12 months' VAT amounting to £10,000;
(ii) 8 months' PAYE amounting to £12,000;
(iii) 100 employees of the company are each owed £900 in wages for the 3 months prior to the winding-up order;
(iv) 12 months' corporation tax is due to Inland Revenue.

Write a report advising the liquidator on each of the above transactions.

(*University of Plymouth*)

3 (*a*) What kinds of liquidation or windings-up are there and what distinguishes them from each other?

(*b*) In what order must a liquidator distribute the assets?

(*c*) Distinguish between fraudulent trading and wrongful trading and say what consequences may follow if a person is found guilty of either of them.

(*Kingston University*)

4 On the liquidation of Technix plc the assets and liabilities of the company are stated as follows:

Assets	£	*Liabilities*	£
Factory	350,000	Alpha plc	300,000
Finished products	70,000	Beta plc	200,000
Computer components	20,000	Delta Bank plc	20,000
Vehicle fleet	30,000	In. Rev. & employees	30,000
Machinery	50,000	Trade creditors	25,000
		Managing Director	10,000
	520,000		585,000

The liquidator of Technix seeks your advice as to the priority of each of the company's creditors. You are given the following additional information:

(i) In 2003 a charge was created over all the company's assets and undertaking, both present and future, in favour of Alpha.
(ii) In 2004 finance was provided by Beta with the company's factory being used as security.
(iii) In 2005 a second charge was created over the company's entire undertaking in favour of Delta, in order to secure the company's overdraft facility of £20,000. The instrument creating the charge specified that Delta was to have priority over any earlier charge.
(iv) Six months prior to the winding-up, the Managing Director secured a specific charge over the company's vehicle fleet as security for loans made in the past which remain unpaid. Owing to an administrative error, his charge was not registered.
(v) Of the trade creditors, Psion Ltd claim that the contract, under which microchips were supplied to Technix at a cost of £10,000, for which Psion has not received payment, contained a reservation of title clause.

(University of Greenwich)

5 You are required to discuss the following liquidation matters.

(*a*) An allegation by a creditor of a company during a winding-up that the directors of the company continued trading when business debts could not be met.
(*b*) A view reached by a company liquidator that certain directors of the company ought to be restricted in their intention to form a new company operating in the same business area as soon as liquidation is complete.
(*c*) The order of priority which a liquidator should afford to claims from company employees for backdated wages, unsecured trade creditors for unpaid goods supplied to the company, and debenture holders secured by way of floating charge for repayment of their loans.

(The Chartered Institute of Management Accountants)

Objective mode

Four alternative answers are given. Select ONE only. Circle the answer which you consider to be correct. Check your answers by referring back to the information given in the chapter and against the answers at the back of the book.

1 A company may go into a members' voluntary winding-up if the directors or a majority of them make a declaration to the effect that the company will be able to pay its debts in full within a period not exceeding:

A 1 year.
B 6 months.
C 2 years.
D 3 years.

2 The members of a solvent company may resolve to wind it up following the passing of:

A an ordinary resolution after special notice.
B an ordinary resolution.
C an extraordinary resolution.
D a special resolution.

3 Thames Ltd is in a creditors' voluntary winding-up. The members and the creditors have nominated different persons as liquidators. What happens?

A An application must be made to the court to decide who shall act.
B The creditors' nominee becomes liquidator but any director, member or creditor may apply to the court to appoint the members' nominee.
C The creditors' nominee becomes liquidator in any event.
D The members' nominee will become liquidator but any creditor may apply to the court to appoint the creditors' nominee.

4 Tees Ltd is insolvent and its directors have made a payment to one of its creditors which is designed to improve the position of that creditor in the event of a liquidation. The creditor is not connected with the company. The company is now in liquidation. The liquidator can recover the payment if it was made within:

A 2 years of the winding-up.
B 12 months of the winding-up.
C 6 months of the winding-up.
D 18 months of the winding-up.

5 What kind of resolution is required to commence a voluntary winding-up when no declaration of solvency can be given?

A Special.
B Extraordinary.
C Ordinary.
D Ordinary with special notice.

6 When does a voluntary winding-up, whether members' or creditors', commence?

A When the relevant resolution is passed.
B When notice of the passing of the resolution is received by the Registrar.
C When the resolution is approved by the court.
D When notice of the resolution is published in the *London Gazette*.

Answers to questions set in objective mode appear on p 577.

APPENDIX: COMPANY LAW REFORM

The Final Report of the Company Law Review Steering Group

Following the publication of a number of consultation documents, the Company Law Review Steering Group published its final report in July 2001. The main proposals and changes are considered below. Copies of the Report can be obtained by telephoning 0870 1502 500 or from www.dti.gov.uk/cld/review.htm.

Modern Company Law for a Competitive Economy: The Final Report

Small and private companies

The report proposes that:

- The rule of common law of unanimous consent (expressed, for example, in *Re Duomatic Ltd* [1969] 1 All ER 161 and other cases subsequently) should be codified in statute law and extended by stating expressly that any decision the company has power to take may be taken, where the members agree unanimously, without observing any of the formalities of the Companies Act or the company's constitution.
- It should be made easier for private companies to take decisions by written resolutions to avoid the need for a general meeting. Unanimity would be abandoned and a 75 per cent majority of those entitled to vote would be enough for a special resolution or a simple majority in other cases. Electronic communication would be permitted.
- Private companies would not be required to hold AGMs, lay accounts in general meeting or appoint auditors unless they positively opted to do so. Elective resolutions would not be required.
- Private companies would no longer be required to appoint a company secretary.
- Private companies would have access to a new, simpler constitution designed especially for private companies as a substitute for the present *Table A*, that is not so specifically designed.
- As regards shareholder disputes, mediation and arbitration alternatives to costly litigation would be encouraged, and in other areas too.
- The small company accounting regime should be extended to the maximum permitted under EU law by increasing the thresholds to cover companies that meet any two of the following requirements: turnover no more than £4.8m (currently £2.8m), balance sheet total no more than £2.4m (currently £1.4m) and no more than 50 employees (as now).
- The threshold below which companies are exempt from the requirement to have their accounts audited (currently £1m turnover) should be raised to the EU maximum (i.e. £4.8m turnover). The government should decide whether to require an independent professional review for companies' accounts where turnover falls between £1m and £4.8m in the light of results which are not yet available of the Auditing Practices Board's field trials of an IPR.
- The content and format requirements for company accounts should be simplified.

- Small companies' ability to file abbreviated accounts should be removed. This is because the Steering Group feels that the form and content of small company accounts should be set entirely by accounting standards and not in part by statute.
- The time limit for private companies to file accounts after their financial year end should be cut from ten months to seven months.
- The rules on capital maintenance should be simplified, including the abolition of the rules on financial assistance for share purchase in private companies and for all companies there should also be the abolition of the need for court approval to a reduction of capital, substituting a directors' declaration of solvency with the opportunity, in a public company only, for a court challenge by creditors.

Directors

The report proposes that:

- There should be a statutory statement of directors' duties that will:
  - give directors clear and authoritative statements of what their duties are;
  - bring the law into line with modern business practice and accepted standards of behaviour;
  - make clear that, in promoting the company's success for the benefit of its membership as a whole, directors must take account of long-term as well as short-term consequences and that they must recognise where relevant the importance of relations with employees, suppliers, customers and others; the need to maintain a reputation for high standards of business conduct; and the impact of their actions on the community and the environment.
- Part X of the CA 1985, dealing with directors' conflicts of interest, should be clarified and updated. New legislation would allow a corporate opportunity to be exploited by a director following approval by a board, independent of the conflicted director.
- Directors' contracts of employment should be limited to three years on first appointment and one year thereafter unless the shareholders authorise a longer period.
- The 'comply and explain' approach of the Combined Code should be preserved but the Code's contents should not be converted into substantive requirements.
- There should be better disclosure on directors' training, qualifications and other relevant information.
- The common law on attribution, contributory negligence and contribution between wrongdoers should be clarified to ensure that the company bears a fair share of the responsibility and the loss where its directors are at fault.

Shareholders

The report proposes that:

- Measures should be taken to facilitate the exercise of membership rights by companies' 'real' or 'beneficial' shareholders, i.e. holdings behind a trust. This would involve the abolition of the rule forbidding companies from recognising a trust on their register of members and so allow a beneficial owner of shares to appoint a proxy.
- Quoted companies should be required to circulate members' resolutions free of charge with the AGM papers where the resolution has the requisite level of support and is received by a clear deadline.

- Companies should disclose in their annual report their major relationships with financial institutions.
- Institutional investors who manage funds on behalf of others should disclose how they have voted their shares.
- Votes on key company resolutions must be audited. There has been some evidence that some chairmen accept the vote on a show of hands if favourable to the board without demanding a poll, while knowing that there is a proxy majority against the resolution.
- As regards the rights of minority shareholders the effect of the decision in *O'Neill* v *Phillips* [1999] 1 WLR 1092, which clarifies the circumstances in which members can take legal action for unfair prejudice under s 459, should be maintained. The decision restricts the ability of members of smaller companies to take action under s 459 to cases where there has been a breach of the company's constitution or some breach of duty or agreement that makes it inequitable for the majority to act in a particular way. The decision discourages the practice that has developed under which minority members have made all sorts of allegations that might possibly sustain a case of unfairness.
- Derivative actions (i.e. actions by shareholders on behalf of the company) should be put on a statutory basis and provision should be made for the circumstances in which a member may take action on the company's behalf where the directors fail to do so. This is designed to remove the vagaries that have surrounded the rule in *Foss* v *Harbottle* (1843) 2 Hare 461.
- The nature of the company's constitution should be clarified and there should be more certainty about what rights are enjoyed and may be pursued by members personally under the constitution.

Company reporting and auditing

The report proposes that:

- Most public companies and larger private companies, i.e. companies of significant economic size, should be required to publish an operating and financial review (OFR) as part of the annual report. This would provide a review of the business, its performance, plans and prospects, and information regarded by the directors as necessary to an understanding of the business, e.g. relationships with employees, suppliers and customers, environmental, community and social impact, corporate governance and management of risk. The OFR would be subject to audit review.
- Where a listed company publishes a preliminary announcement, this should, after release to the market, be published immediately on a website, with notification electronically to those shareholders that want it.
- Listed companies should make available on a website their annual report and accounts, including the OFR, within four months of the year end. More time would be allowed to prepare hard copies but all public companies would be required to lay their accounts in general meeting and file them at Companies House within six months.
- Listed companies should wait for 15 days or more after making the annual report and accounts available on a website before settling the AGM papers for circulation.
- There should be no statutory extension of the duty of auditors on their report nor of the corresponding duties of the directors and their companies on the accounts and

report beyond that set out in the *Caparo* case (i.e. *Caparo Industries plc* v *Dickman* [1990] 1 All ER 568).

- There should be an extension of the duties of directors and employees to assist auditors in the execution of their statutory duties. It is currently a crime for a director or officer of a company knowingly or recklessly to provide misleading, false or deceptive information. The report recommends that employees should be brought within the scope of this duty and its criminal penalty. It is also proposed that for directors the duty should be widened to require them to volunteer information where the normal standards of a director's skill and care would require them to recognise that such information is needed. This enhanced directors' and employees' duty should give rise to civil liability, with vicarious liability for the company, and the directors' or employees' fault being attributed to the company for the purposes of contributory negligence. If enacted, this will be a significant auditors' defence when claims are made against them.
- Auditors should be able to limit their liability both contractually and in tort, to the company and to outsiders. Notwithstanding the decision not to extend *Caparo*, the report recommends that auditors should be able to limit their liability and it proposes the repeal of the current prohibition contained in s 310 of the CA 1985.

Institutional arrangements

The report proposes that:

- A Company Law and Reporting Commission (CLRC) would:
  - keep company law under review;
  - prepare an annual report to the Secretary of State on the state of company law and corporate governance, and any need for reform;
  - issue guidance on company law and governance;
  - advise on secondary legislation and on other matters referred by the Secretary of State;
  - supersede the Financial Reporting Council.
- A Standards Board would:
  - make detailed rules on accounting and reporting, including the OFR and all the form and content rules currently in the CA 1985;
  - make disclosure rules in areas such as the Combined Code and on information to be provided by shareholders;
  - keep the Combined Code under review;
  - make substantive rules on matters such as the conduct of AGMs;
  - publish guidance within its remit;
  - supersede the Accounting Standards Board.
- A Private Companies Committee would examine the impact of company law and reporting requirements on private companies, with the CLRC and the Standards Board being required to take due account of its advice.
- A Reporting Review Panel would:
  - be responsible for reviewing the accounts and reports of public companies and large private companies and for seeking revisions to accounts that do not comply with the requirements of the Act;

– be authorised to apply to the courts for an order requiring revised accounts to be prepared – similar procedures would apply to the OFR;
– supersede the Financial Reporting Review Panel.

Simplifying and streamlining the law

The report proposes that:

- The process of forming a company should be modernised. One person should be able to form a public company, as for a private company. The memorandum and articles should be consolidated into a single document of constitution. Authorised capital should be abolished and there would be no theoretical ceiling on capital.
- The capital maintenance rules should be reformed. This would include:
  – the rules for public companies on giving financial assistance for the acquisition of shares would be simplified and, as already noted, abolished for private companies;
  – an alternative would be provided to the present procedure in court for capital reductions;
  – as we have seen, the requirement for authorised capital would be abolished;
  – the common law rules on company distributions would be codified.
- Public access to companies' registers of members should be preserved but the use that can be made of the information should be restricted to purposes relevant to holding the interests recorded in the register or exercising of rights attached to them and other purposes approved by the company.
- Directors should be allowed the possibility of filing a 'service address' on the public record at Companies House at which they would accept service of documents and correspondence relating to the company. Their residential address would continue to be available to certain public authorities, with others such as members and creditors having the right to apply to the court for access.
- The law on the registration of charges should be reformed and be governed by secondary legislation, and be the subject of a Law Commission study. However, the report favours a notice system similar to the USA model, where there is no particular time for registration of a charge before it ceases to be valid but its priority dates from filing notice, not from creation. Also filing of notice makes it valid against an insolvency practitioner from the date of filing notice.
- The law on 'trading disclosures' – mainly the information that companies must include in business letters etc – should be updated to reflect modern conditions, e.g. the increasing use of electronic communications.
- Company restructuring should be facilitated. This would include:
  – improvements to the procedures for company reconstructions in Part XIII of the CA 1985 and s 110 of the Insolvency Act 1986;
  – clarifying and modernising the procedures on compulsory purchase of shares following a takeover offer.
- Subject to suitable safeguards, a mechanism should be provided for companies to migrate to and from Great Britain and between England and Wales and Scotland without, as now, having to be wound up. This would include any EU jurisdiction and even non-EU jurisdictions approved by the Secretary of State.

- Companies limited by shares should be allowed to re-register as companies limited by guarantee and vice versa.
- The two existing and overlapping regimes for overseas companies should be replaced with a single set of procedures and the disclosure requirements should be updated.
- The law on unregistered companies should be updated.
- There should be a separate form of incorporation designed specifically for charities.

Meetings and resolutions – further points

- A public company should be enabled to dispense with the AGM where the members so decide unanimously.
- The AGM of a public company should be held within 180 days of the end of the preceding accounting cycle. The AGM of a private company should be held (if at all) within 10 months of the accounting year.
- An AGM should be permitted to be held at more than one location, e.g. by video conferencing.
- Proxies should be permitted to speak at meetings of both public and private companies.
- Extraordinary resolutions should be replaced by special resolutions.

Sanctions

The report proposes that:

- The criminal law for Companies Act offences involving dishonesty, including fraudulent trading by British companies and foreign companies in the UK, should be strengthened.
- Company law on the criminal liability of directors, officers and managers should be modernised and clarified.
- The civil sanctions against directors should be codified.
- Companies should be required to disclose in their annual report any criminal convictions during that reporting year for breaches of Companies Act requirements on the part of the company or its officers.
- The 'phoenix' syndrome should be tackled more effectively to prevent that practice under which company directors may contrive to mislead the public by utilising a company name that is the same as or similar to that of a failed company of which they were directors in order to conduct a virtually identical business. Recommendations are that:
  - the existing provisions on transactions between a company and its directors in the context of insolvency should be strengthened;
  - there should be stronger safeguards where a director of a failed company applies to the court to be a director of or concerned in the management of another company with the same or similar name;
  - where appropriate, there should be interim orders for disqualification of directors in advance of final disqualification proceedings.

The future

In July 2002 the Government published a White Paper containing draft clauses for a Bill. The White Paper is entitled *Modernising Company Law – Draft Clauses*. Consultation will continue. A Companies Bill to implement the whole of the Company Law Review is not likely to be introduced in Parliament until after the general election that is expected sometime in 2005. If a Bill is introduced in the early days of a new Parliament say 2006, it will not reach the statute book until 2007 and it is unlikely to be brought fully into force for one or two years after that.

ANSWERS TO QUESTIONS SET IN OBJECTIVE MODE

Chapter 1

1 (D)
2 (B)
3 (B)
4 (B)
5 (C)
6 (D)

Chapter 2

1 (D)
2 (D)
3 (B)
4 (B)
5 (B)
6 (B)

Chapter 3

1 (A)
2 (C)
3 (C)
4 (C)
5 (B)
6 (D)

Chapter 4

1 (C)
2 (C)
3 (C)
4 (B)
5 (A)
6 (C)

Chapter 5

1 (C)
2 (A)
3 (A)
4 (A)
5 (B)
6 (D)

Chapter 6

1 (C)
2 (A)
3 (D)
4 (A)
5 (D)
6 (C)

Chapter 7

1 (C)
2 (C)
3 (A)
4 (B)
5 (D)
6 (C)

Chapter 8

The relevant questions and answers appear at pp 199–201.

Chapter 9

1 (C)
2 (C)
3 (A)
4 (A)
5 (A)
6 (C)

Chapter 10

1 (D)
2 (B)
3 (C)
4 (B)
5 (C)
6 (B)

Chapter 11

1 (B)
2 (D)
3 (A)
4 (C)
5 (B)
6 (C)

Chapter 12

1 (C)
2 (C)
3 (A)
4 (B)
5 (D)
6 (A)

Chapter 13

1 (D)
2 (B)
3 (D)
4 (A)
5 (C)
6 (C)

Chapter 14

1 (D)
2 (A)
3 (B)
4 (C)
5 (D)
6 (A)

Chapter 15

1 (C)
2 (B)
3 (A)
4 (A)
5 (A)
6 (C)

Chapter 16

1 (B)
2 (D)
3 (A)
4 (C)
5 (C)
6 (A)

Chapter 17

1 (C)
2 (D)
3 (A)
4 (B)
5 (D)
6 (C)

Chapter 18

1 (A)
2 (D)
3 (B)
4 (B)
5 (A)
6 (A)

Chapter 19

1 (B)
2 (D)
3 (A)
4 (C)
5 (C)
6 (A)

Chapter 20

1 (D)
2 (A)
3 (D)
4 (D)
5 (B)
6 (C)

Chapter 21

1 (C)
2 (A)
3 (D)
4 (C)
5 (B)
6 (D)

Chapter 22

1 (B)
2 (C)
3 (A)
4 (D)
5 (D)
6 (B)

Chapter 23

1 (D)
2 (D)
3 (A)
4 (C)
5 (D)
6 (D)

Chapter 24

(No objective test)

Chapter 25

1 (A)
2 (D)
3 (B)
4 (C)
5 (B)
6 (A)

INDEX